REVOLTING CAPITAL

REVOLTING CAPITAL

CAPITAL

Racism and Radicalism in
Washington, D.C. 1900-2000

Gerald Horne

INTERNATIONAL PUBLISHERS, New York

International Publishers, NY 10011

Copyright © 2023 Gerald Horne

CIP data available from Library of Congress

ISBN 10: 0-7178-0036-9   ISBN-13 978-07178-0036-0
Typeset by Amnet Systems, Chennai, India

Table of Contents

REVOLTING CAPITAL

Introduction

It was the peak of a typically steamy summer in Washington, D.C. in 1919 and Carter G. Woodson, dubbed as the "Father of Black History," thought he was about to make history—in the worst way.

He was near Howard University, the historically Black institution within walking distance of the White House, and then there sped by him, he recalled, "'a Negro yelling for mercy,'" as he was "'pursued by hundreds of [white] soldiers, sailors and mariners, assisted by men in civilian attire...'" They collared the young man then "'deliberately held him as one would a beef for slaughter...'" Then they shot him. The stunned historian scurried away furtively— "'as fast as I could without running'" is how he put it, while "'expecting every moment to be lynched myself.'"[1]

Dr. Woodson was not the only person shaken by this turn of events. Hayden C. Johnson was born in 1908 but even by 1985 he remained startled at what he saw at "Union Station," the rail crossroads across from the Capitol, as he was "going up Seventh Street" nearby. "They were going to clean us out," he claimed, referring to "machine guns on both sides"—including "the Negroes!"[2]

Fortunately, he and Dr. Woodson escaped relatively unscathed but the same could not be said of the city itself. This center of power was barely containing a nationwide burst of unrest, driven by an enervating racism, the simultaneous rise of radical political forces inspired by the Bolshevik Revolution, and a global climate suffused with war and violence buoyed by a surfeit of weapons.[3] Thus, the *Norfolk*

---

1. Jill Watts, *The Black Cabinet: The Untold Story of African Americans and Politics During the Age of Roosevelt*, New York: Grove, 2020, 29.
2. Oral History, Hayden C. Johnson, 8 July 1985, *Historical Society of Washington, D.C.*
3. William Tuttle, *Race Riot: Chicago in the Red Summer of 1919*, New York: Atheneum, 1970. See also David F. Krugler, *1919, the Year of Racial Violence: How African Americans Fought Back*, New York: Cambridge University Press, 2014.

Journal & Guide, a Black periodical sited due south from Washington, rebuked these "lynchocrats [sic] in uniform" that had so stirred Woodson but reminded that "this sword worked both ways" as "the Blacks answered the challenge man for man and life for life," a result found "surprising." Still, "white enthusiasm in the lawless slaughter began to freeze as soon as the Blacks began to shoot and cut to kill"; yes, "the hospitals contained quite as many whites as blacks..."[4]

Nonetheless, yet another Black journalist found a uniqueness to this bloodshed in Washington, which distinguished it from other urban nodes. Speaking from Kansas City, John Bruce found the "real cause of these outbreaks" was the "unusually large number of Negroes in public office" in a city that would deliver a Black majority shortly. These "well-dressed, well-housed educated Negroes" were "frequently seen in automobiles on Pennsylvania Avenue," a central artery.[5] In sum, there was a peculiar mixture of racism and class resentment with Dr. Woodson as an ostensible target.

All academics did not react in Dr. Woodson's manner. A Howard professor described as "militant" built a barricade, festooned with guns. He and his comrades then engaged in watchful waiting. As one writer put it, "'the professor, using a rowdy principle, had opened up a new and decent area for Negro habitation. Thousands of fine Negroes live there now,'" as reform emerged from the barrel of a gun.[6]

This tumult also served to illustrate why Washington—the headquarters of an apartheid state—was gaining a well merited reputation as a site of Black Strength, as Negroes (in jujitsu fashion) turned the amplitude of the state back against it: unlike countless pogroms over the decades, these Negroes—often trained militarily by that same state—were willing to take a life for everyone expended. They had weaponry, including machine guns. They had organization with a private code. They had trucks and other vehicles to transport battlers. Their mettle acted to cool the hotheads and the lynchers.[7]

Almost a half century later, there was yet another explosion in Washington, again within hailing distance of the corridors of global

---

4. *Norfolk Journal & Guide,* 2 August 1919, in Robert Kerlin, ed., *The Voice of the Negro,* New York: Dutton, 1920, 17-18.

5. *Kansas City Call,* 16 August 1919 in *Vertical File-Race Riots, Special Collections, Washington, D.C. Public Library.*

6. Nicholas Johnson, *Negroes and the Gun: The Black Tradition of Arms,* Amherst, New York: Prometheus, 2014, 177.

7. Winston James, *Claude McKay: The Making of a Black Bolshevik,* New York: Columbia University Press, 2022, 239-241.

power. John Smith, born in 1945 was there in April 1968 when the city was convulsed in the aftermath of the assassination of Dr. Martin Luther King, Jr. He was residing near 8th Street and N Street, N.W., not far from where Dr. Woodson had been rousted earlier but times had changed. For then he was associating with the Zulus, named in honor of the fearsome South African ethnicity known for its militancy, and which he conceded was part of the "roguish element in the movement," then pressing for the eradication of Jim Crow's legacy. "We had dynamite" and "guns" too, he said and then they traipsed to a grocery store on Georgia Avenue, not far from Howard University, which had eluded their good graces since they "had fired a Black man for having a beard"; in retaliation, "we stuck a stick of dynamite in the door and tried to shoot it from a distance and blow the store up,"[8] apparently failing.

As with 1919, 1968 also was unfolding in the midst of turmoil, including the ascendancy of the Black Panther Party, which quite infamously was not averse to wielding weapons; African liberation movements enmeshed in armed struggle against colonialism; and a war in Indo-China that was undermining the routine cliché from the nation's rulers that violence was not the way to resolve disputes.

These contradictions did not faze local businessman George Kalavitinos, one whit. Speaking before Congress while the embers of conflict had yet to be extinguished, he exhorted that since 1776 the nation had "never been faced with a more critical situation as we are confronted with today..." Born in the District of Columbia in 1921, he acknowledged freely that "what I am called is a slumlord" and presumably from his tenants he learned that "planned guerrilla warfare is now in our land," with key activists "following the same tactics as Fidel Castro"; in fact, he claimed "many of these punks were taught by the Cuban leader...." His temper flaring, he challenged the "many [who] say dictatorship is not the answer. Well," he clucked, "I say we could use some now...."[9]

This self-professed "slumlord" had moved to extremism—he was an exemplar of revolting capital—arguably by the press of events at

---

8. Oral History, John Smith, 16 October 2002, *Historical Society of Washington, D.C.*
9. Statement of George Kalavitinos, in "Civil Disturbances in Washington.... Hearings Before the Committee on the District of Columbia....House of Representatives....Ninetieth Congress, Second Session.....Investigating the April 1968 Rioting, Looting, Damages and Losses and Police Actions and HGR 16941 and HR 16948....May and June 1968..." *Historical Society of Washington, D.C.*

the locus of national and global power. It was not evident if he were part of the powerful Board of Trade, an agglomeration of merchants and various businesses that in the pivotal year of 1963 included almost 400 firms.[10]

They and their national peers were kept busy in the 1960s. More than 200 cities erupted in April 1968 in the aftermath of assassination but according to one study, the eruption in Washington "caused the most property damage, resulted in the greatest number of arrests and was occupied by the largest number of federal troops..." This revealing development, scholar Kyla Sommers suggests, is difficult to disconnect from the point that from 1900 to 1962 the suburbs of the District "flipped from 1/3 to only 6% Black while D.C.'s Black population rose from 25% to over 50%,"[11] as a nation renowned for state sanctioned policies of apartheid, managed to have a center of power that was majority Black.

Being at the center of power, provided assets and liabilities for those victimized by Jim Crow. Philip Elman, the man given credit for principally writing the government's brief in the epochal 1954 high court decision in *Brown v. Board of Education*, observed in a point reflected in the case's unanimous opinion that "'this city'" speaking of Washington "'is the window through which the world looks into our house.'" The picture the world saw was hardly attractive: in 1919, for example, there was fretting that a threatened diplomatic corps would withdraw, further sullying the nation's global image,[12] a prospect that no other city had to endure: this provided leverage for the anti-racist bloc, as shall be seen.

Moreover, increasingly during the 20th century, as Senator Olin Johnston of South Carolina was informed, Washington was not just the U.S. capital but "really of the world."[13] To the extent that this was not hubris, it suggested that the world should and would have something to say about the apartheid policies that reigned there, meaning added leverage for the victims of Jim Crow.

---

10. Haynes Johnson, *Dusk at the Mountain: The Negro, the Nation and the Capital; a Report on Problems and Progress*, Garden City: Doubleday, 1963, 212.

11. Kyla Sommers, "'I Believe in the City:' The Black Freedom Struggle and the 1968 Civil Disturbances in Washington, D.C.," Ph.D. dissertation, George Washington University, 2019, 1. 53.

12. Joan Quigley, *Just Another Southern Town: Mary Church Terrell and the Struggle for Racial Justice in the Nation's Capital*, New York: Oxford University Press, 2016, 196, 82.

13. Gilbert Hahn to Senator Johnston, 26 March 1953, Box 35, *Olin Johnston Papers, University of South Carolina-Columbia.*

It was in the late 1940s that the celebrated Howard University sociologist, E. Franklin Frazier, was made aware of the unavoidable: as Washington became not only a global but hemispheric capital, the ingrained apartheid policies there outraged numerous foreign visitors, at a time when the U.S. was seeking to win hearts and minds abroad. Ethiopians found it next to impossible to book a room a "'white hotel'" while one enraged South Asian proclaimed, "'I would rather be an Untouchable in the Hindu Caste system than a Negro here.'" Those from south of the border with more than a hint of melanin often were targeted, making it difficult to woo them in the twilight battle with Moscow and its allies.[14]

Eventually, Washington's rulers sought to pivot away from horrendousness, as described by the city's doyenne, Mary Church Terrell: "'Indians, Japanese, Chinese, Filipinos and representatives of other dark races can find hotel accommodations as a rule,'" she said, "'if they pay for them. The colored man or woman is the only one thrust out of the hotels of the national Capital like a leper.'"[15]

Being sited in the center of power also meant that African American and left-leaning forces generally had more direct access to those from overseas, which could be leveraged to their advantage. It was in the Spring of 1949 that Howard historian, Rayford Logan, confided to his diary that "two secretaries from the Ethiopian legation came out to the house last night along with [fellow H.U. professor, William Leo] Hansberry...."[16]

Logan, whose acts and thoughts figure significantly in these pages also presents an illustrative case. He was quintessentially a District man, born there in 1897 and expiring in 1982. He graduated from M Street High School there then matriculated at Williams College, Phi Beta Kappa, in 1917, then enlisted in the District National Guard. He was promoted to first lieutenant of infantry by January 1918 and served at the front in the Argonne Forest and was discharged in August 1919. So far, so mainstream—for a Negro: however, he was so angry about Negrophobia in a racist military that he remained in France for five years and assisted Dr. W.E.B. Du Bois in organizing Pan African Congresses, 1921-1924. He symbolized how the

14. "Democracy for Export-From its Own Capital," circa 1947, Box 134, *E. Franklin Frazier Papers, Howard University-Washington, D.C.*
15. Jonathan Scott Holloway, *Confronting the Veil: Abram Harris, Jr., E. Franklin Frazier and Ralph Bunche, 1919-1941*, Chapel Hill: University of North Carolina Press, 2002, 44.
16. Entry, circa 28 May 1949, Box 4, *Rayford Logan Papers, Library of Congress, Washington, D.C.*

nation—and the capital—would have to change lest both create a national security challenge with incalculable consequences.[17]

* * *

A boost for the music now called "Jazz" emerged in the 1930s when the son of a Turkish diplomat, Ahmet Ertegun, opened the doors of the embassy in Washington—circumventing Jim Crow laws—on behalf of Black musicians. So positioned, he went on to found Atlantic Records, becoming a major force in cultural production in the U.S.[18]

On the other hand, the global influence in the District was not always wholesome. In the 1970s, the Iranian legation was notorious for a profusion of orgies, opium and hashish, difficult to quarantine from the surrounding neighborhoods.[19] (Of course, the negative influences in the District did not always emerge from foreign legations: then congressional spouse, Rita Jenrette, recalled a time in the 1970s when the District—a "bastion of male chauvinism," she says—was renowned for creative orgies: "at the first party people were taking off their clothes at the door.")[20]

The Black Washington vicinity was a direct victim of U.S. imperialism and not only in terms of tax dollars wasted on a failed regime in Teheran or on military spending generally. Queen City was a neighborhood of about 150 Black American families, founded in the 1880s, that was disassembled so that the behemoth known as the Pentagon—citadel of U.S. imperialism—could be constructed.[21]

In some ways, Washingtonians were guinea pigs, enmeshed in a massive experiment. Thus, the shadowy Sidney Gottlieb, a crafty intelligence operative, conducted many of his ghoulish experiments involving "mind control" and various elixirs in the metropolitan area, often referred to as the "DMV" (District, Maryland, Virginia).[22]

But when one door closes, another often closes too, and those in the District faced an utterly distinct challenge in light of the felt

---

17. Funeral Program for Dr. Rayford Whittingham Logan, 10 November 1982, Box 219-5, *Merze Tate Papers, Howard University-Washington, D.C.*

18. Gerald Horne, *Jazz and Justice: Racism and the Political Economy of the Music*, New York: Monthly Review Press, 2019.

19. John Ghazvinian, *America and Iran: A History, 1720 to the Present*: New York: Knopf, 2021, 259.

20. Rita Jenrette, *My Capitol Secrets*, New York: Bantam, 1981, 53, 51-52.

21. *Washington Post*, 25 December 2018.

22. Stephen Kinzer, *Poisoner in Chief: Sidney Gottlieb and the CIA Search for Mind Control*, New York: Holt, 2019.

need to fortify the center of power. Just before the tumult of 1968, the youthful reporter Carl Bernstein—a few years away from his reportage on the Watergate scandal that brought down President Richard M. Nixon—alerted readers that the "Federal Government—not the administration of Mayor Walter E. Washington—has developed the strategy for confronting a serious eruption of violence"; this multi-pronged offensive would include "the Pentagon and the Justice Department,"[23] which could also mean the FBI, CIA, and a dozen or more other intelligence agencies, Capitol police, park police, Secret Service—in short, unlike those elsewhere, Washingtonians would confront the full force of state power, in addition to local police, the chief antagonists of urban activists nationally. In adjacent Prince George's County, Maryland, now a bastion of Black working class and middle class robustness, the League of Women Voters had noticed as early as 1969 the presence of "over 30 agencies" with a focus on "law enforcement," including a "county police department" combined with the fact that "26 of the county's 28 municipalities" also provided police protection. "We also have Maryland national capital and planning commission park police, Maryland state police, University of Maryland police and military police.... the Sheriff also participates in police activities"[24]—and that does not include similar entities in Virginia. Recently, the *Wall Street Journal* pointed out that the 2001 Patriot Act gave the Federal Reserve Board—perhaps surpassing even the White House in power—to create its own police force; the Supreme Court, the Smithsonian and the Library of Congress have similar power. In Washington, even the police have their own police: the Federal Bureau of Investigation operates the FBI police. The Secret Service administers a uniformed Secret Service Police. There is Amtrak police.[25] Is it a coincidence that this proliferation of armed force occurs in the city dubbed "Chocolate City"?

Thus, those rubbing shoulders with powerbrokers in this relatively small city were subject to an extraordinary level of surveillance and harassment. This was noticed by Black Panther Party leader, Donald Cox, when he arrived in Washington in the late 1960s and spent time at the residence of a fellow militant then known as Stokely Carmichael. "The thing that always bothered me about being in Stokely's company," he complained was the "constant surveillance;

---

23. *Washington Post*, 2 March 1968.
24. "Briefing Paper," October 1969, Series III, Box 28, *Records of League of Women Voters of Prince George's County, University of Maryland-College Park*.
25. *Wall Street Journal*, 12 August 2022.

you literally couldn't do anything without the authorities right there under your nose...it was ridiculous...."[26]

Other activists found it similarly ridiculous when in 1981 it was revealed that the chief local activist of the 1960s and 1970s—Julius Hobson a founder of what became the left-leaning Statehood Green Party—was a "confidential source" for the FBI and was said to have provided this repressive agency with what a journalist termed "information on advanced planning for the historic March on Washington" of 1963; he was "paid $100 to $300 in expenses to monitor and report" on the monumental Democratic Party convention in Atlantic City in 1964, where the shoots of "Black Power" began to sprout,[27] a philosophy articulated most pointedly by the Howard alumnus then known as Stokely Carmichael and which, minimally, sought more Black control over institutions and entities that shaped their lives.[28]

Of course, before he expired, Hobson said that the "'Washington Star' [newspaper and] the D.C. Metropolitan Police acknowledged that they had undertaken extensive police surveillance activities on me and a number of other people" with "assistance from the CIA"—[29] a prospect that most urban activists did not have to endure.

Surveillance and harassment by the authorities was propelled by the presence of national political leadership that often was supportive of Jim Crow: this also meant that District activists and comrades faced the most formidable foe of any nationally. As NAACP chief, Walter White, was informed in 1938 "there are in Washington," said branch leader Gertrude Stone, that "...not only prejudiced natives but Congressmen and Senators who bring with them the fear and hatred of the Negro engendered in the South. The influence of these southerners in our local government is considerable," she lamented.[30] In sum, Dixie often sent to the District the most hardened white supremacists to the detriment of local residents.

Ironically, the U.S. authorities were forced to confront a formidable African American community, a bloc least susceptible to the

---

26. Donald Cox, *Just Another Nigger: Or Use What you Get to Get What You Need*, Berkeley: Heyday, 2019, 78.
27. *Washington Post*, 22 February 1981.
28. Stokely Carmichael and Charles V. Hamilton, *Black Power: The Politics of Liberation in America*, New York: Random House, 1967.
29. Councilman Hobson to CIA, 21 June 1976, Box 52, *Julius Hobson, Washington, D.C. Public Library*.
30. Gertrude Stone to Walter White, 11 June 1938, Box G39, *NAACP Papers-Library of Congress, Washington, D.C.*

conservatism that undergirded U.S. imperialism. In this inflamed context, it was Howard University that became an object of ire. As early as 1935 when the Depression Decade was serving to push many to the left, this trend had not eluded the self-described "Capstone of Negro Higher Education." One of the few Black Congressmen of that era, Arthur Mitchell of Chicago, was flabbergasted by the remarks of the school's leader, Mordecai Johnson, who thought that Negroes should study the Soviet Union, while adding portentously, "'The Negro is carefully watching Soviet Russia.'" He should be "censured," said the politico scoffingly. A federal agent interviewed Dr. Algernon Jackson of the medical school who agreed that there were a number of "radical" teachers at the school—including Ralph Bunche, then a left-leaning scholar on the fast track to the right and a Nobel Peace Prize for the damage he wreaked in Palestine—but "the most radical person of anyone" there at H.U. was President Johnson, whose role was encapsulated in a 1933 headline: "[Johnson] defends communism...before Harlem audience...."[31]

Howard University was graced by the presence in the 1930s of some of the most stalwart radicals and Communists that this nation has produced. Both W. Alphaeus Hunton and Doxey Wilkerson happened to be African American, like many members of the faculty there. Wilkerson born in Excelsior Springs, Missouri in 1905 was described by the color-obsessed FBI in 1957 as "light tan" in color, about six feet tall and 185 pounds, "balding on top...wears mustache, round face, cleft chin, neat, conservative dresser...." By 1943, he left H.U. to work full-time for the Communist Party.[32] Yet another Black educator, Melvin Tolson, also born in Missouri, captured Wilkerson's—and Hunton's—sentiments when he opined in 1939, "radicalism is the Great Emancipator of Negroes,"[33] a point that has yet to be extirpated.

But before that date Wilkerson and Hunton were a dynamic duo organizing across the District and doing more than most to construct a viable radicalism. The tall and lean Hunton emerged from

---

31. See "Alleged Communistic Activities at Howard University...Letter from the Acting Secretary of the Interior...." 12 May 1936, 74th Congress, 2nd Session, Senate Doc. 217, Box 37, *Jesse Moorland Papers, Howard University-Washington, D.C.* Therein see *New York Age*, 10 May 1933 and *Pittsburgh Courier*, 18 May 1928.

32. FBI File, 3 May 1957 and comment by Lee Lorch on 1943 resignation, Box 3, *Doxey Wilkerson Papers, Schomburg Center-Howard University.*

33. Melvin B. Tolson, *Caviar and Cabbage: Selected Columns from the 'Washington Tribune,'* Columbia: University of Missouri Press, 1982, 37.

a prominent Black Canadian family, that included ancestors that collaborated with militant abolitionists e.g., John Brown and Martin Delany. Labor organizing, anti-imperialist solidarity, and the fight-back against police terror was his—and Wilkerson's—specialties. He too left H.U. in 1943, to work alongside Paul Robeson and W.E.B. Du Bois in the Council on African Affairs—the vanguard of African solidarity in North America—before being driven into exile in Africa a few decades later.[34]

When historian Jonathan Scott Holloway termed Washington "Black America's capital from the end of the nineteenth century to at least the end of World War II,"[35] he had Howard in mind and, I would add the names of Communists like Hunton and Wilkerson. Still, the point remained that for a good deal of its history, which began in the early postbellum era, Howard employed the largest concentration of African Americans with doctorates in the U.S. and the world.[36]

This infusion of petit bourgeois ideology often accompanied this stratum in a city disproportionately comprised of wage workers. But this stratum shaped aspirations and the Black families that dominated the upper reaches of this compact southern town, validated the plaint of the late singer, Leadbelly, that Washington was—most definitely-- a "bourgeois" town.[37]

Scholar Kenneth Janken argues that this elite—"Syphaxes... Bruces, Pinchbacks[,] Terrells and no more than one hundred other families in an African American population of seventy five thousand in 1900"— at "times opposed separate facilities for Blacks and whites on the grounds that this would force them to associate with the lower class of their race."[38]

On the other hand, this stratum—frequent melanin deficiency aside—were nonetheless Black and had to suffer the indignities of

34. Christine Ann Lutz, "'The Dizzy Steep to Heaven': The Hunton Family, 1850-1970," Ph.D. dissertation, Georgia State University, 2001, 86, 292.

35. Jonathan Scott Holloway, *Confronting the Veil: Abram Harris, Jr., E. Franklin Frazier and Ralph Bunche, 1919-1941*, Chapel Hill: University of North Carolina Press, 2002, 36.

36. Kwame Wes Alford, "A Prophet Without Honor: William Leo Hansberry and the Origins of the Discipline of African Studies," Ph.D. dissertation, University of Missouri-Columbia, 1998, 131.

37. Charles K. Wolfe, *The Life and Legend of Leadbelly*, New York: HarperCollins, 1992.

38. Kenneth Robert Janken, *Rayford W. Logan and the Dilemma of the African American Intellectual*, Amherst: University of Massachusetts Press, 1993,. 7, 8.

same. One of the first Negro journalists at the "Washington Post"—a "white newspaper in a Black city" was how Dorothy Butler Gilliam described how her employer was perceived widely—recalled that in the early 1960s how she "would wave frantically for a taxicab mostly driven by white men but all would whiz past me...."[39]

The Communist Party had quite a bit to work with in the District as a result. The metropolitan area doubled in population from 700,000 in 1930 to 1.4 million by 1950, while the number of federal workers increased fourfold from 70, 000 in 1930 to 270, 000 by 1942, as the New Deal and government spending asserted itself. Washington became the nation's ninth largest city by 1940 as it was being termed the republic's "Number one Boom Town." In this climate, it is difficult to dispute the estimate that even in the early 1950s, as McCarthyism was flexing its muscles, there were a reported 1,000 Communist Party members in the District—setting aside the numbers in neighboring Maryland and Virginia.[40]

From the early to mid-20th century, Washington had the most substantial concentration—percentage wise—of African Americans, surpassing other regions. The District, thus, was dubbed "Negro Heaven" and the "Black Capital," both monikers attracting the revolting attention of their detractors[41] and the dedicated attention of radicals.

That formulation is easier to understand when one considers that between 1950 and 1960 the Euro-American population dropped by a third from nearly 65 percent to emerging as a city of about 54 percent Negro.[42] This was occurring—coincidentally—as state forged desegregation was in motion. It was in 1965, says District historian, Constance McLauglin Green, that "for the first time in history... Negro residents of a major American city outnumber[ed] white[s] by more than 10 percent...."[43]

---

39. Dorothy Butler Gilliam, *Trailblazer: A Pioneering Journalist's Fight to Make the Media Look More Like America*, New York: Center Street, 2019, 7.

40. David K. Johnson, *The Lavender Scare: The Cold War Persecution of Gays and Lesbians in the Federal Government*, Chicago: University of Chicago Press, 2004, 43, 87.

41. Treva B. Lindsey, *Colored No More: Reinventing Black Womanhood in Washington, D.C.*, Urbana: University of Illinois Press, 2018, 6.

42. Chris Myers Asch and George Derek Musgrove, *Chocolate City: A History of Race and Democracy in the Nation's Capital*, Chapel Hill: University of North Carolina Press, 2017, 326.

43. Constance McLaughlin Green, *The Secret City: A History of Race Relations in the Nation's Capital*, Princeton: Princeton University Press, 1967, 3.

This demographic change was at odds with the then ruling ethos in that it was occurring at a time of rank anticommunism nationally, not as popular among Blacks as among others—this was being launched from a city that was remarkably at variance with this hegemonic ideology[44]: the results in coming decades were predictable, i.e. "gentrification" or reshaping the racial composition of the capital, bringing the center of power in line demographically and ideologically, which—as shall be seen—would have an impact on jury composition for the politically potent running afoul of the law.

This was occurring as the finance capital wing of the ruling class was rising and becoming ever more influential in the Democratic Party, which also housed African Americans, but whose narrow class interests were not always aligned with those of this Black base.[45] This wing was not necessarily opposed to improving the global image of U.S. imperialism by pushing for desegregation nationally but joined their class brethren in revolting against strengthening of unions, the ultimate savior for the working class constituency of which African Americans were an essential component. This mixed message contributed to Black folk taking to the streets in revolt, once more, in 1968 and thereafter.

* * *

By 1938, African Americans were 10 percent of the labor force of the major employer—the federal government—with the Department of Justice and the FBI maintaining the poorest records at about 3 percent; the Interior Department rate was about 25 percent but since this agency provided guards and elevator operators for all other agencies, this figure is misleading. Cafeteria workers were likely the largest predominantly African American union in the District. By 1947, as the Red Scare was heating up and the CP had yet to be weakened profoundly, Communists, and their allies were in support of a 50 building strike at the heart of power by these workers, which—according to scholar, Mary Elizabeth Harding—was "possibly the only example of an all African American union that supported the refusal of the leadership of the local to sign the non-Communist affidavits and remained

44. See e.g. Gerald Horne, *Black Liberation/Red Scare: Ben Davis and the Communist Party*, New York: International, 2021; Gerald Horne, *Communist Front? The Civil Rights Congress, 1946-1956*, New York: International, 2021.
45. Thomas Ferguson, *Golden Rule: The Investment Theory of Party Competition and the Logic of Money Driven Political Systems*, Chicago: University of Chicago Press, 1995.

on strike for over two months until the issue was resolved"; and, in a signal development that portended the weakening of both unions and the CP, "the NAACP declined to become active in the Citizens Support Committee...in support of the cafeteria workers...."[46]

It was comprehensible why these low-wage workers would be ready to defy the then consensus. Back then it was estimated that about 20 percent of the Negro population lived in the District's alley dwellings and 75 percent of these alley dwelling families earned less than $800 annually.[47] Although the District was relentlessly urban, a premier Negro intellectual declared that "there is not a cabin [in] the state of Virginia," a heavily rural state, "that is so unfit for human habitation as are scores of blocks of alley houses in Washington city."[48] One of Washington's most prominent sons, basketball superstar, Elgin Baylor, found his hometown to be a "hard place. A racist place. Segregated parks, schools, movie theaters, lunch counters," all delivering "ugly unforgettable things." Born in 1934, he recalled barely escaping kidnapping by a bevy of racists, with his escape eased by his speed as a runner—which raises the tantalizing speculation as to how many slower Black children were not as lucky.[49]

There was another barrier for Communists and anti-racists to surmount, often dimly understood. In their scabrously tawdry 1951 book, *Washington Confidential*, the co-authors posited that life in a city dominated by the federal bureaucracy offered a foretaste of what life would be like if socialism prevailed; after all, this new system involved public control, suggesting a substantial role for government, meaning in the eyes of some: Washington, D.C. But this perception was combined with the oft-told notion that the city was a kind of "Negro Heaven" with a twist: bosses supposedly could not fire Black workers for fear of retaliation, a kind of replay of the hysteria surrounding Reconstruction, an era that traumatized numerous Dixiecrats.[50]

---

46. Mary Elizabeth Harding, "Eleanor Nelson, Oliver Palmer and the Struggle to Organize the CIO in Washington, D.C., 1937-1950," Ph.D. dissertation, George Washington University, 2002, 221.

47. Kenneth Robert Janken, *Rayford W. Logan and the Dilemma of the African American Intellectual*, Amherst: University of Massachusetts Press, 1993, 9.

48. Kelly Miller, *Radicals and Conservatives and Other Essays on the Negro in America*, New York: Schocken, 1908 [republished in 1968], 138.

49. Elgin Baylor, *Hang Time: My Life in Basketball*, Boston: Houghton Mifflin, 2018, 1, 9.

50. Jack Lait and Lee Mortimer, *Washington Confidential*, New York: Crown, 1951. See also Landon R.Y. Storrs, *The Second Red Scare and the Unmaking of the New Deal Left*, Princeton: Princeton University Press, 2013, 93.

There were also building trades unions in the District but—predictably, as radicalism was weakened—they were the butt of protests by increasingly militant H.U. students. These were "Jim Crow locals," charged student spokesman, Michael Thelwell in 1963, as they were contracted to build a gymnasium on campus.[51] The absence of Black workers from these ranks was a concomitant of Red Scare purges that simultaneously amounted to blockage of efforts to diversify the ranks.

Although the District itself was marked by a non-proletarian labor force—for the most part—in nearby Maryland, a different situation obtained. At Sparrow's Point there sat a major steel center, unionized, which unavoidably shaped metropolitan politics. Thus, what is described antiseptically as "race relations" in late 19th century Baltimore were viewed as mild, but as white supremacy was augmented by the further ascension of imperialism in Hawaii, the Philippines, Cuba, and Puerto Rico, matters worsened tangibly. Then, perhaps not coincidentally, days before Maryland was to ponder disenfranchisement of Negroes, on 7 February 1904, Baltimore was engulfed in flames for 36 hours in a conflagration that rivaled what occurred in Chicago decades earlier and what befell San Francisco by 1906: 2,000 buildings were burnt to a crisp, including 140 acres of downtown, leaving 50,000 jobless—a state of affairs bound to lead to racist tensions in the absence of broad-based unions.[52]

Also not coincidentally, a national leader of the right-wing populism that was to blossom with the onset of the 2016 presidential election and the rise of Donald J. Trump, was prefigured—according to one study—by Spiro Agnew of Maryland, who as governor, was accused justifiably of "bullying" Negro leaders on camera in the wake of the assassination of Dr. King in 1968; this star turn captured the attention of a key aide to Richard Nixon, leading to his election as Vice President.[53]

Besides, Baltimore was blessed by the presence of a stalwart of the Black Press. The *Baltimore Afro-American*, initiated in 1892,

---

51. *The Hilltop*, 22 February 1963: The unions included Steamfitters Local 602; Electricians Local 26; Sheet Metal Workers Local 102; Plumbers Local 5; Carpenters Locals 132, 1126 and 1590; Cement Finishers Local 891; Ironworkers Local 5; Plumber-Laborers Local 115; and Laborers Local 74.

52. David Taft Terry, "'Trampling for Justice:' The Dismantling of Jim Crow in Baltimore, 1942-1954," Ph.D. dissertation, Howard University, 2005, 5.

53. Charles J. Holden, et.al., *Republican Populist: Spiro Agnew and the Origins of Donald Trump's America*, Charlottesville: University of Virginia Press, 2019, 42-43.

maintained an offshoot in Washington and a scion of the organ's founding family, George Murphy, was a bulwark of radicalism, including the Communist Party.[54]

* * *

The failure of the NAACP to stand with the labor left at a moment of intense struggle was an inflection point shaping events to come, including the arrival at H.U. of racially segregated building trade unions. Yes, there was unremitting pressure on the association to do so but it was a self-inflicted wound, nonetheless. For this grouping, founded in 1909 virtually from the inception had strength in the strategically sited city that was Washington. As early as December 1914, the group held "the most spirited meeting" at H.U.,[55] this campus being "the first college to establish a chapter" with a membership of about 50 early on, but by January 1915 this had ballooned to 250, a truly spectacular rise. It was expected that by March this number would grow to 500 or more or about a third of the entire student body.[56]

By 1919—the year of revolt—the District branch, it was announced, "passed through the most successful and prosperous year of its existence" with "more than 6,000 paid up new members" as "efforts against segregation and discrimination in the federal service have continued without permission...."[57] With its proximity to power, it was hardly revelatory when NAACP leader, Walter White, was instructed in 1934 that the District was "the most strategic point in the country for the NAACP...."[58] By 1937 Roy Wilkins, then second in command at the association, acknowledged that "for many years" the District branch "has been one of the greatest, if not the greatest, money raisers among the branches"; in fact, "for thirteen years—1920-1932 inclusive—the branch has sent in to the national office roughly an average of $2,000 a year...by far the largest sent consistently to the national office by any branch...."[59]

---

54. Hayward Farrar, *The Baltimore Afro-American, 1892-1950,* Westport: Greenwood, 1998.
55. Report from H.U., 1 December 1914, Box G39, *NAACP Papers-Library of Congress.*
56. Annual Report, 26 January 1915, Box G39.
57. Report, 19 January 1919, Box G34, *NAACP Papers.*
58. Robert McGuire, Washington branch to Walter White, 14 April 1934, Box G38, *NAACP Papers.*
59. Memo from Roy Wilkins, 19 April 1937, Box G38.

But by 1948, the NAACP crossed the Rubicon decisively as founder W.E.B. Du Bois was purged unceremoniously on anticommunist grounds, shearing the group ideologically and practically: by 1950, as the purge was applied more broadly on the convention floor, one of the staunchest anticommunists, Attorney Jack Greenberg, was "twice ordered to leave...by delegates who thought he was a Communist...." This was done "because a large number of white people who had opposed the resolution on Communist infiltration" were of European ancestry, meaning "some of the persons who were opposed to the resolution on communism actually resorted to race-baiting themselves" to demonstrate their ideological adherence. The witness to this travesty, Clarence Mitchell, a Negro from a vaunted Baltimore family who went on to become a key figure in Washington, was even queried about his purported Communist ties.[60] As the NAACP tied itself in knots in an attempt to adhere to the latest fashion, the broader movement was weakened, the working class Negro was abandoned, and the stage was set for the inchoate revolt of 1968.

* * *

Historically—and even today—one of the major political issues in the District has been "home rule" which arrived in a truncated sense decades ago but still does not include meaningful congressional representation. Over the decades defenestration of the District politically has been the strategic objective of Dixiecrats in particular, often meaning politicos on Maryland and Virginia borders—and points southward. It was in 1959, as the anti-Jim Crow movement was accelerating that Congressman William Jennings Bryan Dorn of South Carolina, stressed that "being without local political control" in the capital "might minimize the possibility of revolutions arising from the local populace to overthrow the government, similar to those characteristic of Paris...." This putative radicalism was shaped by the "Negro situation," he thought; "these are some of the more practical reasons why Home Rule has not been granted," adding emphatically, "I am bitterly opposed to Home Rule"; the latter "would lead to statehood," meaning "two [U.S.] Senators controlled by socialistic influences...."[61]

---

60. Clarence Mitchell to Walter White, 28 June 1950, Part IX: 47, *NAACP Papers*. See also Denton Watson, *Lion in the Lobby*, Lanham, Maryland: University Press of America, 2002.

61. Congressman Dorn to Susie Wicker of American Association of University Women, 10 April 1959, Box 49, *William Jennings Bryan Dorn Papers, University of South Carolina-Columbia*.

Dixiecrats felt they were preyed on in majority Black Washington. By 1963 a constituent of Congressman William Colmer of Mississippi who was irked about travelling to the District with "Mississippi license plates," a presumed signal to antiracists that could lead to harassment. "Obtain courtesy license plates for us from any state of from [D.C.]," cried Gaulden Smith of Hattiesburg. [62] Yet, Dixiecrats were in no mood for compromise after such incidents and, in fact, were more than willing to punish African Americans further.

The angst borne by the Congressmen may have been realized further in 1970 when Pentagon chief, Melvin Laird, was en route to the White House, possibly to plot further violent maneuvers in Indo-China, when his limousine convoy was halted by a raucous student demonstration. Washington not only had a Black majority, it also contained a significant number of college matriculants enraged by the prospect of being conscripted for war. Even high school students were caught up in the vortex of dissent as the Secret Service—tasked with providing security for those at the highest level—expressed grave concern over the security of the White House itself. Senator George McGovern announced solemnly that the nation was "'experiencing its worst crisis since the Civil War.'"[63]

* * *

What served to define Washington was not only the overwhelming presence of the federal government but—as well, the existence there of universities, Howard in the first instance. And H.U. was not just marked by the presence of Communists, e.g., Hunton and Wilkerson. Historically, there had been a Black Nationalist influence too, which grew in potency as the Red Scare debilitated its intermittent Communist competition. But as early as 1924, Marcus Garvey, the Jamaican leader appeared at Howard, sponsored by the both the Caribbean Club and the NAACP branch: "enthusiasm ran high," said an observer as "students...eagerly pushed their way into the chapel whose seating capacity proved quite inadequate for the occasion. Professors, deans and outside professional men formed a part of the vast audience. The varsity yell followed by voluminous applause resounded...."[64]

---

62. Gaulden Smith to Congressman Colmer, 14 June 1963, Box 443, *William Colmer Papers, University of Southern Mississippi-Hattiesburg.*
63. *Washington Star,* 6 May 1970.
64. *The Hilltop* [H.U. organ], 22 January 1924.

The sponsorship of the Caribbean Club was an emblem of the imbedded Pan-Africanism that existed at Howard, which influenced the campus toward internationalism, then anti-imperialism. By 1928, the future Founding Father of modern Nigeria, Nnamdi Azikiwe told the H.U. community, "we are living in a new era...an age of nationalism"; thus, it was "essential that the African speak and open his mind to his Afro-American brother...." This campus, he claimed rightfully, was "becoming an international center for the diffusion of knowledge among Negroes the world over...."[65]

Actually, the matter was more profound than the Nigerian founder described. By 1937, Bernard Powers, a Negro Howardite, was toiling in the Soviet Union as a highway engineer; he had graduated in 1929 as a civil engineer but racism drove him overseas after waiting tables on a train: "American railways have the most highly educated waiters and porters of any railway system in the world," was the view of his interlocutor, speaking of this Negro corps. This Huntsville, Alabama native arrived in the Soviet Union in 1931 and promptly began work on the Kiev-Moscow highway before moving on to the Pamir Mountains, standing as a symbol of the failed promise of capitalism and the spreading sway of H.U.[66]

By 1960, the announcement was made that "within the past four years the foreign student enrollment" at H.U. had "doubled. During the 1959-1960 school year 706 students from 54 foreign countries were enrolled giving Howard the highest percentage of foreign students...among American colleges and universities...."[67] By 1971, the student newspaper was being circulated in the Caribbean, Soviet Union, Canada, Britain and China.[68]

This was a continuation of past trends. It was in 1892 that the H.U. president announced gloatingly that students matriculated there "from almost every state...while some are from the West Indies, Africa and Japan," making Howard a window through which the world could seek to comprehend the U.S. and not always to the advantage of the republic.[69] Just before this announcement, Senator John Tyler Morgan of Alabama railed viciously against the very idea of home rule in the District. He believed, "'[you] burn down the barn to get rid of the rats...the rats being the Negro population and the barn being

---

65. *The Hilltop*, 7 November 1928.
66. *The Hilltop*, 31 May 1937.
67. *The Hilltop*, 30 September 1960.
68. *The Hilltop*, 19 November 1971.
69. "Report [of] the President of Howard University to the Secretary of the Interior," Washington: GPO, 1892, *Schomburg Center-New York Public Library*.

the government of the District of Columbia,'"[70] words not presenting the republic in an ideal light to those matriculating at Howard.

Howard had to do double duty in part because its peers were drenched in the putridness of white supremacy. From its inception in 1887, Catholic University admitted Negroes—until World War, then desegregated again in 1936.[71] As for Georgetown University, not-withstanding the fact that it was sited in a neighborhood that since the late 19th century had become increasingly Black, the school had never enrolled an African American through the 1940s; it was then that protests erupted at the medical school which Jim Crowed Negro patients and had no Black students or physicians.[72] As for the U.S. Naval Academy, across the border in Annapolis, by September 1941 a commentator found it "ironic that of all southern universities," this training ground was "by far the most intolerant,"[73] quite a claim given the existence of Ole Miss or the University of Mississippi; however, in light of the U.S. Navy and its demonstrated resistance to incorporating Negroes, a reality buttressed by the inbreeding occurring on the float-ing communities that were ships, this was an understandable claim.[74]

And though H.U. was ostensibly a university designed for Negroes, it was the mentor of Martin Luther King, Jr.—Benjamin Mays—who underscored that "for many years prior to 1920 a sub-stantial number of the white women physicians in Washington were graduates of Howard. "The *first woman*," he stressed, "in the United States to graduate from a university affiliated law school was a Black graduate of Howard, Charlotte E. Ray of the Class of 1872."[75] In sum, H.U. was not only a democratizing force nationally—and globally—it was also a solvent eroding multiple forms of bigotry.

Still, the presence of a corps of educated and well-trained Negroes in the citadel of U.S. power, also meant that it simplified the process of recruiting them to serve imperial interests. James Wormley Jones

---

70. *Washington Post*, 21 June 2022.
71. C. Joseph Nuesse, "Segregation and Desegregation at the Catholic Uni-versity of America," *Washington History*, 9 (Number 1, Spring / Summer 1997): 54-70, 54.
72. Robert Emmett Curran, *A History of Georgetown University: The Rise to Prominence, 1964-1989*, Washington, D.C.: Georgetown University Press, 238.
73. Statement by Curt Riess, September 1941, *Odds and Ends of Boxing, Vol-ume V. University of Notre Dame-South Bend, Indiana.*
74. Paul Stillwell and S.L. Gravely, *Trailblazer: The U.S. Navy's First Black Admiral*, Annapolis: Naval Institute Press, 2010.
75. Benjamin Mays, "The Relevance of Mordecai Wyatt Johnson for Our Times," Howard University, 27 January 1978, *University of Virginia-Charlottesville.*

served as a police officer in Washington, rising to become a detective by 1919. Shortly thereafter, as detailed by historian Holly Roose, he allied with J. Edgar Hoover, the pugnacious bulldog leader of the nascent Federal Bureau of Investigation and infiltrated the organization of Marcus Garvey, the Jamaican born mass leader in Harlem. He was the "first Black investigator," she says, "in order to monitor Black radical activity" on Hoover's behalf. Thus, Jones became the "personal confidant" of Garvey who "gave him the position of adjutant general of the African Legion," a major arm of Garveyism. "Without him," says Roose, "we would know relatively little about the inner working of the UNIA [Universal Negro Improvement Association, Garvey's group] today."[76]

Jones was not unique. In the forefront of those subduing Indigenes in the U.S. neo-colony that was Liberia, were Negroes with ties to the District. Eldridge T. Hawkins grew up there and graduated with military cadet training from M Street High School in 1907. By 1913, he was putting down a rebellion by militant Kissis in Liberia. He also served with the National Guard in the District. One of his comrades in West Africa was John H. Anderson of Alexandria who was quite harsh toward the Grebo.[77]

This is a book about the District in its environs over the decades in the scintillating context of racism and radicalism; among other things, it seeks to show how this global gateway allowed for international influence that—ultimately—served to erode Jim Crow locally and nationally but, thereafter, the African Americans freed from the most pestiferous bigotry that was Jim Crow, faced a boomerang: Washington then became a laboratory for racialized repression, enhancing what came to be called the "prison-industrial complex." This occurred as the "Red Scare" began to fade and was complemented by the "Black Scare" or the idea that youthful African Americans should be jailed as a threat to domestic tranquility. Yet, all the while the intended victims fought back with panache and brio, complicating the already limited shelf-life of U.S. imperialism.

---

76. Holly M. Roose, *Black Star Rising: Garveyism in the West*, Lubbock: Texas Tech University Press, 2022, 31-32.

77. Brian G. Shellum, *African American Officers in Liberia: A Pestiferous Rotation, 1910-1942*, Lincoln: University of Nebraska Press, 2018, 61, 73, 75, 105. Other Howard matriculants involved in Liberia were Henry "Harry" Atwood, born in the District and Dr. Joseph Johnson, who graduated from medical school at Howard. See also Char McCargo Bah, et.al., *African Americans of Alexandria, Virginia: Beacons of Light in the 20th Century*, Charleston: History Press, 2013.

Chapter *1*

Borne by Revolt, 1900-1919

From the arrival in 1622 of settlers to the vicinity of what is now Washington, D.C., uproar prevailed. It was then that the invaders spent years executing depredations against unwelcoming Indigenes: stealing corn, torching villages, and leaving their antagonists bereft. This prepared the land for an influx of enslaved Africans with the aim of constructing settlements. Thus, two centuries later the capital of a so-called "revolutionary republic" was a flourishing market for buying and selling enslaved Africans. Yet in a theme that was to drive change in coming decades, this stain on the national escutcheon—especially as it was seen from overseas—provided impetus for transformation of the status quo.[1]

At the same time, another trend emerged as early as 1807 when the news was reported that a "colored school" opened in Washington. This, at a time when often nationally education for Africans was forbidden.[2]

Another trend espied early on in the District was contradiction: not only was there the awkward juxtaposition of the alleged "cradle of liberty" containing the involuntarily enslaved but the institution that came to be the reigning symbol of education and resistance to bigotry—Howard University—was named after a general who ran amok bloodily against the Indigenous. General O.O. Howard in the post-Civil War wipeout, refused to accede to the demand of the newly freed enslaved in Edisto Island, South Carolina for land but, worse, chose on to crush the Nez Perce in the Far West of North America.[3]

---

1. Chris Meyers Asch and George Derek Musgrove, *Chocolate City: A History of Race and Democracy in the Nation's Capital*, Chapel Hill: University of North Carolina Press, 2017. See also Bob Arnebeck, *Slave Labor in the Capital: Building Washington's Iconic Federal Landmarks*, Charleston: History Press, 2014.
2. Undated Clipping, *W.E. MacClenny Papers, University of Virginia-Charlottesville.*
3. Daniel J. Sharfstein, *Thunder in the West: Chief Joseph, Oliver Otis Howard and the Nez Perce War*, New York: Norton, 2017, 173.

With a similar level of contradiction, Barry Farm in the District was built in 1867 when the Freedmen's Bureau bought 375 acres of Julia and David Barry's tobacco farm to sell same to Africans migrating from plantations. In turn the profits helped to fund emerging institutions such as Howard University and within a few years hundreds of Black families—including three sons of Frederick Douglass—were living in what is now Southeast Washington. But again—contradictorily—this neighborhood where streets were named after antislavery heroes, faced demolition by 2019.[4]

It was also during Reconstruction that four Black communities arose in Montgomery County, Maryland and adjacent Northwest Washington—Reno City, Scotland, Tobytown, and Macedonia-Moses, also known as River Road—all signifying how the District was to develop a majority Black population.[5] Something similar can be said about North Brentwood, between Hyattsville to the north and Brentwood to the south, the first incorporated Negro municipality in Prince George's County, Maryland, formed during the era of World War I, albeit with roots in the late 19th century: Randallstown was renamed North Brentwood in 1924.[6]

This was part of the process that created what came to be called—ironically—"Chocolate City," the capital of World Imperialism. Thus, between 1800 and 1900, the District's Negro population increased almost 50 percent to create one of the most significant and arguably largest Black populations in the U.S. For the longest time, the weight of this community existing in sight of the international community also meant that this ordinarily besieged minority was allowed to patronize the Carnegie Library at Mount Vernon Square, board and ride local streetcars, and enjoy sumptuous repasts in federal cafeterias.[7]

The scholar, Eric Yellin, is not far wrong when he argues that the District was the "nation's most important city for African Americans at the turn of the twentieth century," a status consolidated in 1912 when every dollar printed, carried the signature of a Negro, who happened to be Register of the U.S. Treasury. At this juncture, Negroes resided, he says, in virtually every quadrant of the city and it was then that a measure to segregate streetcars was defeated soundly. Racial matters deteriorated after the ascension of William Howard Taft as president, then accelerated with the election of his successor, Woodrow Wilson, in

4. *Washington Post*, 22 September 2019.
5. *Washington Post*, 7 July 2019.
6. *Washington Post*, 6 July 2019.
7. Ibid., Asch and Musgrove, 206.

1916. The latter's party—the Democrats—saw echoes of Reconstruction when they espied Washington, which did not bode well. South Carolina's Ben Tillman actually anticipated apartheid in calling for passbooks or internal passports for Negroes. Thus, shortly, rigid Jim Crow descended on Washington and some African Americans began studying Spanish and considering emigration.[8] Yet Taft's Republicans were no prize: the portly politico segregated census takers by 1910, paving the way for Wilson's more sweeping edicts.[9]

During the Civil War, an aphorism that emerged was whether the nation could exist half-slave and half-free. With enhanced forays abroad by U.S. imperialism in the 1890s—Hawaii, the Philippines, Cuba, Puerto Rico—and the intensification of white supremacy, the point emerged as to whether darker peoples could exist easily in a nation that was rampaging abroad against those that resembled them. Washington happened to be adjoined to Virginia, a Jim Crow fortress whose influence easily crossed the river that divided the two jurisdictions. The Democratic Party machine pioneered by the oligarchy known as the Byrd family—relentless enforcers of Jim Crow—was viewed widely as the single most potent political operation in the entire nation. By 1902 the commonwealth's constitution barred Negroes from the electorate and sought to deny this group education as well. Mississippi, often thought to be the master of disenfranchisement was viewed by analyst V.O. Key as a "'hotbed of democracy'" by way of comparison.[10]

But contradiction ensued for coming to maturity in Arlington at the same time was George P. Cooper who after a stint as an army officer, migrated to the Bureau of Printing and Engraving—which was becoming a hotbed of anti-Jim Crow activism—then wedding Esther Irving, who became head of the local NAACP chapter—then gave birth in 1917 to Esther Cooper, who went on to become a leading Black radical activist of the century.[11]

Unsurprisingly, by 1905 the historian Carter G. Woodson was made aware of a question that emerged from the home of the Cavaliers.

---

8. Eric S. Yellin, *Racism in the Nation's Service: Government Workers and the Color Line in Woodrow Wilson's America*, Chapel Hill: University of North Carolina Press, 2013, 4, 11, 16, 20, 66, 82, 88.

9. Haynes Johnson, *Dusk at the Mountain: The Negro, the Nation and the Capital; A Report on Problems and Progress*, Garden City: Doubleday, 1963, 226.

10. Larissa M. Smith, "Where the South Begins: Black Politics and Civil Rights Activism in Virginia, 1930-1951," Ph.D. dissertation, Emory University, 2001, 7, 30, 33.

11. *New York Times*, 1 September 2022.

There was a "swelling migration of colored men and women from the South," said an observant New Yorker, as "one half of the counties of Virginia have less colored population today than they had ten years ago. Where have they gone to?"[12] They headed northward, not just to the District but as far away as Philadelphia, New York, and Boston, transforming politics as they generally obtained the right to vote as they migrated.

These Negroes may have done well to escape the District too or at least scurry as far away from the Mason-Dixon Line as was possible. Thus, when Baltimore's Negro champion pugilist Joe Gans beat "Battling" Nelson, Euro-American fans of the latter in Washington seized the opportunity to exact revenge by attacking Black residents. Two years later when Nelson beat Gans and claimed the crown of conquest, Negroes—in anticipation of 1919—retaliated by pummeling the victor's devotees. Washington may have bordered Virginia, but it also contained an intelligentsia allowing for the circulation of combative ideas. For not only was the Carnegie Library open to Negroes, so was the Library of Congress, which held a vast assortment of works that could fuel subversion.[13]

Given the proximity of this Maryland metropolis to the District, it may not have been coincidental that Gans' wins and losses struck a chord. Segregationist propulsion there provided impetus to similar trends in the District. In 1911 the City Council barred establishment of Negro churches, schools, and businesses within traditionally Euro-American neighborhoods, which was then echoed regionally, then stretching through Dixie and as far west as Kansas City.[14]

Coincidentally, it was in 1912 that the first NAACP chapter to be led entirely by African Americans was organized in the District [15] and this too was a landmark. The city presented the chapter with multiple issues to confront, especially after the onset of the tenure of President Woodrow Wilson. By 1913, the Baltimore branch of the Association was hosting Oswald Garrison Villard, scion of a prominent abolitionist family and a noted activist in his own right. He

---

12. F. Pitts, Jr. to Whitefield McKinley, 12 September 1905, Reel 2, *Carter G. Woodson Papers, Library of Congress, Washington, D.C.*
13. Ibid., Kenneth Robert Janken, *Rayford W. Logan*, 13, 16.
14. Marvin Chiles, "'Down Where the South Begins': Black Richmond Activism Before the Modern Civil Rights Movement, 1899-1930," *Journal of African-American History*, 105 (Number 1, Winter 2020): 56-82, 68-69.
15. Brett William Beemyn, "A Queer Capital: Lesbian, Gay and Bisexual Life in Washington, D.C., 1890-1955," Ph.D. dissertation, University of Iowa, 1997, 53.

castigated the Bureau of Engraving and Printing for their segregation of "colored clerks" compelled to sit at "separate tables and in
separate sections." At the office of the Auditor for the Post Office
"segregation has gone further than anywhere else," he charged hotly.
This was a "clear illustration of the fact," he added, "that the basis
of the whole segregation is caste and not race...." Wilson, he said,
was "behind the times" as evidenced by his "steadfast opposition
to women's suffrage...." Worse, his backwardness was being emu-
lated in the states, e.g., the "Collector of Internal Revenue at Atlanta"
who announced that there should be "'no government positions for
Negroes in the South; a negro's place is in the cornfield.'" Villard felt
betrayed in that he voted for Wilson for president in 1912. "I worked
for him" in Trenton, he said dismayingly. But repression bred resistance, he concluded hopefully for "not since the Reconstruction
period, perhaps, not since the Civil War has there been such a splendid volume of protest on behalf of the colored people as has just"
been displayed during "these last two months."[16]

Villard was joined by the NAACP's chief operative, W.E.B. Du
Bois, who in 1913 observed that "the very presence of the capitol
and of the federal flag has drawn colored people" to the District but
now with the arrival in force of the Democrats "never before has the
federal government discriminated against its civilian employees on
the ground of color. Every such act heretofore has been that of an
individual state" but nowadays "behind screens and closed doors
they [employees] now sit apart as though leprous."[17]

Still, this was a relatively small city with a heavy concentration
of Jim Crow advocates, distilled from the worst Dixie had to offer.
Predictably, in 1908 Congressman "Cotton Tom" Heflin of Alabama
shot and wounded a Black man with scant retribution who—it
was claimed—had been using salty language on a streetcar.[18] Par-
adoxically, since streetcars were not segregated—unlike most of
Dixie—this created combustibility of a unique sort.[19]

Ostensibly, this was an accidental confrontation but given the
simmering and underlying infra-politics, it was structured by intentionality. For it was in 1907 that Congressman Charles Edwards of

---

16. Oswald Garrison Villard, "Segregation in Baltimore and Washington: An
Address Delivered Before the Baltimore Branch of the [NAACP]," 20 October 1913, *University of Virginia-Charlottesville*.
17. O.G. Villard, W.E.B. Du Bois and Moorfield Storey to President Wilson,
15 August 1913, Box G34, *NAACP Papers*.
18. Ibid., Asch and Musgrove, 209.
19. Ibid., Kenneth Robert Janken, 17.

Georgia, aghast at what he witnessed in this citadel of white supremacy, demanded that all Negroes be removed from holding federal offices, which would have ripple effects nationally too.[20] This was hardly trivial since by the late 19th century out of about 23,000 federal employees in the District, more than 10 percent were Negroes, including 337 out of 6,000 at the Interior Department.[21]

In a repetitive occurrence, Dixiecrats protested the serving of Negroes in a cafeteria on Capitol Hill.[22] When his fellow Democrat Woodrow Wilson from New Jersey by way of Virginia entered the White House a few years later, Edwards' febrile dream crept closer to reality.

Compared to neighboring Virginia, the District was perceived as a "Negro Heaven." There were steady government jobs and, comparatively, educational opportunities often unavailable elsewhere for Negroes. There were fissures however in this celestial constellation, as suggested by trends redolent of New Orleans and Charleston: i.e., a lighter skinned Negro population that often overlapped and coincided with elite status. This phenomenon attracted the attention of the conservative columnist, Thomas Sowell. He observed, "this small group of families married among themselves to such an extent that it became noted for birth defects"; their "fertility rates" were "too low even to replace themselves...." As he saw things, the movement toward desegregation, post-1954 led to the decline of Dunbar High School (formerly M Street High), as more opportunities arose for those who otherwise might have attended this school. Still, during the heyday of Dunbar, says this Negro right-winger, this institution "was as remote from whites as if it were on Mars...."[23]

As noted, this sector was not always enthused about being grouped with their poorer and darker brethren, leaving them more susceptible to the often cruel whims of the Euro-American majority, as solidarity withered. Thus, this sector was notorious for petty skullduggery, envies, malicious gossiping—parodying the petit bourgeoisie. Exacerbating the fraught climate was the untrammeled Jim Crow to which they were subjected, as when realtors refused to show them homes in

20. *Washington Herald*, 21 May 1907, Box 15, *Constance Green Papers, Library of Congress, Washington, D.C.*

21. Constance McLaughlin Green, *The Secret City: A History of Race Relations in the Nation's Capital*, Princeton: Princeton University Press, 1967,

22. *Washington Star*, 14 May 1909, Box 15, *Constance Green Papers*.

23. Thomas Sowell, "Black Excellence: The Case of Dunbar High School," *The Public Interest*, (Number 34, Spring 1974): 3-21, Box 426, *Edward Brooke Papers, Library of Congress, Washington, D.C.*

fashionable Le Droit Park. Again, these malignant trends were solidified as U.S. imperialism attained liftoff and as the high court—housed
in Washington, of course—hardened Jim Crow in the "Plessy v. Ferguson" case of 1896. In response, a number of Negro businessmen
in the middle stratum accelerated their own form of discrimination
against the poorer and darker skinned in barbershops, restaurants
and the like, often at the behest of Euro-American patrons.

Yet Washington was the city of contradiction—capital of a
white supremacist state with a burgeoning Black working class
population—and this was reflected further when in 1898 the National
Afro-American Council convened there, often dubbed as the first genuinely nationwide human rights organization. At the same time, one
analyst opines that "Washington prejudice"—even then—was "more
intense than is found in most cities in the South." Other than the southeast of the city, Negroes were pinned in an area from S Street to Florida
Avenue and from 7th Street to 16th Street, the "Shaw" area in short.
By 1920 there were scores of Black businesses festooned thereabouts
including bistros, drugstores, funeral homes, medics, attorneys, gro-
cers, with Howard University, the Freedmen's Hospital, Dunbar High
School, and the Howard Theater as the joint sun around which these
other planets revolved. The latter was a lodestar of music, creating
an environment from which sprung the premier artist, composer and
conductor: Edward "Duke" Ellington. This auditorium debuted in
1910 and came to seat 1,500, rivalling the better known Apollo in Harlem, which arrived on the scene four years later.[24]

Before both the Apollo and the Howard Theater, African Americans began organized basketball with the District producing some of
the stalwarts of this quintessential urban sport.[25]

Also rivalling Harlem's preeminence as the cultural motherlode is
the credible thesis that the cultural renaissance that bears the name
of this Manhattan neighborhood could just as well be termed the
"Howard Renaissance" or the like. "Many of Black America's future
leaders, writers and scholars were either born, studied or worked in
the shadow of the Capitol," argues scholar Kwame Wes Alford. This

---

24. Elizabeth Dowling Taylor, *The Original Black Elite: Daniel Murray and the
Story of a Forgotten Era*, New York: HarperCollins, 2017, 66, 101, 163, 168, 170,
174, 248, 346. On Ellington see Gerald Horne, *Jazz and Justice*. See also Cam-
eron Logan, *Historic Capital: Preservation, Race and Real Estate in Washington,
D.C.*, Minneapolis: University of Minnesota Press, 2017.
25. Bob Kuska, *Hot Potato: How Washington and New York Gave Birth to Black
Basketball and Changed America's Game Forever*, Charlottesville: University of
Virginia Press, 2004, 7.

lengthy list includes, he says, "Sterling Brown, Jean Toomer, Jessie Fauset, E. Franklin Frazier, Angelina Weld Grimke, Abram Harris, Langston Hughes, Alain Locke, Kelly Miller, Charles H. Wesley, Carter G. Woodson"—and, of course, Ellington. The District, he adds, "served as the center of the African American professional class," not least because of the formidable presence of Howard. Mary Church Terrell, the doyenne of this stratum, argued convincingly that there were more well-educated and well-to-do "'colored people [that] resided in Washington than in any other city in the world.'" Their ranks were augmented annually by an influx of Africans from the Caribbean and the continent itself, with those from the latter arriving there in sustaining numbers as early as 1872. Correspondingly, Howard alumnus John Henry Smyth served as chief U.S. envoy to Liberia as early as 1878. Similarly, by the early 1920s Howard was teaching courses in African history, saluted as "'the first courses of this kind ever at the undergraduate level in Europe or America.'"[26]

Likewise, by 1900 the District had a complement of Negro professionals, outstripping other communities with Howard again being critical in this process. Then there were an estimated 400 Negro teachers; 50 physicians; 90 pastors; 30 attorneys.[27]

Howard, an emerging research university replete with professional schools, including a law school that employed and trained attorneys—e.g., Charles Hamilton Houston and Thurgood Marshall—who led the jurisprudential charge against Jim Crow, was equaled if not exceeded in importance by M Street High School, which was to become Dunbar High School. Alumni included numerous luminaries, including General Benjamin O. Davis, Judge William Hastie, Dr. Charles Drew, and writer Jean Toomer.[28] It was in 1905 that Booker T. Washington himself announced without exaggeration in speaking of this secondary school that "'failure here is not local but national and success here is not local but national,'" indicative of the District's importance to the overall trajectory of Black America.[29]

Washington knew the District well and not only because he was one of the few Negroes allowed to enter the White House as a guest. The "Tuskegee Wizard" relied heavily on the counsel of Whitefield McKinlay, whose roots were in South Carolina, but he

26. Kwame Wes Alford, "A Prophet Without Honor: William Leo Hansberry and the Origins of the Discipline of African Studies," Ph.D. dissertation, University of Missouri, 1998, 65, 66, 72.
27. Ibid., Constance McLaughlin Green, 131.
28. Ibid., Kenneth Robert Janken, 18.
29. Ibid., Asch and Musgrove, 216.

headed northward as Reconstruction was decomposing. In the District, he became a confidant of Washington, who relied upon him for recommendations for various government posts. Typically, he was perceived as "mulatto" with close "octoroon" and "quadroon" ties.[30]

Also ensconced in this pigmentocracy was Richard Greener, also displaced from a decomposing Reconstruction South Carolina, who became Dean of Howard's Law School by the late 19th century, then a U.S. diplomat in Vladivostok by 1904 at a turning point in the tortured history of white supremacy,[31] with ramifications reaching North America: Japan's epochal victory over Russia.[32]

The fissiparousness of Negro Washington often turned on the "colorism" that McKinlay and those of his ilk were thought to embody but also was not absent from the esteemed high school that Booker T. Washington celebrated. Edward Brooke, born in 1919, who attained fame as one of the few Negroes elected to the U.S. Senate in the 20th century—Massachusetts in his case, though he was born in Washington—matriculated at Dunbar High School and happened to be of a lighter hue too. He was popularly elected to this august body in 1966. He chose to retain a newspaper clipping that referred to this school as "the greatest for Blacks that the United States has ever produced...."[33]

One of the stellar graduates of this venerable institution was Nannie Helen Burroughs who graduated with honors but in the 1890s. This orator, activist, and feminist was rejected by the public schools of the District as a teacher: it was "likely"—said a recent analysis—"because of the prejudice of colorism...a preference for the lighter skinned," which did not include this dark-skinned intellectual.[34]

This was hardly minor, for not long after Kelly Miller, soon to distinguish himself at Howard, said ambiguously though pointedly that "there are ten thousand surplus women of color at the National Capital,"[35] at least suggesting mass unemployment.

---

30. Editorial Note, circa 1905, Reel 2, *Carter G. Woodson Papers*.

31. Katherine Reynolds Chaddock, *Uncompromising Activist: Richard Greener, the First Black Graduate of Harvard College*, Baltimore: John Hopkins University Press, 2017.

32. Gerald Horne, *Race War! White Supremacy and the Japanese Attack on the British Empire*, New York: New York University Press, 2004.

33. *Washington Post*, 20 April 2001, Box 700, *Edward Brooke Papers, Library of Congress, Washington, D.C.*

34. *Washington Post*, 28 February 2021 and 1 March 2021.

35. Kelly Miller, *Radicals and Conservatives and Other Essays on the Negro in America*, New York: Schocken, 1908, 187 [republished: 1968]

Like the District as a whole, M Street High School—or Dunbar—too, was contradictory. Colorism aside, this institution was decades ahead of typical U.S. high schools—Negro or otherwise—in its emphasis on African American history and culture. Yet, graduates included not only Sterling Brown, the Howard professor who became a renowned specialist on Black culture and Allison Davis, also a prominent Negro scholar, but the aforementioned novelist, Toomer, who chose to cross the color line—and "pass."[36]

Dunbar's sparkle also attracted the dedicated attention of the conservative scholar, Thomas Sowell. He contended that in 1899 this secondary school "came in first in citywide tests given in both black and white schools...." This was an outgrowth, he said, of the point that "as far back as 1830 half the Negroes in Washington were free" and "before the civil war started, 78 percent of the blacks in Washington were free....." Resultingly, the city attracted Negroes from due south who were seeking adequate education, reinforcing pre-existing strengths of the District. It was "Mecca," says Sowell, "for those free Negroes seeking a better life...." Thus, "the federal government's presence made Washington less oppressive than the Southern Slave states'"[37]—yet another reason for the federal government and the city that housed it to be despised in Dixie.

However, this color cleavage was hardly peculiar to Dunbar; it was an endemic component of the landscape, fueled by the poisonous legacy of enslavement, wherein the offspring of slaveholders or those who resembled them, inherited social capital. In the late 19th century, pupils at yet another local District school complained that a teacher was favoring those of lighter complexion.[38]

Correspondingly, what was described as a "color battle" erupted among Howard students, this one involving not only Negroes but also Euro-Americans who—tellingly—were not sufficient numerically to elect one of their own as a class valedictorian so they moved to their next option: nominating a light-skinned Negro. The darker skinned responded by nominating what was described as an "Indian colored Negro." A deadlock ensued, perhaps an unavoidable result of the politics of the epidermis.[39]

---

36. David A. Varel, *The Lost Black Scholar: Resurrecting Allison Davis in American Social Thought*, Chicago: University of Chicago Press, 2018, 20, 49, 52.

37. Thomas Sowell, "Black Excellence: The Case of Dunbar High School," 1974, Box 426, *Edward Brooke Papers, Library of Congress, Washington, D.C.*

38. *Washington Bee*, 11 May 1889, Box 15, *Constance Green Papers, Library of Congress, Washington, D.C.*

39. *Washington Bee*, 24 December 1887, Box 15, *Constance Green Papers.*

Accelerating these noxious trends was the inescapable fact that the Howard faculty included a number of Euro-Americans.[40]

Given the color obsessed society in which Washington was centered, Euro-Americans' very presence served to create an epidermal hierarchy. At the turn of the 20th century, the District was said to house "18,000 mulattoes" who comprised much of the "middle class"—along with "700 octoroons" and "1,100 quadroons." They were a substantial percentage of the District's Negro population, which amounted to about 30 percent, dropping to 28.5 percent in 1910,[41] helping to set the tone of the area—in more ways than one.

* * *

A crucial element of the anti-racist brigades in the District was the NAACP. And a critical element of the Association there was the branch at Howard. This became clear as early as 1915 when students, staff, and educators launched a protest against the cinematic defamation known as *Birth of a Nation* which justified the rise of the Ku Klux Klan as it libeled Reconstruction, the era following the U.S. Civil War. George Hall, president of this chapter, railed against this "photo drama" and, importantly, delivered his protest directly to his neighbor: President Woodrow Wilson, along with local political leaders and newspapers. "We expect to fight it," speaking of the film, "before it gets here," he warned. He and his fellow militants were inaugurating "discussions of the social, economic and political conditions of the Negro in states from which our members come," which portended protests extending nationally from Howard. Adopting the viewpoint to assault the antagonist at his strength, Hall advised that Mississippi was the "first state chosen" to target. "Tell us what our chapters at Cornell and Lincoln [Pennsylvania] are doing," he instructed Association leaders. He already knew that Virginia Union University, due south, was "disorganized." Complementarily, the branch's next meeting was slated to focus on premier leader, Booker T. Washington: "we expect an interesting meeting," Hall added elliptically.[42]

Revealingly, Howard as a magnet for students from Dixie, leveraged this trend to stand as a citadel for anti-Jim Crow activism. The

---

40. Ibid., Constance McLaughlin Green, 130.
41. Ibid., Constance McLaughlin Green, 141. Cf. Ibid., Asch and Musgrove, 226: The Negro population, they say, was 38.5% in 1910; 25.1% in 1920; and 27.1% in 1930.
42. George Hall to May Childs Nerny, 18 December 1915, Box G39, *NAACP Papers*.

chapter strived to make sure that newspapers from this benighted region were to be found in the campus library. Naturally, the chapter sought to bolster likeminded efforts at Virginia Union.[43] As a result of this activism, by early 1916 the chapter had 121 members who had paid the $.50 cent enrollment fee in full.[44]

The university was the lodestar of Black Washington and within strolling distance was the headquarters of what was to become today's premier African American intellectual organization, then known as the Association for the Study of Negro Life & History. Headed by leading scholar, Carter G. Woodson, who maintained an intermittent relationship with Howard, the group published an outstanding scholarly journal and sponsored annual meetings featuring laypersons and academics alike who trumpeted a version of the Black past and present distinctly at odds with the Negro-phobic consensus that dominated the academy. In considering the flowering of the Renaissance routinely associated with Harlem, again the District should not be ignored, especially when contemplating the handiwork of Dr. Woodson.[45]

His organization's reach extended—importantly—to Africa, including the burgeoning metropolis: Lagos, Nigeria. It was in 1917 that Dada Adeshigbin received the latest issue of the journal and was "pleased to know it was edited and published by my own colour. I am impressed by the excellent form," he gushed, adding, "please enroll my name on your list of subscribers...."[46] Also in West Africa the prominent barrister, Casely Hayford writing from today's Ghana, expressed enthusiasm about the journal.[47] D.E. Carney pledged to "communicate with the Gold Coast, Senegambia, Liberia, Nigeria and other countries in Africa" about Dr. Woodson's handiwork.[48]

From Kamloops, Canada John Smith, also an African, expressed interest in the group's work.[49] Jules Rosemond, a Haitian lawyer,

---

43. Annual Report, 31 December 1915, Box G39, *NAACP Papers*.

44. Report, 14 February 1916, Box G39, *NAACP Papers*.

45. *Washington Post*, 1 February 2022.

46. Dada Adeshigbin, to "Dear Sir," 10 January 1917, Reel 3, *Carter G. Woodson Papers, Library of Congress*.

47. Casely Hayford to Dr. Woodson, 15 June 1916, Reel 3, *Carter G. Woodson Papers*.

48. D.E. Carney to Dr. Woodson, 19 January 1921, Reel 3, *Carter G. Woodson Papers*.

49. John Smith to Dr. Woodson, 18 January 1917, Reel 3, *Carter G. Woodson Papers*.

wanted Woodson to publish a book on his homeland.[50] From Guatemala, M.J. Jaramillo reported on activities of Africans there.[51] Similar correspondence was received from Melbourne, Australia.[52] Making it plain, John Pilgrim reporting from the Panama Canal Zone, observed that a number of the Africans there languishing in the bosom of U.S. colonialism—many with roots in the Caribbean—were interested in hearing more about a "'Back to Africa'" campaign.[53]

The emergence of Dr. Woodson's organization inevitably attracted attention beyond the shores of his homeland, helping to generate a kind of Pan-Africanism that had characterized nearby Howard University from its virtual inception. Thus, there was Stansbury Boyce who moved from Baltimore to Trinidad in the early 1850s, before returning after the civil war. He became wealthy and moved to the District. He was fluent in French, Spanish and "a little Italian" he acknowledged, and was the kind of reader that would keep the journal afloat to this very day.[54]

Nonetheless, Dr. Woodson's enterprise was difficult to separate from its proximity to the intellectual scout that was Howard. For at this growing campus was William Leo Hansberry, born in 1894 in Mississippi, who as early as 1912—well before Dr. Woodson's initiative—moved to form what came to be called the "Moorland Foundation," which created what has been dubbed "the first research library in an American university devoted exclusively to material on Blacks...."[55]

Hansberry notwithstanding, the Woodson organization was flourishing in the midst of world war but as Washington entered this titanic conflict dramatically in 1918,[56] inevitably the political climate chilled. Coincidentally, that same year the Howard curriculum shifted to an emphasis on war, with the campus being reconfigured along this line. Barracks were erected, trenches were dug, sentinels were built, and armed guards were placed at the imposing gates to

---

50. Jules Rosemond to Dr. Woodson, 11 January 1919, Reel 3, *Carter G. Woodson Papers.*
51. M.J. Jaramillo to Dr. Woodson, circa 1921, Reel 3.
52. A. Goldsmith to Dr. Woodson, 6 September 1920, Reel 3.
53. John Pilgrim to Dr. Woodson, 30 January 1918, Reel 3.
54. Stansbury Boyce to Dr. Woodson, 1 November 1917, Reel 3, *Carter G. Woodson Papers.*
55. Kwame Wes Alford, "A Prophet Without Honor," 4.
56. Kelly Miller, *History of the World War for Human Rights*, 1919, *University of Virginia-Charlottesville.*

the campus. To complete the transformation, soldiers were quartered in dormitories and university buildings.[57]

In such a forbidding atmosphere a distorted form of patriotic swelling erupted on campus, which was not conducive to radicalism nor progressivism.[58]

However, the rigor of Jim Crow hardly allowed for any surcease of struggle—at least not for long. As the war in Europe was surging in 1916, the pre-eminent Mary Church Terrell strode to the recently opened People's Drugstore at 14th and U Streets N.W., in the vicinity of what was soon to be seen as the epicenter of the Black community. There she simply ordered a glass of soda water and when the clerk refused, protest—predictably—erupted.[59]

Yet this imbroglio was minor compared to what erupted from 19-22 July 1919, when inflamed press coverage about purported Negro transgressions, led to sharp contestation. Soldiers fresh off the boat from combat in Europe added to the unrest, as some feared "outright race war." Hundreds had bought guns from pawnshops or gun dealers, while others relied upon military rifles they had brought home from overseas. More than 30 died and about 150 were injured after about four days and nights of robust conflict. Unlike past conflicts, Negroes—perhaps buoyed by military veterans—fought back vigorously.[60]

The NAACP leadership was panicking, with leader James Weldon Johnson advised of the peril of this "situation over alleged assaults on white women by Negroes...."[61] It was Johnson, the literary stylist, who ascribed "race troubles in Washington" in large measure to "newspapers" that "use [the] phrase 'attack on white women by Negroes.'"[62] In the midst of the bloodletting the District NAACP branch spent time sending letters to "all four of the daily newspapers here calling their attention to the fact that they were sowing the seeds of a race riot by their inflammatory headlines"—though generally they "ignored our warning." Then these campaigners made

---

57. Lopez D. Matthews, Jr., *Howard University in the World War: Men and Women Serving the Nation*, Charleston: History Press, 2018, 33.

58. *Howard University Record*, 12(Number 4, May 1918): 1.

59. Joan Quigley, *Just Another Southern Town: Mary Church Terrell and the Struggle for Equal Justice in the Nation's Capital*, New York: Oxford University Press, 2016, 82.

60. Elizabeth Dowling Taylor, *The Original Black Elite*, 367, 368.

61. James Cobb to James Weldon Johnson, 21 July 1919, Box G34, *NAACP Papers*.

62. James Weldon Johnson to James Cobb, 21 July 1919, Box G34.

an "energetic protest against the arresting of so many colored men while the white men from whom they were attempting to protect themselves were not molested...." In an age-old tactic, "colored prisoners after being taken into station houses were often beaten up and abused by the police officers...."[63] Vainly, the NAACP demanded that the Department of Justice investigate the *Washington Post* for "incitement to riot," especially on the "day the worst disorders occurred" when their headlines were bloodcurdling. Their writers demanded "'mobilization of every available service man'" with the "'purpose'" of a "'cleanup...that will cause the events of the last two evenings to pale into insignificance....'"[64]

As bloodshed spread, John Shillady of the Association telegrammed the White House about "mobs, including United States soldiers, sailors and Marines which have assaulted innocent and unoffending Negroes...men in uniform have attacked Negroes on the streets and pulled [them] from streetcars to beat them"; "cries" of "'there he goes'" would be swiftly followed by an assault.[65] James E. Scott boarded a streetcar and was "attacked by rioters"; a soldier "put his arm across me and said caustically, "'Where are you going nigger?'" while others screamed "'lynch him,' 'kill him,' throw him out of the car window.'" He leapt away—as the conductor fired "three shots at me," according to his sworn affidavit.[66]

On the other hand, one official consulted by Negro attorney, George Hayes, said that "most of the assaults and aggressions were made by white people"—but revealingly, "most of the gunplay was on the part of the colored,"[67] audacity designed to restrain racist bloodlust. This official, Louis Brownlow, informed the Senate bluntly, "I do not believe...there has ever been a city that [has] a larger problem in attempting to keep the streets safe for young women than Washington has had during the war," due to the rampaging of Negro men.

---

63. Statement, 23 July 1919, Box G34.
64. John Shillady to Attorney General A. Mitchell Palmer, 25 July 1919, Box G34.
65. John Shillady to President Wilson, 21 July 1919, Box G34. In the same box, see also "H.J. Res. 155...66th Congress, 1st Session....House..." 22 July 1919: "authorizing the President to use the military forces to preserve order in Washington"; this was a "national scandal" mandating that the authorities "protect the lives and property of all the people in the city irrespective of race or color."
66. Scott Affidavit, 21 July 1919, Box G34.
67. Conversation with Commissioner Brownlow and George Hays, 22 July 1919, 4:10 P.M. Box G34.

There was the related issue of cops seeking "to augment...income from other or questionable sources," notably bootlegging, which was "going on at a pretty lively rate" and enlivening corruption. A legislator then responded, asserting "we have conditions existing in the city of Washington that do not exist in any other city," which was unavoidably true—"a certain number of policemen have to be stationed at all times at the White House." Prompted, another Senator added, "in certain industrial cities...you have a large alien population, a portion of which is fertile soil for Bolshevism" but, he said off-key, "we do not have that population here"; then a colleague piped up, adding, "No, but a man from Philadelphia comes from Washington and explodes his bomb."[68]

A century later, the *Washington Post*, recalled a time when there were four daily newspapers though it appeared that they were competing vigorously as to who could excel in demonizing Negroes. "'Negro fiend pursued by 1,000 posse,'" bellowed one overly caffeinated scribe. So motivated and doubtlessly driven by similar racist episodes in Charleston, South Carolina and Longview, Texas—and even New London, Connecticut—the emergent Ku Klux Klan was spotted motoring through the capital. By fall, there would be two dozen more racist fracases to attract their attention. By mid-September racist mobs had lynched—minimally—43 African Americans, including seven military veterans from this minority murdered in uniform. So inspired, back in Washington, Negro men, women, and children were dragged from streetcars and beaten mercilessly. Like a tossed down gauntlet to the U.S. elite, Negroes were assaulted in front of the White House and the *Washington Post* too. Guns were being bought as if these weapons were akin to barrels of water in a parched desert—500 in one day. On the roof of the Howard Theater, a brief stroll from the university of the same name, a nest of snipers was spotted. Finally, President Wilson ordered thousands of troops to the city, perhaps because—unlike pogroms of the recent past—this unrest featured a rising number of Euro-American casualties.[69]

Also a century later, the historian Jefferson Morley referred to July 1919 as a "neo-Confederate offensive," as Euro-American women and children shouted encouragement, undoubtedly cheered

68. Committee on Police Salaries, 30 July 1919, U.S. Senate, Box 56, RG 46, *Records of U.S. Senate, Committee Papers, Including Hearings, Committee on the District of Columbia, National Archives and Records Administration, Washington, D.C.*
69. *Washington Post*, 19 July 2019.

by citywide chapters of the Sons of Confederate Veterans and the United Daughters of the Confederacy. On the other side of the barricades, Black men converged at 7th and U Streets NW with guns, knives, and clubs. By 2019 the Pennsylvania Avenue sidewalk in front of the Trump Hotel was a magnet for tourists but a century earlier it was a combat zone, and Negroes were dishing out mayhem as they absorbed same. The melanin deficient father of future high court judge, Thurgood Marshall, was chased by "white" mobs for being Black and chased by Negroes as he was misperceived as being part of the racist riffraff. This Negro aggressiveness startled Congress. Tellingly, Congressman J.W. Ragsdale of South Carolina denounced the unrest as the product of a Communist conspiracy—then dropped dead the next day. Predictably, it led to the passage of the District's strongest gun control—ever. The attackers never breached the self-defense line around U Street.[70]

This inchoate revolt ended after three days, according to Howard historian Rayford Logan.[71] As noted, his fellow historian—Carter G. Woodson—was caught in downtown Washington and barely escaped intact. Woodson, about 5' 8" inches tall and about 175 pounds used his size ten shoes adroitly to scurry out of harm's way. His lighter skin did not save him.[72]

Weapons also arrived from Baltimore and were distributed not far from Howard's campus at 7th and T. Afterwards, the *Washington Post* was blamed but there was pre-existing resentment on the part of many Euro-Americans at the presence of a modicum of Negroes with fashionable clothes and expensive cars, hardly the norm citywide but, assuredly, aberrant elsewhere in the nation. There was a mission from Abyssinia in the District then but fortunately—for them and bilateral ties with the republic headquartered there—no reports emerged of nationals of this independent nation being bashed.[73]

These Africans managed to elude what a subsequent journalist described as a "blazing battlefield," and "night[s] of terror unparalleled in Washington's history," as "colored men and women were pulled from trolley cars, manhandled, beaten." Correspondingly, "Negroes repaid some old debts in blood...." What may have prevented further bloodshed was the fact, said Haynes

---

70. *Washington Post*, 21 July 2019.
71. Rayford Logan, *Howard University, The First Hundred Years, 1867-1967*, New York: New York University Press, 1968, 189.
72. Burnis R. Morris, *Carter G. Woodson: History, The Black Press and Public Relations*, Jackson: University Press of Mississippi, 2017, 12-13.
73. Constance McLaughlin Green, *The Secret City*, 191, 192, 193, 195.

Johnson, "providentially a driving rain swept the city" and "mobs dispersed...."[74]

Thus, news of this startling tumult with far-reaching implications may have reached Addis Ababa, if only by resident Abyssinians in the District. More to the point, a takeaway from this unrest was that a sure way to restrain the racists was to fightback vigorously. This was the message conveyed to Black Kansas City in August 1919. "The Negro means to be as merciless in repelling attacks upon him [self] as the attackers," i.e., "worthy of his steel." Continuing in full androcentric mode, John Bruce demanded emphatically, "let us do it MAN FASHION." Bruce too found that "the great number of Negro men in the United States army uniform," trained in combat, made a difference. He too found the class and status dynamic relevant to understanding the disturbance since there was widespread upset at the "freedom" Negroes "enjoy," e.g., a "colored municipal judge passing sentence on black and white alike," along with "school buildings that surpass architecturally and in school equipment the best white schools in the Southern States...." There was the "absence of the Jim Crow car" on public transportation, a novelty of sorts. Above all, he said, there was the "larger casualty list on the side of the instigators," and "among the victims is included one Southern Congressman Rogers of South Carolina who died of 'heart disease' from the effects of a leaden pellet fired from the trusty gun of one of these 'savage Washington Negroes.'"[75]

Indicative of the turmoil that drew Bruce's rapt attention was the 2,000 federal troops dispatched to the heart of riotousness. But Bruce was an example of what a Negro pastor—who called urgently for buying guns—noticed: "'This is a radical age and the old leaders must go,'" a cry bound to resonate in a city that housed national leadership of various stripes.[76] This pastor likely agreed with the conclusion of a recent scholar who found that "most alarming to the

---

74. Haynes Johnson, *Dusk at the Mountain: The Negro, the Nation and the Capital: A Report on Problems and Progress*, Garden City: Doubleday, 1963, 29, 30, 31.

75. *Kansas City Call*, 16 August 1919, "Race Riots", Vertical File, Washington, D.C. *Public Library-Special Collections*.

76. Joan Quigley, *Just Another Southern Town: Mary Church Terrell and the Struggle for Racial Justice in the Nation's Capital*, New York: Oxford University Press, 2016, 89. See also Death Certificates. Record Range 253500-254249, Box 342, #254036, Date of Death, 23 July 1919 for J.W. Ragsdale, Place of Death—1621 Connecticut Avenue. "Cause of Death...Heart...." *Municipal Archives-Washington, D.C.* This South Carolina Congressman evidently was the politico referenced.

white community" then was "the fact that African Americans had armed themselves with guns"; and, perhaps ineluctably, "the aftermath of the riot, tensions between the races surprisingly lessened." Still, quite sobering was the reality that the *Washington Post*, which had been "running a series of articles sensationalizing black crime" in the prelude to the murderous fray,[77] did not seem to draw the appropriate conclusions, as their pages in coming decades continued to rile up the Euro-American majority on racist grounds.

Rayford Logan, who was to become a stellar professor at Howard, subsequently reported that "some of my friends have told me that it was the killing of whites by negroes that helped to bring the riots to an end...guns were brought over from Baltimore...." The conflagration came as no shock to Dr. Logan. For when he was serving militarily in Europe, he "heard white officers say in France: 'Just wait until we return home. We'll put these damn niggers back in their proper place.'"[78]

These officers may have been taken aback by the turn of events at the seat of power. Their projections were not necessarily in accord with the changing temper of the town. There were other factors at play, or at least that was the thought of the "liquor lobby" then battling to restrain broad forces bent on prohibition of their product. As the embers were still glowing in the District a journalist blamed the upheaval on "anti-prohibition" elements who, it was said, "openly welcomed & to some extent planned a 'crime wave' in the nation's capital," then trumpeted by the local press, in order to "illustrate" the "appalling consequences of bone-dryness," i.e., banning alcoholic beverages. The ostensible casus belli also was questioned given the "suspicion that some attacks on white women may have been committed by white men" with "blackened faces in order to stir up race trouble." Like other commentators, this contemporaneous journalist was struck by the point that "'everywhere one can hear expressions of disgust at expensive clothes of successful [Negroes] in [expensive] automobiles....'"[79]

Hence, despite their best—and stalwart—efforts, African Americans continued to be victimized. Less than a year after the July 1919 turbulence, a bloodthirsty mob sought to lynch a Negro in nearby

---

77. Jacqueline M. Moore, *Leading the Race: The Transformation of the Black Elite in the Nation's Capital, 1880-1920*, Charlottesville: University Press of Virginia, 1999, 211, 212.
78. Rayford Logan to "Mrs. Donald R. Green," 9 March 1960, Box 15, *Constance Green Papers, Library of Congress, Washington, D.C.*
79. *Survey*, 2 August 1919, Box 15, *Constance Green Papers*.

Alexandria, Virginia who reportedly had admitted to a double slaying of Euro-Americans in adjacent Arlington. But then a restraining factor intervened: rumors that enraged Negroes from the District would descend on the state en masse in revenge.[80]

It was in March 1919 that James Davis of the District branch was told that "since the [U.S.] entered the war, 109 colored persons (103 men and 6 women) have been lynched. 38 of those occurred from April 6 to December 31, 1917; 63 during 1918; and 8 since January 1, 1919"—excluding those slain in East St. Louis, "estimated from 40 to 175."[81]

Thus, by 1919, as a result of migratory patterns and the disruptive roiling of war, there were an estimated 100,000 additional Negroes in the District since the onset of the war. This meant more targets for opportunistic Dixiecrats and also more haunted memories of Reconstruction. This did not bode well for African Americans.[82]

---

80. *Washington Star*, 27 May 2020, Box 15, *Constance Green Papers*.
81. Secretary to James Davis, Anti-Lynching Committee, 28 March 1919, Box G34, *NAACP Papers*.
82. Eric S. Yellin, *Racism in the Nation's Service*, 179.

Chapter *2*

Aftermath of Revolt, 1920s

30 May 1922 was a festive day in the District: the Lincoln Memorial was dedicated on the National Mall. Among the dignitaries assembled was William Howard Taft, former president and then Chief Justice. But the most consequential role that the corpulent politico played was editor—or censor—in-chief. For the roly-poly politician decided that the words of the only Negro speaker, which stridently objected to the insidious Jim Crow that toxified the land were wholly inappropriate: Robert Russa Moton, the son of a man born into slavery, was muffled. Equality was off the agenda and so were the words of Moton, who followed Booker T. Washington in leading the Tuskegee Institute. Appropriately for the moment, the seating, too, was subjected to racist segregation.[1] This insult was predictable. After all, just before this spectacle, President Warren Harding travelled to Birmingham, Alabama and backed Jim Crow laws.[2] It was in late 1922 as Harding still rode high in the presidential saddle that NAACP leader, Walter White, argued, "segregation is more prevalent in the Departments at Washington today than ever before...."[3]

Vigilantly, the NAACP had sought to bar their constituents' exclusion from this solemn occasion. "Such a ceremony should not be held without the participation of our group therein," insisted District branch leader, Shelby Davidson.[4] "Segrega[tion] [of] the colored people," said the NAACP vainly, "has not therefore been practiced in this city by the Government at such gatherings,"[5] a narrowly legalistic interpretation. But it was all for naught for as Davidson averred,

---

1. *Washington Post*, 29 March 2022.
2. Jill Watts, *The Black Cabinet*, 31.
3. White to Shelby Davidson, 19 December 1922, Box G34, *NAACP Papers*.
4. Shelby Davidson to W.E.B. Du Bois, 7 March 1922, Box G34, *NAACP Papers*.
5. Resolution on Lincoln Memorial Dedication, 1922, Box G34.

it was the "most shameful and disgraceful" display "in the annals of history"; for "placed at the entrance to the seats were Marines who were distasteful, discourteous and abusive" forcing Negroes to recline "in weeds with rough hewn benches without backs or supports" forcing many to hastily depart.[6] This was a customary counter-revolutionary impulse for which the capital of the republic was well-acquainted; as this insult at the Lincoln Memorial was enforced rudely racist segregation was imposed on Rock Creek Park. According to the *Washington Tribune*, a Negro press stalwart, Jim Crow "signs were printed and placed by instructions from Colonel C.O. Sherrill, who has charge of all federal grounds and buildings in the District. He was appointed by President Harding" and was an infamous "Southern Man," meaning that "110,000 colored people of Washington are without public bathing facilities...."[7]

The counter-revolution continued when "Southern Men"—and women—sought to construct yet another monument, this one in honor of a so-called "Mammy." The NAACP was flummoxed, however, reluctant to protest since—said Davidson—"our organization" has been "styled by some...enemies as 'high browed'" and objection would "give them the opportunity for them to try to prove to the illiterate Negroes of the South and nearby that our antagonism was directed against them as a class...."[8] The branch did not hesitate to object to a proposed statue honoring the treasonous Robert E. Lee, revealing their strategic role as the eyes and ears for the organization—and Negroes—nationally.[9] The growing importance of the federal capital caused the NAACP to make local leader, Shelby Davidson, "Regional Director for the District of Columbia...in consequence of the number of cases occurring in Washington and the necessity of having someone at the National Capital empowered to act in behalf of the National Office,"[10] then sited in New York City.

Branch officer, Neval Thomas, knew this well; there were "many federal employees in our group," he said and "'to no other group of Negroes in the nation is given the opportunity for such service

6. Likely from Shelby Davidson to James Weldon Johnson, 31 May 1922, Box G34.
7. *Washington Tribune*, 22 April 1922.
8. Shelby Davidson to James Weldon Johnson, 2 February 1923, Box G34, *NAACP Papers*.
9. Neval Thomas to Architect of U.S. Capitol, 24 March 1926, Box G35, *NAACP Papers*.
10. Press Release, 19 January 1923, Box G34, *NAACP Papers*.

as ours. Here at the seat of government our enemies [have] concentrated their effort"[11]—and his side was compelled to respond accordingly. By then his group had about 300 branches nationally and 90,000 members.[12]

It was a protracted slog with the ascension of President Calvin Coolidge not improving matters appreciably. "You will find segregation in every department where there are enough Negroes to fill a room," groused Thomas, stressing that "the Treasury…is rotten," and the same held true for Commerce: "restaurants in all of the departments are…all closed to Negro employees and Negro citizens from the outside," while the "Senate has closed its restaurant to us…." Yet amidst the darkening clouds, there were glimmers of light: the "Treasurer of the United States extended segregation three years ago to sightseers" but "my visit there made him recall the order…."[13] Perhaps in preparation for his own race for higher office, by 1928 Commerce Secretary, Herbert Hoover, was congratulated "for your action in abolishing segregation by race and color in your department."[14] This won Hoover no applause from Senator Cole Blease of Dixie who was pressed by a constituent who said, "'I wonder how Mr. Hoover would like to have the women of family use the same toilet that colored people use,'" adding contemptuously, "'we call these colored people Hoover's chocolates…'"[15]

The Ku Klux Klan, seemingly one of the more potent politicized groups in the District, controlled a baseball team there that termed itself an auxiliary to the police department.[16] A few years later, Negroes were being warned to stay at home "on Saturday, August 8, 1925 because the city has been turned over to the Ku Klux Klan…." This stark warning came from Francis Wells, a clerk in the Office of the Commissioners of the District. A local editorialist captured the outrage of many readers when he asked plaintively "why should colored people who pay taxes to the District Government be required to spend a day indoors or be restricted to any particular area"; this relevant and piercing query was punctuated with a veiled warning:

---

11. Annual Report, 20 January 1928, Box G36, *NAACP Papers*.
12. Joe William Trotter, *Workers on Arrival: Black Labor in the Making of America*, Berkeley: University of California Press, 2019, 129.
13. Neval Thomas to James Weldon Johnson, 22 March 1928, Box G36, *NAACP Papers*.
14. James Weldon Johnson to Herbert Hoover, 20 April 1928, Box G36.
15. *Wilmington News-Dispatch*, 1 October 1928, Box G36, *NAACP Papers*.
16. Paula C. Austin, *Coming of Age in Jim Crow D.C.: Navigating the Politics of Everyday Life*, New York: New York University Press, 2019, 27.

"the colored people of Washington will not start anything but they certainly will help finish anything which is started!"[17]

Behind the scenes Professor Kelly Miller of Howard suggested that his comrade, NAACP leader, James Weldon Johnson protest the issuance of a parade permit to the hooded villains: "Use the inside touches of your organization," he advised, "to connect up with the Jews and Catholics"—adversaries of the Klan.[18] Inevitably, the NAACP had grown alongside their antipode, the Klan; as late as 1913, it was said that there was "no official branch" of the former in the District but a few years later driven by the misdeeds of the Wilson regime, this had changed dramatically.[19]

This upset at the mass arrival of hooded Klansmen illustrated a major theme of this book and a major flaw in the construction of a white supremacist state: how could this be done in a capital city that included so many of African descent willing to object militantly? In the prelude to the dreaded appearance of Klansmen, anti-white supremacist gatherings proliferated; one meeting in particular, said an observer, "will most likely be crowded."[20]

Also complicating the continued flowering of a white supremacist state was precisely Washington's status as a global city, site of foreign embassies and the like. As the Klan was descending on this town in August 1925 Professor Miller of Howard was informed of the impending arrival of "Andre Siegfried" of the Sorbonne in Paris who was in the District "studying the various interracial questions concerning the American people"; Miller's correspondent, George Arthur, leader of the YMCA in Chicago, knew that Siegfried would receive an eyeful and earful as a result of his journey.[21] Coincidentally, at the Pan African Congresses of the early postwar era in Western Europe, in frequent attendance was the French speaking Rayford Logan, a pre-eminent Howard historian for decades to come, along with Channing Tobias, who served on the school's board for decades, along with celebrated sociologist, E. Franklin Frazier, an

---

17. *Washington Daily American*, 5 August 1925, Box 1, *Eugene Davidson Papers, Howard University*.
18. Kelly Miller to James Weldon Johnson, 18 June 1925, Box 9, *Kelly Miller Papers, Emory University-Atlanta*.
19. Chairman of Committee on Branches to Carrie Clifford, 19 August 1913, Box G34, *NAACP Papers*.
20. *Washington Daily American*, 21 July 1924, Box 1.
21. George Arthur to Professor Miller, 31 August 1925, Box 9, *Kelly Miller Papers*.

alumnus from the Class of 1916.[22] It was Logan, billed by the District branch as a "former [U.S.] officer and Assistant Secretary of [the] Pan African Conference" who was summoned to "tell of six years' experience in France...."[23] Well aware of the impact of the global on the domestic, Howard allotted an honorary degree to Paris' Marshall Ferdinand Foch in earnest of his treatment of U.S. Negro troops in his nation, just as the U.S. authorities sought to keep him away from thankful African Americans during his visit.[24]

There was a downside to the District attracting those from abroad, an eventuality which became clear when the purported Dutch anthropologist H.M.B. Moens was ensnared in a scandal in the District in the early postwar era. He was snapping numerous nude photograph of young Black girls on the premise that this was for his "research" with NAACP branch leader, Charlotte Hunter, accused of being complicit.[25] Apparently, even foreign nationals sought to use captive Negroes as guinea pigs.

Still, as Professor Siegfried was descending upon the District—with evidently unbenign intentions—Professor Miller filed away a report reflective of the dilemma faced by an influential capital straining to maintain white supremacy in the face of a growing corps of Black intellectuals and activists sited at Howard. Until recently the District "contained the greatest number of Negroes" but the influx of Africans from the Caribbean during the Great War meant that New York City had "forged ahead." Washington "used to be called the Negroes' Heaven" and this exalted position had yet to dissipate, population shifts notwithstanding. For the "Negroes in Washington occupy a place in the nation that makes this group the most significant of any other in the country" since "here we have the largest proportion of Negroes which is found in any other city," i.e., "25 percent of the total." Sure, in New Orleans "the relative number of Negroes is greater than in Washington" but it was devoid of the probing eye of embassies and the international press.[26]

---

22. Rayford Logan, *Howard University, the First 100 Years, 1867-1967*, New York: New York University Press, 1968, 539.

23. *Washington Sentinel*, 11 October 1924.

24. Michael R. Winston, "The Howard University Department of History, 1913-1973," Washington, D.C.: Department of History-HU, 1973, *Schomburg Center, New York Public Library*.

25. Dickson S. Bruce, *Archibald Grimke: Portrait of a Black Independent*, Baton Rouge: Louisiana State University Press, 1993, 231.

26. "The Negro at the Nation's Capital," 1925, Box 16, *Kelly Miller Papers*.

In his inaugural address in 1927 President Mordecai Johnson of Howard, reminded that "what is done as regards the Negro in this country is a signal and unfailing indication of the American spirit"—and, he added insightfully, "it will resound in the halls of the world."[27]

This ricochet sounding globally often commenced precisely in Washington. It also sounded in the consciousness of Nigerian Founding Father, Nnamdi Benjamin Azikiwe, a Howard alumnus, who in 1928 argued that the Diaspora and his homeland were "pledged to each other. If we succeed," he proclaimed, "we shall have done our duty to Howard University and to the Negro World."[28] It was not only Azikiwe who espied the ties between and among the vast legions of the "Negro World." In 1923 A.S. Pinkett of 748 Harvard NW instructed Helen A. Waller of the Panama Canal Zone that the "discrimination being practiced by government officials" there was "laid before" the District branch for action.[29]

Ultimately, the travesty of a massive Klan march in the self-proclaimed capital of the "free world" became an unsustainable proposition. And even in 1925, it was a bitter pill to swallow. During this anti-Klan upsurge, the *Daily American* was edited by Eugene Davidson, who died in 1976 at the age of 79 and had graduated from Harvard in 1917 and Howard Law School in 1925. An erudite physics major as an undergraduate, Davidson later led the NAACP branch from 1952-1958 and was subjected to a terroristic cross burning at his home in 1957. In sum, the presence of Howard which served as a magnet attracting a corps of skilled Negro intellectuals cum activists further compromised the ability of Washington to lurch even further to the right than it did.[30]

For Davidson's periodical maintained a steady fusillade targeting Jim Crow. After the Klan march the *Daily American* castigated the praxis that meant "colored passengers are not allowed to ride on the buses operating between here and Baltimore"; in fact, he carped "not even servants of white passengers were permitted to ride on the buses...." Adopting lawyerly tones, he reminded that "interstate passengers cannot legally be barred or segregated...."[31]

---

27. Mordecai Johnson, "Inaugural Address," 10 June 1927, Box 35, *Jesse Moorland Papers, Howard University.*
28. Letter from Nnamdi Azikiwe, *The Hilltop,* 7 November 1928,
29. A.S. Pinkett to Helen A. Waller, 31 July 1923, *Alexander Files.*
30. *Washington Post,* 7 March 1976; for Davidson as a physics major, see *Washington Star,* 7 March 1976.
31. *Washington Daily American,* 16 October 1925.

Innovatively, it was Davidson who argued for the imposition of a "segregation war tax," an impost on the football game between Howard and Lincoln universities in order to accumulate a war chest to combat Jim Crow. Yet Jim Crow was an article of faith among many Congressmen, a reality illustrated when legislators found it wise to ban even desegregated swimming at the Tidal Basin beach, as even this "liberal" compromise would presumably bring those of diverse ancestries in too close contact.[32]

Such outrages meant the local NAACP chapter was working overtime. By 1920 leaders were engaged in ritualistic self-congratulation for their role in insuring that those accused in the aftermath of the 1919 uproar "received suspended sentences" because of the "efforts of the legal committee...." "Not one person," it was added boastingly, "appeared in court without counsel...." Desegregation was imposed on the police force too: "during the year 1919 after more than ten years in which no colored applicant was appointed to the force, two were appointed and it appears that others will follow...." Even "in the new District courthouse our efforts were more successful and colored lawyers and their clients may now, thanks to the branch receive the same treatment accorded to other taxpayers...." As such, branch leaders rejected the criticism that was to dog their group for years, i.e., "the criticism of the branch that it is not interested in the great mass of people who live by working with their hands or in trying to develop business of their own...." Leaders were, however, "encouraging colored people to patronize their own artisans" and inspiring "co-operative buying organizations and other enterprises...."[33]

In their 1922 annual report the branch reported that it had held 35 meetings, distributed 10,000 pieces of literature and was in regular contact with the "Colored Press."[34] By December 1923 the branch sponsored what was termed modestly as a "monster anti-lynching mass meeting" marking the birthday of the late abolitionist William Lloyd Garrison. This took place, as did many of their gatherings, at the John Wesley A.M.E. Church at 14th and Corcoran Streets, N.W. Invoking the rhetoric of the past, they cautioned Negroes roughly that the community should "hang together or hang separately...."[35]

---

32. *Washington Daily American*, 9 June 1925.
33. Report, 5 April 1920, Box G34, *NAACP Papers*.
34. Annual Report, 1922, D.C. Branch, [Notes in the Possession of Shawn Leigh Alexander from Research on Elliott Rudwick and August Meier], *University of Kansas-Lawrence*. [Hereinafter denoted as *Alexander Files*]
35. Leaflet, 2 December 1923, Box G34, *NAACP Papers*.

Proceeding in a Pan-African manner, the branch then secured the legal services of A.P. Holly of West Palm Beach—and former Consul for Haiti to the Bahamas—to work on lynching cases.[36] "I am one of the sons," he said of the "late [James] Holly," a U.S. Negro emigrant to Haiti and clerical potentate.[37]

"You are among the few who can get close to Senator [William] Borah," was the message passed to Whitefield McKinlay from James Weldon Johnson. "I want you to use all of the influence that you can bring to bear on him for the purpose of speeding up the Anti-Lynching Bill...Borah has his ambitions and if the colored people of the United States should rightly gain the impression that Senator Borah championed this anti-lynching measure,"[38] it would help his campaign.

The branch was confronting racist violence of all sorts, including the defense of Howard alumnus, Dr. Ossian Sweet, who became a folk hero after he confronted a racist mob, weapon in hand, menacing his Detroit home in 1925, leading to a charge of murder.[39] The branch raised $2,768.27 for the Sweet defense and of that $1,753.23 was from the Women's Committee, this from a membership of about 3,000. "Race battles are fought against great odds," it was said with accuracy and "we have a united enemy without and snipers and lethargy within."[40]

The Sweet crusade reputedly seeded the emergent NAACP Legal Defense and Education Fund, which played a huge role in decades to come in the anti-Jim Crow campaign.[41] Arriving in the District in early 1927 was Dr. Sweet's counsel, the fabled attorney, Clarence Darrow; introduced by Neval Thomas, he spoke to an enthusiastic assemblage of 3,000 with many others striving unsuccessfully to gain admission. Darrow told the cheering masses that the "'intelligentsia and artists of the world are all friends of the Negro and the morons of the world his enemies....'"[42] Looking back, branch leadership concluded that Darrow's appearance amounted to the "greatest

---

36. A.P. Holly to Walter White, 1 May 1924, Box G35, *NAACP Papers*.

37. A.P. Holly to Walter White, 1 May 1924, Box G35, *NAACP Papers*.

38. James Weldon Johnson to McKinlay Whitefield, 22 March 1922, Reel 1, *Carter G. Woodson Papers*.

39. Chair of Association Board to Neval Thomas, president of District Branch, 11 January 1926, Box G35, *NAACP Papers*. See also *Washington Post*, 8 January 1926.

40. Annual Report, 21 January 1927, Box G36, *NAACP Papers*.

41. Nicholas Johnson, *Negroes and the Gun*, 201.

42. *Washington Eagle*, 18 March 1927.

outpouring of our group yet to be recorded in this city" and, besides, "resulted in more than 500 memberships and stimulated in interest which cannot be measured in terms of dollars...."[43]

The branch also raised funds for those victimized by the disastrously torrential Deep South flooding of 1927; it was a "splendid thing," marveled Association leader, James Weldon Johnson.[44]

The District branch was viewed widely as the largest and most active branch nationally and with the presence of Howard likely had more brain power to draw upon as well.[45] This formidable presence helped the branch to configure the face of the capital; thus, by late 1924—according to the *Afro-American*—the "Office of the Register of the Treasury [was] no longer defaced by a memorial tablet for whites and one for colored," which had been dishonoring those who had perished during the war.[46] Then the branch won again when, said Neval Thomas, "all of the 42 colored employees who had been segregated in the Department of the Interior have been ordered back to their old and unsegregated posts of duty," amounting to an "unprecedented backdown" he chortled,[47] adding yet another feather to the cap of this man who also taught at Dunbar High School.[48]

These conquests may sound impressive at first blush but given the challenges faced by Negroes in the District, these seem less imposing. To cite one bleeding sore amongst many, postwar executives at the Library of Congress, racially segregated Negro workers in the cafeteria and excluded Negroes generally from the public restaurant.[49] James Weldon Johnson of the NAACP, with justifiable irritation had protested such blunderbuss measures with little noticeable effect.[50] Soon NAACP staffer, John Shillady, publicly protested his exclusion from the Library bistro.[51]

Such exclusions were part of a pattern and practice. Chair Ovington was told as much. A new courthouse had just opened, she was

---

43. Annual Report, 20 January 1928, Box G36.

44. James Weldon Johnson to Neval Thomas, 3 June 1927, Box G36.

45. Dickson S. Bruce, *Archibald Grimke: Portrait of a Black Independent*, Baton Rouge: Louisiana State University Press, 1993, 232.

46. *Afro-American*, 24 November 1924.

47. Clipping, November 1927, Box G36, *NAACP Papers*.

48. Boston Clipping, 17 June 1927, Box G36.

49. Secretary of Association to Frank Brandegee, 24 November 1919, Box C280, *NAACP Papers*.

50. James Weldon Johnson to President Wilson, 28 November 1919, Box C280, *NAACP Papers*.

51. *New York Sun*, 29 January 1920, Box C280, *NAACP Papers*.

told, with "eloquent orations on 'democracy'"—just as "colored people and ...colored lawyers" were barred from the restaurant there. This was a "great hardship and humiliation upon the colored lawyers and colored litigants" who had to scramble elsewhere for victuals meaning they were "often late for the afternoon session." Formal protests up the chain of command were unavailing [52]—at least for a while. A 1925 congressional study flagged by the NAACP found that "four thousand four hundred patients and one thousand two hundred attendants" of various ancestries, all crammed into a hospital deemed to be "greatly overcrowded."[53]

The leader of the National Urban League, Eugene K. Jones, was stirred to investigate St. Elizabeth's Hospital "for the insane" which recently had witnessed the "death of 3 colored men...murdered by attendants who kicked in their ribs...."[54]

Moreover, postwar Washington was flooded with the arrival of disabled veterans, many of them Negroes facing the added burden of racism. Their presence highlighted the point that the federal capital was a hub for dispensing of aid, thus attracting miscreants of various sorts, including those seeking to traduce the formerly enslaved. By 1922, Cornelius J. Jones of 1311 Q Street N.W. was dispensing circulars "representing himself as being the 'Chief Counsel' for the colored people, sponsoring a bill...to give a bonus to all colored people or their descendants who worked in the cotton fields of the South from '61 to '65."[55]

Again, disabled Negro soldiers were conspicuously vulnerable. Association leader, James Weldon Johnson, was alerted to the "fleecing of the ex-service men," many of whom had been "gassed and shell-shocked" and were hardly in a position to resist crass exploitation.[56]

Then there was the quotidian Jim Crow that was miasmic in effect. As disabled veterans were fending off assault, NAACP Board Chair, Mary White Ovington, recalled a time in 1922 when in the District

---

52. Neval Thomas to Mary White Ovington, 22 November 1919, Box C280, *NAACP Papers*.

53. Report, Senate Resolution, 69th Congress, 1st Session, 18 December 1925, Box C276, *NAACP Papers, Library of Congress-Washington, D.C.*

54. Memorandum from Eugene K. Jones, 14 April 1926, Box C276, *NAACP Papers*.

55. Secretary of National Negro Farmers Association, Atlanta, 200 Auburn Avenue to Dean Kelly Miller, 6 March 1922, Box G34, *NAACP Papers*.

56. Myrtle De Montis to James Weldon Johnson, 3 May 1926, Box C276, *NAACP Papers*.

Helen Curtis, a "colored woman, started to buy a house on S Street, NW from Mrs. Irene Corrigan, a white woman. Before this, Mrs. Corrigan had entered into an agreement with certain property owners, her neighbors, not to sell to a colored woman. She, however, decided to break this agreement," igniting a tsunami of litigation, culminating in a victory for so-called racially restricted covenants, depriving Negroes the opportunity to move from designated neighborhoods, leaving them susceptible to gross exploitation by landlords and real estate brokers in the blocks to which they were consigned. As for Ovington, she was grubbing for "three thousand dollars for this case."[57]

More funding would be needed. For, said the NAACP, months later, there were proliferating "agreements among white property holders not to sell to any person of Negro race or blood"; leading the charge against this pact were Association leaders Arthur Spingarn and W. Montague Cobb.[58] Dr. Cobb, physician and anthropologist who opined relentlessly on the fraudulence of white supremacy, was provided with chapter and verse as a NAACP official. Segregation cases in at least five states turned on District praxis, he contended, given the capital's prominence and example: the "entire question of residential segregation of colored people and other groups in America," said this Washington born scholar, trained at Howard's Medical School and a long-time faculty member at the university.[59] Following up, James Weldon Johnson maintained that "residential segregation by exclusion paragraphs in deeds has already been invoked against Jews...."[60]

Despite this attempt at coalition building, the balance of forces leaned against anti-racism then. It did not take long, said the NAACP, for Euro-American property owners in the District to organize what was described as the "entire National Capital so that colored people will be unable to buy or occupy property in any but the districts assigned to them". Apparently flush with resources, they were publishing a newspaper, the "North Capitol Citizen."[61]

However, as matters evolved, Helen Curtis was able to live in the 1700 block of S Street NW; as the local Negro newspaper put it, while "lawyers have been arguing in the courts [regarding her] right" to

---

57. Mary White Ovington to Charles Tilton, 18 June 1925, Box C260, *NAACP Papers*.

58. Press Release, 15 February 1924, Box D98, *NAACP Papers*.

59. Press Release, 12 February 1924, Box D98, *NAACP Papers*.

60. James Weldon Johnson, 24 September 1924, Box D98, *NAACP Papers*.

61. Press Release, 27 February 1925, Box D98, *NAACP Papers*.

live there, "nearly all the white people have moved" and "all colored people have moved in...."[62]

The branch was buoyed by the presence of Howard University, the most significant concentration of Black intellectualism nationally. It was during this time that Marcus Garvey arrived on campus and was greeted rhapsodically with faculty and students alike swarming the stout Jamaican, competing to shake his hand. Professor William Leo Hansberry, a pioneer in the teaching of the history of Africa, then decamped to the scholar's office where they whiled away the afternoon reviewing pictures of old Abyssinian culture.[63] This welcome to Garvey did not amuse certain forces within the NAACP since his group at this point had an "astounding membership" increase at this juncture, according to Joe William Trotter.[64]

L.M. Hershaw of 2215 13th Street, N.W. expressed "surprise" and "amazement" at the prospect of "a definitely planned campaign by the NAACP against Garvey"; for "even if he is an imposter, defrauding ignorant and benighted Negroes of their meager earnings," destabilizing his movement was not the Association's job.[65]

This venture into academic freedom by Professor Hansberry was not welcome on Capitol Hill. Shortly thereafter the House of Representatives voted to slash $207,500 from the school's budget because a professor was said to have castigated the "anti-Christ attitude of white people of this country." Future U.S. Secretary of State James Byrnes led the charge, underscoring the importance of the rebuke. It is likely that legislators would have been unhappy to hear of the communication to students by Max Yergan, soon to be notorious for his ties to Communists in both New York and his then residence in Cape Town.[66]

This was an emblem of a trend that was to be even more pronounced in coming decades: Howard's connections to Africa. By 1924 the school was recommending the offer of six scholarships to Liberian students. It is unclear if the non-U.S. students then matriculating were participating in an incipient boycott of stores along Georgia Avenue, the thoroughfare fronting the university, and those en route to downtown too, which were accused credibly—said a

62. *Baltimore Afro-American*, 16 January 1926, Box D98, *NAACP Papers*.

63. *The Hilltop* [Howard University], 22 January 1924.

64. Joe William Trotter, *Workers on Arrival: Black Labor in the Making of America*, Berkeley: University of California Press, 2019, 129.

65. L.M. Hershaw to James Weldon Johnson, 31 August 1922, Box G34, *NAACP Papers*.

66. *The Hilltop*, 4 February 1924.

student reporter—of "not cooperating with the students who spend over a million dollars in the city during the school year...one of the outrages of the 20th century." Similarly, these merchants were not advertising in *The Hilltop*, Howard's periodical.[67]

Students from Liberia were far from being the only non-U.S. students. Soon, Brazilian students at Howard had taken to the streets, according to one commentator, in order to "protest the reign of imperialism...."[68] Attentive to global obligations of imperialism, the Rockefeller Foundation funded the matriculation of three Haitian physicians to study at the Medical School.[69] By 1928, also present on campus was the man then known as Malcolm Nurse of Trinidad—actually, he had arrived some months earlier—who went on to become known as George Padmore, intrepid Pan-African organizer.[70] By 1929, he occupied the front page of the student newspaper. "Comrade Malcolm," said this reporter archly, was an "honest-to-goodness beardless Communist" who addressed wondrous students. "Mr. Nurse objects to Mister or [even] being called a gentleman"; no, "this individual was none other than he who advocated a Communist Party in the Student Council candidates' political campaign of two years back...." Nurse—or Padmore—"had held a group of almost four score professors spellbound for almost an hour in a stump speech in front of the administration building...." His topic? "Comrade Nurse pointed out that Communism holds many attractions for Negroes," with its "international character" being notably appealing. At that juncture Nurse was enrolled in the law school but was "truly" moonlighting on campus as "an instructor in the Communist conventions in Germany, Russia and France..."[71] Coincidentally, days later receiving maximum publicity on campus was the "acclaimed" Paul Robeson, soon to be hailed—or excoriated—as an exemplar of the ideology that Nurse was nursing.[72]

What helped to propel this campus activism was a renewed feminist vigor District-wide. Early on Addie Hunton, mother of the future Howard teacher, W. Alphaeus Hunton, was listed as a Field

---

67. *The Hilltop*, 4 February 1924.
68. *The Hilltop*, 20 January 1927.
69. *The Hilltop*, 8 October 1928.
70. *The Hilltop*, 24 October 1928. See also James R. Hooker, *Black Revolutionary: George Padmore's Path from Communism to Pan-Africanism*, New York: Praeger, 1967.
71. *The Hilltop*, 7 November 1929.
72. *The Hilltop*, 21 November 1929.

Secretary of the local NAACP.[73] It was she who during the convention of the National Women's Party in the District in 1921 who reportedly "organized and directed the colored women in their efforts to bring about through the [NWP] a federal investigation of violations of the intent and purposes of the 19th Amendment" to the U.S. Constitution ostensibly delivering the right to vote across gender lines.[74]

The "new emancipation of women" was trumpeted in October 1924 in the face of a controversy wherein "all traditions of the organization have been bitterly opposed to the acceptance of female students...." At the center of the matter was the "Kappa Sigma Debating Society, the oldest student organization on campus," it was reported; revealingly, it was said, "all traditions of the organization have been bitterly opposed to the acceptance of female students," a reactionary wave that was to fall victim to an upsurge of progressive and radical activism. At issue then was a race for Student Council leadership and, tellingly, "for the first time in the history of the university, the several conflicting male elements, usually at loggerheads with each other, combined to resist this invasion of masculine prerogatives."[75]

However, this testosterone drenched offensive did not deter a student described as "feminist" who rebuked "insinuations that cast upon the females of the university as [being] responsible for immorality existing," a masked reference to fluxing norms concerning sexuality.[76]

Remarkably, a student denied that male supremacy was at hand and pled instead that "medieval chivalry still actuates us and our respect for women forbids us to engage with them in public battle."[77]

However, deflating sexism could not fully suppress student activism for the predictable occurred when students went on strike, the ostensible reason being compulsory military training—the ultimate expression of male chauvinism. A student journalist reported by May 1925 that the plan was "to attend no classes until the expelled students were reinstated"; just as predictably a "mass meeting called by the Student Council" was described understatedly as "fiery."[78]

---

73. Stationery of D.C. Branch, 10 March circa 1920, Box G34, *NAACP Papers*.
74. Inez Richardson, Secretary-D.C. Branch to Dr. Bagnall, Director of Branches, 15 March 1921, Box G34, *NAACP Papers*.
75. *The Hilltop*, 10 October 1924. See also Janet Sims-Wood, *Dorothy Porter Wesley at Howard University: Building a Legacy of Black History*, Charleston: History Press, 2014.
76. *The Hilltop*, 20 March 1926.
77. *The Hilltop*, 13 March 1925.
78. *The Hilltop*, 8 May 1925.

As with the faculty, there was also objection to compulsory chapel attendance with others renouncing the notion of the singing of spirituals—a commentary on the purported religiosity that inheres in Negroes.[79]

The campus was deluged with broadsides warning "Don't be an Uncle Tom" and/or posing the query: "what is this going to be—an army or a university?" As was to occur repeatedly in coming decades, Congress—dominated by Dixiecrats—which held tight the university's purse strings, was irked as a direct result.[80]

It did take much to inflame overly sensitive members of Congress. Senator Reed Smoot of Utah took to the floor at Capitol Hill and demanded the removal of a book at Howard's library by Albert Rhys Williams concerning the emerging Soviet Union and vowed that he would never "'vote for the appropriation of another dollar'" for the school unless his ukase was observed. President J. Stanley Durkee of the university said he agreed with the Senator and promptly ordered that the book be removed.[81]

Not only students were in an uproar during the Roaring 1920s. In a "confidential" message, Carter G. Woodson, yet to be ousted from the faculty, continued to grouse about the school's final "white" leader, James Stanley Durkee and his policy enforcing "chapel attendance of teachers"—a complement to compulsory military training for students who could then be subject to an elder prayer for their well-being in battle zones. Philosopher Alain Locke, he said, was "being driven to wall because he does not attend chapel...." This rigidly religious policy was simply "one of his many faults," sniffed the man to be designated as the "Father of Negro History." Contrary to best practices of management, he "acts on rumors, condemns men thereon without giving them a hearing" and as to this star historian, perpetually he was "trying to browbeat and bludgeon me...." Dr. Woodson was not above circulating unconfirmed stories either, contributing to managerial chaos in that he floated the "rumor that he cannot get along with well educated colored men," not an asset

79. Rayford Logan, *Howard University, the First Hundred Years, 1867-1967*, New York: New York University Press, 1968, 220.

80. Zachery Williams, *In Search of the Talented Tenth: Howard University Public Intellectuals and the Dilemmas of Race, 1926-1970*, Columbia: University of Missouri Press, 2009, 29, 30. See also Walter Dyson, "A History of the Federal Appropriations for Howard University, 1867-1928," *Howard University Studies in History*, Number 8, November 1927, Washington, D.C.: Howard University, 1927, *New York Public Library-Schomburg Center*.

81. Rayford Logan, *Howard University, the First Hundred Years, 1867-1967, 189.*

at the institution with likely the largest number of this cohort worldwide. "His general attitude is that he can do no wrong and can never
err," meaning "no thinking man can stand him very long...." Durkee,
concluded Woodson with horror, was "the most ignorant man I have
ever seen in a responsible position," the essence of a "dogmatic and
domineering czar."[82]

Exasperatingly, Dr. Woodson asked Durkee's ostensible supervisor, "will you permit such inefficient white leadership to bludgeon
well educated Negro instructors into submission to their medieval methods...." This was his dismissal of a man who was a "slave
driver" who sought to "masquerade as an educator...."[83]

If anything, Dr. Woodson may have been overly mild in denouncing Durkee. He was also accused credibly of physically assaulting
faculty and misusing funds.[84] Durkee, according to long-time Howard historian Rayford Logan, was sacked in part because he was not
a Negro but,[85] certainly his rank incompetence was the overriding
factor in his ouster. On the other hand, his successor—Mordecai
Johnson—also ruffled feathers during his lengthy tenure. Early on
one Boston critic complained that in a notably acerbic speech, President Johnson "talked too long"; worse, it was said, his remarks were
to a "large degree an arraignment of the white South and the white
race generally...as it has been unjust to the Negro...." As so often
happened, when Euro-Americans were lectured about the sins of
white supremacy, the Howard leader "lost the crowd"[86]—an alleged
shortcoming he was to be accused of repeatedly in coming decades.

* * *

The working class of the District and the surrounding states was
impacted by the atmospheric Jim Crow emanating from Capitol
Hill, the White House, and the high court. The Washington Central
Labor Union, an umbrella federation of groups, had a combined
membership of 80,000, making it potentially the most potent body
in the District. It was all the more powerful since it did not automatically bar Negroes in that the "Colored" barbers were affiliated and

82. Carter G. Woodson to Jesse Moorland, 11 May 1920, Box 34, *Jesse Moorland Papers, Howard University*.
83. Carter G. Woodson to Jesse Moorland, 15 May 1920, Box 34.
84. Zachery Williams, *In Search of the Talented Tenth*, 33.
85. Rayford Logan, *Howard University, the First 100 Years*, 240.
86. Rolfe Cobleigh of Boston's "The Congregationalist" to Jesse Moorland, 8
July 1927, Box 34, *Jesse Moorland Papers, Howard University*.

admitted on the same terms as others. Leadership concurred that this praxis was "essential to the success of the labor movement... very much so as they are used by employers to defeat the aims of the unions," when they were barred from membership. This was noticeably worrisome, said an official since "Negro members always put other organizations ahead of the labor organizations. They seem to join lodges of all kinds except the labor unions...." In fact, it was said with bafflement, they "will join all church organizations and fraternal organizations but they lack interest in labor organizations...." Thus, in the District "we find that they are working for all the non union contractors. We haven't had any strikes in this city for some time but if we should have, we know full well they would act as strike breakers."[87]

In 1928 union official, Thomas Dabney, spoke of Washington as a "respectable middle class city" with "very few industries," though more than a few "public works" tended by "building trades" (hod carriers; electricians; truckers; etc.), along with "domestic service, laundries, department stores" and a bevy of clerical workers. At that juncture there were "more than 30,000...unemployed," while a "large number of Negroes are employed by the government, 8,000 perhaps...." There were at least "75,000 organized workers" in the District, perhaps an underestimate, with only "1,500" being "Colored." The latter were concentrated at the bottom rungs of the socio-economic ladder and, predictably, "unions in the unskilled trades are very weak...." Where Negroes were scarce—"railway workers" (beyond porters)—"strong locals" persisted. "Barbers are well organized," too. A sign of the times was embodied in the Federal Employees Union where Negroes felt "slighted" and, thus, "withdrew some time ago and formed their own local #71."[88]

Tragically, this simple lesson was not absorbed consistently by the Central Labor Union—or labor writ large—as white supremacy at times vitiated class solidarity.

In 1925 Lovett Fort-Whiteman, subsequently renowned as one of the earliest Black members of the U.S. Communist Party, inquired about the demographic composition of the Laundry Workers International Union. "We make no discrimination against colored people," was the point made by H.L. Morrison, Secretary-Treasurer. "We have, however, one Local Union located in Washington, D.C. with about 100 members and all of these members are to the best

---

87. Survey, 20 June 1928, Part I, Box F87, *National Urban League Papers-Library of Congress.*
88. Report from Thomas Dabney, 31 March 1928, Part I, Box F78.

of my knowledge Colored people," mostly toiling in the "Laundry Department of the Bureau of Printing and Engraving...."[89] Laundry Workers Local #110 was overwhelmingly Negro and was organized in 1916 and, as of 1928, had a total membership of 100: "this is a government union so that the workers are not permitted to strike," was the message from the leadership, a clear suppressant of class consciousness and militancy. On the other hand, "all colored workers in Bureau and Engraving belong to the local," said the official, Thomas Dabney.[90]

This union, unfortunately, was not the norm. More to the point was Bookbinder's Local #4 where it was conceded openly that "there are none [Negroes] eligible for membership" in this District entity with 390 members. "Have there been strikes within the past five years in which Negroes were involved," was the inquiry put to them in 1926? "No," was the terse response. "Has your organization made effort[s] to get Negro membership?" Again, "no" was the reply.[91]

Reading from a similar script were the International Federation of Technical Engineers, Architects and Draftsmen. Although "nothing in [our] constitution to prevent [Negroes]" from joining their union of 3,000, the point was there were no Negro members in a city that over the decades was to enjoy a building boom that would benefit this local. "No," it was replied bluntly the local "made no effort to get Negro membership...." Asked to "comment on the relations of white and Negro members of your organization," the haughty response was the "condition does not exist,"[92] the question was entirely irrelevant.

Washington was a city that produced reams of volumes of documents, especially on Capitol Hill, not to mention daily newspapers and newsletters of various sorts. Typographical Union #1 was critical here and they did admit Negroes to full membership. There were 2,140 members but only 15 were Black, well below this group's percentage of citywide population. For whatever reason none of these Negro members were recorded as participating in "strikes within the past five years" but not as "strike breakers" either. "Are Negro and white members on the same terms?" "Yes" and, moreover, interracial relations of members were described as "generally very good."[93]

---

89. H.L. Morrison to Lovett Fort-Whiteman, 9 May 1925, Part I, Box F87, *National Urban League Papers, Library of Congress-Washington, D.C.*
90. Survey, 31 March 1928, Part I, Box F87.
91. Survey, 18 January 1926, Part I, Box F87.
92. Survey, 25 January 1926, Part I, Box F87.
93. Survey, 9 January 1926, Part I, Box F87.

Federal Employees Union, Local #23, admitted that Negroes were "admitted to full membership" in their 1,100 strong ranks— though somehow there were only 35 Black members. Like a number of other locals in town this one too was a "no strike organization" which was not conducive to building class militancy. In any event, it was thought that there was a "disinclination" of Negroes to join this local since it could be interpreted as "forcing themselves on white membership...." Perhaps evasively—or accurately—when asked to "comment on the relations of white and Negro members," the reply was: "as good as is usual between Negroes and whites anywhere...."[94]

This ambivalent reaction reflected the overall checkered pattern of class solidarity in conflict with white supremacy. This too was refracted in the response of the Teachers' union. "Public schools in D.C. are separated," it was explained "and Negro teachers have their own unions." Still, "all unions meet through representatives where cooperation is necessary for [the] whole system." Thus, this body officially had "no Negro members but affiliated action" occurred in a climate of "cordial, sympathetic [and] generous cooperation...."[95]

Federal Employees Local #2 had 4,000 members but only 75 were Negro, though—supposedly—they were admitted on the same terms as others.[96] This equivocation was generated because it was also admitted that their membership was discouraged. Separate locals, it was explained, was because this was something that the Negroes tended to "prefer"—though "once interested, they make excellent members."[97]

As for Federal Employees Local #260 at the Bureau of Standards, the four Negro members were admitted to full membership in a body of 160. A tad inconsistently, it was added that "we have a separate Negro local (#71)" with "salaries usually lower than [that of] whites...."[98]

Nevertheless, Local #261 at the War Department sheds light on this apparent inconsistency in that Negroes were admitted to full membership though at the same time there was a "Negro local in Washington to which most Negro members belong. They are at liberty to join either our local or the Negro local" and in the former there were 236 members all told and three Negroes. "Negroes had a

---

94. Survey, 17 December 1925, Part I, Box F87.
95. Survey, 25 January 1926, Part I, Box F87.
96. Survey, 31 March 1928, Part I, Box F87.
97. Survey, 1 February 1926, Part I, Box F87.
98. Survey, 14 January 1926, Part I, Box F87.

separate union before white locals were formed" and saw little reason to abandon this formation. Still, "officers of this [racially mixed] local are opposed to [the] attitude of some unions in barring Negroes as we feel that such action deprives the Negroes of their share in bettering conditions and compels them to become scabs...." Perhaps over-optimistically, this official—William S. Kinney—admitted that "few of our members know we have Negro members. Those who know it are friendly to the Negroes."[99]

Local #72 of the federal employees' union was organized in 1919 as a "Colored" formation. What happened was that following the war many Negroes were dissatisfied with Local #2 of which they had been a part and, thus, formed their own local. Local #2 was not unenthusiastic about accommodating them, as white supremacy bested class solidarity—again.[100]

The postal service was to become a major employer of Negro workers, and this too was the case in the District in the 1920s. There was a "colored local" among the postal clerks, organized as of 1916. "Practically all colored clerks organized" but there were "only 140 in the city" and, it was underscored, "colored preferred to have their own local, besides most of the colored clerks work together."[101]

The "Colored Local" of the Barbers—Journeyman Barbers Local #305—was organized in 1903 and by 1928 had a membership of 100; this meant that 70 percent of Negro shearers were organized. The remaining 30 percent were said to lack funds for a "joining fee" or were deemed to be "indifferent." Unsurprisingly, the response was affirmative when the question was posed: "do you regard the organization of Negroes as essential to the success of the labor movement."[102]

Musicians, too, were segregated racially. Local #710 was the Negro unit and smaller than the "white" Local #161 of the American Federation of Musicians which had 1,100 members—and no Negroes. Somehow—and again possibly with a surfeit of optimism—Local #161 concluded that "relations between the two locals are thoroughly friendly."[103]

The Sheet Metal Workers had an affiliate in the District. Their Secretary, William L. Sullivan, explained that his members "take

99. Survey, 10 January 1925, Part I, Box F87.
100. Survey, 31 March 1928, Part I, Box F87. See also Charles Johnson, 1922, Part I, Box E28, *National Urban League Papers*.
101. Survey, 31 March 1928, Part I, Box F87.
102. Survey, 31 March 1928, Part I, F87.
103. Survey, 9 January 1926, Part I, F87.

the raw materials and fabricate it into manufactured materials...
they make the steel products that go into fireproof buildings." It
was unclear if the pattern in Washington mirrored that of other cities where although there were "few colored men in the trade...in
some communities they outnumber the white workers...." Thus, in
Charleston and Savannah there was a "union of colored men" with
"no affiliation" with Sullivan's grouping. There were "white locals"
in Charleston and Savannah, however: "Colored workers work
9 hours and the white worker 8 hours," leading inexorably to more
wear and tear on the former. In Pittsburgh there was "one colored
man," said Sullivan "in a large local" but again, it was not evident
where the District stood in this congeries.[104]

---

104. Interview with William Sullivan, no date, circa 1920s, Part I, F87.

Chapter 3

Working Class Revolt, 1930s

As the nation's capital, the District distilled the very essence of a republic that countenanced Jim Crow at home and imperialist aggression abroad. Howard University housing as it did fierce opponents of both domestic and foreign policies with a budget dependent upon the good wishes of Congress, was an inevitable target of the Dixiecrats. Furthermore, as the 1930s descended into economic crisis, inexorably radicalism in the form of the Communist Party roiled further already tempestuous waters.[1] And, as ever, what the NAACP leadership was told in 1934 remained true: "Washington at this time," said Robert McGuire of the branch, "seems to be the most strategic point in the country for the NAACP."[2]

By 1930 the District was said to have a total population of 486,869, which included 132,068 African Americans. This was an increase from the 86,702 total for the latter in 1900 or 31.1 percent of the overall populace, which was larger than the 27.1 percent of 1930. Negroes constituted 44.8 percent of those out of work with the situation for women of this group being particularly awful: there were 31,383 Negro women in Washington gainfully employed in domestic and so-called "personal service" labor. But given the parlous economic conditions, Euro-American women were now grasping to enter this field, jeopardizing the ability of Negro women to cling to this bottom rung of the socio-economic ladder. (Of course, office jobs where the

---

1. See, e.g., Joseph T. Elvove to H.C. Byrd, Vice President of University of Maryland, 7 November 1934, Box 1, VII, *Records of the President's Office*: As for antiwar students, "All three...are Communists...engaged in Communistic activity in Washington, D.C.", e.g., "the recent troubles with the Bonus Army, the Hunger Marchers and the constant [amongst] the Negro population in Washington."
2. Robert McGuire to Walter White, 14 April 1934, Box G38, *NAACP Papers*.

former group of women were sited, was not open to the same degree to the latter.) Washington was accused by one observer of lethargy in opening the doors of employment opportunity to Negroes except as elevator operators—cruelly, a rare venue for upward mobility for this besieged group—and charwomen, or as unskilled laborers and messengers, the niche for Negro men. By 1932 as the economy plummeted, there were numerous incidents of Negroes being ousted from jobs to provide work for others. This lengthening list included the usual redoubts of Negro employment, e.g., dairies, window cleaning businesses, laundries, and hotels. In any case, Negro workers received less for their work than their Euro-American peers doing the same kind of work. This rapacious racism led to the funneling of Negroes into the growing ranks of the indigent and their complement—the jailed and imprisoned—In spiraling numbers. Furthermore, the death rates for Negroes was higher than that of other groups, as was the infant mortality rate.[3]

Necessarily, to keep this often obstreperous sector of the working class in line, violence was unleashed against them. With a nod towards hyperbole, one commentator argued that the police mandate was to "shoot down Negroes often on sight," as "brutality enthroned" was their mantra—"with apologies to the animals" who often were treated better.[4] A major reason why Communists gained traction among Negroes was because of this party's emphasis on police brutality, exemplified on 9 July 1938 when thousands marched at their behest against this scourge, with thousands more lining the route. Typical of how Black Washingtonians carried a special burden was the point that a Dixiecrat from Louisiana on the floor of the U.S. Congress endorsed the use of police brutality in the District.[5]

---

3. Remarks by Campbell C. Johnson, 3 December 1932, Box 31, *Ralph Bunche Papers, New York Public Library-Schomburg Center*. See also Mary-Elizabeth Murphy, *Jim Crow Capital: Women and Black Freedom Struggles in Washington, D.C., 1920-1945*, Chapel Hill: University of North Carolina Press, 111: 81 % of Black women "labored in domestic and personal service," while 75% of the District's relief budget purportedly was allocated to African Americans—the "highest proportion in the nation." As of August 1932, as a sign of distress, in the past six months 10 Blacks had committed suicide: 35 tried.
4. Harlan E. Glazier, "Brutality Enthroned (with apologies to the animals) Sponsored by the Inter-Racial Committee of the District of Columbia," Box 31, *Ralph Bunche Papers, New York Public Library-Schomburg Center.*
5. Mary-Elizabeth Murphy, *Jim Crow Capital: Women and Black Freedom Struggles in Washington, D.C., 1920-1945*, Chapel Hill: University of North Carolina Press, 2018, 98, 104.

Reflecting nervousness, Walter White of the NAACP was told of the "propaganda…regarding the killing of a certain number of people in Washington by the police…inspired by subversive forces…."[6] This reproach was made by Congresswoman Mary Norton of the District Committee of the House, meaning it could not be ignored easily. However, the *Washington Tribune*, a local Negro newspaper rebuked her for her "most astounding statement…regarding the killing of 30 colored men" which had little to do with so named "'Communist forces.'" The fact was that "50 men, instead of 30, have been killed here" by cops "in the last ten years, 10 of them white and 40 of them colored…and even if the NAACP and the *Tribune* were allied, with the Communists, would that be a justifiable reason for not giving attention to the facts in the case…."[7]

As for unions defending the rights of their actual or potential members, the American Federation of Labor was missing in action while the competing left-leaning Congress of Industrial Organizations was engaged in battle.[8]

Radicalism spiraled accordingly. The focal point for national anger and activism was—understandably—the nation's capital and (inexorably) the local population was impacted and energized. Not long after the Wall Street crash that set the tone for the decade, it was on an unusually wintry day on 6 March 1930 when thousands gathered in front of the White House, a leisurely stroll from Negro neighborhoods. Police disrupted the amassed with deftly wielded batons and teargas, as President Hoover peered nervously through the window. There was a complement of Negroes along with Euro-Americans, not the norm in an apartheid society; they were brought together by the Communist Party. Perhaps coincidentally, on the same day the Commerce Committee of the U.S. Senate slated its first hearing to contemplate an unemployment insurance bill—by 1932, seven states had initiated similar legislation, though not without stiff resistance.[9]

---

6. Mary Norton to Walter White, 16 December 1936, Box G38, *NAACP Papers*.
7. *Washington Tribune*, 9 December 1936.
8. Harlan E. Glazier, "No Negro Need Apply: A Brief Glance at the Employment Situation in the District of Columbia as Related to Colored Citizens," Box 31, *Ralph Bunche Papers*. Lawrence J. W. Hayes, "The Negro Federal Government Worker: A Study of His Classification Status in the District of Columbia, 1883-1938," *Howard University Studies in the Social Science*, 3 (Number 1, 1941): 1-156, Box 12, *Ralph Bunche Papers, University of California-Los Angeles*.
9. *Washington Post*, 7 March 2021. See also Roger Baldwin memo, 27 November 1931, Box 1, VII, *Records of the President's Office, University of Maryland-College*

Hoover had reason to be anxious about unwelcome visitors at his door. The Iowan had approved a plan to segregate Negro so-called "Gold Star" mothers of World War I veterans during a state sponsored journey to France.[10]

Assuredly, the hilltop campus that was Howard continued to outrage conservatives by providing a forum to radicals, including the leading Negro economist Abram Harris, who lectured dispassionately on "Russian Communism" at the beginning of the Depression Decade.[11] He was followed by Howard Ross, a Canadian academic, who addressed the same topic weeks later.[12] Six years later, Harris reappeared to address students on the same topic—but this time he had just returned from Soviet Russia.[13] In that vein the Russian hero of African ancestry, Alexander Pushkin, received tribute from Professor Sterling Brown—a future mentor of both Toni Morrison and Amiri Baraka/Le Roi Jones—who was joined by a Soviet envoy.[14]

"Campus women hear socialist" was a typical headline.[15] Soon organized students had proceeded to Chicago and were demanding curbs on militarism and diplomatic recognition of the Soviet Union, under the influence of Scott Nearing and Jane Adams.[16] Howard students were present at a New York City confab that featured socialist leader Norman Thomas and his British peer, Fenner Brockway. "Big student rally against war set," blared *The Hilltop*, with "steps toward ousting ROTC from all colleges...."[17] Next students described as "liberal" headed north to attend an antiwar conference at Johns Hopkins University.[18] First hand reports from Addis Ababa were delivered

---

Park: "The Communists are arranging a National Hunger March...the Legion and Matthew Woll of the American Federation of Labor are putting pressure on the authorities to break up the demonstration by force."

10. Jill Watts, *The Black Cabinet: The Untold Story of African Americans and Politics During the Age of Roosevelt*, New York: Grove, 2020, 33

11. *The Hilltop*, 16 October 1930. William Darity, ed., *Race, Radicalism and Reform: Selected Papers of Abram Harris*, New York: Transaction, 1989. See also "National Conference on Students and Politics," 29-31 December 1933, Box 1, VII, *Records of the President's Office:* Harris to speak on "State Ownership or control of Private Industry."

12. *The Hilltop*, 30 October 1930.

13. *The Hilltop*, 25 November 1936.

14. *The Hilltop*, 3 March 1937. For more on Pushkin, see the edition of 31 March 1937.

15. *The Hilltop*, 23 October 1930.

16. *The Hilltop*, 19 January 1933.

17. *The Hilltop*, 24 November 1932.

18. *The Hilltop*, 9 November 1934.

by alumnus, Cyril Price, while a Chinese lecturer expounded on the difficulties unfolding in Manchuria.[19] Such messages were bolstered by the lecturing of Professor William Leo Hansberry who, as tensions rose with Italy, instructed students that Abyssinia was the "second most powerful nation in Christendom...from the sixth through the twelfth century" and that it was the ill-considered European sponsored Crusade against Islam that led to religious attacks on this polity.[20]

Simultaneously, the student, Lyonel Florant—who went on to labor on behalf of the Carnegie Corporation of New York, helping to produce sociological studies of the Negro—was one of 375 delegates at an antiwar gathering in Brussels, attended by representatives of 31 nations. Dismayingly for Dixiecrats, he reported that "foreign students have manifested great interest in the Negro problem,"[21] a message conveyed directly to the student body.[22]

Also reporting to students about Europe was Communist leader, Ed Strong, who had just visited Spain during their epochal civil war—just before enrolling as a graduate student in Political Science at H.U.[23] Nearer to home, four H.U. students traipsed to Chicago to attend a national convention of the left-led National Negro Congress, leading a student commentator to term the "gathering...one of the most brilliant ever witnessed in the entire history of the American Negro...."[24] In these different days, NAACP leader Roy Wilkins joined with President Johnson and youthful Communist hero Angelo Herndon—and 10 H.U. students—in launching what was seen as the youth affiliate of the NNC: the Southern Negro Youth Congress.[25]

The influence of campus Communists was suspected when the popular fraternity, Alpha Phi Alpha, held a fundraiser for the Scottsboro Nine,[26] a global campaign with direct Moscow influence designed to both free young Negro men in Dixie facing execution over spurious charges of sexual molestation of two Euro-American women—and place U.S. Jim Crow in an international spotlight.[27] The

19. *The Hilltop*, 17 December 1931.
20. *The Hilltop*, 31 October 1935.
21. *The Hilltop*, 16 January 1935.
22. *The Hilltop*, 15 February 1935.
23. *The Hilltop*, 19 October 1936.
24. *The Hilltop*, 21 April 1936.
25. *The Hilltop*, 27 January 1937.
26. *The Hilltop*, 28 April 1933.
27. Gerald Horne, *Powell v. Alabama: The Scottsboro Case and American Justice*, New York: Scholastic, 1997.

growing and influential Liberal Club was among those who urged action on this trailblazing case.[28] Campus radicalism was buoyed by local bolstering. George Murphy of the noteworthy Black Baltimore family—writing from the headquarters of the Scottsboro Committee at 1333 U Street NW—held what he described as a "mass meeting" in the District in February 1936.[29] Speakers included Professor Ralph Bunche and the left-wing Congressman from East Harlem, Vito Marcantonio.[30] This was followed by a fete at the Memorial Home of Frederick Douglass.[31]

"We, the students of Howard University, the leaders of intellectual life of the Negro people," began the Liberal Club portentously in demonstrating their backing for a case that had Communist leadership.[32] Naturally, a core of H.U. students endorsed the Communist-led National Negro Congress and were addressed by Bunche.[33] So inspired, the student council president protested lynching and urged President Johnson to join—which surely would have outraged lyncher comrades on Capitol Hill.[34] Led by Professor Bunche, students marched to Capitol Hill to lobby on lynching in conjunction with the NAACP.[35] As protests mounted, the cry arose in Congress to "investigate radicalism in Negro universities...."[36] So inspired, when hundreds of antiwar students gathered on campus in 1935, a student journalist was struck by the "belligerent attitude of a few ROTC students who threatened to break up" the amassed due to "what they termed...a Communistic meeting...."[37]

It was unclear if Dixiecrats had a role in arranging a campus visit by a delegate from the embassy of the odious German regime; an observer reported that this was "his first contact with Negroes on a large scale. He was elated over the singing in [the] chapel."[38] A rebuke

---

28. *The Hilltop*, 16 January 1935. See Leaflet, 1934, "War Versus Civilization... the Liberal Club...meeting will be opened with spirituals by the Morgan State College Glee Club..." Box 1, VII, *Records of the President's Office, University of Maryland-College Park*.
29. George Murphy to Mary Fox, 31 January 1936, Box H8 Addenda, *NAACP Papers, Library of Congress*.
30. Broadside, 10 February 1936, Box H8 Addenda.
31. Invitation, 26 September 1936, Box H8 Addenda.
32. *The Hilltop*, 15 February 1935.
33. *The Hilltop*, 20 January 1936.
34. *The Hilltop*, 20 October 1933.
35. *The Hilltop*, 22 December 1934.
36. *The Hilltop*, 5 June 1935.
37. *The Hilltop*, 13 November 1935.
38. *The Hilltop*, 10 November 1933.

was not long in coming: "fascism no solution to Negro problem" was the message from journalist, George Streator.[39] No such reprimand emerged when Professor Alain Locke arranged a talk on "Oriental customs" by a Japanese student at George Washington University,[40] perhaps because Tokyo's reputation—depredations then unfolding in China aside—was ascendant in Black America. Then further sanitizing Tokyo's image a Japanese exhibit of prints were displayed on campus for weeks on end.[41] But what was awarded a page one banner headline was the appearance on campus of the purported "Chinese 'Joan of Arc,'" Loh Tsei, 22 years of age, declaiming on Japanese depredations in her homeland.[42]

Inevitably the various protests motivated some students to address issues closer to home, i.e., what was described as a "100% strike effected" against room and board costs with "women students residing in the dormitory" leading the way.[43] This was just one of many strikes that activist H.U. students had launched to the consternation of some on Capitol Hill.[44]

The hegemonic right-wing on Capitol Hill did not blandly accept this state of affairs. Matters came to a head in the Spring of 1936 when the U.S. Senate decided to probe "alleged Communistic activities at Howard University." Albert Bushnell Hart of Harvard, who counted Du Bois and Woodson as students, sought to reassure that President Mordecai Johnson was no Communist and that this absurd allegation was driven by the "intense jealousy" felt toward him by Professor Kelly Miller, who besides had an inflated sense of his own importance: "in his own mind he remains the most important and significant African in the United States...."

Others begged to differ, recalling a time when Johnson presided over a campus session that included "avowed Communists." Investigators were not assuaged by the presence of Du Bois; Black Communist leader, James W. Ford and his fellow Red, James Allen; and Socialist Party leader, Norman Thomas. As for Johnson, he pointed the finger of accusation at junior faculty member—and future Nobel Laureate—Ralph Bunche, who turned over his "personal files" to the investigators after Charles Thompson of the *Journal of Negro Education* refused to do so. One evening the attendance at

---

39. *The Hilltop*, 22 December 1934.
40. *The Hilltop*, 22 December 1934.
41. *The Hilltop*, 12 December 1935.
42. *The Hilltop*, 27 January 1937.
43. *The Hilltop*, 20 January 1936.
44. *The Hilltop*, 25 November 1936.

this gathering was so crowded that attendees felt compelled to move from an auditorium to the chapel, an indicator intense interest. Du Bois admitted, "I was once a member of the celebrated local in New York City" of the Socialist Party. "I am convinced," he asserted in words assured to raise hackles, "of the essential truth of the Marxian philosophy," though unlike other comrades he conceded "there is no automatic power in socialism to override and suppress race prejudice" and "the analogy of the Jews in Russia is for our case entirely false and misleading...." To that end, he argued controversially, "one of the worst things that Negroes could do today would be to join the American Communist Party" since "for American colored men [that would be] suicide...."

Du Bois' admonition was hardly solace to legislators who were aghast at the words of President Johnson cited in the *Pittsburgh Courier* of 18 May 1928 where he was cited for the proposition that his Negro readership should study the Soviet Union—"'the Negro is carefully watching [the] Soviet Union,'" he advised. Legislators were further alarmed with the presence on campus of Professor Emmett Dorsey, a "Communist" said to have "recently attended a meeting of the Third International," meaning Marxist-Leninist parties globally.[45] Worried alumni nervously addressed this tinderbox [46] and by the mid-1930s articulated "the case against President Mordecai W. Johnson," lamenting that "evidences of unrest within the student body" were "widespread," motivated by an "unwarranted increase in room rent" and a football strike.[47]

Still, it was President Johnson who was fingered repeatedly as the top Red at the pinnacle of the Hilltop campus,[48] which may have been a factor in his denunciation by leading Black Republican, Perry Howard—who in turn was scorned by Woodson.[49]

Professor Miller sought vainly to suppress hysteria that he helped to generate by reassuring that the "Negro is not 'Red' or radical by

45. Report, "Alleged Communistic Activities at Howard University," 12 May 1936, 74th Congress, 2nd Session, Senate Doc. 217, Box 37, *Jesse Moorland Papers, Howard University*.

46. "Howard University Alumni Journal," Commencement 1936, Box 2, *Eugene Davidson Papers, Howard University*.

47. Report from Alumni, circa October 1937, Box 25, *Ralph Bunche Papers, New York Public Library-Schomburg Center*.

48. *New York Herald*, 16 April 1931.

49. *Washington World*, 24 April 1931, Box 36, *Jesse Moorland Papers, Howard University*.

nature" [50]—congenital arguments were hardly comforting to those in power. Nor was it soothing to the hawkish local press, understandably sensitive to the presence of Communists within walking distance of the citadel of power. Communists were "flourishing" not just at Howard but Georgetown and George Washington universities too, said a local scribe, adding with asperity that it was "known that most Communistic bodies throughout this country have many colored members...."[51]

As suggested, Howard professor and future Nobel Laureate, Ralph Bunche—then left leaning—was often at the center of this rancorous dispute. By 1935 he was slated to appear at a Socialist Party forum on academic freedom, but the authorities did not allow it because there was no "occupancy permit" held by the sponsors; a similar forum on the Italian invasion of Ethiopia was stymied for similar reasons.[52] As early as 1934, Bunche was pegged by the FBI as a Communist, which allowed the agency to pressure him adroitly a few decades later.[53] According to the FBI, by the early summer of 1935 as conferees met to form a National Negro Congress affiliate at Howard, on the "same day"— coincidentally—top leaders" of the Communist Party "fraction" on campus met: "informant stated that Dr. Bunche was introduced... as a Communist Party member" by Harry Haywood, no less, the self-proclaimed "Black Bolshevik." Bunche's purported "membership" was "only made known to the Central Committee" and "a few of the top level members, as it was believed he could be more valuable to the [CP] if he was not openly known to be a member" of the CP cell at Howard. James Ford, the premier Black Communist leader, supposedly "acted as liaison between Dr. Bunche" and the top party leadership. This provided Bunche with plausible deniability if queried about his radical ties. Allegedly, Bunche was seen at a "caucus meeting of the Communist fraction" that was "open only to leading Negro Communists." This was in the 1930s but, alarmingly—said the FBI—as of 1953, while serving at the top table of the United Nations, he "may still be under Communist Party discipline...." Reputedly, the Black Communist writer,

---

50. *Philadelphia Tribune*, 16 April 1931, Box 36, *Howard University.*
51. *Washington Times*, 18 May 1931.
52. "The Socialist," November 1935, Box 52, *Ralph Bunche Papers, New York Public Library-Schomburg Center.*
53. Report by Assistant Attorney General W.F. Tompkins, 30 August 1954, Box 1, *Ralph Bunche FBI File, New York Public Library-Schomburg Center.*

Abner Berry, called Bunche "one of a number of Negro intellectuals that have become [a] Marxist...."[54]

Accuracy aside, these ruminations reflected a wider point: Black Washington—ala Black America writ large—was undergoing a transformation in the 1930s, as the Party of Lincoln (the Republicans) lost popularity amidst the ravages of economic distress and the New Deal ascended. The Communist Party, which proved to be quite supportive of many of Roosevelt's initiatives, were instrumental in this process. Thus, in 1932, 77 percent of the Negro vote went to the GOP's Herbert Hoover and 23 percent to FDR—figures that were to be reversed in coming election cycles. Still, reflective of the frequently exercised ideological hegemony of the Black petit bourgeoisie in the District, by 1936, Negro voters there favored FDR only marginally over the defeated Kansan, Alf Landon. This occurred though an initial Social Security proposal would have excluded 87 percent of all Black women and 55 percent of all Black wage earners—the price of an alliance with a Democratic Party in thrall to Dixiecrats thirsting for revenge against Negroes.[55]

Still, even Robert Weaver, a future Cabinet Secretary, said the early New Deal was "neglecting" Negroes, as "few...had secured jobs" at any level in the midst of an employment desert. His peer, Will Alexander, thought given its strategic location and the dire plight of Negroes "the next stage in race relations in the country would center around what happened in Washington."[56]

Writing from his office at 513 F Street NW, CP leader, Robert E. Ray, saluted an initiative of double barreled consequence: he demanded that the Belasco Theatre, "which is now showing Soviet and other films," enforce non-racially segregated seating. "A successful campaign for the admittance of Negroes in the Belasco," he insisted, "will enable us to further the campaign to all the movie houses in the city,"[57] which happened to be accurate.

Ralph Bunche was being prompted to think along parallel lines. It was in 1936 that Todd Duncan, actor and baritone singer, writing from the appropriately named, Hotel Grand of Chicago, told the professor of a similar Jim Crow pattern. "Our opera, 'Porgy and Bess', is to be presented in Washington, D.C. at the National Theatre," an

---

54. Report by "Informant of Unknow Reliability," 29 October 1953, *Ralph Bunche FBI File, New York Public Library-Schomburg Center*.

55. Mary-Elizabeth Murphy, *Jim Crow Capital*, 115, 117, 152.

56. Jill Watts, *The Black Cabinet*, 62, 75

57. Report by Robert E. Ray, 5 March 1935, Box 25, *Ralph Bunche Papers, New York Public Library-Schomburg Center*.

edifice marred by the "ghastly policy of the management of keep-ing Negroes away from its doors." Unfortunately, he confided, "our hands are tied in that we are bound by contract to the Theatre Guild" and "Actors Equity," too. His remedy—"dropping a personal note (confidential) to Mrs. Roosevelt"—was likely insufficient.[58] Illus-trating how Jim Crow was perceived occasionally as a means of circumventing exclusion altogether, Duncan also proposed that "at least a portion of the House should be set aside for Negroes...."[59] The wider point was the creeping influence of Bunche, a Howard profes-sor with left-wing leanings.

This was hardly the first time that Howard had attracted the negative attention of Congress. A Mississippi legislator referred acidulously to "persistent reports from the press" about "unrest and turmoil" on campus, leading to "frequent resignations and violent separations...."[60] Thus, Congressman Robert Hall of the bastion of Jim Crow that was Mississippi, demanded that Howard be scruti-nized carefully.[61] That was predictable. However, more troubling was that a similar call emerged from Congressman Arthur Mitchell, one of the few Negroes to attain such a lofty post. This signaled what was to emerge: Negro liberals seeking to undermine Black Communists in a shortsighted attempt to attain ideological hegemony.[62] Certainly, the presence at Howard of Paul Robeson, soon-to-be notorious Com-munist sympathizer, was bound to stir anxiety on Capitol Hill.[63]

Complicating matters was the point that as Howard's law school became more sophisticated, switching from mostly evening instruction and securing the leadership of the estimable Charles Hamilton Houston—who trained a generation of litigators: a num-ber of Euro-American professors, deemed to be not up to snuff, were ousted, which too did not win plaudits on Capitol Hill.[64] Meanwhile,

---

58. Todd Duncan to Ralph Bunche, 26 February 1935, Box 12, Folder 5, *Ralph Bunche Papers, University of California-Los Angeles.*
59. Memo from Todd Duncan, 6 February 1936, Box 12, Folder 5, *Ralph Bunche Papers, UCLA.*
60. House Resolution 160, 72nd Congress, 1st Session, circa 1934, Box 36, *Jesse Moorland Papers.*
61. *New York Amsterdam News*, 2 March 1932.
62. Report, 25 May 1935, Box 39, *Ralph Bunche Papers, New York Public Library-Schomburg Center.*
63. *Howard University Bulletin*, March 1931, Box 36, *Jesse Moorland Papers.*
64. *Philadelphia Tribune*, 16 April 1931, Box 36, *Jesse Moorland Papers.* See also Genna Rae McNeil, *Groundwork: Charles Hamilton Houston and the Struggle for Civil Rights*, Philadelphia: University of Pennsylvania Press, 1983.

Thurgood Marshall and his comrades beavered on at the school's three story brownstone at 420 Fifth Street, NW.[65]

A problem was the antagonist within the gates: Kelly Miller, who informed the U.S. Senate in 1935 that he had been "connected" with the school "as student, professor, Dean, and alumnus since 1880," and was dismayed by the presence on employment rolls of "prominent Communists, Socialists, Reds and Semi-Reds of varying degrees of radicalism." And as he saw it, the problem began at the top: with President Johnson who "presided at the session on Sunday evening when several speakers openly advocated the overthrow of existing order by revolution and bloodshed...." He seemed to long for the past when Senator Reed Smoot of Utah demanded that a book on the Soviet Union be tossed from the library and "the book was withdrawn that same day."[66] Fortunately for President Johnson, Secretary Ickes of Interior with oversight of the campus, expressed "unwillingness" to even talk with Miller, as his repetitive "tissue of misstatements...demonstrate...you to be a man more eager to break into the newspaper columns than to tell the truth...."[67]

All this placed President Johnson of Howard in a ticklish position, seeking to defend academic freedom while vitiating Dixiecrat lancing. With the skill of a diplomat, he complimented lavishly Secretary of the Interior, Harold Ickes, whose agency had oversight of the District. This occurred after a new building housing chemists was unveiled on campus: "in the entire history of the education of Negro youth," he exhorted, "this is the first time that such a teaching staff in a single science has been provided with a building adequately equipped in quantity and in quality for first rate...graduate instruction and research," an "event of national significance."[68] Not only do movements matter but individuals do too and, according to an early Black journalist at the *Washington Post*, Dorothy Gilliam, it was Ickes who laid the "public foundation" for desegregation in the District "by insisting that the facilities under his jurisdiction be used without

65. Margaret Edds, *We Face the Dawn: Oliver Hill, Spottswood Robinson and the Legal Team that Dismantled Jim Crow*, Charlottesville: University of Virginia Press, 2018, 35.

66. Kelly Miller to "Dear Senator," 28 May 1935, Box 12, *Kelly Miller Papers*. Original reference to "revolution" is underlined.

67. Secretary Ickes to Kelly Miller, 26 September 1935, Box 12, *Kelly Miller Papers*.

68. President Johnson to Secretary Ickes, 15 September 1936, Box 14, Official File, 6L-6P, *Department of the Interior, Franklin D. Roosevelt Presidential Library, Hyde Park, New York*.

discrimination."[69] Ickes was a kind of envoy to Black America, seeking to wangle an invitation to speak at Howard, for example.[70]

His supervisor was not necessarily held in high esteem by a number of well placed Negroes. This coterie included Truman Gibson who had worked for Black Congressman William Dawson and as an attorney worked on the Hansberry housing case in Chicago. He was friendly with Black Communist leader, Ishmael Flory, in the Windy City. But he also knew the White House: FDR aide "Phileo [Nash] and I were socially friendly. He lived a few doors from me in Washington," and both were involved with "Georgetown Day School...the first integrated school in the history of [D.C.]." His progressive credentials notwithstanding, he found Roosevelt to be "really remote, a racist."[71]

This was not a yeasty response. Negro voters had in large numbers cast their ballots for President Franklin D. Roosevelt and were entitled to some spoils. This in turn bolstered the building of a Black intelligentsia—at times with leftist leanings—which served to erode a calcified bias for overall betterment and progress. A reinforced Howard could then fulfill its educational mission contributing to the virtuous circle.

However, it was not just the proximity of Howard's purported "nest of radicals" to seats of power that rankled all too many. Howard's students arrived from 38 different states and 14 different nations as of the mid-1930s with both figures bound to increase in coming years,[72] suggesting that campus radicalism could be transmitted nationally, if not globally. A telling signal occurred during this period when the well-connected Abyssinian (Ethiopian) Malaku Bayen admitted that "'my belief in Race Solidarity caused me to select Howard University for my studies, in order that I might have a closer contact with my people'"; he also gushed that he was proud "'to be married to an American girl of the Black Race,'" the ties of special intimacy that bonded Africa and African Americans and an emblem of their potent mutual solidarity.[73] Congruent with

---

69. Dorothy Butler Gilliam, *Trailblazer: A Pioneering Journalist's Fight to Make the Media Look More Like America*, New York: Center Street, 2019, 10.
70. Harold Ickes to Kelly Miller, 26 February 1935, Box 12, *Kelly Miller Papers, Emory University-Atlanta*.
71. Truman Gibson, Oral History, 27 July 2001, *Harry S. Truman Presidential Library, Independence, Missouri*.
72. *Wisconsin Gazette* [Janesville], 12 February 1935, Box 34, *Jesse Moorland Papers*.
73. Nadia Nurhussein, *Black Land: Imperial Ethiopianism and African America*, Princeton: Princeton University Press, 2019, 147.

the spirit of the era, District NAACP branch leader, A.S. Pinkett, was "eager that we have a public meeting here with [M.K.] Ghandi [sic] as speaker...."[74]

Leading Black publisher, Claude Barnett of Chicago, whose Associated Negro Press had global reach, found a "keen interest of the reading public in the welfare of Howard University,"[75] a cohort that decidedly included Addis Ababa.

Ostensibly, Congress was quite concerned about the presence of Communists on Howard's campus. There was something to this but there was also general concern about the proliferating spirit of protest on campus and citywide, generated precisely by antics on Capitol Hill. When the demagogic South Carolina Senator, "Pitchfork" Ben Tillman spoke of "'the colored woman [as] the more deadly of the species'" it both energized an already engaged core of Black women to protest further but, contrarily, it contributed to the insulting and renewed campaign to build a "'Mammy Memorial'" in supposed honor of their purported fealty to white supremacy. Howard students were in the forefront, as they were when the NAACP accelerated its crusade against lynching. This was manifested when an assemblage of 5,000—mostly Black—engaged in a "Silent Parade Against Lynching." It was asking too much to request that besieged Negroes turn a cold shoulder to Communists, not least because of Reds' global connections, which was precisely what was needed to corrode encrusted bias. Logically, by the early 1930s Negroes and Communists formed the "Washington Provisional Committee Against Lynching." Not for the last time, the center of power had to consider the national security implications of barely containing a disgruntled African American community that was not averse to forging ties with Reds, who in turn had ties to Moscow. On cue, educator Nannie Helen Burroughs thundered, "'there are enough Negroes in Washington...to make Pennsylvania Avenue tremble.'"[76]

Tremblingly, ascendant anticommunists in Washington were forced to contemplate the stirring words of influential Negro publisher in Baltimore, Carl Murphy, who declaimed passionately in May 1931 that Communists were "'as courageous as the Minute Men or the volunteer firemen [and] seem everywhere ready for a

74. A.S. Pinkett to Walter White, 22 October 1931, G37, *NAACP Papers.*

75. Claude Moorland to Jesse Moorland, circa 1931, Box 34, *Jesse Moorland Papers.*

76. Mary-Elizabeth Murphy, *Jim Crow Capital: Women and Black Freedom Struggles in Washington, D.C., 1920-1945*, Chapel Hill: University of North Carolina Press, 2018, 38, 41, 50, 53, 62, 69.

demonstration against race prejudice.'" Ultimately, this compelled an agonized retreat from the more egregious aspects of Jim Crow by the 1950s with the undermining of Communists as the price to be paid.[77] This praise bespoke collaboration with Communists, as reflected when—not necessarily congruent with national policy— the District NAACP branch sponsored a fundraising concert for the Scottsboro defendants featuring native son, Duke Ellington, that garnered $425; as important, a news item on the same event was sent "to the two hundred odd colored newspapers of the country," as the branch leader put it.[78]

Murphy was well-positioned to sense these important trends. On the eve of the Depression, the NAACP in the District had enjoyed a successful recruitment campaign. Branch Secretary, A.S. Pinkett beamingly recounted to him how "this year, as in no other for some years past, the pastors or churches, large and small, welcomed three minute speakers at their regular Sunday services," while "interest taken by Congressman [Oscar] De Priest in local activities gave incalculable impetus to the cause…"[79] With brimming confidence, Pinkett envisioned a "roster of three thousand memberships solicited and paid between December 1, 1930" and the following months.[80]

Du Bois, not ordinarily profligate with praise, hailed District branch leader, Shelby Davidson—also a Harvard alumnus—as "very aggressive," befitting a "dealer in real estate" and "instrumental in procuring a better class of homes for colored people in Washington" and akin in his militancy to his son, Eugene Davidson.[81]

The NAACP in Murphy's Maryland metropolis was moribund by the mid-1920s and shortly thereafter. It had revived by 1935 to include 100 members, many of whom were lawyers, clerics and teachers. However, by mid-1936 the branch grew to over 2,000 members, driven by the emerging ethos of radicalism symbolized by the Communist sponsorship of the defense of the Scottsboro Nine. Soon the Baltimore branch reported 2,700 members, second only to Detroit and by late-1939 the membership exceeded 4,000. Still, an early campaign caused sparks to fly. Seven of the top nine department stores

77. Andor Skotnes, *A New Deal for All? Race and Class Struggles in Depression Era Baltimore*, Durham: Duke University Press, 2013, 45.
78. Secretary of D.C. Branch to Shepherd Allen, 21 October 1931, Box G37, *NAACP Papers*.
79. A.S. Pinkett to "Afro-American," 15 July 1929, Box G37, *NAACP Papers*.
80. A.S. Pinkett to "Dear Friend," 27 February 1931, Box G37.
81. Du Bois to "Mr. Seligman," 13 January 1930, Box G37, *NAACP Papers*.

were Jewish-owned—as were most of the stores hit with a boycott by the early-1930s because of Jim Crow practices, including selling lesser quality goods at exorbitant prices to Negroes; some of these merchants were implicated in allied charges that Jewish American landlords and real estate brokers were enmeshed in similar shady methods. Murphy was in the vortex of these heated protests where he could draw upon his array of contacts at Howard for sustenance: holding an M.A. in German from Harvard, he studied for a year in this European giant and thus was well aware of the perfidy of anti-Semitism—which was transmitted to his students on the hilltop where he had taught the language.[82]

But Murphy's newspaper was hardly an island of tranquility in that as he and his organ were sounding the tocsin against Jim Crow in downtown Baltimore, workers at his shop were railing furiously against "intimidations" including the firing of George Murphy, his close relative, who was to become a leading Communist in succeeding decades. Ralph Matthews who replaced the latter Murphy scion as top administrator of the newspaper, vowed that he would "'smash the union,'" a disturbing trend that would reach efflorescence by the 1950s.[83]

Robert Weaver also matriculated at Harvard—this before his youthful years spent in Washington, all of which led to his becoming a member of the Cabinet of President Lyndon B. Johnson in 1966 as the first Secretary of Housing and Urban Development. His elite credentials notwithstanding, Weaver—born in the District in 1907—by the 1930s was informing his fellow recusant from the hoi polloi, Howard professor Ralph Bunche, that "we lived in a neighborhood containing few negro families," making it "necessary for me to use the streetcar to go to a colored school," although there "was a public school within two blocks of our house." It is worthwhile to consider what impact this had on his subsequent rise to the pinnacle of career success in that he confessed that his "usual approach" involved "avoiding white people as much as possible...." He was born into modesty—his father was a postal clerk—though this did not stunt his academic rise; but what did leave a "lasting impression" was an experience at Dunbar High School where at an oratorical contest the

82. Thomas Anthony Gass, "'A Mean City:' The NAACP and the Black Freedom Struggle in Baltimore, 1935-1975," Ph.D. dissertation, Ohio State University, 2014, 11, 41, 105, 116, 126, 128, 129.
83. Constance Daniel of "Afro" union to Howard Teachers' Union, circa 1938, Box 3, *Eugene Davidson Papers*.

Euro-American judges ignored him callously: "I realized what a terrible barrier race prejudice was,"[84] he concluded.

Bunche could well commiserate. As a newly minted faculty member, he and his growing family moved into a residence at 1510 Jackson Street, N.E. "'When we moved in,'" he recalled, "'my daughters had to go three miles to school—I had to hire a driver to take them—even though there was a school for white kids just around the corner.'"[85]

The horrors of Jim Crow were no revelation to Howard students: with a sense of the dramatic that was not exclusive to Communists, these students were photographed with nooses around their necks in 1934 in protest against widespread lynching of Negroes. This photo was so moving that in 2019 Black students at the University of North Carolina chose to replicate this image in protest against yet another spate of executions of African Americans in a manner that mimicked lynchings of yore, indicative of the continuing impact of Howard demonstrations.[86]

That year, 1934, was a kind of high water mark for the NAACP. They picketed a so-called "National Crime Conference" at Constitution Hall as they pressured the Attorney General to include lynching on that confab's agenda. The legendary Charles Hamilton Houston, architect of the juridical attack on Jim Crow, was active with the branch and lukewarm at best toward anticommunism. Still, it was thought that the District branch, "located in the most strategic and most important spot in [the] country has fallen short,"[87] buffeted as it was by biting winds from Virginia and Dixie more broadly.

A vulnerability still for Dixie is that energized Negroes in the citadel of power focused incessantly on the region's cherished Jim Crow praxis. It is not as if this infestation was invisible. Washrooms in government buildings were racially segregated and often elevators were too.[88] The presence of embassies and an international press guaranteed that this bleeding wound would receive maximum attention.

Although Red hunters and anticommunist birddogs routinely spied on President Johnson and faculty members like Ralph Bunche, if they had been diligent they would have flyspecked more carefully

---

84. Robert Weaver to Ralph Bunche, 25 September 1939, Reel 1, *Robert Weaver Papers, New York Public Library-Schomburg Center.*
85. Sandra Fitzpatrick and Maria R. Goodwin, *The Guide to Black Washington: Places and Events of Historical and Cultural Significance in the Nation's Capital,* New York: Hippocrene, 1999, 69.
86. *Washington Post,* 14 January 2019.
87. Memo by Roy Wilkins, 19 April 1937, Box G38, *NAACP Papers.*
88. Jill Watts, *The Black Cabinet,* 119.

an early actual party member: Doxey A. Wilkerson. Born in 1905 in Excelsior Springs, Missouri, he grew to maturity in neighboring Kansas City and by 1921 was enrolled at the University of Kansas in Lawrence. By 1935 he was ensconced at Howard but departed in 1942; he encountered stiff challenges when he clashed with the Swedish social scientist, Gunnar Myrdal, appointed by the U.S. powerful to pronounce on domestic racism. Wilkerson became a fulltime Communist cadre during the halcyon anti-fascist era embodied in 1943, before departing from Red ranks by 1957 in the wake of internal disputes driven by a bombshell report on the misdeeds of the recently deceased Soviet leader, Josef Stalin. Yet Wilkerson's tenure at Howard occurred during a time when this school was becoming an epicenter of protest, not least because of his ministrations. The experience he received in Washington then led to an epochal chapter when he clashed in 1948 in Harlem with Max Yergan, a former Communist heading steadily to the right, eventuating in rationalizing of Pretoria's apartheid and colonialism.[89]

Wilkerson brought a wealth of varied experience to the hilltop campus. Before arriving in Washington, he had worked in a packinghouse in Kansas City and as a dining car waiter on the Chicago, Burlington and Quincy Railroad. From 1927-1935 he taught at Virginia State University in Petersburg and in the summer of 1935 taught at Hampton Institute. While officially on the faculty at Howard, he spent the years 1937-1939 at the Works Projects Administration of the federal government and then from 1942-1943 toiled at Washington's Office of Price Administration. Those sojourns prepared him well for his serving from 1943-1944 as the Educational Director of the Communist Party in the District and Maryland. [90]

W. Alphaeus Hunton, yet another Communist,[91] also emerged from Howard and too became involved in anti-apartheid protests. Born in 1903, he graduated from Howard in 1923 before taking a M.A. at Harvard, obtaining a doctorate in English literature from New York University in 1938 (his specialty was the study of the

---

89. Shante Julian Lyons, "The Radical Evolution of the Communist Educator, Doxey Wilkerson," Ph.D. dissertation, University of Missouri-St. Louis, 2015, 18, 47, 52, 53, 107, 109. See also Charles Denton Johnson, "African Americans and South Africa: The Anti-Apartheid Movement in the United States, 1921-1955," Ph.D. dissertation, Howard University, 2004, 124.

90. FBI File, various dates, Box 3, *Doxey Wilkerson Papers, New York Public Library-Schomburg Center*.

91. Christine Ann Lutz, "'The Dizzy Steep to Heaven': The Hunton Family, 1850-1970," Ph.D. dissertation, Georgia State University, 2001, 13.

British poet, Alfred Lord Tennyson). He taught at Howard from 1926-1943, soaring to the leadership of the union and becoming an indefatigably tireless activist on a range of issues. Then he decamped to Manhattan, working side-by-side with Robeson and Du Bois in the Council on African Affairs, the premier organization combating colonialism, then falling victim to an ascendant McCarthyism which led to his exile in West Africa (both Guinea-Conakry by 1960 then joining Du Bois in Ghana) and eventual death in Zambia, Southern Africa by 1970, where President Kenneth Kaunda wept openly at his gravesite.[92]

Hunton's sturdy familial roots well-prepared him for the heights to which he climbed. In Chatham, Ontario in the 1850s Stanton Hunton was renowned as a close comrade of the sainted John Brown, who could be found at his Canadian abode. Hunton was one of the selected convened by Brown on 8 May 1858 in preparation for the 1859 insurrection in Virginia.[93] His 19th century forebears were loyal to London, not least because of the rancid racist slavery that stained the U.S. Eventually his ancestors moved from Ontario to Atlanta, where he was born. Perhaps the solitude that allowed him to focus intently on the literature that he loved, stemmed from the difficult circumstances of this Deep South metropolis which was not "too busy to hate" at that juncture, forcing him to turn away abruptly from the ugliness that permeated. His Houston Street home was quite close to the point at which the infamous Atlanta pogrom of 1906 erupted, as the family fled to Brooklyn by 1907. His mother was influential in Protestant ranks which meant he traveled with her to Germany as a child, exposing both to influential socialist forces. As World War I was grinding to a bloody halt, Addie Hunton was being surveilled by the U.S. authorities, perhaps because of her adamant devotion to peace and Pan-Africanism: she joined Howard luminaries at the Second Pan-African Congress in 1921 convened in London, Brussels, and Paris. By 1927, as her son was settling into his campus office, she was told that she should become more clandestine about her global activism, lest the authorities object more

---

92. Birth Certificate, circa 1903 and C.V., 28 January 1967, Reel 1, *W. Alphaeus Hunton Papers, New York Public Library-Schomburg Center*. See also Hollis R. Lynch, *Black American Radicals and the Liberation of Africa: The Council on African Affairs*, Ithaca: Africana Studies Center, Cornell University, 1978.
93. Memoir of Dorothy Hunton, Reel 3, *W. Alphaeus Hunton Papers*. See also Donald Earl Collins, "'A Substance of Things Hoped for': Multiculturalism, Desegregation and Identity in African American Washington, D.C., 1930-1960," Ph.D. dissertation, Carnegie Mellon University, 1997.

strenuously.[94] It was on 3 September 1926 that he received a tele-gram from Howard official, Emmett J. Scott, who was "authorized" to offer him $1,800 annually as an instructor in English literature.[95]

Hunton's upbringing prepared him for both the cosmopolitanism of Howard and a post-university life in the anti-colonial trenches. Before Howard he resided in Europe and like Du Bois became fluent in German. His stature—6' 4-1/2" inches—caused him to stoop to appear shorter, an aspect of his overall modesty. Though his parents were Episcopalians and proselytizers too, he described himself as an agnostic, which prepared him for the rigors of socialism.

Despite his roots in Atlanta, Washington's rigid Jim Crow was bracing for him, competing with Pretoria in this disreputable respect. The Library of Congress was one of the few sites where this was not the case, fortifying his desire to study.

At Howard he was in charge of English classes for frosh, and he lectured—appropriately—in the Victorian style, instructing from behind a desk (though this too may have been a function of his shyness with the desk intruding as a natural barrier between himself and students). This caused some to view him as aloof and anti-social, which was not wholly inaccurate. He was friendly, though—dialectically—withdrawn. He shared an office with Ster-ling Brown, who became a friend, though this fellow professor knew he was "'uncomfortable with small talk....'" One of Hunton's stu-dents "'couldn't understand...how Dr. Hunton whose interests were known to center on explicit contemporary problems, could ever have taken the time and trouble to become an authority on what seemed to me, a dull prose of very distant English gentlemen.'" Hunton countered by explaining that his study of emergent British imperial-ism aided him enormously in understanding Africa,[96] the core of the final chapter of his storied life.

And understanding colonial Africa aided his comprehension of the plight of African Americans. After all, exploitation of both was the critical issue and both sides benefited from mutual backing. So imbued, while teaching at Howard, Hunton simultaneously became chairman of the Labor Committee of the National Negro Congress. This Communist led formation and incipient challenger to the

---

94. Ibid., Memoir of Dorothy Hunton. See also Christine Ann Lutz, "The Dizzy Steep to Heaven: The Hunton Family, 1850-1970," Ph.D. dissertation, Georgia State University, 2001.

95. Emmett J. Scott to W.A. Hunton, 3 September 1926, Reel 1, *W. Alphaeus Hunton Papers*.

96. Dorothy Hunton Memoir, Reel 3, *W. Alphaeus Hunton Papers*.

NAACP as the premier umbrella grouping of diverse political trends among Negroes, demanded desegregation of the union movement. Hunton led a parallel movement to organize District domestic workers. It was Hunton who fought for the appointment of three African Americans to the local Unemployment Compensation Committee and victoriously insisted upon the right of this minority to register for jobs in the Works Projects Administration. It was Hunton who conducted a mass campaign for an adequate minimum wage for Black laundry workers. It was Hunton who led the organizing of protests to demand jobs for African Americans in the city's public transit system. It was Hunton who shaped yet another campaign, demanding that Black workers be hired at the Glen L. Martin aircraft factory in Baltimore. As this latter crusade unfolded, he directed picket lines at the federal Office of Production Management.[97]

When Hunton felt compelled to exit from Howard and the District, a mighty blow was struck against both.

---

97. Christine Ann Lutz, "'The Dizzy Steep to Heaven': The Hunton Family, 1850-1970," Ph.D. dissertation, Georgia State University, 2001, 291.

Chapter 4

Anti-Fascist Revolt, 1934-1941

As the rise of fascism globally proceeded from the 1930s to the 1940s—with its ricochet in the U.S. itself[1]—a paradox settled in Washington. Certainly, this put wind in the sails of Dixiecrats on Capitol Hill and their obsessively maniacal focus on Howard University, perceived as a nest of Negro radicals. On the other hand, the ascendance of fascism exposed the reality that these same Dixiecrats bore an all too uncanny resemblance to the approaching antagonist in Berlin, which put them on the defensive and created more room for maneuver by the likes of Wilkerson, Hunton, George Murphy, and their comrades. Even as the anti-fascist war unfolded in the 1940s, the two professors departed Howard in search of greener pastures, but then after 1945 were wounded severely in a Red Scare buzzsaw. Their fellow professor, Ralph Bunche, also left Howard—and his erstwhile left-wing posture—for the realm of U.S. intelligence, then the nascent United Nations.

Bunche's move reflected the growing strength of the national security state centered in the District and its vicinity. This factor, along with the New Deal, helped to transform Washington from its historic role as a somnolent Southern town to its role as the fortress of a budding superpower, which meant the U.S. and its otherwise rigidifying Jim Crow had to bend, especially post-1945 with the ideological contestation with Moscow. This did open more opportunity for some Negroes, but it often came at the expense of Negro neighborhoods, not least in neighboring Virginia and Georgetown. This was occurring as the Black population of Washington was growing from 86,702 in 1900 to 187,266 by 1940, but as the Urban League put

---

1. Gerald Horne, *The Color of Fascism: Lawrence Dennis, Racial Passing and the Rise of Right Wing Extremism in the U.S.*, New York: New York University Press, 2009.

it: "during the same period the white population has increased in exact proportion," meaning "areas which Negroes may occupy are rapidly diminishing" pushing the latter group into alleyways and overcrowded climes. There was a noticeable "decrease in the total land area available to occupancy by Negroes," was their discouraging conclusion. Thus, "to complete the road system serving the Pentagon and Navy E Buildings" across the river in Virginia, "some 70 acres of land owned or occupied by Negroes were acquired by the public condemnation" and "displacement exacerbated by restrictive covenants," then legal devices which barred African Americans from vast swathes of territory.[2]

At the same time, the District continued to be a magnet attracting leading Negro intellectuals because of the presence of Howard. A budding doctor or professor of medicine did not have many options. There was Meharry in Nashville. But it was Washington that had an entire Surgeon General's Library containing—as of 1930—one million volumes on medicine and allied topics, not to mention libraries of various agencies and the Library of Congress and the Army Medical Museum, "one of the best of its kind in the world," according to an observer. A Howard publication instructed, "all these libraries are open to the student," a pointed reference to the absence of Jim Crow barriers.[3]

The District was not just a boon to medical researchers. W. Sherman Savage, who went on to become a premier historian, began at Howard in 1913: "I was able to make a great use of the Library of Congress where I spent as much time as possible"; though H.U. was hardly an island of progressivism, it seemed that way to Savage by way of comparison in that this campus "granted more freedom to the student than any other black school...."[4]

* * *

2. "Interim Report of the Study Sub Committee of the Emergency Committee on Housing in Metropolitan Washington," no date, Box I: C40, *National Urban League Papers, Library of Congress, Washington, D.C.* In the same collection, Box I: F9, see Report by Rayford Logan, Chairman of Committee on Participation of Negroes in the National Defense Program. In the same collection, see also Waldron Faulkner, President of Washington Urban League to T. Arnold Hill, 15 May 1939, Box I: D37: Estimated "150,000" Negroes in Washington.

3. Article, *Howard University Bulletin*, 18 (Number 7, August 1930), Box 1, *W. Montague Cobb Collection, Emory University*.

4. "Memoirs of W. Sherman Savage," 1975, *Huntington Library-San Marino, California*.

As fascists were surging to power in Berlin, the political climate in Washington was not altogether unpromising. Or so thought the NAACP when it reported happily that U.S. Senators were "breaking party lines" as they lined up to "promise" aid to H.U. Boldly, the Association warned that to do otherwise would "arouse bitter resentment among colored people which would be reflected in … election[s]…."[5]

This was good news for campus radicals. Hunton found time to become a force in the campus union, along with Wilkerson. The first issues of the "Howard Teachers' Union News" in 1936 revealed that H.U. already had members appointed to top bodies in the national American Federation of Teachers. This included Wilkerson as Co-Chair of the Committee on Federal Aid to Education.[6]

The District NAACP branch cooperated with this Communist, for Wilkerson wanted this effort "to have a solid NAACP coloring…."[7] It was Wilkerson who was depicted as addressing an "enthusiastic audience of more than 275 students" assembled by the seemingly ubiquitous Liberal Club.[8] When the Southern Negro Youth Congress met in Richmond in 1937, H.U. was well-represented,[9] despite the group being excoriated as little more than a "Communist Front," when actually it was a precursor of the better-known Student Non-Violent Coordinating Committee, the valuable shock troops of the 1960s, who valiantly mounted the anti-Jim Crow barricades. Soon the H.U. local union was debating shifting affiliation from the American Federation of Labor to the insurgent Congress of Industrial Unions. A tip-off was the warm praise for the latter in the local's pages. By then eminent sociologist E. Franklin Frazier was president and Hunton was recording secretary, while Wilkerson had become a national Vice President of the AFT, elected—said an observer—"by the largest majority vote cast for any candidate at the AFT convention…."[10] Proudly, the union spoke of "Brother [Albert] Einstein," a "charter member of Local #552" at Princeton.[11]

---

5. Press Release, 11 March 1932, Box C207, *NAACP Papers*.
6. *Howard Teachers' Union News*, 1 (Number 1, 16 November 1936), *Howard University*. See also Lloyd E. Blauch and J. Orin Powers, *Public Education in the District of Columbia Prepared for the Advisory Committee on Education*, Washington, D.C.: Government Printing Office, 1938.
7. John Lovell to Walter White, 1 August 1939, Box G38, *NAACP Papers*.
8. *The Hilltop*, 9 February 1938.
9. *Howard Teachers Union News*, 4(Number 4, 6 March 1937).
10. *Howard Teachers' Union News*, 2(Number 1, December 1937).
11. *Howard Teachers' Union News*, 2(Number 4, March 1938).

As to be expected, the Communist duo—Wilkerson and Hunton— were the dynamos of the union. The latter served variously as president and vice president, all the while continuing his anti-lynch activism. "Life for Alphaeus during those hectic years," recalled his spouse, Dorothy Hunton, "was a never ending round of meetings, rallies, picketing," then returning to an office to face "mountains of school papers." The "grave and gloomy picture" of Jim Crow made buoyancy difficult. "An indefinable sadness frequently overshadowed his few fleeting joys," she contended morosely. "By nature, he was not very optimistic," and, thus, was not often disappointed. Perhaps, the "chronic fatigue dogging him at every step" played a role. At that juncture he was separated from his wife and his ultimate life partner—Dorothy Hunton—felt that "much of his distress and despondency stemmed from his unhappy marriage" combined with a "host of commitments that overworked him and scarcely left time for rest....."[12]

A similar process was enveloping his comrade, Wilkerson, though he seemed to handle the pressure with more aplomb. Both were majordomos of the New Negro Alliance of the District, which in the 1930s unleashed an effective campaign against Jim Crow. On the other hand, Bunche—who was to make his peace with U.S. rulers in the following decades—in 1935 flayed the NNA as "'short sighted opportunists and utterly stupid'"; it was potentially "'strike breaking,'" he contended hotly to compel bosses to hire Negroes; it was "'simply fascism,'" he said, if bosses felt compelled to layoff Euro-Americans and hire African Americans in their stead,[13] which was certainly not the thrust of Hunton and Wilkerson but was more of an expression of ultra-leftism, as has been the historic tendency, masquerading as far-sightedness in preparation for feckless capitulation. Bunche and others objected to NNA protests against businesses that did not hire Negroes as too hostile to the long-term goal of what was being touted as "black-white unity."[14]

---

12. Dorothy Hunton Memoir, Reel 3, *W. Alphaeus Hunton Papers*.
13. *California Eagle*, 19 April 1935, Box 92, *August Meier Papers, New York Public Library-Schomburg Center*.
14. Jonathan Scott Holloway, *Confronting the Veil: Abram Harris, Jr., E. Franklin Frazier and Ralph Bunche, 1919-1941*, Chapel Hill: University of North Carolina Press, 2002, 53. By 1939, Bunche was in close touch with novelist, Saul Bellow, also rapidly moving to the right. See Bunche to Bellow, 24 July 1939, Box 24, *Ralph Bunche Papers, New York Public Library-Schomburg Center*: "The main disagreements I have with [C.L.R.] James revolve about the Trotskyist position...when James suggests there is little or no difference between

It was the NNA that took the lead in protest of noxious cinema, e.g., a revival of the terroristic *Birth of a Nation*, where in the creator of the novel on which the movie was based confessed that his purpose—said the protesters—was to "drive the Negro out of America."[15]

The NNA, which was birthed in August 1933, was a battering ram against Jim Crow. By 1938, they prevailed in a high court case that upheld the rights of picketers, a victory vouchsafed when in October of that same year almost 20,000 Black women participated in a job protest in the District.[16]

Undaunted, by 1939 a local scribe marked a "year of picketing" by the NNA, while noting the participation of Hunton's National Negro Congress. "Doxey Wilkerson, President of the Howard Teachers' Union" also served as "chairman of the committee on arrangements for the anniversary demonstration," a propitious occasion. The essence was a kind of "Don't Buy, Where You Can't Work" campaign targeting retail establishments—and delivering jobs.[17] Still, Hunton was not far behind Wilkerson in boosting this protest, as he was pictured prominently in a local newspaper picketing in front of a chain drugstore in July 1936.[18] Hunton was on the Executive Committee of the NNC, while Wilkerson was Treasurer.[19]

Nevertheless, by mid-1939, Wilkerson—listed as chairman of the NNA—acknowledged that "we face a crisis in our fight for Negro clerks" at this drugstore chain; "after more than a year of picketing we seem far from our objective...." For, "merely to maintain the two picket lines at 14th and U and 7th and M will not, in itself, suffice...." What was needed, he said, was to "stage and publicize spectacular picketing events...." He accidentally exposed the underlying problem: relying on material rather than political or moral incentives: "hired pickets are costing us $32 a week," an "expense which we simply cannot bear any longer...."[20]

London and Berlin, I fail to follow him. After all, James did write his books in London, and he could not have written them in Berlin...." Bunche also found Marcus Garvey "ill advised...whole idea is unrealistic...."

15. George H. Rycraw of NNA to Film Society of Washington, circa 1930s, Box 1, *Eugene Davidson Papers*.

16. Mary-Elizabeth Murphy, *Jim Crow Capital*, 124, 126, 136

17. *Washington Tribune*, 24 June 1939, Box 1, *Eugene Davidson Papers, Howard University*.

18. *Washington Afro-American*, 30 July 1936, Box 1, *Eugene Davidson Papers*.

19. Report, 3 June 1938, Box 3, *Eugene Davidson Papers*.

20. Memo from Doxey Wilkerson, 26 July 1939, *Shawn Leigh Alexander Files*.

The Harvard and Howard trained attorney, Eugene Davidson, worked cheek-by-jowl with these Communists in the NNC, as did future mayor, Walter Washington.[21] A District native, he was also part of the Black Elite in that his father too was an attorney; he burnished his elite reputation further when he joined the "Harlem Hellfighters," the combative Negro warriors, and fought for 191 days at the important "Second Battle of the Marne" during the preceding war.[22]

Davidson was also an example of how District leaders could have national reach simply by virtue of residing in the nation's capital. Executive Order 8802 from the White House during the height of the New Deal was an early exemplar of the all-important policy of affirmative action, mandating the government contractors employ a complement of Negroes. Davidson recalled that when this policy was being negotiated in mid-1941, A. Philip Randolph—the measure's ostensible inspiration—"called me" and negotiations ensued featuring FDR, Mayor Fiorello La Guardia of New York City and others.[23]

Randolph also threatened a March on Washington in order to secure this policy, unwanted in the White House. But it also sparked opposition from Charles Hamilton Houston, albeit for different reasons. This proposal, he said, "disturbed me so much that I want to record the fact that I oppose the exclusion of all white people," a backdoor way to exclude Communists; but this did not sway this talented attorney since this "desire to make it impossible for the charge of Communism to be leveled" was incoherent since "there are no Negro Communists" too, meaning that Hamilton had "doubt whether merely excluding white persons will avoid this charge," suggesting that "remedy is worse than the risk."[24] But Randolph's anticommunism was a precursor of what was to unfold in coming years to devastating effect.

Not far behind in forging the NNA was E. Franklin Frazier, President of the AFT branch at Howard,[25] which sent two delegates to an important NNC gathering in Philadelphia in 1937.[26] When the Retail

---

21. *Washington Tribune*, 1 July 1939, Box 1, *Eugene Davidson Papers*.

22. Jill Watts, *The Black Cabinet*, 114.

23. Eugene Davidson, "The Birth of Executive Order 8802," circa 1941, Box 2, *Eugene Davidson Papers, Howard University*.

24. Charles Hamilton Houston to A. Philip Randolph, 20 May 1941, Box A415, *NAACP Papers*.

25. E. Franklin Frazier to Louis Achille, 26 October 1937, Box 22, *E. Franklin Frazier Papers, Howard University*.

26. E. Franklin Frazier to Sterling Brown, 14 October 1937, Box 3, *Eugene Davidson Papers*.

Clerks Union won recognition as the bargaining agent for workers at this chain drugstore, the "CIO News" reported that Davidson was "instrumental" in delivering victory.[27] These forces often met at their headquarters sited at 1333 R Street NW, especially when pressure on Peoples Drugstore intensified and when the intensely efficient, Wilkerson, served as chairman of the "Picket Committee."[28] Typically, in coordinating picketing on a typical Saturday, Hunton coordinated an early block of time and Wilkerson directed a later and larger block.[29]

By June 1939, the New Negro Alliance marked the first anniversary of picketing at the chain drugstore's affiliate at 14th and U Streets. John Lovell, NAACP branch secretary was elated: Hiring Negro clerks was a major demand, along with promotions of Negro workers. A resolution claimed that "continuous picket line every business hour of every day for a year, has set a record" for the District and "seriously diminished the profits" of the chain besides. The spinoff was that this campaign "resulted in the employment of colored clerks in many other businesses" and "encouraged the opening of new stores with a more liberal attitude."[30]

This was a reference to related campaigns involving George Murphy. The Metropolitan Insurance Office at 13th and H Streets N.W. was segregated racially; another office at 7th and D Streets N.W. had a segregated cafeteria where "only white persons are permitted in the main room, colored persons have been ordered out of or forbidden to use the cafeteria," all of which was creating "suspicion and distrust" as the U.S. and its allies teetered on the precipice of world war.[31] Pressing on, local racists sought to segregate Negroes in Rock Creek Park but here self-help was deployed in that NAACP advocates "tor[e] down ...two signs" and deposited them elsewhere.[32]

However, this militancy combined with collaboration with Communists was not necessarily consistent with the politics of the District, routinely described as a sleepy Southern town. There was a "'rule or ruin'" mentality in the branch, complained the Reverend

27. CIO News, 18 December 1938, Box 2, Eugene Davidson Papers.

28. Report, circa 1930s, Box 1, Eugene Davidson Papers. See also Doxey Wilkerson to "Dear Friend," 10 May 1938, Box 1, Eugene Davidson Papers: Wilkerson is listed here as President of Local 440 of the American Federation of Teachers branch at Howard.

29. Picket Schedule, 23 July 1938, Box 2, Eugene Davidson Papers. See Report, 20 December 1937, Box 3, Eugene Davidson Papers.

30. Statement by John Lovell, 20 June 1939, Box G38, NAACP Papers.

31. George Murphy to C.H. Marshall, 5 July 1939, Box G38, NAACP Papers.

32. C.H. Marshall to Walter White, 6 January 1939, Box G38.

H.B. Taylor of the 15th Street Presbyterian Church at 1715 1st Street N.W.[33] Carter G. Woodson, eminent scholar, though regaling the "local body in Washington" as the "banner branch" of the entire Association, with his customary intemperateness castigated detractors for their tendency to "bulldoze" and "run...roughshod" with "discourtesy" in a "vituperative" manner, akin to "fire-eaters"; dipping into anti-melanin bigotry, they were portrayed as "mad looking as Fiji Islanders" engaged in a "cannibalistic foray...."[34]

Gertrude Stone begged to differ, finding "activities of the branch... have been extremely limited" in that they were "opposed to the 'Buy Where You Can't Work' campaign of the New Negro Alliance": this was "ignored completely," she claimed, just as they supposedly gave short shrift to the "organization of the Laundry Workers, the most exploited employees in Washington." The competition—the Communist-led National Negro Congress, "established itself in Washington through the help it gave to that new labor organization." The branch, she claimed, was quiescent on the all-important anti-lynching front. Their petit bourgeois approach meant, she said, that they focused on high-level posts for select Negroes as opposed to advancing "the entire race."[35]

Whatever the veracity of this critique, the larger point was that the branch did cooperate with Wilkerson, Hunton and Murphy: Communists all. The Association's Labor Committee especially was stalwart in this regard.[36] At that point, Murphy was working in the Manhattan headquarters of the Association as chief of publicity and promotion.[37] John Lovell of the Association branch was also part of the American Federation of Teachers and he was pleased when this body, 33,000 strong, re-elected Wilkerson as a Vice President "by an overwhelming majority," as the "convention greatly applauded Professor Wilkerson's plea for federal aid, especially for Negroes."[38]

Lovell and Wilkerson cooperated on numerous levels. By late 1939, there had been a meeting of teachers' union leaders at Douglass Hall on the hilltop focused on "the organization of Negro teachers in the South" it was "intended to make this a major part of

---

33. Reverend Taylor to Board, 7 February 1937, Box G39, *NAACP Papers*.
34. Carter G. Woodson to National Office, 5 February 1937, Box G39.
35. Gertrude Stone to Walter White, 11 June 1938, Box G39. For more on the internecine conflict see *Washington Afro-American*, 4 February 1939.
36. Report from Labor Committee, 16 June 1939, Box G38, *NAACP Papers*.
37. Stationery, 21 June 1939, Box G38.
38. Memo from John Lovell re: AFT Convention, 21-25 August 1940, Box G38.

this year's work" with the aim of "enlistment of strong white locals in the South" in this regard; thus, "Atlanta white teachers are almost 100% unionized but...the Negro teachers are not unionized at all"; thus, the mandate: "get the Atlanta white locals to lead in setting up Negro locals,"[39] which could have fortified the working class and the union too. These same forces were in the forefront during the victorious 1939 hotel workers' strike.[40]

These same forces were also on the warpath against the Treasury Department. L.E. Graves leader of the Negro workers there, praised C. Herbert Marshall, president of the NAACP branch, for his aggressiveness in "personal conferences with [Secretary] Henry Morgenthau," where he assailed "the systematic campaign of cruel, inhuman and grossly unjust treatment" that was "replaced by a system based on fairness...."[41] Flexing political muscles, Walter White vowed to "take this up with the president" referring to a proposed appointment to the department to which he objected.[42] He was referring to a man known to be "unfair to colored employees," meaning—said Marshall—"this is primarily a local issue,"[43] indicating that what was perceived as national, was not necessarily the case.

Left-of-center solidarity was not limited to Lovell. Future Cabinet member, Robert Weaver, a branch vice-president, was conferring with the National Negro Congress in June 1939 where he "pledged support" of their "campaign against police brutality" and endorsed the companion "program of the New Negro Alliance with regard to the Peoples Drug Stores," and the anti-racist campaign there. It was "agreed to join the picket line."[44]

Lovell reprimanded the *Star*, the Negro-phobic daily, for "building headlines around some ghostly, indefinite individual designated as 'colored man,' 'Negro,' 'burly black,'" the likes of which "have resulted in entirely unwarranted opinions of the [alleged] brutality and savagery of Negroes...the only people placed in this kind of bold relief"; that is, "one never reads a headline entitled 'white man sought,' 'Irish man sought.'"[45]

---

39. John Lovell to Walter White, 2 December 1939, Box G38.
40. "The Socialist," 21 March 1939, Box G38.
41. L.E. Graves, Chairman-Grievance Committee to Dr. C. Herbert Marshall, 18 August 1939, Box G38.
42. Walter White to C.H. Marshall, 29 September 1939, Box G38.
43. C. Herbert Marshall to Walter White, 27 September 1939, Box G38.
44. Minutes, 21 June 1939, Box G38, *NAACP Papers*.
45. John Lovell to D.M. McKelway of the *Star*, 29 September 1939, Box G38, *NAACP Papers*.

Yet despite its victories and campaigns, it was in 1937 that the charter of the District branch was revoked,[46] which was—in part—an allergic reaction to the collaboration with Communists, e.g., Wilkerson, Hunton, and Murphy.

This, too, was a setback for the Association since Wilkerson and Hunton could draw upon the resources of their base, the Howard Teachers' Union. By 1936, they were joined by Sterling Brown, a star of the English Department, on the Executive Committee, while Bunche and Frazier were seconded as delegates to the Central Labor Union in the District.[47] By 1936, the FBI spotted Bunche in an AFT delegation that included Communist screenwriter, John Howard Lawson and young Communist, Ed Strong—and Chester A. Arthur, Jr., grandson of the former president—visiting the State Department about political repression. The issue at hand was the case of Victor Allen Barron who was slain after he was pressed to inform as to the whereabouts of Brazilian Communist leader, Luis Carlos Prestes, in a case where the U.S. Embassy was complicit; adeptly, Bunche chose not to sign the letter of protest.[48] Frazier led the union by 1937, though by 1939 Hunton and Wilkerson were returning to power.[49]

It was Wilkerson who as war was erupting in Africa, Europe, and Asia in 1937, instructed Frazier that a "labor peace committee...is being formed...composed of all union groups in D.C.," which should definitely include Local 440 of Howard.[50] On the other hand, Frazier did not require instruction for he joined Hunton in a recruiting drive for the union which reminded, "we supported the probe of police brutality, the students' demonstration against war and fascism... financial aid in support of the Maritime Union strike...[the] cause of Loyalist Spain," all "since its establishment in January 1936"; importantly, they stressed, "the national organization looks to the Howard Teachers' Union for leadership in the unionization of Negro teachers

---

46. "Chronological Statement of the Facts Leading to the Revocation of Charter of the District of Columbia Branch of the NAACP by the National Board of Directors," 1937, Box G38.

47. Report of the Electoral Committee of the AFT, 23 March 1936, Box 3, *Eugene Davidson Papers*.

48. Memo to J. Edgar Hoover, 16 March 1953, Box 1, *Ralph Bunche FBI File, New York Public Library-Schomburg Center*.

49. Stationery, 15 December 1937, Box 22, *Eugene Davidson Papers*. In the same box see also "HTU News," 1 April 1939.

50. Doxey Wilkerson to E. Franklin Frazier, 3 December 1937, Box 22, *E. Franklin Frazier Papers*.

in higher education,"[51] a potential motherlode of dues paying members and concomitant political muscle. Correspondingly, union foes were displeased when Wilkerson continued to gain influence in the AFT,[52] then used his elevated platform to hail Spanish republicans then embroiled in a death match with fascism—covered avidly in the U.S. Communist press.[53] The union at Howard unanimously adopted a resolution questioning sharply the "embargo" on "Republican Spain while permitting trade with Germany and France...."[54]

Bunche, later to make a splash as a specialist on global affairs at the United Nations, joined with Alain Locke, Sterling Brown, Frazier, Rayford Logan, Lois Mailou Jones, et.al., in forging a demarche to the White House concerning anti-Semitism in Europe, which was part of a wider global foray by faculty. Admirably, this was placed in the wider context of "The Crisis of Modern Imperialism in Africa and the Far East."[55]

However, it was one single, solitary Black woman who grabbed national headlines. Following stormy protest, the sterling contralto Marian Anderson sang before thousands at the Lincoln Memorial in April 1939—a site marred by racist segregation seating when first opened more than a decade earlier. But weeks earlier legal eagle Charles Hamilton Houston had to threaten the District Board of Education before, he said, it felt "impelled to grant permission" for her to perform at one of its sites as a result of "unprecedented public rebuke"—though he conceded that "opinion in Washington is sharply divided."[56]

That it was. NAACP leader, Walter White, was seething after the Board "refused to permit the use of the Central High School Auditorium" for her concert though, tellingly, "cities much farther south, as Richmond, Virginia and Dallas, Texas have opened wide the doors of their finest auditoriums" to her. But neither city contained a corps of Dixiecrats with the power of the purse, who were not accustomed

---

51. E. Franklin Frazier and W. Alphaeus Hunton to "Dear Colleague," 25 October 1937, Box 22, *E. Franklin Frazier Papers*.
52. *Washington Star*, 27 August 1937.
53. *Peoples World*, 25 November 1938.
54. W. Alphaeus Hunton, Secretary of Teachers' Union to Senator Kay Pittman, Committee on Foreign Affairs, 14 January 1939, Reel 1, *W. Alphaeus Hunton Papers, New York Public Library-Schomburg Center*.
55. Ralph Bunche to Dear Colleagues, 22 January 1938, Box 28, *Ralph Bunche Papers, New York Public Library-Schomburg Center*.
56. Charles Hamilton Houston to Walter White and "Hubert", 4 March 1939, Box II: L1, *NAACP Papers*.

to being crossed.[57] White was compelled to deny the "absolute false-hood that the recent situation in Washington was 'a publicity stunt engineered by Miss Anderson's manager'"; actually, he said, "every possible effort was made to induce the DAR [Daughters of American Revolution] to remove from its contracts the provision that the hall shall be used 'only by artists of the white race.'"[58]

White's Board was apoplectic and expressed "vigorous disap-proval of the shameful conditions which the Board of Education granted the use of the Central High School Auditorium," i.e., they did "require" that "they never again ask for the use of a so-called 'white' school auditorium" in the District.[59] The so-called Daughters of the American Revolution had blocked her use of the commodious Constitution Hall, yet Eleanor Roosevelt, the First Lady, admitted that "it worries me very much" that anti-racists were considering picketing the DAR. "Washington is a city where one could have seri-ous trouble," she warned, an acknowledgment of its potent caucus of bigots: "leave well enough alone," she advised.[60] Succumbing and not pressing the advantage, White chose to "agree wholeheart-edly" and went further in "telephoning key people in Washington" counseling restraint.[61]

White would have done well to heed the counsel of his comrade, the top attorney William Hastie who found the First Lady and her coterie "'very really naïve.'"[62]

Columnist Louis Lautier informed White directly that Vice Pres-ident John Garner "failed to attend the Marian Anderson concert before the Lincoln Memorial or even to acknowledge the invita-tion" though the politico from Jim Crow Texas likely disagreed with the point that this omission of his "may ruin his chances for the presidency...."[63]

It is likely that Garner was more concerned with the concurrence of his Jim Crow supporters in Texas. For, Capitol Hill itself was a bastion of bias, with negligible reaction from the executive branch where he wielded responsibility. It was left to one of the scant few

57. Walter White to Geraldine Farrar, 17 February 1939, Box II: L2, *NAACP Papers*.
58. Walter White to Mr. Cameron, 10 May 1939, Box II: L2, *NAACP Papers*.
59. Minutes of Board of Directors, 13 March 1939, Box II: L2.
60. Eleanor Roosevelt to Walter White, 12 April 1939, Box II: L2.
61. Walter White to Eleanor Roosevelt, 14 April 1939, Box II: L2.
62. Jill Watts, *The Black Cabinet: The Untold Story of African Americans and Pol-itics During the Age of Roosevelt*, New York: Grove, 2020, 187.
63. Louis Lautier to Walter White, 19 April 1939, Box II: L2.

Negro Congressman, Oscar De Priest of Chicago, to object to Negroes being barred from the cafeteria in the House, where Negro low-wage workers were allowed to toil. Proudly, Congressman Lindsay C. Warren of North Carolina brayed that this exclusion was perpetrated "'under my orders...the restaurant has been operated by [my] committee since 1921. It has never served colored employees or visitors, so long as I have anything to do with the restaurant....'" Others contended that the Jim Crow ban only arrived recently.[64] De Priest's staffer, Morris Lewis, was irate, telling Walter White of the NAACP, "my son and I were seated in the coffee shop when the cashier came over and tapped me on the shoulder, announcing that the restaurant was exclusively for white people and that colored people would not be served...." By his own furious admission, Lewis "exploded" and "gave him a piece of my mind,"[65] a frequently applied solvent to bigotry that over time was serving to erode it.

He and his son escaped relatively unscathed. Mabel Byrd was not as lucky. This Negro woman activist had attended the hearing on an anti-lynching bill at the Senate Office Building—and barely escaped being an exhibit for why this legislation was needed when she sought a meager repast at the cafeteria there.[66] As the NAACP chief told the attorney, Charles Hamilton Houston, she endured "assault,"[67] actually a "brutal assault" was his amendment[68]—this after being refused admittance to this inner sanctum.

What was happening in part was that Congressman De Priest was doing more than voting on and devising bills. He was a congressional insurgent intentionally bringing guests to segregated restaurants on Capitol Hill, creating a predictable backlash; however, as the NAACP's Roy Wilkins argued, the "situation was aggravated...by the presence of a great number of colored witnesses at the hearings on...[the] anti-lynching bill...." The intense sessions lasted "two whole days...." But there was "another factor" which was to reap rich dividends for anti-racism in coming years: there was a "growing determination of colored people generally to combat every form of humiliation and insult and especially to combat it under the dome of the nation's capitol...." This meant a "showdown" in the District, in which local residents would play a starring

---

64. *Washington Post*, 24 January 1934 and H Res 236 in Box C280, *NAACP Papers*.
65. Morris Lewis to Walter White, 23 January 1934, Box C280.
66. Walter White to Charles Edward Russell, 16 March 1934, Box C280.
67. Walter White to Charles Hamilton Houston, 13 March 1934, Box C280.
68. Walter White to Mabel Byrd, 13 March 1934, Box C280.

role.[69] However, De Priest undermined his case and disrupted the anti-lynching coalition when he insisted "I am against Communism and all Red propaganda...."[70]

At this deadly moment in time, a typical "liberal" approach was offered by Jonathan Daniels of the *Raleigh News & Observer*. Yes, he believed in "racial integrity," i.e., he opposed to miscegenation among consenting adults, but it was a "mistake" to "attempt...to draw a color line in the Capitol...."[71]

Why the anti-lynching bill was needed and why Byrd was brutalized in the process was revealed inferentially by Congressman Sterling Strong when callously he told the NAACP that "most of the lynchings of colored people were caused by them [Negroes] being under the influence of liquor. Since we had prohibition," he explained, "you will note very few lynchings of colored people in the South," for "drinking of liquor makes a beast of any person... prohibition in the South was adopted mainly on account of the colored people" was his historiographical intervention.[72]

Meanwhile, up the road at Howard where first-rate historians plied their craft, a different message was propagated. Eventually, one of these scholars, Rayford Logan, was to write about H.U. at length wherein he recounted the radical intervention of that era, featuring inviting Ben Davis, Jr., leading Black Communist to share wisdom with students, contravening Congressman Strong's weak words and the hundreds of H.U. students who went on strike against the prospect of war as embodied in Mussolini of Italy.[73]

Kelly Miller of the H.U. faculty continued to rail opposingly, but he was countered by the former faculty member and premier historian, Carter G. Woodson, who derided this critic, trained as a mathematician but speaking as a sociologist, he noted dismissively. Woodson had arrived in Washington in 1909 and taught French and Spanish in local schools before decamping to H.U. and founding the esteemed scholarly *Journal of Negro History* and housed within the Association for the Study of Negro Life & History, a hybrid of academics and buffs. He was also active in the NAACP and thus could not be dismissed when he defended President Johnson against charges of being a Communist.[74]

---

69. Roy Wilkins to J.E. Mitchell of *St. Louis Argus*, 23 May 1934, Box C280.
70. Oscar De Priest to Kelly Miller, 17 June 1935, Box 12, *Kelly Miller Papers*.
71. Jonathan Daniels to Walter White, 5 April 1934, Box C280.
72. Congressman Sterling Strong to Roy Wilkins, 29 January 1934, Box C280.
73. Rayford Logan, *Howard University, the First Hundred Years*, 278.
74. Burnis R. Morris, *Carter G. Woodson*, 38, 39, 59, 68.

Before the onset of the Red Scare in the post-1945 era, the political climate was not as toxically conducive to routing those like President Johnson. Instead, H.U. students were in the streets, lambasting the cinematic pro-slavery defamation that was *Gone with the Wind*. Dr. Woodson buttressed their activism by blasting the movie's "subtle propaganda," while faculty member, Howard Thurman, said it was an "endless stream of propaganda."[75]

On the one hand, the District was served well by the proletarian consciousness delivered from Maryland, with its steel mills and coal mines,[76] serving as a counterpoint to the often petit bourgeois orientation of the leadership brought by the so-called "Colored Elite." This trend had been noticed by the FBI, which in March 1941, reported with angst unbound about the National Maritime Union, "...the largest and most effectively controlled Communist domi-nated trade union in the Baltimore territory...." The agency was also reproachful of the local Negro newspaper, a family owned business whose scion had included the Communist, George Murphy, since it was "extremely bitter in expressing its dislike for any semblance of discrimination. Many Negroes and whites have characterized the 'Afro-American' as the greatest single contributor to racial discrimi-nation in Maryland...." Going to the source, the agency detected that even the otherwise staid National Urban League was working hand-in-glove with the CP, shedding light on why "nearly two-thirds of all persons recruited during its last membership drive were Negroes. Numerous mixed dances have been sponsored by the Party," with an "average attendance" of "about three hundred persons with approximately twenty to twenty five white girls who make it a point to dance with the colored men continually." Seemingly proud, it was noted that "no white men have taken part in dancing with colored girls," as if yielding to desegregation was a gendered phenome-non. All was not rosy since "there are two inter-racial altercations daily aboard the public carriers," ranging from "heated arguments to actual fights...." As streetcars and buses traversed "dense Negro areas," drivers had to navigate adeptly as "missiles are hurled" in their direction; "robbing of these public carriers" was not uncom-mon. The "most popular ruse" was that "one Negro engage[s] in a heated argument with a white operator just as a Negro is about to leave [the] carrier and then strike[s] the operator, who will immedi-ately give chase, while another Negro proceeds to take the money changer...." Also disturbing, thought the agency, was that "labor

---

75. *The Hilltop*, 26 March 1940.
76. See, e.g., *George Meyers Collection, Frostburg State University-Maryland*.

unrest has resulted from the greatly increased amount of Negro employment...."[77]

One study finds that by 1930 both labor and the anti-Jim Crow movement were at a "low ebb" in Baltimore, but as the decade unwound, it was not long before there was serious reference to the "'Baltimore Soviet,'", a phrase still invoked by 1940.[78]

On the one hand, e.g., when Wilkerson left the relative comfort of Howard for a seemingly unsteady CP leadership post in Maryland, the denizens of Capitol Hill thought they had reason to believe that there was good reason to keep a close eye on radicals at the heart of state power. A similar dilemma was presented by Virginia, home of the political machine of the Byrd family and the quondam cradle of the confederacy. Indubitably, the Cavalier state dragged the District to the right. On the other hand, the very harshness of the state helped to produce first-rate radicals, e.g., the dynamic couple James and Esther Cooper Jackson.[79]

She was a brilliant writer and editor; he was a skilled organizer and theoretician: both were Communists. He was forged in the crucible of struggle that was Howard, she at Oberlin but both were Virginians. Like a general, in 1936 he sketched a path toward full voting rights at the CP state convention, just south of the District. "Guaranteeing that we have a good 'international press'" was—wisely—high on his list of priorities, which would augment the "morale of our own troops."[80]

District authorities were hardly indifferent as Communists with their ties to Moscow, were increasing their sway locally. By the Summer of 1940, CP Secretary Martin Chancey was complaining to the District police that "every request made by the...[CP] for outdoor meetings this summer has been denied...often on the most

77. FBI Report, 14 March 1941, MDMS #4008, *University of Maryland-College Park*.

78. Andor Skotnes, "The Black Freedom Movement and the Workers' Movement in Baltimore, 1930-1939," Ph.D. dissertation, Rutgers University, 1991, ii.

79. On Ms. Jackson, see, e.g., Charlene Burden-Stelly and Jodi Dean, eds., *Organize, Fight, Win: Black Communist Women's Political Writing*, New York: Verso, 2022. See also Sara Rzeszutek Haviland, *James and Esther Cooper Jackson: Love and Courage in the Black Freedom Movement*, Lexington: University Press of Kentucky, 2015.

80. James Jackson, Report to CP State Convention, 1936, *James E. Jackson and Esther Cooper Jackson Papers, New York University*.

ridiculous grounds,"[81] as the First Amendment became functionally a dead letter where it was designed to operate.

The comrades were longing to protest vigorously a spate of police outrages against Black Americans. Signifying the breadth of the coalition, future federal judge, William Hastie, apparently had not gauged the impact on his career trajectory when he too joined with the NCC at a rally occurring at Second Baptist Church, 3rd Street between H and Eye Streets N.W. The summary was sharp, observing that "between 1926 and 1938 sixty...persons were killed by Washington police," i.e., "more people than were lynched in the entire [U.S.] during the same time...." The lesson, too, was clear: "two years of mass activity by the people of Washington has resulted in no police killings in Washington in the past...12 months..."[82]

There was the case, for example, of Wallace McKnight, a young Negro killed by the police, the 16th in this ignominious category in about a dozen years: the "general average was one Negro killed by the police every three months,"[83] said the NNC, where Hunton was then serving as Vice President. Chiming in, George Murphy demanded that "Police Terror Among Negro People Must be Stopped!"[84]

By the Spring of 1941 perennials were arriving on time in the District: cherry blossoms and a student strike at H.U. The issue was war, more precisely students forced into a replay of 1917-1918. They chose to "down their books at 11 a.m. Wednesday morning April 23 and march across campus, placards held high, shouting slogans, singing songs...as they insist in unison," said the overly enthused student reporter, "1941 SHALL NOT BE 1917...."[85] The continuing willingness of these activist students to roil the waters long had engendered irksome concern on Capitol Hill and beyond. As early as 1929, even the National Urban League wondered about the "social consequences of giving high school education to large numbers of boys and girls while the avenues of employment in which they may use

---

81. Martin Chancey to Melvin Hazen, District Police, 29 July 1940, Box 58, *NAACP-DC Papers, Howard University.*
82. Statement, circa 1939, Box G39, *NAACP Papers.*
83. Statement by Arthur Gray, President of the Washington Council of NNC and W. Alphaeus Hunton, Vice President, 12 June 1939, Box 58, *NAACP-DC Papers.*
84. George Murphy, Chair of Joint Commission of Civil Rights for the District to D.C. Commissioners, circa 197, Box G39, *NAACP Papers.*
85. *The Hilltop,* 21 April 1941. Emphasis in original.

this education are so limited...."[86] A fortiori this applied to providing college education—a perception that grew as it became evident that Negro college students were determined to not just absorb passively book learning but shape actively the world in which they resided.

In a sense, these student protesters were inspired by Professor Hunton himself who during the same period scorned the House Un-American Activities Committee after it flayed the peace movement.[87] Hunton's telegram to HUAC demanded the "right [to] testify before your committee...I categorically deny charges of communism against me," he added ambiguously.[88] HUAC may have been overly concerned with the anti-fascist confab in Washington in October 1941 targeting "defeat of Hitler and Hitlerism."[89]

Like many Communists, Hunton recognized the dialectical connection between the struggle for peace and the struggle for economic security at home—weaknesses in the latter fed the imperialist notion of rapacity abroad to compensate. Thus, he was in the forefront of protesting the mere $60 a month for those on the dole, sentiment expressed via the NNC and the Citizens' Committee on Jobs and Welfare in the District.[90] Hunton was also Chairman of the Jobs Committee of the local NNC whose activism delivered 7,000 jobs for African Americans at the Glenn Martin aircraft plant in Maryland.[91]

These jobs descended on Black people like manna from heaven, because the news otherwise on the employment front was grim. At the same time Negro employees of the "Frazee-Potomac Laundry" seemed to be reverting to the antebellum era in that "several hundred" of them, said the Urban League, were victimized when the boss had "difficulties in meeting their payroll...several hundred Negro workers" were at a loss, "most of whom are in arrears on their wages...." Simultaneously, African Americans were "gradually being pressed out of the hotel, restaurant and barbering picture in Washington...all of the colored waiters at the Union Station were suddenly replaced by white waitresses...." Liberal poseurs, "management agreed to take under advisement the gradual integration of colored waitresses...." At this point there were "close to 3,000 Negro

86. Annual Report of the Executive Secretary-Baltimore Urban League, January 1929, Box I: E8, *National Urban League Papers*.

87. Hunton Statement, 22 May 1941, Reel 1, *Hunton Papers*.

88. Hunton to HUAC, 22 May 1941, Reel 1, *Hunton Papers*.

89. Report, 26 October 1941, Reel 1, *Hunton Papers*.

90. Clipping 12 December 1940, Reel 1, *Hunton Papers*.

91. Statement, 15 April 1941, Reel 1, *Hunton Papers*.

men in the Building Trades in the District," said Urban League official, George Goodman, but given what had befallen "colored waiters," the prognosis for them too was equally grim.[92]

While Hunton the actual Communist was under siege by his detractors, the imagined Communist—his supervisor, President Johnson—was likewise dodging various brickbats. Faculty member, Kelly Miller, who proudly and repetitively referred to the "fifty five years as boy and man, teacher and official" he had spent on the hilltop, opined that the advent of the Johnson era marked a new low on campus. The "state of turmoil and confusion" stemmed from the unavoidable reality that Johnson was "constitutionally unable to get along with his co-workers...." Problematically, Johnson was "essentially a prophet, an evangelist, a moral and social reformer," while "his mind does not move on the educational axis...."[93] "The morale of faculty and student body is at the lowest ebb in the history" of H.U., he moaned.[94] As early as 1935, Miller demanded his prompt resignation.[95] This demand would have had a better chance of being implemented if Johnson's supervisors had agreed with Miller; instead Abraham Flexner of the school's Board of Trustees warned the faculty—as Miller put it—that "if they were not satisfied with the way in which things were going, they could resign."[96]

Robert Vann, publisher of the *Pittsburgh Courier*, which shaped Negro opinion nationally, also dismissed Miller's concern. He asked sarcastically, "What would you do if Doctor Johnson should happen to die?"—the professor would have nothing to write about. "Find another subject, the Howard University theme has grown dull. It is threadbare; it is worn out."[97] Miller was nonplussed, suggesting that Vann "try out" his progressive theories on the "Mellon supported University of Pittsburgh in your hometown," referring to the school's mogul backer.[98] For it was "Communism among Negroes"

---

92. George Goodman, Executive Secretary's Annual Report, circa 1940, Box I: E12, *National Urban League Papers*. In the same collection and box, see also Report of Urban League of Washington, D.C., 1 May 1935 to 1 July 1935.

93. Kelly Miller to Harold Ickes, 27 February 1935, Box 12, *Kelly Miller Papers, Emory University*. In the same vein and in the same box, see Kelly Miller to U.S.G. Pierce, 2 March 1935.

94. Kelly Miller to George Bell, 3 March 1935, Box 12.

95. Kelly Miller to Mordecai Johnson, 27 February 1935, Box 12, *Kelly Miller Papers*.

96. Kelly Miller to Anson Phelps Stokes, 2 March 1935, Box 12.

97. Robert Vann to Kelly Miller, 7 June 1935, Box 12.

98. Kelly Miller to Robert Vann, 17 June 1935, Box 12.

that framed his one man crusade and, so moved, he put his concern "in affidavit form at the request of Senator Millard E. Tydings" and "gave a requested interview to the 'Washington Post.'"[99] Miller was affirmed importantly by philanthropist, Anson Phelps Stokes, who "personally stated to President Johnson that he is too prone to discuss radical social theories...."[100] Miller's campaign was so intense that he had to deny that those like himself were "trying to break up Howard University...."[101] Curiously, Miller asked General Amos Fries of the U.S. military then enmeshed in "stamping out Communism in the public schools" to turn his gaze toward H.U.: "I have done all I know how to check [it] from the inside but seemingly without much success,"[102] he added wistfully but accurately.

Miller may not have endeared himself to Flexner when he pooh-poohed his "outraged feelings because of what the 'Afro-American' has to say about the Hebraic invasion" of Howard, a barbed reference to the presence of Jewish American faculty there.[103] Miller did not seem to realize that as long as the likes of Hunton was President of the faculty union, which was the case as late as 1939,[104] when Miller expired, President Johnson would receive a measure of protection from professorial assaults. While Miller was solitarily generating a blizzard of anti-Johnson messages, the union included the two leading Communists—Hunton and Wilkerson—as leaders, once serving under the leadership of the left-leaning President E. Franklin Frazier.[105]

As so often happens, Miller may not have gauged properly how the campus—and the nation—had moved to the left during the depression decade. For earlier, the Black Communist dentist Arnold Donawa, who was to go on to be wounded in Spain and also fought the fascist invasion of Ethiopia, was suspended from his post as Dean of the School of Dentistry. This maneuver, he said, occurred as he was "cross-examined" without counsel by the Board.[106]

---

99. "An Open Letter to the President of [Howard]" from Kelly Miller, 17 June 1935, Box 12.
100. Anson Phelps Stokes to Kelly Miller, 17 September 1935, Box 12.
101. Kelly Miller to Harold Ickes, 28 September 1935, Box 12.
102. Kelly Miller to General Amos Fries of 3395 Woodley Road, Washington, 30 October 1935, Box 12.
103. Kelly Miller to Abraham Flexner, 21 March 1935, Box 12.
104. Note, 10 October 1939, Box 37, *Jesse Moorland Papers.*
105. Note, 15 December 1937, Box 22, *E. Franklin Frazier Papers.*
106. See, e.g., Minutes of Semi Annual Meeting of the Board of Trustees, 27-28 October 1931, See also *Afro-American*, 16 January 1932.

Weeks before Tokyo's attack on Pearl Harbor, which drove the U.S. into the global war, L. Greeley Brown, President of the General Alumni Association of Howard, informed Senator Dennis Chavez, who wielded influence on campus, about the "incompetence, the maladministration and waste, if not dishonesty, of the present administration of Howard University...."[107] This signaled that eventually the hilltop campus would have to adjust to the chilly political winds that were to attain gale force by 1945.

---

107. L. Greeley Brown to Senator Chavez, Box 88, *Dennis Chavez Papers, University of New Mexico-Albuquerque.*

Chapter 5

Fascism Means War, Racism—and Revolt! 1940-1944

Of all the problems Black folk endured in the District, few loomed as large as housing, or what could be called the precursor of today's "gentrification."[1] This was a combination of the federal government expansion driven by the exigencies of war and depression, bringing in more workers—mostly Euro-American given Jim Crow hiring practices—as the Negro working class was hemmed into "ghettos" and barred from moving elsewhere. In decades to come Pentagon spending was to drain national coffers, revenue that could have been directed toward addressing Negro needs: of late even the *Washington Post* was struck by the coincidence that the Queen City neighborhood in Arlington, Virginia, walking distance from the District, which was founded in the 1880s was razed in 1942 in order to facilitate building the Pentagon, displacing at least 150 African American families and contributing to a housing crunch for this besieged minority.[2]

This massive project exposed the growing contradiction of allowing the nation's front yard to decline precipitously, a crisis Dixiecrats were unmoved to address in light of persistent hostility to a federal government that had vanquished their secessionist impulse, then seized without compensation their most valuable property—enslaved Africans; their persistent animus toward the latter then ignited their indifference as the obligations of war and depression heightened that same government's responsibilities. This rancor was embodied in a message to Jim Crow's epitome, Senator James Eastland of Mississippi, wherein he was told in 1943 that the District

---

1. Sabiyha Prince, *African Americans and Gentrification in Washington, D.C.: Race, Class and Social Justice in the Nation's Capital*, New York: Routledge, 2014.
2. *Washington Post*, 25 December 2018.

was "governed by the New Deal" and, thus, had "gone from bad, very bad and then worse," as it had become a "seething caldron of disease, drunkenness and crime."[3]

A pentagon was a shape used by fortresses for centuries and was much too large to place downtown. Angry hearings erupted about Arlington, seen as a casual abandonment of the District though the "Hell's Bottom" neighborhood of the former was hardly a prize: this swampy neighborhood contained District itself, as ousting Negroes took precedence despite angry congressional hearings.[4] The needs of the burgeoning national security apparatus harmed Negroes in more ways than one.

That is, because of its proximity to enslaving Maryland and Virginia, it was unavoidable that the Black population of Washington would increase over the years. By 1800, there were 783 Free Negroes and 5,244 of the enslaved—about 30 percent of the entire population. By 1860, there were 11,131 Free Negroes and 3,185 slaves, a reflection of antislavery politics which in turn would help to generate civil war. Another trend that augured ill were measures in 1830 and 1850 barring Negroes from running businesses, a clear blow against Free Negroes and an emblem of racist solidarity on behalf of their antagonists. The ampler point was Negroes were residing in virtually every quarter of the city, a trend that would tend to dissipate—ironically—with emancipation. Post 1865, a trend that was to become prominent in the early 20th century began to emerge: alley dwellings—informal abodes, terribly cramped, incapable of adequately resisting harsh weather. By 1872, the alley population was an estimated 25,000—more than 90 percent Negro. As war approached in Europe by 1939, a growing percentage of African Americans were alley-dwellers. As so often happened with harsh exploitation, this unfortunate tendency was profitable—to some: as early as 1870, alley dwellings paid a higher rate of return than street property. By 1934, there were 10,000 alley dwellers, only 500 were not Negro.[5]

A survey conducted during this latter period, found that vacancies were rarer in Negro neighborhoods, providing leverage to landlords. Non-Negro areas were more likely to have standard heating and

---

3. W. Hume Logan to Senator Eastland, 3 July 1943, Box 55, File Series 3, Subseries 1, *University of Mississippi-Oxford*.

4. *Washington Post*, 26 April 1999, *Vertical File-Washington, D.C., FDR Library*.

5. Bernard Braxton, "Some Notes on Negroes in the District of Columbia," no date, Box A874, *Records of U.S. Works Projects Administration, Library of Congress-Washington, D.C.*

running water, for example.[6] By early 1941, the District authorities moved to terminate alley-dwellings, but this was unrealistic given the prevailing conditions of Jim Crow and federal land grabs.[7] Howard scholar, Rayford Logan, hinted at one of the stumbling blocks such noble aims encountered. He found District agencies to be "like Negroes are supposed to be. I have never heard reports of such bickering, feuding and backbiting,"[8] perhaps because the irresistible force of anti-racism was confronting the immovable object that was white supremacy, with friction emitted as a result.

Of course, this grim portrait did not encompass the experience of all Black Washingtonians. Assuredly, it did not capture the youthful life of the future prominent attorney, Charles T. Duncan, whose father was a celebrated artist, and who resided in affluence. As noted, the presence of Howard University and a growing influx of federal government employees, e.g., William Hastie, kept their neighborhoods afloat and, in turn, propelled the presence of adequate schools, mostly served by Negro workers keeping their neighborhoods vibrant.

"When I went away to prep school," said the younger Duncan, speaking of posh and tony Mt. Hermon in New England, "I was equal to or ahead of the other kids there...all of whom were white...." By then his father was teaching at Howard where George and Ira Gershwin recruited him to star in "Porgy and Bess," the original "Porgy" at that. "From the time I was born," he confessed unashamedly, "we had a live-in maid...I was raised in a very elite way...." Thus, the younger Duncan, well-prepared in District schools, by his own admission, had a "very good academic record" in Massachusetts: he was "class salutatorian" and managed to become part of the ski team, too. This record led him to Dartmouth, then Harvard Law School and a stellar career. Tellingly, in New Hampshire, out of a student body of 3,000 there were a mere "four, five, six Negro students," of which "two or three" came from his hometown: a commentary on certain high schools of Washington and the declension of those elsewhere.

Yet, perhaps his most revealing memory is his recollection of anti-Jewish fervor in Washington. "There was a lot of anti-Semitism," he recalled. This was partially an offshoot of the bigotry generated

6. Survey of Vacancies, no date, Box A1038, *Records of U.S. Works Projects Administration.*
7. Memo From Alley Dwelling Authority, 19 March 1941, Box B77, *Records of U.S. Works Projects Administration.*
8. Entry, August 1941, Box 3, *Rayford Logan Diary, Rayford Logan Papers, Library of Congress-Washington, D.C.*

by anti-Blackness in that the District was "strictly, strictly, strictly segregated," he stressed. "The only white people that I knew, forgive me," he added apologetically, was the "'Jew's store...that's what we used to call it, 'the Jews' store.'" Only those perceived as not fully "white" were consigned to function in Negro neighborhoods. Thus, until arriving at Mt. Hermon, Duncan, a certified member of the Negro elite, "didn't have any contact with any white people...ever, ever, ever, ever," he insisted; as for department stores "you couldn't try clothes on," so, why bother? "You couldn't go to the bathroom." There was a library exception, however, in that one was allowed use the lavatory at the "main branch of the D.C. public library." Yet, his parents' bankroll notwithstanding, "I couldn't join the Boy Scouts... the local Boy Scout colored troops was not made up of the same class of kids that I came from," and, thus, joining was verboten. Like Marian Anderson, he remembered being "taken to Constitution Hall and had to sit in that little segregated section up in the balcony"—he did not note that similar sections in movie theaters were dubbed derisively as the "crows' nest." But when his father took him to Great Britain in the late 1930s, it was liberating: "it was totally different," he mused, "no racial segregation based on color...."

Duncan knew what those on Capitol Hill and the White House often neglected: Jim Crow had national security implications. "This business of going down and signing up after Pearl Harbor did not exist in the black community," he said with a scoff. "I stayed out of the military as long as I could," said this man of the Negro elite.[9]

Duncan's reflections on his interaction with Jewish Americans is similarly worthy of consideration. There was an unavoidable impediment in that any merchant was structurally impelled to wring profits from customers and in Duncan's neighborhood the latter did not enjoy racial privilege that might cushion the blow. On the other hand, Jewish Americans were impelled in the settler colonial setup in the U.S. to enter into the hallowed halls of "whiteness," which could mean racial privilege at the expense of those not so endowed. Hence, Professor Rayford Logan of Howard was hostile to the *Washington Post*, dismissing this "Jewish owned paper" with "strange policies. Consistently opposed the anti-lynching bill, it practically stood by the DAR [Daughters of the American Revolution] in the Marian Anderson controversy...."[10]

9. See Charles T. Duncan, Oral History, 11 May 2002 and 23 April 2003, *Historical Society of Washington, D.C.*
10. Entry, 27 January 1941, Box 3, *Rayford Logan Diary, Rayford Logan Papers, Library of Congress*.

Professor Logan knew that the living arrangements of Duncan were hardly sui generis. By February 1941, he northward to the "palatial home" in Philadelphia of the prestigious Negro lawyer, Raymond Pace Alexander: "they keep a maid and a butler," he noticed.[11]

As Jim Crow began a halting retreat in the following decade, this disrupted ultimately collaboration across class lines by Negroes, as those like Duncan and Alexander were able to make more ties with the overall U.S. elite, whose interests often clashed with those of the Black working class. That is, they could continue to collaborate with said working class on the bloody matter of police terror and, to a degree, affirmative action but less so—given the simultaneous weakening of the union movement—on radically redistributive tax policies, which the less affluent needed so desperately or foreign policy, for that matter.

Intriguingly, after departing Philadelphia, Logan was "more and more impressed by the widening gulf between our bourgeoisie and our 'masses.'"[12]

Logan was well positioned to make this judgment, being a member of the Negro elite; in the year of Pearl Harbor, he told an assembled crowd that "Europe's distress is America's gain," positing how the U.S. could take advantage of creaky colonial empires. He went on to add the subversive corollary that "the white man's distress is [the] black man's gain" and though "some were reluctant to follow" his logic, its articulation pointed to how Jim Crow compromised national security.[13] By October 1941, Logan accompanied President Johnson and New Dealer, A.A. Berle to Rankin Chapel on campus. The latter "twisted and squirmed when I criticized the government," said the historian, "but almost beamed when I said that some of us must not even admit the possibility of a Negro victory or a stalemate" in this unfolding global conflict.[14]

This was an unsustainable system, designed to alienate Jewish Americans and African Americans alike. Yet, it did not disappear instantaneously postwar because it was so deeply rooted in the nation's history and traditions. This bracing reality was acknowledged by Rayford Logan when he contemplated a book by Martha Dodd, whose brother was the U.S. ambassador in Berlin in the 1930s

---

11. Entry, 16 February 1941, Box 3, *Rayford Logan Diary*.
12. Entry, 19 March 1941, Box 3, *Rayford Logan Diary*.
13. Entry, January 1941, Box 3, *Rayford Logan Diary, Rayford Logan Papers, Library of Congress*.
14. Entry, 18 October 1941, Box 3, *Rayford Logan Diary*.

as fascism was percolating. She praised her sibling's "hatred of fascism, his great liberalism," but "young Dodd was at Harvard with me," he said as he looked back with anger and "never spoke to me even when we passed each other on narrow Dunston Street. Miss Dodd was greatly shocked by the poverty in Russia and the treatment of Jews in Germany," he added contemptuously. "She must have been blind when living in the United States."[15]

Logan had reason to realize what the NAACP leadership knew: as "mainstream" schools of higher education—e.g., medical schools—capitulated to anti-Jewish fervor and barred this minority, Howard did not emulate their bigotry. Typical was the outreach from Ethel Would, who described herself as "Jewish" who requested that Walter White of the NAACP flex his formidable organizational muscle on behalf of her application to Howard Medical School (of course, that she was a woman, too, would have handicapped her application to this school's counterparts).[16]

It was not just members of the local Black elite who maintained ties with Howard and its companion, high-performing secondary schools that groomed the likes of Duncan. Jean Bellegarde was a Howard student, whose father was a high level official in Haiti as the U.S. occupation was declining; his very presence on campus sensitized fellow students to the defects of Washington's foreign policy.[17] By 1942, Haiti's president, Elie Lescot, was on campus addressing what was described as the "racial consequences of this war" and, perhaps, raising expectations unrealistically high by claiming that this gargantuan conflict "will result in universal race equality,"[18] a not uncommon prognosis, revealingly. Haitian leadership was able to disseminate this potentially subversive message to an ever wider audience in that by November 1942 Howard was said to enjoy "student enrollment" that amounted to the "largest in [the] history of Negro colleges."[19]

Howard had the advantage of employing the French speaking historian, Rayford Logan, who facilitated contact with one of the few ostensibly independent nations comprised of those of African descent. It was in 1941 that Professor Logan confide[d] to his diary that "Richard Pattee of the State Department phone[d]...[to] invite

---

15. Entry, 27 June 1941, Box 3, *Rayford Logan Papers*.
16. Ethel Woul to Walter White, 16 April 1940, Box A318, *NAACP Papers, Library of Congress*.
17. *The Hilltop*, 10 November 1933.
18. *The Hilltop*, 15 April 1942.
19. *The Hilltop*, 5 November 1942.

me to a luncheon to be given…at the Mayflower [Hotel] for M. Maurice Dartigue who is here to study rural education." Logan had met him in Haiti in 1934, underlining how the strategic location of the capstone of Negro education that was H.U.[20] served to forge global bonds that were to become essential in the coming decades when Jim Crow came under systematic assault. Logan was called upon repeatedly to intercede with foreigners of African descent who had been subject to the sharp edge of Jim Crow. Such was the case when Haiti's Dr. Felix Buteau and a colleague arrived in the nation's capital: "they are greatly distressed," Logan admitted, "by the treatment they have received" including shabby hotels in "colored" districts where they were forced to reside.[21]

This trend was detected at the highest level. In August 1941, Logan was summoned to the State Department to confer with Nelson Rockefeller, scion of a major fortune then moonlighting as a bureaucrat, concerning racism in the hemisphere[22]—previously not a major concern at Foggy Bottom. Instead, Logan wound up at the scion's abode at 2500 Foxhall Road, an apparent attempt at wooing, where he was administered to by "three colored waiters. Henry Luce," the magazine tycoon, was also there, but Logan was distracted by the "impediment in his speech." Logan left unimpressed by this anti-racism, conspicuously antebellum employment of Negro help aside: "my general impression was amazement at the lack of coordination within the government" on this crucial matter—though he liked and admired Rockefeller.[23]

He met with Rockefeller and his colleagues at H.U. months later, with Haiti again on the agenda. There President Johnson referred to the close relations between the school and this nation and the tactful Rockefeller, Logan observed happily "said a few words in praise of me."[24] Logan was a clear example of how the presence of Howard in the District—a relatively small global capital—opened doors for Pan-African solidarity. By early 1943, there was a typical occurrence as the networking professor "had breakfast with…Mrs. Okala, American colored wife of an African prince from Nigeria."[25]

Irrespective of his admiration for the oily tycoon, there were wider matters that occluded this relationship. By early 1942, Logan

---

20. Entry, 27 January 1941, Box 3, *Rayford Logan Diary*.
21. Entry, 29 September 1942, Box 3, *Rayford Logan Diary*.
22. Entry, 5 August 1941, Box 3, *Rayford Logan Diary*.
23. Entry, 22 August 1941, Box 3, *Rayford Logan Diary*.
24. Entry, 16 January 1943, Box 4, *Rayford Logan Diary*.
25. Entry, 8 February 1943, Box 4, *Rayford Logan Diary*.

was in Cuba and he could not help but notice that "there has been some increase in racial prejudice resulting from the influence of Americans and of Cubans who have studied in the United States"; besides, he remarked, "many Communists are Negroes," which was bound to warp the vision of the heavily racist and anticommunist visitors from due north.[26] The well-networked Logan then travelled to Haiti, where he was "received by the president" and "by the American Minister," while adding "I am glad that [I] talked with [Juan] Marinello and [Nicolas] Guillen, Communists [both] because apparently there are none in Haiti or the DR [Dominican Republic]," often driven into exile or premature death at the behest of Washington.[27] Logan did not consort with those at the highest level in Jamaica but was close enough to see that premier leader, Alexander Bustamante, was a "damn fool, quite the Father Divine type,"[28] a reference to a charismatic Negro religious leader well-known in the District.

The Black Elite of Washington sought to take advantage of their location—sited in a relatively small city with a presence of those of African descent, e.g., Haitians, who wielded state power. One plan anticipated the 21st century proliferation of chains of coffee shops. Located at 1005 U Street NW, this enterprise came into existence in June 1936 and was, it was said, "the first of a proposed chain of retail coffee stores to distribute coffee grown in Haiti and sold by an all-Negro company in America"; this, according to their prospectus, was an "outgrowth of the Colored Man's Better Business League" that was spearheaded by "Elder Lightfoot Solomon Michaux and Major R.R. Wright...." Selling coffee by the bulk and the cup was the idea, coordinating with a likeminded business in France. The enterprisers included such Washington eminences as Emmett J. Scott, late of Howard but renowned for his service to the late Booker T. Washington; fraternal leader, J. Finley Wilson; Judge J.A. Cobb and scholar / administrator Dr. Robert Weaver. However, despite their

---

26. Entry, 20 April 1942, Box 8, *Rayford Logan Diary*.

27. Entry, Circa May 1942, Box 9, *Rayford Logan Diary*. See also Entry, 13 January 1943, Box 4, *Rayford Logan Diary*: Logan also met in Haiti with "Colonel Laroche" who bore "three and a half rows of service ribbons. I wonder whether they are evidences of his campaigns against the American Marines!!," a reference to the lengthy U.S. occupation that had concluded—formally—in the previous decade.

28. Entry, 11 June 1943, Box 4, *Rayford Logan Diary*. See also Gerald Horne, *Red Seas: Ferdinand Smith and Radical Black Sailors in the United States and Jamaica*, New York: New York University, 2005.

class status they still had to engage the Jim Crow barriers that complicated mightily the climbing of the socio-economic ladder.[29]

But even before the advent of the 1950s, Logan was sensing the value of these global bonds. Repairing to Alexandria, Virginia with Dartigue, he felt compelled to "wonder whether any white persons would have entertained colored guests...in Alexandria ten years ago," as the State Department shepherded the duo. "The program of establishing cultural relations with Latin America," the historian with the long view reflected wisely, "may break down some of the racial barriers in the U.S."[30]

To that end, it was in mid-1941 that Howard unveiled a bust of Black Cuban hero, Antonio Maceo. Eric Williams, then part of the H.U. faculty and, ultimately, Founding Father of independent Trinidad and Tobago, was upset when President Johnson—perhaps sensitized to the claim that he was much too tolerant of radicalism—"made him cut short his speech...when he had introduced 'the class struggle,'" or so recalled Logan.[31]

But disrupting class struggle could mean reversion to race struggle. Months before Pearl Harbor, Logan commented, "Hikida my Japanese friend, came up to the office by appointment to buy an autographed copy of my book on Haiti"—the historian's book examined diplomatic relations between his homeland and the island. Now "at least 100 copies will be sold in Japan," endearing him to Tokyo. But this "Japanese friend" went further as he "urged the 'demilitarization of Hawaii' and pointed out the possibility of an eventual alliance between the United States and Germany against Japan!"—a union of two leading racist states to the detriment of Logan and his interlocutor.[32] Logan was leaning in this direction in any case, suggesting that in a China "under Japanese domination there would be no signs" blaring "'Chinese and dogs not allowed,'" but "if there were signs they would read: 'white men and other dogs not allowed,'" a prospect that seemingly left him unruffled.[33]

But as 1941 unspooled, Logan by October came to regard the "situation in the Far East" to be "extremely grave."[34] On the hinge date of 7 December 1941, Logan conceded—as if he were speaking to an unacknowledged investigator, not his diary: "[I] knew nothing of the

---

29. Report, no date, Box A874, *Records of U.S. Works Projects Administration*.
30. Entry, 16 February 1941, Box 3, *Rayford Logan Diary*.
31. Entry, Circa June 1941, Box 3, *Rayford Logan Diary*.
32. Entry, Circa 1941, Box 3, *Rayford Logan Diary*.
33. Entry, 20 May 1941, Box 3, *Rayford Logan Diary*.
34. Entry, 16 October 1941, Box 3, *Rayford Logan Diary*.

Japanese attack until I came home at nine thirty. Although I had long expected war, I am nonetheless stunned."[35]

Logan was a prism of how the authorities responded to the changed circumstance delivered by Pearl Harbor. He was summoned by the FBI for interrogation about his presumed loyalties—and was then invited to confer with Eleanor Roosevelt. This, he said, was his "first meeting" with the First Lady, suggestive of the change brought by war. The appreciative scholar found her to be "much more attractive than her pictures indicate," though she communicated a bit of ugliness: "Mrs. R doubted that we could see the president because both Steve Early and General Watson"—gatekeepers—"are Southerners...."[36]

In other words, the "beans and rifles" approach Washington took toward pacifying paradigmatic Guatemala in the 1950s,[37] was foreshadowed in Black Washington a decade earlier. That is, the disgruntlement of Negroes at the prospect of making the ultimate blood sacrifice for an apartheid regime necessitated repression—plus enticements to undermine the basis for this alienation. As for the latter, the Negro attorney William Hastie was seconded to the War Department by early 1942, but Logan was irate at his "failure to accomplish anything"; it "took Bill three weeks to see [Robert] Patterson, the Under Secretary. Apparently he never sees [Henry] Stimson," the agency's leader: he was "colored" window dressing and "ought to resign." Perhaps worse, "were it not for the fact that Bill is a close personal friend of Walter White's, the NAACP would have been constantly criticizing Bill."[38]

This too became a pattern: Negro ornaments parachuted into purportedly elevated posts, but their tie to certain organizations meant that this risible state of affairs escaped scrutiny.

Still, ultimately, this high-level stitch-up was not sustainable for reasons also adumbrated by Logan when days after this excoriation he was passing through the train station in Philadelphia. "Most passengers were soldiers" and though there was "not the slightest evidence of ill-feeling between white and colored soldiers," more significant for the teamwork that war demanded was that there was

---

35. Entry, 7 December 1941, Box 3, *Rayford Logan Diary*. See also Gerald Horne, *Race War! White Supremacy and the Japanese Attack on the British Empire*, New York: New York University Press, 2003.
36. Entry, 22 February 1942, Box 3, *Rayford Logan Diary*.
37. Greg Grandin, *The Blood of Guatemala: A History of Race and Nation*, Durham: Duke University Press, 2000.
38. Entry, 14 January 1942, Box 3, *Rayford Logan Diary*.

"not the slightest evidence of friendship" between the two groups: "they lived in separate worlds,"[39] not boding well.

Confirmation of this troubling trend arrived at the White House in 1942. FDR was told directly that "Many Negroes…are complaining that their race is not being treated fairly in the armed services. This sort of talk does not help our sales of War Bonds and Stamps," certainly true. The remedy? Recruit boxing champion Joe Louis and give him a "'commission'" to "Major." However, even the popularity of the "Brown Bomber," adding to his commendations, was not guaranteed to erode centuries of compounded bigotry.[40] Moreover, commissioning Louis raised at the same time why it had not happened to that point, unlike the garlanding of other boxing champs, e.g., Gene Tunney and Jack Dempsey—a point swiftly bruited by the recently christened fiery Harlem Congressman, Adam Clayton Powell, Jr.[41] However, Louis' rhetorical demarche—"'we will win this war; we're on God's side,'" just as swiftly pushed this story in a different direction to the point that FDR aide, Stephen Early, was advised to tell the president that if he were to "discuss the Detroit trouble or anything connected with Negroes, he might wish to use this quote,"[42] as verbal sleight-of-hand substituted for effective policy.

Actually, it was more reprehensible than it appeared in that the FBI seemed more interested in rooting out purported Communist influence in the military, as opposed to racism itself. A "confidential informant" told J. Edgar Hoover of plans for the National Negro Congress—where Hunton played a paramount role—to form an apparatus in the District "under the direction of Edward Strong," known to be close to the comrades, with the express purpose of targeting military bigotry.[43]

Still, Logan had outlined one of the many problems of the NAACP, problems exacerbated postwar when it plunged headlong

39. Entry, 20 January 1942, Box 3, *Rayford Logan Papers*.

40. Sumner A. Sirtl, Chairman Fort Greene Park District, Brooklyn and War Savings Staff of the Treasury Department to President Roosevelt, 2 June 1942, Box 1, *OF 4879-4904, OF 4905, Manpower Commission, Franklin D. Roosevelt Presidential Library-Hyde Park, New York*.

41. Undated Clipping, same Box in FDR Library as footnote immediately above.

42. Memo to Stephen Early, 17 March 1942, Same Box in FDR Library immediately above.

43. J. Edgar Hoover to Harry Hopkins, 12 October 1943, Box 151, Group 24, *Harry Hopkins Papers, FDR Library*.

into anticommunism, further compromising a militancy so neces-sary to tackle the malignancies confronted. Too often the Association descended into influence peddling on behalf of middle class constit-uents, rather than a fighting force for a community that was largely working class. Hence, just as Walter White was lobbying Congress for allocations to Howard, he was lobbying their medical school to admit favored candidates.[44]

Howard Medical School was hardly a cipher. Its noteworthy fac-ulty included Dr. Charles Drew, whose pioneering work on blood plasma was to save many a life though neither Columbia nor the Red Cross nor the U.S. Army offered him employment, so he returned to Howard in 1942 (segregated blood transfusions was normative in the U.S. then, even in the military). His contribution to humanity led to his receiving the NAACP's highest honor, the Spingarn Medal, which he received in 1944.[45] Actually, coming to Howard was not nec-essarily viewed as a demotion. It was not just the ineffable point that Jim Crow brought an esteemed corps of Negro academics—without many options—to Howard: Logan believed that the facilities there and Atlanta University, too, were "far superior" to "dormitories in even the richest schools," his alma mater, Williams College, for example.[46]

Yet cooptation of pre-eminent Negroes became more feasible once ominous clouds of war materialized and the need for national unity was concretized. A harbinger occurred when Ralph Bunche—who was to ascend from his status as leftist H.U. professor to global heights—was nominated at the American Federation of Teach-ers convention in Buffalo to challenge Wilkerson for the post of Vice-President. Soon, as Bunche moved from U.S. intelligence to the United Nations and untold notoriety, his former leftism was left far behind.[47]

As for Wilkerson, Logan paid tribute to him in the pages of the *Daily Worker*.[48] Energized by clear anti-fascist currents, he thought by joining the ranks of Communist cadre, he would be instrumental in aiding in the push to the left of the nation. But just as he was

44. Walter White to Dr. Numa Adams, 1 May 1940, Box A318, *NAACP Papers, Library of Congress.*
45. Report, circa 1970s, Box 1, *W. Montague Cobb Collection, Emory* University. See also Spencie Love, *One Blood: The Death and Resurrection of Charles R. Drew,* Chapel Hill: University of North Carolina Press, 1997.
46. Entry, 20 April 1942, Box 4, *Rayford Logan Diary.*
47. Report, 18 March 1942, Box 3, *Doxey Wilkerson Papers.*
48. *Daily Worker,* 8 August 1943.

arranging his move, the *New York Times* reported the alarmist news that Congressman Jennings Randolph of West Virginia had uncovered "'hundreds'" of Communists ensconced in the federal government headquarters in the District—not necessarily an exaggeration—including Wilkerson in the Office of Price Administration.[49] By December 1943, he was listed as leader of the CP in Baltimore.[50] His comrade, Hunton, departed the groves of academe for Manhattan and the Council on African Affairs, the premier anti-colonial grouping that included such notables as Paul Robeson and W.E.B. Du Bois—an occurrence noticed by Congressman Martin Dies of Un-American Activities Committee.[51]

Both former professors may have thought they were heading toward a rosy dawn of progressive—even radical—uplift but instead, Hunton was first jailed, then fled into exile while Wilkerson was forced to migrate back to academia. As early as 1944 a report viewed those who had worked alongside Hunton and Wilkerson at Howard with suspicion, including those who went on to play a role with the NAACP, including Hastie, William Ming, Leon Ransom and others deemed "prominent."[52]

Like many Communists, Hunton and Wilkerson tended to have illusions about the U.S., especially after the Teheran summit between leaders from Moscow and Washington, as if this signaled a long-term entente between the two powers then yoked in an often awkward alliance.[53] Instead, the dust had hardly settled in Nagasaki, Japan in August 1945 before the Red Scare against those like Hunton and Wilkerson was launched. Logan had few such illusions. By early 1943, he had concluded that his nation "appear[ed] to be preparing public for a peace to save Germany and the rest of Europe from Russia!"[54]

Typically, the response of certain authorities to Negro protest about this lamentable state of affairs was to shoot the messenger. The pugnacious bullying FBI leader, J. Edgar Hoover, routinely ordered detailed reports of the conditions of every issue of the *Afro-American* be delivered to his desk; this included every edition in every city in which it was published from 1941-1944 which would include

---

49. *New York Times*, 14 August 1943.
50. *Daily Worker*, 10 December 1943.
51. *Afro-American*, 4 September 1943.
52. Report, 23 May 1944, Box 3, *Doxey Wilkerson Papers*.
53. Gerald Horne, *Black Liberation/Red Scare: Ben Davis and the Communist Party*, Newark: University of Delaware Press, 1994.
54. Entry, circa 25 January 1943, Box 4, *Rayford Logan Diary*.

Baltimore and Washington. He was suspicious of the Murphy family that controlled this enterprise—which included the Communist, George Murphy—viewing it as a model of sedition.[55] The Works Projects Administration, a federal agency thought to be to the left of the FBI, reflected its mindset when their local Washington office counselled in 1941 that "news articles...written by Negroes...are therefore colored by the Negro's psychology of approach to the news," an unclear meaning that did not mean well.[56]

Not just journalists but those Negroes who trafficked in ideas were in potential jeopardy. It was in April 1941 that the historian, Rayford Logan, noted his encounter with a "colored detective," who "said that he was on the subversive activities detail" and "had checked up" on Logan and Howard more generally. The gumshoe was "convinced that I was preaching no subversive doctrines,"[57] wrote the historian with palpable relief. However, things had changed by February. "I am being investigated by the FBI for alleged communistic activities," said this liberal, middle class intellectual. He did "surmise that the faculty at Howard were being simply taken in alphabetical order" in a dragnet betraying guilty hysteria about the intentions of Negro intellectuals. Thus, the economist Abram Harris, too, was "called downtown by the FBI."[58]

Among those flyspecked by this agency were—inevitably—actual Communists, e.g., Hunton and Wilkerson and their comrade, Gene Holmes.[59] As for Hunton, the surveillance of him was an insignia of his effectiveness as an organizer. By April 1940, he was presiding over a NNC convention in the District attended by a formidable 1,300 delegates from 29 states—and, importantly, Haiti. Locally, he continued to irk police by targeting the ignoble reality that monthly, hundreds of Negro boys were not just stopped and frisked but brutalized, beaten, and detained as vagrants. However, by 1943 the NNC quietly closed its doors,[60] a victim of harassment and misperception by the comrades of the rapidly changing political climate delivered by anti-fascism.

---

55. David Taft Terry, "'Tramping for Justice': The Dismantling of Jim Crow in Baltimore, 1942-1954," Ph.D. dissertation, Howard University, 2002, 77.
56. H.B. Dillard of WPA-DC office to Alston Field, 1 May 1941, Box B7, *Records of U.S. Works Projects Administration*.
57. Entry, circa April 1941, Box 3, *Rayford Logan Diary*.
58. Entry, 22 February 1942, Box 3, *Rayford Logan Diary*.
59. Entry, 4 November 1942, Box 3, *Rayford Logan Diary*.
60. Dorothy Hunton Memoir, Reel 3, *Hunton Papers, New York Public Library-Schomburg Center*.

Soon, another exceedingly curious Washington official called Logan "to get information about Japanese activities among Negroes," including "translations into Japanese of 'Fire in the Flint,'" by NAACP leader, Walter White and Wendell Phillips' study of Haitian hero, Toussaint Louverture. The FBI wanted to know about the National Federation for Constitutional Liberties, thought to harbor Communists (but since Washington itself was then in bed with Moscow, it was unclear if the authorities had reconceptualized anticommunist priorities). As for Logan, he found it more than passing strange that "Communists have called me a 'militant, imperialist and warmonger.'"[61]

If the authorities had queried Hunton their worst fears may have been realized. For, according to his spouse, "middle class Negroes" harbored a none too novel notion: "they want Japan to win," an idea that "shocked him," she averred.[62] Of course, postwar those like Hunton were persecuted while many of those whose ideas shocked him, were able to benefit handsomely.[63]

For sufficiently spooked, frightened Washington bureaucrats were hiring Negroes that only recently would have been shunned. "Three young colored men" were sent promptly to "do counter-espionage in Australia," also a Tokyo target, as Logan told the story. The professor candidly told his nosy interrogators that "Hikida had been active for many years; that he had offered me $1,500 to write a book on the Monroe Doctrine in Asia...I reported the offer to the State Department," which apparently did not stir. When asked how "effective" Japanese propaganda had been, he was forthright: "'Very effective' I replied" for "colored orators could almost nightly be heard...saying that 'the Japan[ese] are the best friends of the Negro,'" not a message designed to soothe frayed nerves in Jim Crow Washington.[64] He was also privy to a "highly confidential report" prepared by the "Bureau of Military Intelligence" that exposed how "'Negro children show pronounced inclination in their play to pretend that they are Japanese soldiers...imagining that they are in a position to avenge themselves against white oppressors.'"[65]

---

61. Entry, 26 May 1942, Box 3, *Rayford Logan Diary*.

62. Dorothy Hunton Memoir, Reel 3, *Hunton Papers*.

63. See e.g., Gerald Horne, *Facing the Rising Sun: African Americans, Japan and the Rise of Afro-Asian Solidarity*, New York: New York University Press.

64. Entry, 14 June 1942, Box 3, *Rayford Logan Diary*.

65. Entry, 6 September 1942, Box 3, *Rayford Logan Diary*. See also Gerald Horne, *Facing the Rising Sun: African Americans, Japan and the Rise of Afro-Asian Solidarity*, New York: New York University Press, 2018.

It was comprehensible why Negro children masqueraded as Tokyo avengers. As of October 1941, the Western Electric plant in neighboring Maryland had no Negro employees and when pressure ignited a change from this mossback policy, use of the lavatory was subjected to racist restrictions. Perhaps because of the pressure on Washington to present a more favorable image, as it was the front yard of the republic, this metropolis at times was more advanced than neighboring Baltimore—which nonetheless exercised a malignant local pressure regionally. Baltimore refused to hire Negro firefighters, singular in this regard in the ten largest U.S. cities. It did not even deign to maintain an all-Black regiment of firefighters, unlike some of its peers, whereas Washington had 71 Negro firefighters during the 1940s—in segregated detachments tasked to serve segregated neighborhoods.[66] Still, as war erupted in Europe, Negroes—who were a reported 27 percent of the District's population—constituted about 2 percent of the firefighters and 3 percent of police officers.[67]

Where Negroes were employed—e.g., the Celanese facility in Maryland—veritable riots took place in protest spearheaded by their Euro-American peers. By early 1942, this had captured the attention of the FBI which noticed—with seeming relief—that this would mean it would be "difficult to get [Communist] Party candidates elected" to union offices and "the Negro situation will not make it easier," as this left-wing group was the rare antiracist force.[68]

Pinned into exploitative "ghettoes," deprived of entire categories of employment, subjected to virulently quotidian racism, many among the Negro poor were reduced to "crime"—or so it was thought—meaning intensified harassment of young Negroes, leading to more arrests, detention—and brutalization. This led to Doxey Wilkerson leading a mass march to 10th and U NW in September 1941—the Communist periodical, Daily Worker, counted 3,000 assembled,[69] the Post counted 300.[70] But here, too, Capitol Hill was unforgiving. Senator John Overton of Louisiana was among those

---

66. David Taft Terry, "'Tramping for Justice': The Dismantling of Jim Crow in Baltimore, 1942-1954," Ph.D. dissertation, Howard University, 2002, 125, 147.
67. Griffenhagen Proposal to Reorganize District Governance, no date, Box 29, Ralph Bunche Papers, New York Public Library-Schomburg Center.
68. "General Intelligence Memorandum', 2 January 1942, MDMS #4008, University of Maryland-College Park.
69. Daily Worker, 20 September 1941.
70. Washington Post, 15 September 1941.

in 1941 who—in the words of Negro journalist, Louis Lautier—were "very much concerned about the percentage of crimes committed by colored people in the District," a step toward increased incarceration. Yet, as pressed Negro youth turned toward sports as a way out of grinding poverty, there too were roadblocks. Lautier knew that the "boxing promoter[s]" were "instructed not to put more than two mixed bouts on any of their boxing shows," placing "an additional restriction on opportunities of colored boys to earn a livelihood."[71]

That same year, 1941, the Uline Arena seating about 11,000 opened at 1132-1146 N.E. Yet even Negro brawlers were restricted, while African Americans could only attend matches—not circuses or rodeos or basketball or hockey or tennis or ballet: not even midget car races were deemed worthy to admit Negroes.[72]

Ultimately, this perniciousness would yield to protest—and the favorable winds provided by anti-fascism and national security, blows with special resonance in the District, from which national power was executed. By 1940, the fabled "Homestead Grays" of the Negro baseball league and Pittsburgh decamped to Washington and often attracted more customers than the often sorry Washington Senators of the so-called major league. Griffith Stadium where the latter played, along with St. Louis' Sportsman's Park were the two ballparks that mandated racist segregation. Emblematic of an anti-Blackness, meant to punish descendants of mainland enslaved Africans and their penchant for revolting against U.S. white supremacy and oppression, the Griffith family who owned the Senators were willing to employ what was described as "olive-skinned Cubans" but not African Americans of a similar hue. The Grays owner, Cumberland Posey, opposed desegregation of baseball which—from his viewpoint—made sense in that the arrival of this trend devalued his franchise, just as it led to enhanced incomes for workers—e.g., infielders and pitchers and outfielders.[73]

---

71. Louis Lautier to Major Ernest Brown, District Police, 7 July 1941, Box 44, *NAACP-DC Papers, Howard University*. See also Gerald Horne, *The Bittersweet Science: Racism, Racketeering and the Political Economy of Boxing*, New York: International, 2021.
72. John McNamara, *The Capital of Basketball: A History of DC Area High School Hoops*, Washington, D.C.: Georgetown University Press, 2019, 8
73. Brad Snyder, *Beyond the Shadow of the Senators: The Untold Story of the Homestead Grays and the Integration of Baseball*, Chicago: Contemporary, 2003, xi.

The insultingly named professional football team—the Washington Redskins—was also one of the last squads in the league to accept Black players. This not only deprived these ebony athletes of well-deserved wages, it also may have meant their being denuded of the illicit wages of corruption that some of these athletes were said to enjoy[74] in the ultimate horrific expression of Jim Crow, which anti-fascism had forced into retreat.

---

74. Testimony of Sidney Brodson, 24 March 1951, Executive Session. Hearing of Special Committee to Investigate Organized Crime in Interstate Commerce, Box 87, *Estes Kefauver Papers, University of Tennessee—Knoxville*: Speaking of Washington's star quarterback, he said: "You can bet your last dollar that Sammy Baugh was diving...definitely manipulating those games...[he] could influence the score very easily...by substitutions" during his subsequent coaching career.

Chapter 6

Fascism Retreats/Radicalism Rises— Does Racism Recede? 1942-1945

The departure of Wilkerson and Hunton from Howard was a stinging blow to District radicalism. The continuing existence of Negroes languishing in alleys while those like Charles T. Duncan resided lavishly was an indicator that there was a sharp class divide in this otherwise oppressed community. Wilkerson and Hunton with their tightened focus on job bias and police terror in particular, were able to bridge that yawning class chasm. When Bunche, the other left-leaning professor defected to U.S. intelligence, it was an indication that other avenues were available that were to become more prevalent in the postwar era—to the ultimate detriment of Black Washington. This trait mushroomed during the war as the District was flooded with increased government spending. "The war has certainly brought prosperity to hotels and nightclubs" was Logan's wondrous comment about his hometown in early 1943.[1]

Complicating the policies of the anti-Jim Crow front was what the *Washington Tribune* noticed: "one group of Negroes in Washington is seeking to be integrated into all departments of the District Government while another seeks to maintain Jim Crowism,"[2] e.g., Negro baseball team owners and the like. But even with favorable anti-fascist currents flowing from abroad, Jim Crow was so ingrained and inured that maximal unity was a must to repel it. The Trinidadian intellectual, C.L.R. James, found to his chagrin that the only place where inter-racial groups of comrades could gather was—perversely—at a Negro funeral home.[3]

1.. Entry, circa 14 February 1943, Box 4, *Rayford Logan Papers*.
2. *Washington Tribune*, 9 December 1944.
3. John L. Williams, *C.L.R. James: A Life Beyond the Boundaries*, London: Constable, 2022, 170.

As noted, despite their general insight into the interstices of U.S. society—and imperialism—the postwar turn to the right was not altogether anticipated by the comrades, who maintained the illusion that the Teheran summit in 1943 of the wartime allies—including Moscow—represented the dominant global trend not just in war but also in peace. In that regard, there were contrasting signals: by 1943, the District branch of the NAACP had ballooned to a humongous 10,000 members and, as important, was not averse to working with those like Hunton and Wilkerson—a tendency that was to dissipate postwar. Similarly, by 1943 the federal government, too, had ballooned in size, employing a whopping 283,000 workers,[4] and many were Negroes with the wherewithal to pay Association—and CP—dues. However, postwar with the implementation of so-called "loyalty oaths," the District labor force was drained systematically of any hint of radicalism—or root and branch undermining of Jim Crow as well.

The over-estimation by the comrades of the global balance of forces tipping toward progressivism said to be brought by the war was sensed by Rayford Logan when he prepared an edited volume summarizing Negro demands then.[5] "The surprising thing," said the Howard academic "is that Doxey, like other Communists, is now all-out for the war and is more enthusiastic about the progress the Negro has made during the war than is any other contributor" to this trailblazing volume.[6] The U.S. authorities thought they had sensed this over-estimation for as the war was in its final year, they reported that the Frederick Douglass Club, "the most important Negro branch" of the CP in Baltimore, which had a membership of 225 was "able...to re-register only thirty seven members...."[7]

Logan knew better, too. The contradictorily liberal University of North Carolina Press commissioned a volume seeking to divine Negro demands and, of course, this minority says ditch Jim Crow—which "frightened" the editors who then sought to "revise" what they prompted.[8]

Thus, Congressman Adam Clayton Powell, Jr. had been elected in tandem with Black Communist lawyer, Benjamin Davis, Jr., who

---

4. Mary-Elizabeth Murphy, *Jim Crow Capital*, 182, 192.
5. Rayford Logan, *What the Negro Wants*, Chapel Hill: University of North Carolina Press, 1944.
6. Entry, 29 August 1943, Box 4, *Rayford Logan Papers*.
7. General Intelligence Summary, 2 January 1945, MMDS #4008, *University of Maryland-College Park*.
8. Entry, 23 November 1943, Box 4, *Rayford Logan Papers*.

then supplanted him in the City Council. But by 1949, the latter was on trial and soon would be cooling his heels in federal prison as his comrades were routed. As the left-wing of his coalition withered,[9] the unmoored Powell began floundering, staggering from backing U.S. imperialism at the all-important conference of developing nations at Bandung, Indonesia in the mid-1950s before becoming a tribune of "Black Power" in the 1960s.[10]

This devolution was hardly foreseen in November 1942 when the FBI reported ominously to the White House about Powell's appearance at a Negro Baptist church on Vermont Avenue in the District—which once again illustrated how this town, unlike others, became the recipient of militance honed and polished elsewhere. "A very large crowd was in attendance" was the claim of the bulldog-like leader, J. Edgar Hoover, who knew his hometown all too well. Powell was the "principal speaker," he groused and his inflamed words were "bordering on sedition." He "urge[d]" FDR to pressure Capital Transit, major transport for often auto-less Negroes, to hire more African Americans. Even Hoover knew that "in other large cities Negro bus drivers and streetcar operators were employed by local transit companies…"; yet, this simple demand was met with a brusque rejection. Hoover was at pains to detail that the "Committee on Jobs for Negroes in Public Utilities is located at 2001 Eleventh Street, NW and its membership committee is under the Chairmanship of Doxey A. Wilkerson…."[11] Hoover found it curious that local Communist leader, Martin Chancey, was conspicuously present at this Baptist church when some of the same parties reconvened in January 1943, once more to protest job bias.[12]

Hoover did not mention Hunton, though he too was deeply involved in this struggle. In fact, by late 1942, the FBI prepared "an investigation concerning you," speaking of the tall, stoop shouldered academic: they found nothing "subversive or disloyal," as he was "exonerated"[13]—at least temporarily. Hunton remained a leader of the National Negro Congress in the District and only recently had

---

9. Gerald Horne, *Black Liberation/Red Scare*.
10. Gerald Horne, *The Rise and Fall of the Associated Negro Press: Claude Barnett's Pan-African News and the Jim Crow Paradox*, Urbana: University of Illinois Press, 2017.
11. J. Edgar Hoover to Harry Hopkins, 6 November 1942, Box 151, Group 24, *Harry Hopkins Papers, FDR Presidential Library*.
12. J. Edgar Hoover to Harry Hopkins, 29 January 1943, Box 151, Group 24.
13. Report from Arthur McLean of Federal Security Agency, 10 November 1942, Reel 1, *Hunton Papers*.

visited a chain store to demand Negro clerks where they were only hired as porters and laborers. Suggestive of the inured bias, even in Negro neighborhoods, management refused adamantly to budge, despite what he described as "'threats and picketing and boycott....'" Then, about half of the 2,000 workers were Negro as 63 hotels went on strike—while a majority of strikebreakers hailed from this minority. Possibly shedding light on why he fled Howard, a number of students there chose to join this ignominious group of scabs. Yet before exiting Washington, Congressman Dies of Texas was harassing him and Wilkerson, claiming that their campaign to compel Glen Martin Aircraft to hire more Negro workers was little more than "sabotage" via "infiltration of Black Communist workers."[14]

Soon Hoover was reporting on the maneuvers of this Wilkerson led group as if they were saboteurs sent from Japan. Days after the Powell peroration, Harry Hopkins of the White House was informed that a "group of Negroes" had arrived in the District from Detroit, led by a Reverend Charles A. Hill," known to cooperate with Communists, "and one Eddie Tolan"; their "numbers" were "approximately fifty,"[15] seen as suspiciously sizeable. As if a five alarm fire had erupted in the bowels of Capitol Hill, Hoover then reported with anxiety about "delegations composed of members of the Negro race" that arrived in Washington from "Chicago, Detroit and New York," all "Communist inspired" with the mandate to "protest against the filibuster in the Senate" and push an "anti-poll tax bill." Delegates included not only Ben Davis, Jr., but Communist union leader, Ferdinand Smith, also of New York City.[16]

This burst of politicking was propelled in part by the anti-fascist war, which placed Dixiecrats on the backfoot insofar as they eerily resembled the antagonist in Berlin. By early 1943 Walter White of the NAACP was alerted when top Black union leaders arrived in the District—led by representatives of Wilkerson's and Hunton's American Federation of Teachers but including the Brotherhood of Sleeping Car Porters; hotel workers; and postal workers, too. "Many leaders of Negro labor will be coming," was the message to White, "and the eyes of the nation will be centered here,"[17] which was not far wrong.

---

14. Dorothy Hunton Memoir, Reel 3, *Hunton Papers*.
15. J. Edgar Hoover to Harry Hopkins, 21 November 1942, Box 151, Group 24.
16.
17. Secretary-Treasurer of Council of United Negro Labor Leaders of Washington to Walter White, 7 January 1943, Box 457, *NAACP Papers, Library of Congress*.

Hoover was further distracted when comrades then began pushing for home rule in the District, a reality that was not to materialize for decades; for the longest this democratic initiative was thought to jeopardize national security if the grip of Capitol Hill on the city was loosened, especially if power then was seized by Negroes in league with Moscow's ally—Communists.[18] The epigone of Jim Crow, Senator Eastland of Mississippi, made it clear that home rule "would be tragic" and "you may be assured that I will do everything I can to defeat it"[19]— and he was far from being alone in either his objective or his animosity.

Hoover's FBI was not just preoccupied with Reds and unions and political governance. By 1943, eagle-eyed agents could be found at a dance in Baltimore sponsored by the Young Communist League at the "Colored Odd Fellows Hall," a popular fraternal organization once led by Ben Davis, Sr., father of the then Communist leader from Harlem. There were "300 people, some 25 of that number being white," said the racially numerate observer. Deviously, "the method of recruiting was that of having a white girl dance with a negro boy and during the course of the dance the girl would ask her partner to sign a membership blank," pointing to women of the still self-described "ruling race" being the weaker link in the chains of white supremacy; supposedly, "about 150 new applications for memberships" were "filled out" through such deception. By then, said the agent, speaking of this urban node, "90% of the new members recruited" to Communist ranks "were Negroes...."[20]

By July 1943, Wilkerson—only recently departed from the relative cocoon that was Howard—was at yet another Communist sponsored dance in Maryland, the favored recruiting site for radicals in the eyes of the FBI. He addressed those assembled and for whatever reason, said the observant agent, "very few white men danced with the negro girls but a considerable number of negro men danced with the white girls...."[21]

The agency's monitoring of interracial socializing was an aspect of a wider surveillance, notably of the 1944 conventions of the CP in Maryland and the District.[22]

---

18. J. Edgar Hoover to Harry Hopkins, 8 November 1943, Box 151, Group 24.
19. Senator Eastland to Hon. Walter M. Oates, Alexandria Civil Defense, circa 1943, Box 55, File Series 3, Subseries 1, *James Eastland Papers*.
20. General Intelligence Memorandum, 4 August 1943, MDMS #4008, *University of Maryland-College Park*.
21. General Intelligence Memorandum, 3 July 1943, MDMS #4008.
22. Call to the 6-7 May 1944 and 4 June 1944 Conventions of the Communist Party of Maryland the District, MDMS #4008.

Wilkerson's former colleague at Howard, Rayford Logan, also paid careful attention to gender cum racial ratios. By early 1943, he was addressing an assemblage at the YWCA but huffed that there were "too many colored girls attending," meaning that "if too many colored girls come to the conference, there will be a tendency for white girls to drop out...."[23]

Hoover, no tyro in re-circulating questionable "intelligence," took time from assigning agents to fetes, and informed the White House that a random taxi driver had told him that "FDR has a blueprint for putting Jews in [the] best places backed by Negroes."[24] Hoover sprung into action when Frank Prince of 2450 Belmont Road N.W. sought employment at the White House. He had deployed numerous aliases, said the FBI leader and had an "extensive criminal record" stretching back to the time when he was hired by a "'loose group' of influential and wealthy Jews" to investigate the Ku Klux Klan in Indiana with paramount leader, D.C. Stephenson imprisoned on "evidence framed" by Prince and "that in fact Stephenson was not guilty." Besides, Prince was an "associate and friend of Al Capone," notorious gangster and, disturbingly, "played an important role in the campaign to defeat Gerald B. Winrod of Kansas in the Fall of 1938," a reference to the similarly notorious neo-fascist politico. Prince also supposedly played a role in unveiling the KKK membership of FDR ally and Supreme Court Justice Hugo Black of Alabama.[25] As District progressives were being sidelined, inexorably their right-wing antagonists rose, as if on a seesaw.

This rise was not the ostensible reason that Hunton chose this moment to engage in transformative change. In July 1944, he resigned from Howard, while adding elegiacally, "I shall always remain close to Howard in spirit"[26]—though this feeling was not to be reciprocated inevitably. The then Dean at Howard registered "surprise and shock" at this resignation and added that Hunton "in all his dealings seems to be actuated by ethical principles rather than by mere expedience"; the "loss" of this "honest gentleman" would be "especially...heavy" in the realm of "faculty integrity...."[27]

---

23. Entry, circa 14 February 1943, Box 4, *Rayford Logan Diary*.
24. J. Edgar Hoover to Harry Hopkins, 19 September 1942, Box 151, Group 24.
25. J. Edgar Hoover to Harry Hopkins, 13 January 1943, Box 151, Group 24.
26. W.A. Hunton to Dean St. Clair Price, 18 July 1944, Reel 1, *Hunton Papers*.
27. Dean St. Clair Price to Hunton and Howard Board of Trustees, 1 August 1944, Reel 1, *Hunton Papers*.

On Easter Sunday in 1943, he married for the final time in Alexandria. His newlywed, Dorothy Johnson, then Hunton, later argued, "he was eager to leave Washington and the confining classroom" which "increasingly seemed to stifle his expanding spirit." By July, he was residing in New York City, an asset for Gotham and a clear loss for the District. The increased anonymity of the former probably was a better fit for his personality than the smalltown that was Washington. He was "naturally modest, retiring and somewhat shy," said his spouse, referring to his "habitually silent manner, a trait that annoyed me," she admitted. He "always wanted me around when he was home and I often sat with him for two hours while he worked without exchanging a single word...but he never failed to turn around if I got up...to go out, asking 'where are you going?'" Perhaps, this laconic mien served to fuel his energetic activism? Whatever the case, there were enough commonalities between the two to unite them until he passed away decades later in Zambia. "Seldom did we miss the Sunday afternoon symphonic concert on the radio," although this mutual enjoyment, too, required mostly mutual silence. "TV never graced our home," depriving them of a stream of popular culture, while "to get him on the dance floor was like drilling a well," possibly more complicated than that. Yet his taciturn nature also meant "no detail was too small for his attention," a boon for political organizing. When he turned to gardening—another pursuit that could benefit from solitude—he insisted that they "plant...plugs in our backyard" with the "distance between each piece of sod...[be] measured with a ruler so that the space be exactly as directed...." Although "gregariousness was not part of his makeup," she added unnecessarily, he was a "good listener" and "his analytical mind enabled him to see all sides of any position...." In addition to toiling at the Council on African Affairs, he returned to the classroom, teaching at the Communist inspired Jefferson School for Social Science in Manhattan, where the youthful Lorraine Hansberry matriculated. There he was able to display his mettle as a "Marxist scholar," which meant that he "naturally disagreed" with his spouse's "philosophy, but we always maintained a healthy respect" and the same was true for her "conservative Republican" family and even his "very religious...mother." His philosophy included the too often neglected fundamental: he "firmly believed that one should understand one's society first, before one could really understand oneself—and others."[28]

---

28. Dorothy Hunton Memoir, Reel 3, *Hunton Papers, New York Public Library-Schomburg Center.*

When Wilkerson and Hunton bid a fond adieu to H.U., it was reasonable to infer that they thought they were leaving behind a formidable Communist machine. The ill-intentioned House Un-American Activities Committee likely would have agreed. Just before Pearl Harbor they charged that there were 17 so-called "front groups" of the Party in the District and even given the elastic definition of this slippery term, this bespoke widespread influence as evidenced by what HUAC counted as "'hundreds'" of CP members working for the burgeoning federal government. They knew this, it was said, after membership lists displaying 1,200 dues paying members were seized from the CP bookstore at 916 Seventeenth Street NW.[29] As they saw it, even the Bituminous Coal Commission contained Reds (Hugh B. Miller and Benjamin Karanerk), as did the Federal Security Administration (Sam Schmerler).[30]

Conspicuous attention was devoted to Wilkerson's brief tenure with the Office of Price Administration—viewed by some as an unwarranted government attempt to curb profiteering and price gouging: the right wing insisted that this agency was "taken to town" by him.[31] To a degree, HUAC was engaged in inflation of the importance of the CP in order to undermine antagonists—or so contended Harold Ickes of the Department of the Interior. [32]

Earlier, Martin Chancey, the District leader of the CP, was quoted for the proposition that "'he knew of not a single Government employee who is a member'" of his party. But this denial was dismissed since it took place after a raid on party headquarters. It was then that HUAC Chairman, Martin Dies of Texas, asserted that there were "'over 2,000'" Reds in the District (Chancey said then there 325, "'one third of whom are colored,'" and their budget was a mere $2,500 annually). Unsettling to Dixie barons was his contention that their "chief activities were among colored persons 'against police killings' of which he said there had 60 in the past few years," an astonishing number in retrospect.[33]

The response was the police seeking to bar outdoor rallies on this matter, which elicited a furious rebuke from the District party.[34] Press reports indicated that HUAC was deathly fearful of Communist

29. *Washington Post*, 18 May 1941.
30. *Washington Daily News*, 21 May 1941.
31. *Washington Daily News*, 22 June 1943.
32. *Washington Post*, 23 May 1941.
33. *Washington Post*, 7 October 1939.
34. *Washington Tribune*, 10 August 1940.

membership among Negroes, an implicit acknowledgment that Jim Crow was backfiring and creating radicalism.[35]

What HUAC should have recognized is that if they were interested sincerely in undercutting Communists, they not only should have sought to crackdown on out-of-control head-bashing cops, but moved to isolate their close colleague, Senator Theodore Bilbo of Mississippi, possibly the heavyweight champion of Capitol Hill white supremacists and the so-called "ex officio Mayor" of a District with a growing Black population. The CP, with their incessant focus on him, gained immense popularity with African Americans.[36] For, with his thick Dixie accent, his roots in the heart of darkness that was the Magnolia State and his antediluvian views, Bilbo seemingly emerged from Central Casting as a villain. Likewise, Bilbo in a maneuver that was endemic among Dixie politicians, used his post on the Hill to bludgeon Reds and Blacks to the delight of his constituency back home. As the District then had a plethora of both, it was tailor made for his demagogy, especially warning of the perils of expanding voting rights. If Negroes voted in the District, he told legislators in Jackson, "'the alleys would be completely outvoting the avenues.'"[37]

Aline Wharton Appel (who identified as Mrs. Leonard Appel), objected from her fashionable District residence at 2730 Wisconsin Avenue NW. Speaking as "a native born white...resident" she expressed stringent "disapproval of the action you propose to abolish Negro alley dwellings...." Senator Bilbo was unrepentant, adding curiously that "I'm the best friend the Negro has got" in that "I want him to get into the habit of moving [i.e.,] to be ready for... movement to West Africa," through the deployment of carrots and, especially, sticks. Ms. Appel while noting the idea of "forced exile of [District] Negro residents," wondered if he also had a "plan for the removal of Jewish residents."[38]

The Senator made it clear subsequently in addressing Rabbi Stanley Brav of Vicksburg that "many of the outstanding Jewish citizens have served in campaign after campaign as my county campaign managers"; making it plain, he declaimed, "they are white folks

---

35. *Washington Tribune*, 14 October 1939.

36. *Washington Star*, 13 May 1944.

37. Senator Bilbo to Mississippi Legislature, 21 March 1944 in "The Influence of Congress on the Nation's Capital," no date, Box 134, *E. Franklin Frazier Papers, Howard University*.

38. Aline Wharton Appel to Senator Bilbo, circa 1944, Box 1015, *Theodore Bilbo Papers, University of Southern Mississippi-Hattiesburg*. In the same box see Bilbo's bill on alleys: S1066

just like I am," i.e., "Jews who believe in the white race and white supremacy—Jews who are not Communists," in other words.[39]

Bilbo may have been keen to engage in vigilantly patrolling the perimeter of race since he may have been "Hispanic," a group routinely demoted from the hallowed halls of whiteness, insofar as his surname had been reputedly of Basque origins: "Bilbao."[40] The Senator may have been overly sensitive as well, since a NAACP leader charged that he was the "father of three children by a Negro [woman]."[41] Or maybe he was simply seeking allies to confront more effectively charges that he was involved in "shakedowns" of war contractors, which led to his driving away with a Cadillac sedan.[42]

Bilbo had much to complain about as far as the District was concerned. The local government was largely mired in Jim Crow and during the war the overstretched Fire Department balked at hiring Negroes, even for segregated units. Yet at the office of the Recorder of Deeds, there was the violation of prevailing racial etiquette in that some Euro-Americans were supervised by Negroes.[43]

Official hysteria did not cease when news emerged that Eleanor Roosevelt had hosted "'four or five leading Communists'" at the White House at a gathering of youth leaders.[44] Then a Navy Yard worker was accused of being a Communist.[45] The supposition was that the latter was just one among a capacious group. There were cells among District teachers and the Government Printing Office, too. Chancey was quoted as saluting the "'very excellent comrades in the Street Car Men's Union, the musicians, Office Workers and Iron Workers...the Barber's Union, the Retail Clerks...the Painters...generally,'" he contended with confidence "'our faction in the AF of L [American Federation of Labor] increased from some 45 to 80,'" of late, while he

39. Senator Bilbo to Rabbi Brav, 21 July 1945, Box 1047, *Theodore Bilbo Papers*. Subsequent historiography notwithstanding, relations between Jewish Americans and African Americans were not always ideal. See, e.g., Entry, 13 January 1945, Box 4, *Rayford Logan Diary*: "Ira also told me that the Jews have a blacklist of Negroes who are 'anti-Semitic' that is, who publicly criticize some Jews. He said that Dr. Du Bois is on the list. I suspect that I am too."
40. Report, 12 August 1945, Box 1047, *Bilbo Papers*. In the same collection Cf. Unidentified Essay, 1950, Box 1178: Bilbo is of French Huguenot descent.
41. Frederick Johnstone, Brooklyn NAACP to Walter Winchell, 25 February 1946, 4ZG40, *Walter Winchell Papers, University of Texas-Austin*.
42. Memo on Bilbo, no date, 4ZG40, *Walter Winchell Papers*.
43. "Segregation in the District Government," circa 1944, Box 134, *E. Franklin Frazier Papers*.
44. *Washington Star*, 9 October 1939.
45. *Washington Star*, 12 October 1939.

heaped praise on a hotel strike as an "'outstanding struggle.'"[46] Perhaps, in response to CP strength among teachers, Congress sought to bar funding to any schools that employed Communists.[47]

The local authorities found it difficult to accept the changed political climate that by 1943 allowed the elite National Press Club to host Chancey; CP hero and former political prisoner Angelo Herndon; and CP patriarch, William Z. Foster, as they exhibited and discussed Soviet cinema, alongside a popular novelist, Ruth McKenney, whose signature work, "My Sister Eileen," was soon to become a major motion picture out of Hollywood.[48]

The nervousness of the authorities decidedly included the local press, said Howard sociologist, E. Franklin Frazier. At that juncture, he said, the *Star* was the "richest" among these organs but the worst offender, too—as far as racism was concerned—though the *Post* was not far behind, as both covered up a "near race riot" that rocked the District in 1943.[49]

White House aide Phileo Nash was aware of this near conflagration. This he knew through his relationship with the well-known humorist, Leo Rosten, who was instructed unfunnily of "race riot rumors" which had recurred "some 18 or 20 times in the past 30 years"; the "relation of the rumor to the announced FEPC [Fair Employment Practices Committee] hearing scheduled…is not clear," as it would air disturbing stories of rank racism. "Taxi men and government employees" were fingered as being "especially prominent in the mongering," leading to the companion idea that the White House should recruit these two cohorts to conduct an "anti-rumor program…." It was not evident what was meant by "check with people like Doxey Wilkerson" about this initiative, except that it likely flagged his political importance, CP membership notwithstanding.[50] The idea reached the White House to draft an "anti-rumor poster" that blamed these stories on "Japanese spies," adding "we're fighting the Axis not each other" was the official line, contrary to the machinations of Jim Crow and lynching: "never repeat a rumor—not even to deny it," was advice hard to operationalize.[51]

---

46. *Washington Star*, 8 October 1939.

47. *Washington Post*, 31 October 1935.

48. *Washington Star*, 12 February 1943.

49. "Newspapers and the Segregated Pattern," circa 1944, Box 134, *E. Franklin Frazier Papers*.

50. Eugene Horowitz to Leo Rosten, 11 May 1943, Box 30, *Phileo Nash Papers, Harry S. Truman Presidential Library, Independence, Missouri*.

51. Eugene Horowitz to Leo Rosten, 22 June 1942, Box 30, *Phileo Nash Papers*.

Hylan Lewis, who had taught at Howard too, well knew of this "flood of rumors…that a race riot was brewing and was expected to break that night," i.e., circa 13 May 1943. "Negroes have brought up all the ice picks in town," as the idea of revolt was thought to be in the air. The Department of Justice "received 70 calls on Friday," said this prominent Negro sociologist: the "NAACP, the press and the local schools were likewise beleaguered with calls," while "guards in federal buildings, supervisors," and, yes, "taxi drivers" were vectors of ever wilder rumors. The harried cry in the local press—"'don't spread rumors!'"—probably had the opposing impact in that "baseless and malicious stories of brewing racial clashes between Negro and white citizens," continued to percolate. Lewis suspected that these rumors were "inspired and are a part of an insidious smear campaign designed to discredit the Committee, short-circuit the job campaign and create an atmosphere unfavorable to the holding of the proposed FEPC hearing."[52]

The thinking was that the notion of Negro revolt was so credible—generated by decades of atrocious maltreatment—that racists floated rumors to that effect for their narrow benefit.

With hundreds of members seeded throughout the city and with the winds of antifascism blowing vigorously, Red optimism was not far-fetched—as evidenced by the idea in the White House to "check" with Wilkerson about the city erupting. This idea was reinforced when in September 1944, James Ford, one of the Party's top Black leaders, arrived at the clubhouse of the Negro Elks, a leading fraternal organization; 100 men and women greeted him with only half being African American. An observant reporter heard James Branca of the CP call his party "inspiring" and supportive of the "Hunger Marches" and the "Bonus March" and the other large scale demonstrations in previous years that routinely featured a goodly number of District residents. Washington Reds, he said, were quite effective in curbing a wave of "police brutality, especially against Negroes" and with a possible excess of tact uttered kind words for the Chief of Police, a possible reflection of this moment when the CP had devolved into a loose association, a misstep corrected the following year.[53]

Fortunately, one did not have to be a perceptive Communist in order to be moved to activism by Jim Crow. The lawyer, scholar, and queer activist, Pauli Murray, was no Red but she rapidly surged to the forefront of theorizing—and destabilizing—this spiteful system.

---

52. Hylan Lewis to Clarence Glick, 13 May 1943, Box 30, *Phileo Nash Papers*.
53. *Washington Daily News*, 28 September 1944.

In early 1941, Thurgood Marshall on behalf of the NAACP, recommended her admission to his alma mater: Howard Law School.[54] As a student there she was far from cloistered: by January 1943, along with two other women, she confronted management at a store on Pennsylvania Avenue after being overcharged for hot chocolate. Police quickly arrived and they were arrested. Despite being admonished by cautious Howard administrators, what ensued was a campaign against Jim Crow in the District that was to eventuate in victory—after a protracted and bitter struggle. Murray opined that the "prominent role of women in the leadership and planning" of this titanic effort was a "byproduct of the wartime thinning of the ranks of male students." The "youngest member of that little band of demonstrators," she recalled was Patricia Roberts, who as Patricia Roberts Harris became a U.S. ambassador and Cabinet Secretary.[55]

Sufficiently inspired, by April 1944 about 30 H.U. students in league with the NAACP picketed Thompson's Restaurant for four hours in the 100 block of Pennsylvania Avenue NW.[56]

Murray's fellow Bison, Logan, was involved in his own way in a likeminded struggle. As Murray and her colleagues were assaulting the ramparts, he was dueling verbally: "So many white men out of a job," he said disgustedly, "think they are doing us a favor by helping us to solve our problems"; yet, as so often happened, their ignorance vitiated any—potential—good intentions. His dialogist "did not [know] what the FEPC [Fair Employment Practices Committee] is, who Walter White or [A. Philip] Randolph is; had never heard of the March on Washington Movement"; thus, "everyone became disgusted but remained very polite" as Logan was mired in responding to "the biggest damn fool that I have wasted an evening with in a very long time"—a common vignette endured by many Negroes as they tottered from rigid Jim Crow to a newer dispensation.[57]

Repetitively, a recurrent trend manifested: ugly happenings strained against the leash of would-be reality. "I listened in astonishment" to a "commencement speaker, Rabbi [Hillel] Silver of

---

54. Thurgood Marshall to Leon Ransom, 26 February 1941, Box A318, *NAACP Papers, Library of Congress*.

55. Pauli Murray, *The Autobiography of a Black Activist, Feminist, Lawyer, Priest and Poet*, Knoxville: University of Tennessee Press, 1990, 202, 203, 205, 208, 209, 226. See also Anne Firor Scott, ed., *Pauli Murray & Caroline Ware: Forty Years of Letters in Black and White*, Chapel Hill: University of North Carolina Press, 2006.

56. *Washington Star*, 23 April 1944.

57. Entry, 6 April 1943, Box 4, *Rayford Logan Diary*.

Cleveland. He assured that this war has revivified democracy" and "'the rights of man!,'" even as Jim Crow persisted. "His eloquence did not greatly move the audience—the applause at the end was strictly formal," and it is not evident if the freckle faced professor granted even that.[58]

But Logan also knew that there were other Blacks unwilling to tolerate the usual rhetorical folderol; he discovered this after arriving in New Orleans in May 1943: "there had been rumors of a Negro uprising on May 1," intriguingly the worker's holiday globally, "and that 14,000 troops had been brought into the city," at a moment when the fate of the war was unclear.[59]

The authorities in New Castle, Delaware thought they had sensed a similar trend: "six .45 caliber automatic pistols" were "stolen" from an Army base there and, suspiciously, "the only individuals who had access to these weapons were Negro soldiers stationed in the Air Base...."[60]

The multi-lingual Logan continued to serve as an unofficial special envoy for Black America, taking advantage of Washington's role as headquarters for embassies. The war created more possibilities for him to play this role as the U.S. sought to play down domestic apartheid. After returning from the unrest in Louisiana, he upbraided Senator Tom Connolly of Texas, who chaired the Foreign Relations Committee since this "goddamn son-of-a-bitch did not attend the dinner given by President Roosevelt at the White House...in honor of President Barclay of Liberia...." This "disgusting exhibition of race prejudice" was hardly unusual, even though Logan was quite willing to go to bat for U.S. imperialism: a "'colored' Bolivian visited our campus this week, but again, we have not been invited to anything downtown," he said with disappointment: "we are invited only to affairs for Haitians."[61] The snub to Monrovia was notably untimely for it was in 1944 that six scholarship students from this West African nation arrived at Howard, "the first time a government sponsored group has studied in this country," said The Hilltop.[62]

Eventually, this apartheid policy began to erode, as the U.S. sought to posture as a paragon of human rights virtue and as it eroded in Washington, it did so nationally.

58. Entry, 2 June 1943, Box 4. Rayford Logan Diary.
59. Entry, 9 May 1943, Box 4, Rayford Logan Diary.
60. General Intelligence Summary, 3 November 1944, MDMS #4008.
61. Entry, circa 30 May 1943, Box 4, Rayford Logan Diary.
62. The Hilltop, 17 October 1944.

U.S. Negro tourists encountered difficulty in finding unbiased lodging in the District and so did their African counterparts. This included Ethiopians seeking lodging at the posh Mayflower hotel, who might be able to receive meals via room service but, lamented Logan, "moving through the lobbies" was problematic.[63]

Logan solidified his diplomatically consequential ties with these African visitors when he inscribed one of his books for His Imperial Majesty Haile Selassie.[64] Still, the irascible Logan thought at the same time that "immediate independence for Africa is nonsense."[65]

Washington politically was the equivalent of the plains of Nebraska when a cold front met a warm front: a tornado of disruption ensues. Officials in the District writ large were preening on the global stage in juxtaposition to Berlin's noxiousness but had trouble in confronting its own citizenry who sought Jim Crow uber alles. Paul Douglass served as President of American University in the District, a brisk jog from Howard and in 1944 was fielding complaints that illustrated the actual chasm that separated the two schools. For the prominent attorney, F. Murray Benson of Baltimore, whose firm included Senator Tydings intermittently, objected stridently to desegregation racially of this institution. "I don't think anybody can fairly say that God intended an amalgamation of the races"; how else to explain, he pondered querulously, why "the half breed is the pariah throughout the earth"? Why did the Negro emit "odors which are repugnant to other races," he posed odoriferously. He was part of the inner councils at A.U. and could not be ignored easily: "in the event that I am unable to attend the meeting," he counseled, "I would appreciate it if you will see that my views are communicated...."[66] To his consternation, a few months later, Lillie Jackson, leader of Baltimore's NAACP branch, on behalf of her reported "25,000 members" chose to "commend" A.U. for "opening the University to all students" and now they were "asking [for] the removal of F. Murray Benson" from all posts of influence that he then enjoyed.[67]

Douglass turned to his neighbor, Catholic University, for advice on desegregation, which needed consul itself on this sensitive matter. (Turning to Georgetown or George Washington universities would

---

63. Entry, 2 June 1943, Box 4, *Rayford Logan Diary*.
64. Entry, 28 June 1943, Box 4, *Rayford Logan Diary*.
65. Entry, 30 October 1944, Box 4, *Rayford Logan Diary*.
66. F. Murray Benson to A.U., 10 August 1944, Box 8, *Paul Douglass Papers, American University-Washington, D.C.*
67. Lillie Jackson to A.U., 20 December 1944, Box 8, *Paul Douglass Papers*.

have been a waste of time.)[68] Actually, Douglass confessed "we have Negro students" but in microscopic numbers, stashed away in "our School of Social Sciences and Public Affairs"—this entity overall was "three percent of our student body...."[69] C.U.'s man was at a loss: "after a considerable amount of difficulty," he began unpromisingly, "we finally are getting along very well with that difficult problem"; but "the more difficult problem," he admitted, was "in connection with our dormitories and representation on varsity athletic teams"— this, "has not yet been faced."[70]

While university heads were commiserating, a group of local Negro pastors were not inert. A.U. was affiliated to the Methodists and there were similar problems of racism at Trinity Methodist Church; these clerics were "deeply concerned about the reported position" of the church "regarding racial discrimination," a grave concern: "this congregation has taken the initiative in a forthright campaign," said the pastors, "directed toward the exclusion of Negro students...." Then they wielded their trump card, which provided Negroes in the District more leverage than elsewhere: the Methodists and A.U., they thundered, were seeking to "sow the seeds of racial war within our own Nation's Capital,"[71] sweet music to the ears of Tokyo and their domestic colleagues, but potentially catastrophic for the U.S. itself. This leverage lubricated the path toward a retreat of Jim Crow as the war was unfolding—and thereafter. Ironically, the Communists, who had made a veritable fetish of protesting at the Japanese legation in the District as early as 1932—with pitched battles erupting at times—[72] became a primary victim of the victorious U.S. postwar.[73]

But W.C. John, Secretary of the Board of Trinity provided contrastingly stern orders to his peer, Horace Cromer of A.U.'s Board: "by a unanimous vote," he said with a throttle, "we record ourselves as

---

68. "Institutions of Higher Learning...." Circa 1944, Box 134, *E. Franklin Frazier Papers*: From 1878 to 1882, Georgetown was headed by a "Negro"—albeit one who was not often identified as such then. GWU was hardly different than AU on racial matters.

69. Paul Douglass to Roy Deferrari of Catholic University, 24 August 1944, Box 8, *Paul Douglass Papers*.

70. Roy Deferrari to Paul Douglass, 28 August 1944, Box 8, *Paul Douglass Papers*.

71. Reverends I.M. Gray, W.H. Jernagin and R.M. Williams to Paul Douglass, 13 October 1944, Box 8, *Paul Douglass Papers*. Cf. depiction of Alexander Willbanks, the "'Black Billy Sunday,'" no date, A874, *Records of U.S. Works Projects Administration*.

72. *Washington Star*, 26 March 1932.

73. *Washington Post*, 26 March 1932.

being opposed to the enrollment of Negro students in the American University...." After all, Howard University was "thoroughly capable of providing all educational requirements desired by any Negro student" and, further, it would be manifestly "unwise and detrimental to the best interests of [A.U.] to continue the enrollment" of the negligible number of "negro students...."[74]

Ideologically, the leaders of both the Trinity and A.U. were compatible with their presumed antagonists in Berlin. The Communist founded periodical, *New Masses*, garnered headlines in the mainstream press when it charged that the socially prominent District matron, Evalyn Walsh McLean—fabulously wealthy and once possessor of the famed Hope Diamond—regularly entertained dinner guests ranging from Cabinet Secretaries to Senators to Supreme Court Justices: they rubbed shoulders with seamier types that the *New Masses* charged amounted to a local version of London's infamous "Clivenden Set" or Berlin appeasers.[75]

Still, one did not have to be an oracle or possess a sturdy crystal ball to recognize as early as 1945 that a new world was coming, the only question being what would be its dimensions and content?

---

74. W.C. John to Horace Cromer, 4 August 1944, Box 8, *Paul Douglass Papers*.
75. *Washington Times-Herald*, 21 February 1942.

Chapter **7**

Fascism Defeated/Racism Next?
1944-1947

The end of the epochal war also ignited a dramatically altered political landscape for the U.S. and the District, where these trends were
distilled. Antifascism from 1941-1945 had placed gusty winds in the
sails of Reds and Blacks alike. As Moscow had carried the heaviest
burden in this conflict and was perceived as the major obstruction
to U.S. imperialist hegemony, it was inexorable—especially after
left-leaning Vice President Henry A. Wallace was dislodged in 1944 in
favor of the clubhouse pol and manipulable Harry S. Truman—that
the CP would be pulverized. This in turn weakened labor, especially
in the District, making this massive shift to the right easier. At the
same time, anti-Jim Crow concessions were granted, which sated
the NAACP, making it simpler for this mass organization to turn
against those to their left, including the patriarchal founder: Dr. Du
Bois. These concessions were facilitated by the increasing arrival in
the District of representatives of independent Caribbean and African
nations, making it difficult to distinguish them from African Americans, thereby complicating the execution of Jim Crow. Moreover,
as Blacks leapt over Jim Crow hurdles, their relative empowerment
meant they were more likely to be seated on juries: a major issue in
the prosecution of powerbrokers up to and including Capitol Hill
and the White House. However, these concessions were met with
massive resistance, not least in neighboring Virginia, which washed
across the border into the District. The attempt to throw up a kind
of wall between the two jurisdictions descended in 1946 to the level
of implanting Daylight Savings Time in the federal capital—but not
Maryland or Virginia, with scant attention to the resultant confusion
to commuters: and others.[1]

---

1. Transcript of Hearing plus Letters, 3 April 1946, Box 260, Record Group
233, HR79A-F7.2, *Records of the U.S. House of Representatives, 79th Congress,*

Still, there were agitative trends that were not just District-wide but broader in scope. Bayard Rustin, the queer activist, told Howard's Rayford Logan that in Manhattan, "there are gangs of Italian youths who beat up any interracial couple they see in Greenwich Village...." However, this deranged trend was not just social but political in that Rustin also argued that this "gangsterism stems from the all-out attack of Catholicism upon Communism...."[2]

* * *

The titans of the Negro press—the *New York Amsterdam News*, the *Afro-American*, and the *Pittsburgh Courier*—in 1944 all endorsed New York's Thomas Dewey over the re-election of FDR. This was a last gasp of the then fraying idea that the "Republican Party is the ship, all else is the sea." This was also a reaction to the disastrously catastrophic replacement of Vice-President Henry A. Wallace by Harry S. Truman of Jim Crow Missouri.[3] This debacle was an ominous omen for what was to come.

The skepticism in the giants of the Negro press of the current occupants of the White House was validated to a degree in that by mid-1944 Phileo Nash—who was to coordinate Truman's civil rights initiatives—noticed that the "proportion of Negro to white populations dropped in nearly all of the old Southern States," e.g., in South Carolina from 58.4 percent in 1900 to 42.9 percent in 1940, with a similar "substantial drop" next door in Virginia.[4] The Byrd machine set aside, the Cavalier State presented particular difficulties for those who admired Jim Crow. For, although they were often part of unions that were not progressive, the fact remained that historically there had been a complement of Negro stevedores in the Norfolk area, who had the potential to shape the political economy of this strategic region.[5]

Still, the flight of Negroes from these racist citadels was not a vote of confidence in U.S. policies, as administered by the White House—even though many of them wound up precisely in Washington, to the consternation of Dixiecrats.

Committee on the District of Columbia, National Archives and Records Administration-Washington, D.C.

2. Entry, 25 November 1946, *Rayford Logan Diary*.
3. Thomas Anthony Gass, "'A Mean City'," 229.
4. Phileo Nash to Jonathan Daniels, 10 June 1944, Box 30, *Phileo Nash Papers*.
5. George Millner, Vice President of International Longshore Association to Dr. Woodson, 6 April 1928, Reel 3, *Carter G. Woodson Papers*.

The need to respond to depression and war led to an increase of African American employment in federal jobs ascending from 50,000 to 82,000 from 1930-1938—and further upwards thereafter. However, the dissatisfaction with the New Deal—which was marked indelibly by Dixiecrats—meant that 90 percent of this seemingly sizable cohort were assigned to custodial duties, while secretaries and clerks made up 9.5 percent. Apparently, even these insulting figures were too threatening to Congressman Martin Dies of the Un-American Activities Committee since as Negro employment increased, HUAC turned increasingly to investigating Negro radicals. Since FDR moved to bar the use of photographs in hiring, as a way to circumvent bias in hiring, this may have inflamed even more those who insisted upon same. Yet somehow the White House still managed to exclude Black reporters from press briefings and the same held true for congressional press galleries, too. In the final slap in the face, when FDR's funeral was held in the East Room of the White House, Mary McLeod Bethune, was the only Negro invited.[6]

Unsurprisingly, the ascension of Truman of segregationist Missouri did not represent a major shift on anti-racism—except to the extent that global pressure combined with insistent domestic demand mandated such. Thus, by Spring 1948 James Gordon of 4209 Hayes Street N.E. chided the president for not inspecting "first [your] own back yard" since "there has never been a Negro member of your White House Police Force,"[7] reflecting the long-time trend of suspicion of authorizing Negro men to carry weapons.

The demographic turn suggested that—minimally and crudely— the Palmetto State reactionaries did not have to fear being outvoted numerically. (In any event, U.S. ally, South Africa, then showed that numbers are not necessarily the key metric when considering elections.)[8] Simultaneously, the drop in Negro numbers also made it simpler to wield the cudgel and truncheon to keep this feisty minority in line, which was deemed mandatory postwar for those African Americans who had swallowed the propaganda line that their wartime allegiance would be repaid with enhanced democratic rights.

As the years unwound, the District too had to confront the vexed matter of numbers as it adopted the moniker of "Chocolate City."

---

6. Jill Watts, *The Black Cabinet*, 254, 281, 322, 390, 424.
7. James Gordon to President Truman, 10 May 1948, Box 476, *Official File, Harry S. Truman Presidential Library.*
8. Gerald Horne, *White Supremacy Confronted: U.S. Imperialism and Anticommunism vs. the Liberation of Southern Africa, from Rhodes to Mandela,* New York: International, 2019.

But as the nation's front yard, it was neither easy nor simple to wield tactics there that were suitable for Birmingham, Alabama, or Oxford, Mississippi.

On the other hand, the District's global visibility did not necessarily compel city leaders to confront the proliferation of rats—the non-human variety—placing children sleeping on floors at risk, along with their being warehoused in the absence of parents. This ugly situation caused Harry Wender, Chair of the District's Recreation Board, to charge heatedly in May 1945—as Nazi rule was crumbling—that "our public officials generally have become as callous about conditions of these [Negro] homes [as] the German people became callous about Buchenwald and Dachau"; these poor excuses for shelter were a "disgrace not only to this city but they are a disgrace to the whole nation...." Yes, "V-E is today," i.e., Victory in Europe, he reminded. Thus, "there would not be a better time in the world for all of us to dedicate ourselves to a mission of this kind...." [9]

Such was the heady postwar rhetoric with the atmosphere dripping with the mantra that a new world was birthing. The NAACP was subject to this barrage, with one unnamed official announcing portentously in July 1945 that "Washington as the national capital must serve as the model for all other American communities," a longstanding trope: "As the capitol city of the United States, Washington becomes the key center for the United Nations which our country assumes to lead...." The District as the "nerve center of our Democracy" had to become a model city, especially since "80,000 persons from 59 nations have come to Washington in the last five years," likely an undercount. "As more non-white officials visit us in the difficult times," it was stated perceptively and farsightedly, the District perforce would change. In the short term, it was "impossible to arrange their every movement in advance in such manner as to rule out all possibility of their suffering humiliation and insult as a result of their being mistaken for American Negroes," a potential diplomatic disaster. "During the San Francisco conference," recently organized to initiate the United Nations, an "organized campaign had to be waged warning all San Franciscans to be courteous to any darker skinned person"—but would such enforced niceness work in a neighbor of Jim Crow Virginia? [10]

---

9. Statement of Harry Wender, 8 May 1945, Box 260, Record Group 233, HR79A-F7.2, *Records of the U.S. House of Representatives, 79th Congress, Committee on the District of Columbia, National Archives and Records Administration-Washington, D.C.* [Hereinafter denoted as "D.C. Records-House"].
10. Memo, 17 July 1945, Box II: B67, *NAACP Papers, Library of Congress.*

Capitol Hill likely knew that simply encouraging courtesy was insufficient to address a potential foreign policy crisis. For in January 1946 the Speaker of the House was told that over the past year the number of foreign countries sending students to Howard had increased from 12 to 18, while the number of students from these sites had increased from 92 to 151—with 89 coming from the British Caribbean and 35 from the Virgin Islands, Panama, Cuba, Puerto Rico, Cuba, Haiti, and the Dominican Republic: all with a plethora of the "darker skinned" and susceptible to be mistaken for a U.S. Negro at a glance, leading to embarrassing diplomatic controversies. Overall, H.U. was growing which meant this trend was likely to continue; over the past decade enrollment had soared from 1,963 students to 4,628, a whopping 135.6 percent increase.[11]

In concert with this growth at H.U. was a concomitant interest in global affairs on campus. The columnist, Max Lerner—a liberal who backed internment of Japanese Americans—deigned to address an audience at the hilltop. Rayford Logan was unimpressed in that "one of the keenest minds in America," purportedly, could declaim at length about "world revolution and not include Africa"—at Howard, no less. Perhaps because there was a "very good sprinkling of white people" present wrong-footed him.[12] Then Logan found himself at a meeting in the office of Mary McLeod Bethune, a reputed confidante of Eleanor Roosevelt, alongside Walter White and Charles Hamilton Houston with Channing Tobias presiding with the postwar dispensation at issue.[13] Bethune, thought Logan, was bravely maintaining pretenses: White was soliciting contributions for her, since she was "broke...I sent ten [dollars]" said the generous scholar[14] of a woman thought to be at the pinnacle of Negro society, indicating the parlous nature of these assumed heights.

This outlay did not deter his conferring with Leon Damas, poet and politician, with roots in French Guiana [Cayenne]. Like Logan, he too was "interested in building up contacts between Negroes in various parts of the world," said Logan. This gathering alliance was taken seriously among the U.S. ruling class since Damas was "shadowed in New York, especially when he went out with Richard Wright,"[15] the erstwhile Communist writer.

---

11. Office of the Administrator, Federal Security Agency to The Speaker, 15 January 1946, Box 258, Record Group 233, *D.C. Records-House*.

12. Entry, 14 April 1944, Box 4, *Rayford Logan Diary*.

13. Entry, 24 June 1945, Box 4, *Rayford Logan Diary*.

14. Entry, 9 September 1944, Box 4, *Rayford Logan Diary*.

15. Entry, 30 April 1946, Box 4.

However, if the authorities had surveilled Logan and those in his high-flown circle, they may have found less to fret about since these often feuding intellectuals and leaders, seemed to spend an inordinate amount of time baiting and berating each other, often rendering them less effective than they could have been. After hearing Bunche speak, a mutual colleague told Logan "that he was going to be a diplomat," like the departed professor, "so that he could make a speech without saying anything."[16] Both Tobias and Bunche were aspiring to climb the class ladder to bourgeois success but, said Logan, the former had an intense "dislike" of the latter. As for Logan himself, he admitted, "I do not make friends easily. I am too independent."[17] He was "certainly a bit deaf," which allowed Logan to tune out inconvenient conversations.[18]

Logan and Company may have been influenced by the prevailing climate as anticommunist hysteria tended to discredit dissent generally making room for backbiting as a milquetoast alternative. Although Howard had a justifiable reputation for generating student unrest, by 1947 a turndown in activism was ascertained by NAACP leader, Ruby Hurley. The "chapter has made a very poor showing in membership," she lectured, "you should have a larger membership than the 198," and should "get at least a thousand members...." Sadly, "not too much has been done since Pauli Murray was a student at Howard and chairman of the NAACP chapter of the Civil Rights Committee"—five years previously. Yes, "picketing restaurants...caused the concern of the administration," eternally anxious about congressional budget cuts in reaction to activism. The trick was to "capitalize on the interest in social activities if you wish to make the chapter a success"[19]—e.g., recruiting through fraternity and sorority networks.

* * *

Days after the surrender of Tokyo's force on the battleship Missouri, a dispiriting report was issued. Negroes were 28 percent of the District's population but were encased in a racially segregated school system, a systemic defect that encompassed the Fire Department. Some stores, restaurants and dining cars from which Negroes were

---

16. Entry, 26 July 1946, Box 4, *Rayford Logan Diary*.
17. Entry, 26 July 1946, Box 4.
18. Entry, 4 August 1946, Box 4.
19. Ruby Hurley to Loxie A. Williams, President of HU NAACP chapter, 18 August 1947, Box II: E20, *NAACP Papers*.

barred before the war, reluctantly had opened their doors to them. Yet, Capital Transit adamantly refused to employ Negroes in key posts. The relevant American Federation of Labor union violently opposed substantive change at a time when the competing and Communist influenced Congress of Industrial Organizations, was being subjected to systematic attack. This systemic barrier crippled service as workers were left stranded at bus stops for interminable periods, even as streetcars passed them by loaded beyond capacity: many buses were resting idle because of an insufficient number of drivers. The Citizens Committee on Race Relations that authored this study argued that "federal policy" was more lenient in bypassing Jim Crow in, for example, recreational facilities, but it was the local authorities—doubtless influenced by Virginia—that dug in their heels. Also anomalous, it was said, was that since 1941 the number of Negro cops had increased from 42 to 132—while structurally there was "no segregation" in this force, unlike the Fire Department.[20]

For the most part echoing the above was a report by Truman's Secretary of the Interior, Oscar Chapman, head of an agency with much sway in the District. Like others, he was "steadfastly mindful of the special significance" of the city as "symbol to all the world of America's democratic [sic] ideals...." As Chapman saw it, the era after 1925—as the KKK was in the process of marching in the thousands through the city—marked a turning point for a city that "never had a rigid or complete pattern of enforced segregation," but then the city changed course. As he saw it, his agency "inherited" Jim Crow by 1933 for the local park system, but by 1939 "ordered the discontinuance," at least, in "picnic groves." Then in 1940, tennis courts in West Potomac Park "and the 17 courts on the Mall" were desegregated. By 1941, golf courses were opened to all. Swimming pools were harder to change for the specter of barely clad bodies stirred lustfully the imagination of miscegenation. As he saw it, the local Recreation Board was unwilling to change Jim Crow praxis, though his agency prodded relentlessly. By June 1945, the RB re-articulated the enforcing of Jim Crow over the Agency's objection, which had desegregated the cafeteria in headquarters by 1937. Under Harold Ickes, it was reported, the agency's "auditorium was recognized...as

---

20. "Race Relations in the District of Columbia...Second Annual Report of Citizens Committee on Race Relations," 18 September 1945, File-"Blacks-Segregation and Discrimination," *Special Collections, Washington, D.C. Public Library.*

almost the only place in which interracial events could be staged," as "Interior led the way...."[21]

Self-praise set aside, activist Eugene Davidson found "discrimination in the granting of concessions in public buildings by the National Park Service," a branch of Interior. "Such concessions are to be granted to persons physically handicapped but that applications of colored people are never acted upon favorably,"[22] another sign of the special persecution of the latter that even Ickes and Interior were unable to overcome.

Self-congratulation aside, Washington remained an emblem of Jim Crow. The baseball team, which took the name Senators and was not far from the contrasting campus of Howard, by 1944 had nine athletes from Cuba and one, Alex Carrasquel, from Venezuela, all of varying hues even as the owner, Clark Griffith, staunchly refused to hire Negro players.[23] This was further confirmation of the point that Jim Crow—in part—was punishment targeting African Americans for being historically rebellious, willing to revolt, and who had the temerity to fight in a civil war that defeated Dixie and led to their self-liberation and liquidation of the massive investment in their bodies: without compensation to their "owners."[24]

By way of explanation of these local vs. national discrepancies, the *Washington Tribune* offered the explanation that with apparent anomalousness some Negroes were reluctant to overturn Jim Crow for various reasons, while many local Euro-Americans were more willing than the federal authorities to mount the barricades in order to keep this system of iniquity intact.[25] What helped to change the calculus was the defeat of fascists, which simultaneously was a defeat for local racists; and this was accompanied by a growth in prestige by the forces of socialism, perceived accurately as the major predator of fascists. It is also fair to suggest that the horrors of fascism—death camps and barbarism unleashed—led to uncomfortable parallels with Jim Crow, to the detriment of the latter.

---

21. "Progress in the Movement to Guarantee Equal Rights for all Citizens in the National Capital," Circa 1949, Box 68, 85065, *Oscar Chapman Papers, Harry S. Truman Presidential Library.*
22. Eugene Davidson, New Negro Alliance to NAACP-D.C., 24 March 1939, *Shawn Leigh Alexander Files.*
23. *New York Times*, 15 April 2021.
24. Gerald Horne, *The Counter-Revolution of 1836: Texas Slavery & Jim Crow and the Roots of U.S. Fascism*, New York: International, 2022.
25. *Washington Tribune*, 9 December 1944.

The problem was that many Euro-Americans in the District were unwilling to sing—or even hum—"Kumbaya, My Lord." At least, Rosa Cooley of 65 Randolph Place N.E. did not claim knowledge of this hymn. Instead, she complained directly to Senator Bilbo of Mississippi about the Negroes moving into her neighborhood in the face of a restrictive covenant barring same. Ms. Cooley "went to court," and did not receive an embrace but, "was insulted by a half white-Negro lawyer...asking all the ladies if they were white and if they had any way to prove it...." She was horrified: Negroes, she lamented, "live next door to me and they are very annoying...." With mounting fury, she exclaimed, "in the name of God can't something be done about the Negroes...moving in all white streets...if something isn't done & done quick," she advised angrily, "[this] city is going to be polluted with Negroes. Everywhere you go you just [see] them in all directions," as if she was trapped in a science fiction movie. "If this wasn't a covenant street," she said referring to deed restrictions that soon would be unenforceable, "I would never write" since "by law no Negroes should [have] moved in this street till February 7-1946...."[26]

As federal construction—e.g., the Pentagon—continued to eliminate low-cost housing, the movement to build low cost public housing was disrupted by the insistent cry that this was little more than constructing the road to socialism[27]: a must to avoid, in other words. Inevitably, African Americans were less influenced by this siren song of pernicious deception, which meant they would be viewed even more suspiciously as anticommunism took on the trappings of a holy crusade.

The Pentagon was not unique in this regard. Langley, Virginia, the home of the infamous Central Intelligence Agency, sat on the former plantation of the treasonous Robert E. Lee. Then it was adjacent to a Free Negro community post-Civil War: Lincolnville, then Odrick's Corner. Ironically, the work crews that laid the foundation for the construction of this headquarters that perpetrated so much deviltry in Africa, were primarily African American. Then after the building rose, fewer Negroes still were to be found in these corridors of power.

---

26. Rosa Cooley to Senator Bilbo, 8 October 1945, Box 95, Record Group 46, *Records of the U.S. Senate, 79th Congress, Committee on the District of Columbia, National Archives and Records Administration-Washington, D.C.* (Hereinafter denoted as "D.C. Records-Senate."
27. Sterling Tucker, *Beyond the Burning: Life and Death of the Ghetto*, New York: Association Press, 1968, 84.

The Cavalier State bitterly held on to the poll tax when other states in Dixie were retreating and the same holds true for anti-miscegenation statutes. Just as the Negro population in South Carolina dropped, something similar occurred in Fairfax County, Virginia—just across the river from the District—whose Black percentage there fell from 16 to 4 percent. Eleanor Dulles, scion of an elite family that was to dominate both the CIA and the State Department, was essential to the development of McLean, Virginia, which became a renewed citadel of Jim Crow.[28]

Baltimore and Maryland were little better. During the war Paul Robeson refused to perform in this charmless city because of its deeply entrenched Jim Crow seating policies. Juanita Jackson Mitchell, a long-time NAACP leader recalled this unpretty era with a dearth of fondness: "'When I was in high school,'" she said, "'we would go to downtown…and speak French to get waited on…black foreigners were served, black native Americans, not…'"[29] Again, U.S. Negroes were being punished for their repetitive inclination to revolt against the status quo to the point that enslavers suffered massive capital loss in their bodies at the conclusion of the civil war. If only racism was at issue, presumably even a French speaking Negro would have been turned away.

It did seem that Black Americans forced to sacrifice life and limb during wartime while being subjected to propaganda about human rights, were unwilling to return to the status quo ante. Phileo Nash retained a newspaper clipping that detailed a typical event: in Manassas, Virginia, where in the lifetime of some, blood was shed copiously in order to battle those who resembled eerily those just vanquished in Berlin, a reporter there described a "four hour riot" amidst "10,000 Negroes at their annual Labor Day horse show…one Negro was killed, five others arrested and the county sheriff and his deputy were severely injured," as they were administered severe "beatings."[30] Another scribe wrote of "3,000 dispersed" at this horse show, as state troopers were "armed with tommy guns."[31]

The Jim Crow ethos was being reinforced in the face of ever stiffer challenges. Just before this fracas, Senator Bilbo took note of

---

28. Andrew Friedman, *Covert Capital: Landscapes of Denial and the Making of U.S. Empire in the Suburbs of Northern Virginia*, Berkeley: University of California Press, 2013, 34, 42, 43, 44, 45, 66, 11

29. David Taft Perry, "'Tramping for Justice:' The Dismantling of Jim Crow in Baltimore, 1942-1954," 225, 268.

30. Clipping, 4 September 1945, Box 30, *Phileo Nash Papers*.

31. *Washington Times Herald*, 4 September 1945.

a Chicago editorial that demanded his impeachment.[32] Regaining its footing after the disastrous interregnum with their now deposed leader, Earl Browder—blamed for converting the party into a looser association, allowing the lamb (worker) to recline alongside the lion (capitalist)—the Communists in the District reached the pages of the *Washington Post*, with their demand for the ouster of James Byrnes of South Carolina, a Jim Crow tribune who had served on the U.S. Supreme Court, then as Truman's Secretary of State[33] and, in essence, was little different than Bilbo.

Yet the Dixiecrats were hardly ready to surrender. As President Truman was commuting a death sentence for Nazi spies, Senator Bilbo received a postcard embossed with a swastika, spewing bile: "remember after all those spies are white men and we expect you to keep your promise and help us. We are depending on you as in the past."[34] But the Senator was then on the defensive because of the credible accusations of his wrongdoing, i.e., accepting illicit payments from military contractors.[35]

The nonplussed Senator was not one to be thrown off course by a mere scandal. By 1946, Marie Richardson Harris of the National Negro Congress of the District, was reproving him for asserting that providing a full menu of voting rights to Washingtonians "'would mean the nation's capital would be turned over to the negro race to control and operate.'" This was just "buffoonery" on his part, she responded.[36] Although the issue often was portrayed as a matter of home rule, the underlying issue was more thorny: who shall rule at home? Negroes who had proven themselves to be susceptible to Communist blandishments—or others?

Bilbo responded thusly: Au contraire, countered the chief Dixiecrat. In words that would govern the District for decades to come, he proclaimed that "if the negroes ever get the right to vote in Washington in less than six months they will flood [the city] with enough negroes to elect a negro mayor, negro board of aldermen, negro chief of police and negro everything."[37] How could white supremacy

---

32. *Chicago Sentinel*, 2 August 1945, Box 1047, *Bilbo Papers*.

33. *Washington Post*, 5 December 1945.

34. Unsinged postcard, 1945, Box 1108, *Bilbo Papers*.

35. Richard C. Ethridge, "The Fall of the Man: The United Senate's Probe of Theodore G. Bilbo in December 1946 and its Aftermath," *Journal of Mississippi History*, 38 (Number 3, August 1976): 241-262, 249.

36. Marie Richardson Harris to Senator Bilbo, 14 May 1946, Box 1016, *Bilbo Papers*.

37. Senator Bilbo to Henry Brehlert, 23 July 1946, Box 1016, *Bilbo Papers*.

operate in the old way given such a political makeup? Continuing his maniacal crusade against Black Washington, the Senator scribbled frenziedly on a newspaper article: "The negro is to Washington what the worm is in the core of the apple...."[38] Woefully, Bilbo's rantings often were reinforced by the likeminded in the District. Attorney William Conlyn of 1935-35th Street N.W. told him, "Washington is well governed until you get up around Howard University."[39]

Thomas Auchinloss of 3002-12th Street N.E. was even more explicit, informing the disgraced legislator that he was "determined to insure [sic] your re-election"; the man who bore the surname of a prominent U.S. family and spoke "as a licensed mortician," was "especially grateful [for] the fight you have waged and are yet conducting to prevent mongrelization of the white race...." He took particular umbrage at the presence of a bus stop near his residence since it was "used almost exclusively [by] the colored...." It was hurting his business since he had "lost five cases during the past six months because of the conviction of many of my neighbors"; his was a "colored funeral home" and "none but the colored are ever seen standing before [the Auchinloss] home...."[40]

But these Bilbo fanboys were swimming against a crushing tide for as long as Virginia and the Carolinas were to the right of the District socio-politically, while the latter was growing due to the logic of the national security state, jobs—even of the custodial and secretarial variety—would be created that would attract Negroes northward like iron filings to a magnet. And given obtaining political currents globally, this would create momentum for extending the electoral franchise in a manner that would cause Bilbo to glisten with nervous sweat. A congressional committee in 1946 presented yet another twist on this vexed matter. These investigators found that a "high percentage of congressional time is devoted to matters of a purely local or petty importance. More time is consumed in serving as the City Council for the District of Columbia than is spent on matters involving great importance to the Nation"—this "extraneous workload" was terribly inefficient and, more than this, was a detriment to the all-important national security.[41] When U.S. imperialism was confronting Moscow and attempting to prop up tottering colonial

---

38. Undated clipping, Box 1016, *Bilbo Papers*.
39. William Conlyn to Senator Bilbo, 16 July 1946, Box 1016.
40. Thomas Auchincloss to Senator Bilbo, 7 February 1946, Box 95, Record Group 46, *D.C. Records-Senate*.
41. Report of Joint Committee on Organization of Congress, 4 March 1946, Box 171, Folder 4, *Morris Udall Papers, University of Arizona-Tucson*.

empires in Africa, did it really make sense to have well-paid legislators immersed in the modalities of urban garbage pickup?

With a figure as odious as Bilbo wielding influence in the District,
reinforcement was provided to those who preferred to acquiesce to Jim
Crow. Such was the case at George Washington University—understandably the alma mater of FBI Director, J. Edgar Hoover—where
by 1946, a contretemps erupted because of their refusal to admit African Americans to a campus auditorium. It was in October 1946 that
members of this minority sought to buy tickets to an event at Lisner
Auditorium but were turned away. A stellar cast that included Ingrid
Bergman was featured in a production of "Joan of Lorraine"—and she
too joined the spirited protest. She was joined by Tennessee Williams,
George Abbott, Irving Berlin, Ira Gershwin, and Lillian Hellman, too.
The university responded by voting to admit Negroes—but moving
to discontinue commercial theatrical performances that might draw
an interracial audience. In sum, Jim Crow on campus continued and
did not yield until 1954.[42] Indicating how ostensibly local issues
were of national import because of their global implications, Truman
aide—Phileo Nash—monitored this controversy.[43]

Involved in these protests were also military veterans who took
note of the role of Hoover on the school's board. Aware of the District's role as a venue for global visitors, they highlighted the point
that local hotels "generally follow [a] general discriminatory program," but also aware of the tug-of-war that resulted from this
contradictory role of being the gateway to both Jim Crow Virginia
and a nation with a purportedly contrary vision, they underscored
the point that in this city there was "no consistent or established
community policy in respect to racial discrimination...."[44]

This tug-of-war was also exposed when Dorothy Barnard of
1010 Fourth Street N.E. chose to contradict the veterans, reminding
campus leaders in an "originalist" twist, that "this is a white man's
country," recalling that "we did not have any Negro problem when
it [the U.S. Constitution] was written." Then with a flourish, she
exhorted: "Down with mixing the negroes with the white...."[45]

---

42. Letter from Ruth Horland Wells, 21 March 2001, Box 1, *Lissner Auditorium
Collection, George Washington University.*
43. Newsletter of Committee for Racial Democracy, 15 February 1947, Box
48, *Phileo Nash Papers, Truman Presidential Library.*
44. Pamphlet by GWU Veterans, circa 1946-1947, Box 1, *Lissner Auditorium
Collection.*
45. Dorothy Barnard to Lissner Auditorium, 9 December 1946, Box 1, *Lissner
Auditorium Collection.*

Her tirade was consistent with G.W.U. policy. President Cloyd Heck Marvin, who served from 1927-1959, announced proudly in the 1930s that "there are no colored students" at his campus within walking distance of the White House. "Students of any race or color," he argued, "perform their best educational disciplines when they are happily situated in a homogeneous group"; hence, his school—he noted with disdain—"does not register colored students."[46] Months after the pathbreaking Supreme Court decision, *Brown v. Board of Education*, he reversed field and allowed Negro students to be admitted to his sanctum sanctorum.[47]

It must be understood that G.W.U.'s policies were consistent with those of their neighbors. Georgetown, Catholic, and American universities were hardly different.[48] The Dahlgren Terrace Citizens Association, one of many such bodies in a smalltown of smaller neighborhoods, was mulling if "violence" or "money"—i.e., power of elitism and the logic of the marketplace—would be sufficient to keep Negroes from residing in their locality. The panic that gripped residents suggested a mix of both: "'You're having a scourge here,'" said one homeowner, as "'you see colored real estate agents scurrying up your streets,'" he asserted disgustedly: "'too bad you can't take a nice healthy club or a crowbar and lay them in the gutter....'" Just as the stated priority on Capitol Hill was to keep Reds from "infiltrating," in these recalcitrant neighborhoods the goal was to keep Blacks "'from infiltrating into white neighborhoods....'" Negroes not yet hospitalized may have been less discomfited with the consensus among residents that "'you're not being asked to use violence like we once had to use on R Street,'"[49] site of a mini-pogrom.

Mr. Truman's neighbors were not thrilled with his initiative on equal civil rights for Negroes, sensing correctly that it could undermine their opposition to desegregation. Clifford H. Newell, former president of the Federation of Citizens Associations—a conglomeration of block associations—found these maneuvers to be based on "'false'" and "'biased'" conceptions.[50] Thus, it was Newell who called for "'natural'" Jim Crow in the District since "'the uninformed Negro...is an easy march for schemers who are interested in him

---

46. Memo by President Marvin, circa 1938, Box 27, *Records of the Office of the President, George Washington University*.
47. *Washington Evening Star*, 8 July 1954.
48. Constance McLaughlin Green, *The Secret City*, 262.
49. *Washington Post*, 18 September 1947.
50. *Washington Post*, 14 December 1947.

only to make him a pawn or dupe that in the name of Social Democracy, which is but another name for Communism,'" allowing the CP to "'carry out their plans to bring about...the same conditions that befell France and other European countries,'"[51] then grappling with resurgent Communist parties.

John Connaughton, who followed Newell into this exalted post as president, upped the ante, denying that racism existed in the District: "'there is no discrimination in Washington,'" he insisted. His words suffused with sophistry, he asked querulously, "'Is it discrimination because I want to live here with certain people and you want to live there with certain other people.'" But like his predecessor he denounced unreservedly the Report of the President's Committee on Civil Rights.[52]

Jenny Grayson of 132 B Street S.W. put a different spin on this latest controversy, informing the *Afro-American* that "many white persons have worked for colored and thought nothing of it," but with the new focus on equality in 1947, hardly seen since Reconstruction, a backlash had been engendered. This she knew since she was actually born in the District in 1876.[53]

E.B. Henderson of Falls Church, Virginia was of a different view. Looking three years ahead to 1950, he felt that with the "present trend, a greater percentage of the permanent residents of Washington will be our colored citizens...[but] because of poor schools in Northern Virginia, many colored parents send their children to Washington"; plus, "there are almost no new homes being built for tenancy in the metropolitan area" outside of the District, forcing more movement to this city. "Over 150 children from Fairfax County alone come into the high schools of Washington since there is no high school to which they may go in the county," thanks to Jim Crow. "The nearest Virginia high school admitting these children is at Manassas in Prince William County, which requires as much as a 40 to 60 mile trip daily for many...."[54]

The discrepancy between the District and Virginia was driving more Negroes into the former, at a time when the White House was under global pressure to erode the more egregious aspects of Jim Crow—which too would drive more Negroes to this town. This would impact employment patterns, too. The *Pittsburgh Courier* reported that PEPCO, "one of the city's wealthiest utilities,"

---

51. *Washington Daily News*, 15 October 1947.
52. *Washington Daily News*, 9 December 1947.
53. *Afro-American*, 19 July 1947.
54. *Washington Post*, 28 April 1947.

"barred" Negroes from "white collar jobs,"[55] as capital continued to revolt against equality. But with the influx, more momentum would be created to reverse this pattern, thereby possibly creating more donors to civil rights organizations—and more resentment at their multi-faceted activity.

All told, the steady flow of Blacks into the District was a result of a push administered rudely by Jim Crow due south and the pull of employment and education (soon certain Virginia schools would be closed altogether rather than bow to desegregation). A problem for guardians of the status quo is that Washington was not just another big city, it was the seat of national power at a time when the U.S. was enmeshed in a twilight struggle against the forces of socialism and—to a degree—national liberation. This was not a moment for wobbliness or experimentation but to hardline conservatives this precisely seemed to be the result of desegregation. One of the early Red Scare / Cold War trials unfolded in the District involving the prosecution of Carl Marzani—Communist, veteran of the Spanish Civil War, documentary filmmaker, publisher. He was to serve a term in prison for supposedly concealing his CP membership. However, conspicuous in his 1947 trial was an empaneled jury of six men and six women "nine of whom are colored," said an observant reporter, though this minority was notorious for being less anticommunist than others.[56] Was this verdict a one-off or did it signal that "integration" of Negroes into U.S. society also portended acceptance of bedrock principles, e.g., anticommunism? Or did the rightward nature of anticommunism serve to buttress racism at the precise moment when fascism—abroad—was defeated? Did the ascendancy of anticommunism portend the marginalizing of the tallest trees in our forest—Paul Robeson in the first place—which then served to compromise severely the antiracist struggle?

Unfortunately, postwar changes were proceeding with such rapidity and momentum that rudimentary questions were hardly posed, let alone answered.

---

55. *Pittsburgh Courier,* circa 1947, File- "Blacks-Segregation and Discrimination," *Special Collections, Washington Public Library.*
56. *Washington Star,* 12 May 1947.

Chapter **8**

Anticommunists Revolt, 1946-1950

1948 was an election year with the former FDR Vice President, Henry A. Wallace, challenging Truman for the White House, with Thomas Dewey of New York upholding the GOP banner and South Carolina's favorite son, J. Strom Thurmond, embodying national angst at the prospect of desegregation.

But this was also the year that Dr. Du Bois was sacked from the NAACP along with his portfolio of being a kind of Minister of Foreign Affairs for the group, as anti-Jim Crow concessions proved sufficient to toss overboard the octogenarian along with the very idea of the Association intervening in a muscular manner in global politics.[1] Withdrawal from this important battle station allowed for more latitude by hawks, contributing to debacles in Korea, Vietnam, Grenada, Panama, Iraq, Afghanistan, Libya—and other sites too numerous to note. The reduced portfolio of the Association did not lead to membership growth, at least not in what had been the bellwether branch: the District. For just before the Du Bois sacking, Thomasina Johnson there told leader, Walter White worriedly, "for us to get only 7 or 8 thousand members in a town this size seem[s]... ridiculous."[2]

Ms. Johnson may have overestimated the potential of the branch in that beginning the in the late 1930s, when radicalism surged and Communist strength waxed, the District had trouble keeping pace with this trend, possibly because of the strength of petit bourgeois elements there. There was constant internal dissension and perpetual conflict with the national office in Manhattan. The national office revoked the branch's charter and it ceased to exist from 1937 to 1939

---

1. Gerald Horne, *Black and Red: W.E.B. Du Bois and the Afro-American Response to the Cold War, 1944-1963*, Albany: State University of New York, 1986.
2. Thomasina Johnson to Walter White, 26 December 1947, Box A 318, *NAACP Papers*.

and limped thereafter.[3] The Du Bois sacking could be interpreted as the triumph of anticommunist and opportunist forces eager to partake at the trough of anti-Jim Crow concessions.

This retreat was the equivalent of Negroes tossing away a potentially potent weapon. For it was in 1948 that it was reported officially that in Washington racially discriminatory praxis had been visited upon an "African Foreign Minister," a "Puerto Rican Senator," a visitor from Panama, and a "'Hindu woman.'"[4] But this was the year that the NAACP chose to adopt the line that the nation was moving progressively—Thurmond's stunning sweeping of the Deep South aside—and naked white supremacy was headed for extinction, a wildly premature projection in retrospect and destabilizing at the time. So, Negro leaders instead of making common cause with these fellow victims of bigotry, chose to rationalize the misdeeds of the wrongdoers.

Thus, as the notion of working class solidarity began to fade, Negro leaders—spokesman for a community disproportionately of this class—drifted into clientelism and lobbying for middle class appointments. Congressman William Dawson, of Chicago, was uppermost among these.[5] Hence this product of the Chicago machine was lobbying intensely for Negro appointments to high-level posts, not a negligible concern but it was not balanced by equal concern with, for example, police terror in the District, which cut across class lines. It was in 1949 that a White House staffer—citing Dawson—expressed the "opinion that it would be of both national and international significance if the P [Truman] would appoint a Negro as a Commissioner of the District of Columbia."[6]

Even Congressman Adam Clayton Powell, compelled to break ties with his anointed successor in the New York City Council—Black Communist Ben Davis—found difficult sledding. It required the Communist influenced party of the left, the American Labor Party of New York City, to reprove the Truman White House since Congressman Powell in 1947 "alone was neglected to be invited to a

3. Gregory Borchardt, "Making D.C. Democracy's Capital: Local Activism, the 'Federal State' and the Struggle for Civil Rights in Washington, D.C.," Ph.D. dissertation, George Washington University, 2013, 120.

4. Paula C. Austin, *Coming of Age in Jim Crow DC: Navigating the Politics of Everyday Life*, New York: New York University Press, 2019, 75.

5. Christopher Manning, *William L. Dawson and the Limits of Black Electoral Leadership*, De Kalb: Northern Illinois University Press, 2009.

6. Memo from "RHG", 4 April 1949, Box 477, Official File, *Truman Presidential Library*.

White House reception," which was deemed to be "extremely shock-ing" and a "deliberate snub"—and was "very insulting" besides.[7] Although Truman rhetorically was seeking to move beyond the old time religion of apartheid, old habits died hard, especially when Powell was known to consort with the enemy du jour: Communists.

Another missed opportunity was the NAACP reluctance to intervene in the case of the deportation of Black Communists, which could have meant closer ties to the Caribbean. Progressive women, e.g., Muriel Draper and Gene Weltfish, and the Congress of American Women, were stalwart in their 1948 defense of Clau-dia Jones, slated for shipping either to her native Trinidad or the colonizing power: Britain. Their appeal to the White House was unavailing.[8] At the same time, Ferdinand Smith of Jamaica, once a leading trade union official spearheading seafarers, was being shipped to his former homeland, a wounding blow to workers at the port of Baltimore.[9]

The ouster of Du Bois was part and parcel of a galloping Red Scare that was to amputate the Black Liberation Movement ideolog-ically, which made it easier to execute anticommunist adventures, especially on the Korea peninsula in mid-1950. This devastating demarche also eviscerated left-leaning leadership among labor in the District, in addition to constricting the ideological space that could have allowed the Black Liberation Movement to gravitate toward not just civil equality but redistribution of the wealth.

Initially, the NAACP—even after Du Bois' ouster in 1948—sought to intervene to protect their constituency, then being whipsawed by Truman's "loyalty" program, designed to root out subversives from federal employment, especially in the post office. Frank Reeves, a pioneering Negro litigator in the District, headed this effort.[10]

Again, this was the poisonous complement to the White House's ballyhooed attempt to deliver civil equality to this same constituency. But seeking to ride two horses heading in two different directions simultaneously was unsustainable and, soon the NAACP snapped

---

7. Florence Garden, Legislative Director of American Labor Party, to Presi-dent Truman, 5 March 1947, Official File, Box 476, *Truman Presidential Library*.

8. Muriel Draper, Gene Weltfish and Congress of American Women to Pres-ident Truman, 20 January 1948, Official File, Box 476, *Truman Presidential Library*.

9. Gerald Horne, *Red Seas: Ferdinand Smith and Radical Black Sailors in the U.S. and Jamaica*, New York: New York University Press, 2009.

10. Thurgood Marshall to Clarence Mitchell, 11 November 1948, Box IX: 197, *NAACP Papers*.

into line and began turning its back on victims of the Red Scare, a distressing signal embodied when the eventual ideological leader of the Congressional Black Caucus—George Crockett of Detroit—was jailed after the pivotal trial of his clients in the 1949 trial of the Communist Party leadership in Manhattan: Thurgood Marshall refused to rise to his defense though he and his corps of lawyers had much to lose if aggressive advocacy were penalized.[11]

These trends converged at the congressional hearing that summoned Henry Thomas, 716 L Street S.W., president of Building Laborers Local Union 74 of the International Hod Carriers, Building and Common Laborers Union. However, by the time of this inquisition—December 1950—labor was on the backfoot given the passage of the Taft-Hartley bill of 1947, designed to not just rout the left but handcuff unions generally. Thomas had been a Communist but as the climate shifted, so did he. He joined the party during the halcyon days of 1937, but before Congress sang like a canary about what he knew. The immediate focus was on the Young Communist League, which had branches not just at the major universities—including H.U., A.U., and G.W.U.—but high schools too. He provided chapter and verse on an important meeting of 25 comrades gathered in 1939 at 509 G Street N.W. on the third floor. He joined the military in August 1943 and departed by December 1945. He detailed his Communist education, taught by the legendary Jacob "Pop" Mindel, in classes that included Dr. James Jackson of Virginia. A telling sign, albeit maybe induced by the fearsomeness of his inquisitors, is that he claimed, "dialectical materialism" was "a little too deep for me...." Predictably the party cell—or club—had "disintegrated" within the union by 1948, and by 1949 he signed an anticommunist affidavit mandated by Taft-Hartley.

"I went to the fifth grade in school. The Communists taught me quite a bit of what I know now," he admitted. But his dearth of formal credentials led him to blurt out, "I don't know where I will get my next job...." However, he was sufficiently sophisticated to tell his interrogators what they wanted to hear: "When I discovered...the Communist Party had engaged in espionage, sabotage, spying...this I couldn't stomach...." Now he confessed religiously, "my destiny rests in the hands of God...."[12]

---

11. Edward J. Littlejohn and Peter J. Hammer, 'No Equal Justice': The Legacy of Civil Rights Icon George Crockett, Jr., Detroit: Wayne State University Press, 2022, 56.
12. Testimony of Henry Thomas, 6 December 1950 in "Hearings Regarding Communism in the District of Columbia-Part 2...Hearings Before the

The uproar about his testimony was hardly quelled when he admitted that he had followed "'instinctively'" the Communist line for years even after quitting the party officially and signing a non-Communist affidavit, per obtaining law. Did this suggest that extirpating Communist influence was more difficult than imagined if even those without current membership cards almost robotically continued to adhere to Marxist doctrine? That by December 1950 the party was said to have 3,000 members in the nation's capital was even more grounds for concern—or so it was thought.[13]

However, the report that thousands of Communists hovered in the District as Washington was fighting the same force in Asia, seemed to leave the authorities shaken. By December 1950, the *Washington Post* was moved to proclaim that the police had "grossly libeled" the city by claiming that there were actually 20,000 Reds in the District. However, their competing claim that the accurate figure was 2,000 was hardly assuring.[14]

Repercussions emerged quickly from the hearing featuring Thomas. He promptly fell ill. Then at union headquarters at 525 New Jersey Avenue, storminess erupted. The stricken, Thomas seemed as if he was about to faint, suffering a dizzy spell—though beyond the turbulence, few were willing to entertain Thomas' qualifier that no more than a handful of the 2,000 union members were Communists, at least between 1946 and 1950. His co-leader, Thomas Sampler, also a Negro and Secretary-Treasurer of the union—and also a Communist—was energetically backpedaling on the advice of his pastor, as the claim emerged that it was actually Thomas who persuaded him to become a Communist.[15]

As matters evolved, Washington was not just another big city pilloried by the Red Scare; it was the seat of power and challenges there had to be taken more seriously. Not coincidentally, one of the more celebrated stoolpigeons during this conflicted era was Manning Johnson, who told HUAC on Bastille Day in 1949, "I am a graduate of the Lovejoy Elementary School, [Lovejoy] Junior High School and the Armstrong Technical High School in Washington, D.C." He

---

Committee on Un-American Activities, House of Representatives, 81st Congress, 2nd Session," 6, 11, 12 and 13 December 1950, Washington: Government Printing Office, 1950, Box 10, Folder 18, *Robert Kerr Papers, University of Oklahoma-Norman.*
13. *Washington Post*, 12 December 1950.
14. *Washington Post*, 16 June 1950.
15. *Washington Star*, circa 7 December 1950, Vertical File-Communism, *Special Collections of Washington, D.C. Public Library.*

had been a card carrying Communist for a decade until 1940, then became a repetitive witness against them.[16]

Away from Capitol Hill in the teeming neighborhoods that produced Thomas, it did not appear that the capitulation to anti-communism was delivering benefits. Truman aide, Phileo Nash, was told in late 1947 that there was upset in Black Washington though there had been the "transfer" of five "schools to use by Negroes"—on a segregated basis, of course. "Colored tax-payers object to being given sub-standard plants and equipment," said Charles Durham: "during the war, at least one of the school buildings in question was condemned as unfit for an air-raid shelter."[17]

But Negro youth could now huddle there as they dodged the exploding bombs of indifferent callousness and bigotry. The promise of the antifascist war was delivering inconclusive results. Catholic University deigned to begin admitting Black students in 1943, followed by Georgetown in 1948, and American University in 1949—appropriately, given that it was named for a major slaveowner, George Washington waited until after the *Brown v. Board of Education* case in 1954, to run up the white flag. G.W.U., also appropriately, was grouped alongside its peers in Dixie—Duke, Wake Forest, Emory, Vanderbilt, etc.—in its laggardness.[18] Even the University of Maryland-College Park, on the immediate border of the District, in 1948 yielded reluctantly and for the first time permitted a Negro team from Howard to compete in an athletic event on campus.[19]

At the hilltop, Howard was not left unaffected by this turn to the right. Clark Foreman of the left-leaning Southern Conference for Human Welfare had asked Rayford Logan to address the pro-colonial implications of the founding of the North Atlantic Treaty Organization in 1949 but the historian, no stranger to the left, balked: "When I read in the newspapers, the pro-Communist affiliation of some of the speakers," he assayed, "I concluded that I had acted wisely."[20]

---

16. Testimony of Manning Johnson, "Hearings Regarding Communist Infiltration of Minority Groups-Part 2...before the Committee on Un-American Activities of the House of Representatives," 81st Congress, First Session, 14 July 1949, Washington: GPO, 1949, AF 216, *University of Maryland-College Park*.

17. Charles Durham to Phileo Nash, 13 November 1947, Box 30, *Phileo Nash Papers, Truman Presidential Library*.

18. Attached Summary, circa 1953, Box 35, *Records of Office of the President, George Washington University*.

19. *The Hilltop*, 20 May 1948.

20. Entry, 26 May 1949, Box 4, *Rayford Logan Diary*.

This was understandable—to a degree. Perhaps because of the suffocating Jim Crow, faculty often frustratedly turned their anger against each other, complexifying the ability to engage in objective analysis. This, Logan knew, musing at one point that President Mordecai Johnson and star professor, Alain Locke, "heartily despise each other."[21] Logan was no fan of his supervisor either, observing that "nearly every member of the faculty tries to imitate President Johnson's oratorical, somewhat (at times) pompous tones."[22] Logan and Carter G. Woodson were often at odds, particularly after the former decided to work with Du Bois on a vaunted Encyclopedia.[23] Postwar Johnson was under more fire than usual when he defended Charles Hamilton Houston and Leon Ransom after charges of Communist ties were hurled at both.[24] An informant for the FBI had reported in 1948 that for the longest Howard had a popular "Liberal Club" that was "considered to be a Communist organization,"[25] as evidenced by the past prominent roles of Hunton and Wilkerson.

Then Logan's brother died—"blue eyes and a skin so white as that of almost any white man"[26] (like his sibling)—and his mother expired in quick succession: "work is the best comforter,"[27] he remarked, but his sadness was exported to an already chafing workplace. He continued to be burdened by his dealings with insensitive publishers: "my experiences with the [U]NC press have not been too pleasant," but since for one of his latest books, "few Negroes are buying, by comparison with whites,"[28] options for change were limited. Besides, the industry was still enduring the aftereffects of a paper shortage delivered by world war,[29] limiting options further.

However, Ralph Bunche's jet propelled career trajectory—from U.S. intelligence to the United Nations and a Nobel Peace Prize because of his role in Palestine—suggested that ditching left-wing allegiances could be remunerative, contributing to the frustration of

---

21. Entry, 12 April 1947, Box 4.
22. Entry, 23 January 1944, Box 4.
23. Rayford Logan to Carter G. Woodson, 28 November 1936 and Carter G. Woodson to Rayford Logan, 24 November 1936, Part II, Reel 8, *Carter G. Woodson Papers, Library of Congress-Washington, D.C.*
24. Zachery Williams, *In Search of the Talented Tenth: Howard University Public Intellectuals and the Dilemmas of Race, 1926-1970,* 54.
25. Report, 9 April 1948, Box 3, *Doxey Wilkerson Papers.*
26. Entry, 18 September 1945, Box 4.
27. Entry, 23 February 1946, Box 4.
28. Entry, 17 April 1946, Box 4.
29. Entry, 31 December 1944, Box 4.

some of his colleagues left behind on the hilltop, Logan among them. "Ralph has not written a single book,"[30] said the prolific historian disdainfully, a master at producing the coin of the realm of academia, but obviously the absence of which was no bar to his colleague's ascension, exacerbating Logan's anxiety. Bunche, a major beneficiary of the halting turn from Jim Crow, turned down an offer from the State Department. Logan's newly arrived Howard colleague, John Hope Franklin, thought he had "missed a golden opportunity," but Bunche was eager to escape the doldrums of Jim Crow Washington. But the younger Franklin was quoted by Logan as adding to the acidity by claiming that "naturally Ralph would not jeopardize his future by a forthright statement on segregation," while Du Bois— purportedly—tagged Bunche with the ultimate Negro insult: he was "'the No. 1 white folks' nigger.'" Supposedly above the fray, Logan "did not join the chorus of denunciation when Ralph was supporting the [Count Folke] Bernadotte Plan,"[31] divvying up historic Palestine. Yet, this Logan forbearance was repaid when he continued to receive "too many reports of Ralph Bunche's belittling my name."[32]

Despite their similarities as left-leaning lighter skinned professors who sought to move away from radioactive Communists, Logan was exasperated perpetually by his colleague. Earlier he was grousing about what he was just told: Bunche was "trying as usual to belittle anyone who is not in his gang ([E. Franklin] Frazier and [Abram] Harris" being among the future Nobel Laureate's circle[33]— supposedly. Apparently, future Founding Father of Trinidad and Tobago, Eric Williams, told Logan—"as I had always suspected," added the freckled teacher gruffly—that "Ralph Bunche had told the Political Science Department to turn thumbs down whenever my name was mentioned."[34]

After the dust had cleared in the early 21st century, the well-connected Negro attorney, Truman Gibson, remarked that Bunche was "disabled. In his athletic days he had banged his knees up. He was a great basketball player"[35]—except that Gibson may have downplayed the kneecapping Bunche perpetually endured from captious critics.

---

30. Entry, 12 April 1947, Box 4, *Rayford Logan Diary*.
31. Entry, 28 May 1949, Box 4, *Rayford Logan Diary*. Du Bois expressed a similar sentiment to Logan directly in 1941: "'Ralph Bunche is getting to be a white folks' nigger.'" Entry, 9 September 1941, Box 3, *Rayford Logan Diary*.
32. Entry, 28 May 1949, Box 4.
33. Entry, early 1940s, Box 3, *Rayford Logan Diary*.
34. Entry, 24 September 1944, Box 4, *Rayford Logan Diary*.
35. Oral History, Truman Gibson, 27 July 2001, *Truman Presidential Library*.

Again, what was at issue was a frustration borne from a constricting political space that did not allow the kind of full-throated denunciations of white supremacy and imperialism that the moment demanded, so anger was directed at similarly relatively powerless colleagues, especially those who seemed to be flourishing in the new dispensation which privileged careerism and personal success above all. As has been said, academic politics at whatever venue can be so vicious because the stakes are so low—the paradox for Howard was that the stakes were high: acting as the intellectual vanguard for a terribly oppressed people when straying beyond crudely drawn lines could bring fierce retribution.

Logan particularly had difficulty in making the transition from "Popular Front" politics where Communists were allies to the Red Scare when this trend was verboten. Eventually, as politics took yet another leap he was placed in the anomalous position of despising the descriptor "Black," even after it was accepted widely, leaving him with a dearth of popularity on a campus there this trend was hailed if not incubated. He had difficulty in adapting in a manner that would contradict what his colleague Professor Frazier articulated profoundly as early as 1934: "'what was radical and militant twenty years ago is not radical and militant today.'"[36]

With accusations and imprecations being hurled as subjectivity was unbound, while labor and the left were under assault, Howard dropped 30 faculty members by 1949—allegedly because of an enrollment drop[37]—further debilitating the ability of this political and intellectual lodestar for Black America to play its historic role. This drop was a turnabout from a few years previously when enrollment soared, news announced as both Eleanor Roosevelt and Norman Manley of Jamaica addressed the campus.[38] But as the political climate became more conservative, Howard found fewer friends on Capitol Hill—certainly Bess Truman was less likely to visit the hilltop.

In the immediate postwar scenario, it appeared the good news would not cease: in 1946 *The Hilltop* announced the "largest enrollment in its history, 5,236 students" and "for the first time in years, the female students are outnumbered almost three to two."[39] Even

---

36. Zachery Williams, *In Search of the Talented Tenth: Howard University Public Intellectuals and the Dilemmas of Race, 1926-1970*, Columbia: University of Missouri Press, 2009,

37. Entry, 26 May 1949, Box 4, *Rayford Logan Diary*.

38. *The Hilltop*, 27 October 1945. See also Faculty Minutes, 1948-1953, Box 68, *Caroline Ware Papers, Roosevelt Presidential Library*.

39. *The Hilltop*, 23 October 1946.

then, this news was announced as yet another visitor arrived, Ms. Rajan Nehru of India, spouse of the Prime Minister, to christen an exhibition on "'The Art of India.'"[40]

But if Rip Van Winkle had awakened in 1948 from a slumber beginning in the tumultuous 1930s, he may have been taken aback by the turn of events. Thus, early Sunday morning of 2 October at 516 Second Street N.W., a police raid ensued, as the authorities entered and searched without a proper warrant. Guests were arrested that were attending an orderly social event. The local chapter of the Civil Rights Congress, led by the fiery Communist attorney, William L. Patterson, charged that the trigger for the bruising confrontation was its inter-racial character. A book by Communist historian, Herbert Aptheker, was confiscated while the only person searched for a weapon was the sole Negro guest. An "anti-Semitic remark" polluted the atmosphere while the police argued that prostitutes were present. But symptomatic of the then prevailing and ultimately destabilizing ethos in these left-wing circles was the coda: "while they were waiting," said the CRC leader, "two homosexuals were let in. As a result of hearing the detailed description of their indecent and obscene acts, one of the girls became violently nauseated...."[41]

This overwrought response merits further interrogation. To be sure, Communists—e.g., Harry Hay—were instrumental in the rise during this period of what was called a "homophile" movement.[42] Near the time of the above incident, the Washington police claimed that "'quite a few perverts'" attend meetings of purported "'Communist front organizations,'" not unlike the Civil Rights Congress. It is likely that this police concern reflected a reality that a harassed sexual minority flocked to the banner of radicals—who, in turn, were unwilling to embrace them, possibly because it provided a further rationale for official harassment and obloquy.[43]

Simultaneously, the predominantly heterosexual and "cis-gender" leadership and membership had difficulty in absorbing the surging development that Hay embodied. In one of the premier anticommunist cases of this era, the lapsed Communist, Whittaker Chambers,

---

40. *The Hilltop*, 20 May 1948.
41. Thomas Buchanan to Robert Barrett, 5 October 1948, Box 62, *NAACP-DC Papers, Howard University.*
42. Stuart Timmons, *The Trouble with Harry Hay: Founder of the Modern Gay Rights Movement*, Boston: Alyson, 1990.
43. Brett William Beemyn, "A Queer Capital: Lesbian, Gay and Bisexual Life in Washington, D.C., 1890-1955," Ph.D. dissertation, University of Iowa, 1997, 218.

had accused the elite Alger Hill of conspiring with Moscow—and much was made by the latter of the sexual orientation of the former.[44]

As anticommunism accelerated, there were those who had thought they detected a trend when the "closeted homosexual," Roy Cohn—eventually the combative attorney for Donald J. Trump—led the charge against Communists in Washington in the 1950s under the supervision of Senator Joseph "Tailgunner Joe" McCarthy,[45] who, too, was thought to have veered from the heterosexual mainstream.[46]

Then there was the peculiarity of Washington, a smalltown with capacious chasms separating a mostly Black working class and a powerful corps of Euro-American men, not to mention embassies with diplomatic immunity, meaning—generally—escaping the snare of domestic criminal law. With many of these European men forced into a kind of sexual underground, Negroes became at times their pawns and victims. Yes, this was not necessarily the norm altogether but in an era of sexual panic and repression, this was the story that captured headlines and influenced the distorted perceptions of the CRC in 1948.

And this brings us to the case of Sumner Welles, of a wealthy New York City family who rose to the top level of the State Department. As the CRC in 1948 was seeking to comprehend a complex reality, Welles purportedly became inebriated and had seen a Negro man taking a shortcut across his property and propositioned him for sex—and the man promptly knocked him unconscious.[47] Apparently, this was no surprise to the Truman White House which—for whatever reason—maintained a file on "Sex Perversion."[48]

Before this episode, there was another that caught the eye of the FBI. J. Edgar Hoover, who too had been accused of deviating from the sexual mainstream,[49] was acquainted with the "allegation" that

---

44. James Kirchik, *Secret City: The Hidden History of Gay Washington*, New York: Holt, 2022, 101.

45. Roy Cohn with Sidney Zion, *The Autobiography of Roy Cohn*, Secaucus: Lyle Stuart, 1988.

46. Andrea Friedman, "The Smearing of Joe McCarthy: The Lavender Scare, Gossip and Cold War Politics," *American Quarterly*, 57 (Number 4, December 2005): 1105-1129

47. Irwin F. Gellman, *Secret Affairs: Franklin Roosevelt, Cordell Hull and Sumner Welles*, Baltimore: Johns Hopkins University Press, 1995, 392.

48. See "Confidential File," Box 26, *Phileo Nash Papers, Truman Presidential Library*.

49. Anthony Summers, *Official and Confidential: The Secret Life of J. Edgar Hoover*, New York: Putnam's, 1993.

the elite diplomat "had made improper proposals, involving perversion, to colored male employees of the Southern Railway Company... on board the presidential train while en route from Washington, D.C. to Jasper, Alabama."[50] A similar scandal involved Brigadier General Philip Faymonville, described as "head of the American Lend-Lease Mission in Moscow."[51]

---

50. See Memo for J. Edgar Hoover, 22 January 1941, *Edwin D. Watson Papers, University of Virginia-Charlottesville*: Welles "had been drinking" and "took the waiter into his, Welles,' compartment, locked the door and told the waiter to pull off his clothes, to lie down and offered him twenty dollars, then fifty dollars and finally one hundred dollars" to the "frightened" worker—who finally managed to flee. Then Welles beckoned yet another worker, speaking to him in French, which the man did not understand. Both workers were from Washington. In the same file, see also Deposition of Samuel Mitchell of 154 W Street NW, 9 January 1941: This 43 year old man was born in Honey Path, South Carolina and had been a Pullman porter for 14 years. Welles had rung for him on the day in question and "at that time when I went into his room he had on no clothing excepting the pants of his pajamas. He asked me to close the door, but I did not. He then asked me did I want to make twenty dollars...." He did not. Welles rang for another porter who "remained in there just a few seconds and backed out of the compartment with a strange expression on his face...." In this statement signed by Mitchell, Dwight Brantley, and M.J. West of the FBI, the statement was made that Welles sought to "blow my whistle." See also Statement by Alexander Dickson, 50 and Harry Lucas, of 5333 E. Capitol Street and for two years before that: 1827 Florida Avenue #102. He had been working on presidential trains since the years of Warren Harding. He was 47, married, born and bred in Washington. Walter Calloway had told him that Welles had offered twenty dollars "if he would let Mr. Welles 'go down' on him...." Also speaking "on oath" was Walter Brooks of 5520 33rd Street NW, 59; with Pullman 36 years, 34 as a conductor. An inspector for Pullman, David Gahagan, 52, spoke "on oath" and described Welles as "pale and haggard." Speaking "on oath" was James Hewitt, 34, a married waiter: "I was suspicious of him. I thought he was 'funny' [gay]. I did not think he was a 'he-man'" because he "could 'French' me." In another statement provided by Luther Thomas, Assistant to the Vice President of Southern Railway Company, Mitchell asserts that Welles "curse[d]" him saying "'You will have to do as I tell you on this train.'" Another worker said that Welles was "the worst he had ever encountered." Another worker claimed that Welles "shut the door and locked it... pulled his...bow tie loose and attempted to unfasten his collar...."
51. In the same collection as above, a 1943 file will be found on this case: The undated memorandum asserts that this officer "associated with homosexuals" and was "probably himself a sex pervert...." His office in the Soviet Union had "virtually been turned into a house of prostitution" and this was not unique since Alexander Kirk, "now American Minister to Egypt"

Perhaps because of political reasons, it was the State Department of Welles that suffered more grievously than the Pentagon in light of real and imagined homo-erotic transgressions. The scholar, Irwin F. Gellman, avers that the perception that Welles' presence was not unique led to a change in the line of succession to the presidency, leading to a demotion of the Secretary of State.[52] One can presume profitably that the right-wing with their maniacal obsession with Moscow, alighted naturally on the State Department when pursuing demagogic purges. Roy Blick, the chief of the "Vice Squad" during this difficult era, asserted that there were "'1,000 bad security risks now walking the streets of Washington, D.C.,'" with 75 percent toiling in government agencies and almost 400 in the State Department alone.[53]

However, the dynamics and constructions that may shed light on Welles' vamping on Black men, are not necessarily applicable to Odessa Madre, a darker skinned lesbian described as "'Queen of the Uptown Underworld.'" From 1930-1950, she was one of the District's wealthiest Negroes, dubbed the "Female Al Capone." By 1946, she operated six brothels and employed about 20 women as prostitutes or sex workers. "'I practically ran that damn police department,'" she said of her corrupted relationship with the authorities. Her Club Madre at 2204 14th Street N.W. was the place to see and be seen. Like other wealth accumulators among District Negroes, she too graduated from Dunbar High School, formerly M Street High School. The knowledge she gleaned about mathematics facilitated her operating a "numbers" racket that grossed $3,000 daily. Tellingly, she was detained by the authorities in the hinge year of 1949, as Jim Crow was ostensibly in retreat and expired in 1990 penniless when this process had proceeded.[54]

---

was "reportedly a homosexual." Faymonville "walks with a slight sway to his hips. In his contacts with men, he seems very effusive, grasping and shaking hands warmly...[he] avoids women...certain apartments in the Embassy resemble a brothel...liquor is plentiful...wild orgies [prevail]...[like a] house of prostitution...Moscow is regarded as the city of 'free love' [and] the same women who have been visiting the Embassy quarters over a period of years...under the control of and report to the NKVD [Soviet intelligence]...." Note: As the lawyers might say, I do not present the foregoing as evidentiary of the truth of the matter asserted but more so, to indicate the state of mind of critical actors on a crucial matter.

52. Irwin F. Gellman, *Secret Affairs*, 392.
53. Ibid., Brett William Beemyn, 218.
54. James Kirchik, *Secret City: The Hidden History of Gay Washington*, New York: Holt, 2022, 84, 85, 86.

There may have been another factor at play in Washington. Even today metropolises tend to attract those seeking to elude and evade the narrow-minded Babbitts. At the same time this smalltown of severe power imbalances in the middle of a relative cultural desert, provided a recipe for various hijinks and, more precisely, pursuing alternatives to the status quo. The celebrated chemist at Howard, Percy Julian, discovered this reality to his dismay when his illicit affair with the wife of a laboratory assistant became grist for the gossip mill.[55]

Like many campuses, Howard housed freethinkers of various sorts, unrestrained by the bonds and cant of society. And this school was in a city where—according to Kelly Miller—the "masses and the classes of Negroes in Washington" was "more pronounced than in any other city,"[56] a trend accentuated by limousines depositing diplomats and would-be statesmen, especially in the northwest quadrant of the city where Blacks were hardly absent. In such an atmosphere, it became harder for many Negroes to accept normative propaganda about the U.S. as a just society, which predisposed some to diverge further from the conventionally conformist. Lucy Diggs Slowe, a tennis champion who also was the first Black woman to serve as Dean of Women at any U.S. university—Howard in her case—shared a home with her companion, Mary P. Burrill, for 25 years: Slowe provided a rousing keynote address at a gathering of the National Negro Congress in 1936, when consorting with these progressives was shunned by many of her colleagues.[57]

She was also a founder of the leading sorority, Alpha Kappa Alpha and balked at residing on campus before moving to the Brookland neighborhood, 1256 Kearny Street N.E.[58] Howardite Rayford Logan contended that homosexuality was hardly absent at his campus and was "widespread" at Morehouse in Atlanta: "President [Benjamin] Mays had spoken publicly about it...."[59]

In the hothouse atmosphere that was Washington, especially when the Red Scare constricted political space, attention was diverted unavoidably to social matters; thus, the biographer of historian—and

---

55. See File on Percy Julian, Box 12, *Ralph Bunche Papers, University of California-Los Angeles.*

56. Genny Beemyn, *A Queer Capital: A History of Gay Life in Washington, D.C.,* New York: Routledge, 2015, 50.

57. Carroll L.L. Miller and Anne S. Spruitt-Logan, *Faithful to the Task at Hand: The Life of Lucy Diggs Slowe,* Albany: State University of New York, 2012, 335

58. *Washington Post,* 30 March 2019.

59. Entry, 23 June 1953, Box 5, *Rayford Logan Diary.*

former Bison—Carter G. Woodson, was taken by the fact that "news-papers remained fascinated by his bachelorhood,"[60] as if singlehood was a social reproach.

Then there were the legations, stacked with foreigners often from posh backgrounds and U.S. nationals there who were influenced by them. The gay man known as "Dash Dasham" had a purported affair with a staffer at the Portuguese embassy, who subsequently was arrested on separate grounds.[61]

Ideological regression could not obscure the wider point that in a complicated political environment, anticommunism unfurled as anti-Black rhetoric was increasingly viewed as all too reminiscent of the recently vanquished foe in Berlin: thus, progressive and radi-cal forces continued to campaign against Jim Crow. It was an uphill climb, nonetheless. By late 1948, possibly because of the reaction unshackled by the surge of anticommunism, led significantly by Jim Crow advocates, a reporter found that segregation was mounting in the District. It was more entrenched than "half a century ago," shock-ingly enough. The power behind the throne was the Board of Trade, local merchants, and burghers—barons from real estate, finance, and commerce—unwilling to repel the asphyxiating scent from Virginia that wafted across the river.[62]

It was worse than a scent. It was during the Summer of 1946 that Mamie Davis found herself at the airport that served Washington, sited in Virginia. Her flight was delayed, so she ambled to a coffee shop which curtly and peremptorily informed her, "'This is the state of Virginia and I can't serve you.'"[63] Washington had to contemplate what would be the impact when African and Caribbean diplomats were treated thusly, and could the U.S. absorb the stiff price the Cold War was delivering.

Backed against the wall, by mid-1949 the National Lawyers Guild, once the sole racially integrated bar organization before being ham-mered as a "Communist front," demanded enforcement of an 1872 law banning Jim Crow in restaurants, bars, hotels, and barber shops; the initiative too was integrated, pushed by Joseph Forer, often

---

60. Burnis R. Morris, *Carter G. Woodson: History, The Black Press and Public Relations*, Jackson: University Press of Mississippi, 2017, 69.
61. Ina Russell, ed., *Jeb and Dash: A Diary of Gay Life, 1918-1945*, Boston: Faber and Faber, 1993, 185.
62. *Christian Science Monitor*, 13 December 1948.
63. Mamie Davis to P.S. Damon of American Airlines, 8 August 1946, Box II: B218, *NAACP Papers*.

recruited to defend Reds and Charles Hamilton Houston, the premier advocate for Blacks.[64]

This laudable maneuver coincided with the heat of the 1948 presidential campaign when Henry A. Wallace's Progressive Party declared "'all out war'" against Jim Crow in the District.[65] Soon, the *Afro-American* printed a legal brief from Forer's National Lawyers Guild, underscoring that Jim Crow in the District was patently illegal,[66] then crowed that the NLG had created "'sudden death'" for this spiteful system of iniquity.[67]

This declaration which evidently influenced President Truman to move in a similar direction, also may have influenced press coverage, especially in the dismally retrograde—now defunct—*Washington Star*. As Forer and Houston were in the process of marching into court, this scandal sheet which was not renowned for coverage of the ravages of Jim Crow, carried a sympathetic article about the dilemmas faced by Ralph Bunche when he rejected an offer from the State Department.[68]

The story struck a resonant chord at a moment when Washington was seeking to undermine the propaganda victory for Moscow delivered by Jim Crow. A resident of Salisbury, Connecticut was so upset that he contacted the White House directly, informing the president, "we no longer send our high school students to Washington because of the segregation of…colored students," depriving impressionable teenagers of direct knowledge of the capital. And the losses endured were not just in the Nutmeg State nor Washington, as the "situation reaches out like an octopus with all parts of our land."[69]

The District was in a bind: this close neighbor of Virginia happened to be placed on the cutting edge as the nation moved slowly away from Jim Crow but many residents were not necessarily accepting of the Olympian rationales for this transition—and reacted

---

64. *Washington Star*, 3 June 1949.
65. *Washington Star*, 8 July 1948.
66. *Afro-American*, 1 October 1949.
67. *Afro-American*, 11 June 1949.
68. *Washington Star*, 2 June 1949: Bunche said, "'I built a house,'" while at Howard, in an area where Euro-Americans predominated; he "'spent 18 months going over plans,'" yet still his "'daughters had to go 3 miles to a school—I had to hire a driver to take them—even though there was a school for white kids just around the corner'…."
69. M.A. Warner to President Truman, 27 April 1949, Box 477, Official File, *Truman Presidential Library*.

accordingly. During the Spring of 1949 when Negroes began to move into a "white neighborhood" in the northeast quadrant of the city, deftly launched stones greeted them rudely.[70] The *Afro-American* quickly adopted the ascendant political line arguing that "White bigots['] acts" were "grist for Communists…." They were simply "softening up the minority groups for Communist infiltration…." They were responding to a four foot blazing cross, emblem of the terrorist Ku Klux Klan, which in recent memory had marched in formation through the District, placed near the residence of Ralph Sneed of 1700 M Street, S.E. This fiery demonstration was punctuated by the shattering of his windowpanes with adroitly tossed projectiles. Naturally, it was reported that the police "shrugged the attack off," as this was the price to be paid for desegregating a "previously…all white community."[71]

Also aiding this project was NLG member, Louis Rothschild Mehlinger, a friend of the "unceasing militant," Mary Church Terrell and her attorney spouse. They and other members of the besieged progressive movement were engaged in strict solidarity alongside mostly Black members of United Cafeteria and Restaurant Workers, Local 471 after they went on strike in early 1948. These 1,200 workers were on strike for about 78 days during a frosty winter. Washington was seeking to purge Communists and their sympathizers from the ranks and the response from Robeson and the Civil Rights Congress was to organize a benefit of 2,500 raising a hefty $7,000.[72]

The "loyalty" initiative launched by President Truman, along with its companion, the Red Scare, and the anticommunist Taft-Hartley law of 1947, were in part a tool to hammer local labor in line. Generally, the FBI and Department of Justice were the most flagrant transgressors of what came to be called equal employment opportunity. About three percent of these agencies' workforce was Black—compared to 25 percent of Interior. As noted, the latter figure was misleading since this department supplied guards and elevator operators for virtually all other agencies, who were mostly Black. Normatively, the Department of Labor had 2,290 employees and 150 were African American. To their credit, the Congress of Industrial Organizations sought to transform this iniquitous system, but for its troubles was torched by the Red Scare. Still, one of their leaders, Oliver Palmer in early 1947 led a 50 building strike in the District and

---

70. *Washington Post*, 4 April 1949.
71. *Afro-American*, 17 September 1949.
72. Alison M. Parker, *Unceasing Militant: The Life of Mary Church Terrell*, Chapel Hill: University of North Carolina Press, 2020, 264, 271.

even the alcoholism of one of his closer comrades did not slow him and Local 471 down appreciably.[73]

To be sure, the anticommunist offensive was national—indeed, international—but it was not coincidentally launched from Washington, D.C., which had problems all its own confronting the supposed "Red Menace." In this smalltown of concentrated power, estimates of Communist strength varied, with one source claiming that there were as many as 2,000 card-carrying members at the party's zenith in the 1930s. But the growth had been so startlingly spectacular— before the Wall Street collapse of 1929, one scribe saw the CP as a "joke," hardly worth confronting—that this was bound to frazzle strained nerves. Indeed, this same scribe then cited the police for the proposition that there were actually 3,000 Reds in town[74] and by 1949, the House Un-American Activities Committee claimed that the CP in the District was "one of the most important affiliates of the party in the country,"[75] which was no exaggeration. Potentially reassuring—in a perverse manner—was the testimony of Alvin Stokes who instructed HUAC in July 1949—that "Colored Communists" were "fewer than 100 here"; it was noted that Stokes himself was "colored," adding credibility—presumably—to his estimate.[76]

It did not take long for the dragnet to sweep up "Colored" — and other—supposed Communists. Born in Jaffa, Palestine in 1898, Samuel Rodman denied he was included in this latter category; this graduate of Columbia University was naturalized in New Brunswick in 1927 and by the time of this allegation in July 1949 was residing at 3700 Massachusetts Avenue, NW.[77] Months earlier Red hunter, Howard Rushmore, claimed that "150 U.S. workers in D.C. spy for Reds," which led to a noisome clamor of alarm bells ringing.[78]

So prompted, hysteria reigned when during the midst of the precedent shattering presidential election 400 amassed, paying 50 cents each, at a CP rally at the National Press Club. Black Communist leader, William Taylor, claimed that 200 District police officers were assigned to monitor his organization and they were hardly absent on this occasion. They were left with quite a bit to digest. A reporter

---

73. Mary Elizabeth Harding, "Eleanor Nelson, Oliver Palmer and the Struggle to Organize the CIO in Washington, D.C., 1937-1950," Ph.D. dissertation, George Washington University, 2002, 114, 194.

74. *Washington Times*, 21 July 1934.

75. *Washington Star*, 24 September 1949.

76. *Washington Star*, 13 July 1949.

77. *Washington Star*, 28 July 1949.

78. *Washington Times-Herald*, 23 July 1948.

noticed attendees "ranging in age from bobby-soxers to bewhiskered grandfathers...amicable and well-dressed" all, as opposed to the scruffy and bedraggled thought to populate Red ranks. "A third of those attending were colored," remarkable in retrospect in this Jim Crow bastion. "Among the big givers" of donors solicited were the "Mid-City and Petworth branches of the party...."[79]

This event was preceded by the impaneling of a grand jury in Manhattan that happened to investigate the CP in the District too. Among the scores questioned, were witnesses who affirmed that a headquarters for the comrades was a violin studio on Connecticut Avenue. The most prominent "cell got its first toehold," said the breathless reporter who observed this proceeding, "in the old Agriculture Adjustment Administration, a hotbed of Commies and fellow travelers during the 1930s. A Washington druggist who died last year was a kingpin in the cell and his pharmacy was used as a mail drop," and, yes, the "cell" was said to be infested with Soviet agents[80]—and not U.S. nationals concerned about Jim Crow and workers' rights.

The U.S. ruling class was in a quandary. Siting the seat of power near Virginia, was seen decades earlier as a timely concession to this so-called home of presidents. But as relations with Moscow suffered a downturn, with the latter's local comrades able to influence Negroes and others upset with slavery's legatee—Jim Crow—this fateful decision did not seem wise. The number of federal workers had grown in the 1930s from 63,000 to 93,000, then 166,000 by 1940—with the upper limit not in sight—providing more room for Red recruitment in a compact town and, correspondingly, more demagogic campaigning against federal spending and growth, which became a kind of proxy for racist anxiety. Likewise, the city's population had grown by more than a third, topping 663,000 by 1940, larger than 12 states and adding substance to the nascent notion that the District should become a state with requisite voting rights and the ability to elect a Negro Senator. Understandably, Communists ascended to the leadership of the United Federal Workers and campaigned vigorously and relentlessly against Jim Crow. In response, Bilbo of the Magnolia State became the senatorial overseer of the District. "'I wanted this position,'" he yelped, "'so I could keep [D.C.] a segregated city.'" But that demented wish was contrary to his nation's global responsibilities postwar. This contributed to yet another response. The city's population peaked at 900,000 in 1943 then began a repetitive decline,

---

79. *Washington Star*, 3 May 1948.
80. *Washington Times-Herald*, 9 December 1947.

as the example of the Pentagon demonstrated, federal spending was spreading increasingly to Virginia and Maryland, meaning the District's portion of regional population declined from 68.5 percent in 1940 to 36.9 percent by 1960. Part of this process meant "white flight," as by 1960, the Negro population of the District was 53.9 percent headed toward its moniker of "Chocolate City"—up from 35 percent in 1950. Suburban—meaning Virginia and Maryland outskirts—had grown by a whopping 330 percent.[81]

Still, there was no gainsaying that the anticommunist revolt had wounded severely the progressive—and radical—movements. However, the immediate postwar years provided only a brief foretaste of what was to come.

---

81. Chris Myers Asch and George Derek Musgrove, *Chocolate City*, 251, 280, 290, 291,

Chapter **9**

Contested Waters/Gusty Winds, 1946-1950

Oscar Chapman was nervous.

The telephone of the Secretary of the Interior had rung insistently in 1949. "I got a phone call, an anonymous phone call," he recalled decades later, "about 11 o'clock Saturday morning [claiming] that the Communists over in Baltimore were planning to raid the swimming pools" in the District "when I opened them the next day on Sunday and that they were coming over here in cars; they were going to park down here [near] the Progressive [Party] headquarters," i.e., "park their buses." He did not reflect on why District Communists were not part of this planned civil disobedience, intended to desegregate forcefully a Jim Crow pool.

In any case, their plan—purportedly—was to induce a "black boy" to be "amorous with a white girl," a casus belli to be sure. Their plan, it was said, was to park their vehicles near the "Anacostia Bridge," so the checkmate devised by the Secretary was "to keep the bridge tied up. We kept that traffic tied up there...then we blocked another incoming road on the other side the same way...." Beamingly, he added, "not more than five or six blacks got in there and they got out of their cars and walked over there...."

Like the anti-love police, the Secretary, his timbre narrowing, proclaimed, "we had it organized to the extent that if a black boy would get amorous with a white girl, or attempt to [do so] in any way, a black policeman would tap him on the shoulder" in a bout of premature affirmative action, "and just quietly say, 'I'm a policeman. Now, we don't allow that in here, in this pool.'" But flummoxed, "then a white boy got amorous with a black girl," and matters "played itself out just like a stage play," or the maunderings of a fabulist, for that matter.

"We had more policemen, or as many policemen in that pool as did anybody else swimming that day. I had policewomen in there, white

181

and black, and always a black policewoman or policeman would call attention to the black person that was trying to get amorous with a white girl and vice versa" and instantaneously "[they] stopped that thing in five minutes...[as] we made one black get out of the pool," blocking desegregation. "We stopped that thing," he boasted strangely, "I was so organized...the public never did know...."

But the crafty Reds did not give up easily, as there was a similar incident near "Hains Point...I had had a meeting with all the newspapers...I had asked them not to play up the pool opening, just give it a little opening..." He told newspapers: "'[I] don't want an exciting story about it.' Just 'the pools will open.' They did," he concluded, while adding morosely, "I never could get [Harold] Ickes [his predecessor] to do that."[1]

Katharine Graham, celebrated publisher of the *Washington Post*, had a different recollection. Yes, there were "riots" at swimming pools, but her recollection was that it was the Progressive Party—not the Communists—led by Henry A. Wallace himself who "led black children to swim [at] Washington's previously all-white public swimming pools," leading to "pitched battles" as "emotions ran high." But her remembrance dovetailed with that of the Secretary when she wrote that her staff wanted the story to be displayed on the front page, but she wielded her veto and insured that this explosive story would be "buried in the paper." At the time her paper, soon to bury the competition—especially the *Star*—was under siege for supposedly being insufficiently hawkish in confronting Communists, a preposterous allegation echoed by the *Times-Herald* and the voice of Midwest reaction: the *Chicago Tribune*. "The war between McCarthy and the *Post* was vicious and frightening,"[2] she lamented—and she could not allow Wallace and his party to appear to be in the vanguard of desegregation on her newspaper's front page, allowing the left to steal a march in the battle for Negro affections to the dismay of her right-wing challengers.

However, she may not have been the ultimate decider at this juncture in that this inflamed incident occurred before her spouse's suicide years later and as of 1949, it was Philip Graham who was mostly calling the shots. And he seemed to be more attuned to ruling class leanings, according to historian Gregg Herken: his "sympathy for the poor and downtrodden was actually rooted in a larger concern—namely that it would be impossible for America [sic] to win the Cold War if the country were seen as indifferent to the plight of its minorities."[3]

---

1. Oral History, Oscar Chapman, 2 August 1972, *Truman Presidential Library*.
2. Katharine Graham, *Personal History*, New York: Knopf, 1997, 186.
3. Gregg Herken, *The Georgetown Set*, 209.

By June 1949 Ben Bradlee, soon to be catapulted into fame because of the Watergate scandal of the 1970s that brought down President Richard M. Nixon, was a cub reporter in Washington. He too was critical of the *Times-Herald*—a "jazzy, scrappy and right wing daily owned by Eleanor Medill 'Sissy' Patterson, daughter of the legendary Colonel Robert McCormick" of the *Tribune*. But there was no guarantee that this competitor would go belly up—which it did—particularly if the *Post* was seen to play up the story of civil disobedience at public pools.

By 1995 in the twilight of his career, Bradlee admitted, "I covered the race riots in Anacostia," which his periodical termed coyly "'incidents...disturbances...demonstrations.'" The "fight was over who could swim in what public pools," he remembered. He saw the Progressive Party and "Young Wobblies" or anarcho-syndicalists joining with Negroes and "once six black kids managed to get into the water briefly at one of the white pools, until they were booed and splashed out by about fifty whites...." His paper—and others—were "scared to death of the story," especially since the "black community was barely covered." Yet agape, he "watched a pitched battle between whites and blacks...waves of whites would periodically break out of the crowd to chase those whites they believed to be responsible for trying to integrate the pools, or to corner blacks." Responsively, "blacks would go after isolated whites...." All told, there were "about four hundred persons...involved" with "twenty cops...in the middle."

But, he said sarcastically, "the great liberal *Washington Post* was afraid to tell the story," and he found out why when he was summoned to a meeting with the tuxedoed grandee Clark Clifford, a key aide to President Truman, accompanied by Chapman and Julius Krug of Interior. Bradlee ascertained that the newspaper executive—Graham's spouse—"cut himself quite a deal with the big shots: close the Anacostia pool immediately and promise that all six pools will operate the following years on an integrated basis or Bradlee's story run[s] on page one tomorrow. Krug...had made the deal on the spot." And Bradlee's employer, which had a skimpy circulation of a mere 160,000 then and in coming months would record losses of about $1 million annually, was willing to oblige and evade alienating right wing competition and readership which often tended to be more affluent.[4]

---

4. Ben Bradlee, *A Good Life: Newspapering and Other Adventures*, New York: Simon & Schuster, 1995, 117, 120, 125, 126, 127, 128

Even after 1949, desegregating swimming pools continued to be a bedeviling issue for federal authorities. A year later, Chapman "learned through his contacts with the Subversive Squad of the Metropolitan Police" that a "group of Young Progressives were planning to hold a demonstration at the Anacostia pool," with a "mixed group, 100-150," with fireworks sure to follow.[5]

Naturally, the NAACP claimed this victory as its own, when the parties on the frontlines included left-wingers,[6] who they had begun to shun. Yet, what Chapman, Graham, and Bradlee did not seemingly realize was that swimming pools—with the scantily clad post-pubescent flocking together—were inexorable flashpoints whenever desegregation loomed ominously.[7]

William Patterson, the Black Communist leader of the Civil Rights Congress, which had an active chapter in the District, found the "rioting around the swimming pool there in Washington" reprehensible. A keen consumer of news, Patterson tied this latest discord to similar events then unfolding in St. Louis and "on the pattern of the East St. Louis riots of some years back, which spread from East St. Louis to Chicago and other sections of the country...."[8]

Clarence Mitchell of the NAACP groaned about the "sporadic scuffles which have occurred at the swimming in Anacostia" and excoriated the fact that the "hoodlums who chased various persons at the pool escaped arrest while those who were being pursued were taken into 'protective custody' by the police"[9]—a result that should not have surprised him.

The Association's Capitol lobbyist, Clarence Mitchell, rebuked Senator Andrew Schoeppel after this Kansas Republican descended into the morass of redbaiting, lambasting Oscar Chapman of Interior for supposedly having Communist ties.[10] This reflected continuing unease about how this agency handled the 1949 swimming pool controversy, perceived as a defeat for Jim Crow. An irate Mitchell then upbraided the *Post* for their piling on Chapman from the right and

5. Department of Information, 3 July 1950, Box 68, *Oscar Chapman Papers, Truman Presidential Library*.
6. Press Release, 7 July 1949, Box II: B67, *NAACP Papers*.
7. Jeffrey Wiltse, *Contested Waters: A Social History of Swimming Pools in America*, Chapel Hill: University of North Carolina Press, 2010.
8. William Patterson to Thomas Buchanan, 29 June 1949, Reel 24, Part 2, *Civil Rights Congress Papers, New York Public Library-Washington, D.C.*
9. Clarence Mitchell to Julius Krug, 30 June 1949, Box IX: 226, *NAACP Papers*.
10. Clarence Mitchell to Senator Schoeppel, 6 September 1950, Box IX: 226, *NAACP Papers*.

wondered why they were—seemingly—interested in justice except "on your front doorstep."[11]

It was also a response to the never-say-die attitude of Jim Crow defenders in the District, still peeved about how this crisis evolved. According to Roy Wilkins, who was to succeed White within a few years as the group's chief leader, hardliners executed a "deliberately staged brawl" at a desegregated pool, and the spooked Interior Department, folded and returned control to the local Department of Recreation, comprised of ultras who said that Jim Crow would be reimposed. This was followed by Dixiecrats who promptly filed legislation making this move permanent. The lesson was that anti-Jim Crow victories were hardly permanent when those who had helped to deliver these conquests—the left—were being eviscerated at the same time.[12]

The journalist, Carl Bernstein, a native of the region, recalled that "when I was in grammar school, all the public swimming pools in the District of Columbia had been drained by order of the City Recreation Board [sic] rather than allow Black Families to swim," a defeat for the anti-Jim Crow movement but, as well, a setback for all who relied on this public service (of course, the more affluent could rely on pools in their backyards).[13] The obvious distaste for consorting with Negroes, memorialized in law and designed to demean, reached a nadir when Euro-American workers objected to sharing toilet facilities at work with Negroes which one scholar shockingly asserting that this odoriferous matter "more than any other has given us trouble between colored and white employees." That this general point was gleaned from a specific depiction of a jet bomber plant in Maryland, at once implicated the national security implications of the U.S. seeking to maintain Jim Crow while pontificating about human rights.[14]

It appeared that the ultras in the District felt that they had struck an emotive chord when they campaigned against desegregation at locales where children might have encounters across racial lines. Association attorney, Robert Carter, reported that "Negro children [were] not being allowed to play in Rosedale Playground" in the northeast quadrant of the District.[15]

---

11. Clarence Mitchell to *Post*, 17 April 1950, Box IX: 226, *NAACP Papers*.

12. Roy Wilkins to Branches, 4 May 1950, Box IX: 226, *NAACP Papers*.

13. Carl Bernstein, *Chasing History*, 119.

14. David Taft Terry, "'Tramping for Justice,'" 152. *Afro-American*, 12 January 1952.

15. Robert Carter to Clarence Mitchell, 14 May 1951, Box IX: 226.

The chairman of the Department of Recreation just happened to be Harry Wender, the former resident of racist South Africa and chief of the Federation of Civic Associations, bulwark of Jim Crow on a block-by-block basis. When Mitchell implored him that "colored children are barred" from Rosedale, the pasty faced, rosy cheeked epitome of regression, likely smiled—or smirked. Undaunted, Mitchell pressed on: "I visited the area personally and observed that a great many small colored children," he said with a seeming choke in his voice, "who live in the neighborhood were forced to remain outside of an iron fence while white children were admitted to the play area."[16]

Mitchell and the NAACP should have recognized that the issue of pools and playgrounds was imbricated in the larger question of demographic reality. Anacostia was at the heart of a so-called "Black Belt" of residential neighborhoods that like a boa constrictor encircled downtown from Foggy Bottom—the State Department—to the Anacostia River, raising discomfiting questions of security given the ordinary restlessness of Negroes. What to do about this contributed to fissures among elite forces. There was the Federation of Civic Associations which plumped for the status quo, including enforcing of racially restrictive covenants barring the transfer of property so designated to Negroes; one of their leaders, Harry Wender, son of a Jewish merchant who had won and lost a fortune in racist South Africa earlier in the 20th century before settling in Southwest Washington—soon to undergo a demographic transformation—in 1909. Then there was the National Committee on Segregation in the Nation's Capital, which included Eleanor Roosevelt; future Vice President, Hubert Humphrey; future high court justice Abe Fortas; union boss Walter Reuther; the spouse of leading pol, Adlai Stevenson; and the District's own Charles Hamilton Houston. They denounced racist segregation and in turn were castigated by Congressman John Rankin of Mississippi. Coincidentally, these blue ribbon leaders may have contributed to the dispersal of Negroes, lessening hysteria about national security implications of having an often disgruntled minority residing near crucial chokepoints; but it also might have just moved the problem as Negroes amassed in Prince George's County, Maryland as this vicinity began to house key federal agencies.[17]

---

16. Clarence Mitchell to Harry Wender, 1 May 1951, Box IX: 226, *NAACP Papers*.

17. Bell Clement, "Pushback: The White Community's Dissent from 'Bolling,'" *Washington History*, (Fall/Winter 2004-2005): 87-109, 87.

At the heart of the controversy locally was Wender. The *Afro-American* assailed this "chief champion of Washington's diehard and poor trash bloc," backing Jim Crow, though he was Jewish and not necessarily poverty-stricken.[18] Chapman was well aware that the pugnacious Wender had "declared that any attempt to operate the pools on a non-segregated basis...would result in riot and bloodshed"—and he was true to his word.[19]

Nor did most analysts sense a closely related matter concerning the lifeblood that was water. Somehow this elemental issue did not elude the analysis of the myrmidon of anticommunism: Senator Pat McCarran of Nevada. He instructed his fellow reactionary, Senator Olin Johnston of South Carolina, that District "residents pay too much for city water...private residents of the District must carry the cost of providing free water for all the departments and agencies of the Federal Government which are located here,"[20] yet another encumbrance carried heavily by Negroes.

However, the District did have an advantage of sorts as far as Congressman John McMillan of South Carolina was concerned. It was the "only city in the United States without bonded debt," he said in mid-1949 and his opinion was that it was the "cleanest city in the world," too, appropriate for the nation's front porch.[21]

Coincidentally, just as the building of the Pentagon disrupted a historically Black neighborhood, a similar postwar push added to a similar result in Georgetown, now a synonym for the stylishly fancy upmarket enclave but which had been a fortress for this increasingly scattered minority[22] and before that this oldest part of the District was the site of a village of tranquility known as Tahoga to the Nacotchanke. Dean and Alice Acheson—he was Secretary of State under Truman and, in many ways, architect of the Cold War—settled at 2805 P Street. Ben and Tony Bradlee were sited at 3321 N Street. Premier diplomat David Bruce and his spouse Evangeline resided at

---

18. *Washington Afro-American*, 15 April 1950.

19. A.E. Demaray to Oscar Chapman, 4 April 1950, Box 68, *Oscar Chapman Papers*.

20. Senator McCarran to Senator Johnston, 29 December 1945, Box 6, *Olin Johnston Papers, University of South Carolina-Columbia*.

21. Congressman McMillan to "Constituent," 18 June 1949, Bo 194, *Records of Republican National Committee, Dwight D. Eisenhower Presidential Library-Abilene, Kansas*.

22. Carroll R. Gibbs, et.al., eds., *Black Georgetown Remembered: A History of the Black Community from the Founding of the 'Town of George' in 1751 to the Present Day*, Washington, D.C.: Georgetown University Press, 2022.

1405 34th Street. Allen and Clover Dulles—he led the Central Intelligence Agency—were ensconced at 2723 Q Street. Felix and Marion Frankfurter—he sat on the Supreme Court—were at 3018 Dumbarton. Phil and Katharine Graham, of the *Post*, were at 29th and R Streets. Averill and Marie Harriman—he was a tycoon and political operative—lived at 3038 N Street. Joseph and Susan Alsop—he was a prominent columnist—resided at 2720 Dumbarton and his brother and fellow chronicler of the derring-do of the foregoing Stewart (and his spouse Tish) were at 3130 Dumbarton. This power elite lived within walking distance of each other and as far distant as possible from adjacent Negroes in this smalltown. As one observer put it, "'more political decisions get made at Georgetown suppers than anywhere else in the nation's capital, including the Oval Office.'"

Naturally, capers were part of the landscape Joseph Alsop had been ensnared in a gay tryst in Moscow causing diplomatic ripples—his marriage was a kind of clandestine "cover"; he was also a gentrifier, claiming to be "among the first white people on the block" in 1935—though others were soon to follow. The lascivious writer also kept an eye on this tiny domain since it was a "'haven for rich widows protecting their investments.'" George Kennan, the man who devised the blueprint for the Cold War captured the sentiments of fellow gentrifiers, may have taken the District too literally when he envisioned Negroes and other disenfranchised forces being governed by an "elite."[23]

Oscar Chapman, Secretary of Interior, was part of this elite, albeit playing a different role in presiding over an agency that employed more Negroes than most—admittedly in low-level positions—while administering a city that contained African Americans not unwilling to raise their collective voice. More than most, he was aware of the hallmark Truman's highly publicized 1947 report, "To Secure These Rights," a hinge moment in the federal incursion against Jim Crow,[24] as well as being part of a Cold War counter-offensive.

And what the NAACP and many of their elite supporters did not grasp altogether was that the U.S.—and its headquarters in the District, most notably—was under unremitting pressure to radically reform its rancid racist regime, which propelled these swimmers. Instead, the NAACP turned its back stiffly against Wallace and his party, though they were instrumental in taking advantage of a

23. Gregg Herken, *The Georgetown Set*, xiii, 20, 38.
24. "Progress in the Movement to Guarantee Equal Rights for All Citizens in the National Capital," circa 1950, *Oscar L. Chapman Papers, Truman Presidential Library*.

changing global climate. It was Progressive Party leader, Senator Glen H. Taylor of Idaho who dared to enter the lion's dean that was Alabama and learned that violation of the draconian Jim Crow regime meant that he would be termed an obnoxious "Nigger Lover" which could mean he would be "beaten to death."[25]

As the NAACP rebuffed allies, they constricted ideological space to their own detriment. When the PP and their labor ally, the National Maritime Union, were ousted from influence in Baltimore, it hardly improved the anti-racist climate.[26] Similarly, when Du Bois was bounced out of his lofty NAACP post in 1948 precisely because of his failure to rebuke the PP generating vigorous opposition from on high, even Rayford Logan did not raise a hue and cry, though as an otherwise perceptive historian he should have known better.[27]

These winds of change were blowing incessantly. These gusts buoyed Crystal Malone Brown, a 1943 graduate of Dunbar High School who then matriculated at the University of Vermont. This lighter skinned Negro woman then sought to desegregate the Alpha Xi Delta sorority since "'feelings after the warm made me think it was possible,'" but her quest was rebuffed. A controversy erupted that did not cease when Robeson arrived in October 1946 for a concert. So stirred, sorority sisters revolted, burned the group's charter, with the group then dissolving a year later. She then married Wesley A. Brown, who in 1949 became the first Negro graduate of the U.S. Naval Academy at Annapolis before joining Howard's staff. She was a product of a changing climate whereby Jim Crow had difficulty in flourishing.[28]

But these gusty winds had to be of testy velocity in order to overcome the massive resistance faced. Just across the river from the District there loomed forebodingly Virginia. But repression breeds resistance, and such was the case there. As noted, the ultimate top Black Communist leader, James Jackson and his talented spouse Esther Cooper Jackson emerged from this state. And Charles Hamilton Houston exploited the state as a litigative battlefield, while residing in the District. Attorney Oliver Hill attended Dunbar High School, then Howard, before traipsing across the water to become Houston's companion in legal warfare. The NAACP grew

---

25. Glen H. Taylor, *The Way it was With Me: A Personal and Political Memoir*, Secaucus: Lyle Stuart, 1979, 350.
26. David Taft Terry, "'Tramping for Justice': The Dismantling of Jim Crow in Baltimore, 1942-1954," 272.
27. Entry, 10 September 1948, Box 4, *Rayford Logan Diary*.
28. *Washington Post*, 9 March 1921.

accordingly, spurting quickly in the 1930s and by the end of 1941 had 39 branches with 5,441 members; but even this impressive figure was to jump during the antifascist war—thus exploding in 1943, jumping to 48 branches with 12,818 members and by 1945, 69 branches and 19,733 members. Similarly, by 1946 as "Operation Dixie" was launched, a mass labor organizing drive, the state had a sizeable 100,000 union members, an earnest of the Jacksons' toil in tobacco plants especially in and around Richmond; 24,500 of these were tied to the left-leaning CIO and 44,336 by 1948. Complementarily, by 1946 the NAACP had mushroomed to 91 branches and 24,843 members. However, the Red Scare punctured this balloon as labor organizing plummeted and NAACP membership flattened.[29]

This was concomitant with the undermining of Communists. "Any of us who spoke or worked for racial equality could expect to be smeared with the Red brush," sighed Virginia activist, Marvin Caplan. "'Integration is the southern version of Communism,'" was the motto. This was happening although by the early postwar era "there were hardly any Communists in Richmond"; "only three," he could recall: "Alice Burke...ex-sailor Louis Kalb," and "Kalb's patient wife, Mary."[30]

As time passed and the second half of the 20th century emerged, it appeared that the local and national authorities were executing a deft two-step: promulgating soaring rhetoric from the White House particularly, about equality, prompted by global pressures and necessities—while on the ground, massive resistance to this new paradigm unfolded. Among those caught in the vortex was Odis Von Blassingame, his spouse and their six month old son. Their house at 3303 Ames Street N.E. was stoned after they moved in[31]—soaring rhetoric blocks away aside.

Part of this new strategy also involved a bashing of the organized force which—theretofore—had campaigned tirelessly against Jim Crow. The question rarely entertained was if this echoing at the White House of a political line thought to be the exclusive domain of Communists—after all, Truman's predecessor, FDR, remarked that Confederate traitor, Robert E. Lee was "the most Christian like

---

29. Larissa M. Smith, "Where the South Begins: Black Politics and Civil Rights Activism in Virginia, 1930-1951," Ph.D. dissertation, Emory University, 2001, 86, 151, 165, 225, 281.

30. Marvin Caplan, *Farther Along: A Civil Rights Memoir*, Baton Rouge: Louisiana State University Press, 1999, 35, 36.

31. Clipping, June 1949, Vertical File-"Blacks-Segregation and Discrimination," *Special Collections, Washington, D.C. Public Library*.

American who ever lived"[32]—was sufficient in the long term to guarantee Negro equality in the face of massive resistance and the absence of non-Black grassroots pressure.

For the other prong of White House strategy was an unremitting offensive against Communists, which not only eroded a sturdy shield upon which Negroes had relied, but also destabilized the labor movement which a mostly working class Black community depended upon. This left this besieged community in the anomalous position of gaining the right to eat at a restaurant but bereft of funds to pay the bill.

The District was trapped between two fires. From one shore was right-wing bulldozing from the Cradle of the Confederacy: Virginia. On the land border was similar coercion from Maryland. In 1948 the state constitution was amended barring reputed Communists from public office and imposing ultimately all manner of persecution: it was ratified by an unnerving vote of 202,910 to 84,132. It was opposed even by the ritualistically anticommunist Americans for Democratic Action, an important force within the Democratic Party and too was rejected by the CIO. Except for the *Baltimore Sun*, the statewide press was generally supportive. Wildly enthusiastic were veterans' groups, especially Veterans of Foreign Wars.[33] Soon dragged into court was local leader Philip Frankfeld as the leadership was routed.[34]

Yet this was not just an onslaught against Communists, it was also targeting labor. This was the conclusion of Thomas Buchanan of the Civil Rights Congress of the District, scorned by its many foes as little more than a "Communist Front." In March 1949, he assayed that the "loyalty investigation against federal workers have been aimed chiefly against Negroes and Jews" and the "Post Office as a whole," known to have a complement of both. Thus far, there had been "loyalty charges brought against a total of 130 persons, of whom 73 were Negroes, 45 were Jews and only 12 were white gentiles...."[35] Of course—as the saying goes—one only had to beat one slave

---

32. "Robert E. Lee" in Samuel W. Mitcham, Jr., compiler, *The Encyclopedia of Confederate Generals: The Definitive Guide to the 426 Leaders of the South's War Effort*, Washington, D.C.: Regnery, 2022, 384-387, 384.
33. William B. Prendergast, "Maryland's Anticommunist Law," *University of Maryland-College Park*.
34. On the litigation in Maryland concerning this legislation see various briefs and correspondence in Box 3, Folder 20, *Abraham Unger Papers, New York University*.
35. Thomas Buchanan to William Patterson, 7 March 1949, Reel 24, Part 2.

to keep the entire plantation in line: pummeling a host of workers on anticommunist charges was generally sufficient to restrain most workers. Hence, it was also in 1949 that CRC chapter leader Buchanan confided that "our major disappointment this week— Mary McLeod Bethune changed her mind and wrote me she 'felt she was doing everything she could [to] fight segregation in…D.C.' and therefore could not join in our test case… [She] evidently figured it might embarrass the Truman Administration" if this comrade of Eleanor Roosevelt continued to consort with a so-called "Communist Front."[36] She had reason to be anxious. Even before the war she had been recommended for FBI detention in a national emergency.[37]

Besides, like many others she may have felt insecure about navigating complex issues involving national security. Rayford Logan had encountered her at a Pan African Congress gathering in New York City in 1927; she "knew practically nothing about international problems," he said with contempt and "little about domestic issues"; she even had an amanuensis, Constance Daniel, who penned numerous items under the great woman's name.[38]

Thus, as postal and other workers were trampled, groups like the CRC chapter became collateral damage, as those like Bethune cut and ran. The cost of operating a Washington Legislative Bureau, necessary to keep an eye peeled on the latest anti-labor and anticommunist demarches, was about $493 monthly with $238 comprising salary,[39] but by mid-March 1949 top leader, William Patterson, admitted that the "financial situation here is grave."[40] At the same time, the local chapter was said to have a piddling $24 in the bank with liabilities of about $138.[41] If it were any consolation, the District affiliate of the National Urban League, which long since had made peace with corporate elites, by 1950 was enduring a deficit of $1,100, a matter of "much concern" according to officialdom.[42]

"I have received no pay since April," was Buchanan's dour pronouncement in June 1949, referring to the District's CRC leader. But amidst the gloom and doom, evidence emerged as to why the

36. Thomas Buchanan to Len Goldsmith, 6 January 1949, Reel 24, Part 2.
37. Diane Kiesel, *She Can Bring Us Home: Dr. Dorothy Boulding Ferebee, Civil Rights Pioneer*, Lincoln: University of Nebraska Press, 2015, 154.
38. Entry, 7 September 1950, Box 5, *Rayford Logan Diary*.
39. Thomas Buchanan to William Patterson, 1 March 1949, Reel 24, Part 2.
40. William Patterson to Thomas Buchanan, 15 March 1949, Reel 24, Part 2.
41. Thomas Buchanan to William Patterson, 24 January 1949, Reel 24, Part 2.
42. Julius Thomas to "Administration," 10 August 1950, Box I: C63, *National Urban League Papers*

authorities continued to bludgeon the CRC and their Communist patrons. For at the same time, Buchanan was gloating about a local rally in defense of Communist Party leaders, then on trial in New York. It was "the best attended meeting any progressive organization has held in Washington since the war excluding the open air rally for Wallace last year...[the] National Press Club Auditorium was nearly filled" and "without heckling of any sort," their usual bane. George Murphy of the eminent Baltimore family that controlled the local Negro press, "was an excellent chairman," while best-selling novelist, Howard Fast, "was terrific...." And polemicist, I.F. Stone provided an "excellent statement...." Nervousness was the prelude to this event since "some of the Progressive Party leaders were afraid the local chapter would lose some of its supporters by taking part," but this proved to be specious reasoning—in the short term.[43]

To be fair, at least in the incipient stages of the Red Scare, there were anguished voices arising among certain Negro leaders, among which was Lester Granger of the otherwise staid National Urban League. As early as 1945, he informed an audience at Howard University that "there were Negroes who were misled by wartime racial gains to the point of feeling that the longer that the war lasted, the more secure became the situation of Negroes"—a questionable presumption in his estimation. However, contrary to normative posturing, "America is not a democracy," he roared, and "never has been a democracy—and probably will not be for a long time to come...." Instead, he fulminated, "within this country democratic and fascist impulses are at war with each other today as they have been for generations long before the word fascism had been coined...." Yes, he uttered with a slump, the "hysteria that accompanies a war can possibly excuse many Negroes for the drift toward racial neuroses, separatist thinking and defeatist attitudes that have characterized too many of us during these frenzied [times]," not to mention, "too much talk among members of our race regarding the hopelessness of ever solving racial problems in this country...."[44]

The problem was that this kind of frank talk about the unforgiving climate in the U.S. became virtually forbidden with the Red Scare upsurge that celebrated chauvinistically the imagined virtues of settler colonialism—a term, too, in disuse. Granger was able to be

43. Tom Buchanan to William Patterson, 20 June 1949, Reel 24, Part 2, *Civil Rights Congress Papers.*
44. Address by Lester Granger at Fall Convocation, in "Howard University News...Howard University Bulletin," 24 (Number 11, 1 February 1945): 3-5, 8-9, Box I: A261, *National Urban League Papers.*

candid during an epoch of anti-fascism when the exigencies of war allowed for more candor.

According to their theory of the case, it was the Communists who were supposed to be clear-eyed about the vicissitudes of capitalism, but it is arguable that despite the ouster of their leader, Earl Browder, that vestiges of his illusions about the progressivism even of elements within the ruling elite persisted. Why? There were deeper reasons having to do with illusions about the origins of the republic, which tended to privilege the U.S. as a sanctuary for Europeans fleeing persecution and to downplay the role of Indigenous dispossession—especially—and, to a degree, enslavement of Africans in this overall ugly process.[45] In sum, even Communists were not able to escape the suffocating miasma of Euro-centrism—though, admittedly, they were far superior to their counterparts in other parties.

Again, this latter trait was manifested where it counted: on the ground. This was noticeably the case for the left-wing shock troops, the Communist-led Civil Rights Congress. By December 1948, complementing the contemporaneous offensive in the courts their local leader Thomas Buchanan announced that his chapter would be "the organizer of a carefully planned test of the District's anti-segregation law," then blared, "WIPE OUT JIM CROW IN WASHINGTON IN 1949...."[46] Earlier he had told paramount leader, William Patterson that "we are about to launch a campaign here to establish a real mass basis for the D.C. branch," referring to this anti-Jim Crow initiative, but he was realistic enough to know in the face of a beginning Red Scare that "up to now...about 10 of us have carried the entire load...."[47]

Ambitiously, the chapter "reorganized" in the midst of a flurry of activity. Buchanan opined that the brunt of work was borne by "not more than a dozen workers, none of whom were themselves actually dues paying members"; thus, "as of last Monday," he said

---

45. Gerald Horne, *The Counter-Revolution of 1776: Slave Resistance and the Origins of the United States of America*, New York: New York University Press, 2014; Gerald Horne, *The Apocalypse of Settler Colonialism: The Roots of Slavery, White Supremacy and Capitalism in Seventeenth Century North America and the Caribbean*, New York: Monthly Review Press, 2018; Gerald Horne, *The Dawning of the Apocalypse: The Roots of Slavery, White Supremacy, Settler Colonialism and Capitalism in the Long 16th Century*, New York: Monthly Review, 2020.
46. Thomas Buchanan, Executive Secretary to "Member," 23 December 1948, Reel 24, Part 2, *Civil Rights Congress Papers*, New York Public Library-Schomburg Center.
47. Thomas Buchanan to William Patterson, 20 September 1948, Reel 24, Part 2.

remorsefully in late 1948, "our dues paying enrollment was zero. Today it is 15 and by the end of the month we hope to have several hundred," he said in a burst of optimism.[48]

This hearty ten—or fearsome 15—had quite a load to carry for not only was there the burden of confronting citywide Jim Crow but, per usual, the police were wielding their batons and pistols with frolicking abandon. It was also in 1948 that a CRC leader observed that "in the District police brutality has been on the increase in recent months...." This too was part of an elongated process of the ruling elite: conceding to certain reforms but wielding the mailed fist eagerly so that activists did not proceed but so far.[49]

But it was also part of another process that preceded this onrushing era of reform. The issue of crime and the supposition that Negroes were the vector of this phenomenon was deployed to keep this restive community off kilter, immobilized, incapable of pushing back against a super-exploitation that consigned them to low wage havens. This was not news to close District observers, especially the role of the so-called mainstream press in disseminating propaganda. The scholar, Carter G. Woodson, retained a 1931 study that said as much, while pointing out that a problem that was to persist for decades—a dearth of Negro reporters—was a pressing issue even then.[50]

Interestingly, Eugene Meyer, controlling shareholder of the *Washington Post*, was the Honorary President of the Washington Criminal Justice Association, which was quick to repel the common claim: it is "not a vigilante organization," was their huffy motto. They were alarmist, however, pointing to 8,002 "serious crimes" in the District in 1947, referring to felonies, an "increase of 1,843 serious offenses or 23 percent over 1946." They were keen to underline that as for murder, there were 19 "colored male" victims and "30 colored male accused" and "11 colored female" victims and "4 colored female accused."[51] Did not this justify roughhouse tactics to keep this obstreperous community in line?

---

48. Thomas Buchanan to Felix Kusman, 1 October 1948, Reel 24, Part 2.
49. Joseph Cadden to Gertrude Evans, 6 February 1948, Reel 24, Part 2. See also *Daily Worker*, 7 October 1948.
50. Lynette Mulholland, "Survey of the White Press in Washington, D.C... Relative to News Concerning the Negro," 28 May 1931, Reel 20, Part II, *Carter G. Woodson Papers*.
51. "Crime in the Nation's Capital...Twelfth Annual Report" by "Washington Criminal Justice Association...1420 New York Avenue...." May 1948, Box 13, *Olin Johnson Papers*.

The scholar, Kyla Sommers, critiques the "false narrative that D.C. was rampant with crime," which "was politically useful to integration opponents" since "Southern lawmakers claimed crime in D.C. was the outcome of integration...."[52]

Burtell M. Jefferson, the first African American police chief in the District, was no stranger to these tensions. When he joined the force in 1948, he noticed that Euro-American booking officers took credit for arrests by their Black counterparts, driving down the "productivity" numbers of the latter, harming their chances for promotion—this at a time when the District was 35 percent Negro (officially), though a paltry 10 percent of the force was from this group.[53]

Besides, this fabricated crime wave also kept the push for home rule and voting rights off balance. Just before the swimming pool crisis, home rule advocates felt compelled to brand as "misconception" the commonly accepted notion that voting rights for the District meant "domination by Negroes"; no, said these lobbyists, as of 1947 the city's population was "72%" Euro-American and was about the same in 1940 and 1910, it was contended and had changed barely since 1880.[54]

But it was not just Negroes who were the bete noire as far as home rule was concerned for there was too a rouge noire—or so thought Congressman McMillan of the Palmetto State: "I have not had twelve letters," he declaimed in mid-1949, "from people in Washington in favor of Home Rule; and these, with the exception of two or three, were all people who had Communistic tendencies and were interested in securing control of the Federal Government"—through alliance with Negroes unavoidably.[55]

Reverberations of this process were felt at the hilltop. Somehow, by 1948 Reginald Ruggles Gates was teaching at Howard but then faced a petition to remove him, which he felt was an outgrowth of the "International Jewish Conspiracy"; further, he argued that "only a few 'ignorant Negroes' were fit to be in a university at all...."[56] Howard students demanded the swift dismissal of this zoologist.[57] Also awakening from slumber were Howard teachers, who began

---

52. Kyla Sommers, "'I Believe in the City': The Black Freedom Struggle and the 1968 Civil Disturbances in Washington, D.C.," 61.

53. *Washington Post*, 20 March 1921.

54. "Home Rule" pamphlet, circa 1948, Box 17, *Olin Johnston Papers*.

55. Ibid., Congressman McMillan to "Constituent," 18 June 1949.

56. Angela Saini, *Superior: The Return of Race Science*, Boston: Beacon Press, 2019, 54.

57. *The Hilltop*, 19 February 1947.

a belated organizing drive meant to overcome the debilities that ensued when both Hunton and Wilkerson fled northward[58]—and which allowed a scoundrel like Ruggles to be hired.

The assault on Ruggles demonstrated that the postwar dispensation could serve to undermine those who may have been embraced earlier, indicative that reforms were hardly nugatory.

Rayford Logan did not have to be convinced of this in that his forays into global affairs likely accelerated postwar as he was a symbol of the new order: the Negro sufficiently trusted to be accorded a role in the execution of U.S. foreign policy, as opposed to being kept far away from this portfolio, seen widely as a living refutation to Washington's pretensions. As of 1948 he was jousting with Addis Ababa because of his ambivalence in backing their claim to Eritrea. "I took the same position," he recounted, "when Hikida [of official Japan] some years ago, wanted me to write a book on the Monroe Doctrine in Africa...."[59]

Logan was straddling a shifting line. He wanted to maintain positive relations with the State Department and the White House on the one hand, but the latter were often less than willing to alienate European allies, many of whom were major colonizers of Africa—and, contradictorily, he sought positive ties with anti-colonial forces too. The latter included Sylvia Pankhurst, the British exile in Addis Ababa who questioned if Truman's heralded "Point Four," an essential element of his, was "imperialism" or maximally "an enigma."[60] Unabashedly, Logan admitted, "I was later named by [Socialist leader] Norman Thomas to serve on the coordinating committee to win popular support for Point IV,"[61] the heart of Truman's foreign policy.

Such a posture was nothing new for the flexible Logan. As early as 1940, when many were fretting that the war in Europe was simply a replay of the disappointing World War I, Logan served as Chairman in an official body: the "Committee on Participation of Negroes in the National Defense Program."[62] He was in sync with others on the hilltop. For it was then that Mordecai Johnson served on the National Committee on Defense of the American Council; Dr. Charles Thompson, Dean of the College of Liberal Arts, joined

---

58. *The Hilltop*, 7 November 1947.
59. Entry, 10 September 1948, Box 4, *Rayford Logan Diary*.
60. *New Times and Ethiopia News*, 11 June 1949, Box 5, *Rayford Logan Papers, Library of Congress-Washington, D.C.*
61. Entry, 6 January 1950, Box 5, *Rayford Logan Papers*.
62. Report, 19 October 1940, Box I: F9, *National Urban League Papers*.

the wartime Commission of the U.S. Office of Education and the Sub-Committee on Education, Joint Army and Navy Committee on Recreation and Welfare; and, of course, Bunche took a job of head of the Sub-Division on Africa and Native Affairs in the British Empire Section of the Office of the Coordinator of Information; Physics professor Frank Coleman and his colleague, James Nabrit, served on draft boards for the District with the former as chair. This was occurring as 3,000 Howard students and alumni served in the military.[63]

This blood sacrifice occurred during the ignominious reign of Jim Crow, generating fury, barely suppressed. Now there was a Cold War erupting with similar sacrifices expected, at a time when Washington—capital and city alike—was being bruised ideologically in its attempt to preen and posture as a paragon of human rights virtue. This contradiction created an opening for the erosion of Jim Crow.

63. Lopez D. Matthews, Jr., *Howard University in the World War: Men and Women Serving the Nation*, Charleston, South Carolina: History Press, 2018, 41.

Chapter 10

Anticommunism Leads to War, 1950-1951

By 1950 the U.S.—and the District—crossed the Rubicon into a darker night of anticommunism. That was the import of the midyear intervention on the Korean peninsula, the repercussions of which continue to percolate. Increasingly, the rationale on Capitol Hill and the White House was that it made little sense to combat Communists in Asia while tolerating same in Washington. Thus, further purges and execrations of Reds in the region—and those that were said to resemble them—proceeded apace. This decimated the Progressive Party, where Du Bois and Robeson had served and as the swimming pool controversy of 1949 demonstrated, this force served as stalwart opponents of Jim Crow. But with the left dazed and on the defensive, anti-Jim Crow concessions were dribbled out—many of which evaded the bedrock question of economic equality or even union rights.

The linkage between the toxicity of anticommunism at home and abroad had not escaped the attention of the then dwindling ranks of the organized left in the U.S. By March 1951, the feisty "American Peace Crusade" had gathered 2,000 strong at the "Tenth Street Triangle"—10th and U streets N.W.—in the District; delegates came from 36 states and numerous foreign nations. Their cry for an end to the war in Korea attracted—ominously—a record assemblage of police officers, according to the *Pittsburgh Courier*.[1]

By 1950 Elgin Baylor, soon to be celebrated as a basketball icon, was a teenager grappling with the contradictions of his hometown of Washington, which supposedly was the bastion of democratic rights—while he dismissively and verminously referred to it as "Rat City." Indeed, he contended, still miffed in his dotage, "a lot of

---

1. *Pittsburgh Courier*, 24 March 1951.

people who grew up in D.C. at the same time as I did feel the same way. They love the people; they don't love the city. Something about it makes you uneasy. You're always looking over your shoulder." If he had examined his birthplace through the acute lens of history, he might have perceived that Washington was writhing in the contradiction that it was the center of state power for the nation, but was surrounded by a population, African Americans, who over the decades had proven themselves to be quite amenable to cutting deals with the real and imagined foes of the republic. Besides, Washington continued to attract the likes of Senator Bilbo, the most dedicated "Negro-phobes" in sum, those whose constituencies reviled in both bashing the capital—which did spearhead the vanquishing of the Confederacy during the lifetimes of some—and pulverizing the descendants of their former property, expropriated without compensation. As for Baylor, whose athletic prowess included seemingly hanging in mid-air interminably, he was able to launch an airborne escape for Seattle University, then the Los Angeles Lakers and glittery stardom at an early age. His speed, honed in racing away from bloodthirsty cops, aided his mastery on the court. It gave him an "identity," including his early nickname, "Rabbit," testament to his ability to scurry away from opponents. "In all my years on Heckman Street," referring to his old neighborhood, "I never [did] see one black police officer," exacerbating a pestiferous trait: "we all fear them." But this was justified, he thought: "I hear about a guy who gets picked up by the cops and disappears...."[2]

Baylor's reminiscences were reflected in the contemporaneous remarks of Black Communist leader, William Patterson: it was in 1950 that he complained sharply that "there is no end to such cases,"[3] referring to a skein of police brutality episodes.

While cops were running amok in the District, Senator Estes Kefauver of Tennessee, a Democratic Party leader, was said to be cracking down on crime nationally in dramatically televised hearings. Yet, an unnamed spectator chided him and fellow legislators, asserting that none had "the nerve to look into the crime situation in Washington," referring to organized crime bosses, not to mention normalized grift and graft. "It is now plain it didn't have the nerve. Crime is too big here for weaklings to fool with...." The local police chief, it was said, "has a beach home" on a relatively meager salary

2. Elgin Baylor, *Hang Time*, 2, 10, 11. See also *Wall Street Journal*, 30 June 2018.
3. William Patterson to Muriel Paull, 18 May 1950, Reel 24, Part 2, *Civil Rights Congress Papers*.

and ventures on "expensive fishing trips," as "the chief's 'take' is somewhere between $1,000 and $5,000 per week."[4]

Presumably, Baylor was writing about the Metropolitan Police Department of the District, but one of the utterly unique features of the District was the proliferation of police authorities, making Blacks one of the most heavily surveilled communities on earth, given the penchant to confuse crime fighting and Negro hunting. The famed journalist, Carl Bernstein, who grew up in the vicinity, pointed to the "Park Police...Capitol Police...Federal Aviation Police...National Zoo Police...Foreign Embassy Police"—and he could have added their peers in Maryland and Virginia, not to mention the Federal Bureau of Investigation and various intelligence agencies who viewed Negroes skeptically—at best.[5]

Arguably, what Baylor was depicting was the bitter fruit of the anti-Jim Crow path taken by the Negro leadership. Ultimately, it did lead to the formal erosion of U.S. apartheid, but it infuriated those diehard racists, often speckled in police forces resistant to reform, who then exacted fierce retribution. With the Progressive Party and Civil Rights Congress then under assault, the "Rabbit" and those like him were left defenseless, with those able fleeing and those unable often simply suffering.

An insignia of this troubling trend arose as 1950 was winding down; former Howard faculty member, W. Alphaeus Hunton was snagged by legal troubles that led to his jailing. He had moved on to Manhattan to work alongside Robeson and Du Bois but also William Patterson, foremost Black Communist who led the CRC. Hunton was a trustee of their bail fund and refused to be a stoolpigeon and provide to the authorities the names of those who had contributed to this kitty after four Communists had absconded after being bailed out of prison. This was a dramatic signal to the hilltop that a stiff price could be imposed on those so bold as to confront the status quo frontally. His sister, Eunice Hunton, a rising attorney refused to speak with her brother, a searing personal cost. She had joined him in 1942 and Robeson and Du Bois and Adam Clayton Powell and then Communist chief, Earl Browder, in signing a petition demanding that the U.S. and its allies bring self-determination to Africa—but times had changed.[6]

---

4. Memorandum, 19 June 1951, Box 200, *Records of Special Committee to Investigate Organized Crime in Interstate Commerce, CR9 [Rackets] and CR10 [Juvenile Delinquency]*, National Archives and Records Administration, Washington, D.C.

5. Carl Bernstein, *Chasing History: A Kid in the Newsroom*, New York: Holt, 2022, 78.

6. Christine Ann Lutz, "'The Dizzy Steep to Heaven,'" 292.

Her grandson, novelist and Yale Law School professor, Stephen L. Carter—one of the most amply compensated Black intellectuals today—was unsparing in his spearing of his left-wing relative. He acknowledged the trauma of his having survived the pogrom in Atlanta of 1906 as a toddler, but wrote that this tall, stoop shouldered Communist played a central role in harming her trajectory that meant "her career" as a highly publicized crime-busting New York attorney was "wrecked," as anticommunists did not make meaningful distinctions between and among siblings when imposing retribution. She sought to display her mettle, as Carter put it, by seeking to "reinvent herself as an internationalist," or as a Negro who would carry water for Washington overseas when it was being pelted by antiracists. "Once Alphaeus went to prison," says her wealthy scion, "Eunice knew that her own career as a public figure in the United States was over"; the "estrangement between the siblings was complete. They never spoke again," as her "younger brother's radical activities destroyed her career." Carter—rather speculatively—writes that Hunton may have been "running little errands for intelligence officers on the staff of the Soviet consulate." More to the point, the authorities were furious with Hunton for his Communist activism, e.g., pressuring the federal government to hire more Negroes and, in league with Du Bois, preparing a memorandum on maltreatment of Negroes and Africans that Moscow used to attack London and Washington at the United Nations.[7]

Howard staff, faculty, and students hardly needed the Hunton reminder to refresh their recollection about the pressure that could be exerted against them. In the Spring of 1950, Rayford Logan observed that his employer was planning to "drop nineteen members of the faculty as [of] June 30 because of an anticipated drop in enrollment of 302 for next year,"[8] in turn generated by parsimony on Capitol Hill, which held tightly the purse string of the campus. As the campus budget constricted, tempers flared, the latest squabble being between star sociologist E. Franklin Frazier and President Mordecai Johnson, the ostensible conflict being expanding doctoral programs. "There are 13 states," countered Logan, "with populations smaller than that of the District with state universities that offer the Ph.D."[9]

7. Stephen L. Carter, *Invisible: The Forgotten Story of the Black Woman Lawyer who Took Down America's Most Powerful Mobster*, New York: Holt, 2018, 3, 269, 271, 272, 204, 226, 239.
8. Entry, 17 April 1950, Box 5, *Rayford Logan Diary*.
9. Entry, 14 April 1951, Box 5.

By November Logan was supping with Du Bois who regaled him with tales "about his recent trips to Moscow and Prague. I marveled that the State Department" permitted such, he mused, especially since the NAACP founder cursed his former comrade O. John Rogge, who like so many had turned with a vengeance against former comrades, and "bitterly criticized Wallace for leaving the Progressive Party."[10]

Soon Logan need not wonder about Du Bois' mobility, as he fell under indictment and barely escaped imprisonment because of his peace activism—yet another not so subtle message to Howardites.

Thus, Logan had to tread carefully. An operative from the U.S. propaganda arm, the Voice of America, asked him "casually, almost too casually" about Hunton's Council on African Affairs. Bravely, Logan praised their publications, then added quickly he had joined with them initially "in order to help the liberals"—not because of sympathy for Communists.[11]

This year, 1950, also marked the expiration of some of the stauncher forces, including the combative litigator, Charles Hamilton Houston— who balked at adhering to the Red Scare; and another Howard man who resisted segregated blood banks: Dr. Charles Drew. The latter fortunately left behind a daughter, Charlene Drew Jarvis, who carried the progressive torch into the 21st century; also expiring was Dr. Carter G. Woodson, whose historical excavations created a foundation for a stronger tomorrow.[12] These three losses were almost too much to bear.

Like Dr. Drew, Dr. Woodson, too, left behind a rich legacy in the form of an organization now known as the Association for the Study of African American Life & History (full disclosure: some years ago, they awarded me one of their highest honors for scholarship). His Stakhanovite regime included routinely 18 hour days often in the three bedroom house that he bought for a mere $8,000 in 1922, sitting in the shadow of Howard University, providing students and faculty alike a model to emulate. Early on a youthful Langston Hughes, soon to be a renowned writer, toiled as an assistant to Dr. Woodson imbibing lessons of perseverance that held him in good stead over the decades. On 3 April 1950, months before the Korean intervention was to mark a new stage in U.S. and world history, Dr. Woodson expired on the third floor of his headquarters at 1538 Ninth Street NW, now a national historic site.[13]

---

10. Entry, 22 November 1950, Box 5.
11. Entry, 7 February 1951, Box 5.
12. Report, 1950, Box 1, *W. Montague Cobb Papers, Emory University*.
13. *Washington Post*, 6 February 2022.

As for Houston, the impact of his loss on Howard Law School that he had helped to propel, was irreparable. Days before he died, reports emerged from recent graduates that the bar examination, qualifying them to practice, was rife with bias, explaining "reasons"—said the *Pittsburgh Courier*—"for the small proportion of colored applications" passing muster.[14]

The remarkable simultaneity of the felling of three Sequoias— Houston, Drew, and Woodson—ill prepared Negroes in the District to comprehend, let alone combat the downside of the Copernican changes just over the horizon.

Complicating matters further was the District galloping headlong to its future role as "Chocolate City." This also meant a kind of residential desegregation not accepted blithely by those Euro-Americans who thought this meant a decline in property values at a time when the home was beginning to resemble a piggybank, the major repository of family wealth. But their often violent reactions to changing demography could give Uncle Sam a purplish blackeye not conducive to winning hearts and minds abroad.

Truman aide Phileo Nash retained an article detailing that by late 1951 "increases of white and negro populations in Metropolitan D.C. are nearly parallel...." From 1940-1950, it was said, the area grew by 496,104 or 51.3 percent, as the mandate of New Deal spending and the growth of the national security state both became more pronounced. "Whites in the population increased from 737,158 to 1,222,206 or 52.2. percent" while "non-whites increased from 230,827 to 341,883 or 48.1 percent" in a region that also encompassed Northern Virginia and Maryland. In the District alone, there was a population gain of 139,087 or 21 percent, although Euro-Americans there grew by 9.2 percent—compared to "non-whites," mostly Negroes, who increased 50.3 percent.[15]

The NAACP in the District was straining to adapt. "You know how anxious we are to get a segregation case in the District of Columbia," said Thurgood Marshall.[16] In support of the anti-Jim Crow lawsuit propelled initially by the left-leaning National Lawyers Guild and their advocate, Joseph Forer, they counselled to their members to "patronize the restaurants that obey the 1872 law" this litigation was

---

14. *Pittsburgh Courier*, 4 March 1950.
15. *Washington Post*, 19 December 1951, Box 30, *Phileo Nash Papers*.
16. Thurgood Marshall to Frank Reeves, 10 July 1951, Box IX: 226, *NAACP Papers*.

designed to uphold.[17] In unison, the Communist led Civil Rights Congress, confided that it was "pressing this issue" likewise.[18]

Initially, this left-wing campaign brought success. It was in February 1950, during the early stages of this serpentine litigation that Tom Buchanan of the CRC was ecstatic, saluting "the long CRC campaign to compel the District government to enforce the 1872-1873 laws against Jim Crow in restaurants has brought results! The Commissioners say they intend to test the law in court," although— he noted correctly—this "didn't come as a gift," since "they never wanted to enforce this law" but were pressured to do so.[19]

Buchanan had in mind the activism of his comrade Annie Stein. She solicited a "generous contribution" from Dr. W. Warrick Cardozo of the District—likely a relative of Eslanda Robeson—"to cover the cost of printing 2,000 of our Boycott Kresge leaflets...our leaflet distribution outside of Kresge's at 7th and E has been very effective both in keeping trade out of Kresge's and in diverting trade to Woolworth's, Grand's and McCrory's, nearby stores that are now consistently serving Negroes without discrimination at their sit-down counters...."[20] This mass action brought results. A few days later Stein happily informed left-wing union leader, Ewart Guinier, that "after 8 weeks fights, Kresge's finally gave in." It was "tragic" to consider, however, "to think that in the nation's capital it takes eight weeks of picketing and a big mass boycott to win the right to sit down in a dirty old dime store...we now have changed the policy of every single dime store in the city (except one small place we're still working on—Neisners')."[21]

Still, by July 1951, even global heroine, Josephine Baker—French national, though born as a U.S. Negro—was refused service at Kresge's neighbor, Hecht's at 7th and F.[22] But this mulish obstinance was doomed, especially when Congressman Adam Clayton

---

17. Survey of Bistros, 18 May 1950, Box IX: 226, *NAACP Papers*.
18. Thomas Buchanan to Annie Stein, 2 June 1949, MS 404, Box 2, *Records of the Coordinating Committee for the Enforcement of the D.C. Anti-Discrimination Laws, Historical Society of Washington, D.C.*
19. Tom Buchanan to "Dear Friend," 22 February 1950, Reel 24, Part 2, *Civil Rights Congress Papers*.
20. Annie Stein to Dr. Warrick Cardozo, 5 January 1951, MS 404, Box 2, *Records of Coordinating Committee for the Enforcement of the D.C. Anti-Discrimination Laws.*
21. Annie Stein to Ewart Guinier, 29 January 1951, MS 404, Box 2.
22. "Progress Report," July 1951, Box 2, MS 404, *Records of the Coordinating Committee for the Enforcement of the D.C. Anti-Discrimination Laws.*

Powell, Jr., increasingly a growing force in the District, given his accumulation of seniority, weighed in, backing this campaign.[23]

"The Negro press has been very cooperative," said Stein effusively. "The 'Courier' making the Hecht…boycott a major civil rights project of the newspaper…." Stein was "speaking before meetings of organizations daily, 34 meetings have been covered since the 1st of May," was message by 21 May 1951: "we have sent out material to over 4,000 persons…."[24]

When preliminary rulings rebuffed their ambitious lawsuit meant to complement mass action, Walter White sought to leverage the Cold War to the organization's benefit—as opposed to fighting this global crusade: "This is a bad 48 hours for American prestige abroad," he said with lamentation. "Soviet Russia will jubilantly tell Koreans of the defeat of cloture and also of Judge Myers' ruling that Jim Crow still reigns in the Nation's Capital."[25]

Bolstering Jim Crow as a gift to Moscow became a constant refrain by the NAACP in coming years. Months later, White's words were echoed by those of Stephen Spottswood of the District branch, arguing that the "bill to prevent integration of the [D.C.] Fire Department" meant—once more—that Moscow "rejoices."[26]

But as U.S. imperialism sank into a Korean quagmire, pressure grew to buff and burnish her deteriorating image. Thus, months after White's remonstration, Mary Church Terrell, doyenne of District progressives and a comrade of Communists, delivered good news in her capacity as Chair of the Coordinating Committee for the Enforcement of the D.C. Anti-Discrimination Laws: "The end of segregation in D.C. restaurants is at least in view," she reported happily in June 1951. "Our two year fight for the 'lost' laws of 1872 and 1873 was crowned with victory when the Municipal Court of Appeals decided last week that it is the law that all well behaved [sic] persons must be served…." But even then the city's Corporate Counsel demurred, requesting that all appeals be exhausted before celebration ensued.[27]

Terrell, who by then was approaching her 90s and had lived in the District since the 1880s, knew that "'in the 1890s colored people

23. Annie Stein to Congressman Powell, Box 2, MS 404: "You have been kind enough to help our Committee in the past in its efforts to end discrimination in D.C.…"
24. Annie Stein to Dr. John O'Connor, 21 May 1951, Box 2, MS 404.
25. Report from Walter White, 12 July 1950, Box IX: 226, *NAACP Papers*.
26. Stephen Spottswood to Honorable James Davis, 13 October 1941, Box IX: 226.
27. Statement by Mary Church Terrell, 1 June 1951, Box IX: 226.

could dine anywhere in the nation's capital but near the end of the century, these rights were wrested away from us,'"[28] as imperialism surged in Hawaii, the Philippines, and Cuba, and now with a different global climate, Jim Crow was retreating formally. It was left to Annie Stein, presumed Communist who shared leadership with Terrell, to remind Max Winkler of Longchamps Restaurant of the financial imperative that undergirded desegregation: "Since one third of the population of the District is colored," she said, "and the income level of this group is high compared to the rest of the country," that suggested that "non discrimination is good business"[29] and illustrated, too, why the District was in the vanguard of this process.

Both Stein and Terrell were well within the orbit of the Communist Party. The latter even travelled to Manhattan to work on the case of Rosa Lee Ingram, one of the CRC's premier campaigns, featuring a Black woman in Georgia charged with felonies after beating back attempted sexual molestation by a Euro-American landowner. She "did a magnificent job,"[30] enthused William Patterson. But Terrell was that rare figure capable of maintaining fruitful ties across the political spectrum, working with the NAACP at a fancy fundraiser in Manhattan's Hotel Statler designed to raise $50,000 for a fund to fight Jim Crow in Washington.[31]

However, the right wing was sufficiently attuned to the political zeitgeist to realize that they possessed an effective weapon with which to riddle their detractors, referring to the double-barreled fusillade of the Red Scare and Cold War.

Still, sweeping Negroes from certain neighborhoods was a priority in enforcing what came to be called "ethnic purity." By October 1950, Samuel Davis, described as a "colored bricklayer," a union then being purged of purported subversives, found an unpleasant surprise at his new home at 716 Hamlin Street N.W.; as noted in the *Star*, "2 kerosene smelling jars" were "found at the scene of Davis'

---

28. Beverly W. Jones, "Before Montgomery and Greensboro: The Desegregation Movement in the District of Columbia, 1950-1953," *Phylon*, June 1982, Vertical File: "Blacks-Segregation and Discrimination," *Special Collections, Washington, D.C. Public Library.*
29. Annie Stein, Secretary of Coordinating Committee for the Enforcement of the D.C. Anti-Discrimination Laws, to Max Winkler, 6 June 1952, Box IX: 226.
30. William Patterson to Tom Buchanan, 29 June 1949, Reel 24, Part 2, *Civil Rights Congress Papers.*
31. Announcement, 10 October 1953, Box 457, *NAACP Papers.*

home fire."[32] Restaurants, thought to be on the verge of desegrega-tion, were not exempt. By July 1951, in Capitol Heights a mob of 1,500 Euro-American amassed at what was depicted as a "new lunch room for Negroes...stones were thrown and at least one window was broken...."[33] Interviewed by the Negro press, Revella Clay was less restrained: "I watched race hating white supremacists turn a peace-ful interracial business venture into mob fodder in Capitol Heights," she cried in her denunciation of "bestial, bloody thirsty rioters" and where maddened "white mobsters beat up two of their own race," while others merely chose to "throw rocks."[34]

There was also a legally sanctioned churn that led to a similar result: Negro removal. Roger W. "Whitetop" Simkins, a Negro, had been known as the "Czar" of rackets, especially gambling in the District, administering a "numbers" game from the Georgia Ave-nue home of his paramour, Sarah "Dimples" Mears Hall. In Foggy Bottom and Georgetown, the game was directed by the Warring brothers, formerly bootleggers—and Euro-American, while Sim-kins' territory extended out from U Street and 14th Street. By 1951 Congress had had enough and Hall was one of the first witnesses. Ambling to Capitol Hill in a mink trimmed Persian lamb coat, she caused quite a stir as she provided detail on how $4,000 a day was absorbed. Her colorful comrades—"Little Joe, Sporty Johnson, Jack the Bear, Sunshine Boldware...Piggy Leake, Geechee Charlie" and, particularly the aforementioned Odessa Madre, the lesbian lady of the night—caused quite a stir. Shortly Simkins and five others went on trial, charged with bribery and conspiracy and were found guilty and imprisoned.[35]

The Warrings also were not left unscathed for it did seem that the elected grifters and grafters resented competition.[36]

Verbal rocks continued to be tossed at certain government agen-cies thought to be promoting desegregation, which at the same time heightened anti-Washington sentiment nationally. Interior was sus-pect perpetually because of its reputation—largely undeserved—as being pro-Negro: the assault on this agency also made it simpler to then attack the State Department, suspect not least since it super-vised diplomatic ties with the presumed ogre that was Moscow.

32. *Washington Star*, 24 October 1950.
33. *Washington Star*, 7 July 1951.
34. *Pittsburgh Courier*, 21 July 1951.
35. *Washington Post*, 28 February 2021.
36. Leo Warring, *The Foggy Bottom Gang: The Story of the Warring Brothers of Washington, D.C.*, Cleveland: Parafine Press, 2020.

By mid-1950—days before conflict erupted in Korea—the son of Maryland's Senator Millard Tydings, who too was to serve in that body, filed stories concerning Senator Joseph McCarthy's allegations regarding Red penetration of Foggy Bottom.[37] The younger Tydings—Joseph—was also aware of the explosive charge from a constituent that while working in a government building at 18th and New York Avenue N.W. with State Department personnel files being his specialty, "we were instructed to remove all derogatory material,"[38] a coded reference to possible Red connections. Frances Eugene O'Brien, 25, of Arlington, confirmed this story.[39]

Within strolling distance of Rosedale playground, yet another site of contestation, was the hilltop campus where some of these "colored" children would venture to matriculate in coming years and there they too would be susceptible to being influenced by international currents that McCarthy found questionable. Howard continued to maintain global ties, which by their very nature pressured official Washington to cloak or erode an odious Jim Crow. By early 1950 President Mordecai Johnson had just returned from India,[40] a frequent haunt for Negroes since independence in 1947.[41] After his return, taking off for India was faculty member, Flemmie Pansy Kittrell, the first African American woman to receive a doctorate in nutrition, at Cornell in her case.[42] Weeks later Nnamdi Azikiwe, Founding Father of modern Nigeria, reappeared on the campus where he had studied earlier, briefing those assembled at Rankin Chapel on the latest news from the ancestral continent.[43]

His presence was buttressed by the fact that intermittently serving on the faculty was W. Mercer Cook, who taught Romance Languages and as Jim Crow began to erode was able to serve as U.S. Ambassador to Gambia, Senegal, and Niger (Negro diplomats in African nations became de rigeur in coming decades). Cook, described pleasingly by a student journalist as possessing a "voice" that is resonantly "deep," was actually born in the District and attended Dunbar High School.[44]

---

37. *New York Herald Tribune*, 22 June 1950 and *New York Times*, 22 June 1950, Box 7, *Joseph Tydings Papers, University of Maryland-College Park*.
38. Handwritten letter, 7 July 1950, Box 7, *Tydings Papers*.
39. Letter from Francis Eugene O'Brien, 11 July 1950, Box 7, *Tydings Papers*
40. *The Hilltop*, 13 January 1950.
41. Gerald Horne, *The End of Empires: African Americans and India*, Philadelphia: Temple University Press, 2008.
42. *The Hilltop*, 15 October 1951.
43. *The Hilltop*, 17 April 1950.
44. *The Hilltop*, 25 October 1950.

He was remarkably similar to Rayford Logan, who too was flu-ent in French and was born in the District. By October 1951, he was pursuing a path not unlike that of Cook, in that he was en route to Europe on a quasi-diplomatic mission, representing the NAACP at a time when William Patterson was lobbying the U.N. seeking an indictment against U.S. imperialism for genocide against African Americans. After landing, Logan conferred with Negro diplomat Rupert Lloyd, one of a number who were promoted to deflect atten-tion from U.S. apartheid. He was candid, Logan said, in sketching an "observation that the United States has been posing as the champion of colonial peoples"—patting London, Lisbon, and Paris on the back with one hand and picking their pockets with the other—"in order to cover up the failure to pass civil rights legislation at home"; Logan said that this was the "most perspicacious comment I have heard in a long time" indicative that these intellectuals were to the left of their Foggy Bottom counterparts,[45] which would cause problems for them and the capital they served alike. From a certain perspective, there was reason for these counterparties to suspect these Negroes recently admitted into the sanctum sanctorum. For months before sharing opinions with Lloyd, the gregarious Logan was doing the same with Tadao Yanaihara, Dean of the Department of General Education at Tokyo University, who "pointed out that there is much interest in Japan about the Negro in the United States…I got the impression that he feels that the colored peoples of the world should know and understand one another better,"[46] not exactly the message conveyed by apartheid Washington, as it was too soon after the searing episodes of the Pacific War, often described as a "Race War." Logan simply had a wider range of experience that informed his views, compared to those in Foggy Bottom. Days after repasting with a Japanese col-league, Logan was listening intently to the words of a "colored Baptist missionary from Italian Somaliland who came over on his own to try to raise funds for a school there and to encourage American Negroes with technical and professional skills to settle there."[47]

Besides, his opinions of State Department leaders was hardly ele-vated. By September 1950, Logan' was at the White House rubbing shoulders with President Truman and Eleanor Roosevelt marking the formation of the United Nations. Stretching his legs, he walked there and en route he saw Secretary of State Dean Acheson. He was "not immaculate," said the perpetually well-turned out historian.

45. Entry, 29 October 1951, Box 9, *Rayford Logan Diary*.
46. Entry, 1 June 1950, Box 5, *Rayford Logan Diary*.
47. Entry, 18 June 1950, Box 5, *Rayford Logan Diary*.

"His sleeves and trousers needed pressing," he was "very thin" and was "putting on weight around the middle, for his coat button was straining."[48] To Logan, Acheson was no stranger; shortly after this encounter he was conferring with him in Foggy Bottom about hiring more Negroes for the Foreign Service, a strategic ambition for U.S. imperialism in the face of rising independence movements in Africa and the Caribbean and the need for U.S. diplomats to deodorize Washington's smelly profile.[49]

The candor of Logan and Lloyd may also have reflected the cynicism and subjectivity that inheres when those who are performing a mission do not believe in it altogether. Logan epitomized subjectivity, once deriding his colleague in the History Department, John Hope Franklin, for being "too aggressive. He is trying to see how much he can dominate me...."[50] Though on the surface, the two eminent historians were imbued with mutual bonhomie, behind the scenes Logan held tightly to the "fear that Harvard, Princeton, Williamsburg, etc. are grooming Franklin as a 'safe' man just as Ralph Bunche has been built up." As for the recently deceased Carter G. Woodson, Logan rationalized his "break" with this prolific historian since "he wrote a number of letters denouncing me" after he worked alongside Du Bois on the abortive "Encyclopedia Africana." Still furious, he rebuked the deceased scholar since he "would not even permit a book I had written to be reviewed in the 'journal,'" referring to the bible of the field: Woodson's *Journal of Negro* History.[51]

After an occupational hazard in the field—a negative review of one's book—an irate Logan was "tempted to write" the reviewer: "I knew that you are Ralph Bunche's flunkey," was his intended riposte, "but I did not know that you are his toady."[52] His anger toward Bunche—on the surface—remained incandescent though he had little negative to say about what may have been the Nobel Laureate's major blunder: aiding the dispossession of Palestinians in the runup to 1948. In fact, Logan recalled proudly, "I served as chairman of a faculty committee that screened applicants for a trip to Israel this summer to work on a kibbutz."[53]

Neither Bunche nor Franklin should have taken Logan's reprimands personally. The prickly historian, marinating in

---

48. Entry, 7 September 1950, Box 5.
49. Entry, 14 April 1951, Box 5.
50. Entry, 22 January 1950, Box 5, *Rayford Logan Diary*.
51. Entry, 6 May 1950, Box 5.
52. Entry, 4 February 1950, Box 5.
53. Entry, 21 May 1950, Box 5.

subjectivity and despite his vast knowledge was unable or unwilling to comprehend fully the retreat from Jim Crow, often descended into nettlesome quarrels. As for James Nabrit, a worthy civil rights lawyer and valued faculty member at Howard Law School—and eventually school president—Logan found plenty of "evidence of [his] unscrupulousness."[54]

Logan's mission was notably tense given the Cold War stakes. "Every stranger I meet is either an FBI agent or a Communist,"[55] was the message he received early on in Paris, not a good sign. Fed up with being asked about the Patterson-Robeson *We Charge Genocide* initiative, Logan exasperatedly fumed, "Negroes in the U.S. are not the victims of genocide," remarks undesigned to forge global solidarity with Negroes.[56]

However, Logan was unimpressed with those with whom he shared a trench, especially Edith Sampson, who represented the U.S. abroad. "Her knowledge of international affairs is not held in too high esteem" by fellow U.N. delegates, he said. The Howard academic was feeling besieged, conflicting with Communists and liberals like Sampson, too. There was a "sheer necessity," he moaned at one point, "for us American Negroes to have our representatives moving constantly around the world," seeking to shed light minimally. "I sent a letter today," he said as Thanksgiving 1951 hovered, "to the Paris edition of the *New York Herald Tribune* commenting on the article in the special Belgian Congo supplement praising segregation," a typical assertion by those in the U.S. elite that Logan was ostensibly serving. Even when he buried the hatchet and lunched with Bunche, the former Howard man and Logan seemed to agree in denouncing the "'weasel like'" attitude of Washington toward apartheid Pretoria—though neither man at that point dared to say so publicly.[57]

This was so since Logan and his cohort often agreed with the most primitive anticommunist tropes, constraining African independence and development; near the same time, he hailed the *Post* and the *Herald Tribune* when both referred to Africa as the "West's bastion" against socialism: "this is the point that I have frequently advanced," he said proudly, seemingly unaware of the wider consequences.[58]

---

54. Entry, 2 June 1950, Box 5.
55. Entry, 31 October 1951, Box 9, *Rayford Logan Diary*.
56. Entry, November 1951, Box 9.
57. Entry, 25 November 1951, Box 9, *Rayford Logan Diary*.
58. Entry, 26 February 1950, Box 5, *Rayford Logan Diary*.

Logan, however, was the man who knew too much: he was too aware of the depredations of colonialism to buy altogether the primitivism he often espoused. He not only was able to read the increasingly popular writings in French of Frantz Fanon, the Martinican cum Algerian firebrand, but while in Paris months later he met Paul Bouteille, who he described as a "high official in Madagascar at the time of the 1947 revolt" against Paris' rule. "I asked," he said naively, "whether the Communist charge that 89,000 ...had been slaughtered" was accurate. "He did not deny the figure" and instead painted a dire portrait of Africans "buried...alive" and how "French had fired point blank into crowds...." A dismayed Logan then noted that apartheid "is worth 50 divisions to Stalin, as is the Belgian Congo...I also slipped in the point that Belgium is prosperous in large measure because of the wealth of the Congo," sounding suspiciously like a Communist himself. His interlocutor pointed to the "coal in Belgium and the port of Antwerp" itself also being dependent upon the draconian regime in Congo.[59]

For months after hostilities had erupted in Korea, Logan was in a defensive crouch, lambasting the "snooping, smearing and hysteria sweeping the nation and especially the capital"[60]—where power was concentrated and scrutiny was most intense, especially surveillance of Negroes suspected inveterately of being willing to ally with real and imagined foes. At one point, Logan exposed the frailty of such a dispensation and how it could rupture potential bonds when he concluded mournfully that "any strange white woman is an FBI agent."[61]

The U.S. Negroes consorting and gallivanting in Paris were suggestive of a new trend whereby some amongst them—at least overseas—were not accorded their customary polecat status. By December 1951 Logan was enmeshed in conversations with Eleanor Roosevelt. "She recognized me," he gushed; "she had seen Mercer [Cook]," fellow Bison, "but had not seen Franklin Frazier," the eminent sociologist.[62] The busy Logan then jetted to Stockholm for another diplomatic soiree, financed by Washington.[63] Then it was back to Paris—"I chatted for a few minutes with Ralph Bunche," he said in passing. But in those different days, he could hardly escape the specter of Communists, for "a group here had presented [Bunche]

59. Entry, 17 May 1950, Box 5.
60. Entry, 7 September 1950, Box 5.
61. Entry, 1 October 1950, Box 5.
62. Entry, 6 December 1951, Box 9.
63. Entry, 11 December 1951, Box 9.

with 90,000 francs for the family of Willie McGee, a young Negro executed in Mississippi,"[64] and a signature case for Patterson's and Robeson's CRC.

Logan's Paris journey was haunted by the CRC—but with the continuing diminution of their influence, foreign junkets by Negroes would be spared such in the near future. Finally, on 19 December 1951, he went to a lunch at 45 Avenue de Friedland the residence of an influential U.S. couple, described as "Mr. and Mrs. Chester Williams," to discuss the CRC's genocide petition—and "what should be done" about it. Present at this paradigm setting gathering were Sampson, Negro powerbroker Channing Tobias, and a few others, including "an official of the Voice of America," Washington's propaganda arm. "We spoke for almost two hours" about the dilemma faced. Sampson insisted that the Negroes "should not be called upon to answer the charges made against the U.S.—but Tobias and Logan dissented vigorously, causing Sampson to backtrack, then "agreed with me that we should not accept the entire burden but that we should accept our share...." Logan would prove to be an articulate spokesman, deriding the CRC petition—without descending into the grimy details—as an "exaggerated one-sided indictment." Rehearsing the repetitive mantra of coming years, he hailed the "measurable progress toward first class citizenship" for Negroes "in recent years"—even as apartheid barriers persisted stickily. Voice of America, conventionally, "wanted to emphasize the shortcomings of the Soviet bloc" followed by a "general reply" from "Mrs. Roosevelt." Then awkwardly the question was raised of what to do about Richard Wright, the famed novelist—and former Communist—then exiled in Paris. Logan expressed a "reservation" about enlisting him while Tobias tactfully added that since the writer was an "expatriate one might question his right to speak...." The chanteuse, Josephine Baker, too, was discussed. There was fretting all about "as to the effect of the [petition] on American Negroes," with the consensus emerging that "it would have great effect." Walter White was "afraid to attack too vigorously the charges," and there was "general agreement" on this point, possibly for fear as if they would seem to be "Uncle Toms," apologists for barbarity. The coda: all were "warned that we must not underestimate Patterson," a fair assessment.[65]

---

64. Entry, 17 December 1951, Box 9. On McGee see Gerald Horne, *Communist Front? The Civil Rights Congress*, London: Associated University Presses, 1988, passim.

65. Entry, 19 December 1951, Box 9.

So armed, Sampson proceeded to a formal session of the U.N. on the petition: "she has a slight tendency to talk too long,"[66] was Logan's ungenerous review of her remarks. Logan was among those who opposed her appointment. This phalanx was led by Crystal Bird Fauset, who was to become the first Negro woman elected to a state legislature—Pennsylvania in her case. She was "calling me every day," Logan groused, complaining about Sampson; Fauset "accused Negroes of 'betraying' the whole race by not protesting the appointment," of a woman who could easily be dubbed Madam Malaprop. Others disagreed and carried the day, feeling that "the appointment would answer charges made by the Soviet Union that Negroes were maltreated in the United States"—which they were. Walter White, according to Logan, "said he could not oppose" Sampson for "his opposition would have been looked upon as a betrayal of Negro women."[67]

There was hardly unanimity within official U.S. ranks in any case. Logan cited "the two representatives of the American Jewish Congress" who "pointed out the importance that European papers attach to incidents of violence against Negroes in the U.S.," a phenomenon that has yet to disappear, while Sampson was irate since she felt that there had been "pussyfooting" among fellow delegates who "declined to sign a joint cable to the [U.S. Attorney General] urging prompt action" in the assassination of Florida's NAACP leader, Harry Moore.[68]

There were balms to calm frayed nerves. Logan then traipsed to a "quiet but enjoyable evening at the home of E. Franklin Frazier, 1 Place d'Lena," toasting his new role with the United Nations Educational, Science and Cultural Organization [UNESCO]."[69]

By 1965, the imprisoned future leader of the Black Panther Party—Eldridge Cleaver—would espy such maneuvers and angrily conclude with emphasis that "THE CIVIL RIGHTS MOVEMENT, ANALAGOUS TO A COLONIAL LIBERATION MOVEMENT LED BY THE NATIONAL BOURGEOISIE, WAS THE BLACK BOURGEOISIE'S DEMOCRATIC REVOLUTION."[70] This was a bridge too far, given the ineffable point that countless ordinary Negroes did benefit from the erosion of Jim Crow, not to mention that Cleaver,

---

66. Entry, 21 December 1951, Box 9.
67. Entry, 7 September 1950, Box 5, *Rayford Logan Diary*.
68. Entry, 27 December 1951, Box 9.
69. Entry, 1 January 1952, Box 9.
70. Eldridge Cleaver to Beverly Axelrod, 10 September 1965, Reel 1, *Eldridge Cleaver Papers, University of California-Berkeley*. Original text is underlined.

the presumed radical, managed to ignore the eclipse of those like Patterson in sketching his thesis. Yet, it remains true that it was at least ironic that the major theoretician of the "Black Bourgeoisie"—Frazier—was being skewered for hijacking the movement, along with other well compensated colleagues. The wider point was that some Negroes were allowed to profit handsomely from the titanic transition away from the more egregious forms of Jim Crow and this helped to dull justifiable outrage since these figures—Logan, Sampson, White, Bunche, et.al.—were often perceived as articulate and legitimate spokespersons for the besieged minority from which they had emerged.

Chapter 11

Anticommunism Feeds Conservatism, 1950-1953

By the time President Truman's term was expiring by early 1953, whatever popularity he had enjoyed was dissipating. Setting the tone was William Patterson, whose genocide petition at the United Nations had evoked veritable hysteria in official circles. He objected stridently and rebuked the Missourian when Major General Ulysses S. Grant, descendant of another former president, was being slated for reappointment as Chairman of the National Park and Planning Commission, one of the more potent agents shaping the District's future, because he backed Jim Crow in Washington.[1]

In response the Missourian was feinting and dodging like a champion boxer as he sought to placate his Dixiecrat base while pandering to the growingly strategic Negro voting bloc. A 1951 meeting with Truman included the issue "Segregation in the District of Columbia" and Negro labor boss, A. Philip Randolph, was said to be "insisting on this quite strongly," meaning desegregation. Truman—or whoever spoke for him—sought to satisfy Randolph by simply pointing to earlier boilerplate on this matter and the allied issue of "home rule," but this was hardly sufficient.[2]

Alice Dunnigan, one of the few Negro reporters on the White House beat in her capacity with the Associated Negro Press, was similarly in revolt. She had written Truman directly "recalling work" she "performed" during the tumult of the 1948 presidential campaign, including a "trip she took with him, at her own expense" and her purpose was not necessarily dispassionate, impartial press coverage but "to help win the Negro vote," for the Kansas Citian,

---

1. William Patterson to President Truman, 27 April 1949, Box 477, Official File, *Truman Presidential Library*.
2. Memorandum, 11 June 1951, Official File, Box 477, Truman Presidential Library

she emphasized. She was "promised she would be compensated by way of a position" with his team but was rebuffed instead; she was furious.[3]

Coincidentally, a few months later Dunnigan chose to attend a meeting—involving the Communist led Civil Rights Congress—designed to challenge the District's Jim Crow laws.[4]

Similarly furious were many of her fellow Negroes in the District. Yes, change in the racist status quo was proceeding but not fast enough for a nation that styled itself as the paragon of human rights virtue. By February 1951, Robert Carter of the legal staff of the NAACP, was reporting happily that "as a result of suits brought by us, the University of Maryland has been forced to admit Negroes into its School of Nursing, School of Engineering, the Graduate Department of Sociology, as well as its Law School."[5]

Thus, as Truman's tenure at 1600 Pennsylvania Avenue was expiring, his aide, Phileo Nash retained an analysis which averred that "all the major universities and colleges in the District except George Washington University," alma mater of FBI chief, J. Edgar Hoover, "now admit Negroes to professional and graduate courses and to many of the undergraduate courses." This was a shift from an unsustainable status quo, but the point remained that "medical facilities for sick Negroes" were "generally deplorable" as "several hospitals do not admit Negroes at all"; as for employment, "no Negro gets a job operating streetcars or buses, or as a switchboard operator for the telephone company or as a sales clerk...." The public schools were one—limited—exception in an otherwise grim picture.[6]

But even here the scenario was hardly unblemished as school board member Robert K. Faulkner was raising a hue and cry about supposed "socialism...creeping into the school system" in that there were "too many services and specialized classes," along with "medical and dental clinics" deemed too plush for Negroes.[7]

---

3. Memorandum from Alice Dunnigan, 22 March 1949, Box 476, Official File, *Truman Presidential Library*. Emphasis in original.

4. Postcard from Alice Dunnigan, circa September 1949, Box 2, MS 404, *Records of the Coordinating Committee for the Enforcement of the D.C. Anti-Discrimination Laws, Historical Society of Washington, D.C.*

5. Robert Carter to Walter White, 16 February 1951, Box A318, *NAACP Papers*.

6. Phineas Indritz, "Racism in the Nation's Capital," *The Nation*, 18 October 1952, Box 30, *Phileo Nash Papers*.

7. *Washington Daily News*, 6 October 1952, Box 36, *Stephen Spingarn Papers*, *Truman Presidential Library*.

The *Washington Post* claimed contrarily that this dual school system—one for Negroes, yet another for "others"—was costing District taxpayers almost $8 million annually and that desegregation would be considerably less pricey.[8]

Increasingly, the contradictions of Jim Crow were becoming all too evident, especially as U.S. imperialism claimed to be waging wars on behalf of human rights and democracy. This high-mindedness was rejected by the woman identified as "Mrs. Warren J. Strudwick," who asked plaintively: "One wonders whether it is a crime to be an American Negro. I always was puzzled as a college student," she said quizzically, "when dark skinned classmates from foreign countries could venture forth in all parts of the city with no fear of embarrassment because they were not American Negroes." Unfortunately, the ideological trajectory of even the most advanced had yet to reach the realization that this likely had something to do with her ancestors failing to fight in sizeable numbers for a slaveholders' revolt in 1776 then contributing mightily to the defeat of this class by 1865 and being forced to pay a stiff price as a result.[9]

This outrage was occurring as segregated schools designed for Euro-American youth sat virtually empty where those for Negroes were jammed to the rafters and often operating part-time as a result. Negro children were walking past these empty schools in order to reach their overcrowded schools. Undaunted, Virginia Attorney General justified this waste of resources expectorating viciously about the "'livid stench of sadism, sex immorality and juvenile delinquency infesting the mixed schools of the District of Columbia.'"[10]

It was hardly inevitable that the steely forces of Jim Crow would retreat. Their roots were too deeply implanted in the loamy soil of slavery, a defining institution still fresh in the living memory of many. To the advantage of progressives was the opinion captured by the otherwise conservative *Washington Star*: "What goes on here," it was said of the District, in words preserved by the Interior Secretary, who had oversight of the city in 1952, "makes news in Stockholm, Cairo, in Singapore"[11]—which was all too accurate. Indicative of

---

8. *Washington Post*. 26 March 1952.

9. *Washington Post*, 28 September 1952. See also Gerald Horne, *The Counter-Revolution of 1776: Slave Resistance and the Origins of the United States of America* and Gerald Horne, *The Counter-Revolution of 1836: Texas Slavery & Jim Crow and the Roots of U.S. Fascism*, New York: International, 2022.

10. Carl F. Hansen, *Danger in Washington: The Story of Twenty Years in the Public Schools in the Nation's Capital*, West Nyack: Parker, 1968, 10, 47.

11. *Washington Star*, 22 April 1951, Box 68, *Truman Presidential Library*.

this issue's importance, soon after moving into the White House, President Eisenhower reminded Washingtonians that "visitors of all races from the entire world" arrive at their doorstep and "among these visitors are representatives of nations whose goodwill will be needed to win" against the despised Reds; "our Nation's Capital," he said accurately, "is the most damaging place to let racism flourish...."[12]

But the president' seemingly anodyne remarks were not viewed as such by those in the region. James Gannon of Maryland sternly informed the *Washington Star* that "the white race is outnumbered by the other races in the world," thus, "I am against society intermingling."[13] Responding implicitly was Thurgood Marshall who argued that "army officials reached the conclusion that segregation in education almost cost us World War II,"[14] but that was speculative and even if it were not, it was unclear if those who had grown accustomed to Jim Crow were willing to retreat—for any reason, even being defeated in war.

President Eisenhower's paeans of sympathy for antiracism notwithstanding, he echoed his predecessor in continuing the crackdown on Negroes' most battletested allies: the organized left, notably Communists. His Executive Order 10450 mirrored Truman's "loyalty" oath mandate.[15] And despite his rhetorical flourishes, Eisenhower continued to wrestle reluctantly with the sensitive matter of home rule, a matter of significance to Maryland, Virginia, and Dixie generally. Weeks after being sworn in, his top aide, Maxwell Raab reported that he had a "long discussion" on Capitol Hill with this delicate matter, finding that legislators and their staff "feel that it would be advisable to have a three-man commission with one of the commissioners a Negro,"[16] a kind of affirmative action that within decades would be virtually forbidden. One of the proponents of this approach, Senator Francis Case of South Dakota, told the chief executive that he should consider Mordecai Johnson of Howard, whose purported pro-Communist leanings decades earlier had been forgotten apparently. "Selection of the right person," he said, "would not only yield dividends in good government for Washington but also for freedom's cause throughout the world," amounting to a "potent

---

12. *Washington Post*, 18 October 1952.

13. *Washington Star*, 31 March 1953.

14. *Afro-American*, 12 December 1953.

15. David K. Johnson, *The Lavender Scare*, 123.

16. Maxwell Raab to Sherman Adams, 21 February 1953, Box 237, WHCF, OF 71, *Eisenhower Presidential Library*.

weapon the Cold War...."[17] In that different moment, Congressman Sam Yorty of Southern California, who was to become a staunch anti-Negro advocate as Mayor of Los Angeles by 1965, then was blasting away at Jim Crow.[18]

He was echoed by a representative of the American Friends Services Committee, i.e., the Quakers. Though an "unbelievable number of neighborhoods are mixed," said Ralph Rose, and there was no racist segregation on streetcars, Negroes were "barred from most movie houses," while the "largest cab companies have no Negro drivers," ditto for Capital Transit buses.[19]

But as was the case in Tuscaloosa within a few years, many of the Euro-American locals in the District were not as taken with this relatively new-fangled notion of desegregation. This included leaders of the president's party there or at least that is what Eisenhower's chief aide, Sherman Adams, was told: "they are most opposed to a Negro Commissioner and for some very valid reasons, I believe."[20]

However, as noted, that same White House had to cater to a gaggle of Dixiecrats who developed an antipathy to the District that was grounded in part on lingering grievances against the federal government which had defeated their vaunted confederacy decades earlier—and was to morph in coming years into general hostility to federal spending generally, if it could be somehow linked to assuaging the needs of the formerly enslaved.

By 1952 Senator Olin Johnston of South Carolina was being briefed about a plan for mass distribution of this legislator's intemperate remarks opposing home rule for the District. His inflaming words were "distributed to the Mayors of cities of 100,000 and over, in the densely populated states and 25,000 and over in the smaller states," along with the "various Chambers of Commerce" and "to the Political Science Instructors at our colleges and universities...."[21]

Edward Collady, General Counsel of the Washington Board of Trade, the parliament for capital in revolt against progress, praised the "scholarly presentation made by Senator Johnston," remarks

---

17. Senator Francis Case to President Eisenhower, 7 February 1953, Box 237, WHCF, OF 71.

18. Congressman Yorty to President Eisenhower, 23 March 1953, Box 237, WHCF, OF 71. See Gerald Horne, *Fire this Time: The Watts Uprising and the 1960s*, Charlottesville: University of Virginia Press, 1995.

19. Ralph Rose to White House Staff, 2 July 1953, Box 237, WHCF, OF 71.

20. Charles Willis to Sherman Adams, 24 January 1955, Box 237, WHCF, OF 71.

21. Harland Wood of Washington to Senator Johnston, Box 30, *Olin Johnston Papers*.

with which he chose to "agree most heartily" since his words were—supposedly—"strong and amply documented...."[22] Putting his money where the organization's mouth was, Duane Strawbridge of the Board of Trade, sited conveniently at the building that housed the conservative *Washington Star,* subsidized generously "printing for ten thousand copies" of Senator Johnston's inflammatory words: "we can address them and return them to you for the stuffing and sealing of the speech," he offered.[23]

This spending was welcomed by mossbacks concerned with Negroes coming to power in the nation's capital during a moment when Jim Crow had yet to be extirpated. Hence, Harry Klinefelter and Willis Smith of neighboring Baltimore, turned their attention from their own city's immense problems, to focus on the District. Mass influence was their concern, especially that which included Negroes. The "tremendous influence the galleries have upon the delegates," was how they expressed it, referencing political conventions where the stampeding chant arises of "'We Want Roosevelt'" or "'We Want Willkie'" can be transmuted to the District in that there was a "perpetual daily galley plus lobbying and buttonholing pressure that could not but produce a tremendously bad influence so close to the throne...." More to the point, "Negroes comprise about 30% of the population and voters," it was said in January 1952, which was a "very bad and dangerous simply because both Republicans and Democrats would turn Heaven and Earth to secure the Negro vote...." Unavoidably, this "would produce a Negro dominated Washington" and most assuredly, they demanded, "the capital of the country should not be dominated in this manner...."[24] Alarmingly, Senator Johnston concurred.[25]

All sides watched census figures concerning the District with the single-minded scrutiny of a hungry bird-of-prey. For more Negroes would influence—potentially—jury pools, not to mention the possible ascension of Black political Power. By the early 1950s it was the Urban League's turn, as the population of the District was said to grow from 663,691 in 1940 to 802,178 by 1950, but the population defined as "white" increased from 475,326 to 517,865, while

22. Remarks of Edward Collady, 17 March 1952, Box 30, *Olin Johnston Papers.*
23. Duane Strawbridge, Assistant Executive Vice President of Washington Board of Trade to William Alexander, Johnston staff, circa 1952, Box 35, *Olin Johnston Papers.*
24. Harry Klinefelter and Willis Smith to Senator Johnston, 18 January 1952, Box 30, *Olin Johnston Papers.*
25. Senator Johnston to Harry Klinefelter, 22 January 1952, Box 30.

their proportion fell from 71.5 percent to 64.5 percent: Negroes grew from 187,266 in 1940 to 280,803 in 1950 with the proportion growing from 28.2 percent to 35 percent—[26]creeping steadily to "Chocolate City" status, a brand with manifold consequences often dimly perceived.

Complicating further the fever dreams of opponents of home rule was the lingering presence of a cadre of Euro-American Communists in the District, along with those in their orbit. The contemporary journalist, Carl Bernstein, who rose to maturity in the region, recalled the apartment complex in the southeast quadrant, Trenton Terrace, which he termed a "'wretched new development of small Colonial Style brick apartments,'" which the House Un-American Activities Committee described as a "'leftist nest'" insofar as it housed for a while the activist Annie Stein and the left-wing attorneys, Joseph Forer and David Rein, notorious for defending the civil liberties of Communists. It was built on a hillside in 1945 and included twenty three story brick buildings encircled with a green ridge of foliage. Stein's fellow activist, Marvin Caplan, was among those who were convinced that the complex was under surveillance by the authorities, up to and including tapping of their phones, because of the presence of presumed Communists.[27]

They were part of a dwindling legacy. For as the Red Scare continued on its decimating path, this coincided with a kind of "white flight" as the antiracist consciousness brought by a modicum of Communists, shriveled. Carl Bernstein, a son of Communist parents, recalled a time when the southern quadrant of the city was the "closest thing to ghetto that existed in the capital. Its narrow streets were crowded with the commerce of immigrant experience: notions traders with their carts, egg men in their horse-drawn wagons, rag vendors, carpet merchants, building tradesmen," in the midst of an area that was "overcrowded, dirty, rough, run-down...." By 1910, he said, 4 percent of the District were Jewish, and their material conditions of existence often drove them to the left: this included his family. His mother attended Central High School and, he said, "only five white schools in Washington then—Eastern, Western, McKinley Tech, Business and Central," the latter being the "elite school in the city" for Euro-Americans. By 1950, she was representing the beleaguered Progressive Party—late of the swimming pool controversy—as she testified before the school board urging that

---

26. Nelson Jackson, Evaluation of the District Urban League, 15 December 1953, Box I: B30, *National Urban League Papers*.
27. Marvin Caplan, *Farther Along*, 122-123, 131.

Central with its "tiled swimming pool and greenhouses and terraced gardens and mahogany paneled library with fireplace and leaded glass windows, be transferred to the Negro Division. Which it was and its name was changed to Cardozo...." The younger Bernstein was matured in the crucible of struggle, fleeing "in panic from the charge of the Park Police cavalry during the battle to integrate the swimming pools...." His father was in the middle of Truman's "loyalty oath" purge of the left in the federal government, which trickled down to states and cities. Truman requested a substantial $25 million for the first year of this purge brought by Executive Order 9835. Swept up in the dragnet were those who conducted a sit-down protest in the counting room at the Bureau of Engraving and Printing, where—as Bernstein recollects—"hundreds of Black women counted the dollar bills" with "huge fans whirring in the heat of the counting rooms" as sheets of uncut bills fluttered. Their union, United Public Workers, was victimized, just as it was enrolling Negro war veterans often unwilling to accept the Jim Crow status quo. Between 1947 and 1953, there were 12,859 of such cases in Washington, says Bernstein, and of these "more than five hundred were handled by my father," who then paid a price as he too was purged. Like other similarly situated leftists, he migrated to running a neighborhood laundromat. This transition from staunch defender of the working class to small businessman was simultaneously a blow administered against the Black working class desperately in need of defense and less in need for someone to receive their coins for laundry.[28]

This attack on the left weakened the anti-Jim Crow movement ultimately, especially as it meant the routing of the Black Left within labor, who often provided the wherewithal for the movement. Hysteria about Communists arose as comrades even began to flee to suburban Maryland. Supposedly there were hundreds of Reds in the vicinity of College Park and the authorities were determined to uproot and harass each and every one of them, constitutional protections be damned.[29]

This was occurring as their sturdy shield—the Congress of Industrial Organizations, too, was walking the plank. It was during the Truman regime that Thomas G. Sampler of 1661 Gales Street N.E., Secretary Treasurer of Building Laborers Local 74, was dragged before the House Un-American Activities Committee. He had served in the military from June 1944 to January 1946 and joined

28. Carl Bernstein, *Loyalties: A Son's Memoir*, New York: Simon & Schuster, 1989, 33, 43, 44, 46, 47, 86, 175, 193, 204.

29. *Washington Star*, 12 July 1952.

the Communist Party in May 1947 and assumed his union post in 1948. His unit in the CP—the Frederick Douglass Club—had nine or ten members and a number, including himself, were also active in the Civil Rights Congress. "I was active in the Progressive Party," too, said this native Alabamian, besides acting as a bodyguard for Robeson during his forays into the District. But soon he was seeking employment elsewhere. The same held true for William Gray, of 1208 Quincy Street N.W., Business Agent for Local 74, born in Charlotte in 1896. Also snared by HUAC was Norris Hammond, born in Virginia in 1911 and a construction worker, a category kept busy by the postwar building boom. Then there was Roy Wood, born in Idaho in 1914, a seafarer with experience in Western Europe and fingered as the Chairman of the District CP. He was then residing at 1517 Wisconsin Avenue and his dewy eyed references to his ancestors fighting in 1776 and his great grandfather being an abolitionist, fell on uncomprehending ears. The grim reaper also fell on Ernest Chambers of Local 74, a military man from January 1944 to November 1945 and also a Red. Likewise, construction worker McKinley Gray of 53 ½ Hanover Place N.W., born in Chester, South Carolina and in the District since 1941, also was hounded because of this CP membership since 1948. Robert Paul of 5345 M Street N.E. was born in Cherokee City, Oklahoma in 1910 before matriculating at Tuskegee then Howard, then the University of Denver Law School; the latter may explain why he was accompanied by counsel, Joseph Forer of the National Lawyers Guild. Alice Stapleton was the only woman grilled during this marathon session.[30]

As so often happens, Truman's listing to the right served to pave the way for the victory of the opposition party. His bipolarity on Jim Crow—rhetorically opposing it while undermining those, e.g., Robeson, most determined to combat it—was a reflection of his reliance on Dixiecrats and Negro voters both and, to a degree, demobilizing both: adroitly gilding the lily for Dwight David Eisenhower. This racial mood swing was refracted in the successor ticket of Truman's Democrats, led by Adlai Stevenson of Illinois—and influenced by Black Chicago voters—and John Sparkman of Alabama, where Negroes were disenfranchised. Typically, in 1952 Sparkman agreed to address the soiree of the Federation of Civic Associations, Jim

---

30. Testimony, "Hearings Regarding Communism in the District of Columbia-Part 2. Hearings Before the Committee on Un-American Activities, House of Representatives, 81st Congress, 2nd Session," December 6, 11, 12 and 13 1950, Washington, D.C.: GPO, 1950, Box 10, Folder 18, *Robert Kerr Papers, University of Oklahoma-Norman.*

Crow Washington's event of the season.[31] On cue when President Eisenhower was inaugurated in January 1953 the report emerged that "when black units veered into camera range," the ABC-TV affiliate in the District instantaneously called for a station break or a "commercial." Near the same time Justice William Douglas of the high court, viewed as "liberal"—though he eventually became a strident opponent of affirmative action—fretted that Communists or the CRC were funding civil rights litigation, rendering this campaign questionable. In the midst of this front-lash against Negro progress, the NAACP—in the person of their premier litigator, Thurgood Marshall, went along to the extent that he (and they) threw in their lot with the anticommunist crusade. Yet he admitted frankly in 1953 that "'no one would deny that the basic reason for withholding the vote to the citizens of the District of Columbia is that a sizeable portion of these voters are colored,'"—which begs the question of how a formidable bloc of opposition would be overcome.[32]

This was the dilemma rarely faced by the NAACP leadership. They knew instinctively that the correlation of forces domestically were not favorable, given the persistence of Jim Crow and support for same. They also knew that the changing global scene was in their favor but what would occur if the world balance of forces changed for the worse while domestic opposition continued to reign? This rudimentary inquiry seemed to be beyond their imagination.

Shortly after Eisenhower's inauguration, Walter White was speaking at a testimonial dinner for Mary Church Terrell, slated to raise funds for anti-Jim Crow efforts in the nation's capital. Although White intended for his remarks to be moving, Rayford Logan was unmoved since he "injected his own experience a bit too much,"[33] typical of the NAACP chief. Still, White pressed on: "One year ago," he began, "the doors of most of the hotels and all of the restaurants of Washington were barred to dark skinned patrons," though exceptions often were carved out for non-Negroes. But then, he continued, "Thava Rajah, a distinguished labor leader of Malaya [Malaysia]" arrived and "went into a drugstore located in the building in which the State Department cultural activities division has its offices, he and another guest [from] Burma were bluntly refused an ice cream soda." As if that indignity were insufficient, the following evening "Mr. Rajah and yet another visitor were told by a well known Washington restaurant that 'We don't serve Negroes here.'" But thanks to

31. Bell Clement, "Pushback," 90.
32. Joan Quigley, *Just Another Southern Town*, 200, 214.
33. Entry, 10 October 1953, Box 9.

those like Terrell, a winding road of litigation had altered the racist landscape in the District. "Today," said White, "thanks to the decision in the United States Supreme Court in the Thompson Restaurant case, dark skinned visitors and even loyal American Negroes, can be fed and housed in Washington" —even "moving picture houses in downtown Washington," he added wondrously, "have recently dropped the color line."[34]

At one point, John Bates, District branch leader of the NAACP at 1227-Eleventh Street N.W. informed his members proudly, "we have the largest concentration of men and women endowed with creative thinking,"[35] yet somehow this facility was hardly evident in understanding the major issue of the day: the intersection of Jim Crow with global imperatives and how to leverage the latter to erode the former.

White could have and should have told his entranced audience about what quickly became evident. African American customers continued to be unwelcomed in District bistros despite their being ordered to serve them by 1953.[36] He also probably knew from intelligence shared by Terrell, that the sparkplug of desegregation, Annie Stein—a presumed Communist—had chosen this moment of apparent victory to leave the District, moving to Brooklyn: a telling moment.[37]

Revealingly, the prominent Negro attorney, Belford Lawson, hosted a farewell reception for the presumed Red, Annie Stein, at the headquarters of his equally prominent Negro fraternity, Alpha Phi Alpha. With candor it was pointed out that in the 1930s she was Chair of the Women's Trade Union League where "she helped organize the lowest paid women workers in the city," involved in both "laundry" and "domestic" sectors, along with "restaurants and hotel employees too." The frank depiction of her mentioned that she was "Secretary of the Progressive Party's Anti Discrimination Committee" whereby "she was one of the first persons to suggest that a test case be launched to determine if the anti-discrimination lost [sic] laws of 1872 and 1873 were still in force...in 1951 the 'Afro-American' named her to its annual roll....." The lengthy list of sponsors included the National Lawyers Guild, the National Council of Negro Women, the Progressive Party affiliates in both the District

---

34. Remarks by Walter White, 10 October 1953, Box 457, *NAACP Papers*.
35. Memorandum from John Bates, 17 January 1951, Box IX: 226, *NAACP Papers*.
36. David K. Johnson, *The Lavender Scare*, 164.
37. Alison M. Parker, *Unceasing Militant*, 281.

and Northern Virginia, and the *Pittsburgh Courier*.[38] This remarkable array suggested that even as the biting winds of the Red Scare were snapping, some Negroes were seeking to remain vigilant—thus far.

For as White was regaling his audience in wonder, his comrade Clarence Mitchell was informing Attorney General Herbert Brownell, one of Eisenhower's early and most important appointees, that "dark skinned individuals from foreign countries have been refused service because of their color" while "on official business for their countries." Admittedly, this latest atrocity was before the judicial opinion celebrated by White; however, the willingness of the NAACP to not only throw internationalists like Robeson overboard—their ramified global networks notwithstanding—while throwing in their lot with "liberals," who hardly had hegemony at home, was breathtaking in its naivete. This was occurring, as Mitchell was lamenting how this shabbily treated "student from Egypt... became hysterical when he was denied service in a Washington hotel dining room...." That they could have leveraged Robeson's popularity in Cairo and elsewhere to place pressure on Washington, simply did not dawn.[39]

With the departure in the previous decade of Hunton and Wilkerson, Howard was hampered in its ability to provide intellectual and political guidance to the NAACP. Shortly after Eisenhower's inauguration, the campus newspaper blared the banner headline: "[Senator] McCarran Eyes HU Reds,"[40] such as they were.

Again, when intellectuals of a persecuted group, e.g., U.S. Negroes, are blocked from expressing fully the panorama of their discontent—especially because of right-wing measures—it tends to create fertile soil for the growth of the kind of backbiting and infighting that seemed to inhere on the hilltop and was a specialty of one of their leading professors: Rayford Logan.

As time passed, he added to his list of pet feuds. There was William Brewer, a "nuisance" who "threatened me over the phone"; it was typical low stakes academic politics, guaranteeing viciousness ironically, involving "rejection of his article," said Logan, from the *Journal of Negro History*. As was his wont, Logan could not leave things there, contemptuously referring to him as a "Georgia 'cracker.' Although

38. Announcement, 8 May 1953, Box 1, MS 404, *Records of Coordinating Committee for the Enforcement of the D.C. Anti-Discrimination Laws, Historical Society of Washington, D.C.*

39. Clarence Mitchell to Attorney General Brownell, 12 March 1953, Box IX: 226, *NAACP Papers*.

40. *The Hilltop*, 18 February 1953.

colored, he passes for white frequently. He did so at John Hopkins before [J.H.U.] began to admit Negroes...I do not hold this against him," said the historian magnanimously, "since he gets expressions, candid, of opinion by white people...a kind of 'intelligence agent' for us," though the tensions inhering in "passing" left him perpetually "embittered and frustrated." And confused, too, for though he owned a Georgia plantation, teaches in District public schools—yet resided in a cubbyhole in the YMCA.[41]

Then Logan sharpened his rhetorical spear at the expense of L.D. Reddick, fellow historian and soon-to-be known as a close comrade of Dr. Martin Luther King, Jr. At the annual gathering of the Association for the Study of Negro Life & History in Atlanta he "alienated most of the people" there.[42]

Virtually every contretemps that captured Logan had involved men but none exceeded in volcanic intensity his disputatiousness with his Howard colleague, Merze Tate, a leading woman scholar. The venting of his spleen took on—eventually—intensely personal terms but seemed to reach a new plateau with an ordinary academic turf battle when, he said, she became "suddenly interested in Negro history," a primary field of his. "She has been wont to belittle and even to sneer at the theses in Negro history that I have been supervising, at John Hope Franklin's and my writings in the field." She had focused on the Pacific, especially Hawaii, where her work was pathbreaking, but then she "received a Fulbright award to teach in India and the subject that the Indians...want her to discuss" was, yes, "the Negro," hence her pivot.[43]

But Logan, an adroit historian, should have been able to sense the wider historical forces that was igniting these pirouettes. As ever, his former Howard colleague, Ralph Bunche, was subjected to censure by him. He, "some years ago went around calling me a 'black chauvinist'" for his defense of Negroes in the face of the future Nobel Laureate's skepticism of the "Don't Buy where you can't work" campaign, but now with the change in the global landscape, Bunche too had pivoted and "was now making speeches about the treatment of colored races in the world at large and of Negroes in the United States."[44]

Bunche should not have felt special in being subjected to Logan's ire. Benjamin Mays was to gain subsidiary renown as a mentor to

---

41. Entry, 2 July 1950, Box 5, *Rayford Logan Diary*.
42. Entry, 7 September 1950, Box 5.
43Entry, 2 October 1950, Box 5.
44. Entry, 28 January 1951, Box 5.

the young man who became Dr. King, but for Logan he was "one of the most overrated men" in the nation.[45] One would imagine that Logan would be sympathetic to those with whom he shared ideological affinities. Instead, he asserted bluntly, "I do not trust Phil [Randolph], Walter [White], Lester Granger, [Channing] Tobias and Mrs. Bethune," the leaders of Black America. The problem was the ideological climate which incentivized mutual undermining, particularly sabotaging those like Logan who only recently had been linked to the now reviled Council on African Affairs.[46]

For those who Logan suspected were similarly under siege. Tobias' son-in-law, Bill Dean, who had been toiling in "Italian Somaliland," had just returned to the U.S. "depressed": he committed suicide.[47] Chastened, when Logan bumped into Tobias in Paris, the latter leader with asperity claimed, "he was not going to be cast in the role of defending the treatment of Negroes in the United States; that he was an American delegate" to the U.N. session "and not a delegate representing American Negroes. Dr. Tobias told me that Mrs. [Edith] Sampson had been used too much in that way last year, sometime against her will."[48]

This suspicion of Logan himself continued, as he confessed that "during this wave of Republican cum Catholic dominated hysteria"—a peculiarity of this historian was his anti-Vatican bias— the FBI "can find enough criticism of U.S. foreign policy in my writings to make it impossible for me to get a Fulbright," i.e., subsidized research and travel abroad, the likes of which had been granted to his colleague, Merze Tate. "I have never been a Communist or a fellow traveler," he told himself warily, while adding superfluously that "Du Bois is vulnerable...."[49] Yet, Logan did not help his bona fides when at a well-attended speech before the American Legion

---

45. Entry, 7 February 1951, Box 5.
46. Entry, 8 April 1951, Box 5.
47. Entry, 9 January 1952, Box 5.
48. Entry, 23 January 1952, Box 5.
49. Entry, 21 April 1951, Box 5. For Logan's anti-Vatican bias, see, e.g., Entry, 17 June 1951, Box 5: "I consider the Catholic Church the greatest threat to the liberties of the American people." His colleague, Professor Frazier told him that the Church "owns whole blocks of whole houses in Bahia and Rio," where enslavement of Africans once reigned: Entry, 4 January 1952, Box 5. Yet despite Logan's denunciations of Catholics, he evidently did not recognize that at a moment when Jim Crow reigned supreme, a member of the District's Negro elite—according to a scholarly investigation—was "not accepted at any white colleges in the District except for Catholic University...." See Elizabeth Dowling Taylor, *The Original Black Elite*, 384.

and the Chamber of Commerce, he served up what he termed "my usual speech, deploring the use of the 'Free World' to designate countries that held 200 million black colonial subjects" in subjugation.[50] True—but this was now seen widely as ideological heresy, i.e., not acknowledging the obvious. "Many of us in the U.S.," he said, "do not want [to] have to make the choice between Bao Dai," the French and U.S. toady from Vietnam "and Communism..."[51] He did not realize that the Cold War mandated such a choice if one wanted to enjoy the full menu of citizenship.

Though Logan was deprived of certain emoluments—e.g., a Fulbright—he was sufficiently on board with the ideological turn to avoid being submerged by choppy currents. By January 1952 he was in France, marking his 55th birthday and though he was in touch with Walter White about the tragic slaying of Florida NAACP leader, Harry Moore, he was sure to take time to meet with "Mr. Irving Brown"—a top U.S. intelligence operative—and "five different groups to discuss labor problems...."[52] Days later Logan and Brown were again shoulder-to-shoulder, this time discussing Communists—then on the march—in Italy.[53] Logan was explicit that U.S. aid—meaning the "Marshall Plan"—"had saved France in general from Communism,"[54] a plus in his opinion. Logan spent an extraordinary amount of time in Europe with the wily Brown, comparing notes on Communists and trade unions in France and Italy.[55]

Then Logan was sighted at the National Assembly in Paris, "famous for its stormy debates," said the professor of this version of class struggle. He was aghast at the "most intemperate statement" that was "made by a colored Communist...." Subsequently, Brown "called me to say" that "we ought to get together with some of his friends,"[56] likely a nest of spies and vipers. They were all on the same page in that Logan simultaneously was seeking to unmask a U.S. national in Paris, while frustratedly noting "of course, if he is a party member... he is too clever to reveal his membership,"[57] making suspicion ironclad veracity—a crass capitulation to anticommunism. And it was not as if Logan were an obscure figure; when he met Colette La Croix, he

---

50. Entry, 11 May 1951, Box 5.
51. Entry, 9 January 1952, Box 5.
52. Entry, 7 January 1952, Box 5.
53. Entry, 14 January 1952, Box 5.
54. Entry, 17 May 1952, Box 5.
55. Entry, 14 January 1952, Box 5.
56. Entry, 25 January 1952, Box 5.
57. Entry, 26 January 1952, Box 5.

commented that she "used to be the secretary of Jean Paul Sartre," paramount French intellectual; "she said she knew about me and showed me her address book with my name and telephone number."[58]

Thus, on Mayday 1952, Logan was to be found at this massive flexing of muscles by labor and the left, then virtually unknown back home. "Scattered among the crowd were some Negroes," he said of this "most impressive parade I have ever witnessed...." He assured himself by observing that he was "confident that the U.S. and other Western Powers had their intelligen[ce] agents on the job and I am sorry that I can not compare notes with them,"[59] he added unnecessarily and ruefully.

This anticommunist vigilance held him in good stead upon his return to Howard; by December 1952, he was witness to a stormy faculty meeting where all were told that "anyone [that] was a member of the Communist Party had better resign at once...." Still, Logan was nervous, recalling "I was one of twenty-two more or less faculty members who had been investigated by the FBI," but his latest sparring partner, Merze Tate, too, was alarmed, telling him, "'You are one of those that the President was talking about,'" referring to the afflicted Mordecai Johnson. "I laughed and laughed so uproariously that Merze said: 'This is serious.'" His response? "I laughed some more,"[60] possibly the mirth generated by anxiety. He was not grinning when in November 1952 "FBI agents came to see me at Howard. Someone said I [might] be able to give information about Dr. [James] Jackson," Howard alumnus from Virginia, "one of the indicted Communists in flight," on the lam.[61]

Likewise, what was happening to Nobel Laureate and former Howardite, Ralph Bunche, was hardly humorous. Though they had clashed, Logan made the pilgrimage to the U.N. and found that his friend "seemed a bit depressed...." One of his colleagues, U.S. national, Jack Harris, had been "suspended from the U.N. for invoking the Fifth Amendment," prohibition against self-incrimination, and Bunche had reason to believe that he would be trapped similarly. "'The hysteria has nullified the Fifth Amendment,'"[62] was his sour message to Logan who replied, "I am more afraid about civil liberties than I am about civil rights"[63]—a wise summary reflect-

---

58. Entry, 4 May 1952, Box 5.
59. Entry, 1 May 1952, Box 5.
60. Entry, 16 December 1952, Box 5.
61. Entry, 9 November 1952, Box 5.
62. Entry, 16 December 1952, Box 5.
63. Entry, 16 December 1952, Box 5.

ing the circumscribing of political association as certain more formal rights were allowed.

The FBI was outraged that in 1935 Bunche—supposedly—had "participated in a student strike against war [at] Howard University" that was "held in opposition to the wishes of university authorities...." In February 1936, "Bunche spoke at a meeting of the Local Professions Scottsboro Committee," known to be tied to Communists.[64] Yes, he was a candidate for vice president on an anticommunist ticket on behalf of the American Federation of Teachers in 1940 but, suspiciously, he was removed when the "Communist faction contested his standing as bona fide union member...." And, yes, his opponent was the recognized Red, Doxey Wilkerson. But actually, J. Edgar Hoover was told, Bunche was identified as a Communist while at Howard and then, was placed at the United Nations by Alger Hiss, convicted of maintaining suspect ties to Communists. Viewed with suspicion was the role of Bunche and his allies playing a role in formulating regulations concerning investigations of U.S. citizens at the United Nations—which allegedly led to a dearth of scrutiny of Dr. Bunche.[65] Also in his FBI file was the tidbit that in 1949 when Hiss was under attack, Bunche was "prepared to vouch" for him, a man he was said to have met in 1944.[66] Hoover was also informed that Bunche was "'susceptible to flattery and [was] a self seeking ego maniac,'"[67] making him similarly susceptible—in their perfervid imagination—to being recruited by a U.S. foe.

Perhaps not accidentally, as this controversy was unfolding in 1953, the FBI chose to highlight a news report from 1948 detailing a so-called Communist "'underground'" in Washington in the 1930s that was said to include Hiss,[68] hence implicating Bunche. Bunche's tenure at Howard repeatedly was used to raise suspicions about him. Hoover himself was told that in December 1943 that Bunche was "'one of the numerous members of the faculty of Howard University who signed a telegram of 'greetings and congratulations'" saluting a wounded veteran of the Abraham Lincoln Brigade, the U.S. nationals, often recruited by Communists, who fought on behalf of Republican Spain.[69]

---

64. D.M. Ladd to J. Edgar Hoover, 10 February 1953, Box 1, *Ralph Bunche FBI File, Schomburg Center-New York Public Library. 949*
65. D.M. Ladd to J. Edgar Hoover, 24 March 1953, Box 1, *Ralph Bunche FBI File.*
66. *Washington News,* 7 June 1949 and Report, 19 March 1953, Box 1.
67. D.M. Ladd to J. Edgar Hoover, no date, Box 1.
68. Report from FBI-New York City, 27 February 1953, Box 1.
69. Special Agent to J. Edgar Hoover, 4 February 1953, Box 1.

Recalled was the intense interrogation of Bunche by the FBI in March 1942 on the cusp of leapfrogging to working for the federal government where he detailed his past ties to the National Negro Congress, the Council on African Affairs, and other entities now viewed banefully as little more than "Communist fronts." He happily recalled his disputes with Communists, e.g., when in 1940 he ran for Vice President of the American Federation of Teachers over the objection of left-wing Howardites: "in disgust," he said with relief, "I withdrew from Local 440 and have not held membership in the American Federation of Teachers" since. Dissatisfied, his interrogators reminded him of a 1935 article from the Communist sponsored journal *New Masses* that assailed Howard but, his sanctimonious response was that "a few of us" were "falsely labeled the '[Abram] Harris School of Marxists.'"[70] Also used against him was yet another interrogation, this of April 1943 where he was on leave as an administrator at Howard—now seen as a den of subversives—though working for the government.[71]

Yet despite this flagellating of the Nobel Laureate, he retained advantages. In his home state of California, the State Senate had concluded that the "overwhelming majority of our Negro people have shown a far greater tendency to follow the magnificent example" of Bunche—as opposed to the oft flayed Robeson.[72]

However, the FBI found it hard to swallow what a Detroit informant had told them, i.e., Bunche was not "indebted" to the Communist Party, but "may be indebted" to Howardites "who particularly during World War II were used by the Communist Party" since "it was widely known that during World War II some Communist Party fronts were organized at the University...."[73] This apparent absence of debt to Communists was viewed with skepticism even though part of his FBI file was a lengthy denunciation of him—precisely by the Black Communist writer, John Pittman. Bunche was "unquestionably a man of great abilities," he said, but "the fact that his abilities could find outlet only in service to the oppressors of his people and the enemies of world peace and progress—this is an unforgivable and monstrous crime of U.S. imperialistic white chauvinism. This crime that deprived the Negro people of a leader and left among them a servant of their oppressors."[74]

---

70. FBI Report of 16 March 1953 including Transcript of 26 March 1942 Interrogation, Box 1.
71. Transcript, 16 April 1943, Box 1.
72. Report from State Senate, 20 February 1953, Box 1.
73. Report, 25 February 1953, Box 1.
74. *Daily Worker*, 5 December 1950, Box 1.

But Pittman's scorching words were reminiscent of the old joke about a cop bludgeoning an apparent picketer, with the latter screaming, "Stop! I'm an anticommunist" with the withering response being, "I don't care what kind of Communist you are, you will continue to be beaten."

This was the hysteria that gripped the U.S. in the early years of the Eisenhower era. And even the formal retreat from Jim Crow signaled by the high court deeming this noxious poison unconstitutional as of 17 May 1954 did not erode altogether this climate of fear.

Chapter *12*

Jim Crow's Reluctant Retreat, 1952-1955

The District was the "camel's nose in the tent," i.e., this city—the nation's front-yard—was under relentless pressure to desegregate as a result of Cold War pressures, but as this was occurring it became difficult to keep the entire animal of antiracism corralled exclusively in Washington. The "Thompson" case of 1953 ("District of Columbia v. Thompson," 346 US 100) desegregating public accommodations in the District prefigured the Civil Rights Act of 1964 and, to a degree, the 1954 high court decisions mandating public school desegregation. Unleashed was a process that like falling dominoes reached neighboring Maryland and Virginia, then southward into the heart of Dixie. This in turn generated stormy anti-Washington maneuvers, metastasizing into a revolt against "liberals" perceived as being the force most in favor of desegregation and much of what they were thought to symbolize, e.g., domestic spending that happened to uplift Negroes, which responsively strengthened the right-wing of both major political parties.

Of concern to anticommunists, inter alia, was the "unanimous" resolution passed under the direction of doyenne, Mary Church Terrell, which "recognize[d] our debt of gratitude to the...D.C. Chapter of the National Lawyers Guild...[including] Joseph Forer, Chairman, Judge James A. Cobb...the late Charles H. Houston," et.al., "for the devoted and brilliant legal leadership given to the District of Columbia in bringing the Act of 1872 and 1873 back to active life...."[1] The NLG was then being flayed as little more than a "Communist front" in one precinct in the District, while in another it was being hailed. Something had to give.

---

1. Minutes, 28 May 1951, Box 3, MS 404.

Unavoidably, the intellectual and political candlepower at Howard was essential to this elongated process, even with the expiration of Charles H. Houston. In September 1953 Rayford Logan and his colleague in the History Department, John Hope Franklin, were aboard a train northward to consult with the NAACP. Their mission? "To give the advice of historians in the preparation of the briefs for the reargument [sic] of the cases in the school segregation cases," speaking of what eventuated on 17 May 1954 in *Brown v. Board of Education*. They resided at the Algonquin Hotel, where Logan was pleased to spot Ethel Waters, actor and singer. Thurgood Marshall presided at the session he attended, taking place at the office of the Newspaper Guild and Logan was impressed: "tall, handsome, cool." Fellow historian, Howard Beale, was also present as was prominent Negro attorney, William Coleman. Historian C. Vann Woodward presented a paper prepared with Franklin and Logan unimpressed: it "seemed too inclined to stress the economic factors" in the 1890s turn in the high court toward ratifying Jim Crow.[2]

Logan's concern set aside, he and other liberals should have contemplated the point that those accustomed to residing in a nation of white supremacy, grounded in enslavement of Africans, then Jim Crow, found it difficult to accept—or even imagine—an alternative.

As the "Thompson" case was on the verge of decision a supporter of Senator Olin Johnston of the Palmetto State was enraged. He congratulated the legislator on his opposition to "home rule" in the District since this "would really mean Negro rule and assault and rape and murder of white girls by Negroes. It happens every 24 hours in D.C.," he cried, to the point that the local press—especially the *Washington Post*—"refuses to print the horrible [details]…in the interests of 'racial harmony'"! Attached was a clipping of an article reporting "man held in attack on two women…charges were filed against Oliver H. Fooks, Jr, colored…."[3]

Senator Francis Case of South Dakota passed on to the White House a likeminded screed from the Capitol Hill S.E. Association, a grouping of homeowners and residents, who sounded an alarm since the "population of the colored race is growing daily," as they continued to "consider…Washington the Promise Land" and, thus,

---

2. Entry, 12 September 1953, Box 9, *Rayford Logan Diary*.
3. Letter to Senator Johnston, 14 February 1953, Box 35, *Olin Johnston Papers*. See also Gregory M. Borchardt, "Making D.C. Democracy's Capital: Local Activism, the 'Federal State' and the Struggle for Civil Rights in Washington, D.C.," Ph.D. dissertation, George Washington University, 2013.

"start trouble" upon arrival. "Enlarging the police force" was a remedy proposed and avoiding by all means "creating conditions that force white taxpayers to leave the city." In fact, the proposer, John McCarran, added further, "if segregation is abolished elsewhere, it should be kept here"—the precise reversal of what was then occurring. "Too many important people live here," he cried, "sent from other governments," referring to Capitol Hill not least; thus "keep the hordes of Negro people" from "rushing into Washington," adding pointedly, "if northern agitators sent to stir up the Washington negroes can be eliminated, it will help"[4]—leaving the means of elimination unclear. The local press reported that these residents "went on record in opposition to any 'forced' racial integration" and furthermore objected shrilly to allotting "the District a non-voting delegate in Congress," which then took decades to arrive.[5]

Henry C. Hallam, Secretary of the Chevy Chase Citizens Association, residing in a tony Maryland suburb, also was among those "opposing home rule legislation for the District of Columbia," along with his "more than 3,300 members."[6]

Nineteen fifty-four and the epochal judicial opinion seeking to invalidate Jim Crow in education should also be seen, retrospectively, as the opening shot in a counter-revolution against the idea of racial equality. That was the import of the raw remarks from Therman Lloyd of Arlington, Virginia who in 1955 warned ominously, "Can you afford to let your young daughter or son associate constantly with boys or girls of different color with the risk of social and emotional conflict...."? He warned unpropitiously of an impending "'block busting' invasion of white neighborhoods...an invasion of District Negroes which a local Negro leader has predicted will occur"; this could not stand, he bellowed, since "Negroes are not on the same intellectual and achievement level as whites," i.e., "integration will mean the lowering of school standards."[7]

Arlington, a former center of African enslavement and Jim Crow did not adjust easily to the promised new order. The Buckingham building there, provided housing for CIA secretaries, clerks, and the like from close by Langley, and though there was stiff competition,

---

4. John McCarran to Senator Case, 10 January 1953, Box 239, WHCF, OF 71, *Eisenhower Presidential Library*.
5. *Washington Times-Herald*, 13 March 1953.
6. Henry C. Hallam to Tom Steed, 29 March 1955, Box 8, *Tom Steed Papers, University of Oklahoma-Norman*.
7. Therman Lloyd to Dear Neighbor, 1 November 1955, Box 3, *James Stockard Papers, George Washington University*.

one scholar assesses this intelligence hideaway as "one of the most vicious local bastions of segregated whites-only housing...."[8]

Frenzied irrationality about the fruits of desegregation—often viewed through a blurry sexualized lens—was occurring in the context of rapidly changing norms of intimacy. As Lloyd was bleating about the purported dangers to Euro-American girls brought by desegregation, police authorities and their supervisors in the District were considering making "perversion" a priority for arrests. "Perversion is a peculiar psychological problem that is little understood by most persons," said an amateur social scientist. "The average policemen feels somewhat ill at ease and handicapped in his ability to deal with it," was the assurance to the Board of Commissioners, the ostensible power in the District beyond Capitol Hill and the White House. Barely containing revulsion, the police railed against "the deviate practices of the pervert...." While detaining those involved in adult consensual activity, the authorities rushed to recommend "the creation of an Intelligence Unit in the [Police] Department," guaranteeing more Red hunting and hurried to reassure that "organized crime does not exist in the District to the extent it does in some other large cities,"[9] likely a surprise to the notorious "Foggy Bottom Gang."[10]

This attitude, mirrored by the FBI, served as a rationale for focusing so intently on hunting Reds. Earlier, another House committee was flabbergasted by the "'shocking enormity'" of organized crime in the District, with crooks leading a "'charmed existence'" due to the "'ineptness'" of police. Breathing sighs of relief as their apparent non-existence was announced were such gangsters as "Jewboy" Dietz and the "Pickle King" and Alfred "Puddinhead" Jones.[11]

McCarran's approach, quite consistent with past practice, was inconsistent with the new line signaled by the Thompson case and the opening era of desegregation. However, this disjuncture between past and present was bound to create turbulence, quickly highlighted by the vigilant Negro press who berated a local hotel for refusing to house baseball star, Orestes "Minnie" Minoso of the Chicago White

8. Andrew Friedman, *Covert Capital*, 182.

9. "The Metropolitan Police Survey for the Board of Commissioners of the District of Columbia," 1955, Box 8, *Tom Steed Papers, University of Oklahoma-Norman*.

10. Leo Warring, *The Foggy Bottom Gang: The Story of the Warring Brothers of Washington, D.C.*, Cleveland: Parafine Press, 2020.

11. Leo Warring, *The Foggy Bottom Gang: The Story of the Warring Brothers of Washington, D.C.* , Cleveland: Parafine, 2020, 156, 162.

Sox, who happened to be of Afro-Cuban descent, meaning that it amounted to a diplomatic incident besides.[12] Those described as "race artists," meaning African American musicians and entertainers, were—said the *Courier*—"sent to separate doors," apparently at the behest of the National Broadcasting Corporation, NBC.[13]

Looking back, it is astonishing to consider the lengths to which the law ordered apartheid nationally and, particularly within the District, where numerous foreign legations were present—with their number growing—potentially compromising U.S. global policy. This bespeaks the deep roots of this system of iniquity, making it difficult to upend. Carl Bernstein, a "red diaper baby," recalled woefully this unlamented era: the "only places downtown where Negroes knew they could sit down to eat were the railroad station and the government cafeterias," but even there, his left-wing parents were "constantly challenging food-service managers who took it upon themselves to designate separate seating areas for blacks. Except for the government buildings, there were few places where colored people were permitted to go to the bathroom." Strikingly, "the only integrated theater in town," he says, was the "Gayety Burlesque House on Ninth Street."[14]

By 1952, Hecht's surrendered and allowed Negro patronage.[15] The slog continued, however, for even then, according to Annie Stein, "of all the hotels...only the Statler has the reputation of being fully non-discriminatory"—other than Negro hotels—while "the regular first run [movie] houses do not admit Negroes" at all.[16]

There were conflicting trends. Local activists took advantage of the proximity of Vijaya Laskhmi Pandit, the ambassador of India to the U.S., to complain to her when Hecht's refused to serve "a lady from India," though the waitress in this incident was "very indignant as the compulsion she is under to refuse to serve persons of her own race and nationality" was infuriating. So moved, the manager "then personally served the lady...."[17] Although, said Stein, "fully a third of the customers of the store are colored and we estimate 8 ½ million dollars was spent by Negroes at Hecht's last year,"[18] she continued to be "surprised that we could keep out only about half

---

12. *Pittsburgh Courier*, 21 June 1952.

13. *Pittsburgh Courier*, 17 May 1952.

14. Carl Bernstein, *Loyalties*, 95, 93

15. Press Release, 19 January 1952, Box 2, MS 404.

16. Annie Stein to Dianne Katz, 6 November 1951, Box 2, MS 404.

17. Annie Stein to Ambassador Pandit, 25 July 1951, Box 2, MS 404.

18. Annie Stein to Dick Seidman, Silver Spring, 25 July 1951, Box 2, MS 404.

of the colored customers," willing to be inflicted with third-class status, a disturbing signal.[19] Similarly troubling was a letter sent to the Hecht family in Baltimore, detailing that a "very serious result of the humiliation and injustice which your store has perpetrated upon my group here is that it is likely to cause colored people all over the country to hate the Jewish people and regard them as their bitter enemies...."[20]

This lingering and blatant form of racist discrimination was proliferating and was mirrored widely in the schools. It was also the Federation of Civic Associations and their Capitol Hill affiliate, which demanded that the FBI investigate the purported "subversive" influence delivered by school desegregation.[21]

By mid-1953 and despite the implication of the Thompson case, Negroes were disallowed from driving buses in the District or working as streetcar motormen; one periodical observed that there was "fear of 'serious' consequences among...white workers—including protests, mass resignations, and possibly [an] organized strike"; their obstruction meant "white drivers being paid overtime...that if the company used the whole labor market it would reduce its overtime and wouldn't need a fare increase...." This flagrant abuse was occurring even as other cities, including Los Angeles, San Francisco, Indianapolis, Chicago, Boston, Detroit, Buffalo, New York City, Syracuse, Cleveland, Toledo, Tulsa, Philadelphia—and others—were pursuing a different course. Nonetheless, J. Godfrey Butler, Capital Transit's director of personnel, predicted that at least 200 of the company's 2,300 drivers and motormen would quit if Negroes were hired,[22] solidifying the wider point that per its founding, the District remained a captive of Dixie. At the same time even Baltimore, routinely the District's twin in perpetuating misdeeds, had begun hiring Negro drivers with hardly any upset.[23]

The District was different. Capital Transit refused to hire Negro drivers or streetcar operators until 1955 although they were short of these workers for the longest time. They were mirroring the amusement park in Glen Echo, Maryland which only admitted Negro patrons under enormous pressure, leaving them unamused. Negro

---

19. Annie Stein to James Wesley, 25 July 1951, Box 2, MS 404.
20. Undated Letter to Samuel Hecht, Box 3, MS 404.
21. *Washington Star*, 30 July 1954.
22. *Washington Daily News*, 27 August 1953. See also Frederick W. Gooding, Jr., "American Dream Deferred: Black Federal Workers in Washington, D.C., 1941-1981," Ph.D. dissertation, Georgetown University, 2013.
23. *Washington Times-Herald*, 29 December 1953.

drivers were then unallowed to use toilets there after dropping off paying customers.[24]

The origin of the District involved a geographic concession to the slavocracy, and it was the center of power as well, meaning that slippage or even concessions could be fatal. The other center of power about 200 miles away—which contained Wall Street—had similar patterns of Jim Crow, to a degree. The fire department in Gotham in the early 1950s, like the District, had Negro firemen serving in separate companies and an attempt to assign these second class firefighters to understaffed "white companies" was resisted fiercely.[25]

They were not alone. By November 1952 Clarence Mitchell of the NAACP was complaining to Maurice Tobin, Secretary of Labor, about "possible work stopping at the Washington Terminal" with "national implications" since the "Brotherhood of Railway Carmen has a constitutional requirement that colored persons must join separate locals under the jurisdiction of the nearest white local." Predictably, Negro workers were furious.[26]

While Washington was wrestling—often unsuccessfully—with desegregation, reverberations abroad continued to resonate. Rayford Logan noticed that Owen Dodson and his corps of Howard thespians had just left Munich where they found that "some Germans do not like the Germans who work for Americans," a nation stained by apartheid.[27] Then he heard from Eunice Lyon, a former student at Howard then in Nuremberg; this Bison told him that at that moment in Japan, U.S. viceroy, General Douglas MacArthur barred "colored WACs [Women's Army Corps] because 'colored women are immoral.'"[28] In nearby Britain, Logan was distressed to find unwanted hints of home: he found it "surprising how frequently the word nigger appears in English whodunits. Agatha Christie seems to take particular delight in using it," redolent it was thought of the spreading malignancy of U.S. culture.[29]

In short, Washington would have difficulty implementing the new line of desegregation and, ostensibly, antiracism when it had spent decades creating an infrastructure for the opposite.

---

24. *Washington Post*, 21 February 2021.
25. Nelson Jackson, Evaluation of the District Urban League, 15 December 1953, Box I: B30, *National Urban League Papers*.
26. Clarence Mitchell to Maurice Tobin, 25 November 1952, Box IX: 196, *NAACP Papers*.
27. Entry, 17 December 1952, Box 5, *Rayford Logan Diary*.
28. Entry, 5 April 1952, Box 5.
29. Entry, 1 May 1952, Box 5.

This basic insight had not dawned altogether on Logan and his view was representative of an emerging trend among Black Intellectuals, who sought to cooperate with U.S. imperialism abroad, while wresting antiracism concessions at home. This was particularly objectionable coming from him since—seemingly—he was more attuned to global trends.[30] In Washington, Logan had rare access to foreign policymakers: in October 1952 he was hobnobbing at a "cocktail party at the home of M. Van Lalthem, First Secretary of the French embassy at his home, 2958 Northampton Street N.W." and "had an opportunity to express some of my views…"[31]

Logan was willing to play ball with the powerbrokers in Washington. Thus, by January 1953, he was conversing with Ruth Sloan at the State Department who wanted him to tour Africa on behalf of the U.S. She did not want him to lecture on the U.S. Negro, possibly fearful of what he might say, but "on general American problems"; she "even said that she was going to arrange for me to go to the Belgian Congo. If I were able to speak Portuguese she would try to arrange for me to go to Angola,"[32] ancestral home of countless African Americans, unbeknownst to most.

There was considerable back and forth about this proposed trip since Logan was suspect because of past ties to the likes of Wilkerson and Du Bois—yet Washington needed him to press the flesh in Africa. By late June 1953, he was still unsure if he could get a passport: "people are beginning to ask in West Africa why I have not arrived," he said, while "African students at Howard are wondering why I have not left…."[33] A flustered Logan ambled to Capitol Hill to discuss this matter with Congressman Adam Clayton Powell who told him that someone from the hilltop told congressional watchdogs that "'Bunche, [Alain] Locke, Logan, Mordecai Johnson,'" and "'someone else,'" perhaps Frazier, "'needed to be watched.'" Logan suspected that Eugene Holmes, thought to be operating as a stoolpigeon, was the culprit.[34]

Nevertheless, by July 1953 Logan was in Dakar consorting with various bigwigs and feeling "greatly saddened by the sight of a company of Senegalese soldiers waiting to board the boat to go on to Indo-China. How many of them will never come home?"[35] Good question. However, he should have known that they were warring

---

30. Entry, 17 May 1952, Box 5.
31. Entry, 12 October 1952, Box 5.
32. Entry, 10 July 1953, Box 5.
33. Entry, 26 June 1953, Box 5.
34. Entry, 30 June 1953, Box 5.
35. Entry, 22 July 1953, Box 9.

in the name of anticommunism, a creed that he questioned rarely. Indeed, Logan was aflutter while in Dakar about a presumed surge of Communists.[36]

Moreover, apparently he did not absorb what he had read; soon he was giving lectures in French—in France—stressing the "importance of Africa in the fight against the Soviet Union," a hegemonic Negro stance. Yet he remained critical of Walter White's NAACP, notably his "egocentrism and his determination that the NAACP shall be the spokesman for Negroes everywhere"—which, as then constituted, would have been catastrophic. Logan was asked "what would be the most effective action in France on behalf of American Negroes," and he had enough sense to acknowledge that a "careful record is kept at the [U.S.] Embassy of public opinion,"[37] implying the registering of protest there, pointing to this legation and displaying a remaining iota of good sense.

Logan, speaking to French audiences, was ensnarled in a spaghetti bowl of contradictions. "Questions were asked," he conceded, "about the degree of interest of American Negroes in Africa"—he did not note the undermining of Robeson's Council on African Affairs in determining this result, an unfortunate result in which he was not inactive. There was "not so much as there ought to be," he admitted about the flagging degree of interest, "but [was] increasing" in that there was "great interest in Seretse Khama" of the nation that became Botswana "and in Gold Coast [Ghana] and Nigeria...." With hope he stressed, "I pointed out that it is possible to bring together nearly every day in Paris a Pan-African Congress with a larger number of participants than we had during the best days of the 1920s"; to his credit, he added helpfully that it was "vitally important to keep up contacts between American Negroes and other Negroes...." For example, in the French colony that was Madagascar, recent site of a stunning massacre of tens of thousands of Africans, it was necessary to generate global condemnation, especially since a "minority of Frenchmen [were] seeking aid from the Union of South Africa in spreading its racist ideas...[a] considerable number of Dutchmen from Indonesia have settled there" and "Frenchmen from Indo-China are arriving in increased numbers...." Unhelpfully, Logan did not add that his own anticommunism was consistent with that of those he had scorned, thereby bolstering them.[38]

---

36. Entry, 29 July 1953, Box 9.
37. Entry, 27 May 1952, Box 5.
38. Entry, 29 May 1952, Box 5. Comment regarding "a Pan-African Congress..." underlined in original.

Instead, he repeated—as if it were a magical incantation—the motto of Negro liberals of that era: "my old cliché 'the white man's distress is the black man's gain'" was applicable; "in brief the Cold War is weakening the colonial powers about as much as the two world wars."[39] He did not seem to notice that this very same Cold War involved the defenestration of Africans bent on redistributing the wealth, these leaders' concern being the order of the day, thereby preparing the path for what Kwame Nkrumah termed "Neo-Colonialism."[40]

Logan was quite familiar with the events in Africa that led to Nkrumah's illuminating conclusions. By August 1953, he was resting comfortably in the "[U.S.] embassy compound" in Monrovia, Liberia. He managed to snag an audience with President William Tubman and provided a preview of one of his soon to be published books on late 19th century U.S. history. As so often happened, it was easier to be insightful in discussing the faraway past as opposed to the complicated present. Perceptively, Logan told the chief executive, "the failure of Reconstruction helped to 'justify' the conquest of Africa and reciprocally the necessity of the conquest of Africa had served to justify the second-class citizenship of American Negroes. But now," he continued, "the improved condition of the Negro in the U.S. had served somewhat to change the attitude of Americans toward Negroes in the U.S. and reciprocally the progress that Liberia is making is helping to improve attitudes toward Negroes in the U.S." While in Monrovia he also met with Colonel Oscar Randall, who he knew from M Street High School in Washington—he was "2 years behind me" and now was "commanding a U.S. Military Mission to train the Liberian Frontier Force," useful in suppressing indigenous revolt against the so-called "Americo-Liberian" elite who in the early 19th century had invaded and appropriated land, not unlike their North American sponsors. Logan also found time to confer with James Duncan, a graduate of the Massachusetts Institute of Technology and, he opined, the "ablest man in the government, after President Tubman"; like many on the continent, he was "most critical of racial discrimination in the United States, especially in the nation's capital...."[41] It would have been well if this "Americo-Liberian" elite had focused as intently on the discrepancies between themselves and the indigenous masses in their nation.

---

39. Entry, 1 June 1952, Box 5.
40. Kwame Nkrumah, *Neo-Colonialism: The Last Stage of Imperialism*, London: Heinemann, 1968.
41. Entry, 3 August 1953, Box 9.

Later Logan conferred with Lagos' mayor who told him that "the inhabitants of Freetown, Sierra Leone, descendants of free slaves, consider themselves superior to the people in the hinterland. They are therefore opposed to a legislature elected on the basis of numbers,"[42] seeding future conflicts, as occurred destructively in Liberia.

By November 1954, Tubman was to be found at the hilltop, addressing students, faculty, and staff as Liberia with its long-term collaboration with U.S. Negroes materializing as a model for the continent as a whole.[43] Liberia was quite familiar with Howard. The spouse of Charles D.B. King, Monrovia's chief envoy in Washington in the mid-20th century, had arrived in the District in 1902 to attend Howard, receiving her degree in 1906—after previously attending Morgan State University in Baltimore.[44]

Logan's lengthy government subsidized journey to the hard-pressed continent was not unique as Howardites increasingly were enlisted in the defense of U.S. imperialism, as opposed to the wholly polecat status they had been enduring. By 1953, Professor Frank Snowden had returned from what was described as a "26,000...mile trek" sponsored, once more, by the State Department. This resident of 1227 Girard Street N.E.[45] was born in York County, Virginia and had a modicum of credibility since his father had served with the Department of War, while stationed in the District.[46]

However, Mr. Duncan should have been familiar with apartheid praxis since it was part of the landscape in Liberia. Logan visited Liberia's Firestone "plantation," a gigantic 80,000 acres, featuring 175 U.S. and European nationals lording over 25,000 Africans; "separate schools for whites and Negroes" was de rigeur, a taste of home. Damningly, Logan "observed that American Negroes would probably take the same position...as have white parents here," i.e., endorsing apartheid schools. As if commenting mundanely on the weather, he noted in passing, "there was a pretty bloody strike some time ago; the Liberian Frontier Forces" of Colonel Randall of Washington, D.C. "put it down...." It seemed that Liberia was crawling with Howardites, including Bernard Coleman, leader of the Booker T. Washington Institute there, who was living the high life in neo-colonial fashion: "as he said he never lived so good in the U.S.: three

---

42. Entry, 17 July 1954, Box 6.
43. *The Hilltop*, 20 November 1954.
44. *Washington Post*, 11 December 1950.
45. *The Hilltop*, 20 November 1954.
46. *The Hilltop*, 13 May 1949.

servants and making a good living," residing in a "modern home" all while preaching the Tuskegee gospel of "agricultural and industrial training...."[47]

Briefly taking his head out of the clouds, Logan acknowledged that "many of the Liberians...resent the fact that Americans (including American Negroes) receive higher salaries than they do...." Besides, "American colored girls practically never date Liberian boys, but almost always go out with Europeans," yet another perceived slight. "Some of them were actually engaged," as the class status of U.S. Negroes provided a kind of social promotion. "Whether it was love or whether the Europeans wanted to marry the colored girl in order to facilitate entry into the U.S.," was a question he was unable to answer, though he well knew—bitterly—that "many Negroes still place a premium on a white face...." Despite their elevated status in Monrovia, "no one with Foreign Service Officer rank at the American Embassy [there] is colored..." The Negro ambassador there, Edward Dudley, "was quite proud of the fact that all of his FSO [Foreign Service Officer] staff is white...."[48]

Possibly the jarring experience of Liberia led him to muse about arriving in neighboring Ivory Coast that "even here I imagine that the Africans could line up and butcher most of the European population...."[49]

More pleasantly, in Lagos, Nigeria he bumped into indigenous officials with "Colored American" spouses, a change from Liberia and also various Howardites serving in high-level posts. Yet here too he was wracked with anxiety about the possibility of Communist strength, especially in unions. And in response, he provided a local leader the address of Irving Brown, notorious U.S. intelligence official, with the aim of him providing "typewriters, mimeographing machines, paper, larger office space" and the like.[50]

Logan was traveling as an informal State Department envoy though it was unclear if he shared details of his meeting with novelist Richard Wright in Lisbon. He "feels if he ever sets foot on American soil he will be instantly investigated by the FBI"; the writer also gave him a preview of a book he planned on Ghana while mentioning juicy details,[51] which would be real fodder for U.S. intelligence. "I have spent some time organizing in my mind my report to the State

---

47. Entry, 4 August 1953, Box 9.
48. Entry, 7 August 1953, Box 9.
49. Entry, August 1953, Box 9.
50. Entry, 24 August 1953, Box 9.
51. Entry, 27 August 1953, Box 9.

Department,"[52] said Logan of a briefing that—hopefully—was edited severely. Perhaps not, since effusively a State Department bureaucrat cackled "'we certainly got our money's worth out of the trip.'"[53]

Perhaps not since upon arrival back home, Logan reported to the State Department, where the leading official, Ruth Sloan was—he said—"unduly disturbed about the reactions of the British to the fact that Richard Wright was staying at the home of Gene Sawyer in Accra," the latter being a U.S. official; "it might hurt Gene in his career," clucked Logan sympathetically. "Ruth Sloan is going to arrange for me to talk with some of the people in the State Department" about this and other sensitive issues.[54]

It seemed that Logan was in the vanguard of carving out a new role for Negroes: no longer to be treated like the skunk at the garden party but as a valuable intermediary in Africa, then rebelling against the cruel restraint of European imperialism—thus allowing Washington to appear to be the reasonable alternative to the status quo. Soon Logan was to be found at fashionable events, turning up at the well-appointed home of Archie Campbell at 5702 Warwick Place in voguish Bethesda, alongside his fellow Bison, Frank Snowden. Before that he was conferring at the Haitian embassy. "There has been a change in Washington," he said astutely—though he was referring not to his altered role but the reality "most of the guests are now Republicans" at the most important social gatherings. He had scribbled a hefty 250 pages during his Africa junket and did not hesitate to share insight with his sponsors.[55]

By October 1953, arriving at Howard was "Mr. McCann" of the CIA. He was "especially interested in communism in Africa," but Logan sought to divert him to concern about "Mohammedanism," which he saw as a "greater danger than Communism"; actually, he stressed the "greatest danger lies in a possible uniting of the forces of communism and Mohammedanism."[56] Danger to whom was the query unposed.

It is possible that Logan's labor on behalf of U.S. imperialism, may have helped the case of the beleaguered Ralph Bunche, still under fire from the FBI because of his left-wing dalliances at Howard in the 1930s. In November 1952, Senator Herbert O'Connor of Maryland who had reason to scrutinize the District, emphasized the "need for eliminating from the United Nations Secretariat any or all American citizens of known Communist affiliation," while adding cryptically: "our efforts to date have produced results,"[57] a shrouded reference to the former Howard professor—who managed to hang on to his plum post.

By January 1953, Logan was on a train heading south from Philadelphia accompanied by fellow Howard man, William Stuart Nelson. "He (and obviously President [Mordecai] Johnson) is very much concerned about congressional investigation of alleged subversion or disloyalty at Howard." Logan was unsparing: "I told him that current members of the Communist Party would have to go," music to multiple ears on Capitol Hill. Logan was told, "Howard would be investigated first in order to provide protection for other schools,"[58] since the hilltop was seen as most vulnerable to Red penetration and administering a beating there would be sufficient to keep other campuses in line.

As Logan's experience in Monrovia suggested, U.S. Negroes were more than willing to collaborate with those involved in the plunder of Africa and it would be sectarianism to exclude them, especially when they were willing to exhibit anticommunist bona fides.

However, it was one thing to subsidize a generally impecunious Howard teacher on an extended junket in Africa, it was quite another matter to countenance a former Howardite with access to the halls of power in Turtle Bay. Assuredly, this was the view of Archibald Roosevelt, son of the early 20th century president, who objected to Bunche receiving an award from the Theodore Roosevelt Memorial Association based on his "'past record of close affiliation with Communism.'"[59] The objecting Roosevelt wondered why not yank the award away from Bunche and give it to the infamous Negro conservative, George Schuyler?[60] Agreeing generally was a woman in Oslo who heard his remarks there. She was then in Iran, in the midst of enduring a U.S. backed regime change but still "fighting mad," said an FBI agent, "at the way [Bunche] denounced the U.S." previously.[61]

---

57. Senator Herbert O'Connor to George McCullough, 12 November 1952, MDMS #4366, *University of Maryland-College Park*. See also Susan Brinson, *The Red Scare, Politics and the Federal Communications Commission, 1941-1960*, Westport: Praeger, 2004.

58. Entry, 22 January 1953, Box 5.

59. *Washington Daily News*, 26 October 1954, Box 1, *Ralph Bunche FBI File*.

60. Archibald Roosevelt to Oscar Straus, circa 1954, Box 1.

61. Special Agent-New Haven to J. Edgar Hoover, 23 June 1954, Box 1.

The objecting Roosevelt and others felt that Bunche's tenure on the hilltop was itself an ineradicable stain. "Dear Foster," was his message to hawkish Secretary of State, John Foster Dulles, as he railed and flailed against Bunche. The "training of [this] man in the 'hard boiled' school of Stalinism," was his embroidered description of Bunche, a man "active in the Communist movement as a professor at Howard University," a school "riddled with Communist members and sympathizers," which immeasurably "contributed largely to the Communist movement among Negroes"[62]—the final point not being inaccurate. Roosevelt's swollen rhetoric was echoed by words shared officially with J. Edgar Hoover, who was told that Howard was a "center for Communist infiltration," though extravagantly, the queer philosopher, Alain Locke was said to be "a Communist Party member...."[63] (Logan thought that the subversiveness of Locke was not necessarily political: in July 1941, he wrote, "I took to lunch at the Union Station my protégé William Willis II. He told me that Alain Locke had invited him to his apartment. Should he go? I told him flatly, NO!")[64]

Howard as a fortress of subversiveness with Bunche often at the controls was a narrative that the FBI found hard to discard. This may have been an outgrowth of Bureau leader Hoover serving on the Board of his alma mater, George Washington University,[65] placing him in a position to be aware of the unique culture of campuses, which did often attract "free thinkers" and dissidents. Veracity aside about Howard, this jaundiced view of the hilltop kept the former professor off-balance, susceptible to being flattened altogether. For four years Bunche was part of the "editorial apparatus" of *Science & Society*, a still extant academic journal initiated by Communists in the 1930s, according to the FBI. He was an official of the now beset Institute of Pacific Relations, viewed similarly as a sock-puppet for despised Reds. Apparently on the cusp of exploding in rage, an FBI official found Bunche's Communist associations "greater overall than the combined evidence [against] Alger Hiss, William Remington, Harry Dexter White and the Rosenbergs," rattling off those who ended either in prison—or executed.[66]

---

62. Archibald Roosevelt to "Dear Foster," circa 28 October 1952, Box 2, *Ralph Bunche FBI File*.
63. Special Agent-New York City to J. Edgar Hoover, 7 July 1954, Box 2.
64. Entry, 25 July 1941, Box 3, *Rayford Logan Diary*.
65. Cloyd Marvin to O.S. Hoebreckx, 5 October 1955, RG0002, Box 48, *Office of the President, George Washington University*.
66. FBI Document, no date, Box 1, *Ralph Bunche FBI File*.

Bunche was fingered as "one of the founders" of the National Negro Congress, once vibrant in the District and attended meetings of the Communist "fraction" therein in the 1930s and "allegedly was introduced as a Communist Party member...." He had the gall to have "listed Alger Hiss as a reference in connection with his U.N. employment in 1946," a damning admission it was thought. In order to exonerate himself, he violated protocol—if not law—by sending "transcripts of the Loyalty Board hearing" on himself to the influential columnists, Stewart and Joseph Alsop, Georgetown potentates both: this, too, was seen as indicative of guilt.[67]

Potentially, the FBI may have moved even more aggressively against Bunche but for realizing that he was busily cutting ties with those in the Communist orbit. This included Du Bois, who Bunche resented and refused to contribute to a "testimonial dinner" in his fellow scholar's honor 1951, when the NAACP founder was about to face trial for his peace activism; conveniently, he had yet to forget that the elderly activist had dubbed Bunche—reportedly—a "tool of the imperialists...traitor to his race...."[68]

Besides, the army of informants the FBI and allies employed in Washington, may have convinced these top gumshoes that percipience dictated that there were larger fish to reel in. One of these characters reported that in 1947—well after Bunche had left the hilltop—he infiltrated "the Students Group, a Communist organization," reputedly, "and at that time there were seven members... including himself," with "two of the members...attending Howard Law School...." They discussed "current events" and planned "distribution" of Communist literature, accompanied by "discussion of Communist activities...." But the group swiftly grew exponentially, soon having "about 18 members," including students from George Washington and College Park. Despite his high station, how worthy was it to allocate informants to bird-dog Bunche when he lived his life in the spotlight in any case? Besides, his comrades in the NAACP—and Howard (see Logan)—were all busily cutting deals with the authorities in any case, shrinking whatever subversive mettle they may have had.[69]

---

67. A.H. Belmont to R.R. Roach, 2 November 1954, Box 1.
68. Report, 7 October 1953, Box 2.
69. Report, 7 July 1954, Box 2. See also "Investigation of Communist Activities in the Baltimore Area-Part 1, Hearing Before the Committee on Un-American Activities. House of Representatives. 83rd Congress, Second Session, May 18, 1954. Committee on Un-American Activities," Washington, D.C.: GPO, 1954, *University of Maryland-College Park.*

In coming years when "Black Power" icons, e.g., Malcolm X and Congressman Adam Clayton Powell, Jr., termed Bunche an "'International Uncle Tom,'"[70] it likely vindicated the notion that leaving him in Turtle Bay to twist slowly in the wind was the "least bad" option.

Still, it was not easy to overcome the qualms of those like Roosevelt, whose anticommunist delirium was buoyed by ongoing events. Congress found it hard to ignore a continuing stream of stories. The transcript of a 1951 hearing of the Un-American Activities Committee was only published in 1954. Forebodingly, "Communism in the District of Columbia-Maryland Area" was the topic and the testimony predictably set hair on fire on Capitol Hill. By mid-1951, Mary Stalcup Markward, then 29 years old,[71] had served as an informant in a beauty shop—where the informal atmosphere often loosened tongues—and joined the Communist Party by May 1943, serving as treasurer as late as October 1949. She sang like an expert contralto pointing to Frank Brown, a Negro laundry worker as chairman; Sadie Chancey as membership secretary. Also named was Will Rosen, implicated in the Alger Hiss bombshell case, not unlike Bunche. Eugene Holmes of Howard and his spouse, Margaret, a beautician, were also seen as Communist cadre. The authorities were not placated by the evident precipitous drop in membership: from thousands in recent years to 230 at the time of her testimony. Viewed suspiciously was the existence amid the decline of a "Civil Rights Club" or cell that included Civil Rights Congress personnel, including Marie Richardson, and was designed to shape what was coming to be called the "Civil Rights Movement," which soon would upend the nation. But the same could be said of the "Frederick Douglass Club" or cell, which too incorporated a bevy of Negro members. There was a club that carried the name of then CP leader, William Z. Foster, which contained various members of American Federation of Labor unions. The Health Club included physicians and other workers. Al Underwood of the party was also viewed suspiciously since he toiled for the Yugoslav legation as a chauffeur. Markward argued that prior to Belgrade's "deviation" a few years earlier, veering away from Moscow's embrace, the Communists did not want their cadre employed by legations of the then socialist camp. The "Students Club" generally was comprised of Howard and George Washington matriculants; in fact, she said in words tailored to accelerate concern about Bunche, there were "quite a large number of members at the

---

70. Jonathan Scott Holloway, *Confronting the Veil*, 158.
71. *Washington Post*, 7 July 1951.

Howard University campus," apparently exceeding the number "at Maryland University," which in turn had close ties with the CP in Baltimore.

HUAC's chief interrogator, Courtney Owens, found it mistrustful that during the Summer of 1946 the party's major activity included anti-lynching and anti-Bilbo campaigns. "There was a tremendous parade down Pennsylvania Avenue," he said querulously "and a mass meeting at the Lincoln Memorial and a picket line around the Mutual Broadcasting Company while Bilbo was making a speech there...." Presumably, protesting a naked white supremacist was beyond the pale, chilling associational efforts of the NAACP, for example. But ears inevitably pricked up when a witness testified that the "decision of district and city committees" of the party "was to concentrate on the AF of L Building Trade Workers primarily" key to the postwar construction boom and "food workers secondarily"; heartening, it was thought, was the caveat that "in the building trades area were only partially successful...." Still, "in the laborers' field... under the leadership of Henry Thomas and other veterans," he was the then defrocked Communist who conceded that he "instinctively" followed the party line nonetheless, "a rather remarkable advance was made...."[72] There may have been audible gasp when these chilling words were uttered, as the hearing room was overflowing with spectators, indicative of local interest.[73] Likewise remarkable and bracing too was the disturbing fact that in a similar 1954 hearing five witnesses refused to testify, the downstream consequences notwithstanding.[74] By mid-1954 one could easily imagine heads bobbing in unison when a HUAC official commented caustically that the "'hard core of the Communist Party'" was sited in the District,[75] an opinion which did not bode well.

---

72. "Hearing Before the Committee on Un-American Activities [,] House of Representatives, 82nd Congress, 1st Session," 11 June 1951, "Ordered to be Printed June 23, 1954," Washington, D.C.: GPO, 1954, Vertical File-Communism, *Special Collections, Washington, D.C. Public Library.*
73. *Washington Daily News*, 11 July 1951.
74. *Washington Post*, 15 July 1954.
75. *Washington Post*, 16 July 1954.

Chapter *13*

Howard University Besieged, 1953-1956

The "Thompson" case in the District of 1953 followed by the "Brown" case of 1954, was thought to mark a rosy dawn in the centuries' long struggle of African Americans. Eleanor Holmes Norton, who was to represent the District in Congress through the 21st century, recalled the ecstasy that erupted when the latter case was decided. Her teachers were weeping openly when it was announced over the loudspeaker at her high school. There was a recognition of the widening repercussions for fresh in memories was the fact, she said, that "'we couldn't try on clothes at Hecht's department store...you couldn't go into any restaurant....'"[1]

However, a simple glance at Howard—the capstone of Negro higher education, the fortress of Negro intellectual firepower—could lead easily to a differing conclusion.

This contradictory skein is reflected in the peregrinations of Rayford Logan. Just before "Thompson" he was to be found on the campus of American University, crosstown. He was serving on a committee on behalf of an African graduate student there but, perversely, the "student had 'cracked up,'" possibly under the strain of residing in a Jim Crow society and was "confined to St. Elizabeth's Insane Asylum," where Logan found it strangely appropriate that "the examination would be at the asylum!!!"[2]

Professor Logan should have realized that this asylum violated the Dixie norm of racially segregated asylums and admitted Negro patients—though the campus was racially segregated until 1954 with the high court rulings. Negro patients also experienced generally an inferior quality of care and substandard living conditions.

---

1. *Washington Post*, 13 July 2020.
2. Entry, 26 January 1953, Box 5.

Queer patients also were subjected to biased maltreatment. Hospital attendants and nurses were exclusively Euro-American for years but contradictorily, Native Americans from federal reservations were admitted[3]—not the norm in Dixie generally, illustrating the District's purported "liberalism."

Ironically, what Logan found so unnerving about this graduate examination was the familiarity of it all. No, it was not because Howard was comparable to an "insane asylum," it was because—said Logan—the "impact of the segregated buildings was not pleasant." As was the maddening norm in such settings with Euro-Americans, "of course, the others said nothing about it"; and "as a native Washingtonian I should have been prepared but somehow I was not," for some things are never acclimating. Exacerbating the alienation, Logan saw fit that "in order to prevent any possible suggestion of favoritism on my part I questioned [him] at greater length and more searchingly than did the others...."[4]

So, in the midst of an off-putting climate infested with apartheid, a Negro professor grilled an African student. If the student had been plunged deeper into mental distress, the result would have been understandable.

This was not the sole encounter Logan had with this "insane asylum." Weeks later, William Brewer then serving as editor of the *Journal of Negro History*, was receiving "mental treatment" at St. Elizabeth's. Then Logan bumped into his colleague, William Willis, at Slowe Hall on campus who told the shocked historian that "he has been under mental therapy" and was "given to crying, thoughts of self-destruction...."[5]

No wonder so many were on edge. Enduring apartheid was deranging, especially when the hegemonic line that the creation of the U.S. was a great leap forward for humanity: did that mean those not enjoying the bounty were unworthy, even inhuman?

In the midst of this madness the FBI came on campus to pay Logan a visit. "It was not until a few days ago," he said in April 1953, "that I learned that the investigation has been under way at Howard for some time...." Tellingly, suspected Communist, Eugene Holmes, "was about to 'crack up' as a result of continued prolonged questioning by one of the congressional investigating committees." The renowned scientist, Herman Branson, who served on the faculty

---

3. Sarah A. Leavitt, *St. Elizabeth's in Washington, D.C.: Architecture of an Asylum*, Charleston: History Press, 2019, 83, 85, 87.
4. Entry, 4 February 1953, Box 5.
5. Entry, 21 March 1953, Box 5.

from 1941 to about 1968, and as a physicist and biochemist served alongside lionized Nobel Laureate, Linus Pauling, at the California Institute of Technology, was "closely connected with the Party at one time," making Logan wonder how this Negro "could have been cleared for his work at Cal Tech," since their Pasadena campus was a hotbed of military and intelligence contracting. Linguist Mercer Cook, a future U.S. ambassador, found that the FBI "had made inquiries" about him "because he had been active" in France during the German occupation "which made him a 'fascist'"—presumably any excuse would suffice to rout Negro intellectuals. "Oh well," said Logan sarcastically, "it is good to know that we have [only] one 'fascist' on the faculty," then added to his anti-Vatican profile by adding that "Mercer is doubly safe at the present time because he is a Catholic."[6]

Then just before he was to takeoff for an African junket to improve the declining image of U.S. imperialism on the continent, he was invited downtown to meet with the FBI, softening him up in case he had considered a double-cross upon landing in Dakar. He described the "post office building" where he was to be interrogated as—appropriately—"more like a prison" than "any other building in Washington." Tradition was followed, as one agent was friendly and his comrade was "stern, almost hostile." He assumed the room was "wired for sound" and proceeded accordingly. Stoutly, he denied present or past party membership. Sure, while at Harvard from 1930-1932 he attended a meeting of "Friends of the Soviet Union." And, yes, he was investigated in 1942 after representing his fraternity—Alpha Phi Alpha—at a meeting of the suspected Communist "front," the National Federation of Constitutional Liberties. "I was questioned somewhat closely about this," he said warily. Eyebrows were probably raised when he confided that there were "blank and blind spots in my memory," because a "shell explosion in World War I" left him with "'retrograde amnesia.'" He felt that the real target was President Mordecai Johnson, whose flirtations with Reds decades earlier had yet to be forgotten, followed by Charles Wesley (yet another historian), Bunche—then himself. Thus, he was questioned about having dinner with Black Communist leader, Ferdinand Smith, just returned unceremoniously to his native Jamaica, and—of course—Robeson's Council on African Affairs was a hot topic for discussion. According to his diary, this elicited a sharp rebuke from Logan: "You gentlemen must understand," he said with a reprimanding flourish, "that

---

6. Entry, 29 April 1953, Box 5.

Negroes joined a number of organizations not because of any affinity with Communism but because these organizations were fighting in defense of Negroes." He did not record the response, but it is probable that agents were hardly satisfied with an implicit defense of repugnant Reds. Then he shifted again, recalling when he spoke at a confab of the Communist led Southern Negro Youth Congress: "I came nearer being booed and hooted at New Orleans than perhaps at any other time in my life," this after he clashed in 1940 with Max Yergan—then backtracking to the depths of anti-communism—after this then Communist adopted the "party line" on the war in Europe. "Is it possible," he asked, "that those who favored war against Germany even before June 1941 are suspect?" Answer: possibly. Logan was asked about his condemnation of the Un-American Activities Committee and about his subscriptions to left-wing periodicals. "As an historian," he responded huffily but not necessarily effectively, "I considered it my duty to know what was going on...." Logan was "incensed" to be asked about the whereabouts of James Jackson, Negro Communist leader from Virginia, then a fugitive. Why did he appear at a Washington bookshop with Doxey Wilkerson? "I had invited him to contribute a chapter" to a book although he added quickly, he was "not...a personal friend...."

He departed uneasily after a harrowing 50 minutes of probing. "The colored woman operating the elevator," with the wisdom of experience, remarked "'They certainly kept you in there a long time.'" Still, fellow Washingtonian Eugene Holmes was "interrogated several times for several hours," so Logan's treatment was relatively gentle. Then it was back to campus and in the men's restroom he was asked about this encounter but then the questioner pointed to the "feet of a colleague" and "I understood I was not to say anything," as Howard was becoming an ever more fearful place, exuding the kind of pressure that could lead to a breakdown. A colleague had "turned informer" and Logan was told that Herman Branson "had given some names that he did not have to give," i.e., identifying past and present Communists and so-called "fellow travelers."

It did not take long for Logan to unburden himself by upbraiding his prime villain: his colleague, Merze Tate. She was "most abjectly intimidated" by this turn of events—as if he were not. The chill infiltrated the classroom when a student asked nervously "if it were true that students at Howard University had been advised not to join the NAACP...." Bravely, Logan replied, "my advice would be not to run: 'the best defense is an offense....'" Thus, he said, at a previous faculty meeting he suggested that faculty "join the NAACP, Merze Tate had advised against it" and was said to have told him: "'The best thing is not to answer back and to admit that [one] had been duped.'"[7]

This anxiety about anticommunism may serve to explain why before heading to a fete at the Panamanian Embassy in October 1953, Logan joined Tate and John Hope Franklin in opposing the hiring of a specialist in Chinese history: "there will probably be few students interested,"[8] said the freckled scholar.

As Logan saw things, Tate was much too gun shy; when in December 1953 "that goddam sonofabitch Joseph McCarthy" made one of his customary flagrancies, Logan signed a petition rebuking him but that "craven coward"—speaking of Tate—refused.[9] The nation, concluded Logan, was "suffering from one of the worst hysterias in modern history" and "teachers are particularly vulnerable...."[10]

Although quite respectably, the NAACP had proceeded systematically to purge its ranks of real and imagined Reds, the group remained suspect, not least since their challenge to Jim Crow itself was perceived as subversive by quite a few legislators on Capitol Hill. Summoned before the Senate in early 1955, Leslie Perry of the District branch testified that in this city alone there were "10,000 currently paid colored and white members," not consoling for those who held Jim Crow dear.[11]

Howard, which contained a number of these card carrying members, was under siege, even before the NAACP branch was reactivated in January 1956.[12] Logan thought that budget cuts mandated by Capitol Hill meant the hilltop was becoming the "curbstone" of Negro higher education, not the capstone.[13] According to hilltop bibliographer, Dorothy Porter, the message from Congressman Adam Clayton Powell, Jr., that it was only Logan who called to thank him for restoring sums that had been snatched from Howard's appropriation[14] was indicative of the fright at the hilltop.

Matters had reached such a nadir that it "dawned" on Logan that "in effect, Senator McCarthy will name the new president of

7. Entry, 4 May 1953, Box 5. (This note incorporates previous paragraphs re: the FBI encounter.)
8. Entry, 17 October 1953, Box 9.
9. Entry, 7 December 1953, Box 9.
10. Entry, 1 April 1954, Box 6.
11. Testimony of Leslie Perry, 22 February 1955, Box IX: 226, *NAACP Papers*.
12. Herbert Wright, Youth Secretary to Harold Bell of Howard, 9 January 1956, Box III: E3, *NAACP Papers*.
13. Entry, 7 June 1953, Box 5.
14. Entry, 2 July 1953, Box 5.

Howard...."[15] Logan "warned" his fellow historian, Clarence Bacote, "that he should be careful" about discussing "his friendly relations with Ben Davis," jailed Black Communist leader, who Bacote knew when both resided in Atlanta in the 1930s. Bacote had attended the trial there that had catapulted Davis into notoriety: his legal defense at the tumultuous trial of Angelo Herndon, a youthful radical. Bacote's opinion that the prosecution was "pitiful" and Davis "masterful" in the courtroom was the kind of opinion that could lead to untoward consequences.[16]

Then Logan made his way to the local barbershop where he saw Judge James Cobb who promptly was ensnared in an argument with a corporate colleague, also there for a trim; again, the suffocating political climate intruded as sparks flew about the failure to grant clemency to Julius and Ethel Rosenberg, Communists slated for execution for—supposedly—sharing atomic secrets with Moscow. "'You and I can't afford to fall out about a couple of damned Jews,'" was the calloused retort of the corporate honcho; Logan turned away—wisely in a sense—to confer with George Hayes, a local attorney, about upcoming high court decisions on desegregation.[17]

But Logan found it hard to turn away from the bellicosity that permeated Washington then. By July 1954 he was lunching with Tom Kelly of the *Washington Star* who opined that the "Air Force is strongly in favor of a preventive war against the Soviet Union,"[18] a hair raising prospect that underpinned the pervasive anticommunism that kept possible dissenters in line, even when planetary extinction was at stake. It is likely that Logan did not share with this journalist his unconvinced view of West Germany's "pledge" not to "undertake manufacture of a-b-c weapons—atomic, bacteriological, chemical and possibly others." Justifying the State Department's view of his ultimate unreliability he said, "anyone who places more faith in this pledge by [German leader Konrad] Adenauer than those given by or demanded of Russia is a plain damn fool."[19]

Akin to some of his colleagues and students, Logan was beginning to display traits of stress, dreaming about being interrogated by the FBI, for example. He wanted to see a book about "intellectuals under McCarthyism" but seemed unable to produce it. He wondered if the larger purpose was to drive him into exile, as would befall Hunton

---

15. Entry, 23 June 1953, Box 5.
16. Entry, 23 June 1953, Box 5.
17. Entry, 23 June 1953, Box 5.
18. Entry, 14 July 1954, Box 6.
19. Entry, 3 October, Box 6.

and Du Bois within years.[20] His nervousness was on display at American University where a "lovely brunette…flirted with me with her eyes and legs. Since there was probably an FBI agent present," said the wary historian, "I gave her only a passing glance."[21]

It seemed that Logan or one of his colleagues was a candidate for St. Elizabeth's. This became clear in December 1954 when at a department meeting, his colleague—Merze Tate—was railing against sexism. "While I was talking," said Logan, "she was muttering to herself" and "on the verge of tears." He recalled that she "had made the threat about using a pistol" against John Hope Franklin. Stoutly, said Logan, "I decided that I could not ignore Dr. Tate's threat to shoot somebody," as he recounted her past sins: she "urged members of the faculty not to join the NAACP"; she "urge[d] that Howard not participate in the intercollegiate debate on the recognition of Red China"; Logan then recalled yet another professor who "had spent two years in an insane asylum," as if Tate were next. This former professor "would call [Logan] up at four o'clock in the morning to complain that no woman would marry him," and then he "threatened to shoot another member of the Department of German…." Logan's spouse told him that "Tate will probably say that I had put her out of the office," which he did, "because I now have a young and pretty secretary, the implication being that I will want to make love to her in the office"—baseless speculation, of course. "Tate will do many mean and vicious things," he proclaimed: "she is capable, I believe, of peddling lies to the FBI," a recurrent game of score-settling that had become popular.[22]

Logan thus reported her to the administration, including her reported comment that if anyone asserted that she was incompetent to teach U.S. history—the casus belli—"'she would get a pistol and shoot him. She added that she meant what she said….'" The nervous and turf protecting Hope Franklin "does not want it to be known that it was his remark last year that prompted Tate's threat."[23] Franklin siding with Logan thought that she would appeal too to the administration and, besides, "peddle lies about all of us in the community. He agreed that she would be capable of peddling lies to the FBI…."[24]

Whether it was prompted by Tate or not, it turned out that the FBI was not finished with him. By July 1954 they returned, inquiring

20. Entry, 7 June 1953, Box 5.
21. Entry, 26 June 1953, Box 5.
22. Entry, 9 December 1954, Box 6.
23. Entry, 11 December 1954.
24. Entry, 12 December 1954.

about James Jackson and various organizations. Naively, Logan thought that the interrogation "strikes me as quite contrary to fair judicial procedure...." Did not Max Yergan recruit him to the Council on African Affairs to "offset the influence of the Robeson-Wilkerson-Hunton group"? Did not the FBI recall that for "a number of years he [Yergan] and Paul Robeson had come down once a year to spend a day with Secretary of State Cordell Hull" to discuss Africa? Maybe this Tennessean should be interrogated? Did not the FBI recall that when CAA split, Logan stood alongside the losing anticommunist side; it was this historian who asked that the liberals deny a quorum by storming out, but "we were soundly thrashed...[and] I left the board shortly thereafter...." Nonetheless, Logan said "that Doxey [Wilkerson] was avowedly a Communist" and that "I was 'scared' to read the 'Daily Worker,'" so he could not be punished; "I believed that Alphaeus [Hunton]" was akin to his fellow former Howardite, Wilkerson. He hedged on if he would say as much at a session of the Subversive Activities Control Board.[25]

Logan had reason to be irked about this grilling. After his 1951-52 sojourn in France, by his own admission he reported dutifully to "agents of the Central Intelligence Agency" about what he had ascertained and squealed to the London legation too.[26] The garrulous historian may have told the latter what he told his diary: the "influence of Moslem agents from Cairo" in West Africa was spreading apace.[27] His presence at a cocktail party at the British embassy was suggestive of his cooperation with them.[28]

Logan was trapped. He was certainly no Communist, but the phenomenon known as "McCarthyism" was not exclusively concerned with routing Reds: the continuing presence on Capitol Hill of Dixiecrats was a tipoff that concern about the onrushing desegregation was rarely far from the calculus of certain anticommunists. After being pressed by the FBI, Logan made his way to the Cosmos Club, an exclusive precinct and listened to a speaker, Charles Tansill, expound on the emerging conventional wisdom that the U.S. "should have supported Germany and Japan against Russia" during the previous war, which Logan found "venomous and vicious," and as was his tendency, descended into subjectivity in response: the speaker was a "hunchback," he sputtered, "his deformity perhaps explains in part his viciousness...." If Dixiecrats had been able

---

25. Entry, 21 July 1954, Box 6.
26. Entry, 31 July 1954, Box 6.
27. Entry, 27 July 1954, Box 6.
28. Entry, 29 May 1954, Box 6.

to peer into his diary, they would have been repulsed by Logan's admission that he was "almost ready to vomit when I had to sign the non-disloyalty oath" just to obtain a passport.[29]

However, as the U.S. authorities were making the complex transition away from Jim Crow, Logan—who spoke fluent French—was trotted out frequently to explain his strange land to inquirers. Just after being questioned by the FBI, he was meeting with "foreigners" who, too, "questioned" him but this time, "the major point" was: "'How could Americans critique Germans for their treatment of Jews in view of the way that Americans treat Negroes,'"[30] a query not easy to answer. Then he met with Georges Creppy, Togolese and former Bison who he found to be "very bitter because of his experience in travelling by bus through the South: segregation on the bus," said this African, "would discourage other Africans from going South," or even sojourn in the District, "as they would become "'blanco-phobes'...haters of white people," a real demerit during the Cold War. He was "also very critical" of U.S. Negroes, since all too many were disinterested when he was "introduced as an African but were much more interested when it was learned that he had studied in Paris."[31]

Still, as long as Africans were alienated by Jim Crow during a hotly contested battle of ideas with Moscow, Logan could play a valued role in explicating the peculiar folkways of his homeland. Moreover, just before jetting to Dakar, Logan joined the leadership of the newly born American Committee on Africa—an anticommunist alternative to Robeson's Council on African Affairs, soon driven into extinction—which was more willing to cooperate with U.S. imperialism.[32] This enhanced Logan's value further.

Speaking of enhancing value, Logan chose this moment to enhance his investment portfolio: "I have bought 175 shares of Remington Arms," said the canny historian, "because it has an affiliate Rem-Cru that is manufacturing titanium,"[33] essential to the military-industrial complex and suggestive of why this historian was more than willing to cooperate with U.S. imperialism.

In a sense, the ascendant Dixiecrats were forced to accept one with Logan's politics for they needed him, as much as he needed— or at least desired desperately—subsidized junkets to West Africa.

---

29. Entry, 21 May 1953, Box 5.
30. Entry, 21 May 1953, Box 5.
31. Entry, 7 June 1953, Box 5.
32. Entry, 27 June 1953, Box 5.
33. Entry, 28 June 1953, Box 5.

By October 1953 with a certain smugness, Logan observed that the "Embassy of the Union of South Africa is about the only embassy in Washington with which the Howard University community"—meaning, himself—"does not have some contact."[34] A tell-tale sign of Logan's heightened profile arrived in November 1953 when Anna Hedgeman, a former Howard administrator who then leapt to closeness to President Truman, ran into Logan at the Hotel Theresa in Harlem and grovelingly asked how she could get a job with the State Department. "I told her to get in touch with Harold Howland,"[35] a low level functionary there, which amounted to a snub.

Hedgman was knocking on the proper door for by January 1954 Logan was to be found at the Haitian Embassy for the 150th anniversary of the triumph of the revolution. A "very large crowd" materialized, including "Secretary of State Dulles"; John Hope Franklin, too, was marking the holiday: Logan visited his home "to meet some guests, one from Germany and the Minister Plenipotentiary of Bolivia and his wife" was his tally of assembled prominence.[36]

Shortly Logan was dining with the mayor of Lagos, a "huge (about 300 pound) Nigerian" who he "needled" about "the fact that women do not vote," and the politico "talked like the Mayor of Charleston, South Carolina" in his biased justification. Grumpily, Logan acknowledged, "I was not invited to affairs for Dr. Azikiwe," former Howard man and Founding Father of independent Nigeria "because the latter did not want me...." Still, he provided counsel to these Africans then studying the federal capital system: "I suggested to them that it would be helpful to them to study the question of the federal capital in Argentina...."[37]

As if he were a diplomat at large, Logan traveled to the Ethiopian legation on Kaloram—truly one of the poshest areas in the District—for a reception by July 1954; there were other U.S. Negroes there, including Mississippi's Perry Howard who he asked "how long...it would take for schools in Mississippi to become mixed"; he replied optimistically in retrospect, "'about fifty years'" and "I told him that I was glad to hear one person express an honest opinion." He was taken by a "saucy eyed, charming Jamaican" who caught his roving eye. "Mrs. Dulles is very charming," he said, referring to the spouse of the hawkish Secretary of State; this was "the first time I have met her" so he "asked her about her recent trips to Geneva and Paris...."

---

34. Entry, 20 October 1953, Box 9.
35. Entry, 1 November 1953, Box 9.
36. Entry, 4 January 1954, Box 9.
37. Entry, 16 July 1954, Box 6.

A "representative of the Russian [sic] embassy was there,"[38] and he wisely steered clear of him.

Earlier the party-hopping historian was at a reception at the Mayflower Hotel for His Imperial Majesty Himself, Haile Selassie, who he found to be "small and frail. His skin is yellow rather than brown or black like that of most of his entourage...." Indicative of U.S. Negroes' seeking to capitalize upon the rise of a sovereign Africa, John Hope Franklin found that some from this minority "just stood around near the hotel so that they could be seen" as they "hoped that it would be believed that they had attended the reception...."[39]

Just before taking off for Dakar, Logan traipsed to the Liberian embassy where he received a cool reception. "I am afraid that I am too light to please" said the melanin deficient scholar, though he admitted that "Liberians are especially critical of what they consider lack of interest on the part of American Negroes in Liberia." Edward Dudley, the former chief U.S. envoy in Monrovia, was also there, as was CIA leader, Allen Dulles. The leading spy urged the diplomat to "take a top level job in CIA on African problems...I very much hoped that he would accept," said Logan. Just yesterday Dudley had a "long talk with President Eisenhower" and informed him bluntly that "the treatment of Negroes in the United States is hurting the United States abroad" and the chief executive pledged that "he is going to do all that he can in the District of Columbia" as a kind of model city for the nation as a whole.[40] Promptly, a leading liberal anticommunist periodical portrayed the District as a "model for the rest of the nation."[41]

Despite the happy talk and official optimism, a few months before the high court desegregation decision, the law school at George Washington University was one of 17 not admitting Negroes among the 110 members of the Association of American Law Schools—and the only one in the District, meaning they were outdone by Georgetown, American, Catholic—and, of course, Howard.[42]

There was growing concern that the presence of so many universities in the District was attracting too many "free thinkers" with portentous implications for national security given academics' supposed attraction to radicalism. By July 1955 the spotlight was

---

38. Entry, 24 July 1954, Box 6.
39. Entry, 6 June 1954, Box 6.
40. Entry, 3 July 1953, Box 5.
41. Douglas Cater, "Washington: A Model for the Rest of the Nation," *The Reporter*, 11 (Number 12, 30 December 1954): 12-15, Box 3, *Walter Tobriner Papers, George Washington University*.
42. Report on Admission of Negroes by Glen E. Weston, et.al. of GWU

focused on Herbert Fuchs, who had joined the law faculty at American University in the midst of joining the Communist Party in 1934 before—allegedly—quitting in the 1940s. By 1936, he was working on a congressional committee headed by Senator Burton Wheeler investigating the nation's railways. He revealed that his party cell was composed entirely of staff members of this committee—himself and three others. Then he moved laterally to the National Labor Relations Board and joined the cell there. As the war exploded he moved to Denver to serve on the War Labor Board—and joined yet another party unit; by 1946, he returned to the NLRB and—no surprise—rejoined his old party club.[43] By 1955, he was fighting his ouster from American University on anticommunist grounds.[44]

It was not seen as coincidence by the authorities that Fuchs wound up on a local law faculty. By November 1956, the law school at Howard, which Charles H. Houston had done so much to build, was shipping membership payments from a hefty 27 students to the NAACP.[45]

As had been the case for some time, those at the apex of the socio-economic pyramid could make lofty declarations of a new dawn in the District but it would take time for those elevated words to trickle down to the grassroots. For within walking distance of Logan's Howard was the office of Walter Tobriner, local potentate within the Democratic Party and eventually on the Board of Commissioners that ruled the District and remarks attributed to him were not necessarily from the same chapbook as the president's. Washington was a "Southern City," it was said, albeit lacking the "homogeneity of culture and background, found in the cities farther South," especially given the substantial international presence on campuses and within legations. "Neither pro nor anti-segregation forces prior to the decision of the Supreme Court had taken a predominant place among the city's ruling factions," not necessarily an accurate assessment but indicative of the idealistic state of mind among elites. Still, it was recognized accurately that "segregation as later events were to prove, may be said to have been a way of life imposed upon the District by earlier Congresses, rather than a deeply conceived and rigidly obeyed way of life."[46]

---

43. *Washington Star*, 10 July 1955.
44. *Washington Star*, 22 September 1955.
45. William A. Smith to Membership Secretary, 4 November 1956, Box III: E3, *NAACP Papers*.
46. Undated Speech, Box 1, *Walter Tobriner Papers*, George Washington University.

This analysis did not consider the revolt against desegregation, especially but not exclusively in the schools, that erupted post-1954. To be sure and as noted repeatedly in these pages, the District historically had contained a considerable complement of Negroes, befitting a space abutting the slave bastions that were Maryland and Virginia. However, so-called "white flight" accelerated at the moment of desegregation, opening entire neighborhoods for an influx of Negroes. Looking back from the 20th anniversary of the *Brown* case, the *Post* still seemed stunned by the events of October 1954 at McKinley High School in that 200 Euro-American students shouted "'integration will lead to intermarriage.'" Echoing President Eisenhower's pledge to have the District serve as a model, Washington was deemed to be the "first major American city to put thousands of previously segregated black and white children into the same schools."[47] If there was subversion in the District, as some darkly hinted, it was emerging from those adults who were encouraging student strikes against desegregation.[48]

Typically, the Federation of Citizens' Associations, demanded that the FBI check the alleged "subversive influence in school integration...."[49] Gladyce G. Museecy of the District's Public School Association, insisted that "integration impairs education and decreases property values"; she warned in 1956 that the "white population in the [D.C.] public school is declining at a phenomenal rate," while "mass exodus to the suburbs in Maryland [and] Virginia is shaking the foundation of property values...." Contrary to President Eisenhower's admonition, this was not a model but a "warning to the rest of the country...."[50]

Agreeing was Senator James Eastland of Mississippi. This scowling, cigar-chomping, Scotch guzzling Dixiecrat growled while addressing comrades in the White Citizens Council, as he rebuked the president whose "own grandchildren have been removed from"

---

47. *Washington Post*, 12 May 1974. As early as 1952, the NAACP had been collecting leaflets concerning "local moving" in Maryland, featuring "our white drivers," underscoring the *Brown* decision may have been an accelerant as much as an instigator: See leaflet, 1952, Box IX: 226, *NAACP Papers*.
48. Margery T. Ware, Community Organization Secretary of the Washington Urban League, "Some Aspects of the Student Strikes Against Public School Integration," 30 September 1955, Vertical File: Blacks-Segregation and Discrimination, *Special Collections of Washington, D.C. Public Library*.
49. *Washington Star*, 30 July 1954.
50. Clipping, 7 July 1956, Vertical File, File-Blacks-Segregation and Discrimination, *Special Collection of Washington, D.C. Public Library*.

District schools "and placed in a private segregated Episcopal school in Alexandria...."[51]—meaning that even the chief executive was not immune from the popular revolt against desegregation, which had appeal across class lines in the Euro-American community.

Of course, there were other factors besides fear of school desegregation that marked the flight from the District. Postwar mortgage rates, construction of expressways, and a propagandistic wave drove the race to Maryland. (I recall growing up in St. Louis during this same time and as "urban renewal"—or "Negro removal"—impelled Black families to flee from the area near downtown, there was a hypnotic murmur then about the desirability of moving "out west": in the near term to the outskirts of the city, in the long term to Los Angeles.)

The parents of Carl Bernstein were dedicated antiracists, but the famed reporter implies that this was not altogether the case for their ethno-religious peers. By 1955 they were under severe anticommunist pressure but still found the means to buy a new home in Silver Spring, Maryland. Washington's Jewish community, he says, "had been concentrated in that little enclave...between Fifth Street and Sixteenth Streets" but there ensued an "inexorable march" of the city's "Jews" to Silver Spring "and Bethesda in the 1960s and 1970s and now out to Rockville and beyond the Beltway, across the river into Virginia. It is largely a tale of flight from black people," was his astringent assessment in 1989, "an exodus from the District of Columbia into the promised land of Montgomery County," which came to possess the "highest per capita income of any county in the nation, even Westchester," just beyond New York City. Like students at McKinley High School, these newly minted suburbanites were unwilling to accede to the newly minted policy of desegregation; "the local ice cream parlor" in Silver Spring "refused to serve blacks" in sync with the "segregated movie theater in Bethesda...." Left wing suburbanites were subjected to segregation of their trash for inspection for suspected subversion. Teenagers were marinating in Jim Crow on the televised dance show hosted by Milt Grant, a local version of the nationally broadcast "American Bandstand." On "Tuesdays and Thursdays black kids danced," said Bernstein of this otherwise lily-white program.[52]

So, while numerous Euro-Americans were fleeing from the District in the wake of the 1954 school desegregation decision, others of a less progressive hue were arriving. Days after the *Brown* decision,

51. Clipping, 27 January 1956, Vertical File-Blacks-Segregation and Discrimination.

52. Carl Bernstein, *Loyalties*, 130-131, 134, 135, 151, 165, 167.

as if he were volunteering for combat, Wade J. Vick of Biloxi made a special request to Congressman William Colmer of Mississippi: "I have always wanted to be a policeman in Washington," he said imploringly, adding unctuously, "I know you can help"[53]—a fair supposition since the legislator promptly responded.[54] Upon arrival, Vick would have been comfortable in the racially segregated National Guard corps in the District.[55]

The White House had reason to be aware of the ultimate impact of this divergence that was desegregation. In 1955 the president's aide, Gerald Morgan, drafted a message to Congress on home rule and there he pointed out that "taxpayers of Washington bear over 85% of the cost of running the city and the Federal Government pays less than 15%," suggesting that "white flight" could reduce revenues leaving devastating impact on schools and city services and making the fall in property values bruited by those fleeing a self-fulfilling prophecy.[56]

"White flight" placed the District on the path to becoming "Chocolate City." By mid-1953 the NAACP held figures that indicated that the District had a population that was 35 percent Negro[57]—this was to change dramatically in coming decades.

The purported intersection between falling property values, desegregation, and schools was chafing irritably during the early Eisenhower years. By May 1956 it was the subject of a congressional hearing featuring Jerome McKee of the Georgetown Businessmen's Association with the transcript making its way to the White House. Rather blandly he recounted that in Blair, Maryland—not unusually— property was conveyed with a deed and covenant saying it could not be "'deeded to anyone of a race whose death rate is higher than that of the Anglo-Saxon race....'" Yet today, he warned menacingly "there are 3,000 to 5,000 cases of scalp ringworm" in District schools, the tip of the iceberg as far as impending mortality of Negroes were concerned. Why these rates? "Morals and standards of living may be low," said this untrained sociologist and revolting capitalist. As if fleeing a breath of pestilence, these worrisome trends had "moved a lot of people away, especially those who have daughters and have

---

53. Wade J. Vick to Congressman Colmer, 30 May 1954, Box 443, *William Colmer Papers, University of Southern Mississippi-Hattiesburg*.

54. Congressman Colmer to Wade J. Vick, 4 June 1954, Box 443.

55. *Afro-American*, 30 April 1955.

56. Draft Special Message, circa 1955, Box 9, *Gerald Morgan Records, Eisenhower Presidential Library*.

57. Census Figures, 21 July 1953, Box IX: 226, *NAACP Papers*.

taken their families to nearby areas...." Thus, "at one of the local high schools where they were going to vote on a dance and they did not realize it would be an integrated dance," causing heartbeats to gyrate. Then there was at "Easter time the riot at Fort Du Pont where the police themselves [were] beaten...and the glass was broken...." He counseled with a sinister flourish that "we may have to call on the troops at Fort Myer as we did when the Bonus Army" marched in the 1930s, if these marauding Negroes did not cease.[58]

Delirium descended with the advent of desegregation in the District, as Negro-phobia merged with anti-federal government sentiment, whose roots were watered when Washington presided over the expropriation of enslaved property without compensation. In 1956 Congressman James Davis of Georgia led a hearing where John Paul Collins, billed as former principal at Anacostia High School and Eastern High School too, was hyperbolic: "At times," he insisted, "I heard colored girls at the school use language that was far worse than I have ever heard, even in the Marine Corps...." There was rampant "fighting including knifings," all "after integration of the schools in 1954...." There were "more thefts," too, and "sex problems" as well, involving "filthy and revolting habits...." These supposed miscreants proceeded to "purge names at the local bank," walking away with misbegotten wealth. He was irate in maintaining that the "lowering of public school standards" was in motion, for "nothing like this had ever occurred prior to integration...."[59]

Following in the odious tradition of Senator Bilbo, Congressman Davis—former Klansman—was quick to join the House committee with oversight of the District, where he served ignominiously as Chairman of the Police, Firemen's, Streets and Traffic Sub-Committee,[60] a portfolio which should have been held by a City Councilman.

With the left on the defensive—notably Robeson and Du Bois—it was not easy to formulate an accurate and adequate analysis of what was befalling the District, subjected to desegregation not least because of global imperatives. The intellectuals at Howard were of little help in filling the ideological vacuum as they were driven to "insane asylums" when not descending into servile backbiting. This was a recipe for chaos which surely was to come in coming years.

58. "Hearing Before a Subcommittee on the District of Columbia. House of Representatives. 84th Congress, Second Session on HR 4993..." 23 May 1956, Box 9, *Gerald Morgan Records*.

59. "Dan Smoot Report," 15 October 1956, Box IX: 226, *NAACP Papers*.

60. Louis Lautier of NNPA News Service, 1 November 1956, Box IX: 226.

Chapter 14

When Black Folk Awaken, 1953-1959

The observer from the *Pittsburgh Courier* was unhappy. Marking the anniversary in 1957 of the high court decision on school desegregation, 25,000 attended a so-called "Prayer Pilgrimage for Freedom," descending in Washington on behalf of the anti-Jim Crow movement. However, this journalist was unsettled in comparing this demonstration to previous manifestations, e.g., in the 1920s when the perception was that more locals were in attendance. But by 1957 the "number of out-of-town pilgrims" outnumbered Washingtonians by several thousands. How could this be "in a city with a Negro population of more than 365,000" featuring the capstone of higher education, i.e., Howard. "Out of a class of 24 students," said this observer speaking of the hilltop campus, "apathy was general and widespread," though as recently as "five years ago their hometown was the most Jim Crow center of America...."[1] This sour perception was all the more remarkable since 1957 marked the District, according to one student, as "the first American city with a majority black population"—a development of magnitudinous proportion.[2]

However, with all of this handwringing, if this reporter had been paying attention, difficult to miss was what a *Post* reporter grumbled about: "Communists seek to infiltrate Negro March in Washington,"[3] the headline growled.

Anticipating that the despised Reds had yet to be purged altogether, the Congress of Industrial Organization—then in the midst of ousting Communists—allotted $25,000 to Howard for Labor Studies. Here "race" and anticommunism intersected when E.E. Lewis of the

---

1. *Pittsburgh Courier*, 1 June 1957.
2. Susan Philpott, "PRIDE, Inc.: Black Power and Black Capitalism in Washington, D.C., 1967-1981," M.A. thesis, University of Maryland-Baltimore County, 2018, 37.
3. *Washington Post*, 12 May 1957.

Economics Department sought to administer the program; the campus administration was "inclined to go along," said Rayford Logan, "partly, I suspect to show that the university is not prejudiced against the white minority" professoriate to which Lewis belonged—and not accidentally he was also "an extreme right wing pro-McCarthy Republican,"[4] undergirding ongoing purges.

If queried, Logan could have added texture to this hyperbolic anticommunist concern. Earlier Noel Story of the Department of Justice, strolling distance from campus, again wanted to discuss the Council on African Affairs, though it was on its deathbed. Thus, Logan found himself in Room 2257 of the imposing headquarters of U.S. law. The "interview," said Logan with relief, was "conducted on a very friendly basis," adding unnecessarily, "I certainly do not want to be cast in the role of a paid informer"—though he did provide details about the political trajectory of Eslanda Robeson.[5]

Yet the compromised Logan continued to rebuke his colleague, Merze Tate from the left: his embattled colleague "said that she was using the word American interest in the Pacific rather than American imperialism because of the danger of criticism. How cravenly coward can a 'scholar' become?"[6]—a question he could easily answer based on his own experience.

Logan had another advantage compared to many Negroes. "With my freckles and closely cropped hair," he said, "I could be a 'Nordic,'" whereas his spouse, Ruth Logan, "could easily be taken for a Latin American...." This presentation meant "the problem of where to eat is no worry now,"[7] a sea change in the District—and also an emblem of privilege that was to dissolve in coming decades, when any Negro could dine anywhere, generally speaking, if ducats were in order: the class barrier remained not least because class warriors were being purged systematically.

Logan was sufficiently savvy to recognize that these profound shifts were not due to some awakening morality in Washington. It was in early 1955, shortly after the school desegregation decision, that he observed that "Catholic University had admitted Negroes in the 1930s as a part of the 'first counter-offensive' against Communism," now being updated in that it was "only some twenty years later that Georgetown University has opened its doors."[8] As late

---

4. Entry, 4 July 1954, Box 6.
5. Entry, 14 June 1955, Box 6.
6. Entry, 8 September 1955, Box 6.
7. Entry, 26 January 1954, Box 6.
8. Entry, 28 January 1955, Box 6.

as 1959, American University was a member of the Mason Dixon Intercollegiate Conference, alongside peer schools in Virginia and Maryland[9]—hence, Jim Crow, though desegregation was soon to follow.

Logan was also sufficiently savvy to try to avoid the pitfalls that enveloped his fellow Negro intellectual, J. Saunders Redding, who—said the Howardite—was treated like a "stooge" during his tour of India "because he said some good things about the [status of] the Negro in the United States."[10] Logan was walking a tight-rope: seeking to stay in the good graces of the State Department, while consorting with Africans skeptical of same. A Liberian woman told him, "the United States knew that if it did not take an interest in Africa Russia would,"[11] spurring Washington to soar to greater heights accordingly—and Logan too. Again, Logan was sited stra-tegically in the nation's capital, a smalltown at that, intensifying his ability to interact with diplomats whose job was to respond to and shape the nation in which they were located. Thus, it was Logan who spoke with Jan Hofmeyr of apartheid South Africa, who was "quite frank about forced labor" on Pretoria's and Lisbon's behalf in Mozambique.[12] Logan was tasked with the job of picking up Dr. J.S. Gericke, Vice Chancellor of Stellenbosch University in the heart of apartheid and gave him a tour of the District: "I wanted him to see that in Washington Negro...guests are welcome...I wanted him to see that a Negro college professor could afford to pay for lunch in a first class restaurant.[13] (His propagandizing was for naught since his guest "said that he was going to visit the Deep South where he hopes 'to find some argument in support of segregation.'")[14] He gleaned from his many conversations with apartheid advocates that the con-sensus was that "American movies have a very bad effect on the South African Negroes,"[15] likely a reference to the growing profile of those like Sidney Poitier, Dorothy Dandridge, and Harry Belafonte especially.

Logan was rubbing shoulders in exclusive territory. When he attended a cocktail party in honor of Garfield Todd, Prime Minister

---

9. Paul Menton to Hurst Robin Anderson, 1 April 1959, Box 26, *Hurst Robin Anderson Papers, American University-Washington, D.C.*
10. Entry, 19 November 1954, Box 6.
11. Entry, 15 January 1956, Box 6.
12. Entry, 17 August 1955, Box 6.
13. Entry, 12 October 1958, Box 6.
14. Entry, 15 October 1958, Box 6.
15. Entry, 12 October 1958, Box 6.

of Southern Rhodesia (now Zimbabwe), there was "only one other Negro guest" present—and he was Nigerian.[16]

Logan was insightful to declare after a visit to London's raucous and "most interesting" Hyde Park; there he "listened to Catholics, Conservatives, Socialists, Colored [activists]...Communists," too. "I believe that we, in the United States," he proclaimed perceptively, "would be wiser if we allowed the Communists to hold public meetings of this nature."[17] As a thaw in the Cold War was emerging in 1955 it was Logan who realized that "when Russia exploded the atom bomb, the chances for world peace were increased for now" since the "two giants (U.S. and U.S.S.R.) know that war would mean the well-nigh destruction of both."[18]

In other words, Washington—the locus of federal power and capital of a superpower—was a frontline metropolis, grappling, often unsuccessfully, with the nagging problem of improving its racial image, for global consumption not least. At the same time the District was purging busily real and imagined Communists, while emitting an air of intimidation that was suffocating activism in the vicinity. It was also in 1957 that Mercer Cook, the multi-lingual Howardite, soon to be recruited as a leading U.S. diplomat, expressed a "very deep concern about the apathy on Howard's campus...many students here are not interested in world or even national events,"[19] he lamented.

Professor Cook should have known of factors constricting activism for an anticommunist pall had enveloped the campus. Or he could have considered the contemporaneous example of former Howardite, Ralph Bunche, still hounded because of activism that had occurred decades earlier. The Communist press was seemingly astounded to report that Bunche was "questioned for 12 straight hours by a loyalty board...."[20]

As 1955 was about to dawn, it was revealed that there was reluctance to invite Dr. Du Bois to campus, given his ties to Communists.[21] Just before then Rayford Logan and Du Bois shared a platform for the first time in a while. Walter White of the NAACP "assured" the warily prudent scholar "that if Du Bois plugged the Communist line, I could take care of him." Afterwards, Du Bois

---

16. Entry, 15 August 1955, Box 6.
17. Entry, 22 September 1954, Box 6.
18. Entry, 16 January 1955, Box 6.
19. *The Hilltop*, 30 October 1957.
20. *Daily Worker*, 1 March 1955.
21. Entry, 18 December 1954, Box 6.

and Logan shared a train ride to Manhattan and the tactful NAACP founder "said nothing about his having been handcuffed" during his recent indictment after being accused of being an agent of an unnamed foreign power, principally Moscow. Tactlessly, Logan was lured into a discussion about the petition Du Bois had prepared for the United Nations indicting Washington for its vast depredations against Negroes. The Secretary General referred the sticky matter to his deputy, Ralph Bunche, and predictably "nothing was done" about it, indicating that the former Howardite had "'made it,'" said Du Bois ruefully. Waxing philosophical Logan admitted that Du Bois' "most important contribution" was "namely, his influence on [Charles] Drew, [William] Hastie, [Charles] Houston and others."[22]

It was not evident if either party recalled what Howard's paper of record noted in 1947 when Logan joined Du Bois during this different time in filing the petition in question. "'It is not Russia that threatens the United States,'" declaimed Du Bois, "'so much as Mississippi; not Stalin and Molotov but Bilbo and Rankin.'"[23] However, by the time of their train ride, such verbiage was verboten, heretical. "I am a little deaf,"[24] Logan complained at one point, not in reference to understanding what he formerly did comprehend.

Then Du Bois was radioactive and when that toxicity seemed to dissipate, it was seen properly as an important sign. When an announcement was made—finally—in early 1958 that the NAACP founder was to speak at Howard, it was viewed by some as a kind of coup.[25] It was George Murphy of the Baltimore newspaper dynasty—though he had a Red tinge—who pushed for Du Bois to speak at Howard. The vote was "unanimous," said Logan, speaking of the relevant faculty, to extend the invitation since "most of the intellectuals of my generation were 'disciples'" of the elderly scholar-activist. "I told President Johnson," said Logan reassuringly, "that Dr. Du Bois would say nothing to embarrass the university. President Johnson said that Dr. Du Bois should not be restricted in what he said."[26] The prelude to Du Bois' arrival was akin to the preparation involved in inviting a Soviet leader to Washington. Logan feared the FBI wanted to interrogate him about the event, yet another demerit on his record. Fearlessly, President Johnson arranged a luncheon on campus in honor of Du Bois and his spouse, Shirley Graham. A

---

22. Entry, 2 May 1954, Box 6.
23. *The Hilltop*, 7 November 1947.
24. Entry, 30 January 1954, Box 6.
25. *The Hilltop*, 28 March 1958.
26. Entry, 19 February 1958, Box 6.

smaller luncheon was held for the paramount scholar, Kenneth Dike of Nigeria, by way of comparison. Judge James Cobb of the District, a Howard alumnus, agreed to confer with Logan beforehand in case there arose a last minute controversy about Du Bois' arrival—though Logan added (perhaps ironically), "of course some might say that I am an undercover agent for the FBI...."[27]

This point was very much on his mind since he suspected that scholar, Harold Isaacs, "may be an undercover agent," which he inferred when he queried Logan "to find out why I had not been aware at the time of the Comintern [Communist International head-quartered in Moscow]" when aiding Du Bois in organizing the Pan-African Congresses of the early 1920s.[28]

Retrospectively, it was a kind of coup in that Du Bois' address in April 1958 drew a crowd of 700 at a time when apathy was said to reign on campus. Perhaps not coincidentally, the NAACP then announced a campus drive seeking 1,000 new members.[29] It was an "overflow crowd" Logan exhorted: "five hundred persons had been turned away," though administrators "were very much con-cerned "about the pro-communistic line in Dr. Du Bois' speech...." In his remarks introducing the speaker, Logan remarked with appar-ent sarcasm that Dixiecrat curmudgeon Senator James Eastland of Mississippi be invited to campus to show how open Howard was to diversity of thought. Predictably, press coverage of Du Bois' visit was massive, not all of it fair and balanced; the Veterans of Foreign Wars were obstreperous in protest.[30]

Also retrospectively, it is difficult to separate the lionizing of Du Bois at Howard from his privileged relationship with Prime Minister Nkrumah of newly independent Ghana, who the State Department was seeking to cultivate. During his 1958 visit, Howard was the only university that he visited.[31] Logan was invited to a reception for the visiting Ghanaian and Secretary of State John Foster Dulles appeared and Logan seized the opportunity to compliment the dour diplomat. Logan thought he could parlay a promotion from his $9,000 annual salary to the post of Assistant U.S. Secretary of State for Africa, an appointment pushed by *Pittsburgh Courier* titans, Robert Vann and P.L. Prattis, though the prospective appointee felt

27. Entry, 30 March 1958, Box 6.
28. Entry, 4 August 1958, Box 6.
29. *The Hilltop*, 14 April 1958.
30. Entry, 13 April 1958, Box 6.
31. Note, *Howard University Magazine*, 1 (Number 1, November 1958): 6, *Schomburg Center*.

there was "practically no chance" of this happening, since "I had not been finally cleared by the FBI"—though the authorities continued to consult him repeatedly. "As a colonial subject living in Washington," Logan said caustically, "I had no political affiliation" that would bring unwanted attention. Nevertheless, as his friend, George Hayes, was driving him home after the Nkrumah affair, he broke the news that "'everybody knows that...Logan is a socialist,'" upsetting to the historian. Customarily, Logan thought that this prospective "offer" was just another plot by his foes in that "some of my 'friends' would be delighted to have me 'mentioned' in order to say"—gleefully—"that I had been 'turned down' for the post." There was a kind of new scramble for Africa, positions that is. The American Society of African Culture was founded just before Ghanaian independence as a kind of counterpoint to Hunton's Council on African Affairs, then being liquidated. To limit competition, "some members did not want whites to participate in any manner," according to Logan. "'Negroes ought to have one organization which we can control,'" said Hope Franklin. More to the point, Logan wanted to know "who [is] pulling the strings of these organizations that are interested in Africa?"[32]

Still, the prospect of a post at Foggy Bottom was too tantalizing to ignore so he importuned the lawyer, Belford V. Lawson, to lobby Senator Kennedy about this post and in turn JFK would speak to his affluent father about advertising in the *Courier* as a kind of lubricant for the deal.[33] This once proud periodical, like a good deal of the Negro press, was in decline as the bourgeois press turned reluctantly toward desegregation, hiring Black journalists who formerly would have been ignored: the ascending Nation of Islam had begun a column in its pages and, Logan proclaimed that the group "bought the opportunity to publish this column by guaranteeing the purchase of a certain number of copies of the 'Courier' each week," a result of the journal's "financial difficulties."[34]

Perversely, Logan had to think his many foes had scored a point against him when the popular magazine *Jet* carried an item about his being mentioned for the State Department appointment[35]—which never was made.

What was asserting itself were external events—Ghanaian independence, the backwash of the Little Rock school desegregation

---

32. Entry, 4 August 1958, Box 6.
33. Entry, 14 August 1958, Box 6.
34. Entry, 31 January 1959, Box 6
35. Entry, 22 August 1958, Box 6.

battle, and the global significance of Sputnik, or Moscow pene-
trating the heavens—which shaped matters to the granular level,
opening doors that theretofore had been shut firmly. Then there
was the continuing arrival of teachers and lecturers with dissident
viewpoints, accompanied by the departure of those like Bunche,
then Hope Franklin to Brooklyn College (he wound up there though
his most discerning book, *The Militant South*, and was accused
wrongly of being hostile to the region, as opposed to being hostile to its peculiarities)[36]; historian Charles Wesley, too, was being
inspected for a high-level government post (an FBI agent queried
Logan about him,[37] etc. Frazier was often in a snit about what he
saw as weaknesses in the research agenda of colleagues like Hansberry, helping to instigate the sociologist's leave from campus.[38]
Frank Snowden, one of Howard's most eminent scholars, was in
demand including for various U.S. government assignments (these
inquisitors wanted to know, said Logan, "whether he got along
with his wife.")[39]

Mordecai Johnson remained under fire, his pro-Moscow remarks
of decades earlier were hardly forgotten—even by Logan, who
recalled a time when the top administrator "repeatedly praised the
Soviet regime"[40]; by the 1950s, Logan thought that the Republicans
were "out to 'get' Mordecai,"[41] not indicating any sign of amnesia in
recalling Johnson's stinging comments of yore that Moscow had done
a far better job of eliminating poverty than Washington.[42] With faculty fleeing and the administration weakened, the door was opened
for the arrival of faculty, e.g., the prolific and militant journalist, J.A.
Rogers, who had been lecturing at the hilltop in any case. "I had
a higher opinion than did some of my colleagues of Rogers," said

---

36. Entry, 9 December 1954, Box 6.
37. Entry, 8 April 1953, Box 5. See also Entry, 13 March 1957, Box 6: Hope
Franklin while a graduate student was asked to review Wesley's book on the
Confederacy's collapse; he "happened to find a doctoral dissertation which
was almost identical with Wesley's book" but was told "he should not reveal
the plagiarisms. John Hope followed his advice." However, when Logan
saw Franklin at a historians' conference the latter had "no recollection of
Wesley plagiarism." Entry, 31 December 1957, Box 6.
38. Entry, 1 March 1953, Box 5.
39. Entry, 23 October 1954, Box 6.
40. Entry, 10 July 1955, Box 6.
41. Entry, 2 January 1953, Box 5.
42. Kenneth Robert Janken, *Rayford W. Logan and the Dilemma of the African
American Intellectual*, 205.

Logan, though "some of his conclusions are documented and some are not. His three volumes on 'Sex and Race' are a conglomeration of pornography and history"—but students were likely attracted to his progressive stances beyond the classroom.[43]

In a precursor of the succeeding decade, also arriving as Howard faculty in the 1950s was Chancellor Williams, an alumnus, who became a Black Power icon because of his excavations of the role of Egypt in Africa.[44] Then there was James Porter, a pioneer in the field of African American art history whose lack of a doctorate caused him to consider migrating to Africa.[45] Ultimately, faculty churn allowed for the arrival of lecturers, e.g., Rogers and faculty, e.g., Williams, who laid the groundwork for the emergence of militancy at Howard, then in Washington in the coming decade. Yet even as some were complaining about "apathy" of Howard students, in late 1955 Logan observed—in a possible indicator of the presence of faculty like Williams—that a Moroccan official addressed his students and ascertained that "questions asked at Howard were superior to those asked at the other schools in Washington."[46] Interestingly, as Morocco was pushing for independence and Algeria was laboring under the weight of a bloody war induced by Paris, the French embassy sought to have a Moroccan speak at Howard,[47] suggesting how the winds of change were also subjecting students to anti-colonial gusts. Coincidentally, the First Secretary at the Egyptian legation as of 1956 was a Howard graduate student.[48]

Despite this optimism, police in the District retained their reputation for brutalization, even as steps were supposedly taken to make Washington a "model" city of anti-Jim Crow initiative. The police chief, Robert V. Murray, pleaded his case directly to Congressman John McMillan of South Carolina, a successor to Mississippi's Senator Bilbo as an overseer of the city. He was able to forward a

---

43. Entry, 4 July 1954, Box 6.
44. *The Hilltop*, 18 December 1952.
45. Entry, 14 July 1954, Box 6.
46. Entry, 17 November 1955, Box 6. Weeks later Logan and George Houser of the American Committee on Africa were at the State Department defending Congressman Adam Clayton Powell after the latter said that the Jewish community in Morocco were "ill treated," though an "investigation...found that the charges were not true...I wonder what the Zionists would have found," said Logan.
47. Entry, 1 November 1955, Box 6.
48. Entry, 16 April 1956, Box 6.

supportive editorial from the soon-to-be-defunct *Washington Daily News*.[49] The NAACP accused Murray of condoning the manhandling and roughhousing of "colored prisoners," and—as well—he "permits a policy of discrimination against colored officers."[50] The rising *Post*, along with the soon-to-be-defunct *Star*, both defended Murray with the latter proclaiming that the NAACP "discredited itself," adding threateningly that "something is wrong with the local NAACP."[51] Exacerbating Negro-police ties was the continuing bias targeting officers of the court: The bar in the District, lamented the NAACP's Roy Wilkins in mid-1958, "has long excluded Negro lawyers as members...."[52]

Nonetheless, no better indicator of a changing city was the state of the police force and the growth of the NAACP. Indicating that the city was awakening from its enforced slumber was the excited report from Eugene Davidson of the NAACP in 1958. The "branch has enjoyed one of its most successful years," he exhorted. "Its membership bids fair to exceed its 1957 total...[as] unsolicited donations from clubs, organizations and churches," poured in. "Life memberships during the year surpassed any year in our history," he said dazedly. Even Negro police officers, accustomed to rough treatment "report that more and more they are being treated as officers and not just Negro officers"—though much room for improvement remained. Still, "for the first time in history a Negro was promoted to sergeant. Today the department has the largest department of Negro corporals in history"; even "integrated squad cars are now," an abrupt reversal of recent praxis. The fire department continued to be the "biggest blot"; "token integration exists,"[53] he said mournfully.

But Davidson would have been likewise exuberant about the report from a social science class at Howard, emerging at the time of his optimistic report: 58 students joined the Association—"the entire class took the unusual action after a lecture on NAACP

49. Robert V. Murray, 19 November 1957, Box 6, *John McMillan Papers, University of South Carolina-Columbia*.

50. *Washington Daily News*, 28 October 1957.

51. *Washington Star*, 8 November 1957 and 3 November 1957. See also Faye Haskins, *The Evening Star: The Rise and Fall of a Great Washington Newspaper*, Lanham: Rowman & Littlefield, 2019. See also *Washington Post*, 1 November 1957.

52. Roy Wilkins to Congressman Herbert Zelenko, July 1958, Box IX: 226, *NAACP Papers*.

53. Annual Report by Eugene Davidson, 14 December 1958, Box IX: 227, *NAACP Papers*.

accomplishments."[54] Inevitably these students had been inspired by an enthusiastic march of about 10,000 in the District weeks earlier, pressing for school desegregation. The NAACP was the instigator and it told hilltoppers encouragingly, "join Harry Belafonte, Mrs. Ralph Bunche, Sidney Poitier," and Dr. King for this demonstration; "Howardites are asked to meet at Founders Library" and "to march as a unit in [the] youth march...."[55] Astonishingly, organizers sought a march of 1,000 and were deluged by the arrival of 10,000. Perhaps it was because of the star wattage of baseballer, Jackie Robinson, who was the marshal for this eventful occasion.[56]

Although the "day was clear and bright and the weather warm" NAACP principal, Gloster Current, groused that there was a "failure of the entire affair. There was little enthusiasm in the entire gathering." Besides, "the Association was [not] treated very courteously as no sooner had its representatives started on the first day of a three page talk, he was told by the Chairman to cut it short...at the end of the first page...."[57] Current lacked the perspicacity to connect the deficit of energy at this march from the previously stated NAACP policy: "anti-American groups not invited to youth march for integrated schools," was the viperish rebuke; "[we] have not invited Communists or Communist organizations...we do not want the participation of these groups, nor of individuals or other organizations holding similar views...."[58] Yet Current was either obtuse or cynical when he perused the financial statement of the march, submitted by Stanley Levison, thought to be—at least—a former Communist and Bayard Rustin—ditto.[59]

Du Bois was soon to join the Communist Party, which helps to account in part for the hesitation in allowing him to speak to impressionable youth. But then student, Tim Jenkins, later a leading civil rights attorney, reported at length on his journey to socialist Yugoslavia.[60] That was the good news. The unfortunate news is that Jenkins

---

54. Press Release, Box III: E3, *NAACP Papers*.
55. Announcement, circa October 1958, Box III: E3, *NAACP Papers*.
56. Dave Zirin, *A People's History of Sports in the United States*, New York: New Press, 2008, 123.
57. Gloster B. Current to Roy Wilkins, 27 October 1958, Box III: A334, *NAACP Papers*.
58. Statement, 17 April 1958, Box III: A334.
59. Financial Statement, 3 September 1958-31 October 1958, Box III: A334. See also David Garrow, *The FBI and Martin Luther King, Jr.*, New York: Penguin, 1983.
60. *The Hilltop*, 17 December 1958.

then languishing under a Jim Crow regime at home took time to broadcast his less than flattering impressions of Belgrade over Radio Free Europe, the anticommunist propaganda arm of Washington, which was translated into ten languages.[61] Simultaneously, like currents in west Africa building up then socking the Caribbean and Florida with hurricanic velocity, the "Beat Generation," with roots in Manhattan and San Francisco had arrived on campus, bringing with it—according to a student reporter—"increasing concern by the students for social problems."[62]

This spirit of dissent had infused Bruce Carver Boyton. He graduated high school at the tender age of 14 and seven years later was a third year law student at Howard. Traveling from campus to see his family in Selma, Alabama, he was detained in Richmond for daring to visit a Jim Crow restaurant at a transportation terminal. As a subsequent litigant in a high court case in the late 1950s, he compelled the justices to rule that segregation violated measures designed to promote interstate commerce, a wounding blow for Jim Crow.[63]

Not as a result of happenstance, Howard students were inspired by the frequent appearances on campus of role models from abroad. As the Cold War escalated, U.S. imperialism growingly deemed it necessary to woo Africans and Asians particularly, many of whom when visiting Washington made their way to the hilltop. Such was the case for the baby-faced Kenyan leader, Tom Mboya, who spoke at Rankin Chapel in May 1958.[64] If Africans were fighting for progress, why shouldn't African Americans follow suit? Thirty educators from India arrived on campus, brought by the State Department although it was likely realized that this visit was inimical to maintaining Jim Crow.[65]

President Paul Magloire of Haiti and his subordinates were such frequent visitors to Howard during the 1950s that their presence hardly caused a ruffle.[66] Even local capital felt constrained to join the bandwagon. The Eugene and Agnes Meyer Foundation, tied to *Washington Post* ownership, felt compelled to sponsor four scholarships for Nigerian students to attend Howard,[67] though conceivably they could deliver on the hilltop a message underlining the escape

---

61. *The Hilltop*, 17 December 1958.
62. *The Hilltop*, 29 November 1958.
63. *Washington Post*, 28 November 2020.
64. Announcement, 8 May 1958, Box III: E3, *NAACP Papers*.
65. *The Hilltop*, 13 March 1957.
66. Entry, 1 December 1954, Box 6.
67. *The Hilltop*, 13 February 1958.

from oppression. The same could be said about the leader of Jamaica, Norman Manley, who communed on campus with Logan.[68]

Manley referred to Logan and himself as "'old friends'" and "my fraternity brother," speaking of the Alphas. Cleverly, these remarks were expressed at the British embassy, likely enhancing the authority of both men. Up for debate was the issue of agricultural exports from Jamaica northward. "Florida is very much concerned." Thus, Senator Spessard Holland of the Jim Crow state, was also present and diplomatically "was very courteous to both Ruth [Logan] and me," said the historian.[69]

When Logan addressed "about thirty foreign visitors," he found—"as usual"—that "questions were designed to show that we [meaning the U.S.] are discriminating against Negroes."[70] This was a regular assignment for Logan then, for example as Jim Crow was being ruled invalid by the high court, the historian "spoke to about 30 Vietnamese in French," the topic being—per usual—the "Negro Problem in the United States...followed with the closest attention"; he was "roundly applauded at the end."[71] A companion lecture he provided on "the implications of the impending crisis of Africa on civil rights in the United States" was similarly timely.[72] The well connected Logan underlined the tragic lynching of Emmett Till in Mississippi by racists to a lecture of atomic scientists, then was told by a Norwegian and Belgian couple, both present, "that papers in their country had carried front page articles on the kidnapping and murder...."[73]

Logan was respected as both a scholar and what would be called today a "public intellectual." The volume he edited with the University of North Carolina Press, *What the Negro Wants*, had sold a sizeable—for an academic text—11,000 copies within a decade of publication in 1944.[74] One of his most popular books, which popularized depicting the post-1876 era as the "Nadir" for the Negro, generated a "very disturbing letter" from his publisher, who insisted on "deletion of two names from [the] bibliography, namely [Herbert] Aptheker," Communist historian and Du Bois: "these authors," he was instructed sternly, "have been linked with Communist fronts

68. Entry, 18 March 1954, Box 6.
69. Entry, 4 August 1955, Box 6.
70. Entry, 4 April 1954, Box 6.
71. Entry, 22 June 1954, Box 6.
72. Entry, 1 March 1953, Box 5.
73. Entry, 7 November 1955, Box 6.
74. Entry, 22 January 1953, Box 5.

and their inclusion would automatically cut down on prospective government sales...."[75] Courageously, Logan responded: "I will not consent to the deletion of the Aptheker and Du Bois items."[76]

As such, Logan was able to spread his influence nationally, especially by dint of invitations to speak at other campuses. There he, too, could gather intelligence, grist for his political mill. At Ohio Wesleyan he spoke briefly to a Nigerian student who told him that he was being shunned by young Euro-American women but "Oriental girls—Chinese, Korean, Japanese-are more willing to accept dates" with him[77]—again, unhelpful to Washington in the wider scheme of things.

This apartheid mindset was not useful during the Cold War and served to undermine Jim Crow, stalwart support for same notwithstanding. The Ford Foundation awarded $50,000 to Howard to bolster African Studies in response but this was paltry compared to what was allocated to Northwestern, as if the hilltop campus was untrustworthy when it came to defending U.S. interests.[78] In any event, leading Africanist, Hansberry, was unhappy since not only was Ford uninterested in his specialty—pre-colonial Africa—but his respected colleague, Frazier, did not respect him.[79] Hansberry went on to charge that his high blood pressure and heart condition were induced in part by the shabby treatment of his specialty.[80] "No question," said Logan admiringly, "but that Mel[ville Herskovits] in Evanston has the very best center for the study of African affairs in the United States."[81]

The preceding notwithstanding, the North Atlantic powers had to pay a price for their previous policy which had shunted Africa and Africans to perceived backwaters, e.g., Howard. Thus, both Logan and his colleague William Leo Hansberry were invited with their spouses to a sumptuous reception in honor of a visiting official in Britain's Colonial Office. Even a sharp exchange on the merits of Richard Wright's recent tome on Ghana could not erode the significance of the invitation.[82] Logan's abject willingness to cultivate positive relations with colonizers led him to the disgrace of sending

---

75. Entry, 25 August 1956, Box 6.
76. Entry, 28 August 1956, Box 6.
77. Entry, 4 May 1953, Box 5.
78. Entry, 26 April 1954, Box 6.
79. Entry, likely September 1954, Box 6.
80. Entry, 15 January 1956, Box 6.
81. Entry, 7 April 1954, Box 6.
82. Entry, 10 October 1954, Box 6.

a virtual apology to Brussels for his past critical remarks about their devastating role in the Congo.[83]

As ever, Logan's cooperation with the State Department continued with direct implications for Howard students. Continuing his close relationship with Haiti, a subject of one of his better known books, he hosted a reception for Dantes Bellegarde, a member of the Ad Hoc Commission on Racial Discrimination in South Africa, a nation whose salience was only to increase in the U.S. in coming years. Hope Franklin and Franklin Frazier also attended.[84] With prescience, Logan detected early on a tie between events impacting apartheid and those impacting Jim Crow.[85]

Logan remained a regular at the Haitian embassy, especially on their "Independence Day" of 1 January; on one occasion Rafael Trujillo, the caudillo of Santo Domingo was present, described as "quite small and quite handsome...the first time I have ever seen Dominicans at the Haitian embassy...."[86]

Frazier was among those who were reproached by Logan after a discussion with a visiting Afrikaner scholar: "As usual," said the historian, "it seemed to me, the sociologists were impolite, intolerant and hot-headed" in confronting this apologist,[87] whereas Logan was more reserved. Ultimately, students would align with Frazier.

He was then invited to the Swiss legation where an attempt was made to recruit him and his spouse to the fervently anticommunist and ultra-religious Moral Rearmament movement, though he was disinclined: "My 'first love' is to the Quakers," he conceded,[88] though colleague, Belford Lawson was said to have remarked, "Moral Rearmament insist that I am 'the one Negro they want to land'"[89] because of his intellectual prestige and vast range of contacts. They wanted to "finance," said Logan, "a trip for me around the world."[90]

Eventually in the 1960s the lid was blown off and, like many campuses, Howard became the site of untrammeled protest which could be seen retrospectively as a direct result of the previous decade's suppression of dissent until the indignant steam of discord built up uncontrollably and exploded thereafter.

---

83. Entry, 6 March 1955, Box 6.
84. Entry, 1 March 1954, Box 6.
85. Entry, 1 March 1953, Box 5.
86. Entry, 2 January 1953.
87. Entry, 8 March 1954, Box 6.
88. Entry, 1 March 1954, Box 6.
89. Entry, 9 December 1954, Box 6.
90. Entry, 13 November 1955, Box 6.

But—as suggested—even before this decade of tumult, already there were signs at Howard that turmoil was nearby.

For in the District and thereabouts the surging energy in the 1950s seemed to be borne by opponents of Jim Crow, not their opposite number. As the "Prayer Pilgrimage" was marked—the name seeming to provide an aura of non-threatening Christian benevolence—on Capitol Hill there was sturm und drang. At issue was the "belligerence on the part of many Negro students," whose specialty was "making fun of teachers," deploying "foul and obscene language," all while being embroiled an "many fights." In response the "white population is leaving Washington," potentially reducing the seat of power to a site of Black Power, with inauspicious implications for national security. Unhelpful, it was said, was the supposed "bias of one of the Washington newspapers in favor of integration," an oblique reference to the ascendant *Post* in the process of driving its competitor, the *Star*, into extinction. A presentiment of the turmoil in the coming decade was the unsober description of the "investigation and subsequent hearings" which "were conducted in an atmosphere charged with abuse and name calling directed at members of the committee and its chief counsel by some of the Washington press" and "some minority pressure groups," in "conduct" that "was constant and deliberate."[91]

Yet as legislators were tearing out their hair about purported transgressions by Negro students even the *Washington Star* seemed stunned to see that African American youth were "denied entry to Arlington schools....."[92]

Washington was paying the price of history and geography. The capital was sandwiched between slave states of Maryland and Virginia as a concession to these flesh peddlers, but by the 1950s the nation felt compelled to move away hesitantly from these states' trademark: Jim Crow. This created a patchwork, legally and politically, and incoherence, too. Since Dixiecrat influence was far from on the wane on Capitol Hill, this provided this bloc with inordinate leverage, allowing them to throw a spanner into the works. However, that was not the analysis of Dixiecrats. As the "Prayer Pilgrimage" was stepping off Senator Olin Johnston of South Carolina

91. "Investigation of Public School Conditions. Report of the Subcommittee to Investigate Public School Standards and Conditions and Juvenile Delinquency in the District of Columbia of the Committee on the District of Columbia. House of Representatives. 84th Congress, 2nd Session," Washington, D.C.: GPO, 1957, Box 2, *James Stockard Papers, George Washington University*.
92. *Washington Star*, 5 September 1957.

was instructed that the time had come to move the U.S. capital, "as far as Cincinnati or better yet, St. Louis"[93]—though it was unclear how moving to yet another border between former slave states and their opposite number would resolve the ultimate dilemma. As this proposal gained altitude, a rationale beyond escaping Washington's racial geography emerged: "newspapers report that because of the danger of atomic bombing," said George Osborn of Geneva, Illinois to Senator Johnston, "you have proposed that the capital be moved"; as if he were involved in a real estate play designed to drive up property values in his backyard, he too agreed that "somewhere in the Middle West" was a prime consideration.[94]

It was not evident how these midwestern metropolises could heighten harshness further toward Negroes—absent a leap toward fascism.

Across the river in Arlington, Jack Rathbone complained bitterly that "toilet and lavatory facilities," along with "knives and forks and spoons, dishes and cups of our white cafeterias are now being used by members of the Negro race," one of countless "nefarious acts" that were driving certain disgruntled Virginians away from this suburb.[95]

In response, Rathbone and his comrades claimed the scalp of a confirmed backer of desegregation. Agnes Sailer had been a Communist from 1933 to 1945 but was fired when this fact was uncovered,[96] a questionable maneuver backed by the school board.[97]

Rathbone's fiery condemnation was bolstered by the words of O.L. Bell of the District's Public School Association. He contacted leading Dixiecrat, Congressman Thomas Abernethy of Mississippi, to express smarting irritation with both Howard and the NAACP, which had the temerity to produce a publication "lauding integration of the Washington, D.C. public schools," when castigation was merited; also drawing reproach was the Anti-Defamation League of B'nai B'rith, which acted similarly.[98]

---

93. William Punkay to Senator Johnston, 10 January 1957, Box 64, *Olin Johnston Papers*.
94. George Osborn to Senator Johnston, 11 January 1958, Box 64, *Olin Johnston Papers*.
95. Jack Rathbone to Arlington School Board, 8 November 1957, Box 2, *James Stockard Papers*.
96. *Washington Star*, 23 May 1958.
97. Jack Rathbone to Ralph Given, 28 November 1958, Box 2, *James Stockard Papers, George Washington University*.
98. O.L. Bell to Congressman Abernethy, 16 March 1957, Box 49, *Thomas Abernethy Papers, University of Mississippi-Oxford*.

Abernethy was told directly by Ganson Purcell of the Washington Home Rule Committee that more than school desegregation was at play in explicating the increase in racial strains. There was the related question of home rule in that school desegregation fueled "white flight" in turn creating a "Chocolate City" at the heart of imperial power. Telling Abernethy what he likely knew, Purcell asserted that "opposition of a few members of the House District Committee to granting the rights of suffrage and citizenship to Washington's Negro minority has for ten years kept bills for Washington home rule bottled up."[99]

Repetitively the idea was broached that desegregation was leading to a moral collapse. Contemporaneously, Congressman Abernethy was also informed breathlessly about a "colored" principal at Shaw Junior High School in the District who was sacked "because of discovery of unnatural relations he had with a 15 year old student at the school"; then adding insult to ignominy a "colored lawyer by the name of Bedford V. Larson," probably meaning Belford Lawson, who in defense said allegedly the accused's "actions were not unusual [,] that he knew of other instances in the public schools here where principals have had such relations...."[100]

Increasingly, fears of racial desegregation merged with nervousness about changing sexual mores—and not just concerning the centuries long apprehensions about inter-racial heterosexual relations.[101] Black Washington leader, Sterling Tucker, was forced to rebut the idea that "school integration leads to inter-marriage."[102] Lawson was said to have committed the supposed outrage of asserting that "homosexual practices are prevalent" in the District's schools, with magnification coming from his ties to Robeson and Henry A. Wallace, inserting in a neat package concern about political radicalism and sexual divergences.[103] It was also Lawson who was said to have told Logan that the then growing Moral Rearmament Movement was suspect and not just on anticommunist grounds since "many of the men are sex deviates. Pressure is still being put upon him," said the historian, "to have me line up with the movement...."[104]

---

99. Ganson Purcell to Congressman Abernethy, 3 July 1956, Box 373, *Thomas Abernethy Papers*.

100. Unsourced Memorandum, circa 1956, Box 48, *Thomas Abernethy Papers*.

101. Jane Dailey, *White Fright: The Sexual Panic at the Heart of America's Racist History*, New York: Basic, 2020.

102. Sterling Tucker to Guichard Parris, 15 September 1959, Box I: E43, *National Urban League Papers*.

103. Unsourced Memorandum, circa 1956, Box 48, *Thomas Abernethy Papers*.

104. Entry, 3 November 1954, Box 6.

Lawson was not easy to ignore. By 1957 his spouse, Marjorie McKenzie, was about to become a judge and to cement the proposal, she journeyed to Las Vegas "at the request of Congressman [William] Dawson," the Chicago Negro leader, to campaign for Senator Alan Bible of Nevada who could pull strings on her behalf.[105]

Logan, a major vector of gossip, was also told that Senator McCarthy himself was "homosexual," leading the Howardite to muse about writing a novel on this matter, featuring the spouse of the legislator denouncing him unreservedly.[106] Logan did not write this proposed fiction; if he had, he might have included what he was also told: Horace Mann Bond, college president and father of Julian, "had been dismissed because of drunkenness and frequenting houses of prostitution...."[107]

Continuing to roil waters on Capitol Hill was the tragic case of Senator Herman Welker of Idaho, a comrade of Senator McCarthy whose claim to fame theretofore was persuading the local major league baseball franchise to sign the Hall of Fame slugger from his hometown, Harmon Killebrew. But then he ran afoul of Senator Lester C. Hunt of Wyoming, among others, as he pressed the man from the "Cowboy State" to leave his seat. Hunt's 20 year old son was arrested for soliciting prostitution from a male undercover cop in Lafayette Park, in the vicinity of the White House. Senator Hunt was told that if he did abandon his seat, his son would not be prosecuted but the legislator stood firm—so his son was dragged into court and at that point the distraught father committed suicide at his desk on Capitol Hill.[108]

Contributing to the frazzled nerves was an aspect of desegregation that extended beyond "white flight." After the publisher and philanthropist—segregated Houston's Oveta Culp Hobby—spoke on campus, Logan exposed a contradiction that was to rock Howard and other schools for years to come: "Some of the most fervent advocates in public of [racial] integration," he reflected, "are the most alarmed over the fear of losing their jobs"[109]—as a direct result of that

---

105. Ella Roller to Senator Bible, 20 June 1957, Box 43, *Alan Bible Papers, University of Nevada-Reno.*

106. Entry, 24 January 1954, Box 6. See also Entry, 4 August 1958, Box 6: He was told that his colleague, Flemmie Kittrell, needs a "'good screw'" and despite the "frank language" of the attestant, "Lee (Mrs. Alonzo) Moron"; her "frank language" notwithstanding said this moral compass, "I believe that she is a good wife...."

107. Entry, 17 May 1957.

108. Leo Warring, *The Foggy Bottom Gang,* 161.

109. Entry, 3 March 1954, Box 6.

very same process. "Some Negroes are 'integration crazy,'" carped Logan, "that is, they have not examined closely the consequences or even the possibility of integration especially in the Deep South. I am not even sure that integration would work over night in Washington," he concluded.[110] The historian was "gravely concerned about the future of Howard, especially in view of the Supreme Court decision of May 17, 1954,"[111] envisioning before many what was already unfolding as Franklin decamped to Brooklyn and Bunche to Manhattan. Yet even Logan was conceptually unclear in not seeing the bright line separating "integration" from "desegregation" or, to put it another way, denuding Howard versus prying open G.W.U. The NAACP flayed two Negro members of the local school board when they refused to second a motion on the inadvisability of Jim Crow in education (the *Star* backed the two), [112] but Montague Cobb of the Association resigned from the board nonetheless.[113]

This incident was symptomatic of the ideological flabbiness that had arrived as two major processes unfolded: Jim Crow retreating as radicals, e.g., Du Bois and Robeson were made marginal. However, overall Black folk were awakening and that did bode well for the immediate future.

---

110. Entry, 21 April 1953, Box 6. Box 5.
111. Entry, 31 May 1955, Box 6.
112. *Washington Star*, 4 February 1954.
113. *Afro-American*, 16 February 1954.

Chapter 15

From Red Scare to Black Scare, 1955-1960

Phyllis Costly, a Negro mother was frightened. It was early 1959 and Stratford Junior High School in Arlington was enduring a painful transformation: desegregation. "'The school was surrounded by dozens of white helmeted police officers,'" she recalled. Chillingly, "'it didn't become frightening to me until the cross was burned in my yard,'" a flaming symbol of racist intimidation. Foreshadowing this dire episode, Nazis in regalia had been attending school board meetings. "'It was like a war zone outside,'" agreed Joseph Macekura.[1]

Not accidentally, Stratford was the first school in Virginia—and in Dixie more generally—to flout the state's rigid policy of "massive resistance" to desegregation;[2] the proximity to Washington, headquarters of an ideological contest with Moscow for "hearts and minds" in Africa, most notably, was consequential. There was "white flight" from the District and now, ineluctably, there would be an exodus from sites like Arlington, hard by Washington, helping to create exurban development, a term and trend that arose—again, not accidentally—in 1955, as school desegregation was taking flight.[3] Also, it was only to be expected that the so-called "American Fuehrer," George Lincoln Rockwell, leader of U.S. Nazis, made his first significant foray into publicized agitation as a fascist in Washington, D.C. near this same time—1959.[4]

Interestingly, the so-called capital of the "land of the free" contained fertile soil for the growth of Rockwell's forces. By the advent

---

1. *Washington Post*, 12 May 2001, Box 1, *James Stockard Papers, George Washington University*.
2. *Northern Virginia Sun*, 16 February 1996, Box 1, *James Stockard Papers*.
3. Auguste Spectorsky, *The Exurbanites*, Philadelphia: Lippincott, 1955.
4. Frederick J. Simonelli, *American Fuehrer: George Lincoln Rockwell and the American Nazi Party*, Urbana: University of Illinois Press, 1999, 46.

of the 1960s, journalists Andrew Kopkind and James Ridgeway wag-
gishly opined that "'like the Belgians in old Leopoldville the whites
live mainly in one large colony of their own; in Washington it is
called Northwest.'"[5]

This unpalatable trait was bolstered by a long-term trend: the
lack of home rule and even congressional representation allowed for
those in Leopoldville's peer neighborhood in the District to continue
a trend that the late Senator Bilbo had accelerated, i.e., Mississippi
legislators as a sounding board for disgruntled Euro-Americans in
the District. The latest embodiment of this reinforcement of the more
horrid aspects of the District was Delbert Payne of 4000 Cathedral
Way—northwest Washington, of course. "This is one city where a
subway should not be built," he insisted to Congressman Thomas
Abernethy of the Magnolia State, "and that is because of the high
rate of Negro crime. As it is, the residents fear to go out after dark
and this [is] above ground, where they can be seen and heard. Think
what opportunities a subway could give muggers, rapists, robbers,"
he claimed darkly. Anyway, he continued, "we do have a subway
in N.W. Washington, up on Connecticut Avenue but I know of no
one who uses it, unless absolutely necessary. The 'planners' of transportation," he declared, "do not take into account the ever growing
Negro population here and proceed as though there were no Negro
crime problem"—he then added, "please do not reply," as if his
claims were self-evident or, perhaps, unwilling to run the possible
risk of having mail from a Mississippi politician delivered to his
mailbox,[6] by a disgruntled Negro mail deliverer.

Even legislators representing jurisdictions far distant from the eastern seaboard were subjected to unremitting pressure to crackdown on
the District. Such was the case for Senator Alan Bible of Nevada. A.E.
Cahlan, general manager of the *Las Vegas Review Journal*, one of the
more influential newspapers in this booming state, sent Bible an article about the purported viciousness of Negro gangs in Washington.
Turning his attention away from the gangsters who dominated the
political economy of his hometown, Cahlan instead pondered reflectively: "the thought immediately occurs to me," he considered, "as to
whether or not white gangs are causing the same amount of trouble."
A Congressman was quoted in his attached article that referred to
these Negro youth as a "'pack of wolves.'" The demand was clear
said this article: "Call out [the] militia—if necessary—to keep order";

---

5. Chris Myers and George Derek Musgrove, *Chocolate City*, 332.
6. Delbert Payne to Congressman Abernethy, 22 June 1960, Box 48, *Thomas
Abernethy Papers, University of Mississippi-Oxford.*

the "assistance of U.S. Marshalls and as many deputies as might be necessary" was the demand. Liberal and moderate squishiness would not do: "The facts must be faced. There are 19 million Negroes in the United States. Their number is exploding because of the high birth rate"[7]—something severe must be done.

As the manacles of Jim Crow were loosened the old reliable—the "Black Scare"—i.e., the idea that unless there was a draconian police crackdown, African Americans would run amok and ignite a crime spree, arose as a substitute. Quite conveniently for ultra-rightists, as the Red Scare wreaked havoc depriving African Americans of their most visionary leaders—Du Bois and Robeson in the first place—a Black Scare arose allowing these vultures to gnaw further on Negro bodies and carrion.

Echoing Payne and Cahlan was Attorney Robert N. Miller of the District who buttressed him ideologically by raising the Red specter in order to evade home rule. He contacted that other Dixie guardian of the status quo in Washington, Congressman John McMillan of South Carolina, reminding him that "if the Communists could manage to infiltrate the police and other agencies in the Federal District, they could of course do a great deal...." But they could not, he thought, when Congress was in control and home rule was blocked and if this were to change, prepare for the Red flag to flutter over Washington.[8]

It was Miller's colleagues in the District Bar Association, who sought to strengthen the already fortified anticommunist scaffolding in Washington. Recent high court decisions seeming to weaken the fervently anticommunist Smith Act, involving plaintiffs Clinton Jencks and Oleta O'Connor Yates, were not greeted with ease among leading members of the local bar, who wanted Senator Johnston of South Carolina to intervene, i.e., "strengthening the government's hand in combating subversion." Their formidable Committee on Un-American Activities, complementing their peer on Capitol Hill, railed against the "'few, clever, well trained and well disciplined Americans,'" of which the District had more than their share, necessitating the "'fight against Communism and the insidious and devious means'" by these forces.[9]

---

7. A.E. Cahlan, General Manager to Senator Bible, 31 August 1959, Box 43, *Alan Bible Papers, University of Nevada-Reno.*

8. Unsourced memo, apparently from Robert Miller, 11 August 1959, Box 6, *John McMillan Papers, University of South Carolina-Columbia.*

9. Report by District Bar Association, 16 May 1958, Box 64, *Olin Johnston Papers.*

Senator Johnston of the Palmetto State was also aware of another factor driving Jim Crow. This viewpoint was reflected in the remarks of C.O. Thompson, president of the Gray Line of Charleston and Haish Turner, president of Carolina Scenic Trailways of Spartansburg, both firms described as "independent, locally owned and operated sightseeing and charter firms" with the former having a District subsidiary. The latter was "getting closer to being forced out of business by the D.C. Transit System," with the situation spiraling "from bad to worse." How could Thompson maintain Jim Crow as this edifice was under assault, especially when his competition was a "secure tax exempt monopoly" destined to "invade other competitive fields—such as helicopter services [and] interstate passenger services"?[10] It was not apparent how he reacted to the nascent plans by incoming U.S. President Kennedy, to construct mass rail transit.[11]

How could a private business like his survive in the face of a government competitor that simultaneously was pressing for desegregation, which would alienate a good deal of those who patronized Thompson's business? Would not an attack on government itself— soon to be seen as commonsense by the presidential election of 1980—at once challenge frontally competition while guaranteeing profitability and Jim Crow?

As ever, that external pressures were driving internal matters in the U.S. was clear. Yet, when Ralph Bunche in early 1959 had the audacity to articulate what was painfully plain, the report was encased in his FBI file. Still, for an international civil servant—or even a U.S. national—his words were quite blunt, reviving memories of the Bunche of the 1930s. "The world of '59 is no longer a white man's," he announced portentously, "as yellows, browns and blacks rise." That he would have the fortitude to announce this in the "Heart of Darkness" that was Birmingham, Alabama, albeit at the "Periclean Club," i.e., an "all Negro study group" did not buffer the sting. "The world of 1959 is not by any means a 'white world' or a 'white man's world,'" said Bunche; today, he asserted "it is overwhelmingly a nonwhite world and a world in which the authority of white men which knew little or no challenge even as recently as a

10. C.O. Thompson and Haish Turner to Senator Johnston, 7 January 1959, Box 64, *Olin Johnston Papers*.

11. "Recommendations for Transportation in the National Capital Region, Finance and Organization, a Report to the President for Transmittal to Congress by the National Capital Transportation Agency," 1 November 1962, Box 100a, Folder 3, *President's Office Files, John F. Kennedy Presidential Library-Boston*.

generation ago, are [sic] rapidly declining."[12] This was a throwback to the hellishness of what had transpired only recently—the Pacific War as a "Race War,"[13] which had ensnared so many Negroes and frightened so many Euro-Americans. This expression also allowed the sly Bunche to evade the sensitive class matters embodied in the Cold War, while still invoking the potency of global confrontation where Negroes were not altogether outnumbered.

Bunche's insight also helps to explain the pigheaded recalcitrance then unfolding in Arlington, for there was the gnawing perception that a way of life with deep roots in chattel slavery was lurching to a juddering close. Unfortunately for African Americans, they were caught in a bloody meatgrinder. For the response of the authorities often was overly sympathetic to those resisting desegregation. This was the case with the FBI—but not only the FBI—which, directed an adjunct of the COINTELPRO or Counter-Intelligence Program, which was devised in 1956 purportedly targeting the Communist Party but also encompassed the anti-Jim Crow movement more generally. There was massive and intense spying on African Americans, a group deemed to be inherently subversive—which had a kernel of truth insofar as many in this besieged community were adamantly opposed to the Jim Crow status quo, which was the law in too many jurisdictions. It was utterly foreseeable that this surveillance and disruption would be extreme in the center of power: the District. "Every agent in [the FBI] Washington, D.C. office was required to recruit at least six 'ghetto informants,'" was the analysis presented by Betty Medsger, a corollary of the point that the FBI leader, J. Edgar Hoover, was born in the District and was well aware of the crevices of insecurity there, thought to be sited disproportionately in Black Washington, especially since this disputatious leader had a "tendency to be particularly cruel to African Americans," according to Medsger.[14]

Certainly, events in the vicinity of the District allowed for plenty of opportunity for Hoover to bare his fangs. Perhaps because a good deal of the fear and loathing of those resistant to change was directed at schools on the presumed premise that these sites were training grounds for intermarriage, youth leapt to the forefront of

---

12. *New York Herald Tribune*, circa 14 February 1959. See also *Birmingham Post-Herald*, 14 February 1959, which carries the story necessarily with a differing spin, Box 1, *Ralph Bunche FBI File, Schomburg Center*.

13. Gerald Horne, *Race War!*.

14. Betty Medsger, *The Burglary: The Discovery of J. Edgar Hoover's Secret FBI*, New York: Knopf, 2014, 226, 227, 347.

the anti-Jim Crow movement.[15] This inexorable trend provided ballast to the Black Scare.

Howard was Exhibit A in this regard as it tossed aside the torpor of the 1950s. By late 1957, Rayford Logan already had begun to notice a "spirit of rebellion" among his students, coupled with a worrisome "anti-intellectualism."[16] The growing cohort of African students he found to be "truculent, belligerent and intolerant," not factoring in how Jim Crow was such a shock to so many of them. "They were suspicious about the reasons why the United States and American Negroes were interested in Africa" and suspected—rightfully—it was because we "were disturbed by the interest of the Soviet Union in Africa,"[17] which they then began to leverage in their multiple protests.

It was in March 1960, weeks after students in Greensboro, North Carolina ignited a new stage in the movement with their protests at lunch counters, that Hayward Farrar—who went on to a distinguished academic career—counselled the regents of the University of Maryland at College Park, that "'[the] time has come for you all to really take steps you should have taken in 1954.'" Described as speaking in a subdued but firm voice, Farrar was reminding that the main campus just across the District line as well as the Baltimore County campus were virtually 100 percent lily-white, while their counterpart in Princess Anne County was overwhelmingly Negro.[18]

"At present there are no Negro students at College Park," was the message from the *Washington Post* in 1948.[19] It was only in 1951 that the flagship campus on the District's border reluctantly agreed to veer away—at least rhetorically—from this degeneracy.[20] Thus, by 1955 the campus rejected Negro recreation workers who sought to enroll in a course—this after being invited to do so.[21] Within a short driving distance in Princess Anne County was the campus for Negroes, described by the *Post* in 1952 as a "ramshackle counterfeit of a place of higher education...."[22]

---

15. V.P. Franklin, *The Young Crusaders: The Untold Story of the Children and Teenagers who Galvanized the Civil Rights Movement*, Boston: Beacon Press, 2021.

16. Entry, 20 December 1957, Box 6.

17. Entry, 14 January 1958, Box 6.

18. *Baltimore Sun*, 22 March 1960, Vertical File- "Black Student Union," *University of Maryland-College Park*.

19. *Washington Post*, 15 November 1948.

20. *Washington Post*, 30 January 1951.

21. *Washington Star*, 9 March 1955.

22. *Washington Post*, 31 August 1952.

College Park was not singular. John Thompson, who was to become a celebrated basketball coach there, spoke of Georgetown University as "basically segregated in 1960 and the basketball team remained entirely white until 1967." This 6'10' tall former hoopster at Providence College and the professional Boston Celtics had not forgotten that this school's "very existence had been secured by the sale of 272 enslaved Black people," nor had he forgotten that growing up in Washington in the 1940s "light skinned kids were treated better than those of us with dark skin,"[23] an ineluctable aspect of hegemonic white supremacy.

Howard continued to be a burr under Washington's saddle. As Arlington was going up in metaphorical flames, appearing at the hilltop was former Secretary of State, Dean Acheson, an architect of the Cold War. There was an overflow audience, generating elaborate discussion, with a notable emphasis on what was termed the "China problem" and the "Berlin crisis...."[24] Tellingly, this inveterate Cold Warrior was sponsored by the campus NAACP chapter, though on the front page of the campus newspaper that carried his appearance was a story of the famed hilltop professor, Bernard Fall, one of the nation's leading specialists on Vietnam, flanked by the writer soon-to-be a Black Power icon then a Marxist—alumnus Le Roi Jones/Amiri Baraka—alongside then fellow "Beats," Allen Ginsberg, Gregory Corso, and Peter Orslovsky, a corps capable of inspiring dissidence.[25]

A few months later, there appeared Tom Mboya of Kenya, a State Department favorite, and even more attended. Those unable to enter the chapel crowded the lawn outside, listening over a public address system. In addition to students and faculty, envoys from various embassies showed up, suggesting that the hilltop was reinforcing its role as a diplomatic crossroads and solidifying Howard's application to be allotted the "Distinguished College Chapter Award" of the NAACP,[26] a prize granted at the Summer 1959 convention.[27] Within weeks recorded was the observation that "record attendance marks first NAACP meeting" for the fall semester of 1959,[28] not auguring well for Jim Crow in Washington.

---

23. John Thompson with Jesse Washington, *I Came as a Shadow: An Autobiography*, New York: Holt, 2021, 45, xi, 14.

24. *The Hilltop*, 27 March 1959.

25. *The Hilltop*, 27 March 1959.

26. Reports, March 1959 and May 1959, Box III: E3, *NAACP Papers*. On Mboya, see *The Hilltop*, 3 June 1959.

27. *The Hilltop*, 22 September 1959.

28. *The Hilltop*, 19 October 1959.

Almost by necessity, Howard had to be in the vanguard of anti-Jim Crow protest. This was illustrated when the hilltop reported the sad story of student, George Cooper, barred from his hometown public library in Lakeland, Florida;[29] how could he advance his studies in the face of such penalty? A few months later, students there in the hundreds participated in the 20,000 strong march for desegregation held in the center of the city: a petition was drawn up to deliver to the outgoing President Eisenhower, a project given heft by the presence of baseballer, Jackie Robinson; actor and singer, Harry Belafonte; Kenyan leader, Tom Mboya; and Congressman Charles Diggs of Detroit, who had developed a decided interest in African affairs.[30]

By early 1960 hilltop students descended on Capitol Hill and picketed, gathering on the west side of the imposing building where laws were debated, displaying huge placards in favor of a civil rights bill then under scrutiny. Commands from police to remove the signs were brusquely ignored; then if President Eisenhower had peered outside his window a few days later, he would have seen almost 400 Howardites protesting, again in support of civil rights.[31]

This was occurring in the context of the startling events in Greensboro, where students sought to desegregate lunch counters, which had knock-on effects, not least at Howard—already primed and moving in that direction in any case. By early April 1960, Vice-President Richard M. Nixon and Speaker Sam Rayburn of Texas refused permission for Howardites to picket on Capitol Hill, though a hilltop student leader argued rightfully that their initiative was of "'international significance.'" A student journalist pointed out that for weeks now "students from Howard University have participated in non-violent picketing of...Woolworth's...stores which are located at 3200 14th Street and 3111 M Street, N.W.," in solidarity with their comrades in North Carolina. A beleaguered employee said sighingly that "'there are more salespeople in here, than customers,'" a sign that victory was certain.[32]

Again, the NAACP chapter at Howard was essential to this early spate of demonstrations before the Student Non-Violent Coordinating Committee (SNCC) began to assert itself. "We have been deeply concerned about the student demonstrations in the South," said

---

29. *The Hilltop*, 15 January 1959.
30. *The Hilltop*, 24 April 1959.
31. *The Hilltop*, 7 March 1960.
32. *The Hilltop*, 8 April 1960.

chapter president, Jeanne Marie Anderson. Hence, her "members have joined in the picketing of the Woolworth stores in Washington and have gone with the pickets to the White House and the Capitol...."[33]

Then as the semester ended students from Howard, which attracted a student body from across the U.S. and the world, seeding protests nationally, if not globally. "Congratulations to those students in the Washington area," read an editorial in *The Hilltop* welcoming returning matriculants back to campus in September 1960, "who participated in the sit-in movement over the summer"; moreover, it was said revealingly, "many foreign students abroad have far more interest and concern for this movement than many of us here...."[34]

What this comment reflected is the symbiosis between anti-colonialism and the fortunes of Howard. For as Caribbean and African nations surged to sovereignty and as many U.S. campuses were perceived as unfriendly to these potential students, many of them arrived on the hilltop, were shocked by the surrounding Jim Crow and took to the streets. Furthermore, foreign students often paid full tuition, absent scholarships, making them that much more valuable. It was also in September 1960 that Ernest Wilson was designated as the first full-time Foreign Student Advisor, a response said a student reporter, to the "growing number of foreign students enrolled...."[35]

These overseas arrivals were influencing Howardites ideologically. Many were stunned by Jim Crow with a reporter underscoring that the "impact of racial discrimination upon the colored foreigner is admittedly so distasteful that it tends to taint every other aspect of life," a distaste they were more than willing to communicate, causing an onlooker to find it "extremely irritating to hear America... termed 'imperialistic,'"[36] a descriptor that had retreated domestically as the Red Scare advanced.

It did not take long for African Americans to detect that global pressure might cause Euro-American shopkeepers and the like to try to carve out an anti-Jim Crow exception for Africans. Route 40 through Maryland was a highway of turmoil as Africans often had to run the gauntlet of bias in order to get a meal or find lodging, complicating U.S. foreign policy. Enterprising U.S. Negro

---

33. Jeanne Marie Anderson to Herbert Wright, Youth Secretary, 3 April 1960, Box III: E3, *NAACP Papers*.
34. *The Hilltop*, 30 September 1960.
35. *The Hilltop*, 30 September 1960.
36. *The Hilltop*, 10 November 1960.

journalists dressed nattily in top hats and formal dress and hopped into a chauffeured Cadillac and sought service—often successfully.[37] It did not take long for U.S. Negro students to dress in West African garb while seeking service in shops that would otherwise be refused: they often were successful, possibly accelerating the trend of adopting this form of dress which became au courant during this decade.[38]

The metropolitan area was changing rapidly but not fast enough given the pace of transformation in Africa and the Caribbean. Just after Ghana's independence in 1957, Howard's Logan took a train to Newport News: "there was definitely no segregation on the train," he noted with wonder; "the curtain and/or the partition are gone," separating Negroes from others—"no segregation. I went to the white men's room," he announced.[39] However, a patchwork was developing in Dixie. By November 1958 he was in Atlanta, where he met fellow scholar, Howard Zinn, and there he found that in the "waiting room" sat a "sign: colored waiting room: interstate passengers."[40]

In 1960 alone, 17 African nations attained independence from Senegal to Somalia to Nigeria and their nationals began arriving in Washington and its vicinity, often greeted rudely. When Malick Sow of Chad was refused service in Maryland, followed by his counterparts from Mali, Cameroon and Togo, with a Euro-American shopkeeper unapologetically arguing as to Sow that "'he looked like just an ordinary run-of-the-mill [n-word] to me...I couldn't tell he was an ambassador.'" Eventually caught up in companion protests was the Howardite with roots in Trinidad then known as Stokely Carmichael who already had spent weeks in a state penitentiary resulting from a "Freedom Ride," taking a train from New Orleans to Jackson, Mississippi. Eventually, Annapolis felt compelled to pass laws restraining this bigotry, preceding the federal civil rights laws of 1964 and, in fact, helping to trigger same.[41]

Yet while Washington was bludgeoning Cameroonians and other Africans with Jim Crow, Rayford Logan happened to speak with Patrick Furlong "who is going to open the American consulate at

37. Faith Wassink, "Meeting in the Middle in Maryland: How International and Domestic Politics Collided on Route 40," M.A. Thesis, University of Maryland-Baltimore County, 2010, 1. See also USA Today, 12 November 2021.
38. Dorothy Butler Gilliam, Trailblazer, 19.
39. Entry, 25 August 1957, Box 6.
40. Entry, 27 November 1958, Box 6.
41. USA Today, 12 November 2021.

Yaounde, French Cameroons...he told me frankly that the Communists are spending a lot of money in the French Cameroons."[42]

This attainment was the result of attritional war as generations of racist praxis were overturned. Norman Bernstein was then tasked with the difficult job of finding 3,500 apartments in Washington and thereabouts for these arriving African dignitaries and he sought assistance from others with knowledge of the market: "'No one stepped up,'" said his son Joshua Bernstein, decades later.[43]

What happened in August 1960 was typical. Four students carrying passports variously from Ghana, Chad, and Somalia were turned away from a Washington apartment, presumably on racist grounds, they were seeking to inspect.[44] This was old hat for Ghanaians: a few months earlier an official from this West African nation was refused lodging—again on presumed racist grounds—at 1426 2lst Street N.W.[45] This was a double-barreled offensive for as Africans were being barred from one set of hotels, there were vice squad raids on what were described as "Negro hotels and tourist homes," e.g., the Pitts Hotel at 1457 Belmont N.W.[46] It was not enough to drain away the latter's patrons, they had to be undermined officially at the same time.

Back at the hilltop, all was not lost for simultaneously studying to become a scholar of Ghana was Ray Kea, one of Logan's students; the senior scholar "helped him to improve the language of [an important application] and typed it for him," indicative of the mutuality between Africans and African Americans as Washington was acting otherwise.[47]

This illustrated the dilemma of Washington, under siege because of a Jim Crow system that so many supported. Logan was trapped in the vortex, unwilling to move too much to the left while capable of influencing Africans who had no such compunction. He was summoned by U.S. ambassador in Ghana, Wilson Flake and with a tinge of sarcasm Logan "made it clear I am no Communist," the obligatory introductory remarks in Washington then; confusion about his membership status "explains why I have been asked

---

42. Entry, 25 May 1957, Box 6.
43. *Washington Post*, 4 October 2020.
44. *Washington Post*, 9 August 1960.
45. *Washington Post*, 23 April 1960
46. *Pittsburgh Courier*, 29 November 1961.
47. Entry, 21 April 1957, Box 6. See, e.g., Ray Kea, *Settlements, Trade and Polities in the Seventeenth Century Gold Coast*, Baltimore: Johns Hopkins University Press, 1982.

so infrequently in recent weeks to lecture" on behalf of the State Department. The envoy "asked me whether I did not believe that Prime Minister Nkrumah would not be well advised to confine himself to the problems of Ghana rather than to try to head up a Pan-African movement...." Logan, quite unctuously, "fully agreed" but then added that "Nkrumah might be forced to become a 'Black Napoleon'" on behalf of more unfortunate nations, including Congo. He analogized that contemporaneously "practically every Southern Negro Baptist minister feels compulsion to be another Martin Luther King." He went on to underline how the U.S. had a material interest in backing African independence in order to undermine "the former metropolitan country," e.g., London, Paris, and Lisbon, a policy exemplified by then Senator Kennedy, promptly continued when he entered the White House. Flake also "was concerned about criticisms in the Negro press concerning the appointment of a white man to Ghana"—this community likely assumed that since Liberia and Haiti were reserved for Negro envoys, this would continue indefinitely, apparently unaware of the Cold War stakes that altered the role of Africa. "I added," said Logan, "that I was certain that Haiti would not accept a Negro as ambassador but that if Argentina did, Haiti would," returning serve adroitly back to Flake. But Logan was understandably skeptical: "chances are that our entire conversation was being taken down on a tape recording machine," since this Howardite continued to be viewed with suspicion. Although Flake remarked insultingly that "some of my best friends are Negroes," it was "only once did [he] pronounce the word Negro in a way that might give offense."[48]

Logan was walking a tightrope seeking to curry favor with emerging Africa and their opponents alike. By early 1959 he had concluded "there is a dictatorship in Ghana," while complimenting Eisenhower: "he looks much better than he does on television."[49]

But these major powers had little option beyond consulting with Logan for insight, given their past ham-fisted policies. "Commander Klein of Naval Intelligence wanted to see [me]...to talk about anti-Americanism in France," was a typical random comment.[50] Thus, he found himself sipping "cocktails" at the home of "Mr. and Mrs. Douglas Williams, British Colonial Attaché" in Washington and, naturally, Francis Wilcox U.S. Assistant Secretary of State asked if he knew Nkrumah. U.S. national, Edwin Munger, considered to

48. Entry, 1 June 1957, Box 6.
49. Entry, 31 January 1959, Box 6.
50. Entry, 14 November 1957, Box 6.

be a leading Africanist, referred distastefully to Ghanaians as "'Gonorrheans,'" indicative of a diseased attitude.[51] Logan's comrade in the American Committee on Africa, George Houser, had "the same doubts about…Munger that I do," though this wordsmith was certainly "shrewd."[52]

These authorities had to consult with Logan despite their doubts because they had been too successful in fully co-opting those of similar rank. This included Professor Helen Edmonds, said Logan, an "apologist for the State Department in her speeches abroad," and, thus, with little purchase in sites like Ghana. The Ku Klux Klan was "gaining more headway in North Carolina," her home—"most of the members are grocery store owners, filling station operators and the like"—yet she soldiered on.[53]

Yet, the granite of Jim Crow had cracked to the degree that when the Martinican born Algerian revolutionary, Frantz Fanon, arrived in Bethesda, Maryland for medical treatment—just before he expired in 1961—high level officialdom was seeking enrollment for his son in Howard's kindergarten.[54]

As so often happens, the activism of students was inspiring to alumni, e.g., the successful human rights attorney in the District, James Cobb, bequeathed the bulk of his hefty $347,000 estate to Howard.[55] Mimicking Le Roi Jones who had returned to campus, so did prolific writer, Julian Mayfield, alumnus of both Howard and Dunbar High School.[56]

However, unlike other major cities, Washington was more subject to the changing tides of electoral politics, a reality that came clear with the arrival of the "New Frontier" in late 1960. President-elect John F. Kennedy already had shown he was willing—quite opportunistically—to break ranks with the French ally and speak more favorably of decolonization in Africa. Similarly, he sensed the direction of prevailing currents domestically. Speaking at Howard in October 1960, he put his Cold War foot forward and asked plaintively, "can we…mobilize and not only endure but prevail over a Communist system," as long as Jim Crow stained the national escutcheon. How could U.S. imperialism "prevail" in sovereign Africa with

---

51. Entry, 20 July 1957, Box 6.
52. Entry, 14 September 1958, Box 6.
53. Entry, 1 September 1957, Box 6.
54. Thomas Meaney, "Frantz Fanon and the CIA Man," *American Historical Review*, 124 (Number 3, June 2019): 983-995, 990.
55. *The Hilltop*, 29 April 1958.
56. *The Hilltop*, 23 March 1960.

African Americans treated so atrociously? How could imperialism prevail with such a wastage of human capital? There was then one Negro federal court judge out of 200 appointees and, according to the incoming chief executive, "we cannot afford in 1960 to waste any talent which we have." The successful 1957 Sputnik launch still weighed heavily and Kennedy noted that "we are producing about half as many scientists and engineers as the Soviet Union," he concluded dourly. Echoing Bunche, indicating that the latter's sourness was not his alone, Kennedy said, "We who are white are a minority in this global world and all those over the world who are colored are now reaching greater and greater power," as "the whole course of history for the past 150 years has been toward freedom"[57]—which perforce must include the District of Columbia.

The presidential hopeful received a standing ovation at Howard with a commentator observing that "the welcome was so enthusiastic that if both candidates had appeared"—referring to Richard M. Nixon—"[Eisenhower] would probably have had to call out the National Guard" to prevent the dour Republican candidate from being mauled.[58] Thus, in a presentiment of the actual election, JFK won a "mock" campus election by a landslide: 755 to 223.[59]

Days earlier Kennedy was sited at the Sheraton Park Hotel in the District and the complexion of those assembled might have changed but not his substantive message. His predecessor, Abraham Lincoln, had announced decades previously that the nation could not exist half free and half slave but now, said the youthful leader, the question was: "can the world exist half slave and half free," adding pointedly "three years ago when I was in Cuba, the American ambassador was the second most influential man in Cuba, today the Soviet ambassador is...." Thus, "Cuba and the Congo and Algeria...[all] judge us abroad by what we do here at home," pressuring imperialism further since "the enemy is lean and hungry,"[60] like a scheming Shakespearean character.

The tall and lanky Alphaeus Hunton was certainly lean. He had travelled from the Howard faculty to the side of Robeson in Manhattan and the Council on African Affairs—with a brief stay behind bars—but by 1960 he was headed eastward: his first stop was

---

57. Speech at Howard, 7 October 1960, Box 1058, Folder 7, *Presidential Campaign Files, John F. Kennedy Presidential Library-Boston, Massachusetts.*
58. *The Hilltop,* 14 October 1960.
59. *The Hilltop,* 10 November 1960.
60. Speech, 20 September 1960, Box 78, Folder 4, *President's Office Files, Kennedy Presidential Library.*

Guinea-Conakry, then he reunited with Du Bois in Ghana soon thereafter before fleeing to Zambia after the coup in Accra in early 1966.
His looming presence was an emblem of the point that it would be
difficult for Washington to sneak fairy-tale propaganda past Cona-
kry, Accra and Lusaka, complicating JFK's mission.[61]

The steadfastness of Hunton created space for Rayford Logan,
though U.S. authorities viewed him uncertainly too. He was summoned by U.S. Naval Intelligence, for example, after reading
Hunton's recent book on U.S. imperialism's policy in Africa. The
subject was French Communists and comfortingly Logan "doubted
that the publication in French newspapers of articles about the injus-
tices inflicted upon Negroes in the United States contributed as
much to anti-Americanism as is generally believed...." He knew this
since he "lived in France from 1919 to 1924. During that time there
had been only a small number of black Negroes in France; most of
them were students and intellectuals. But in 1951 and 1952 the number of black Negroes had increased...." Then Logan flashed before
his curious interrogator a copy of *We Charge Genocide*, the cause
celebre identified with Robeson: "some American delegates to the
U.N. General Assembly in Paris wanted to make a direct rebuttal.
I had been asked to write a working paper." Then Logan "showed
him my copious notes in the book and said that I had planned not
to deny specific charges—which were true—but to give the other
side of the picture," providing aid and comfort to U.S. imperialism.
Logan then displayed Hunton's book which caused the intelligence
agent to request ominously "information about both William Patterson and Alphaeus Hunton."[62] Logan shored up his credentials
by reference to "my conference with Irving Brown [U.S. intelligence
operative] from Paris to Milan in 1951 or 1952," and his association
with Maida Springer, similarly oriented, her union—International
Ladies Garment Workers Union—"and their interest in the trade
union movement in Africa."

Thus, despite unsureness about Logan, he continued to be consulted not least since he—like Bunche—was as complicating as JFK's
own rhetoric. The Bostonian was as responsible as Hunton, Du Bois,
or Robeson for repeatedly linking the conjoined fates of Africa and
African Americans, albeit with a different overall purpose in mind.
It was in early 1959 that after decades of prompting, Howard offered
courses in Ki-Swahili and Yoruba [Nigeria] for the first time.[63] This

---

61. Christine Ann Lutz, "'The Dizzy Steep to Heaven,'" 330.
62. Entry, 18 November 1957, Box 6.
63. *The Hilltop*, 13 February 1959.

would only bring Negroes ever closer to their ancestral homeland, increasing the strength of both.

Kennedy also was seized with grave concern about the unfolding revolutionary process in Cuba, a subject that would lead to his catastrophic decision to overthrow the regime. Howard had noticed and Dr. Allan Taylor of the faculty brought to campus what was described as "two ranking officers in Fidel Castro's army" in order to "provide students with an example of resistance [to] centralization of power," said the perceptive student journalist. "Dr. Taylor has two cousins in Cuba," said this reporter, "who were boyhood friends of Castro and fought in the revolution with him...."[64] Three weeks after the triumph of the revolution, Logan was summoned to the State Department for an "all day session." Proudly, he noted, "I was the only one of 'us,'" present, meaning U.S. Negro. "I had arrived in Havana in 1933 the day after [the leader] had fled. I was impressed by the fact that there was no color line manifest," pointing to an article he had written then for the *Afro-American*. But his first question in January 1959 was whether Chinese-Cubans "had taken an important role in the overthrow" of the regime and was told the answer was negative.[65] The point being that Logan, too, had much to convey about Cuba to his engaged students.

Faculty member, Flemmie Pansy Kittrell could have embroidered his remarks since she toured only recently the nation that was to become Havana's primary ally: the Soviet Union.[66] By November 1959, faculty member Dr. Jose Ferrer was assuring that the "Castro regime" was "not Communist,"[67] remarks made just prior to the arrival of six visiting Soviet students to the hilltop.[68]

It had become de rigueur for certain African and Caribbean leaders visiting the White House or State Department, to make a pit stop at Howard, enhancing the stature of both. Forbes Burnham of what was to become Guyana, the English speaking nation on the northern coast of South America, arrived at the hilltop in May 1959,[69] followed by Norman Manley of Jamaica.[70] A few months later making a grand entrance through the gates of Howard was founding father

---

64. *The Hilltop*, 24 April 1959.
65. Entry, 22 January 1959.
66. *The Hilltop*, 7 October 1959.
67. *The Hilltop*, 23 November 1959.
68. *The Hilltop*, 7 December 1959.
69. *The Hilltop*, 8 May 1959.
70. *The Hilltop*, 8 February 1960.

of independent Guinea-Conakry, Sekou Toure, soon to host former Howardite, W. Alphaeus Hunton. He arrived in an imposing black limousine, followed by a procession of other vehicles, including army cars, all led by a motorcycle escort. As he exited his limousine students assembled, cheered lustily, and cheered further when he announced that Howard was producing tomorrow's leaders.[71] Unbeknownst to the Guinean stalwart, in the vicinity as he spoke— if not in the audience—was Donald McHenry, a future U.S. envoy to the United Nations in the 1970s with whom he was to consort, who was then a graduate student at Georgetown.[72]

The internationalism of Howard was not limited to the Caribbean and Africa; as Kennedy was campaigning for the White House in 1960, Howard students exchanged books with fellow college students in Pakistan.[73]

As ever, Professor Logan played an essential role in this internationalization of the campus, a product of his fluency in French, his research interests, his invitations to foreign dignitaries, and his being called on frequently to address these visitors. His books also instructed; he was pleased that the leading U.S. Communist, Gil Green, cited his proposition that one of the reasons that Reconstruction after the civil war failed was because of the dearth of "effective foreign criticism."[74] He was so engaged with pending civil rights legislation that once he "woke up about one thirty [in the] morning and thought about the disgusting history...."[75] He contested the contention by premier columnist, David Lawrence, who sought to undermine the entire edifice of civil rights reform by alleging that the 14th Amendment to the U.S. Constitution was not ratified legally.[76]

He would have been able to do even more—but for his being bogged down in petty and subjective tussles with fellow faculty, especially Professor Merze Tate. This pettifoggery was partially a result of the inordinate pressure exerted on those like Logan, courted but suspected because of his past association with the Council on African Affairs. Thus, Logan responded awkwardly while rebuking Black Communist leader, James Ford, after he asked Mordecai Johnson to collaborate on a study of "Marxian Principles," —"the

71. *The Hilltop*, 13 November 1959l
72. *The Hilltop*, 10 November 1960.
73. *The Hilltop*, 23 February 1960.
74. Entry, 16 August 1956, Box 6.
75. Entry, 25 July 1956, Box 6.
76. Entry, 6 August 1956, Box 6.

president should have nothing to do with the study...obviously the new party line (after the downgrading of Stalin and the relaxation of the Cold War) is to involve Negro intellectuals as some were involved about twenty years or more ago." No dice—Logan had suffered enough because of his brief dalliance with Communists—though with awkwardness he added, "many persons think that I am white,"[77] as if that were exculpating in the charged environment.

Yet as desegregation seemed to erode whatever advantage Logan's lighter skin brought, he began to suspect that he was enduring a fall in status. He felt that Hope Franklin being "black gave him an advantage over mulattoes (such as me....)[78]

Nonetheless, it was a blow overall to the movement that these Howardites steered clear of those to their left to their mutual disadvantage. For when Johnson and Logan got around to discussing the "downgrading" of Stalin, the latter historian opined that it was linked to the simultaneous "downgrade" of Mao in China and Tito in Yugoslavia.[79]

However, the contretemps with Tate absorbed so much of his mental energy it was even more remarkable that he could get anything done. Before decamping to Brooklyn College, John Hope Franklin was—said Logan—"disturbed by what the feud between Tate and me was doing to the department,"[80] likely a factor in his flight northward. Yet, when Tate held a luncheon on campus for ambassadors from India, Pakistan, and Ceylon, Franklin was the only colleague invited.[81] It was unclear if Frank Snowden, the Classicist, was invited; this was unlikely since Logan confessed to having "affection" for him, possibly making him suspicious in Tate's eyes (Logan quickly claimed that "neither of us is a homosexual," lest there be any doubt. He also surmised that "Frank also keeps a diary" in case prying eyes sought to investigate further.)[82]

---

77. Entry, 3 May 1956, Box 6.
78. Entry, 31 December 1957, Box 6.
79. Entry, 3 May 1956, Box 6.
80. Entry, 7 April 1956, Box 6.
81. Entry, 3 May 1956, Box 6.
82. Entry, 20 December 1957, Box 6. Cf. Entry, 21 January 1960, Box 6: Logan met Earl Schwarz for lunch at the Burlington Hotel and "after much hesitation he told me that he had had homosexual experiences in the Middle East and other places. He then asked me if I had had any homosexual experiences. I told him no and that I wanted none...." He then "pleaded with me to find him a 'sweet intellectual colored boy'"; the "conversation began to be embarrassing" as Logan declined the role of pimp. He then wondered if he

Logan was shunned and collegiality continued in its downward flight. Sterling Brown, another noted professor, was said to have called Tate a "'porcupine'" and, so inspired, Logan "turned" his "back on her and said" contemptuously, "'Woman shut up'" and, worse, from the "corner of my eye I could see her shaken from head to foot.'"[83] "Tate does not hesitate to tell a lie,"[84] he claimed about his eminent colleague—a woman he called a "pathological liar"[85] who "does not hesitate to tell a lie"[86]—and, in addition, was a "fool,"[87] "crazy and demented" besides.[88] Tate reportedly replied that Logan "might need a bullet-proof vest," as Logan recalled how purportedly "Tate had threatened in a departmental meeting to 'get a pistol and shoot anybody' who repeated what John Hope had said about her not being qualified to teach American history."[89] She "made a damn fool of herself again," he argued in early 1959.[90] By early 1960, she was "acting like a damn fool again" and "clearly in need of psychiatric treatment...."[91] Snowden joined the dispute insisting that Tate "stop molesting me" while Logan—who quoted him—said she was "deliberately trying to provoke me into hitting her...."[92]

But it was not just Tate with whom Logan was involved in murderous disputes. "If any violence is done to me," he said at one point, "find out where Professor Harold O. Lewis was at the time."[93] As for William Leo Hansberry, to Logan he was "the skunk."[94]

Once more, I do not see this searing friction as merely titillating but, instead, view it politically, as an example of what happens when otherwise intelligent individuals are thrust into the den of iniquitous wickedness of Jim Crow, then blocked from taking measures to

---

was an "agent for some one or is trying to blackmail me"; thus Logan chose to "record three points: I did not go up to his room...I came directly home and told Ruth [spouse] about the incident."

83. Entry, 26 May 1956, Box 6.
84. Entry, 9 December 1956, Box 6.
85. Entry, 27 December 1956, Box 6.
86. Entry, 9 December 1956, Box 6.
87. Entry, 1 October 1958, Box 6.
88. Entry, 12 October 1959, Box 6.
89. Entry, 21 December 1956, Box 6.
90. Entry, 6 February 1959, Box 6.
91. Entry, 19 February 1960, Box 6.
92. Entry, 6 February 1959, Box 6.
93. Entry, 18 July 1957, Box 6.
94. Entry, 24 January 1960, Box 6.

confront it effectively by deflecting them away from potential allies: they turn with a fury against each other since they cannot assail the true culprits.

And the context was worsened as the Red Scare was bolstered by the Black Scare, which had devastating impact on the hilltop campus most notably.

Chapter 16

Howard Students Revolt, 1958-1962

It was not just energized students and an accommodating global atmosphere that were driving transformational change in the District and nationally. There was also the seemingly frivolous matter of sports. Jackie Robinson's presence at pivotal marches on Washington in the late 1950s was emblematic of the gravitas he brought as the man who had desegregated the national pastime in the 1940s, which too had repercussions far beyond baseball.[1]

Washington's baseball team, as noted, was an outlier as teams rushed to sign contracts with other sepia stars. Their fraternal twin, Baltimore, attracted the St. Louis Browns, renamed as the Orioles, but as of 1955 they were surpassing their District peer insofar as this team was the only American League squad not to offer a desegregated hotel option whereby all players could stay under the same roof. Leading the charge against both teams was the columnist for the *Afro-American*, Sam Lacy, defined as a Negro though he was born as a Shinnecock indigene of the Mohawk nation. When in 1961, Interior Secretary imitated his predecessor Harold Ickes in pressuring the ignorantly named football team—the "Washington Redskins"— to desegregate or risk losing easy access to the football stadium where they entertained fans, Lacy could have claimed considerable credit for this attainment.[2]

But Lacy was just one amongst many. Wendell Paris suggested a boycott of the team because of its "anti-colored policies"; while in Rome for the Olympics he was queried about the team, indicative of the potential reach of a boycott: he passed along a list of District

---

1. See, e.g., Gerald Horne, *Communist Front? The Civil Rights Congress, 1946-1956*, New York: International, 2021.
2. Sam Lacy with Moses J. Newsom, *Fighting for Fairness: The Life Story of Hall of Fame Sportswriter*, Centreville, Maryland: Tidewater, 1998, 82, 15, 111.

footballers who could perform on the gridiron, including Willie Wood,[3] who was to join the Hall of Fame eventually, wearing the colors of the Green Bay Packers.

These gridiron giants who were often featured on live television and enjoying stratospheric ratings in the process, were becoming a magnet for all types of protest. Walter Tobriner, the de facto potentate of the city in his capacity with the hegemonic Board of Trade, was terribly upset after the "unhappy incident involving the threatened arrest of members of the Democratic [Party] Central Committee in connection with their attempt to distribute leaflets urging people to vote…at the D.C. stadium last Sunday during the Redskins-Cowboys football game…."[4]

The obdurate owner of this poorly managed franchise, George Preston Marshall, mimicked the Orioles in that his was the last football franchise in the entire league to desegregate. Marshall was the epitome of the revolting capitalist. After writhing in futile protest, Marshall capitulated in 1962 and sought to sign to a contract star footballer, Ernie Davis who replied angrily, "'I won't play for that [epithet deleted]'" and was traded for another Negro, Bobby Mitchell, who proceeded to star on the gridiron. Aiding the atmosphere for Marshall's surrender was Washingtonian, Elgin Baylor, who in 1959 had received national attention when he refused to play in a basketball game slated for Charleston, West Virginia because of the objection of a local hotel to allow him to obtain lodging under the same roof as his teammates. Reportedly joining the fray was the pugilist then known as Cassius Clay, soon renamed Muhammad Ali, who was said to have tossed his Olympic gold medal in boxing at the 1960 Rome games, after being denied service in a restaurant in his hometown of Louisville, Kentucky.[5]

Again, the changing global climate, the protests of energetic students, the desire from U.S. elites to improve their international image by desegregating, all added gusts to the sails of these initiatives in sports, a subject of maximum interest to a good deal of the U.S. population.

Somehow it was appropriate that the disgustingly named "Redskins" proved to be the most bull-headed and stiff-necked of all in resisting change. Professor Logan of Howard was told in 1958 that Marshall had confessed that not only would he not hire Negro

3. *Afro-American*, 9 August 1960.
4. Walter Tobriner to Joseph Rauh, 7 November 1962, Box 31, *Joseph Rauh Papers, Library of Congress-Washington, D.C.*
5. Dave Zirin, *A People's History of Sports in the United States*, 128, 135.

athletes, he also desired that Negro fans not attend the games[6]: refuting economistic arguments, he did not want tainted money from Negroes. Though born in West Virginia, the tightfisted capitalist spent a good of his youth in the District, soaking up the brine of bigotry. "'When are you going to hire a black football player?'" Marshall was asked by *Washington Post* reporter, Ben Bradlee, to which the crusty entrepreneur replied elusively, "'When the Harlem Globetrotters [all Negro spoof basketball team] hire a white basketball player.'"[7] Even after being dragged every step of the way toward breaking the ban on Negro athletes, Marshall remained implacable. He refused to pose for a photograph with one of his early Negro signees, i.e., Ron Hatcher, arguing that this would constitute "'exploitation....'"[8]

Howardites continued to do their part in generating the flames of unrest that compelled the Interior Department to pressure Marshall. The campus newspaper boasted that it was "the only college publication to have regular coverage of presidential news conferences," a turnabout from the time not so long ago when Negro journalists were barred from this event. When the founder of independent Congo, Patrice Lumumba, was assassinated in January 1961, numerous letters peppered their columns in protest. [9] Still, contrarily and auguring protests to come, the Reserve Office Training Corps of the U.S. Air Force, enrolled 443 male students then topping previous highs and dampening the notion that anti-imperialism was the reigning ideology on campus.[10] Similarly, a charter member of the military-industrial complex—Raytheon—was holding interviews on campus for prospective employees.[11] Given the temper of the times, it was not surprising that soon strident objection was taken to what was called "compulsory ROTC."[12]

Nevertheless, a prime campus activity was a "model" version of the Security Council of the United Nations that discussed Congo, Algeria, Laos, apartheid, and Tibet with future movers and shakers including Gloria Richardson (soon to grab national headlines because of her activism in Cambridge, Maryland), Phil Hutchins (soon to play a starring role in SNCC), and Acklyn Lynch (a future

---

6. Entry, 6 December 1958, Box 6.
7. Ben Bradlee, *A Good Life*, 203.
8. *New York Daily Mirror*, 31 December 1961, Series I, Subgroup 8, Box 16, *Hank Kaplan Papers, Brooklyn College-New York City*.
9. *The Hilltop*, 24 February 1961.
10. *The Hilltop*, 30 September 1960.
11. *The Hilltop*, 9 February 1962.
12. *The Hilltop*, 13 April 1962.

premier professor at the University of Maryland).[13] By then Michael Thelwell, who was to become a key advisor and comrade of the young man then known as Stokely Carmichael, was an assistant editor of the paper that reported these activities[14] and went on to become a prime professor at the University of Massachusetts-Amherst. Coincidentally, with Thelwell's arrival at the periodical, Carmichael began to appear in its pages more regularly, including a recent jaunt that he made to Nashville to join protests there.[15] By early 1962, Thelwell was Managing Editor and, yes, articles by Carmichael accompanied his ascension.[16] Thelwell's stellar performance led to this Jamaican becoming editor within months[17] and coming along with him was a writer who began to pen a "We Shall Overcome" column: Carmichael.[18]

The Trinidadian-American could draw easily from his own experience in order to enrich his columns. By May 1962, H.U. students had flocked to Baltimore where they joined, what a student reporter described as "marching pickets, jeering crowds, flustered innkeepers" seeking vainly to maintain Jim Crow. It was Carmichael who demanded service from a shopkeeper, then the door was closed quickly behind him, and he was not allowed to exit. The "struggle in Baltimore," it was reported, "assumed a new twist when Howard student...Carmichael brought charges against [this] restaurant owner and a patron...."[19]

Though students were prominent, Reverend Logan Kearse of Cornerstone Baptist Church in Baltimore was among the clerics who were involved intimately in what he called the "campaign to test the racial segregation of places of public accommodation along Route 40...."[20]

Looking back from November 1962 the campus newspaper recalled what happened over the past year when "some three thousand students converged in Baltimore...for the largest anti-segregation demonstration on the East Coast," a "complete surprise to the store owners of Baltimore...." H.U. students provided "surprisingly...[a]

---

13. *The Hilltop*, 10 March 1961.

14. *The Hilltop*,24 March 1961.

15. *The Hilltop*, 6 October 1961.

16. *The Hilltop*, 23 March 1962.

17. *The Hilltop*, 11 May 1962.

18. *The Hilltop*, 14 December 1962.

19. *The Hilltop*, 18 May 1962.

20. Report from Reverend Logan Kearse, 25 October 1961, Box 1, *Julius Hobson Papers, Washington, D.C. Public Library*.

representation of over 500 students" and so moved, the "City Council passed a law banning segregation...."[21]

The vanguard roles played by those with roots in the Caribbean was buttressed by the frequent appearances on campus of those like Forbes Burnham of what was to be called Guyana,[22] to the point that Professor Logan "more and more" was "considering a large scale Program of West Indian Studies at Howard...."[23]

Predictably, soon the paper's office was deluged by complaints—possibly coming from ROTC advocates and those aspiring to employment at Raytheon—that too many column inches were accorded to protest.[24]

Or these complaints could have come from the staff. Igor Kozak, an editor, was a critic of the Soviet Union[25]—not a preoccupation of other staff members. The issue was joined when Howard student, Dion Diamond, was arrested in Baton Rouge in an anti-Jim Crow protest and charged with criminal anarchy. SNCC field secretary, Charles McDew, and his comrade, Robert Zellner, were also detained.[26] This was followed by a campus rally in the face of administration opposition where—it was said—Zellner's jailer told him bluntly, "'We'll keep you as long as your people kept [Francis Gary] Powers,'" the U.S. pilot downed and jailed in the Soviet Union; of course, associating Zellner with Moscow was hardly a slip of the tongue. Undaunted, a 17 person H.U. delegation marched to the Department of Justice to plead for aid in freeing Diamond.[27] Because of such ministrations, Diamond was freed after 58 days in jail.[28] However, he was not alone. Entering Howard in 1961 was the future prolific journalist and writer Charlie Cobb, who by October 1962 was described as a "former Howard student" then organizing in Ruleville, Mississippi.[29]

Nor was Rozak the only student of European descent on the hilltop for also present was Tom Kahn, a former lover of Malcolm's debating partner, Bayard Rustin, who was also associated with the founding of Students for a Democratic Society, which shared a trench

---

21. *The Hilltop*, 9 November 1962.
22. *The Hilltop*, 4 May 1962.
23. Entry, 14 July 1962, *Logan Diary*.
24. *The Hilltop*, 9 March 1962.
25. *The Hilltop*, 23 March 1962.
26. *The Hilltop*, 9 March 1962.
27. *The Hilltop*, 23 March 1962.
28. *The Hilltop*, 13 April 1962.
29. *The Hilltop*, 12 October 1962.

with SNCC. He was a frequent contributor to *The Hilltop*, and, like Professor Bernard Fall, who brought Prince Norodom Sihanouk of Cambodia to campus, was also involved in antiwar protests.[30] Fall, who had served in the French underground during the war and was a renowned authority on Indochina, soon to dominate the news, was a notable campus influence.[31]

Kahn's—or Fall's—presence was not extraordinary for as early as October 1958, Logan remarked that of H.U.'s "5000 students... we have a few white students" and, unavoidably, a "considerable number of white students," with the first of this group arriving with the school's opening in 1867, mostly "children of the white professors...."[32]

By the fall of 1961 Howard received what was described as "worldwide notice" after launching its "first nonviolence course,"[33] as if the school was opening training shock troops for the movement.

After Malcolm X was banned from speaking at Queens College, he was invited to the hilltop which—it was reported—was part of "bringing controversial speakers and issues to the campus."[34] A capacity audience filled Cramton Auditorium, at least 500 were unable to enter, as the Minister debated Bayard Rustin, a former Young Communist League member who migrated to anticommunism and a role alongside Dr. King as an apostle of non-violence. "Every seat" was filled, it was said, with even newly appointed President James Madison Nabrit absorbing the "electric excitement"[35]—though Nabrit's "close ties" to Richard M. Nixon,[36] in the words of Logan, suggested that whatever "excitement" he displayed might have been performative.

Not as pleased was Logan who termed the Minister's organization as "a very vicious anti-white organization" though he added quickly, "I knew nothing about" the man on whose behalf Malcolm spoke: Elijah Muhammad. He did say that their headquarters in Chicago, "rooms are covered with posters showing...a Negro being lynched," a possible tipoff to their growing popularity among Negroes, whose brutal history was often submerged—even by the

---

30. *The Hilltop*, 16 February 1962.
31. Bernard Fall, "Vietnam: The Realities," *Howard University Magazine*, 1 (Number 1, November 1958): 8-10, 19, 19, *Schomburg Center*.
32. Entry, 12 October 1958, Box 6.
33. *The Hilltop*, 6 October 1961.
34. *The Hilltop*, 7 October 1961.
35. *The Hilltop*, 10 November 1961.
36. Entry, 1 July 1960, Box 7.

left—in the interest of portraying the founding of the U.S. as a great leap forward for humanity.[37]

"Electric excitement" was an apt descriptor for what was occurring at Howard during the fall semester of 1961, which was the culmination of assiduous tending over the years going back to the halcyon days of Hunton and Wilkerson in the 1930s. Adventitiously, Channing Tobias, who had conspired with Logan against Robeson's Civil Rights Congress in 1951-1952 in Paris and their attempt to charge the U.S. with genocide against Black people, happened to expire as Howard turned the corner toward enhanced activism: he had served as Chair Emeritus of the Board of the NAACP and as a key member of H.U.'s board.[38] When this crafty operator left the scene—combined with the advent of the untested Nabrit regime[39]—the door was opened for the unleashing of a wave of activism.

On the other side of the ledger, when Professor E. Franklin Frazier, a native of Baltimore passed, the campus was deprived of an erudite class analyst.[40] Yet, despite differences the diplomatic Frazier was able to maintain reasonable relations with various forces; when the State Department "wanted at least one Negro at the luncheon" for West Africans, "especially one who could speak French," the often testy Logan recommended the sociologist.[41] By early 1959 Frazier had endured a stroke and was hospitalized. When Logan went to visit him at Freedmen's Hospital, the nurse was reading Frazier's book, *Black Bourgeoisie,* and the attending physician was familiar with it too. "Frazier, like most of us," said Logan in a premature eulogy, had "driven himself too hard…,"[42] an emblem of being a Negro intellectual in an apartheid society.

For Frazier was one of the few intellectuals—at Howard and nationally—capable of tracking the profound metamorphosis then unfolding. As Logan saw things in early 1959, "one group of Negroes desires integration; a second says that it does not but really does and is afraid to say so because of possible reprisals by white people, a third group sincerely prefers to remain segregated"—but "the first group…is increasing because integration itself is increasing,"[43] but

---

37. Entry, 31 January 1959, Box 6.
38. *The Hilltop,* 10 November 1961.
39. *The Hilltop,* 21 April 1961.
40. *The Hilltop,* 25 May 1962.
41. Entry, 27 November 1958, Box 6.
42. Entry, 16 January 1959, Box 6.
43. Entry, 21 January 1959, Box 6. See also Entry, 6 August 1959, Box 6: Months later Logan spoke to a "young white man" at Howard and this point

underlying, often unexamined, tensions persisted to this community's ultimate detriment. Frazier, quite uniquely, could have helped in navigating this troublesome transition. And if Logan had not been so wrapped up in consolidating his ties with a ruling class that was skeptical of him, he too could have made a more substantial contribution to understanding. In early 1960 he was meeting with Al Friendly of the *Post* at the Du Pont Plaza and there he was told that the South African ambassador objected to Thurgood Marshall traveling to London to advise the Kenya delegation there. Logan soaked it all in, then thought to himself, "We Negroes had first been allowed to attend meetings in Washington hotels as members of a group," an exception to rigidifying Jim Crow, but "now we go as individuals," ala South Africa,[44] a weighty point still not interrogated sufficiently.

Still, critical to constructing this passage to freedom—or at least away from invidious Jim Crow—was not only the certitude of Frazier but, as well, the continuing influx of students from abroad,

---

arose, i.e., "Some colored members of the faculty at Howard do not favor integration because of their sense of insecurity," to be fair: this trait has been endemic in faculty of all sorts. But this special cohort was "afraid that integration would mean the loss of their jobs to superior whites...I would give the preference, other things being substantially equal to a Negro applicant so long as Negro professors do not have equal opportunities in northern universities and no opportunity in southern white universities"; then "the thought struck me that some white persons have a vested interest in integration" since "they find opportunities for employment in predominantly Negro universities...Howard University is one of their principal targets... Wolfgang Seiferth, a German refugee who has been on the faculty at Howard for many years has repeatedly recommended to me some European or other white person to teach in the Department of History. I have not recommended any of them." See also Entry, 12 October 1959, Box 6: Logan saw a "real danger, namely that white teachers and administrators are going to try to 'capture' Howard University...." Some of these European faculty were akin to a Trojan Horse. Entry, 22 December 1959, Box 6: Logan recalled a faculty member who "had worked in Germany under Hitler" and "carried out experiments during Hitler's regime...I was the only member of the committee who wanted to examine the evidence," while others took a "Voltaire" view, e.g., I disagree with what you say but will defend your right to say it—or do it, in this case. See also Entry, 31 October 1958, Box 6: Logan retained aspects of the proverbial "Race Man"; thus, when Du Bois advocated "self-segregation...I also did so. The reason is obvious: the Negro was the first to be fired and last to be hired. Negroes, therefore, had to develop their own businesses."

44. Entry, 13 January 1960, Box 6.

many from newly independent nations and unwilling to accept the venom of Jim Crow. And not all were exclusively of African descent: an Indian Student Association was formed during the fall semester of 1961.[45] Nonetheless, matters African continued to generate proliferating concern in the student body. Trevor Huddleston, a comrade of Nelson Mandela arrived on campus,[46] followed by the telling headline: "Africa's rise set as topic" for the school.[47] Another indicator of the influx of students from abroad occurred when Howard, said an excited reporter, "fielded the first Negro soccer team to win a national soccer championship"[48] with students hailing from especially Nigeria and Trinidad.[49]

Further solidifying its role as the unsung champions of the anti-Jim Crow movement, Howardites were also prominent in the organizing of the metropolitan Non-Violent Action Group. On the first day of 1962 they were plotting to deploy to Cambridge, Maryland where Bison, Gloria Richardson, was in the forefront of a difficult struggle. But akin to a general staff, they were also organizing a caravan of "sharecroppers from Tennessee" to descend on the city, while listening to a "report on the struggle for freedom in Kenya,"[50] surging to sovereignty in the next year.

Then their president, William Mahoney of 1116 Girard Street, N.W., cheered the assembled by reporting that the group "participated in every major action in the United States in the struggle for civil rights," including shipping "clothes, food and medicines, donated by local churches, to the sharecroppers in Fayette County, Tennessee who were evicted from their land"; they sent "4,000 and nine tons of material assistance," too. They "picketed the White House during the presidential election" and "participated fully in the CORE [Congress of Racial Equality] Freedom Ride from Washington to Mississippi...." In the Magnolia State "thirteen members of NAG spent time" there—in "jails." They "joined the demonstration in Rock Hill, South Carolina" and, also in 1961, "NAG initiated civil rights demonstrations in Middleburg, Leesburg and Warrington, Virginia, as well as Hagerstown, Maryland." They "participated

---

45. *The Hilltop*, 3 November 1961.
46. *The Hilltop*, 10 November 1961.
47. *The Hilltop*, 17 November 1961.
48. *The Hilltop*, 1 December 1961.
49. *The Hilltop*, 11 January 1963.
50. Minutes, 1 January 1962, Box 1, *D.C. Area Non-Violent Action Group Papers, Schomburg Center-New York Public Library.* (Denoted henceforth as "NAG Papers."

in civil rights action in Jackson, Mississippi; McComb, Mississippi; Monroe, North Carolina; Nashville, Tennessee; and Albany, Georgia. Three NAG members became field secretaries for [SNCC], one member became field secretary for CORE and one member is active in the Jackson Non-Violent Movement" in Mississippi. "Current demonstrations which have and are occurring in Baltimore and eastern sections of Maryland are in part a direct result of NAG members." Thus, as a result of NAG organizing, "ten or more restaurants in Baltimore have desegregated and approximately eleven more than the original 35 of Route 40 have opened to all...." To coordinate better with comrades in CORE and SNCC, a "copy of NAG's minutes" will be forwarded to them.[51]

Yes, there were downsides: "middle class attitudes of our leaders and their willingness to be satisfied with 'token-ism' and piddling results" topped the list. Significantly, the decision was made that "at each meeting a report will be given on a topic relevant to the struggle for freedom in the world" in order to "broaden the outlook of NAG members...." Of similar significance was the decision to "intensify...struggle against the inhumane treatment of 54% of the population of the nation's capital," adding precisely: "note to Howard students: the 1961 Civil Rights Commission reports that Negro college graduates earn less than white high school graduates. It [is] your fight too"—was the point aimed at future Raytheon hirelings.[52]

Despite the headlines grabbed by Carmichael and Thelwell and Kahn, it would be a gross error to assume that their stances were universally embraced at the hilltop. A few days after this lengthy report, Mahoney contacted "Dear Jim," possibly SNCC principal, James Forman, to brief him on a conference that was slated for Howard—however, "because the administration receives millions of dollars from the Congress they might try to block such a program"; admirably, "if Howard shows such cowardice to the Southern Congressmen there are other organizations in this city that would enjoy playing host to SNCC...." To state the obvious, there were "many advantages in having your [SNCC] conference in Washington"; "with civil rights legislation pending a demonstration at the Capitol and the White House," this gathering "is in in order," if not mandated. At this point, NAG had 300 cadre they could call on, a considerable number. Still, said Mahoney, "last semester was rough," exhibiting the burnout that would overtake many cadre soon. "I came from Monroe,

---

51. Report, 13 January 1962, Box 1, *NAG Papers*.
52. Minutes, 13 January 1962, Box 1, *NAG Papers*.

N.C. with nothing. The first month I slept on a floor, ate little...this semester [is] looking better. I am receiving financial aid...."[53]

Strategically sited in the District, NAG sought to pressure the Louisiana congressional delegation because of excessive bail demands in the Pelican State. "Get the home addresses of all the Southern Senators and Representatives," was the instruction, "and keep them on file...NAG might very well institute protest around their houses, when an act of violent injustice [occurs] in the South," was the wise advice from one strategist.[54]

Then with consolidation, Mahoney was elected unanimously as NAG's chairman with Carmichael declining to serve as co-chair. The AFL-CIO and the National Council of Churches were then solicited for funding.[55] Formalizing what was already in motion, next on the agenda was forming a NAG chapter at Howard but this was defeated narrowly, perhaps because of the pre-existence of the NAACP and SNCC, though the upside was that having a chapter meant access to "the facilities" of H.U. and facilitating campus mobilization. A midway proposal was forming a "Civil Rights Discussion Group."[56]

But simple discussion was insufficient for NAG activists, so they then joined a picket-line on 14th Street focused on public transportation—buses in this case—that had crept tortoise-like to three percent Negro employment and 80 percent Negro patronage.[57]

That was April. By August the other shoe dropped. "John, Stokely, Butch and I have given up our apartment in Washington on Belmont Street," said Mahoney and he was now "working in a sweatshop in the Garment District in New York City...." It was a "rare honor in my life," he said modestly, "to have been elected to the SNCC Executive Council," but now that too was up in the air. In a concluding noble gesture, usual for selfless cadre of that era, he "included... money collected by some children in D.C. in return for newspapers and coke bottles...."[58]

Just as it would be mistaken to assume that all hilltoppers were cut from the same cloth as Carmichael and Thelwell and Kahn, it would even more of a blunder to think that their teachers were all pushing them in the direction of activism.

---

53. William Mahoney to "Dear Jim," 1 February 1962, Box 1, *NAG Papers*. [Emphasis in original]
54. Letter from "Jim," 2 February 1962, Box 1, *NAG Papers*.
55. Minutes, 18 March 1962, Box 1.
56. Minutes, 1 April 1962, Box 1.
57. Minutes, 18 April 1962, Box 1.
58. William Mahoney to "Dear Jim," 7 August 1962, Box 1, *NAG Papers*.

Such an assumption would do little to explain the ideological contortions of Professor Logan, likely the most prominent teacher with knowledge of African, Caribbean, and African American history. Archetypal was the incident when he boarded a train to Manhattan and encountered the Sudanese ambassador who introduced him to "'His Excellency,' the Secretary of Foreign Affairs, Mohammed Mahgoub," but Logan then was invested in oil stocks, with this African nation having lush reserves, suggesting that the ensuing conversation was not altogether disinterested.[59]

Eventually, he made it to the home of the tasteful abode of Marietta Tree, the socialite who resided on the trendy Upper East Side of Manhattan—123 East 79th Street in her case. There he chatted amiably with Sylvanus Olympio, chief of the independence forces in Togo, West Africa, which left him "tremendously impressed" though his "flawless English" meant that Logan was unable to display his similarly flawless French.[60]

Logan subscribed to the informative *Central African Examiner* and also was in direct touch with Harold Hochschild, chief executive of the major exploiter of African natural resources, i.e., American Metal Climax, and was keen not to run afoul of his "point of view"[61]—a stance unlikely to be shared with militant students. Then Logan was considering a jaunt to the Belgian Congo where Hochschild had major investments: "I have little doubt that if I should go to Belgium," beamed Logan, "I shall see King Baudouin...." This realization occurred as he conversed with Baron Dhanis of the Brussels legation, who was quite friendly toward him possibly because "I mentioned the fact that the Belgians do not invite 'us' [meaning Negroes] to their cocktail parties and receptions...." The Belgian let drop a point that students would have benefited from hearing: "'My King' must grant one man, one vote in order to defeat the propaganda of the Soviet Union and [G.A.] Nasser" of Egypt. "I did not have the opportunity to ask him about the Chinese in the Congo," was Logan's coda.[62]

Logan also maintained fulsome diplomatic relations with the colonizing power in Congo's next neighbor, i.e., France in Brazzaville. After his repast with the Belgians, he was to be found sipping cocktails in Chevy Chase, Maryland with French officialdom.[63] Part of the problem was that Logan was a creature of Old Washington

---

59. Entry, 31 August 1958, Box 6.
60. Entry, 16 May 1958, Box 6.
61. Entry, 2 March 1959, Box 6.
62. Entry, 2 June 1959, Box 6.
63. Entry, 19 October 1959, Box 6.

as a newer updated version was yearning to be born. Lindy Boggs, spouse of a congressional colossus then a Congresswoman, recalled a time of rigid protocol when "you couldn't leave a formal social event until everyone who outranked you had left": this inelasticity began to yield—coincidentally—as the upheaval of anti-Jim Crow dislodged various norms. But Logan was a creature of the past, too, and was not always capable of changing.[64]

Thus, Logan was positioned to give guidance to H.U.'s diverse student body, but at times his at times volatile temperament got the best of him. In discussions with an African student, he peremptorily dismissed the notion of a West African Federation, especially after this ingenue claimed that all West Africans speak Hausa. "I slapped him down hard," said Logan rancorously, "because of previous experiences with African students."[65]

Logan was more tactful in speaking with Tom Mboya of Kenya; when Howard "gave a dinner in his honor," the historian dexterously "chose a place opposite him."[66] Mboya, too, was well-placed: his younger brother, Alphonse Okoku, became a student at Howard in 1962.[67] Logan was sufficiently agile ideologically to recognize what eluded many in Washington: there was a "widespread belief in Europe and among Europeans that the United States government and American businessmen in Africa are supporting self-government for Africans and African nationalism so that American capital can take over."[68]

As the example of Thelwell and Carmichael and the victorious soccer team suggested, students with Caribbean roots were to be found in profusion on campus and with his still edifying book on Haiti, Logan was well-positioned to educate them. Yet somehow he could "not understand...that Mercer and Vashti Cook, John and Mavis Davis, who are as white and cultured as nine-tenths of the most cultured white people, advocate this 'Negritude' this cult of blackness" in Haiti under "Papa Doc" Duvalier.[69] Logan could not

---

64. Lindy Boggs with Katherine Hatch, *Washington Through a Purple Veil: Memoirs of a Southern Woman*, New York: Harcourt Brace, 1994, 80.

65. Entry, 27 November 1958, Box 6.

66. Entry, 20 June 1959, Box 6: The Kenyan acknowledged that Afrikaners can call themselves "'Africans...I would concede that,'" he asserted, though he "repeatedly referred to the 'immigrant community' in Kenya...."

67. *The Hilltop*, 9 November 1962.

68. Entry, 14 September 1958, Box 6.

69. Entry, 23 October 1958, Box 6. See also Entry, 26 June 1961, Box 7: Logan did "not understand how an intelligent person," e.g., "Mercer Cook, for

quite figure out that this option was motivated in no small measure as a foil against the rise of a local left, glimmerings of which would soon be espied in Logan's hometown.[70] By early 1960 Logan was in Port-au-Prince: "I was known to many Haitians, including President Duvalier...," where apparently his own felt desire to be accepted at the highest level eroded whatever lingering concern he held about "Negritude."[71]

Logan also was positioned to educate Harlem's Congressman, Adam Clayton Powell, who spent a good deal of his free time in the Bahamas. But Logan refused to share a platform with this "flamboyant personality," as he termed him, "not because of income tax charges," he was then battling but because he "said that he had helped to bring Fidel Castro to power in Cuba and that now he was going to overthrow Trujillo in the Dominican Republic," a diplomatic faux pas; besides, Logan wondered why he should introduce Powell, when the professor too was a speaker.[72]

Logan was no neophyte in this realm, given his pathbreaking book on Haiti. The oft consulted Negro journalist, Simeon Booker, called Logan to brief him on a "junket" to Santo Domingo at "Trujillo's expense" and the professor "urged him to go" in order to "look for the 'nexus between race and class,'" insight that could have benefited his students.[73] (Nevertheless, by 1959 his trailblazing book on Haiti, published in 1941, had sold a mere 703 copies—a shame and sufficient cause to leave the already unbalanced Logan even more erratic, resentful of the dearth of recognition he should have been accorded.)[74]

Logan was once quite critical of Ralph Bunche, often from the left, but as politics heated up on campus, he seemed to mellow in his evaluation of this diplomat. He telephoned him and the call was returned promptly, and Bunche then asked him why "I had not been in to see him" causing Logan to remark appreciatively, "I do not know anyone who has been changed less by his eminent position than Ralph has."[75]

---

example, can accept the goddamn claptrap of the Catholic Church," not to mention the "crafty and astute" Duvalier.

70. Gerald Horne, *Fire this Time: The Watts Uprising and the 1960s*, Charlottesville: University of Virginia Press, 1995.

71. Entry, 26 February 1960, Box 6.

72. Entry, 8 January 1959, Box 6.

73. Entry, 22 January 1959, Box 6.

74. Entry, 6 February 1959, Box 6.

75. Entry, 16 January 1959, Box 6.

This switcheroo on Bunche was reflected in his deepening ties to the Negro middle class of the District, which the folksinger, Leadbelly, had satirized as the pre-eminent "bourgeois town."[76] Unfortunately, the singer was no longer alive when in early 1959 Logan and his spouse attended a dinner dance in the tony Du Pont Room of the Du Pont Plaza Hotel, sponsored by his elite fraternity, Boule. It was "colored Washington society in the best sense of the word," he gushed, as "the men wore tuxedos and the women evening gowns." Per usual for this fraternity, there was "only [one] dark brown man" present, "all the rest of the men were light brown or almost white in color." His colleague Frank Snowden, thus, stood out, resembling "an Arab." As for the distaff side, "practically all the other women would be white anywhere in the world except the United States...."[77] Despite this bourgeois preening, Logan rolled up to the hotel in a nine year old Buick,[78] arriving from his humble abode at 1519 Jackson Street, N.E.[79]

While Logan was gallivanting with cream colored Negro elites, he continued his obsession with his colleague, Merze Tate, who happened to be of a similar stratum as himself. As a new stage of the movement was launched in Greensboro, Logan was whining about her "harassing" him. Supposedly their colleague, Dorothy Porter of H.U.'s rich archives, agreed that Tate "'is crazy. I wish that you could have seen her at a meeting a few nights ago.'"[80] As the flames of antagonism leapt ever higher, Logan chauvinistically adopted a new name for his colleague: "The Bitch."[81] Logan was losing a sense of proportion as he then turned on Frank Snowden, referring to this similarly situated colleague as "arrogant" and "conceited." "Snowden must hate me,"[82] he concluded. Possibly if he had taken some political education lessons from his boycotted Communist colleagues—e.g., the now departed Wilkerson and Hunton—Logan would have evaded this moral cul de sac.

* * *

76. Charles Wolfe, et.al., *The Life and Legend of Leadbelly*, New York City: HarperCollins, 1992.
77. Entry, 16 February 1959, Box 6.
78. Entry, 12 October 1959, Box 6.
79. Entry, 27 June 1961, Box 7.
80. Entry, 26 February 1960, Box 6.
81. Entry, 23 March 1960, Box 6.
82. Entry, 26 June 1961, Box 7.

While Logan was seeking to mud wrestle with Tate, student activists were picketing the White House, this time the nuclear showdown with Havana and Moscow that brought the planet to the brink of destruction in October 1962 was at issue.[83] The editorial that emerged from the Thelwell-led team was forceful, reminding readers that "humanity at [the] crossroads" with many ordinary citizens bereft, stranded "pawns in [a] cynical game of 'nuclear chicken.'" *The Hilltop* had "consistently and vigorously opposed the Cold War in all its forms," not the norm locally or nationally but this present confrontation was "the most absurd and obscene development in mankind's long history"; unlike many onlookers, a comparison was made between Soviet missiles in Cuba and U.S. missiles in Turkey.[84]

The turmoil emanating from the hilltop was noticed on Capitol Hill. As 1961 was dawning, Senator Bible was ready to raise the white flag of surrender. He demanded "speedy action by the Nevada legislature in ratifying the proposed constitutional amendment granting" the District the "right to vote for president and vice-president," yet another steppingstone to home rule in what was becoming a "Chocolate City" as the main office of white supremacy, a contradiction that would be difficult to continue in coming years. Senator Bible adopted the cry that was to resound: "How can we fear democracy here and yet proclaim its advantages to the world?"[85]—a de facto capitulation to global currents. Local Negroes were not simplifying his task. His colleague Senator Joseph Montoya of New Mexico retained a report detailing how "400 storm[ed] Capitol for home rule" in the midst of the "first House hearings on home rule in 10 years," occurring in mid-1959. "Another 300 overflowed into the corridors of the Old House Building," with angst-ridden Congressman James Davis, Georgia Dixiecrat, equating "the disgruntled citizens with a Cuban revolutionary model," adding bumptiously that it was the "'same kind of situation as in Havana.'" Apparently, these home rule backers "needed only 'guns, knives and machetes'" to be in sync with Cubans. What next, he added angrily—demands for "'distribution of land and property?'"[86]

Next Hobart La Grone, Legislative Chair of the NAACP state conference of branches in the Land of Enchantment, came to collect. He "congratulate[d]" the Senator "on your sweeping victory in the

---

83. *The Hilltop*, 2 November 1962.
84. *The Hilltop*, 2 November 1962.
85. Telegram from Senator Bible, 17 December 1960, Box 43, *Alan Bible Papers*.
86. *Washington Post*, 29 July 1959, Box 19, *Joseph Montoya Papers, University of New Mexico-Albuquerque*.

recent primary election," a real feat since "so many of the state's newspapers lined up against you," amplifying the importance of the otherwise small Negro vote. "Many of your friends shared our view that you are an able legislator"—and now he wanted payback on home rule, though by May 1960 the legislator "had not signed the discharge petition" allowing the measure to proceed.[87] His constituent, Ellen Bloom, had once lived in the District but was now in New Mexico and she saw the absence of home rule as "undemocratic," demanding that he sign the petition.[88] Nonetheless, NAACP Board member, W. Montague Cobb, recognized that because of congressional and other "bureaucratic layers," it took "longer to get anything done in the District than in other major cities of the United States,"[89] guaranteeing a slow walk to home rule and, hence, commensurate tensions.

Yet, Senators Montoya and Bible did not necessarily represent the alpha and omega of congressional sentiment, especially as far as Dixie was concerned. Early in the JFK administration, the highly regarded 44 year old Negro attorney, Frank Reeves, was grilled by the U.S. Senate as he bid to become a District Commissioner. The hearing room was packed as he made history as the first Negro to be nominated by the White House for this post since this form of government was established in the 1870s. But he was pilloried because of delinquency in satisfying one federal and two District tax liens since 1957 because of alleged inability to pay. Though born in Montreal, he had the requisite local credentials—alumnus of both Dunbar High School and Howard; he was part of the team that crafted the school desegregation victory at the high court in 1954; an NAACP loyalist—he had served as an advisor to Kennedy during his victorious race. But he declined the appointment after the fierce pummeling he absorbed[90]—and after prodding from the White House.[91]

Breaking ranks with the NAACP, Reeves and his law partners, Aubrey Robinson and Charles Duncan, had chosen shortly before this imbroglio to defend the Black Communist with roots in Virginia, Dr. James E. Jackson. Duncan recalled that it was another factor in the disruption of the partnership and that they all "used to hope we never had to face the moral problem of whether to represent a

---

87. Hobart La Grone, 31 May 1960, Box 42, *Joseph Montoya Papers*.

88. Ellen Bloom to Senator Montoya, 29 March 1960, Box 42.

89. Speech, 25 January 1959, Box 128, *Phileo Nash Papers, Truman Presidential Library*.

90. *Washington Star*, 27 June 1961, Box 43, *Bible Papers*.

91. *New York Herald Tribune*, 29 June 1961, *Bible Papers*.

Communist or not. Well, as it turned out the opportunity presented itself as a big-paying case...so we decided to take it." Still, they "couldn't join the Bar Association" in the District; "...you couldn't use the library," for racist reasons hampering the defense. Then, said Duncan, tensions meant that Robinson "just got very impressed with himself...." It cannot be ruled out—mantras about not mistaking attorneys and clients notwithstanding—that their defense of Jackson may have played a role in Reeves' difficulties and Robinson's alienation.[92]

Senator Bible did not represent a large Negro constituency, though their numbers in Las Vegas were not negligible and he may have thought that this provided him with latitude to be statesmanlike or play the high-minded role of pursuing the wider interests of his class, rather than the narrowness of Dixie. Still, the mascot of the university campus in "Sin City" was not named "Rebels" for nothing, homage to the Confederacy. He retained articles on Reeves as a result—and, as well, a detailed one that appeared in the newspaper in the state capital, Carson City. Tellingly, "the Negro" was deemed to be among the "complications in running" Washington. They were "half the population" with numbers not seeming on the decline. The "Southern members of the D.C. directorate look at every new proposal, every new tax, highway or welfare proposal in terms of the Negro," i.e., "will it increase the Negro population?"—a must to avoid. "Washington has House bosses who hesitate to vote money for schools lest it increase the influx of Negroes," despite the obvious drawback; the understated conclusion was that this regression bore a "stultifying effect on the city's basic needs." The House was more "Negro conscious" and "will hold up programs" rather than allot a benefit to this persecuted minority. But the Senate too had a role and, per Bible, were often more elevated in their concerns, which "makes the town comparable to a neurotic family where one family has compassion for the child and the other hates it...." The Chamber of Commerce—Board of Trade often were favorable to Bible, as he helped to arrange capital construction—fattening their wallets— while unwilling to cross the House. The complexity was that if he stepped down, slated to replace him was Senator Wayne Morse of Oregon, a maverick not as predictable as Bible[93] and possibly sending the Board into damaging revolt, as Negroes continued on the march.

92. Oral History, Charles T. Duncan, 11 May 2002, *Historical Society of Washington, D.C.*

93. *Carson Nevada Appeal*, 2 December 1962, Box 43, *Bible Papers*.

The money grubbers of the Board had reason to be wary for they too were in the crosshairs by Negroes in revolt. Richard Norris, arguably the titular leader of the local Big Bourgeoisie in his capacity as President of Riggs Banks, was told in 1960 that in banks—like his—"Negroes have no employment in any capacity other than custodial. The banks have no cashiers, tellers, clerks, managers who are Negro—certainly not in the 'downtown' banks." Indeed, "even in your banks," Norris was told of something he should have known: Riggs' branches "in neighborhoods of substantially Negro population," had no Black employees.[94]

Thus, the District was now a rumbling volcano, virtually destined to explode, which it did in April 1968 when Dr. King was assassinated, and Carmichael was scapegoated. Providing rhetorical ammunition was a steady stream of enlightening speakers, many of them arranged by Kahn and the "Project Awareness." Malcolm X was among them, but he was hardly alone. Until 1955 the paradigmatic writer, James Baldwin, had never traveled below the Mason-Dixon Line—but then he visited Howard and as a subsequent analyst put it, this visit "would prove transformational." There he encountered the cerebral professor, steeped in Negro culture, Sterling Brown[95] and thereafter became a regular sojourner in the District, in many ways the nerve center of the movement. "I was indeed glad to have been at the rally,"[96] was his mid-1961 comment to activist, Julius Hobson in the District.

As the Cuba crisis was gripping imaginations globally, Baldwin came to the hilltop, along with Ossie Davis—politicized creator— and Ralph Ellison,[97] with their imminent arrivals preceded by a ferocious assault on JFK's policies in the campus paper.[98] Then John Oliver Killens, novelist known to be close to the organized left, came—just as the campus was in a tizzy about the nuclear crisis.[99] After that emergency came to an unsatisfactory—though survivable—conclusion, students initiated a campaign that was to continue intermittently for decades: picketing the South African

---

94. R. Hal Silvers to Richard Norris, 26 February 1960, Box 25, *American Veterans Committee Records, George Washington University.*
95. *Washington Post,* 22 August 2022.
96. James Baldwin to Julius Hobson, 23 June 1961, Box 1, *Julius Hobson Papers, Washington D.C. Public Library.*
97. *The Hilltop,* 27 October 1962.
98. *The Hilltop,* 9 October 1962.
99. *The Hilltop,* 2 November 1962.

embassy and the White House, their accomplice, too.[100] Inexorably, such protests were unnerving allies, including Canada, which began to raise a halting voice about maltreatment of African envoys in Washington,[101] which could redound to the advantage of African Americans.

---

100. *The Hilltop*, 7 December 1962.
101. Asa McKercher, "Too Close for Comfort: Canada, the U.S. Civil Rights Movement and the North American Colo(ur) Line," *Journal of American History*, 106 (Number 1, June 2019): 72-96, 77.

Chapter *17*

Thanksgiving Revolt, 1962

On Thanksgiving Day 1962 a high school football game with about 50,000 fans in attendance at the stadium that was to be named eventually for the slain Senator Robert F. Kennedy—a two mile stroll from Capitol Hill—dissolved into what an official report termed "savagery." It was Eastern High School (mostly Black) vs. St. John's (mostly not)—public vs. Catholic—dueling before the largest sports crowd ever assembled in the District (surpassing a professional tussle between the local "Redskins" and Dallas Cowboys). The official reporter found it troubling that "just before the National Anthem was played hundreds of young adults were seen retaining their hats on their heads or sitting in their seats," referring to Negroes who chose—disrespectfully, it was thought—not to doff their headwear, place right hand on heart and stand. They were mostly "youngsters between nine and [18]," a disturbing portent for the future. "Bootleg sale of liquor" was said to lubricate the passions of those assembled. Four hundred were injured in this latest revolt in the capital but less than a dozen arrests were made. The official report stressed "attacks on white persons by Negroes," with notable outrage flowing from the account that "three priests" were "assaulted by a group of Negroes." The melee spread to the streets. "Many were angry because Eastern lost the game," though a sigh of relief was expressed that there was "no link" between the unrest and the growing Nation of Islam.[1]

The then cub reporter, Carl Bernstein, found the scene "terrifying." As he recalled, "mostly Blacks going after whites," a reversal in a sense from what had unwound in the streets decades earlier in the World War I context. "Eight of the forty injured and taken to hospitals were Black." Since Washington then was the "only big

---

1. Report to the Superintendent. Public Schools of the District of Columbia from Special Committee on Group Activities, Washington, D.C., January 1963, *Historical Society of Washington, D.C.*

American city with a Black majority," this was not altogether surprising, a demography often unexamined since the "subject of race
was largely avoided and even suppressed," as reality was too fearsome to confront. In the 1950s, said Bernstein, "almost everything
important in Washington that wasn't about the Communists seemed
to come down to race in one way or another," and as the Red challenge domestically seemed to recede, the Black challenge seemed to
rise: From Red Scare to Black Scare in sum. This also brought into
the spotlight those perceived as the aiders and abettors of the Negro:
during JFK's inauguration, when the limousine of the embodiment
of the school desegregation issue, Chief Justice Earl Warren, navi-
gated the boulevard, there were "loud boos (just like for the Soviet
ambassador) and even some people yelling 'lynch him.'"[2]

Shortly thereafter, the Reverend Duncan Howlett of All Souls
Church in the District sermonized that "the Negro in the District of
Columbia is the most frustrated man in America today," in words
that dissected the "Stadium riot...." This raucous commotion "has
been widely reported across the United States and even in the foreign
press [emphasizing] that our most serious problems are basically
racial. In that sense," he intoned not inaccurately, "the riot was pivotal...." Beforehand periodicals like *U.S. News & World Report* "kept
the pot boiling" as they "virtually advocated defiance of the nation's
integration laws," complicating further what used to be called the
"Negro Question."[3]

The Negro reporter, Dorothy Butler Gilliam, had only reported for
duty at the *Washington Post* as the city was erupting. Her editor, John
Riseling, who had been on the scene during the 1919 tumult, should
have known better but, instead, "refused to publish stories about
murdered black persons because he did not believe black lives mattered. He called them cheap lives." Soon Gilliam was headed toward
burnout, if not a breakdown: "trying to cover news in a city where
even animal cemeteries were segregated overwhelmed me."[4] She
was not exaggerating; her employer reported on a time when cemeteries for "'Negro dogs'" were a thing.[5]

Ben Bradlee, en route to becoming the lead editor at Gilliam's
employer, recollected that "we didn't cover fires or crimes in the
city's black neighborhood," adding "to be blunt about it, I didn't

2. Carl Bernstein, *Chasing History*, 176, 193, 194.
3. Sermon by Reverend Duncan Howlett, 10 March 1963, Box 1, *Richard Dun-
lop Collection on Vietnam War Era Protests, George Washington University*.
4. Dorothy Butler Gilliam, *Trailblazer*, 24, 30.
5. *Washington Post*, 7 May 1964.

know anything about blacks," this "in a city that was 70 percent black and a readership that was 25 percent blacks."[6]

The *Star*—according to Dolph Thompson, President of the Capital Press Club—pursued an explicit policy of "racial exclusion." Put simply, their "policy" was "not hiring reporters who are Negroes and of not using photography of Negro activities when these events are social in nature"; that this was taking place in a town where the "Negro population is almost 70% is atrocious," he said.[7] The paper was founded during slavery's heyday in 1852 and though it shunned Negroes as employees, routinely hired many of its press operators from Gallaudet University, the local school for the deaf since—supposedly—they were unperturbed by the incessant noise from the gigantic presses. The staff also was inbred, with dozens of employees related to the paper's founding families, a number of whom seemed to sit at their desks all day imbibing alcoholic beverages. In 1959 they moved from Pennsylvania Avenue to a dilapidated neighborhood near Capitol Hill and that seemed to sour their collective mood, especially when it came to the blackening city they were covering.[8]

Still, this was a general exclusivist culture that happened to encompass the *Star*. The Gridiron Club, which incorporated numerous press heavyweights, was founded in 1885 and well into the 20th century excluded women.[9]

There was a yawning chasm between the boldly soaring verbiage of the likes of Ralph Bunche and JFK, speaking eloquently about a world transformed, which contrasted sharply with the lived experiences of those who had been the mudsill of society but were now envisioning ever brighter vistas: the ugly reality of Jim Crow meant that the tiniest retreat of this villainous system was exacted at bloodily tremendous cost. This generally unexplained state of affairs also led to the failure to engage in the civic ritual of respect for the National Anthem and the subsequent explosion on the gridiron—and beyond.

---

6. Ben Bradlee, *A Good Life*, 282.

7. Dolph Thompson to "Dear Friend," 10 January 1961, Box IX: 227, *NAACP Papers*.

8. John Norris, *Mary McGrory: The Trailblazing Columnist who Stood Washington on its Head*, New York: Penguin, 2016, 13, 14, 17, 94.

9. Kathryn McGarr, "We're All in this Thing Together:' Cold War Consensus in the Exclusive Social World of Washington's Reporters," in Bruce J. Schulman and Julian E. Zelizer, eds., *Media Nation: The Political History of News in Modern America*, Philadelphia: University of Pennsylvania Press, 2017, 77-95, 77.

Ironically, this report of unrest on Thanksgiving—a faux holiday celebrating the inglorious implanting of settler colonialism—was issued in the keystone year of 1963 when, once more, a new era was said to have arrived with 250,000 marching on Washington and Dr. King orating "I Have a Dream." Less noticed as the marchers were stepping off, was the death of Dr. Du Bois, in exile in Ghana, a member of the U.S. Communist Party, a grouping whose defenestration altered profoundly the dynamics and the political ecosystem of the working class of various stripes, eroding a kind of class solidarity that could have corralled racial tensions among the 50,000 football fans.

Maybe. But it is not evident what impact this would have had among the still powerful Dixiecrats on Capitol Hill who continued to wield influence on the District, as a product of their deeply ingrained Negro-phobia and their runaway hostility to federal power, which pinned their ancestors to the mat during the civil war—then seized their most valuable property without compensation. A few months before the vital August 1963 march, Congressman William Colmer of Mississippi was getting an earful from Terrell Perkins of Bay St. Louis; he railed against crime in the District. Perkins had forwarded the diatribe he had sent to JFK to that end and attached a clipping that asserted, "Negroes make up 54.8 percent of the Washington population" but "of all persons arrested for serious offenses last year 84.6 percent were Negroes...." Colmer was also the recipient of a missive from Perkins to a newspaper where he denounced "the President, Attorney General, Justice Department and Civil Rights Commission" since all were "concentrating on the persecution of the South, especially Mississippi, on voting rights and lawlessness and not looking over their shoulders at the complete disregard of law and order in Washington."[10]

Mississippi legislators were perceived correctly as the hardest of the hardliners when it came to cracking down on Negroes in the District, which sheds light on why Colmer then heard from A.E. Harbison of the curiously named Yankeetown, Florida. "The Negro will take over" soon in D.C. and "their action will be the final course in [eradication] of the white race." He was 87 and "still going strong" and had sufficient energy to fret that there was a plot to "turn Washington over to them, then sit back and watch the fun. The rest of the country will have to witness what really happens where the Negro is in power"[11]—and it wouldn't be pleasant. The

---

10. Terrell Perkins to Congressman Colmer, 5 April 1963, Box 443, *William Colmer Papers, University of Southern Mississippi-Hattiesburg*.

11. A.E. Harbison to Congressman Colmer, 8 April 1963, Box 443.

congressman tended to agree—"you may have something there!," reassuring that he would resist "turning the District of Columbia over to the Negroes."[12]

Like other Dixiecrats, Colmer's conservatism benefited from barring Negroes from voting—in a state where their proportional numbers were higher than any other—which allowed him to accumulate seniority and climb the rungs of exclusion to the chairmanship of the authoritative House Rules Committee, a kind of traffic cop controlling when—and if—legislation would proceed. Thus, as organizing for August 1963 accelerated, Colmer was explicit in expressing his unvarnished "animosity" toward the "hoodlum element of the Negroes in Washington" which "is particularly directed just now at Mississippi and Washington"—"even adults are not too safe on the streets of Washington after dark. Some three or four years ago," he wailed, "a group of teenagers from Mississippi strayed off several blocks from their hotel into a predominantly Negro business section after dark and were mauled...." He had reason to believe that "people with Mississippi tags on their cars have been insulted and embarrassed at traffic lights."[13] Was not the Magnolia State part of the union and did it not merit respect?

The congressman's correspondent, J.P. Floyd of Gulfport, was not assuaged. He was bringing a delegation to the capital and "anxiety concerning possible overt hostile acts against our bus and its occupants due to the current racial situation" was wracking his brain; "certain unpleasantness may arise," he speculated credibly: "we are concerned about extremists and hoodlums."[14]

He was not alone. Gaulden Smith, a businessman in Hattiesburg and, therefore, at the top of the class pecking order, told the congressman that "we feel it mandatory not to travel at this time" to Washington "with two small children"; however, a presumed disparity was animating his imagination: "with all the protection and consideration the colored population seems to be getting," he harrumphed, "isn't it incongruous that the whites seem to need some too?"[15]

There were a multiplicity of factors driving this increasingly hysterical concern: there was fear that the August 1963 march and the prelude to same would open old wounds with unpredictable consequences for those once thought to be the "Ruling Race." And there

---

12. Congressman Colmer to A.E. Harbison, 11 April 1963, Box 443.
13. Congressman Colmer to J.P. Floyd of Gulfport, 4 June 1963, Box 443.
14. J.P. Floyd to Congressman Colmer, 30 May 1963, Box 443.
15. Gaulden Smith to Congressman Colmer, 14 June 1963, Box 443.

was the specificity of the District with the riotous football game thought to augur ever more dire fates for unwary Euro-Americans.

If Dixiecrats had been able to peer into the correspondence of SNCC leader, James Forman, they would have had even more reason for concern. In August 1963 he happened to receive a telegram from China where a rally of 10,000 chose to "voice support to American Negro people."[16] Even the tireless Cold Warrior, Roy Wilkins, chose to respond to Chinese solidarity diplomatically,[17] not acerbically. For this was the kind of global solidarity that provided sustenance to Negro leaders and organizations even when they chose to ignore it for prudential reasons.

Instinctively, Dixiecrats knew of the importance of this kind of solidarity for arriving on Capitol Hill provided a glimpse of a changed balance of forces. Instead of a jaunty vacation to the nation's capital, for certain Mississippians coming to the District was akin to approaching a buzzsaw. Earlier, NAACP Board member, W. Montague Cobb, made a major address to congregants at the District's Wesley A.M.E.Z. church where he argued that the branch in that town was "most strategically located of all the branches,"[18] making it the command post of the movement, with attendant militancy intensified.

This importance was not unnoticed by Dixiecrats, especially the pertinently named Congressman William Jennings Bryan Dorn of South Carolina, who as Cobb was speaking took on an opposing tack. Home rule, he warned, could bring the "possibility of a powerful city political machine"; it could "greatly influence the Federal Government by demonstrations and picketing on orders from the NAACP"; indeed, he continued, a "colored mayor and colored city officials"—soon to be the norm—tasked "to greet all of the visiting dignitaries…would give the people visiting Washington from abroad that this is largely a colored nation": quelle horreur! Echoing Mississippians, Congressman Dorn too thought that home rule and the growing Negro population were an existential threat: "as it is," he concluded, "we are harassed and our families [are] in danger here at night. It would be much worse under local control,"[19] he thought.

---

16. Telegram, 13 August 1963, Box 35, *James Forman Papers, Library of Congress*.

17. Roy Wilkins to Chinese Peoples' Committee, 21 August 1963, Box 35.

18. Speech, 25 January 1959, Box 128, *Phileo Nash Papers*.

19. William Jennings Bryan Dorn to S. Wicker, American Association of University Women, 10 April 1959, Box 49, *William Jennings Bryan Dorn Papers, University of South Carolina-Columbia*.

Senator Olin Johnston was likewise irate, as he told Louis Foster of Cross Anchor, South Carolina: he reactivated "my proposal to move the capitol [from] Washington...."[20] Foster was wholly supportive, agreeing that a "safer site" should be sought, especially since "war with Russia looks more imperative with each passing month," making such a move "ultimately inevitable...."[21]

F.A. Mellush of Overland Park, Kansas, was in concurrence—adamantly—since the District "has become the Nigger Capitol of the world. Bring these niggers out here into the Middle West"—or the vicinity—and, ineluctably, "they [will] start throwing their weight around like they do with nigger vote buyers in Washington" and this "would result in another civil war. We are having enough trouble as it is." Minnesota could substitute since Senator Hubert Humphrey of this state "will welcome the influx of these Negroes," meaning "turning their state into another Sodom and Gomorrah as they have the city of Washington...." He attached a normatively inflammatory article from *U.S. News & World Report* denouncing the "blight" in the District, which also revived memories of the Thanksgiving revolt, then segued into the old chestnut of the "growing problem" of crime. "Many congressional employees have been attacked," he wheezed; "illegitimacy is a real problem." As he saw it, "Negroes are moving into Washington almost as fast as the whites move out...." Yet he was unable to see the bureaucratic madness of his description: the "President is in effect the city's mayor" and "Congress...the city council," as if in the midst of nuclear standoffs, this was efficient. As he saw it, "as the proportion of Negroes in Washington's population grows larger, the talk of 'home rule' appears to diminish," as delirium asserted itself. This Kansan also attached a leaflet castigating the "Black Bastard" as "Breeder Supreme," pointing the finger of accusation at the familiar target: "Unwed Negro Mothers."[22]

The unmellow Mellush was doubtlessly influenced by the dominant narratives in the news media, especially those in Washington which often had national reach. Before his unhinged tirade WTOP, a radio and television empire in the District, editorialized crudely about "Four suspects"—"Negroes" of course—detained on rape charges; this "points anew," it was enunciated haughtily, "to the

---

20. Senator Johnston to Louis Foster, 2 March 1963, Box 88, *Olin Johnston Papers, University of South Carolina-Columbia.*
21. Louis Foster to Senator Johnston, 7 February 1963, Box 88.
22. F.A. Bellush to Senator Johnston, 16 February 1963, Box 88. See also *U.S. News & World Report*, 18 February 1963.

need for a broad program of self-improvement among Negroes," as "blame lies with the entire community," veritably demanding collective punishment for individual misdeeds: a "self-improvement program among Negroes" was their officious demand.[23]

This hallucinatory approach was an indirect response to the growing momentum that was bringing home rule—a nightmare for some—ever closer. By 1959 the *Post* recorded that at least 16 states were demanding this reform, which they saw—correctly—as an outgrowth of the overall anti-Jim Crow movement.[24]

This newspaper's editorialist felt the "tide that swept Alaska and Hawaii into the union," was now impelling home rule, particularly since the District had four times the population as Alaska's. Conceded was the "argument" against home rule, i.e., that a "large percentage of Negroes" resided there but this was countervailed by the "flight of high income families to the Maryland and Virginia suburbs...a result of their disenfranchisement."[25]

By 1961, the 23rd Amendment to the Constitution was certified—only one Southern state concurring—allowing District residents to select Electors for President, a giant step toward actual home rule.[26]

As Jim Crow moved hesitantly toward erosion in the District—a city where militancy was intensified—frustration increased on all sides creating a tinderbox, which was displayed on Thanksgiving Day of 1962. The Urban League was caught in the crossfire, as it sought to represent a stormy constituency while appealing to the Board of Trade, the antipode of same. Even before this tense turning point, Reginald Johnson, the League's Director of Housing, conceded that his group had "lost some community prestige because its course of action was not of the hell-raising variety," the mode of choice then. But the mode was simply a creative adaptation to hellish conditions, as William Harris and his spouse discovered to their dismay. Johnson sent to the main UL office, an article from the *Afro-American* that depicted the Negro couple's attempt to "inspect a model apartment in the swank Capital Parks apartments" but a "rental agent" was "summoned to eject them because of their race...." Perversely, this swankiness was erected on land from which "thousands of colored home owners were displaced"; illuminatingly, the spouse in this case was Patricia Roberts Harris, a future U.S. ambassador and Cabinet member, exposing

23. WTOP Editorial, 14 May 1961, Box IX: 227, *NAACP Papers*.
24. *Washington Post*, 25 March 1959.
25. *Washington Post*, 27 April 1959.
26. Chris Myers Asch and George Derek Musgrove, *Chocolate City*, 344.

the cross-class impact of Jim Crow which tended to unite Negroes across socio-economic lines.[27]

But Washington had to content with problems that were verily singular. For at the same time pouring into the city were African diplomats dickering to buy mansions to be used as legations— Mali, for example, bought the old FDR home at 2131 R Street N.W.[28]—complicating the age-old pattern of sidelining Negroes discriminatorily. Promptly seven neighbors filed suit to block the use of this residence as a chancery—but their protestations were turned aside,[29] creating further grounds for the flourishing of Negro-phobia. These neighbors often were unable to make critical distinctions between the arrival in their vaunted neighborhoods of U.S. Negroes and African diplomats at a critical moment in history. As Malians were negotiating for a mansion, President Nabrit of Howard was informing Rayford Logan—then ensconced in Cold War Berlin— about the visit to Howard University of Patrice Lumumba of the Congo, whose nation too would be seeking a chancery.[30] Guinea-Conakry, the future home of exiled Alphaeus Hunton, sought to buy a building for an embassy for a handsome $250,000.[31]

Unfortunately, in Washington—and nationally—class collaboration was a defining feature of the Euro-American majority, serving to animate the transcendent conservatism amongst them. The *New York Times* got wind of the Urban League's request to the outgoing Vice President, Richard M. Nixon, to lower the boom on the continued exclusion of Negro electricians from federal construction jobs in the District. UL chief, Lester Granger, asserted that this exclusion featured "'collusion' between the builders and Local 26 of the [International Brotherhood of Electrical Workers]."[32] It was in March 1963 that Carmichael presented excoriating testimony about unions' malignant role before the Commission on Civil Rights.[33] It was also Carmichael who led a student rally of 500 at the Labor

27. Reginald Johnson to Lester Granger, 1 October 1959, Box I: C63, *National Urban League Papers, Library of Congress-Washington, D.C.* See also *Afro-American*, 12 September 1959.
28. *Washington Post*, 28 December 1960.
29. *Washington Post*, 5 April 1961.
30. James Nabrit to Rayford Logan, 11 August 1960, Box 6, *Rayford Logan Papers, Library of Congress-Washington, D.C.*
31. *Washington Post*, 1 October 1960.
32. *New York Times*, 29 April 1960.
33. *The Hilltop*, 8 March 1963.

Department in protest against discriminatory hiring at a hilltop construction site.[34]

This protest was occurring as a local journalist was quizzically pointing to the "paradox" that Negroes were jobless as jobs went unfilled—though belatedly underlined what Carmichael and Company were protesting: "exclusion of Negroes from apprenticeship and training...."[35] The District was paradoxical. As of 1963, predominantly Negro neighborhoods had more unemployment than that in mostly Euro-American areas but were relatively better off than comparable communities elsewhere. And even when jobs were landed, other surreal obstacles were strewn about. There was the Negro woman who worked at the Treasury Department but was flummoxed by the color line for obtaining a permit to park in the "virtually lily white parking lots," and, thus, said a furious Negro reporter, "she has to walk five or six blocks to get to work."[36]

Similarly, on the jobs front, intra-racial irksomeness was sparked by what caught the eye of the NAACP's Clarence Mitchell. An advertisement in the *Washington Star* blared that a "'Colored Family' wants refined colored girl, fair complexion....'"[37] This was bound to stoke friction between the darker skinned who believed that their lighter counterparts also discriminated against them. Straining to keep pace, a *Post* ad referred to Negroes as "'boots,'"[38] possibly another allusion to melanin richness and unhelpful to intra-racial unity, not accidentally. It was possible that this fissiparousness could even have overshadowed a similar proposal from the Communication Workers of America, a premier union, that was advertising for employees in the *Post* to staff its national office and—said the NAACP counsel—"would deny colored persons an opportunity to apply,"[39] likely meaning any Negro unable to "pass" for Euro-American. Disrespecting Negroes of all types was the barbershop in the House of Representatives which refused to give a haircut to Negroes, presumably Congressmen Diggs and Dawson, perhaps Powell, too.[40]

---

34. *The Hilltop*, 1 April 1963.

35. *Washington Post*, 11 June 1961.

36. *Afro-American*, 12 July 1961.

37. Clarence Mitchell to 'Washington Star,' 27 October 1960, Box IX: 227, *NAACP Papers*.

38. *Pittsburgh Courier*, 28 April 1962.

39. J. Francis Pohlhaus to Theodore Brown, AFL-CIO, 17 August 1959, Box IX: 227.

40. Clarence Mitchell to Speaker Sam Rayburn, 26 October 1960, Box IX: 227.

They should not have seen this as unique to them. Ronald Gault, then a teenage student—before becoming a noted businessman with interests in post-apartheid South Africa and spouse of noted reporter, Charlayne Hunter—could not get a trim there either.[41]

The *Afro-American*, befitting a journal that included a radical scion, George Murphy, was unrelenting in its scalding reportage of the Jim Crow that bedeviled the region. At the time of the Harris debacle, their editorialist was fuming: the ongoing policy of Negro removal— or urban renewal—which took the guise of "gentrification" in coming decades, a response to a "Chocolate City" embedded in the capital of white supremacy, also created adverse conditions since "overcrowding and lowering of living standards" was the result, when entire communities were "uprooted en masse and literally dumped on other communities...." Betraying Murphy's lingering influence at the paper, the writer mused, "if Premier Khrushchev," Soviet leader, "will have an opportunity to visit...[the] Deep South to see first hand how colored citizens are treated"; to save time, the roly-poly Communist "need look no further than out the window of the White House"—for that would be "Exhibit A" for "Mr. K."[42]

The Urban League was well-placed to assault this barricade with vigor but it was compromised because of its strategy of conciliation with the very same ruling elite that was perpetrating the problem. Johnson informed Sterling Tucker of the District affiliate that the Federal Housing Administration "continues to give its services and grants temporary mortgage commitments to builders who are obviously and blatantly violating a state's non-discriminatory leg-islation"; there was in effect "redistribution of a Negro population out of an area," then their "return" was "denied," depriving them of "the benefits of the improved area"—this "constitute[s] Negro removal,"[43] an accurate assessment.

However, Tucker—like many Negro leaders—had unusual lever-age that was wielded deftly. Unlike a typical U.S. city, Tucker heard from the Bureau of Public Affairs at the State Department, which was "concerned" with "the recent flurry of incidents of violence by Negroes in Washington...." Tucker's mealymouthed response was to craft an "experiment to expedite processes of assimilation and acculturation of the 'uninitiated' segment of the brothers and sisters

---

41. Lillian Gault to NAACP, circa 1961, Box IX: 227.

42. *Afro-American*, 12 September 1959.

43. Reginald Johnson to Sterling Tucker, 18 January 1960, Box I: C63, *National Urban League Papers*.

among us."[44] Translation? Address the matter aggressively as a so-called "Negro Problem" rather than a white supremacy problem or imperialism problem.

Tucker was encouraged in his wrongheadedness by his superiors in New York City. Julian Thomas wanted Tucker to "reach" the "irresponsible Negro population," as he referred to an incident during a recent State of the Union address when often the world's attention turned toward Capitol Hill; on that heady day "two policemen were murdered by Negro thugs," he spat out; yes, "Washington presents a laboratory" for experimenting on Negroes with national implications.[45]

Mulling over the implications of this caterwauling was the Board of the District UL with such eminences present as foremost attorney, Charles Duncan; the future mayor, Walter Washington; and distinguished scholar, Caroline Ware. Akin to other affiliates, the repetitive line was stressed: "full employment of minority group persons up to the limit of their capacity and paid accordingly would insure a burgeoning economy." But unlike other affiliates at issue was the "experiences of visiting foreigners and their impression of our racial attitudes...." Washington was depicted harshly as a "hardship post for colored diplomats," no minor matter during the Cold War, when Africa and the Caribbean were contestants. Lest any spying eyes think otherwise, they emphasized that "in working on these problems we are demonstrating the highest patriotism"[46]—and not, as some Dixiecrats would have it, undermining national security by simply broaching this sensitive matter.

Paramount journalist, Ben Bradlee, a close friend of JFK, revealed that "a few months into his presidency," he "talked to me about how foreign affairs were dominating his life,"[47] a direct result of how this complex matter intersected with pressing domestic concerns. The president was likely aware of what his protocol aide, Pedro Sanjuan, told the press and the NAACP: Route 40, the serpentine byway from Washington into snaky Maryland was presenting ever more nettlesome problems as Negroes demonstrated or even mocked Jim Crow pretensions by pretending to be African diplomats, as the latter fumed about apartheid maltreatment. Diplomats from Sierra Leone were furious after being refused service at the Howard Johnson's

44. Sterling Tucker to Julian Thomas, 21 January 1960, Box II: D73, *National Urban League Papers*.

45. Julian Thomas to Sterling Tucker, 8 January 1960, Box II: D73, *National Urban League Papers*.

46. Minutes, 28 September 1960, Box II: D73.

47. Ben Bradlee, *A Good Life*, 220.

restaurant in Hagerstown; the protocol aide lamented the backlash from the continent: "reaction to these incidents in the African press [was] immediate," especially in oil-rich Nigeria. Frantically, San-juan accompanied by White House aides and the state's governor, traipsed up and down Route 40, lobbying haphazardly. He denied stoutly that Washington was a hardship post for diplomats, the fore-going notwithstanding.[48]

Yet by 1962 the State Department grasped the nettle and conceded the ineffable tie between Africans and African Americans, which delivered racial reform. Equal housing laws were demanded by this agency ostensibly focused abroad since securing homes for African envoys—said a reporter citing their argument—"will be solved only when housing is freely available to the city's Negro Americans...." Lining up to agree was Angier Biddle Duke, the protocol chief and the State Department official and former premier Michigander, G. Mennen "Soapy" Williams. It was Duke who captured the ethos of the era when he said, "'It is not only his own housing problem that concerns the African diplomat. It is, instead, the housing problem of those of African descent" more generally.[49] Williams chimed in adding that housing bias was "detrimental to the effectiveness of the foreign policy" that he was sworn to execute.[50] Even Roy Wilkins of the NAACP noticed that the arrival of African envoys in the District was a boon for the U.S. Negro.[51]

By 1963 such incidents continued to proliferate, the latest involv-ing a Jamaican diplomat who was refused service in Warrenton, Virginia and was subjected to threats and indignities when he object-ed,[52] yet another reason for the passage of a sweeping Civil Rights bill on Capitol Hill in 1964.

To be fair, the League strained to make solid points. Days after the Thanksgiving riot, the UL informed the press that "segregation in housings costs the District's nonwhite tenants approximately a quarter of a million dollars each year in excessive rents," a "segre-gation tax" in other words that included "overcrowded conditions," among the many "causal factors in the high incidence of crime and ill-health within the Negro ghetto."[53] The latter words exemplified the

---

48. "Washington Viewpoint" Transcript, 18 November 1961, Box IX: 227, *NAACP Papers.*
49. *Washington Post*, 13 April 1962.
50. *Washington Star*, 30 November 1962.
51. *Washington Star*, 24 November 1962.
52. *The Hilltop*, 26 April 1963.
53. Press Release, 30 November 1962, Box II: D73.

arduousness encountered by the League when it sought to analyze reality, arising again in scrutinizing "Washington's labor market and the nonwhite [sic] worker." The "unemployed segment [of] Washington's workforce is always lower than the national average and seldom exceeds 3 percent of the total labor supply," continuing to attract migrants from Negro heavy states, e.g., the outer reaches of Maryland and Virginia. Yet, there was a "white collar bias," meaning "a different kind of Negro has been attracted to Washington," accenting pre-existing bourgeois sensibilities. It was not a compliment to the federal government to assert that "the degree of employment discrimination found within government is much less than is common within private industry"[54]—this was more so a condemnation of the latter.

The journalist, Haynes Johnson, presented a bracing portrait of the "segregation tax": rents for Negroes often were about $85 monthly for an apartment—$65 for non-Negroes. One interviewee told him, "'This is one of the reason[s] why so many people are being Communist'"— though what could have been said was "this is one the reasons why Communists were routed" in order to reduce resistance to exploitation. In the prelude to August 1963, Johnson reported that "Negroes are virtually barred from the craft unions" and "cannot get a skilled job." Negroes were battered into accepting this unsustainable status quo to the point where, said Johnson, "hostility toward policemen is almost an ingrained habit among these Negroes." What served to fill the ideological vacuum forged by the routing of Reds was revealed by the 7,000 strong rally of the Nation of Islam at Uline Arena. Minister Malcolm X spoke, described as "a tall rangy man with light skin, a cleft chin and a rapid speaking delivery." Months later the Nation had escalated, rallying at Griffith Stadium and "another large crowd turned out" and this time, Malcolm's mentor, Elijah Muhammad appeared: "a slight man with a lined face appearing more an oriental than a Negro," as the very sight of him "unleashe[d] wild emotions in his followers. It is a frightening experience," said this rapidly balding Euro-American man. As was their tendency, Nation followers were breathing fire, as one recalled the mass rally of the Klan in the 1920s: "'We were ready to fight if they broke ranks. We didn't know anything about non-violence in those days,'"[55] a jab at the then ascending strategy and tactic.

---

54. Statement, 19 November 1962, Box II: D73.
55. Haynes Johnson, *Dusk at the Mountain: The Negro, the Nation and the Capital; A Report on Problems and Progress*, Garden City: Doubleday, 1963, 48, 30, 31, 48, 55, 70, 110, 145, 157.

As suggested previously, it was not just employment that fueled the flames of unrest. From the other shore a favorite whipping boy for the Dixiecrats was public education and the presumed wrath unleashed by Negro youth in the wake of desegregation. Sensational congressional investigations of same was a preoccupation of certain legislators, leading to countless reports nationally, magnifying panic and seizing the attention of Walter Tobriner of the Board of Trade.[56]

By 1963 Carl Hansen, Superintendent of the District school system, was told of a situation that should not have shocked him: the "deplorable condition of the District Public Schools," but as usual, his correspondent was seeking to manipulate a matter that victimized the Negro to their detriment. In the schools, said Eleanor Gedney, "the Negro [is] the ruling race" and, as such, "has most of the advantages in the District..."[57] This rhetorical excess was indicative of the conflict at the highest level of the school system, with one editorialist finding "disturbing evidence that Doctor [Mordecai] Johnson is out 'to get' Doctor Hansen."[58]

More accurately, the Dixiecrats were out to get Negroes. A photographer denied wanly that he had asked students at three predominantly Negro schools to "pose pulling hair, pushing each other or throwing stones"—though he had been hired by the fossilized Congressman F. Edward Hebert of Louisiana[59]—in order to inflame further the routine hysteria of the Black Scare.

Contrastingly, in May 1963 Mordecai Johnson late of Howard, who had the ear of Hansen and the Board of Education, like the Urban League directorate, directed these educators' attention to current journalism "concerning world perspective on the Negro minority situation in America today"; it was "highly significant" he said to the point that "all members of the Board [should] read it."[60] The Board would ignore the impact of the global on the local at their peril.

---

56. Pamphlet by Erwin Knoll, "The Truth About Desegregation in Washington's Schools," series in *Washington Post*, 22-28 December 1958, Box 1, *Walter Tobriner Papers, George Washington University.*

57. Eleanor Gedney to Carl Hansen, 4 February 1963, Box 24, *Mordecai Johnson Papers, Howard University.*

58. Editorial, 19 April 1963, Box 24, *Mordecai Johnson Papers.*

59. *Washington Daily News*, 10 June 1961.

60. Minutes of Board of Education, 15 May 1963, Box 24, *Mordecai Johnson Papers.*

As so often happened, what occurred in Washington was reverberating in Prince George's County.[61] Across the river in Arlington, there were about three or four neighborhoods to which Negroes were consigned informally and one building where they could attend junior high and high school, studying from tattered, discarded textbooks and nubs of chalk.[62]

As of 1962 District Catholic schools felt they were outperforming their peers in New Orleans, then embroiled in tawdry protests against desegregation: "segregation was never an official policy" in District parochial schools said the Archdiocese.[63] The segregationist Citizens' Council in the gulf city sought to send busloads of Negroes to the District, since they seemed not to object to their presence. It was a "Freedom Ride North" cracked an aide to ultra-rightist Leander Perez while Senator Russell Long wondered like a weasel why any would object to this maneuver.[64]

Perhaps the most egregious example of obstruction and objection to school desegregation occurred in Prince Edward County, Virginia where as early as 1959 the decision was made by the authorities to shut the entire school system, rather than share classrooms with Negro children, then subsidize so-called "segregated academies" by various means, including taxpayer money. This meant depriving these ebony youth of education and the District NAACP branch responded. As put by their counsel, J. Francis Pohlhaus, they "offered to provide free room and board for one of the students" from this country "in order that such student could attend school" in Washington.[65]

This conflictual board was reflective of the turbulence then rocking youth—the Thanksgiving revolt, for example—that also had seeped into the marrow of post-secondary education. Weeks after Thanksgiving, three students—one was Negro—from Georgetown University, theretofore not known as a hotbed of dissent, were refused service at an Arlington bistro. Days later they returned with 12 others—and were arrested. The administration basically said they were on their own and balked at rising to their defense. At least the administration was consistent. In the previous decade, when even

61. Statement before Prince George's County, Maryland Board of Education, 6 January 1962, Box 3, *Ruth Wolf Papers, University of Maryland-College Park.*
62. *Washington Post*, 13 April 2019.
63. *Pittsburgh Courier*, 14 April 1962.
64. *Washington Post*, 26 April 1962.
65. J. Francis Pohlhaus to W. Lester Banks, Richmond branch, circa May 1959, Box IX: 227, *NAACP Papers.*

the perpetually staid American and George Washington universities objected to McCarthyite probes, President Edward Bunn of Georgetown "welcomed" the inquisitors.[66]

By mid-1963, the College Park flagship campus bordering the District was said to hold not more than 200 Negro students out of a total enrollment of 15,000.[67]

Activism at Howard stood as both inspiration and stark contrast to the other campuses in the District. The hilltop was the site where in March 1963, Communist historian, Herbert Aptheker was defending the Soviet Union against the imprecations of Socialist Party cadre. The Non-Violent Action Group was collecting funds for Mississippi Negroes with Courtland Cox leading the way.[68] Even Attorney General Robert F. Kennedy, found it necessary to make a beeline for the campus where he discussed civil rights.[69]

Tom Kahn remained active to the point where he and another student—Vernon Gill—were feared to be abducted en route to a campus meeting and did not materialize for four days. Kahn's presence led to yet another April Fools' Day droll headline in the campus newspaper: "university integrates peacefully as two whites register… without incident" at Howard, referring to disgruntled transfers from the University of Mississippi. Suggestive of the creeping advance of sexual heterogeneity on campus, another headline designed to be rollicking trumpeted "frat brother pulls change becomes 'Queen for a Day…wishes to remain anonymous," as he announced: "'I was a Howard woman for 24 hours.'"[70]

Not tomfoolery was a columnist opining—again: weeks before August 1963—about student apathy: "is this the same campus where last year on any given Saturday, one could see scores of students leaving for Maryland to protest the Route 40 incidents."[71] Coincidentally, the future star professor, Houston Baker, chose that moment to run for a post in the student government.[72]

66. Robert Emmett Curran, *A History of Georgetown University: The Quest for Excellence, 1889-1964, Volume II,* Washington, D.C.: Georgetown University Press, 2010, 378, 383.
67. *Cambridge Banner,* 18 July 1963, *Vertical File-Campus Unrest, University of Maryland-College Park.*
68. *The Hilltop,* 8 March 1963. See also *The Hilltop,* 22 March 1963: "Large crowd hears speakers in debate" on Soviet Union.
69. *The Hilltop,* 22 March 1963.
70. *The Hilltop,* 1 April 1963.
71. *The Hilltop,* 27 May 1963.
72. *The Hilltop,* 26 April 1963.

Meantime, Professor Logan continued providing a mottled model for students. He continued to flit in and out of elevated soirees; thus, he could be found at 3317 Q Street, N.W. for an affair honoring Hastings Banda, founder of sovereign Malawi. "Ruth [spouse] and I were the only Negro Americans there," he said with a tad of pride, even as he detected an eavesdropper—"an intelligence agent—CIA, FBI, Army, Navy or Air Force—from the twinkle in his eye, that he knew that I knew...." Undeterred, Logan proceeded to engage Banda; the future dictator "showed knowledge of the early Pan African movements...he also referred to Marcus Garvey and George Padmore," a former operative of the Communist International and of late advisor to Nkrumah.[73] Curiously, he found Banda's "accent" to be "as much American as it is English," a reflection of his prior education in the U.S. or a fashionable affectation betraying his fondness for U.S. imperialism.[74]

Later, "Ruth and I," he said with a touch of haughtiness, "were the only 'representatives' of Washington 'colored society' at the French embassy"; then he gravitated to the Liberian legation where a Bulgarian envoy wanted to discuss "the Negro," a frequent occurrence, leaving Logan with the notion that "perhaps" he should "notify the FBI or the CIA."[75] Logan had to proceed carefully for—apparently—he was being vetted by the JFK regime for a top-level post, ambassador according to Louis Martin, Negro White House aide, to an unnamed African nation. "I know further that I might not be cleared by the FBI or the CIA," he said dampeningly, adding likewise: "I sincerely believe that the students at Howard need me,"[76] partially accurate. Hope Franklin informed Logan that the FBI had "interrogated" him to that end—but he was also being scrutinized by the Internal Revenue Service, too. The apparently nervous Franklin, lowered "his voice occasionally to such a low pitch that I cannot understand him"; he was interrogated especially about Logan's years in France after World War I. Logan surmised that his H.U. aide was also queried about him.[77]

President Nabrit "had just filled out a long questionnaire for the FBI about a member of [the] History Department," (presumably Logan) adding to the list of Howard faculty "who had been or were

---

73. Entry, 15 April 1960, Box 6.
74. Entry, 16 April 1960, Box 6.
75. Entry, 26 June 1961, Box 7.
76. Entry, 25 June 1961, Box 7.
77. Entry, 30 August 1961, Box 7.

on government assignments," indicative that JFK truly had delivered certain hilltoppers to a "New Frontier."[78]

However, Logan did not descend from the hilltop to Foggy Bottom or anywhere else, perhaps because interrogators contacted his colleagues who—to use a word that he would have appreciated—proceeded to blackball him. Merze Tate was christened officially by him as "The Bitch," a colleague agreed that she was "trying to provoke him into hitting her" and Logan had a similar urge. "I do not know when she will begin acting like a crazy woman...."[79] He may have been jealous of her since as he was being "blackballed." Snowden told him that "The Bitch...would probably be asked by the Armed Forces to write a textbook," a lucrative assignment generative of envy. Archivist Dorothy Porter fanned the flames by telling Logan that Tate had been selected over her art historian spouse for a rare H.U. perk.[80] This led him to demoting her further, her status becoming "The Witch-Bitch," a wildly misogynist term "particularly enjoyed" by fellow academic Saunders Redding[81] and as if that insult was too mild, she then became "The Witch Monster."[82] Speculating homicidally, she was "crafty enough to plan to use her many acts of unprofessional conduct as evidence of insanity if she should kill someone."[83] As heavy snows fell in December 1962, he engaged in classic projection, averring that "The Bitch is really unhinged,"[84] adding the note from Sterling Brown that she was "in need of psychiatric treatment...."[85]

Retrospective psychologizing is inherently problematic—I did not know Logan, for example. Yet, it is not difficult to suggest that he was being buffeted by forces he found it hard to comprehend—Red Scare, Black Power—which helped to push him toward ever more subjective approaches to reality. Though he had expressed doubts about the ties of fellow scholar, Harold Isaacs, to U.S. intelligence, he chose to discuss with him whether St. Clair Drake, an anthropologist and ultimately a Stanford professor, had "'diseased'" traits; this was an aspect of his becoming "more and more distressed by

78. Entry, 19 September 1961, Box 7.
79. Entry, 15 December 1960, Box 7.
80. Entry, 1 July 1960, Box 7.
81. Entry, 26 January 1961, Box 7.
82. Entry, 19 July 1961, Box 7.
83. Entry, 31 July 1961, Box 7.
84. Entry, 29 December 1963, Box 7.
85. Entry, 23 January 1963, Box 7.

the emotionalism and the anti-intellectualism in these AMSAC meetings,"[86] a reference to the American Society for African Culture organized in the 1950s and continuing to bear the imprint of the Red Scare. Logan continued to duel with fellow professor, William Leo Hansberry, especially after he was lauded in *Ebony*, the rapidly influential Chicago-based glossy magazine, which portrayed this relative of Lorraine Hansberry favorably and lamented how H.U. had treated him[87]—publicity that Logan thought should have been accorded himself.

As is evident, Logan continued to be a habitue of the plethora of legations popping up in Washington as decolonization proceeded. Soon he was at the Pakistani embassy conversing with Sayed Haq who sought to "convince" him that "Pakistanis are better friends of Negroes and Africans than Indians are," a critical factor as Islamabad and New Delhi jockeyed for Negro support. He dangled before the captivated professor the prospect of "establishing a Chair of Islamic or Muslim Culture at Howard," though Logan thought the "initial difficulty would come from our Jewish friends," concerned both with the steady rise of the Nation of Islam and possible risk to Israel. The university Dean, William Stuart Nelson and the administration more generally were "strong 'Indianists" while students were giving credence to concerns about the Nation of Islam in their discussion of a new club: "'the OMWISE, the Organization to Make White the Symbol of Evil'"—that some students "burst into laughter" at the mention did not allay the underlying concern, since an ideological vacuum had been forged by the Red Scare that disrupted class analysis. Students had ingested the rhetoric of the Nation and rattled off the litany of deploying the term "black" as a symbol of evil: blackguard, blackball, blackmail, black Monday, black Tuesday, black Friday, blacklist"—a powerful argument that somehow had escaped the attention of much of the left.[88]

This historian was ambivalent about this ideological turn, as at the same time he found an "undercurrent expressed implicitly by many of the Africans," i.e., "hostility to light-skinned Negro Americans,"[89] like himself. As the temper of the times hurtled toward "Black Power," Logan became more anxious about his melanin content, once speculating that those like himself and Bunche are "too white"

86. Entry, 27 June 1961, Box 7.
87. Entry, 26 June 1961, Box 7.
88. Entry, 6 May 1960, Box 6.
89. Entry, 27 June 1960, Box 7.

to succeed in Africa, with—somehow—pointing to the Congo as evidence.[90] As Hope Franklin continued to climb the rungs of academic success—the University of Chicago, then Duke—Logan thought "'reverse color discrimination'" was at play in that the dark skinned Oklahoman was "'promoted' by his white friends" as a result of his being "'black'" almost literally.[91]

Logan continued to be recruited by the U.S. authorities for various missions, e.g., lecturing to trade union leaders from Lebanon and Latin America and Japan on racism in the U.S., where he was guaranteed to present a hopeful analysis about retreat of this pestilence.[92] He conferred with Francis Russell, U.S. envoy in Accra, where "Nkrumah's authoritarianism" was the topic du jour.[93]

The broader point was that the landscape was shifting rapidly: a Red Scare now accompanied by a Black Scare; arriving African and Caribbean envoys complicating the ability to maltreat Negroes viciously; and a Thanksgiving Revolt that outraged Dixiecrats and their legions of District followers.

---

90. Entry, 22 June 1961, Box 7.
91. Entry, 16 December 1962, Box 7.
92. Entry, 26 June 1961, Box 7.
93. Entry, 16 December 1960, Box 7.

Chapter 18

African Solidarity with African Americans, 1963-1964

The March on Washington of 1963 was a true turning point, leading directly to the important Civil Rights Act of 1964, which established a federal anti-Jim Crow infrastructure with gigantic implications for the city in which it was crafted: the District.

Local organizers from the NAACP, CORE, and Dr. King's Southern Christian Leadership Conference issued a clarion call for a kind of feeder march, urging protesters to "assemble opposite the White House" on 14 June 1963, demanding that "Mr. President" allocate "no federal funds for apartheid states...don't play politics with human rights...issue fair housing ordinance—NOW!" The creative cadre reminded that "We can't eat Jim Crow," and "we demand fair job rights for all"; further, "end blatant job discrimination in the Justice Department...."[1]

This protest signified how the March on Washington was in many ways the March of Washington in that the ultimate target was Capitol Hill and the intersection of the domestic and the global that was driving events was centered in the District. Symbolic and real was the point that local activist, Julius Hobson, was in charge of the marshals during the march, directing the line of march and maintaining order.[2]

Howard marchers were there in August and the Medical School provided first aid stations ringing the Mall on this steamy August day.[3] Howardites were part of an estimated 35,000 Washingtonians who participated, with the Washington Home Rule Committee

---

1. Leaflet, 14 June 1963, MS 0848, *Johns Hopkins University-Baltimore.*
2. Transcript of WTOP Interview, 8 March 1964, Box 1, *Julius Hobson Papers, Washington, D.C. Public Library.*
3. LaSalle D. Lefall, Jr., *No Boundaries: A Cancer Surgeon's Odyssey*, Washington, D.C.: Howard University Press, 2005, 135.

crediting the "enormous amount of work done by the Reverend Walter E. Fauntroy,"[4] soon to reach Capitol Hill as a congressman. Post-August, a meeting of NAACP activists found housing in Howard dormitories.[5]

On the day of the march, a sympathetic Ontarian reminded the NAACP to "never forget that Negroes, 20 million strong...are greater in number than many countries' total population, Canada included."[6] Even Patrick Duncan, a local representative of South Africa's questionable Pan-Africanist Congress, pledged that he would "be able to participate in the march."[7] In Africa itself Hunton was among a group of U.S. expatriates who picketed the legation of his homeland in Accra.[8] Basketball superstar, Bill Russell of the Boston Celtics, was among the celebrities present in Washington—their stature, too, was global.[9]

The same held true for Sidney Poitier, the extraordinary cineaste who was recruited by the NAACP to lobby Senators and the president for the final push for the 1964 Civil Rights Act, which the march was designed to propel.[10]

Although the very name Howard continued to trigger a kind of trauma among Dixiecrats, wiser elements in the U.S. ruling class were coming to see its value in Cold War contestation. Senator Abraham Ribicoff of Connecticut, who was to serve in JFK's cabinet knew that it was the "'only comprehensive complex institution in the world dedicated primarily to serve the Negro student,'" and, quite importantly, "'14 percent of its nine thousand students come from fifty different countries,'" an appropriate transition for this former site of a plantation.[11]

This insight had not been absorbed by all. In the runup to the pivotal year of 1963 Vincent Okobi, a Howard student of Nigerian origin, was arrested after walking against the traffic; he claimed that the sidewalk was too dark for perambulation. This was the sort

---

4. Minutes of Washington Home Rule Committee, 12 September 1963, Box 1, *Julius Hobson Papers, Washington D.C. Public Library.*

5. Memorandum, 31 December 1963, Carton 58, *NAACP Papers, University of California-Berkeley.*

6. "Mrs. C. Canham" to NAACP, 28 August 1963, Box IX: 154, *NAACP Papers.*

7. Patrick Duncan to NAACP, circa August 1963, Box IX: 154.

8. Christine Ann Lutz, "'The Dizzy Steep to Heaven,'" 331.

9. Dave Zirin, *A People's History of Sports in the United States,* 153.

10. Walter Sutler and Ed Hailes, District Branch to National NAACP, 6 May 1964, Box VI: E19, *NAACP Papers.*

11. Haynes Johnson, *Dusk at the Mountain,* 185, 186.

of petty offense that often ensnared U.S. Negroes. He also charged that the officer who detained him pushed him against a car—not demurely—and he was put behind bars on a charge of disorderly conduct. But times had changed. Riding to the rescue were two State Department officials; a Nigerian diplomat; a Howard administrator—all conferring with the police for two hours, before he was released.[12]

How could the police continue to manhandle ordinary Negroes when they could not necessarily distinguish them from expatriate Nigerians? Laws and customs had to change as a result—which brought marchers to Washington in August 1963.

Nigeria was to become a major supplier of energy to the North Atlantic bloc and the same held true for sovereign Algeria to the north, which had fought a bitter war of liberation against France. The experience of the latter's envoys in the District were hardly reassuring in Algiers, almost guaranteeing what occurred a few years later, when doors were flung open for the Black Panther Party, which established a legation there. For it was in 1964 that Robert O. Clouser, Planning Director of the District Zoning Commission, was compelled to deny that he called the Algerians "'a smelly, messy people, unclean in their personal habits....'" He did not ease the gravity of the problem when he claimed that actually he was quoting what opponents of the Algerian application for a chancery had stated. It is not clear if Algerian ire was assuaged when his superiors argued that this view did not reflect the views of the citizens of the District government.[13]

This was just one more example of how African independence altered the landscape in the U.S. itself—apologizing to Africans did not come naturally and easily in the republic. Previously, the "Islamic Republic of Mauretania" was in the news, as this Algerian neighbor in northwest Africa sought a zoning variance for what was termed an "Islamic chancery." Instantaneously, strong opposition erupted from neighbors near Nouakchott's building at 2737 Cathedral Road N.W., an upscale vicinity of course. Naturally, the State Department backed Mauretania, engendering more hostility toward a federal government which seemed to side with outsiders against citizens.[14]

This cascading alienation was reflected on campuses. The chief executive at the flagship campus in College Park, Maryland sought to bar student from attending the August 1963 march.[15]

---

12. *Washington Post*, 6 April 1962.
13. *Washington Daily News*, 20 October 1964.
14. *Washington Star*, 17 May 1962.
15. Carl Bernstein, *Chasing History*, 250.

Georgetown alumni appealed vainly to President Bunn and his comrades to sponsor a campus procession for the march but, said a subsequent analysis, the administrators "did not wish to be identified with the civil rights movement"[16]—not a surprising view, subsequent hagiography notwithstanding. The Catholic initiated school had no compunction, on the other hand, about hiring Stephen Possony as a professor—while he served as a full-time intelligence officer for the Air Force.[17] Nor was Georgetown or its nearby neighbor, George Washington, pulling their weight in addressing other local needs, including health care, where their respective medical schools had seen fit to admit one Negro student each by 1963, contributing to dismal health outcomes: the District said the Urban League "has the highest rate for cities of its size," speaking of venereal disease.[18]

For Logan at Howard, the exclusivity of these crosstown rivals was a bit much. Alan Pifer of the Carnegie Corporation told him George Washington was "'second rate; American is third rate; Catholic University is strong in some departments,'" while "he said nothing about Georgetown,"[19] damned with silence.

Still, hospitals were under fire because of discriminatory praxis which guaranteed poor health outcomes, a point made by Lizbeth Bamberger of the AFL-CIO. Approvingly, she cited NAACP official—and physician—Dr. Montague Cobb, who said he was "tired of surveys—he wants some action NOW!" This was in concert with the temper of the times. Just before August 1963, the Association picketed the American Medical Association in Chicago. Bamberger also mentioned that "Freedmen's Hospital," the Howard affiliate, "is government subsidized and costs patients less. This means fewer Negroes will want to go to 'white' hospitals."[20]

Maybe. But other District hospitals were not exactly rolling out a red carpet to welcome Negro patients, suggestive of why Black Washingtonians turned out for an anti-Jim Crow march in their hometown.

Contrarily, on Capitol Hill, there were numerous congresspersons—despite the dedicated purging of Communists—who were unwilling to accept the bona fides of desegregation. Arguably, these purges ultimately weakened anti-Jim Crow forces making them more vulnerable as the political climate changed, especially after the collapse

---

16. Robert Emmett Curran, *A History of Georgetown University, Volume 2*, 378.
17. Robert Emmett Curran, 247.
18. Study, circa 1963, Box II: D17, *National Urban League Papers*.
19. Entry, 3 April 1964, Box 7.
20. Interview, 26-30 August 1963, Box II: D67, *National Urban League Papers*.

of the Soviet Union less than three decades later. Certainly, it weakened ideological rigor among anti-racist forces, in some senses
freezing them in place in terms of their understanding as of the
obtaining situation in, say, 1954.

At that moment, the resurgent Ku Klux Klan was capturing headlines. They portrayed themselves as the staunchest advocates of the
renewed civic religion: anticommunism. This was the appeal from
their branch in Del Mar, Virginia months before the August march:
"We shall not succumb to the Communist plot of a mongrel race,"
it was announced resolutely, as they eviscerated "humiliation by
integration" perpetrated by "Jew Negro Communism."[21] Their comrades, led by foremost Nazi, George Lincoln Rockwell, echoed their
genocidal appeal: "Fellow Virginians!" was the luring message as
Rockwell, the Fuhrer announced, "We are still here and growing
stronger every day," as suggested by the "display at our headquarters [and] signs and the swastika banner of the White Race" at 928
North Randolph Street; they also had an office in Arlington at the
well-trafficked Buckingham Shopping Center. They, too, were apoplectic about the "COMMUNIST APPARATUS IN THIS AREA...."[22]
It was unclear if the ban on school dances in Arlington was somehow related to the racism-mongering occurring there.[23]

These toxic fumes were taken advantage of, as Dixiecrats and
their allies unleashed a series of lurid hearings focused on crime in
the District—and nationally—with Negroes targeted and blamed.[24]
Bellowed was the allegation that by 1964 crime did rise in the District.[25] An aide to Congressman McMillan of South Carolina, told
WWDC radio of the "police need for detention for questioning," a
response to "unquestioned crime conditions" in the District.[26] Just
days before the march, the American Civil Liberties Union was
lobbying intensively against a crime bill on Capitol Hill. There

---

21. Broadside, 15 April 1962, Box 1, *James Stockard Papers, George Washington University,*
22. Brochure, 1963, Box 1, *James Stockard Papers.* Emphasis in original.
23. *Washington Post,* 17 August 1962.
24. "Joint Hearings Before the District of Columbia Committee of the Senate and the House of Representatives on the Increasingly Serious Crime
Situation in the District of Columbia," 6, 25 February and 4 March 1963,
Washington, D.C.: GPO, 1963, Box 96, *Office Files of Charles Horsky, Lyndon
Baines Johnson Presidential Library-Austin, Texas.*
25. Kyla Sommers, "'I Believe in the City'," 67.
26. James Clark, Clerk to Ben Strouse of WWDC radio, circa 1963, Box 6, *John
McMillan Papers.*

were many far-reaching provisions," said their representative, David Carliner, including verbiage that would "overturn a unanimous decision of the Supreme Court (the 'Mallory Rule') which is intended to protect persons under arrest from forced confessions," the erosion of which infuriated Dixiecrats where this gruesomeness often was exerted against Negroes. The draconian bill "would restore the power of the police to arrest persons, without probable cause, solely for investigation...." It was a "desperate, vindictive measure," he complained, supposedly "to cope...with the problem of crime in the District"[27]—but with clear national implications—as Washington elevated its historic role as a laboratory for ghoulish remedies, targeting Negroes in the first instance, before exported elsewhere. Ominously, Congressman McMillan of South Carolina with oversight in the District was pursuing the perilous procedure of "investigative arrests...."[28]

In this stinging context that the *Afro-American* advised worryingly that certain Washingtonians "read the 'Daily News,' [to] learn how to hate colored people," a not singular periodical which "entrenched racial antagonism among the District's white citizens...."[29] What was at play was the Black Scare arising to supplement the Red Scare, which drove many young Black men either to premature graves at the hands of trigger-happy cops or into the maws of the aptly named prison-industrial complex.

Generating and taking advantage of this luridness was Senator Barry Goldwater of Arizona who garnered the GOP nomination for the White House in 1964—then was defeated soundly. Still, as the subsequent rise of Nixon, then Ronald Reagan suggested, it was evident that this campaign prepared the ground for a range of conservative views that boded ill for progress in the District. Approaching the 1964 party convention in San Francisco's Cow Palace, the Arizonan's troops were well-organized with inside intelligence on opponents. One backer for William Scranton was listed as a "wealthy fundraiser" who was "militantly" for the Pennsylvanian. Another delegate was denoted as "screwy, perhaps

---

27. David Carliner, Chairman, National Capital Area Civil Liberties Union to "Dear Congressman," 8 August 1963, Box 3, *Cornelius Gallagher Papers, University of Oklahoma-Norman,*

28. David Carliner to Congressman McMillan, circa 1963, Box 6, *John McMillan Papers, University of South Carolina-Columbia.*

29. *Afro-American,* 23 March1963, Box 81, *Julius Hobson Papers, Washington, D.C. Public Library.*

senile" and a "friend of [Senator] Karl Mundt's wife," he of the audacious anticommunism.[30]

J. Franklin Wilson of 1020 U Street N.W. was a Senior Vice Chairman of the party and one of three Negro delegates and was irretrievably hostile to the Senator. "I'll never vote for him in the convention," he vowed. "I couldn't face myself and I couldn't face my friends" to vote for a man who "would be beaten 10 to 1 in Washington...I doubt if he'd get 100 Negro votes in [the] District,"[31] possibly an over-estimation and indicatory of the cross-class collaboration among Negroes, a legacy of a heritage that included necessary solidarity—to forestall even more persecution—among unpaid workers.

In the midst of a taxing campaign, the Arizonan found time to lobby Professor Logan for support who pressed him on his weak record on civil rights. The ruddy politician sought to impress his interlocutor by telling him that he had been invited to speak at 280 colleges and universities—but Logan did not flinch and refused the implicit request that he receive an invitation from the hilltop.[32] The Senator was scrounging for a H.U. invitation because he said neither Roy Wilkins nor Whitney Young of the Urban League would speak to him because, said Logan, they were afraid of a "black backlash" if they capitulated. Logan told him bluntly, "many Negroes believed that he was planning to build a white Republican Party based on the white backlash in the North and white segregationists in the South," a pithy summary of what was to grip the GOP in coming decades. "Our interview lasted so long," said Logan, "that a member of his staff came to tell him that he was keeping other persons waiting."[33]

Contrastingly, Julius Hobson, rapidly becoming a premier local activist, in the prelude to August, reminded the authorities—as if he were warning against a replay—of what occurred "on Labor Day 1961" when 200 members of CORE, his organization, "picketed the main police [headquarters] on Indiana Avenue in protest against the unwarranted use of dogs in this precinct"; these officers of the law "turned their dogs on a young Negro couple and their baby on Upper 14th Street NW...."[34] This was in the midst of a torrent of protests led by the peripatetic Hobson, which included leading a march of

---

30. Delegate List, 1964, Box 138, *Barry Goldwater Papers, Arizona State University-Tempe*.
31. Memorandum, circa 1964, Box 138.
32. Entry, 17 September 1964, Box 7.
33. Entry, 17 September 1964, Box 7.
34. Julius Hobson to District Commissioners' Council on Human Relations, 11 March 1963, Box 1, *Julius Hobson Papers, Washington, D.C. Public Library*.

3,000 on the District building—the equivalent of City Hall—in June 1963, yet another stream that flowed into August. He was a fixture on picket lines at downtown stores unwilling to accept the emerging racial order and negotiated about 60 different accords mandating more hiring of Negroes. It was Hobson who threatened to launch a disruptive "Freedom Ride" along Route 40, the latter day trail of tears where public accommodations in Maryland were barred to resident Negroes and visiting African dignitaries alike.[35]

As noted earlier, Hobson's enhanced profile was not only because of the dramatic protests he led. He became a "confidential source" for the FBI at the same time, providing—inter alia—intelligence on the planning for the August march and then was paid up to $300 in expenses to monitor on their behalf the Democratic Party convention in Atlantic City of 1964. He died of cancer in 1977, though his later life marked the grave concern held by the authorities about raucous protests at the seat of power.[36] (Formally, he was expelled from CORE in May 1964.)[37]

Thus, at the pinnacle of his popularity, Hobson was contacting Secretary of State Dean Rusk in "regard to dinners at the embassies of Austria, Ireland, Nyasaland and Pakistan." Retrospectively, it is not easy to understand if this were simply yet another manifestation of his becoming a "confidential source" or suggestive of the growing influence of local activists.[38] These circumstances were all the more curious since during these Red Scare times, Hobson confessed that he was a "'Marxist Socialist but not a Communist.'"[39]

For Hobson was far from being a one-man band. Another experienced organizer was Douglas E. Moore, who—unlike many treading water in the swirling currents of Black Nationalism—actually had resided in Africa, serving as a Methodist missionary in the Congo.[40]

What was clearer was the point that other leaders conspired with the authorities aboveboard. Or at least that was the point made by Nelson Jackson of the Urban League who apprised affiliates, a few days after 28 August 1963, of the "role that was played by Whitney Young," his boss in New York City and Roy Wilkins of the NAACP "in changing the emphasis of the March from one of civil disobedience

35. *Washington Star*, 16 April 1967, Box 79, *Julius Hobson Papers,*
36. *Washington Post*, 22 February 1981, Box 75, *Julius Hobson Papers.*
37. Minutes, 22 May 1964, Box 1, *Julius Hobson Papers.*
38. Julius Hobson to Dean Rusk, 6 November 1963, Box 1, *Julius Hobson Papers.*
39. Chris Myers Asch and George Derek Musgrove, *Chocolate City*, 333.
40. *Washington Post*, 5 September 2019.

to that of responsible [sic] leadership," which was "bringing order out of chaos."[41] This mode of thinking was reflected in a meeting on 11 July 1963 between the Reverend Fauntroy, future Congressman, and Bayard Rustin sitting across from the Metropolitan Police Department. Minutes revealed that Rustin denied adamantly that "people would be lying down in the streets" or "lying on railroad tracks" or "lying in front of planes...." Yes, said Rustin downplaying the significance, "responsible leaders"—meaning Wilkins and Young—"have talked about one hundred thousand people...there could be less...."[42]

Apparently, the authorities did not take him seriously; that is the inference of the recollection of reporter, Carl Bernstein, who recounted that present the day of the march were "fifteen thousand soldiers, including a thousand military police," accompanied by "two thousand guardsmen."[43]

Nonetheless, whatever legerdemain was executed by Young and Wilkins, the momentum of 250,000 marching under the banner of "Jobs and Freedom" could not be sidelined easily. This was because local mossbacks continued to hand weapons to their adversaries. The Benjamin Franklin Secretarial School was sited a stone's throw from Moscow's legation—yet, it refused to accept Negro students, so District Commissioners told city agencies to limit their contact with this entity. Yet somehow police were deployed to arrest those who protested the school's policies. The journalist from the *Afro-American* summed up matters nicely when it charged that this police policy was "tantamount to upholding" Jim Crow and was "ridiculous. And the Russians across the street must be laughing"—and providing grist for their propaganda mills worldwide.[44] And this was occurring months after August 1963 when it was thought widely that this ridiculousness was in the rearview mirror.

These absurdities also buoyed Hobson, who despite his Marxism or suspicions about where his ultimate allegiances rested, remained in the spotlight during the upheaval of the 1960s. Ostensibly affiliated with CORE, he came into conflict with James Farmer, the group's kingpin. Yet by mid-1964, he expressed "surprise" to "see first in the newspapers that I had been expelled from CORE," which meant—he

41. Nelson Jackson to Affiliates, 25 September 1963, Box II: D30, *National Urban League Papers*.
42. Minutes of Meeting, 11 July 1963, Box 6, *John McMillan Papers, University of South Carolina-Columbia*.
43. Carl Bernstein, *Chasing History*, 215.
44. *Afro-American*, 23 November 1963.

said accusingly: "you have effectively destroyed a very good group. The racists are very happy," he argued, adding "the movement needs a CORE, not another NAACP or Urban League."[45]

Just before this, Hobson was accused by fellow CORE member, Dolores Pelham, of making "alleged anti-Semitic remarks,"[46] with journalist Charles Sumner "Chuck" Stone, accused likewise. Other members attacked Hobson as "undemocratic," meaning a "massive turnover of Chapter members." It was "impossible to work with Mr. Hobson," complained his co-workers, which was a missed opportunity since "Negroes constitute 57% of the population of the city," meaning we have a most fertile area for the Negro Revolution."[47] Intriguingly, an objection to this demarche came from the "City Wide Detective Agency."[48] But this objection was hard to entertain for as CORE principals James Farmer and Floyd McKissack put it, Hobson was "expelled" by "unanimous action...."[49]

Hobson staked out a position to the left of the mainstream of the civil rights leadership. He engaged the Reverend Walter Fauntroy on the efficacy of a boycott of the schools which the latter opposed, arguing it "is not justified at this time," this was the "overwhelming reaction [from] the civil rights groups, from the NAACP, the Urban League, from the Ministers and from the Civic Associations"; this was "indicative that the people who will conduct the work have not been consulted...."[50]

Hobson turned up on television where his interlocutor seemingly grouped him with the increasingly brash Congressman Adam Clayton Powell, Jr. The suave and slippery Harlem pastor tended to "make fun of Negro audiences in Washington because they were more interested in their private lives and their private welfare than they were in the civil rights cause...." Hobson tended to concur: "I don't think that the middle class Negro is going to ever come out in the District of Columbia for any kind of action which is going to 'jeopardize his economic or whatever kind of security,'" a common plaint which also reflected that Negroes had more to lose—see Bunche—as doors of opportunities were opened for them in the seat

45. Julius Hobson to James Farmer, 22 June 1964, Box 1, *Julius Hobson Papers*.
46. Dolores Pelham to James Farmer, 9 April 1964, Box 1.
47. Ad Hoc Subcommittee for an Effective Washington CORE to James Farmer, 8 May 1964, Box 1.
48. City Wide Detective Agency to James Farmer, 30 June 1964, Box 1.
49. James Farmer and Floyd McKissack to "Dear CORE Member," 24 June 1964, Box 1.
50. Debate on School Boycott, 15 March 1964, Box 1.

of power that was the District. Hobson pooh-poohed the school boy-cott, suggesting that "all of the support for this boycott is coming from the white middle class [of] CORE," since "not a single mid-dle class Negro mother has come to the aid of CORE," which was "very strange." In fact, he said, "CORE is not a Negro organization... we have 700 members in Washington...and at least 75 percent...are white"—last year "85 percent of the members of the Washington CORE were white" and "national CORE itself has 55 percent white members...." This distinguished CORE from its peers in that—as he saw it—the NAACP was not "dominated by any white people. I was on the executive committee here in Washington for five years and...I know of no domination by any white person" in the Associa-tion. Per Powell's rebuke, "it is indeed dominated [by] middle class Negroes who are not activists...." Critically, Hobson thought "Negro teachers in the D.C. public schools...dislike themselves [and] see the under-privileged, poor Negro child as close to the stereotyped Negro" and therefore "dislike and mistreat these children," in a spiteful expression of "self-hate...."[51]

But Hobson was not the most credible of analysts, his intermit-tent insight notwithstanding. Thus, the scholar, Gregory Borchardt, wrote, "'Washington Negroes take pride in their individualism and small cliqueism [sic],'" which dovetails with Hobson's view. Yet he was expelled from Howard and, says Borchardt, his "openly Marxist views did not sit well with the leaders of the NAACP and Urban League," not to mention his atheism and vocal critiques of Chris-tianity. He resigned from the NAACP in 1960 and his expulsion from CORE in 1964 was largely due to an abortive school boycott. However, he did not lose many Black fans when he charged that the Beltway—the ring road circling the District—was a noose around the neck of what increasingly was called "the ghetto." Nor did he lose popularity with his lancing assaults against Congressman Joel Broy-hill, the Republican warhorse from Northern Virginia, who served ignominiously from 1953-1974: his family owned a large real estate business and he was opposed adamantly to fair housing legislation, along with others in his class in that few apartment complexes in that region were open to Negroes, be they civilian or even those in the armed forces. Besides, Hobson's fondness for socialism was not held by him alone; there was not only the lingering memories of Hunton and Wilkerson and the ongoing reality of George Murphy, part of the elite Negro publishing family. Then there was the anti-freeway

---

51. Transcript of WTOP Interview, 8 March 1964, Box 1.

movement which was inspired by a venerable activist in Takoma Park, Maryland—rapidly becoming a redoubt of progressivism: Sammy Abdullah Abbott was the grandson of an Arab Christians and, ala Hobson, was a vocal Marxist—and a former labor organizer, too. Whatever his philosophy—or Hobson's—issues mattered to Negroes, especially when freeways were diverted from non-Black Northwest Washington to the predominantly Black Northeast.[52]

Whatever criticism Hobson absorbed, the fact remained that he was seen as a prominent figure. In the prelude to the pivotal Democratic Party convention in 1964, it was Hobson who was providing instruction to Bob Moses, on the ground in Mississippi. "I am turning down the chairmanship of the delegation to Atlantic City," he said modestly, "and asking instead to be put on the Credentials Committee. As such, I can be both an inside and an outside part of the drive for the [Mississippi Freedom Democratic Party]," which was challenging the credentials of the Jim Crow delegation. "I will be able to argue the legal case inside the Credentials Committee."[53]

Hobson was up to his eyeballs in activity in Atlantic City but so was the virulently anticommunist liberal lawyer, Joseph Rauh, who billed handsomely the Brotherhood of Sleeping Car Porters for his services, thereby solidifying a political alliance with the boss of this union, A. Philip Randolph, who was oriented in a similar political direction.[54] The audacious Rauh had the temerity to reprimand incoming Vice President, Hubert H. Humphrey, who too was no

---

52. Gregory Borchardt, "Making D.C. Democracy's Capital," 120, 127, 131, 132, 148, 194, 204, 212.

53. Julius Hobson to Bob Moses, COFO, 8 May 1964, Box 31, *Joseph Rauh Papers, Library of Congress-Washington, D.C.* Washington attorney, Joseph Rauh, was heavily involved in the MFDP struggle. See, e.g., Rauh to Julius Hobson, 8 February 1964, Box 31, *Joseph Rauh Papers*: "I fought against seating of racist Mississippi delegations at the Democratic conventions in 1948, 52 and 56 and would have fought against their seating in 1960 except that no rival delegation appeared." This was in response to Hobson to Rauh, 27 February 1964, same box. See also Minutes of Democratic Party Central Committee, 5 October 1964, Box 32, *Joseph Rauh Papers*: "Dick Lyon moved that the CC commend Joe Rauh for the wonderful way in which he carried out the mandate of the CC to support the seating of the [MFDP]...unanimously adopted." See also Report, circa 1966, Box 56, *James Forman Papers:* The "MFDP challenge is essentially a narrow political focus—one state and one basic issue—SNCC ought to implement a systematic program around Title VI of the 1964 Civil Rights Act."

54. Joseph Rauh to A. Philip Randolph, 9 February 1954, Box 57, *Joseph Rauh Papers.*

slouch in the realm of anticommunism, because of the latter's apparent faux pas in reaching out to the left-leaning National Lawyers Guild. Rauh denounced the NLG as no more than a "Communist Front" and he was shocked that Humphrey would "actually write" them.[55]

Rauh was a practiced anticommunist knife-fighter, ironically rivalling his presumed antipode: Richard M. Nixon. As early as 1954 he boasted, "I represented the Polish Government in 1946 at a time when there was still an internal struggle between the Communists and the anti-Communists and our State Department was seeking wean Poland away from the Communist orbit"; quite rightly, he termed himself a "real (as distinguished from 'political') anti-communist," a sturdier brand, he thought.[56] He need only point to his vicious attacks on Henry A. Wallace's challenge for the White House from the left in 1948 from his perch in the recently minted Americans for Democratic Action—the prototypical "liberal" Red Scare creature—in order to validate his boast.[57]

However, Rauh was instrumental in cementing anticommunist liberalism by solidifying ties with A. Philip Randolph and the NAACP. In 1957 Robert Carter, a talented attorney on behalf of the latter group, was "desirous" in seeking Rauh's aid in fighting Dixie, finding his "vast experience...helpful."[58] Rauh also contributed his "vast experience" to the United Auto Workers, which had undergone its own purge of Communists.[59] He was active in seeking to place distance between Yugoslavia and its erstwhile comrades in the region,[60] setting the stage for the violent breakup of the nation in the 1990s. However, Rauh was not necessarily a favorite of President Johnson going into the 1964 convention, as he opposed him strongly when he was competing for the vice-presidential nod in 1960.[61]

Hobson may have had a point in his critiques of the civil rights movement mainstream but as a self-proclaimed "Marxist"—and a leader to whom others looked for guidance—he should have sought to provide a more objective analysis. Rare was the occasion when

---

55. Joseph Rauh to John Stewart, aide to Hubert Humphrey, 13 October 1964, Box 31, *Joseph Rauh Papers.*

56. Joseph Rauh to A. Stauffer Curry, 27 May 1954, Box 38, *Joseph Rauh Papers.*

57. See items in Box 44, *Rauh Papers.*

58. Robert Carter to Joseph Rauh, 6 May 1957, Box 38, *Joseph Rauh Papers.*

59. Joseph Rauh to Veljko Kovacevic, 5 December 1957, Box 64, *Joseph Rauh Papers.*

60. *Washington Post,* 4 October 1957.

61. *Washington Post,* 6 February 1960.

Hobson or any other with command of the airwaves acknowledged what even the *Post* publisher, Phil Graham, detected: the District was a "sleepy southern town that became the capital of the free world."[62] Interpretively, this meant that the forces of "ordinary" U.S. conservatism were magnified in the center of imperial power at a time when nerves were frazzled, as the October Crisis in 1962 over Soviet missiles in Cuba, indicated. Rarer still was any invocation of the meaning of routing the previous generation that Hunton and Wilkerson symbolized, and the impact on the hilltop, leading to the careerism and subjectivity of those like Logan. Sparse and scarce to the point of evanescence was any analysis—even by those who invoked the term—of the local "power structure" and what this portended. Thus, in 1964 even Walter Tobriner, overlord of capital in the capital, was upset when the Federation of Civic Associations, a kind of local version of Dixie's notorious Citizens Councils, chose to expel units that opted for desegregation. This was based on a reading of their constitution limiting membership to those defined as "white."[63] A tug-of-war ensued with the FCA initially reversing field,[64] then digging in their heels as if they were in Montgomery, Alabama.[65]

An unshackled Hobson then surged to the vanguard as 10,000 in the District mourned the murder of little Black girls in Birmingham, as he led a march from 16th and Harvard N.W. to Lafayette Park, across from the White House.[66] Even President James Madison Nabrit—described by one who knew him as "fair skinned" with "reddish hair and freckles" and "deliberative speech" and "big cigars"[67]—felt compelled to lead a march on campus in the wake of the terrorist bombing.[68] Coincidentally, shortly thereafter an announcement of a scholarship to H.U. to another Black girl—future mayor of the District, Sharon Pratt [Dixon]—was announced.[69] Soon she was preparing for higher office by running for a student government post.[70] She was joined in this quest by Togo West, who

---

62. Ben Bradlee, *A Good Life*, 249.

63. *Washington Post*, 16 May 1964.

64. *Washington Star*, 13 November 1964.

65. *Washington Star*, 10 December 1965.

66. *Washington Star*, 23 September 1964, Box 1.

67. Dovey Johnson Roundtree, *Mighty Justice: My Life in Civil Rights*, Chapel Hill: Algonquin, 2019. 96.

68. *The Hilltop*, 27 September 1963.

69. *The Hilltop*, 1 November 1963.

70. *The Hilltop*, 30 April 1964.

went on to become a top Negro official at the Pentagon and Secretary of Veterans Affairs in the 1990s.[71]

Hobson touched a sensitive nerve when he assaulted Jim Crow in Annapolis, site of the U.S. Naval Academy and, thus, a linchpin of the all-powerful military-industrial complex, thereby eliciting an anguished reply from Paul Fay, Jr., Under Secretary of the Navy.[72]

The apparent radicalism of Hobson was mirrored on the Howard campus where he formerly matriculated. In September 1963 students returned from Cuba redolent with praise songs for what were termed "Castro's socialist reforms." A student reporter rhapsodized about what occurred in that "this past spring and summer has been the most exciting for civil rights progress since the original 'Freedom Rides' in 1960. A few Howard students," it was announced proudly, "devoted their whole summer vacations to further the cause of equality." For good measure, in a nearby column was further elaboration by the epitome of this trend: Stokely Carmichael.[73] Appropriately, the organization that was to transport Carmichael into the ionosphere of leadership—the Student Non-Violent Coordinating Committee—chose to hold a summit of their principals on campus.[74]

Carmichael's close comrade, Michael Thelwell, headed the District office of SNCC while also serving as a founder of "Project Awareness," whose mission was to bring controversial speakers to campus.[75] Galvanizing student sentiment was the arrival on campus of James Baldwin, James Farmer of CORE, and antiwar activist, the Reverend William Sloane Coffin.[76]

Still, with all of this buzzing activity, there was a sorrowful resignation on campus that the assassination of JFK in Dallas on 22 November 1963 was horrible news, given the skepticism of his successor—the Texan, Lyndon Baines Johnson. "Disbelief and amazement permeate[d] the student body after the...murder." One journalist saw "many people with tears in their eyes. Groups of thirty to forty students...gathered to listen to the radio report."[77]

That apparent setback notwithstanding, the hilltop was gaining a global reputation as a site of excitement. By early 1964 a report

---

71. *The Hilltop*, 23 October 1964.
72. Paul Fay, Jr. to Julius Hobson, 18 March 1964, Box 1.
73. *The Hilltop*, 20 September 1963.
74. *The Hilltop*, 15 November 1963.
75. *The Hilltop*, 23 November 1963.
76. *The Hilltop*, 15 November 1963.
77. *The Hilltop*, 23 November 1963.

indicated that H.U. was leading U.S. colleges in foreign enrollment—16.2 percent of the total fall semester of 1963 student body of 6,780. Actually, the hilltop had led the nation's colleges and university in the percentage of foreign students enrolled for the previous four years; 67 nations were represented including students from Gambia, Mali, Swaziland, and Zanzibar arriving for the first time, as African nations deprived of higher education took advantage of what H.U. had to offer. There were 26 African nations altogether as this continent supplied the greatest number of foreign students, with the Caribbean not far behind—although strikingly West Asia (the "Middle East" and "Near East") were heavily represented. The six nations with the largest number were: Jamaica, 240; India, 172; Trinidad & Tobago, 153; British Guiana, soon to be known as Guyana, 85; Nigeria, 74; and Iran, 63. The African enrollment at Howard more than doubled in the past three years.[78]

Correspondingly, the recently constituted Office of Foreign Student Services, reported that as students from abroad arrived on campus, H.U. hosted about 50 foreign dignitaries within a span of a few months, representing various governments, businesses, and other universities.[79]

Howard's global reach influenced allied organizations, including the Urban League. By December 1964 their executive in the District, William Johnson, escorted the Minister of Education for the then "West Cameroons," in Africa on a two week tour to Los Angeles and Manhattan. The increased international contact necessitated an expansion of staff from two in 1963 to five by the time of the African junket.[80]

Former H.U. professor then serving as Prime Minister of Trinidad, Eric Williams, was among those appearing on campus—though his former colleague, Rayford Logan, thought his two hour peroration on "Intellectual Decolonization" was one of the "worst" he had heard in his lifetime. Logan also conferred with Jean Daridan, former French ambassador to Japan about the book he was penning on Negroes.[81]

The influx of Africans provided a distinct challenge to trigger-happy cops, overly accustomed to manhandling U.S. Negroes but now running the risk of sparking an international incident if the

---

78. *The Hilltop*, 20 February 1964.
79. *The Hilltop*, 17 April 1964.
80. New Year's Message from Johnson Family, 21 December 1964, Box iv: 8, *National Ur*
81. Entry, 1 May 1964, Box 7.

roughhoused individual was—for example—Nigerian. This sped up the process whereby laws were passed—and customs altered—to facilitate these foreign nationals being able to visit public accommodations without being assaulted or insulted, which then redounded to the benefit of beleaguered U.S. Negroes.[82]

Beleaguered was also an apt descriptor for H.U.'s most eminent professor: Rayford Logan. He threatened to resign if Howard marked its centenary by ditching the term "Negro" ("Black" was ascending as a substitute).[83] Already he was clashing with Sterling Brown in composing the contents of a centennial volume for their mutual employer.[84] He was reluctant to use a dictaphone: "Who knows whether my office is 'bugged,'" he wondered, with suspicions directed per usual to Merze Tate, now regarded as the "Number One Fool."[85] Logan expressed suspicion not sympathy when headlines blared that she was stabbed after a teenager knocked at her door—he thought it was fakery, a ruse to escape her teaching load.[86] It was a "preposterous story" akin to her "'paralytic stroke'" a year or so earlier. Finally, Logan resigned with relief as department chair after a 22 year tenure—"a chapter in my life is closed."[87] He could not resist poking at Tate, as he departed, lambasting her "fantastic story about the alleged stabbing," typical of a "pathological liar" who "cannot keep her lies straight."[88]

But going out the door, he could not escape controversy as Logan insisted that "the head of the Department of History...should be a Negro," as the tentative replacement had the further liability that he "drinks too much," as he "frequently smelled liquor on his breath in the morning"; this candidate also had "the shakes, a sure sign of incipient alcoholism."[89]

Tate might have received a reprieve from him as he turned his venom toward Brown—"increasingly difficult...more imperious... unreasonable...profane...abusive"[90]—though, resolutely Logan retained "great admiration and affection" for this "woman crazy" colleague afflicted with "emotional instability" who—in one of the

---

82. *The Hilltop*, 17 April 1964.
83. Entry, 24 March 1862, Box 7.
84. Entry, 5 April 1963, Box 7.
85. Entry, 10 April 1962, Box 7.
86. Entry, 29 February 1964, Box 7.
87. Entry, 11 March 1964, Box 7.
88. Entry, 19 March 1964, Box 7.
89. Entry, 15 April 1963, Box 7.
90. Entry, 4 May 1963, Box 7.

historian's inquisitive preoccupations—was not "homosexual...at least I doubt that he is...."[91] However, he did have a "serious mental disturbance...."[92]

* * *

The District was a ball of contradictions: an emerging "Chocolate City" as the capital of white supremacy, for example. In 1964 the momentum of these contradictory forces came to a head with the murder in Georgetown of a woman who—purportedly—was JFK's mistress, a still unsolved tragedy worthy of cinematic treatment. A Negro man was accused but—luckily—he was able to draw upon the expertise of the capable attorney, Dovey Johnson Roundtree.

She led the first law firm in the District to be shepherded by a Black woman. She was inspired to ever greater heights by the deplorable conditions she witnessed, e.g., Negro students forced to attend overcrowded schools, while the well-appointed schools for Euro-Americans stood half-empty. She plied her trade on 11th Street N.W. between U and T, within hailing distance of her law school alma mater: Howard. Born in 1914 and expiring in 2018, she was also a minister in the African Methodist Episcopal church. She was present at the high court, a stroll from her office, on 17 May 1954 when the desegregation decision was rendered: "Somewhere behind me," she recalled, "I heard muffled sobbing," an expression of centuries of grief. She was no stranger to controversy, stirring same when before her most publicized case she instigated—by her own admission—"bitter protests when my name had been proposed for membership in the all-white women's bar association...."[93]

This was an insignia of the fact that she was banned—like most Negro attorneys—from the wider bar association, shunned by their members and hardly tolerated by judges. Still, she soldiered on in her office sited within a necklace of narrow rowhouses and scrimped along, taking just about every client who made it to her door. That included Ray Crump, accused of the infamous murder of Mary Pinchot Meyer, whose former spouse was central CIA operative Cord Meyer, making her intimate association with JFK even more curious. Crump's attorney thought that she was being surveilled during her expert defense of him, that led to his release. In a scene straight out of Hollywood, the *Post*'s Ben Bradlee evidently

91. Entry, 26 May 1963 and 22 September 1963, Box 7.
92. Entry, 17 April 1965, Box 7.
93. Dovey Johnson Roundtree, 106, 120, 145, 197.

confronted [94] what he called, the "CIA's most controversial counter-intelligence specialist" who "had been caught in the act of breaking and entering" Meyer's home "and looking for her diary...." Bradlee also asserted the acquitted defendant, Mr. Crump, was "escorted to the city limits" and "told never to set foot in the District of Columbia again," yet another putative violation of the civil liberties of Negroes,[95] just as some were celebrating a new birth of freedom in the aftermath of August 1963 and passage of the 1964 civil rights legislation on Capitol Hill.

94. Katie McCabe and Dovey Johnson Roundtree, *Justice Older than the Law...*, Jackson: University Press of Mississippi, 2009, 119, 120, 190, 195, 206.
95. Ben Bradlee, *A Good Life*, 270.

Chapter *19*

Prelude to Revolt, 1965-1967

By 1965 after tireless organizing and protesting, a civil rights bill and the Voting Rights Act had been ratified, supposedly marching Negroes toward a new dawn. Yet by November of that determinative year, Negroes in the District would have been hard-pressed to assess that even a lesser version of Valhalla had been reached. The Urban League found that "some 25,000 Negro families in the District [city] limit[s]" had "incomes of less than $3,000 annually—below the poverty line," while "another 42,000 families" were "barely above the poverty line...just under $6,000 a year"; moreover, "of each 100 Negro workers, 31 are presently engaged in domestic work" compared to "just six out of each 100 white workers. A large number of these workers [were] primarily women" in that "51 percent of Negro workers in the District are engaged in domestic, laboring, unskilled or related job categories compared with just 13 percent of all white workers."[1]

But as so often happens, there were detectable rumbles that were to explode in April 1968 in the aftermath of the assassination of Dr. King; these vibrations were also flowing from the February 1965 assassination of yet another leader, Malcolm X in this instance. In the District this led to the formation of the Black United Front, ostensibly encompassing diverse classes and strata within the community but mostly projecting a kind of Black Nationalism that the hilltop's Stokely Carmichael served to articulate in his call for "Black Power." Doug Moore, with experience—as noted—in the Congo was a principal, as was the so-called "Blackman's Volunteer Army of Liberation led by Colonel Hassan Juru-Ahmed Bey; SNCC, especially

---

1. Urban League Report, 17 November 1965, Box IX: 228, *NAACP Papers*. See also Elizabeth Clark-Lewis, *Living in, Living Out: African-American Domestics in Washington, D.C., 1910-1940*, Washington, D.C.: Smithsonian Institution Press, 1994: See especially Chapter 8.

their latest operative, future mayor, Marion Barry, was close to this formation, too, and these diverse streams were to flow into a river that buoyed the emergent Black Panther Party, which was launched in the midst of these ideological cross-currents.[2]

Barry was appointed Director of the SNCC office in September 1965 and quickly became involved in the "Free D.C. Movement" in February, yet another lurch toward home rule. However, SNCC was splitting on the axis of "Black Power," or at least an interpretation of this often ill-defined notion, and the office at 107 Rhode Island Avenue began to lose altitude. Hilltop students remained stalwart, however, but were often preoccupied with their studies. As one operative put it in September 1967, "I have no money, no car, can't get a plane ticket...." This was occurring as a bus boycott was launched, not an ideal confluence.[3]

The District provided these newly surfacing forces with quite a bit of raw material. It was also in 1965 that Washington was said to have the fastest growing crime rate in the nation, a reliable campaign issue on Capitol Hill[4] and providing momentum for the mounting Black Scare.

U.S. Senator Ernest "Fritz" Hollings of the Palmetto State was thought to be a Democratic Party lion who—unlike fellow Dixiecrats—purred like a pussycat when it came to playing the typical demagogue. Yet, it was Senator Hollings who claimed in 1967 that "crime and the courts are completely out of hand...in the District of Columbia the crime rate has risen 80%."[5] Echoing the soon-to-be silver maned legislator, the *Spartanburg Herald* forwarded their histrionics disguised as an editorial declaiming with pulses racing about "terror in the capital...."[6] Senator Hollings loosened his already flapping tongue to indicate that there was "little question but that the preponderance of crimes committed here in the District are committed by Negroes...."[7]

---

2. John Preusser, "Exceptional Headwinds: The Black Panthers in D.C.," in Judson Jeffries, ed., *The Black Panther Party in a City Near You*, Athens: University of Georgia Press, 2018, 52-88, 53, 61, 62.

3. Report, 17 January 1967, Box 56, *James Forman Papers*.

4. Lauren Pearlman, *Democracy's Capital: Black Political Power in Washington, D.C., 1960s-1970s*, Chapel Hill: University of North Carolina Press, 2019, 44.

5. Senator Hollings to T.D. Truluck, 23 March 1967, Box 128, *Ernest Hollings Papers, University of South Carolina-Columbia*.

6. *Spartanburg Herald*, 3 March 1967.

7. Senator Hollings to E.L. Alexander, Secretary and Treasurer of Columbia Supply Company, 26 May 1967, Box 106.

So prompted, his constituent from the former slave state, mimicked his rhetoric, arguing that "more than 80% of the crime...stems from Negro people" and things were getting worse: "the Negro feels he can demonstrate, he can sit down, he can sit in, he can parade, he can disregard the rights of others" with impunity. This outrage was occurring though "the Negro is not an equal of the white man" and the so-called "war on crime," so proclaimed, lacked authenticity since it "never once mentions the relationship between the crimes and the races involved...."[8]

The blather and bloviating about Negro crime provided a rationale for sweeping aside this community from the District. Often lost was the point that by dint of sitting on juries, African Americans were exercising considerable sway as to who held the reins of power. In early 1967, for example, a 12 member jury with 11 Blacks—six men, five women—convicted Bobby Baker, a crony of President Johnson for various transgressions.[9]

It was an issue also not ignored in various neighborhoods, serving to fuel ever stauncher opposition to home rule, a process that led to eventually to the election of Mayor Barry. However, these opponents were in a kind of bind, as the discourse on the Negro was being transformed by the changing global climate—including a sovereign Africa and Caribbean, many of their future leaders represented at the hilltop—meaning a reinvigorated ideological barrage had to be mounted, which was possible but contained the downside of backsliding into the odiousness of the recent past with resultant diplomatic disadvantage. Thomas Quinn headed the Chevy Chase Citizens Association in chic Maryland—speaking for what he called "2,200 residents and businessmen"—yet he opposed home rule across the border; but in a cringeworthy gesture toward the "Chocolate City," he hastened to add, "our opposition is not based on race...."[10]

Closer to home, John R. Immer, who led the scandalous Federation of Citizens Associations of the District, too expressed stridently unyielding opposition to home rule. However, his message was more up to date in that he dared not to mention the sensitively explosive matter of "race." Instead, he adopted the modern lingo warning of "financial chaos, irresponsibility and bankruptcy as we had in 1873,"

---

8. E.L. Anderson to Senator Hollings, 22 May 1967, Box 106.
9. *Los Angeles Sentinel,* 16 February 1967.
10. Thomas D. Quinn, Jr. to "Mr. Congressman," 21 September 1965, Box 3, *Cornelius Gallagher Papers, University of Oklahoma-Norman.* This same letter can be found in Box 13, *Harvey Machen Papers, University of Maryland-College Park.*

the last time Negroes exercised a modicum of power. "Leaders of the local Democratic Party," he complained, "have shown more concern for the criminals on our streets than they have for the victims. Already our courts are ineffective," he groaned. "The first act of a 'popular' government," he said dismissively, "will be to destroy the effectiveness of our Police Department."[11] It was Immer who from his office at 1638 19th Street N.W. boasted of the FCA's origins in 1910 before arriving at yet another assault on home rule, wherein he argued that proponents happened to be "the strongest supporters of the rights of accused criminals."[12]

M.T. Harrison of 3850 Tunlaw Road N.W. informed Senator Daniel Brewster of Maryland that "I vote in Maryland, I reside in the District" and "home rule would be a great mistake"; there was too much "hysteria in improving the lot of the Negro," he insisted and home rule "would accelerate the pace toward a completely black Washington," a must to avoid since the "crime rate, illegitimate births, relief rolls" all needed to be considered, all of which Negroes were said to deliver.[13] Frances Green of 1708 New Hampshire N.W. cried that home rule "would give Negroes undeservedly the upper hand...and take one more step on the downward course of this government...." This was just a "wave of insanity" and, she seemed to shout: WOULD MEAN 'NIGGER RULE' for the District" in that "Washington would become the Black Capital...a comic opera, Catfish Row" and, horribly, an "anti-climax for a great white civilization...." Worse, "more and more negroes would flock to this city where there are too many already. We could expect more Adam Clayton Powells and Nkrumahs of the black tribe to rise with corruption...." Starkly, it was emphasized, "there is no way to give the Negro more freedom in this country without eroding the white man's rights...." Indeed, harking back to the past, there was "no satisfactory solution to the Negro problem except to ship them back to Africa," i.e., "Lincoln's policy" of yore. "WHITE PEOPLE WANT THEIR FREEDOM TOO...FREEDOM AT LONG LAST FROM THE NEGRO...."[14]

---

11. John R. Immer to "Mr. Congressman." 28 September 1965, Box 3, *Cornelius Gallagher Papers.*
12. John Immer to "Dear Congressman," 20 August 1965, Box 1, ACC. No. 2014-3, *Records of the History of the University of Maryland, University of Maryland-College Park.*
13. M.T. Harrison to Senator Brewster, 5 February 1965, Box 31, Series II, *Daniel Brewster Papers, University of Maryland-College Park.*
14. Frances Green to Senator Brewster, 5 October 1966, Box 31, Series II. Emphasis in original.

A.W. Fawke of La Plata, Maryland thought it "insane to turn the government of Washington over to the Negroes, a large percentage of whom are criminals and the others belonging to...Negro organizations dominated by Communists...." (I had thought that issue was dispensed with in the previous decade.) Fawke, undaunted, thought that "after Los Angeles," meaning the revolt in Watts in 1965, "I should think the whole country would agree...."[15] George Wendt was blunter, cautioning that if home rule "passes, we will never vote democratic again," so he was "strongly opposed" since he didn't "want our nation's capital governed by colored people."[16]

As matters evolved, opponents of home rule had difficulty confronting an issue that arose in suburban Maryland. It was "estimated that our U.S. Congress must spend 10% of its valuable time," it was said, "in running the government of Washington," debating such weighty matters as "whether ice cream bars and trading stamps are illegal" in the midst of Cold War implicating human survival.[17]

Congressman Thomas Abernethy of the Magnolia State, strained to acknowledge that as to home rule, "I opposed it long before the proponents made it a racial issue,"[18] thereby flipping the script— charging that anti-racists were the true racists—in a manner that had become customary by the 21st century. Wisely he had liaised with the District's Board of Trade, the king of local capital and the power behind the throne, as F. Elwood Davis, then leading this august body told the legislator that his group "and quite clearly most of the responsible business and professional people of Washington... are opposed to the so-called home rule."[19]

The District powerbroker, Joseph Rauh, heard from Forbes Shepherd of Chicago who reminded him of a disturbing undercurrent, rarely surfacing in the ongoing debate. "'The situation has [never] existed,'" he began balefully, citing the words of a Dixie journal, "'in which a race contributing a small minority of a nation's people has won control of the national capital.'" Menacingly, "the young Nazi who disturbed the House of Representatives today," he was writing in September 1965, "was more explicit. 'Sieg Heil,'" he shouted

---

15. A.W. Fawke to Congressman Machen, Box 13, *Harvey Machen Papers*.
16. George Wendt to Congressman Machen, Box 13.
17. Press Release, no date, Box 1, ACC. No. 2014-3.
18. Thomas Abernethy to Robert Rall, 10 October 1965, Box 265, *Thomas Abernethy Papers, University of Mississippi-Oxford*.
19. F. Elwood Davis to Congressman Abernethy, 6 October 1965, Box 265, *Abernethy Papers*.

forbiddingly, before racing to his main agenda item: "'Down with Home Rule.'"[20]

Apparently this ill-omened display had effect. A few months later, Rauh opined that "shortly after the defeat of the home rule in September 1965, we picked ourselves up off the floor and decided to go after the 41 Northern Democratic Congressmen who had deserted us,"[21] a reflection of the impending electoral success of Governor George Wallace of Alabama, who pledged revanchist gains if sent to the White House, with particular momentum in neighboring Baltimore. Still, a version of "home rule" arrived in 1967 when Walter Washington, a former Student Council President at Howard, became the District's mayor.[22]

This Maryland metropolis—Baltimore—which historically had exerted influence on its smaller neighbor miles away, was grappling—always successfully—with myriads of problems. In 1966 the Black Panther Party headquartered in Oakland had come into being and it did not take long for these militants to be castigated by the larger NAACP. Yet this Association chapter in Baltimore soon was to contain an ample 5,205 members and 828 youth members, third largest in the organization behind Detroit and Chicago and, thus, could not be ignored easily,[23] adding impetus to the home rule struggle.

* * *

With the passage of the civil rights reform in 1964 and the ratification of voting rights in 1965, home rule was next on the District agenda but—as noted—this had ignited a hailstorm of opposition.

It was then that Rauh reached White House aide Jack Valenti and apprised him that "if the Negro community comes to believe that the President is no longer working for home rule...I do not believe it will be possible to avoid disruptive demonstrations," signaling a vow if not a threat; "the longer the delay in accomplishing home rule the less influence the white liberal-moderate Negro leadership of the

20. Forbes Shepherd to *Chicago Tribune*, 24 September 1965, Box 31, *Joseph Rauh Papers*, The periodical cited was the *Richmond Times-Dispatch*.

21. Joseph Rauh to Karen Flynn, 30 November 1966, Box 32, *Joseph Rauh Papers*.

22. *The Hilltop*, 15 November 1967.

23. Thomas Anthony Gass, "'A Mean City': The NAACP and the Black Freedom Struggle in Baltimore, 1935-1975," Ph.D. dissertation, Ohio State University, 2014, 421, 431.

local Democratic Party will have. At the moment," he advised, "I believe the leadership could elect a moderate Negro mayor," meaning Walter Washington, "but I do not know how much longer this will be true," meaning the rise of former SNCC organizer, Marion Barry. "The longer the delay in accomplishing home rule the less influence the white liberal-moderate Negro leadership of the local Democratic Party will have...."[24]

It was not just principals of the Magnolia State or Rauh correspondents that were quite concerned with who ruled in the District. From faraway Hobbs, New Mexico the correspondent identified as Mrs. Jack Maddox informed her congressman about her worries: "So many people employed in government offices vote in their own states," though residing in the District, "and so many others are connected with the embassies; that those that will be voters will turn the crime ridden city over to the NAACP" was her overriding concern.[25] Lillian Coy of Santa Fe was not so sure; though she did "agree that the national capital is a special case." Her own hometown "struggles with some of the problems of running a city which is also a capital,"[26] suggesting she was more interested in extracting lessons from the District experience. But D.R. Trolinger, Executive Secretary of the Temperance Union in Albuquerque, had a differing complaint about the District, objecting to the "bill to legalize Sunday liquor sales" in the capital; after all, this city "where in all the world we need the clearest heads and the steadiest hands, already has the infamous title as the drinkingest [sic] place in the nation with the highest per capita consumption of alcohol" and "the highest incidence of alcoholism" nationally while competing globally.[27] Others cross-referenced this analysis with crime rates.

Opponents of home rule were often perceived as thinly veiled Jim Crow advocates and this was contrary to the then prevailing zeitgeist featuring the city enveloping a multiplicity of arriving African and Caribbean diplomats, skeptical about the bona fides of this country in the first instance. This had created a palpable antiracist momentum impacting related realms but ultimately constraining

---

24. Joseph Rauh to Jack Valenti, 9 December 1965, Box 32, *Joseph Rauh Papers*.
25. Mrs. Jack Maddox to Congressman Morris, 20 September 1965, Box 373, *Thomas Morris Papers, New Mexico State University-Las Cruces*.
26. Lillian Coy to Congressman Morris, 11 October 1965, Box 373, *Thomas Morris Papers*.
27. D.R. Trolinger to Congressman Morris, 25 August 1967, Box 396, *Thomas Morris Papers*.

the chances of success for opponents of home rule. It was also in 1965 that Glenn Seaborg, chairman of the Atomic Energy Commission, a federal agency, informed the president of American University that he wanted "assurances" that this school with a checkered history of antiracism would not discriminate—assurances "required" of "recipients of financial aid."[28] A.U. received similar stern reminders from the National Aeronautics and Space Administration[29] and other agencies too.[30] Even *U.S. News & World Report*, not usually friendly to anti-Jim Crow efforts, took note of this "crackdown" in an article retained by A.U. administrators.[31]

In short, anti-Jim Crow activism had bled into home rule advocacy and that—as Rauh adumbrated—propelled further Howard's favorite son (Carmichael) and his SNCC comrade, Marion Barry. James Forman, SNCC's chief, thought that his organization should have a Negro—make that Black—director. "'That's not right,'" he said of the group having a Euro-American leader in a "'majority Black town,'"—at least, that is what Barry recalled as he was dispatched there after the September 1965 defeat of home rule in Congress. Barry, with roots in Mississippi and academic training in Nashville, had an intellectual bent for chemistry, which allowed him to gauge expertly compounding reactions that could mean explosions, which was a District specialty. He was also a boxer, meaning he knew the value of a head-snapping jab combined with fancy footwork. Despite the soaking anti-Moscow atmosphere, Barry was not shy in paying obeisance to Dmitri Shepilov, the Russian crafter of propaganda who was also a scientist with an often astonishing memory, leading the future mayor to dub himself Marion "Shepilov" Barry, hardly reassuring to his growing list of detractors. "At Fisk," he recalled, "we studied the international struggles of India and South Africa," which prepared him to reside in a small Southern town, overflowing with Asian, African—and Caribbean—envoys. So, by January 1966 he had launched a protest against the five cent hike in the bus fare and it did not take him long to identify his main antagonist: the "Board of Trade," the often revolting local nabobs "represented big white business and they

---

28. Glenn Seaborg to President Hurst Anderson, 8 January 1965, Box 6, *Hurst Anderson Papers, American University-Washington, D.C.*

29. T.L.K. Smull, Office of Grants & Research, NASA to President Anderson, 30 March 1965, Box 6.

30. William Crockett, Deputy Under Secretary for Administration to A.U., 30 March 1965, Box 6.

31. *U.S. News & World Report*, 3 May 1965, Box 6.

would not support our fight."[32] There had been a 25 percent fare hike leading to this boycott with a massive 75,000 participating, indicating that early on Barry had displayed mettle as an organizer. Within hours, the transit agency ran up the white flag of surrender embellishing Barry's credentials.[33]

The courageous Barry took his seditious message into the lion's den, telling Congressman Abernethy of Mississippi directly that "Southern white segregationists," like himself but "led by John McMillan [of South Carolina] have gotten together with the money-lord merchants of the city to oppose our right to vote."[34]

At the same time, the wily Congressman Abernethy was plotting with Mayor Pat Dunne of Greenville, Mississippi—in the vicinity of Barry's birthplace, Itta Bena—exposing his inner Machiavelli by asserting that "it might be a good thing to just have the Negroes tear up this town as well as allow them to carry through with their boycott,"[35] in order to leverage their power in the realm of capital: revolt and crush them.

It was not just the bumptious bigshots who had disdain for Barry and his campaign. Ruth Crawford Jackson of Arlington was also part of this caucus, as she informed Congressman William Jennings Bryan Dorn of the Palmetto State: "someone should shut Barry and Carmichael up," she screeched, and she had another assignment for both: she presumed "they couldn't possibly pass a physical and be sent to Vietnam" to dodge incoming projectiles. What upset her, she stressed was that "they scream Home Rule, Home Rule" and she had had it up to her keister with their antics.[36]

Ms. Jackson's view was not hers alone. A telling sign appeared when Congressman Emmanuel Celler of Brooklyn, a potent liberal force on Capitol Hill, was unreserved in arguing, "'I loathe Stokely Carmichael and his ilk'"; chillingly, he added with brio, "'if I were a hangman or a gravedigger there is no one I would rather do a service

---

32. Marion Barry and Omar Tyree, *Mayor for Life: The Incredible Story of Marion Barry, Jr.*, Largo, Maryland: Strebor, 2014, 6, 20, 36, 41, 65.

33. Lauren Pearlman, *Democracy's Capital: Black Political Power in Washington, D.C.*, 34.

34. Statement by Marion Barry, Jr., 21 February 1966, Box 265, *Thomas Abernethy Papers*.

35. Congressman Abernethy to Mayor Dunne, 21 February 1966, Box 265, *Abernethy Papers*.

36. Ruth Crawford Jackson to Congressman Dorn, 27 July 1966, Box 75, *William Jennings Bryan Dorn Papers, University of South Carolina-Columbia.* Emphasis in original.

for.'"[37] Understandably, the intended victim chose to leave the U.S. for an intermittent exile in Guinea-Conakry, following in the footsteps of Alphaeus Hunton.

This sojourn was wise on Carmichael's part for it was likely unbeknownst to him that one of his comrades, Julius Hobson, was cooperating with the authorities. A "Special Agent" of the FBI reported that "Hobson stated Carmichael lived in Hobson's home for a year while [the SNCC leader] attended Howard"; he "used to 'baby sit' with Hobson's son...Hobson is Carmichael's godfather...." As of mid-1967 when Carmichael was marching through Dixie and other distant climes, this spectator did "not think [he] will come" back to the District, a real fear given tinderbox conditions. "Carmichael generally contacts him when he comes" to town. In a veiled threat cum prediction, he asserted that Carmichael's "presence" in town "permanently would not be welcomed by the local racketeers such as the number writers and gamblers who would fear police scrutinization of their activities...."[38]

This interaction between Hobson and the FBI was not unique. It was understandable from a certain viewpoint that this nest of spies would keep a close eye trained on Black folk given their growing strength at the seat of central power. Even J. Edgar Hoover was apprised when Hobson was "contacted by this office in cooperation with racial matters since 1963...has furnished much and accurate information" in that he was "the first and sometimes the only person to advise us of coming events...."[39]

But even if the military draft had been manipulated to allow for the dispatching across the Pacific to an uncertain fate of these two young militants, there were others more than willing to take their place. There was J. Charles Jones, for example. Hailing, too, from South Carolina, he was a founding member of SNCC, a tireless Freedom Rider, a graduate of Howard Law School who garnered headlines in 1966 when he campaigned against segregated housing near military installations ringing the District. Beginning in June in this year of the proclamation—by Carmichael of "Black Power"—he walked around the Beltway counter-clockwise as some drivers jeered and shouted obscenities at him. Organizing sit-ins at the Pentagon was also part of his bulging activist portfolio.[40]

---

37. *Washington Star*, 20 July 1967.
38. Special Agent to Washington Field Office, 17 July 1967 Box 75, *Julius Hobson Papers*.
39. Special Agent to J. Edgar Hoover, 3 June 1966, Box 75.
40. *Washington Post*, 22 January 2020.

Jones, Barry, Carmichael, and others were confronted with a many headed hydra of Jim Crow determined to strangle the Black working class. Clarence Mitchell of the NAACP instructed J. George Stewart, Architect of Capitol Hill, that "colored persons employed at the Senate Office Building are discriminated against on the basis of race...."[41] Ashby Smith of the National Alliance of Postal and Federal Employees told the NAACP glumly that anti-discrimination measures "for the 250,000 Negroes working in Federal Civil Service cannot be achieved" as matters stood in early 1967. The "Postal Service is the largest employer of Negroes having approximately 100,000 Negro employees," an astonishing figure retrospectively indicative of how this minority was essential to the political economy; yet, he added, "this number will be doubled within the next few years...."[42]

It was Jones who told Secretary of Defense, Robert McNamara, in the process of marching the nation into a quagmire in Southeast Asia, about a problem that should have engaged his distracted attention. Speaking for the Coordinating Committee to End Segregation in the Suburbs, Jones sounded the tocsin about the plight of "Negro servicemen in the Washington area," who "suffer great pain and indignity because of housing discrimination," assailing the Pentagon's tepid response to "areas surrounding six major military installations in the Washington metropolitan area"; with urgency he insisted that "action is required and that action must come from you...." With barely disguised sarcastic insight, he told McNamara that his regime was "willing to send Negro servicemen to fight and possibly die...[but it] is not willing to do anything concrete about" housing at home.[43]

The alma mater of Jones and Carmichael—Howard—continued to be an intellectual and political engine for transformation. The cancerous and cankerous transgressions of the Federal Bureau of Investigation caused the campus journal to declaim that "it is now time to end the [J. Edgar] Hoover version of the FBI,"[44] a stinging slap at the agency's chief. Then the FBI struck back as a page one banner headline reported that "Khaleel S. Sayyed...[a] former engineering student" was "among suspects charged in attempt to bomb national

41. Clarence Mitchell to J. George Stewart, 15 February 1966, Box IX: 228, *NAACP Papers*.
42. Ashby Smith to Roy Wilkins, 17 April 1967, Box IX: 228, *NAACP Papers*.
43. J. Charles Jones to Secretary McNamara, 23 June 1967, Box IX: 228, *NAACP Papers*,
44. *The Hilltop*, 4 December 1964.

monuments." Detained with him was Walter Bowe, also with ties to the hilltop, as an attempt to tie both to an emerging Black Power and leftist militancy arose, including the Fair Play for Cuba Committee.[45]

There had long been signs that said militants did not enjoy unchallenged sway on campus, despite the prominence previously of Thelwell and Carmichael. One bookend of this era was the assassinations of Malcolm, which set the stage for "Black Power" as a number of activists strained to fulfill his perceived legacy. However, a dissenting view was expressed by a campus editorialist, who found that "probably only a few people could find tears to shed at this man's tragic passing," given his "venomous diatribes." The Nation of Islam, from which he had defected, were a "vicious hate organization. The sooner the government clamps down on their activities, the better...."[46] In a similar vein when a reporter asked random students if the U.S. should depart Vietnam, all asked said no.[47] There was no consensus which was manifested when 400 attended a debate on U.S. policy in this tempestuous region. "Most in attendance were against the present U.S. policy," said an observer, unsurprising given the orchestrating presence there of Nathan Hare,[48] the controversial sociologist who was to wind up at San Francisco State University battling for Black Studies, alongside student Paula Giddings,[49] who was to make her mark as a feminist writer. She revealed her predilections when she waxed poetic about the dilemma faced by her generation: "I ride down the highway shadowed by pinnacles of progress on one side and the abyss of bias on the other."[50]

William K. Nelson, a senior student from Los Angeles, espied the abyss when he reflected that "a popular topic among college men today is how to avoid the next ship of fools to Vietnam" to participate in "this horrible undertaking."[51] Predictably when the former high court justice then diplomatic envoy—Arthur Goldberg—spoke on campus, a number of students and at least five faculty organized a walkout.[52] Forty students joined this protest of the U.S. war in Vietnam.[53]

---

45. *The Hilltop*, 19 February 1965.
46. *The Hilltop*, 19 February 1965.
47. *The Hilltop*, 19 February 1965.
48. *The Hilltop*, 10 December 1965.
49. *The Hilltop*, 10 December 1965.
50. *The Hilltop*, 28 January 1966.
51. *The Hilltop*, 25 February 1966.
52. Entry, 11 February 1967, Box 7.
53. *The Hilltop*, 17 February 1967.

By April 1967 students were hanging effigies of President Nabrit, Dean Snowden, and burning one of General Lewis Hershey, Director of the Selective Service System—the draft, i.e., shipping the flower of youth to possible death in an unjust war. The two Howardites were termed "Uncle Toms."[54]

An observant reporter heard someone shout "America is the Black Man's true battleground" and a few dozen voices chimed in appreciatively, as placards of protest appeared almost magically. Some of these demonstrators carried large photos of ragged and horridly beaten Negroes both hanging limply from the same tree surrounded by a smiling lynch mob. A goodly number of the 300 assembled began cheering and clapping as General Hershey grabbed the arm of his host and beat a hasty retreat backstage. Lights were doused and students exited. Irked congressmen suggested that if students continued to exercise their First Amendment rights, all draft deferments could be cancelled—and the current budget of the campus would be reviewed.[55]

Future well-known feminist writer, Pearl Cleage, practiced her craft by informing campus readers that "congressional hold up stops university budget."[56] This intimidation did not work in that soon hundreds of students joined a protest against four student hecklers, which then led to about 25 students scuffling with members of the Alpha Phi Omega fraternity.[57]

Administrators did not sense that times had changed. They preferred to discuss how about 3,000 students and alumni served during the previous world war and harped on the seemingly inflated figure that 90 percent of all Negro officers then had hilltop ties. But such claims were not impressive to students in 1967 staring down the barrel of deployment overseas, nor was it necessarily impressive to students enrolled in the Reserve Officer Training Corps (ROTC), awakened for reveille at 5 a.m. Their very presence on campus had been a matter of contention since 1962 and only rose further in the hothouse atmosphere of the 1960s. Soon some of these disgruntled students were enrolled in courses entitled "Revolution and Theories [of] Guerilla Warfare and Military History,"[58] as if they were

---

54. Entry, 20 April 1967, Box 7.
55. *The Hilltop*, 7 April 1967.
56. *The Hilltop*, 3 November 1967.
57. *The Hilltop*, 21 April 1967.
58. Lopez D. Matthews, Jr., *Howard University in the World War: Men and Women Serving the Nation*, Charleston, South Carolina: History Press, 2018, 46, 62, 84, 87.

preparing for another kind of war. Soon first year students were demonstrating against the ROTC.[59]

Friends of Logan thought he too was being targeted when a fire erupted in the corridor opposite his office, as gasoline was poured down a chute—then exploded in a fireball. Perhaps a tad optimistically, he opined that it was all "coincidental,"[60] despite his polemicizing against the turn toward "Blackness." This was preceded by two fires outside Douglass Hall on campus, bringing roaring firetrucks and with them the dire suspicion of arson, a perception not doused when graffiti was scrawled nearby on columns fronting Douglass Hall: "Join the Black Guards,"[61] a possible homage to the Red Guards then inducing turmoil in China. Presumably, they were not to be confused with the "Black Man's Volunteer Army of Liberation"; four were arrested in October 1967. Among other things, they were accused of distributing a pamphlet that the *Star* said was "anti-Jewish in nature."[62] By December 1967 Douglass Hall had endured its third fire within the past seven months.[63]

An indicator of the gathering muscular militancy was seen at a rally in 1966 at 9th and V N.W., not far from the hilltop, where the Deacons for Defense of Louisiana, ballyhooed because of their lack of hesitancy in wielding weapons, made an appearance alongside Julius Hobson, Jesse Gray—the politico and tenants' leader from Manhattan—activist entertainer, Dick Gregory, and journalist, Charles Sumner Stone.[64]

The proliferation of such groups was a product of an altered political climate delivered by the Red Scare, the resultant political vacuum, and the recrudescence of new varieties of Black Nationalism—witness: Black Power—that in turn generated metastasizing hysteria. More to the point, Hobson had a point when he analyzed the ascending Black Nationalism as a reaction to the often unanalyzed "'White Nationalism,'"[65] essential to the nation's founding. Summer 1967 featured what were termed "false rumors" that "included the National Guard streaming" into town, that a key bridge was torched; this led

59. *The Hilltop*, 13 October 1967.
60. Entry, 22 May 1967, Box 7.
61. Entry, 27 March 1967.
62. *Washington Star*, 22 October 1967.
63. *The Hilltop*, 15 December 1967.
64. *Washington Star*, 16 November 1967.
65. *Washington Post*, 22 June 1966. See also Gerald Horne, *The Counter-Revolution of 1776: Slave Resistance and the Origins of the United States of America*, New York: New York University Press, 2014.

to a stampede for weapons by the citizenry—though this may have been just another false rumor, along with the companion notion that a "riot" in the District was "scheduled" that involved a "'battle plan' calling for the burning of all the bridges." Yet "one store did sell some hand guns to Middle East diplomats...And so it went...."[66]

Other groups rushed to the District to occupy the vacuum but according to Clarence Mitchell of the NAACP, "most of the new so-called organizations that have come to Washington soon...run out of things to do and become somewhat spontaneous,"[67] a word often used as a substitute for chaotic.

This rebuke of Malcolm was greeted with harsh reaction subsequently, but the point remained that there was a wide spectrum of opinion on campus.[68] Sociologist Nathan Hare exemplified this spirit of sharp critique when he proclaimed, "'I think Martin Luther King is an Uncle Tom and I wish he was here so I could tell him to his face.'" Dr. Lonnie Shabazz of the Nation of Islam then proceeded to denounce Malcolm in similar terms, leading to an outburst from the audience defending the slain leader, which was greeted with applause.[69] Dr. Shabazz, who grew up in the District and received a doctorate in mathematics from Cornell University and a M.A. from the Massachusetts Institute of Technology, was unmoved.[70]

Nonetheless, then student and future film festival impresario, Anthony Gittens, denied adamantly that the student body was "apathetic"—or worse. He singled out his classmate, Sondra Kinder, who had just learned Hindi, allowing her to become a bridge to this historic ally of Black America: India.[71] Gittens could have added that the hilltop was becoming an engine of influence on allied campuses, e.g., when S.E. Anderson of Lincoln University in Pennsylvania, weighed in on the rapidly evolving matter of "beauty" standards among Black women,[72] which was to emerge as a flashpoint for progress. Alice Walker, ascending writer—and formerly of Spelman College—was cited for her wisdom on "homosexuality" with

66. *Washington Post*, 29 July 1967.
67. Clarence Mitchell to Cenoria Johnson, 8 June 1966, Box IV: 7, *National Urban League Papers*.
68. *The Hilltop*, 1 October 1965.
69. *The Hilltop*, 7 April 1966.
70. *The Hilltop*, 17 February 1967. *The Hilltop*, 17 November 1967.
71. *The Hilltop*, 23 October 1965.
72. *The Hilltop*, 7 January 1966.

Paula Giddings demanding that this human relation should be legalized—"with the same restrictions imposed on heterosexuality."[73]

A further rebuke of those excoriating Malcolm's evolution occurred when Dr. King spoke to an overflow audience at H.U.'s Cramton Auditorium. Accompanied by actor and playwright, Ossie Davis, he too was joined by President Nabrit lending an official air to the event.[74]

The press of horrors off-campus was sobering, making it problematic at best to focus on the real or imagined peccadillos of Malcolm. Thus, a few days after Dr. King's stirring address, future Pentagon official but then a student, Togo West, joined with Nabrit in lamenting the slaying of James Reeb at the hands of racist sadists in Selma, Alabama. He was "a former colleague of ours," said Nabrit, "through his work with the University Neighborhoods Council," arriving at the hilltop in 1961 and departing in 1964. His brutal murder was triggering, leading directly to what Rauh had predicted: an unprecedented sit-in at the White House itself, protesting the lack of federal intervention in Alabama; there were five hilltop students among the ten protesters sitting in the vaulted Arch Corridor of the East Wing while outside 500 Howardites rallied to protest police terror in Selma, an embarrassment to Washington before the eyes of the world. For as Reeb was breathing his final breath, another hilltopper—former student, John Harris—was beaten senseless while picketing a proposedly segregated library in Indianola, Mississippi.[75]

African hilltoppers also rose up, as a number of students with roots in the nation that became Zimbabwe, marched on the British Embassy after European settlers in their homeland—in their estimation, mimicking 1776—issued a "Unilateral Declaration of Independence."[76] Similarly, the South African poet, Keorapetse Kgositsile, informed students about the travesty of apartheid.[77] Then "some Howard Ghanaian students" were reported to be "very upset" about the overthrow of the Nkrumah regime—though the non sequitur was added that "this could be the beginning of Communism in Africa,"[78] suggesting that political acuity was not a virtue on all corners of the campus.

---

73. *The Hilltop*, 25 February 1966.
74. *The Hilltop*, 15 March 1965.
75. *The Hilltop*, 26 March 1965.
76. *The Hilltop*, 10 December 1965.
77. *The Hilltop*, 2 December 1966.
78. *The Hilltop*, 4 March 1966.

Strikingly, as the campus erupted, Walter Reuther—the vividly anticommunist leader of the United Auto Workers—spoke before a sparse audience at Rankin Chapel,[79] as if hilltoppers were turning thumbs down on his archaic approach. Richmond Flowers, an Alabama politician thought to be opposed to Governor Wallace likewise attracted a sparse crowd though he had the audacity to say that he agreed with the precepts of "Black Power" as he understood it.[80]

A chastisement of another sort occurred when Robert Welch, founder and president of the virulently anticommunist John Birch Society appeared at Cramton. This time 1,300 assembled but he was greeted with laughter, boos, and a bit of applause when he argued that the anti-Jim Crow movement was "'Communist inspired,'" that Bayard Rustin was a "'sexual pervert,'" and that Communists were demanding a "'Negro Soviet Republic.'" In any case, the reporter noticed that the crowd included "many visitors"—as opposed to student and staff—with Welch's comrade, George Lincoln Rockwell of the Nazi Party and several of his party members amongst them.[81]

International guests continued to arrive, including Gilberto Freyre of Brazil, accompanied by H.U.'s archivist, Dorothy Porter and her spouse, the art historian, James Porter, who compared racism in his homeland with the local version.[82] Soon the campus was bustling in preparation for a visit by His Imperial Majesty, Haile Selassie of Ethiopia, with Mercer and Vashti Cook coordinating the complex protocol.[83]

By the fall of 1966, more international matriculants were among the 11,500 students that arrived on campus, the largest number in the school's history, providing more fodder for protest, including more than 2,500 first year students, yet another record. Ewart Brown who was to pursue a distinguished career as Premier of Bermuda, primed the pump of protest by writing, "May I be the first to introduce the topic of Black Power," then being popularized by Carmichael.[84] Relatedly, Senegalese president, Leopold Senghor, expounded on the philosophy of "Negritude" at a special convocation at Cramton—providing an official imprimatur—with translation provided by the professor (and future U.S. ambassador) Mercer Cook.[85]

79. *The Hilltop*, 4 June 1965.
80. *The Hilltop*, 16 December 1966.
81. *The Hilltop*, 12 November 1965.
82. *The Hilltop*, 15 January 1965.
83. Entry, 11 February 1967, Box 7.
84. *The Hilltop*, 14 September 1966.
85. *The Hilltop*, 30 September 1966.

Unsurprisingly, as this ideological trend—Negritude cum Black Power—began to grip the campus, an editorial found it "disheartening" that Dr. King, Randolph, Whitney Young, and Wilkins were under pressure to disavow it.[86] Carl Moultrie, president of the District branch of the NAACP, capitulated and denounced "Black Power"—or what he thought it meant.[87] Bucking up the troops, Carmichael arrived to address a "closed session" on campus where he termed Professor Hare his "mentor,"[88] speaking of a soon-to-be elected leader of the American Association of University Professors.[89] Then the embodiment of "Black Power" was joined by Marion Barry and Julius Hobson before a wider audience on this increasingly popular topic.[90]

Climbing aboard the bandwagon were Floyd McKissack of CORE and the Reverend Fauntroy, ostensibly of SCLC; the latter was making his third appearance on campus this year, i.e., 1966, solidifying his credentials since he was the first organizer, it was said, of the "Project Awareness Committee" in 1961, designed to bring non-mainstream ideas to campus. Their session, too, was "packed."[91]

By October 1966, Carmichael received front page coverage as he once more trumpeted "Black Power" and yoked this topic to a denunciation of the U.S. war in Vietnam.[92] "Black Power not Vietnam" was "our hottest political issue," was a claim contradicted by those like Carmichael who joined the two.[93] But, as ever, amidst the unrest sparked by Black Power were favorable mentions of icons of propriety, e.g., the only Negro U.S. Senator, Edward Brooke of Virginia, a native of Washington and an alumnus of both Dunbar and Howard.[94]

Off campus Marion Barry was generating a movement that too was to shape the hilltop. He formed a group called PRIDE, dedicated—inter alia—to youth employment and funded by the Labor Department, a federal agency. With his gumption and flair for protest, Barry was attracting ever more attention—not all of it positive: "I even had to carry a pistol with me." He was arrested

---

86. *The Hilltop*, 14 October 1966.
87. *Washington Post*, 12 August 1967.
88. *The Hilltop*, 21 October 1966.
89. *The Hilltop*, 3 February 1967.
90. *The Hilltop*, 21 October 1966.
91. *The Hilltop*, 21 October 1966.
92. *The Hilltop*, 28 October 1966.
93. *The Hilltop*, 10 October 1966.
94. *The Hilltop*, 2 December 1966.

for jaywalking by the police, but this did not blanch his robust style. "We even had a saying about white men and segregation," he recalled later, "if he red, he scared," as blood rushing to the temples was a giveaway. But his following continued to flourish, not least because officialdom's bigotry aided him objectively. "In the past at the District Building downtown on Fourteenth Street, Black people were not allowed above the second floor unless they were cleaning up the offices and the bathrooms."[95]

It was not just the bureaucrats. Leonard Downie, Jr., who was to serve as the top editor at the *Post*, recollected that judges then "appeared lest competent to hold court than I would have been," as these figures cloaked in black were "sometimes visibly intoxicated." Their awakened wrath was often directed at Black youth before them and rarely did the judiciary interfere when "grifters going door to door…talked the victims into overpaying for shoddy home improvements with loans secured by high interest second mortgages…then sold to finance companies that threatened foreclosure."[96]

Tenants were confronted by empowered landlords who did not hesitate to charge a six or seven dollar fee if the rent was only technically tardy—on top of exorbitant rents already in the areas to which Negroes were consigned. Apartments with gaping holes and cracks in the walls and rooves ushered in cold air during the winter and heating costs soared. Retaliatory evictions for reporting violations was not uncommon. Stores avoided government workers because of the abject difficult in garnishing wages; these sharks desired customers who would buy more than they could afford and tended to ignore those with good credit as they were harder to loot. Ubiquitous pawnshops encouraged burglary and theft generally.

Southwest Washington, blocks from Capitol Hill and the White House, was once described as "'overcrowded, incredibly primitive'"—and, yes, it was mostly Negro: of 23,500 residents about 77 percent were Black. Then urban renewal—or "Negro Removal"—socked the vicinity, uprooting thousands and tossing them to the four winds, as thousands of homes were razed. As they fled, attitudes still calcified. Carl Rowan, a Negro who was to serve as U.S. ambassador in Helsinki, recalled his mowing the grass in his exclusive, upmarket neighborhood and a Euro-American woman in a limousine asked how much he charges. His tart reply? "'I don't charge the lady in this house anything. She lets me sleep with her!'" Such tartness did

---

95. Marion Barry, *Mayor for Life*, 71, 76, 78, 79.
96. Leonard Downie, Jr., *All About the Story: News, Power, Politics and the 'Washington Post'*, New York: Public Affairs, 2020, 36, 42.

not halt the ongoing effort to ban Negroes from the sacred territory west of Rock Creek Park. To the extent that schools were limited to those in the neighborhood, this often guaranteed inferior education for Black children. Black folk knew that the role of the police was to uphold if not exacerbate this unjust status quo, causing many to see them as an occupying army. By September 1966, African Americans were 63 percent of the population and 18.6 percent of the police force; until 1962 Blacks held three of nine seats on the Board of Education. The 1954 high court decision ordering desegregation—albeit at a leisurely pace—ignited "white flight" and correspondingly in the coming decade or so there was a startling 88 percent increase in the number of District Blacks, creating what came to be called "Chocolate City." These overlapping contradictions—increasing Black population; erosion of radical left-wing interracial influence; recalcitrant Euro-American conservatism; the proliferation of "Black Power" ideology—not only were to come to an explosive head in the April 1968 revolt but according to mainstream Negro leader, Sterling Tucker, it contributed to sharper ideological fissures. There were "many Negroes who remain unsympathetic to both the Black Power advocates and the integrationists," especially the latter since "as it is presently practiced, [it] is a white man's handout. It is not a sharing process." Mainline Christianity was hardly immune from these forces since "ever since the March on Washington the Church has grown more conservative."[97]

The federal authorities often seemed impotent in the face of these formidable forces but one issue they were more willing to address was confronting the prospect of revolt. By early 1967 President Johnson was told by Charles Horsky, who advised him on capital matters, that a proposal afloat was "giving you power to assume command of the District of Columbia police in an emergency"[98]—as if revolt against an unsustainable status quo was unavoidable.

Serving to keep afloat this trend contrary to militancy was Professor Logan, then on the downslope of his career. The problems he encountered in 1965—his spouse's leg amputation combined with "troubles with Tate and with Sterling Brown added" to his "own heart and vascular condition"—abbreviated his lifespan.[99] His addled state of mind—"Sterling Brown is even more of a stinking bastard

97. Sterling Tucker, *Beyond the Burning: Life and Death of the Ghetto*, New York: Association Press, 1968, 20, 21, 29, 30, 85, 92, 97, 128, 133, 146, 148.
98. Charles Horsky to President Johnson, 27 January 1967, Box 115, *Office Files of Charles Horsky, Lyndon B. Johnson Presidential Library-Austin, Texas*.
99. Entry, 17 April 1965, Box 7.

and liar than Merze Tate is a lousy bitch and liar"[100]—was likely not helpful to enlivening physicality. His rhetorical escalation—Brown was then dubbed "evil"—possibly hastened the historian's eminent decline.[101] Yet, Logan was still dashing about town, slated to visit the Soviet Embassy in February 1967 for a reception for a fellow scholar, though the continuing chill of the Cold War caused him to "wonder how soon FBI agents will be paying me a visit."[102]

This latter point was not the best advertisement for Washington, then seeking to portray itself as a paragon of human rights virtue in the ideological contestation with Moscow, yet—as the Pentagon exemplified—bashful about eradicating the racist disfiguration of the national escutcheon.

Unfortunately—for Washington—arriving envoys often had developed ties of singular intimacy with African Americans. In one example amongst many, Sarah Lou Harris, born in North Carolina and a graduate of that state's all Black women's institution—Bennett College—was the spouse of Ambassador John Carter, representing the nation to be known popularly as Guyana.[103] Earlier, there was Jacques Antoine, Haitian ambassador to the U.S., who then went on to teach French at Howard; his California spouse—Caroline Antoine—taught French and Spanish at Dunbar High School in the District.[104]

Tellingly, Leopold Senghor, a renowned writer and leader in his native Senegal, in 1966 wanted to hold a "World Negro Arts Festival" in Harlem, which would have been a Cold War coup for the State Department. He had written about this Manhattan neighborhood: "'I was so struck by it,'" was the gushing remark of this comrade of the Harlem Bard, Langston Hughes. What about Washington? "'I haven't been struck by it to the point of writing poetry,'" he sniffed condescendingly.[105] Whatever the case, Professor Logan chose to skip the reception for Senghor at Howard.[106]

Protestations notwithstanding, for many diplomats of African descent, an assignment in Washington was akin to being a stranger in a strange land. That was certainly the perception of Douglas Hembas of the Nigerian legation who was driving and became lost and

---

100. Entry, 29 June 1965, Box 7.
101. Entry, 24 June 1967, Box 7.
102. Entry, 11 February 1967, Box 7.
103. *Afro-American*, 11 June 1966.
104. *Afro-American*, 23 October 1948.
105. *Washington Post*, 30 September 1966.
106. Entry, 5 February 1967, Box 7.

wound up next door in Montgomery County, Maryland, a region unaccustomed to welcoming melanin rich men, as the ground itself continued to resonate with the muffled moans of the dead, once enslaved. He had to endure an unpleasant encounter with a police officer and, according to an inquiring reporter, he was "critical of the treatment...he had received," to the point that he too would not be writing poetic elegies honoring the District.[107]

Nigeria's next door neighbor on the continent—Niger—was experiencing a different kind of unpleasantness, though increasingly common for Africa's emissaries. Their attempt to establish a chancery in a sumptuous neighborhood was resisted by neighbors—though it was unclear if they would have been hesitant if, say, Switzerland or even Albania, had made the request.[108] For the Sudanese envoy in Washington—Mohammed Ali Adris—was cited for a proposition likely shared by many African envoys generally: Negro journalist, Ralph Matthews, observed that "because of their own struggle against foreign domination," these delegates "have a deep sympathy for darker people, both in America and in Africa in their fight for self-determination and equality." In a further reversal, he had hired a German secretary, Lotte Leuders, further upsetting the delicately wrought race-class balance [109] which began to unravel shortly thereafter.

---

107. *Washington Post*, 16 April 19
108. *Washington Star*, 10 August 1965.
109. *Afro-American*, 2 March 1957.

Chapter *20*

Revolting Capital, 1967-1968

In April 1968, revolt inexorability arrived in the District: the ostensible trigger for this mass revolt was the assassination of Dr. King but keen readers thus far should be able to discern other causes, including police terror; dilapidated housing choices; an unpopular war that was dispatching the flower of youth across the Pacific; and the general crisis of everyday living embodied in this town's perennial: starkly malignant racism. The detonation of 1968 "forever changed the trajectory of the city," according to one study.[1] Further, not unlike 1919, it demonstrated that what occurred in the District—unlike many other cities—was of national, if not global significance.

There were about 7,500 arrests and the deployment of 15,000 troops. As one analyst put it, "only thirteen citizens died" while "only two were at the hands of the police...." Congressman Bourke Hickenlooper of Iowa was not singular in comparing those who took to the streets to "Viet Cong." Clyde Aveilhe, Director of Student Activities at Howard, asserted that "'anywhere from 65 to 80 percent of the most 'militant' students on our campus have working involvement with off campus organizations and individuals who are in the revolution,'" the latter phrase being the synecdoche for the accelerating pace of anti-Jim Crow transformation. Taking note, GOP presidential candidate Richard M. Nixon accelerated his campaign against the District and crime—and both combined—which was to deposit him in the White House within months. "No knock" provisions in criminal law, allowing the authorities to enter homes unannounced, was part of his signature regression, as he took the Black Scare to new heights. Marion Barry enhanced his already glowing reputation as a

---

1. Amber Wiley, "A Right to the City," *Journal of American History*, 106 (Number 1, June 2019): 128-130, 130.

tribune for the disaffected when he pointed the finger of accusation at the police—an "'alien occupying army'" in his estimation.[2]

Howard, which supplied a good deal of the political and intellectual energy of the new dispensation emerging, was roiling in the prelude to April 1968. Fanning the flames was the coincidental opening of "Drum and Spear" bookstore in the District in 1968, with a publishing arm there—and, revealingly, in Dar es Salaam, indicative of activists' global ambitions. They supplied the literature that fueled dissent, including the works of Trinidadian elder statesman, C.L.R. James and—predictably—were subjected to harassment by the authorities.[3]

Eventually, the erstwhile Trotskyite himself, celebrated in militant circles for his prematurely perceptive book highlighting the grandeur of the Haitian Revolution, moved near the bookstore, then taught at the newly opened Federal City College, before residing at a massive, formerly grand apartment building sited conveniently at 16th and R Streets, N.W. His was a voice that galvanized and shaped an emerging revolutionary fervor.[4]

A scant year before this pivotal year of 1968, students amassed on the steps of Douglass Hall in an unrehearsed, impromptu three hour long debate on aspects of Black Power and awareness, punctuated by the astringent comments of Professor Hare.[5] By then SNCC had an office at 1234 U Street, N.W. which included an anti-draft initiative; tellingly, said activist Lester McKinnie, they were "getting quite a lot of support from the Black Bourgeoisie on the police issue," since the moneyed in their Mercedes were hardly exempt from this plague. Their staff also included Linda Smith, who also toiled at the nearby Ghanian embassy.[6] SNCC importantly provided a good deal of the energy that suffused the hilltop.

Campus morale was boosted when the defrocked heavyweight boxing champion, Muhammad Ali, arrived to address 2,000 students under the auspices of the aptly named "Black Power Committee." His association with the Nation of Islam and opposition to the war embellished his magnetic appeal. He was followed

---

2. Lauren Pearlman, *Democracy's Capital*, 77, 83, 144, 168.

3. Joshua Clark Davis, *From Head Shops to Whole Foods: The Rise and Fall of Activist Entrepreneurs*, New York: Columbia University Press, 2017, 4, 58, 68.

4. John L. Williams, *C.L.R. James: A Life Beyond the Boundaries*, London: Constable, 2022, 371.

5. *The Hilltop*, 14 April 1967.

6. Lester McKinnie to SNCC staff, 5 May 1957, Box 56, *James Forman Papers*.

by alumnus, Amiri Baraka, the poet laureate of Black Power.[7] He was to be followed to the rostrum by the man to be known as Maulana Karenga who addressed 1,000 assembled—including Carmichael—as he sought to "define" the "U.S. Cultural Revolution."[8] (Even before his role was highlighted in April 1968, Senator Robert Byrd of West Virginia had threatened the Black Power tribune with 20 years in prison on an unnamed charge.[9] Wisely, he wed South African exile Miriam Makeba in 1968 and decamped to self-imposed exile in Guinea-Conakry. Douglas Moore, a former Methodist missionary in the Congo officiated.)[10] Karenga's advice? "Form political coalitions with the Third World and play politics of disruption." He saluted Reies Tijerina as a model, speaking of the reigning symbol of Chicano Nationalism who made ambitious demands about reclaiming land in New Mexico. "No people on earth have a religion that says that they are not the chosen people except Black Christians," said the balding, mustachioed intellectual. Applauding "loudly" was the crowd at Cramton. He rehearsed his Kwanzaa holiday, still marked today in late December of every year (the word itself was from the Zulu but "'the Zulu word was too hard to pronounce.'") To his credit, he reminded the students of their importance, as they were "'strategically located on three different levels. Geographically, he [sic] is halfway between the South and the North...politically, the possibility of his exposure to national and international figures makes his position very, very strategic....'" However, he did caution those assembled not to "'waste himself away into Black Greekdom,'" the fraternities and sororities that dominated social life.[11]

The student newspaper beamed when Howard was accorded a "prominent place in a current 'Esquire' [magazine] article...[on] The Black Power Establishment." This was not puffery on the part of either organ. Baraka, novelist John Oliver Killens, and writer Claude Brown were all former students listed, while others with hilltop ties included John Hope Franklin; Whitney Young; Ralph Bunche; Senator Edward Brooke; psychologist Dr. Kenneth Clark; and liberation theologian, Albert Cleage.[12] It was "no accident," said a student

---

7. *The Hilltop*, 28 April 1967.
8. *The Hilltop*, 15 December 1967.
9. *The Hilltop*, 12 January 1968.
10. *Washington Post*, 5 September 2019.
11. *The Hilltop*, 3 January 1968.
12. *The Hilltop*, 20 October 1967.

reporter that Carmichael "chose Washington as his headquarters upon returning from his tour of the Third World."[13]

Indicative of the balance of forces was the stern reprimand of critics of Black Power administered by student, Wade Henderson[14]—who distinguished himself in coming decades as a mainstream civil rights lobbyist. Henderson's reproach notwithstanding, there were students who questioned this new consensus. Thus, showing up at the hilltop was Tommy Jacquette, who had captured headlines during the transformative Watts Revolt in Los Angeles of 1965[15]; congruent with the new ethos, he argued that "Black youth should not be exposed to white leadership" and pointed to the soldierly Father James Groppi of Milwaukee who had led many an anti-Jim Crow protest.[16] More disturbing was the maunderings of the man called "Colonel Hassan Jeru-Ahmad" of the "Blackman's Army of Liberation"—sited at 910 Kennedy Street N.W.—who disapproved of the proposed march on the Pentagon and instead reproved "'American Communist[s]'" and "'Zionist Jews'" as the true instigators of this protest.[17]

Students were rallying on behalf of Congressman Adam Clayton Powell, Jr. of Harlem who had become a totem of Black Power and, coincidentally, his colleagues were seeking to remove him from his seat on Capitol Hill.[18] At least 500 students participated and also sought appointments with congresspersons from districts across the country to register their dissent.[19] Diplomatically, they chose—per a spokesperson—to "'walk softly'" to Capitol Hill, as opposed to the usual raucous pattern.[20] This was one among many visits to the site of legislative power. They proceeded to launch a campaign against the "crime bill," which targeted District residents especially. Steve Abel of the United Black Peoples Party captured the sentiments of many students when he warned, "'You better get your thing together and quick. If you don't, you will see this city torn apart by the angry Black masses,'" words that would seem prophetic within a few months. "'Since the Black people are the majority in D.C. we

13. *The Hilltop*, 15 March 1968.
14. *The Hilltop*, 5 May 1967.
15. Gerald Horne, *Fire This Time: The Watts Uprising and the 1960s*, Charlottesville: University of Virginia Press, 1995.
16. *The Hilltop*, 29 September 1967.
17. *The Hilltop*, 20 October 1967.
18. *The Hilltop*, 3 February 1967.
19. *The Hilltop*, 17 February 1967.
20. *The Hilltop*. 10 February 1967.

should take advantage of our numbers and rise up in a violent revolution.'" The crowd cheered again as he paid homage to the late Martinican-Algerian revolutionary, Frantz Fanon.[21]

Hundreds of law students and faculty rallied against CIA recruiting on campus,[22] their presence seen as being at odds with the campus' implicit mission of aiding African liberation on a campus that featured a Ghana Students Union; a Sierra Leonian Students Association; an East African Students Union; a Zimbabwe Students Union; a General Union of Congolese Students; and a Nigerian Students Union—among others.[23] Since the agency continued to advertise on campus,[24] the CIA might have thought that financially desperate students might be in need of a lush stipend. It is possible that recruiters liaised with the Chair of the Government Department known variously as "Dr. D. George Kousoulas" and "Demetrius Kousoulas" who seemed to endorse the right-wing coup in Greece and consulted with Athens to that end.[25]

This sprawling African presence was embodied—once again—when coming to campus was His Imperial Majesty, Haile Selassie of Ethiopia. This was described as a "surprise visit" by this diminutive ruler who in 1954 had received an honorary doctorate from H.U.; gratefully, he contributed to the school's scholarship fund.[26] His Majesty was not the only prominent "alumnus," for this growing list would also include Aaron Mitchell, then serving as Chief Architect in Liberia.[27]

Students continued to protest the attempt to discipline those who disrupted the appearance of General Hershey; an estimated 500 of them barged into the administrative offices of Locke Hall.[28] By May 1967, students had launched a boycott of the school, deemed to be 80 percent effective; "thousands of students cut classes simultaneously" and, instead, held a "teach-in," described by one observer as a "bongo-in."[29] Activism spread as high school students shortly formed their own Black Student Union.[30]

---

21. *The Hilltop*, 12 January 1968.
22. *The Hilltop*, 10 March 1967 and 17 March 1967.
23. *The Hilltop*, 5 May 1967.
24. *The Hilltop*, 27 October 1967.
25. *The Hilltop*, 16 February 1968 and 24 May 1968.
26. *The Hilltop*, 17 February 1967.
27. *The Hilltop*, 5 October 1967.
28. *The Hilltop*, 28 April 1967.
29. *The Hilltop*, 12 May 1967.
30. *The Hilltop*, 16 February 1968.

Administrators were not resting recumbent as this turbulence proceeded. There were about 200 students from the future Zimbabwe in the U.S. then and about 15 were at Howard. Sanders Bebura of this Southern African nation was distraught when considering this altered landscape: "'Every time I come to campus,'" he lamented, "'the incredible abundance of armed guards makes me feel as if I had gone back to Rhodesia.'"[31] This intimidating presence was accompanied by a faculty purge.[32] Students were purged too, including future film impresario then staunch activist, Anthony Gittens.[33] Soon Bebura became Managing Editor of the student periodical, injecting an African liberationist impulse into its already progressive pages.

The hilltop was figuratively—at times literally—on fire in 1968. Early on Anthony Gittens, raised the provocative slogan, "'We're going to get things straight in '68'" and to that end, the U.S. flag was lowered where it had fluttered in the middle of campus and taken to the office of President Nabrit. Howard was termed a "'contemporary plantation'" in protests on the steps of Douglass Hall led by Gittens and Bermuda's Ewart Brown. Fiery denunciation greeted the news from Orangeburg, South Carolina, the site of the slayings of three young Black male college students in the midst of anti-Jim Crow protests. An editorial linked this tragedy with another, this time in Rhodesia, where of late "three black freedom fighters" were slain.[34] Highlighted were the remarks of Carolina militant, Cleve Sellers, who blasted "'Negro leadership [who] joined the white folk in the conspiracy'" against those like himself: they were "'responsible to the needs of the poor Black community.'"[35] Militancy was confirmed when Howard students declared that the February birthday of Dr. Du Bois, who died in exile as a Communist in 1963, should be a holiday.[36]

In early March 1968 students disrupted Charter Day, an otherwise solemn occasion, in order to press their demand that the school, as the *Post* put it, "'meet the needs of America's and the world's oppressed peoples.'"[37]

The students then backed a proposal to endorse a march to be led by Dr. King in a 13 to one vote.[38] At the same time, well-connected

---

31. *The Hilltop*, 5 October 1967.
32. *The Hilltop*, 3 January 1968.
33. *The Hilltop*, 23 February 1968.
34. *The Hilltop*, 8 March 1968.
35. *The Hilltop*, 15 March 1968.
36. *The Hilltop*, 23 February 1968.
37. *Washington Post*, 2 March 1968.
38. *The Hilltop*, 1 March 1968.

columnist, Marquis Childs, cited both Joseph Rauh and Bayard Rustin to the effect that neither "would have no part" of this "Poor Peoples' Campaign" designed to propel massive civil disobedience toward a redistribution of wealth.[39]

Finally, days before the city was to erupt in flames, about a 1,000 students dominated what was said to be "nationwide and international news" by seizing the campus' administrative nerve center in protest of a raft of festering problems. The newly minted Black United Front, backed by Carmichael, hailed their initiative,[40] while the students then sought to spread their example by aiding a companion demonstration at Bowie State in Maryland.[41] Local authorities keenly monitoring the crisis chose to report the presence of "female students inside of [the] Admin Bldg." and "1000 students" altogether: "they need food desperately...only enough left to last until tomorrow."[42]

Appropriately, Dr. King preached his final Sunday sermon in Washington, D.C. days before the city exploded after his assassination.[43] A few days later, surveillance of the Black United Front deepened with agents planted in a meeting that lasted 50 minutes with 125 attending. The agent reported disconsolately that "newspapermen and cameramen were asked to leave, including all white people"—magnifying the importance of Negro agents: "All white persons left except two white women who were harassed during the meeting."[44]

This friction presaged what was to blow up by 4-5 April. Retrospectively, it is stunning how disordered and chaotic the citadel of national power became in April 1968. This should not have come as a shock in that in 1967 alone there were various disorders occurring in 164 U.S. cities, as Negroes' limit of tolerance and absorption of pain had been breached. Armed men had to be sent to Capitol Hill just in case the idea was broached of retaliation against this regnant symbol. Like a gushing leak in a dyke, stories began to pour out

---

39. *Washington Post*, 6 March 1968.

40. *The Hilltop*, 22 March 1968.

41. *The Hilltop*, 29 March 1968.

42. Report, 22 March 1968, Box 2, RG 23, *Office of Emergency Preparedness Records re:...Demonstrations, Civil Disturbances and Special Events, 1965, 1968-1978, Washington D.C. Municipal Archives.*

43. *The Hilltop*, 5 April 1968.

44. Report, 2 April 1968, Box 1, RG 23, *Office of Emergency Preparedness Records re:...Demonstrations, Civil Disturbances and Special Events, 1965, 1968-1978, Washington, D.C. Municipal Archives.*

detailing the pain that generated disruption. John Hope Franklin by 1964 was teaching in College Park and rented a house in Hyattsville, Maryland, compelling the History Department to organize teams to guard the residence to insure he and his family were unmolested. The local newspapers—part of the problem—epitomized their complicity even as the flames leapt ever closer to their doors by sending 14 Negro reporters and photographers to cover the unrest, while Euro-American colleagues from the safety of their offices staffed the phones, receiving the reports—and bylines.[45] Intra-class tensions also emerged when President Johnson was told at the height of the conflagration that Black protesters were marching on Georgetown with mayhem in mind; he was reported to have said of this affluent enclave, "'I've waited thirty-five years for this day....'"[46]

On 6 April 1968 at 3:30 p.m., as frazzled leaders gathered in the Situation Room at the White House, the unusually rattled FBI briefed those assembled on a "plan to hit Georgetown area tonight."[47] Black protesters should not have taken the president seriously since earlier he had warned that "'if the Negroes started moving in [on] the White House,'" Vietnam style, then the authorities should deploy "'the same kind of gas,'" then used in profusion in Indo-China.[48]

William Banks was to become Chair of African American Studies at Berkeley, but in April 1968 he was in Washington. Later he recalled the "stress" of that era and the case of Robin Gregory, elected Homecoming Queen in 1968 but since she was "militant" with a "big Afro," President Nabrit "refused to crown her," to his dismay: "you take a deep breath," he sighed. As the city detonated in April 1968 "we weren't sure of our safety in this white complex" sited on New Hampshire Avenue, near Georgia Avenue, the thoroughfare abutting the campus, though—admittedly—his residence was "way out there," far from the center of the Black community. "I was worried about what they [could] do to me," he said worriedly. "That was in the revolutionary days, you know, a race war was about to break out," conceivably "and I didn't want to be out there with a wife and

45. J. Samuel Walker, 'Most of 14th Street is Gone': The Washington, D.C. Riots of 1968, New York: Oxford University Press, 2, 3, 18, 163.
46. Lawrence Wright, God Save Texas: A Journey Into the Soul of the Lone Star, New York: Random House, 2018, 154-155.
47. Report, 6 April 1968, Gen Hu 2 Ex HU2/FG 216, Box 20, Johnson Papers, Johnson Presidential Library.
48. Stuart Schrader, Badges Without Borders: How Global Counterinsurgency Transformed American Policing, Oakland: University of California Press, 2019, 201-202.

child int that context," so he made a temporary move: "we stayed about a week" at another site "until things calmed down...."[49]

A dilemma for many Black folk then was the proliferation of numerous armed men in uniform—defined as "white"; this did not just include the police. Befitting the center of power of a superpower there were all manner of troops nearby, many with expertise in what was described loosely as "riot control": the Third Infantry at Fort Myer; the 91st Engineers at Fort Belvoir; the battle-hardened Marines at Quantico; the bloodied Sixth Cavalry at Fort Meade; not to mention park police, zoo police—and a wide array of others. This was a formula as unstable as nitroglycerin: for these men were facing off against a heavily Black community in the majority since about 1957 and constituting two-third of the population by 1968, the highest for any major U.S. city. Indicative of trends to come, by then the proportion of Blacks enrolled in public schools was over 90 percent. Consequently, given the population density, the relatively enclosed space, the formidability of the force encountered, all this led to what was called "vandalism, looting and setting of 1,000 fires," causing destruction more pervasive than, possibly, its peers in Watts 1965 and Detroit 1967. Resultantly, the number of forces called on to suppress the discord exceeded that of the western and midwestern counterparts.

At the hilltop, the U.S. flag, unsurprisingly, was lowered and replaced by the red, black and green flag of Black nationalism, while student chief—Q.T. Jackson—was clubbed. By 5 April—Friday late afternoon—suburbanites and routine commuters, overwhelmingly Euro-American, were panicking, leading to one of the most congestive traffic jams in the region's history: they fled in dread from Capitol Hill and downtown, with the overflow reaching Anacostia. This area was heavily Euro-American before 1960, but by 1968 this section contained about 200,000 souls—about 150, 000 being Black—of the city's 830,000 population.

Firefighters were overwhelmed and called for backup from about 60 companies from Maryland and Virginia—even Pennsylvania—not fortifying inter-racial comity. But since 500 fires were breaking out as of Friday, it was unclear if this posse would be sufficient. That flaming day hundreds of fires were burning simultaneously, often fueled by gasoline, all of which astounded those sworn to halt the conflagration. One confounded onlooker said this was the most serious challenge to federal rule since the early 1930s when military veterans arrived in a quest for funding.

---

49. Oral History, William Banks, 16 September 2005, *University of California-Berkeley*,

Quickly, radio communications broke down, allowing protesters to listen to presumed confidential conversations. Public telephones had to be used to reach the White House, the military and city principals necessitating the presence of jingling coins in pockets. From a certain viewpoint, it was problematic that the National Guard was about 25 percent Black and that one military police unit was 40 percent Negro and that there were some integrated units under the command of these ebony warriors too.

During these days of tumult, police alone fired about 8,000 cannisters of teargas, an enormous

quantity for a battlefield, let alone a crowded urban node. All this was occurring about ten blocks from the White House, then seeking to direct a war in Vietnam while confronting Moscow and backing allies bent on suppressing national liberation movements in Africa—and elsewhere.[50]

The atmosphere at the White House was understandably nervous and harried, faced by what amounted to a domestic insurrection. Ears pricked up at 10:50 a.m. on Friday when word arrived that Carmichael "made an inflammatory speech at Howard University" and less than three hours later "Army Intelligence" reported that local police were "unable to cope" with the cascading uproar, as "looting and fires had spread" uncontrollably.[51]

A recent study reveals that, yes, 5 April was not just the "height of the upheaval" but, possibly a day unlike any the District has endured before—or since. Of the 500 fires set that day, a few hundred were still burning simultaneously before sunset, raising the distinct possibility that the capital would be immolated, challenging national cohesion—and security. Credible allegations emerged that there were multiple "pay or burn" incidents—threats to torch businesses if a bounty was not paid. As matters evolved, there was $33 million in property damage, taxing the insurance industry a bulwark of capital, and 1,352 business were damaged, displacing thousands from employment, straining the tax base. There were not just traffic jams but also phone jams, perhaps unintentionally but creating disarray, nonetheless. A perversely ironic statement from a soldier

---

50. The preceding paragraphs were based largely on Ben Gilbert, et.al., *Ten Blocks from the White House: Anatomy of the Washington Riots of 1968*, New York: Praeger, 1968, 2, 3, 32, 39, 63, 71, 72, 82, 85, 88, 91, 99, 105.

51. "Chronological Sequences of Events Commencing" with Dr. King's assassination, 7:30 PM, 4 April 1968; Report, 5 April 1968, 10: 50 a.m., Human Rights, Gen Hu 2, Ex Hu/FG 216, Box 20, *Lyndon B. Johnson Papers, Johnson Presidential Library-Austin*.

revealed the danger endured in the capital when he claimed "'Only the teenagers harassed us...and that really didn't seem to be racial, just against authority.'" This was not necessarily accurate, but if real it sketched a formidable problem for the near future. Some other claims seemed far-fetched too, e.g., the military only firing 14 rounds of ammunition throughout the uprising where in 1967 troops in Detroit fire 156,391 rounds. Perhaps the apparent discrepancy can be explained by reference to the military using 5,258 CS grenades, dangerous to any unlucky enough to come into contact. Most deaths—it was said—came from smoke inhalation and immolation. Negro men—contrary to the above—were blamed mostly for the depth of this entire occurrence. Barbershops were rarely damaged, suggesting intentionality of protesters. Nevertheless, Congressman Joel Broyhill of Virginia counselled that fire next time meant that next time the authorities should fire—and "'shoot to kill.'" April 1968 arrived as the crime rate was said to be accelerating with the murder rate purportedly tripling between 1960 and 1969, an indicator a wider malaise; instances of rape were 50 percent higher than in 1967. This all was like manna from heaven for the GOP and their presidential nominee, Richard M. Nixon, who compared what was occurring to the British invasion of August 1814, in what he termed the "'crime capital of the world.'"[52]

The District's fabled cherry blossoms were about to display their beauty on this squally Friday but in the White House there was the concern of causticity about another kind of blossoming. By 3:10 p.m. on that afternoon, President Johnson was told that "live television coverage" was slated for the "Cherry Blossom Ball...scheduled for tonight" with this perennial pitched to an "almost totally white population": said aide, Larry Temple tersely, "I agree."[53]

Temple agreed because he had a close eye on Carmichael on that stormy day. He had been told that the Howard alumnus had "just completed" what was "described as 'a very ugly speech'" on campus, punctuated by his pulling out a pistol and declaiming, "'We will go out tonight. Don't loot—shoot.'"[54] Carmichael was apparently

---

52. Kyla Sommers, "I Believe in the City: The Black Freedom Struggle and the 1968 Civil Disturbances in Washington, D.C.," Ph.D. dissertation, George Washington University, 2019, 105, 106, 107, 115, 117, 119, 120, 152, 184, 210, 218, 221,252, 265.
53. Larry Temple to President Johnson, 5 April 1968, Gen HU 2, Ex HU2/FG 216, Box 268, *Johnson Papers, Johnson Presidential Library*.
54. Larry Temple to President Johnson, 5 April 1968, Gen HU 2, Ex HU2/FG 216, Box 20, *Johnson Papers*.

moving through the city like a general rallying troops; soon he was to be found at 16th and F Streets, N.E., speechifying.[55]

Rumors were flying fast and furious on that day. As White House principals huddled in the Situation Room, the FBI told one and all that "reliable sources with contacts with militant black leaders reported that Chicago's Mayor [Richard] Daley [w]as 'marked for assassination.'" Was the District's influence spreading? Were "Militant Black Leaders" elsewhere taking advantage of the central authorities' local preoccupation to launch an offensive in the provinces?

Prior to the devastation of the District, numerous U.S. cities had gone up in flames—but Washington was different: this is where central power rested. And as a result, the authorities were powerfully unnerved—and it was not just the FBI. District officialdom was running around like decapitated chickens. Gun stealing from pawnshops proliferated, or so it was thought. Once more, Carmichael was bathed with floodlights as he reputedly "told the Negroes to arm themselves and take to the streets...[as] Black Power advocates tore down the American flag at half mast and raised their own, at Howard University." There was a "man with a rifle on top of the [National] Archives building facing Pennsylvania Avenue" not far from the Department of Justice. Just in case, the White House and Capitol Hill were "surrounded by machine guns."[56]

Recollections of this tumult are similarly disquieting. Reuben Jackson moved to 5322 5th Street, N.W. in 1959 when there were still "lots of Jewish kids," though "they were not allowed to play with us," souring relations. Nonplussed, he developed a serious crush on Sarah Goldfarb and his grandmother from Florida countered, "'That boy's going to end up like Emmett Till,'" referring to the Chicago youth slain in Mississippi for supposedly broaching the barbed race-gender divide. By 1961 the neighborhood had been transformed, as almost all those defined as "white" had evacuated—"most of the whites were gone," he said. "This was a time when the 171 form used for government employment still had that rider about being a member of the Communist Party," an association—per Carl Bernstein—that many of these families were also fleeing. By April 1968 disorderly ferment reigned: "You couldn't cross the

55. Report, 6 April 1968, 1:30 P.M. and 12:40 P.M. Gen HU2, Ex HU2/FG 216, Box 20

56. Report, 5 April 1968, #0101, Box 1, "Operation Band-aid," Record Group 23, *Office of Emergency Preparedness records re:...Demonstrations, Civil Disturbances and Special Events, 1965, 1968-1978, Washington, D.C. Municipal Archives.*

bridge that leaves town...they searched your car to make sure you weren't bringing gasoline in and out"; suggestive of the chaos, even "Opening Day baseball was delayed...."[57]

Virginia Ali present at the creation of the District's famed eatery, "Ben's Chili Bowl," also recalled the chaos of April 1968. Born in 1933, she had worked at the Industrial Bank, a Negro institution and by 1952 lived in Columbia Heights in Washington. Then Euro-American neighbors used to say to the melanin deficient woman, "'That fella you went out with. He's too dark for you.'" At Virginia Union University due south in Richmond "we rode the back of the bus. And Africans from Africa with their [tribal marks]...they would sit in the front and talk to [passengers] because people were interested in hearing about their culture...." It was "pretty ugly," she recalled years later, "didn't like that...." She wound up marrying a Trinidadian, Ben Ali, and found that "banks were reluctant to provide funding" to this dark-skinned man for a business that was to attain celestial success. Yet, by April 1968 their homeland tie to Carmichael, viewed as the embodiment of the mounting Black Power ideology, was paying dividends in that he dropped in "two or three times a day, every day" from his "office across the street." Similarly, "Dr. King [had] a satellite office" at 14th and U Streets, N.W., also nearby. The fact that her spouse was Muslim—she converted and journeyed to Mecca—did not harm relations at a time when this religion was growing boundlessly among Blacks. As was the pattern nationally, a number of Black businesses were "spared" as arson rose—an emblem of the arable "Black Power" ideology.[58]

Recall our earlier account of John Smith's experience in April 1968 and his references to "dynamite" and "guns" deployed. His neighborhood, a stroll from Capitol Hill, was "inundated with liquor stores all around...I started drinking early," a process facilitated since "my best friend's mother was a bootlegger...." Besides, "there were more liquor stores in our neighborhood than anything else...." The alcohol instigated combativeness and "fighting was the thing that kept you alive"; as for intellectual pursuits, "if you had too many books on you, you were a faggot...a chump," a reflection of how anti-intellectualism had been used to propel enslavement then Jim Crow. His "first experience...about hating white folks was in '55," seared as he was by the lynching of Emmett Till. "I used to go [to] Kenwood

---

57. Oral History, Reuben Jackson, 13 October 2002, *Historical Society of Washington, D.C.*

58. Oral History, Virginia Ali, 12 February 2003, *Historical Society of Washington, D.C.*

Country Club to caddy" in Montgomery County, Maryland, "the only time I would hear the term 'Nigger.'" Hence, he was hyperactive in April 1968—and before, "threatening people who wanted to march...we wanted people to be violent...." Even the Black Panthers did not meet his exacting standards—they "never took hold in D.C." He was aligned with the "Black Revolutionary Army" and often "we were shooting at each other," perhaps overdosing cinematically on the "Battle of Algiers," influential then as any novel. He had looked to Carmichael for inspiration but when he departed for Africa, Smith "felt disillusioned" and chose to "run for cover." Before then, he conceded "we wanted a revolution" and this "kept the flames going," that and the reality that the District "was just as racist as it was in Mississippi,"[59] perhaps more so in that the Magnolia State's hardest hardliners often spent considerable time on Capitol Hill nearby.

Fath Davis Ruffins wound up at the heralded African American Museum in the District, but she had lived in Lamond—or Lamond-Riggs, N.E., blocks from Maryland, arriving in 1957 in time to witness "white flight." It was a "fast turnover," she mused. "Racial turmoil characterizes these years between '65 and about '75," which she saw as "equally as important [as] the Vietnam War...." There was a forbidding "idea that there could be a race war in the United States...." She was shaped by the convulsions: "up until '68 I had straightened hair. And in '69 I insisted on getting an Afro...."—a typical pattern. When the National Guard arrived in her neighborhood, she sensed instinctively the fretful "concerns about the seat of government" and its questionable stability. This, too, "hastened white flight...."[60]

John D. Jackson was a cop, enlisting in 1957, and his spouse was a teacher in Anacostia. He was present at the 1963 March on Washington—"three fourths of the people in that march were white people," he estimated and it "wasn't a quarter of a million people, it was probably more than that...." Just before April 1968 he detected "professional agitators" who did "arrive to stir up Negroes" and "we caught them" (apparently, not all). Like Reuben Jackson, he recollected that during that time "there were mostly Jewish merchants," whose numbers were thinning. Ironically, the National Guard was "bivouacked" at the Langston Golf Course, named after Negro congressional solon of an earlier era, John Mercer Langston and an inspiration for Blacks on the links. He helped to enforce "partial

---

59. Oral History, John Smith, 16 October 2002, *Historical Society of Washington, D.C.*
60. Oral History, Fath Davis Ruffins, 2 November 2002, *Historical Society of Washington, D.C.*

martial law," a glancing phrase that would include suspension of ordinary civil liberties—justified since there were "snipers everywhere" and the "sounds of gunshots everywhere." Displaying the improvisational finesse that still characterizes racist bullies, "all of a sudden" police cars were "integrated," thought to be a shield for Euro-American officers. Yet this only exposed deeper maladies since "a pretty wide cultural gap between black officers and white officers" persisted in that "a lot of white officers didn't want to work with black officers," safety be damned. Likewise, a "lot of black officers didn't want to work with white officers." He "didn't have any riot gear," meaning he was exposed further since the "whole city was on fire." As for "Arab merchants," just beginning to arrive in town, there were "not that many," subtracting a key flavor from the ethnic stew.[61]

The *Post* was caught by surprise by the ferocity enveloping neighborhoods they ignored routinely. The tone deaf editor, Ben Bradlee, oddly boasted that his paper "pioneered in hiring...black journalists" with Simeon Booker in 1952—though soon he defected to the Negro press, where he stayed—and the patrician editor did not deign to explain why this "pioneer" move took place only in the second half of the 20th century. Yet, since the singular Booker was "the first black reporter on a white newspaper in Washington," perhaps his boast was not as empty as it seemed. As for Booker, he tearily confessed, "'God knows I tried to succeed at the 'Post.' I struggled so hard that friends thought I was dying...after a year and a half [I] had to give up. Trying to cover news in a city where even animal cemeteries were segregated overwhelmed.'" As late as the Summer of 1965, Negro reporters on the staff included the centrist William Raspberry and Jesse Lewis—who became a U.S. intelligence agent in what was called the "Middle East." (Dorothy Gilliam was then on leave, taking a breather from this snake pit.) Bradlee conceded, "we didn't cover fires or crimes in the city's black neighborhood," adding offhandedly as he mimicked Professor Logan's anti-Vatican attitude, that the "powers-that-be on the business side were Catholics...." Naturally, by April 1968 the *Post* saw fit to cooperate with the authorities. "Each morning," said Bradlee, "we sent them [police] over an 8-by-8 print of whatever photo had appeared in the paper," identifying those to be surveilled—or worse.[62]

---

61. Oral History, John D. Jackson, 27 March 2003.
62. Ben Bradlee, *A Good Life*, 279, 280, 282, 283, 291. See also Carl Bernstein, *Chasing History*, 220: Here Clarence Hunter is designated as the first Negro reporter and by 1963 there were five.

Bradlee's nonfeasance and malfeasance was not his alone. Black influencer, Sterling Tucker, argued properly that the "Communications industry has done more to create and promote a negative image of the Negro than any other single group or industry of American Society."[63] The flames approaching the White House and Capitol Hill served to illuminate the unavoidable reality that this industry simply was not doing its job if it were unable to report accurately and adequately on communities routinely disparaged and ignored, since the affected and damaged had the means to retaliate damagingly. It did not take long for the daily newspapers to be assailed over what was referred to daintily as their "racial coverage,"[64] forcing overdue reform.

---

63. Sterling Tucker, *Beyond the Burning*, 129.
64. *Washington Star*, 16 June 1969.

Chapter *21*

Revolting Capital Redux, 1967-1968

The White House was in the unenviable position of combating an insurrection that could be seen while peering from the window at a time when the GOP was in the process of decomposing the "Solid South" or yanking Euro-Americans across class lines away to presidential candidate Nixon who was pursuing his own "Southern Strategy" devised to accelerate this vitriolic reaction to the anti-Jim Crow movement.

Before the eruption, there were signs of spreading discontent. By May 1967 Johnson's assistants had filed away an editorial from WMAL-AM, a radio station in the District; they were alarmed by Carmichael's "decision to make Washington his 'target city' this summer...." Press spokesman, George Christian, congratulated the editorialist on his insight.[1] Yet another of the legions of Johnson aides, spotted by early 1967 an "incredible increase in car thefts" in the District,[2] which suggested that something was awry. Even speaking to Congress in mid-1967, President Johnson advised that "today's Washington has a population of 800,000" and was the "center of the country's fastest growing metropolitan area,"[3] which unavoidably delivered strains that could easily tip into unrest that should have been addressed—except the White House was busily expending tax dollars on a losing war in Vietnam.

President Johnson who—jocularly?—welcomed a march on Georgetown may have had second thoughts when he began to receive an anguished outpouring from constituents. (Similarly,

---

1. Editorial, 5 May 1967, Box 21, Human Rights Gen HU2 ExHU2/FG 216.
2. Charles Horsky to Marvin Watson, 19 January 1967, Box 266, *White House Central Files,* Ex FG 211/A, 11/22/63, *Johnson Papers.*
3. Remarks by President Johnson, 1 June 1967, Box 267, *White House Central Files,* Ex FG 211/A 11/22/63, *Johnson Papers.*

Henry Kissinger once remarked of the District, "'I really hate this city,'" a scorching comment worthy of further parsing.)[4] It was on 8 April 1968 when the embers had yet to be suppressed, when Steve Guback of the *Star*, informed the chief executive that "I have never been as ashamed—or as angry—with my country as I have in the last few days"; bringing him to the "point of tears" was a "ride down Anacostia freeway early Saturday morning, at dawn, on my way to work and to see between the capitol and the Washington Monument a column of smoke curling up into the sky from the destructed area of Washington...." That was not all, he exclaimed: "When before have we had complete takeovers of Howard, Virginia Union and Bowie State colleges by militants?" "How in the name of justice and common sense can we allow a [Carmichael] to enflame the population with treasonable statements?" Worse, "if they can get away with in Washington," the citadel of power, surely "they can try it in Alexandria and Fredericksburg." He thought he knew what to do: "They say that we must draw the line abroad against Communism"— that was insufficient: "I say let's draw the line at home too and get tough...."[5]

Concurring were Joseph and Julie Brown of Lanham, Maryland who asked rhetorically, "are the law breakers a front for Communistic activities...."[6] Margaret Nieman of Shady Side, Maryland was able to ferret out the revelation that the "vast majority of riots, strikes and demonstration and the recent rash of assassinations are <u>instigated</u> by Communists intent upon destroying this country from within" and they were "succeeding in tearing this country apart; between half our defenses [are] situated in Vietnam and the other half [is] putting down internal riots and preparing for possible riots...this country has never in history suffered so much internal turmoil"— (the Civil War?)—"thanks to the Communist instigators...they are into everything, the unions, the colleges and universities...." As for the monument to Dr. King's legacy, "Resurrection City," it was a "big farce." The remedy? "Rid this country of all Communists" and "lower the immigration quota" and "place more stringent regulations on overseas travel" and "screen...union officials and members...for

---

4. Gregg Herken, *The Georgetown Set*, 369.
5. Steve Guback to President Johnson, 8 April 1968, Box 21, Human Rights Gen HU2 Ex Hu2/FG 216, *Johnson Papers, Lyndon Johnson Presidential Library-Austin, Texas*.
6. Joseph and Julie Brown to Congressman Machen, 30 April 1968, Box 11, *Harvey Machen Papers, University of Maryland-College Park*.

Communist affiliations...."[7] Coincidentally, enough random shots were fired at Resurrection City, a deterrent to participation.[8]

Congressman Harvey Machen from just across the District line in Maryland had his eyes on Carmichael too, with even the mundane seeming sinister. His district included Prince George's and Charles' counties with the former billing itself as the District's largest suburb with the highest percentage of working class residents—including a sizeable number of Washington cops and, reputedly, one of the highest crime rates. Beginning on the evening of 4 April the county stationed heavily armed officers at the borderline with the capital.[9]

Early in 1968 the Black Power advocate was present at an "invitation only" meeting attended by the Reverend Fauntroy, intellectuals like Sterling Tucker and Nathan Hare and C. Sumner Stone—and, worryingly, NAACP president, Carl Moultrie—somewhat belying the claim that the "bulk of those attending were Black Power advocates."[10] The congressman found Fauntroy's presence "imprudent"—it was "incumbent upon [him] to consider his position in the city government carefully in his contact and dealings with Black Power organizations," as if the latter should be treated like Communists of the previous decade.[11]

A few months later, Machen was more explicit demanding that responsible leadership must choose between city government and the Black United Front—but could not choose both.[12] He was prompted by G. Garrett Carpenter of St. Matthew's Church in Seat Pleasant, Maryland who was horrified when the Front, which included Fauntroy, Channing Phillips, Sterling Tucker, and other mainstream Negro leaders, were said to have termed the "brutal slaying" of a cop to be "'justifiable homicide'"—this was "intolerable" he charged.[13]

---

7. Margaret Nieman to Congressman Machen, 28 June 1968, Box 11. Emphasis in original.

8. Clipping, 3 May 1968, Box 3, RG 23, *Office of Emergency Preparedness Records re: Demonstrations, Civil Disturbances and Special Events, 1965, 1968-1978, Washington, D.C. Municipal Archives.*

9. Undated Clipping, Box 11, *Harvey Machen Papers, University of Maryland-College Park.*

10. George Miller to Congressman Machen, 10 January 1968, Box 13, *Harvey Machen Papers, University of Maryland-College Park*: Attached is a *Post* article with detail about the meeting referenced.

11. Congressman Machen to George Miller of Adelphi, Maryland, 21 February 1968, Box 13.

12. Congressman Machen to G. Garrett Carpenter, 17 July 1968, Box 13.

13. G. Garrett Carpenter to Congressman Machen, 5 July 1968, Box 13.

Machen's constituents in Maryland were obsessed with Carmi-chael. George Miller of Adelphi co-signed a missive with eight others and forwarded a cartoon and editorial from the—fortunately—soon defunct *Washington Daily News*, providing the "correct perspective," featuring Adolf Hitler giving a Nazi salute and Carmichael seeking to replace him with the caption: "'Move over honkey!'"[14]

The couple described as "Mr. and Mrs. Marvin Lohr," also of Adel-phi, wondered why a local "white agitator" was "jailed" but "King, Rap Brown and Carmichael" were "allowed to carry on"; though the "root of all this evil is the welfare program,"[15] was their considered opinion. They thought that cracking down on activists would help things too. This perception that those defined as "white" were the real oppressed was rampant.

Nixon—and Machen too—were preaching to a local choir of authorities. By 6 April at 9:10 a.m. there had been 2,000 arrests, 700 injuries, and six dead but about 45 minutes later there had been 2,123 arrests and 734 injuries, indicative of the aggression expended. By 1:55 "Soul Brother Number 1," the fancy-footed singer, James Brown, appeared on television and radio urging those within range of his voice to "go home" but listeners were not necessarily hearing him. Ten minutes later a machine gun nest was affixed on Capitol Hill and 70 minutes later "three Negroes," it was said, were spotted "setting up a machine gun on Rock Creek Parkway...." By 7 p.m. there had been 2,899 arrests with 900 for looting along with 781 inju-ries, including 26 cops, 17 firefighters, and two soldiers. The next day Baltimore was being rocked, but did "not have sufficient fire equipment to control outbreaks" and that was followed rapidly by another report about an "uprising in Maryland correctional institu-tion; six ambulances have been dispatched...." The ultra-right, too, was not recumbent: "Military Intelligence advises of unconfirmed report of organization (Minutemen) planning uprisings throughout the nation after or on the day of [Dr. King's] funeral...." There were said to be "arms cache[s] at Stone Mountain, Georgia and Montpe-lier, Vermont...."

By Monday a "Negro male, about 20-21 years of age" was spotted "impersonating military...[in] green fatigues," no less, and "accom-panied by male and female Negroes...." Marion Barry was then quoted to the effect that his constituents "realize the troops must be

---

14. George Miller, et.al. to Congressman Machen, 9 April 1968, Box 11, *Har-vey Machen Papers*. See also *Washington Daily News*, 8 April 1968.
15. Mr. and Mrs. Marvin Lohr to Congressman Machen, 22 April 1968, Box 11.

there and prefer them to D.C. policemen, whom they do not like" perhaps shedding light on the presence of the young man in "green fatigues...." Then noticed were "three Negroes dressed in army field clothes. Believed to be Marines, armed with M-16 rifle[s]; last seen walking near Benning Rd. & Anacostia area." By 10 April, perhaps the most stressful news of all was delivered to the authorities: "Russians are linking, as propaganda, the assassination of [Dr. King] with the war in Vietnam."[16]

It was not just Moscow who broached the still sensitive issue of the slain prophet. Adabelle Welch of Adelphi, Maryland felt that "disregard for lawfulness is perpetuated by every leader in the U.S. who eulogized Dr. King as non-violent...."[17]

If Guback had been able to interrogate certain protesters he would have been angrier. Said one, "the news didn't report how many white people got fucked over...how many white people crawled back to Maryland and Virginia...."

Guback was not alone in being upset. Negro attorneys in the District, many of them trained at Howard and still carrying the ethos of the late Charles Hamilton Houston, were distraught. J. Francis Polhaus of the NAACP, weeks after the height of the inferno, spoke "as one of the lawyers involved in the defense of persons arrested during the recent civil disorders" and found lamentably that "burglary II (housebreaking) charges have been brought rather indiscriminately...[by] using the threat of felony prosecutions to induce guilty pleas to lesser offenses...."[18]

A number of jurists felt that certain Euro-American judges were visibly antagonistic toward Black defendants and their attorneys by setting astronomically high bonds, meaning detention without trial. About 90 percent of those detained were Black and about 9 percent were women—or so it was estimated. Judges argued that they could not conduct business as usual as the nation's capital came under siege. The A&P grocery store on Benning Road was reportedly dynamited and this was not the only case of this sort. One protester claimed that he and his comrades had "long guns" while another substantiated this point by asserting that "you can get them right on

---

16. Reports, 4-10 April 1968, Box 1, RG 23, *Office of Emergency Preparedness Records re:...Demonstrations, Civil Disturbances and Special Events, 1965, 1968-1978, Washington, D.C. Municipal Archives.*

17. Adabelle Welch to Congressman Machen, 10 April 1968, Box 11, *Harvey Machen Papers.*

18. J. Francis Polhaus to Director, Legal Interns, Georgetown Law, 8 May 1968, Box IX: 228, *NAACP Papers,*

the block. Cats that are in the war," meaning Vietnam, "right in this country," can obtain them from "their camps" that ringed the otherwise secure urban center. "The brothers took them off the base...." The "brothers" did not dwell on the almost 700 dwelling units that were damaged, exacerbating the affordable housing crisis. Liquor stores were ravaged; in fact, no other single category of stores felt the kind of damage they endured: 37 burned, 82 looted, 52 partially looted—and, yes, only Negroes owned liquor stores. Fortunately, there was a noticeable absence of scrawled swastikas and other emblems of anti-Jewish fervor—at least according to *Post* reporters, not prone to suppress the news if it were otherwise. Near the epicenter of the revolt, these journalists assayed that there were about 20,000 in the streets or about 12 percent of residents in the affected area,[19] redolent of the mass character, impact, and ideological resonance of April 1968.

In this chaotic context tensions began to spark at the top. Congressman Hickenlooper was "extremely worried about Mayor Washington's desire to withdraw troops from the District of Columbia...." Why? "Local thugs are waiting for troop removal," he groused "and are particularly hopeful it will happen over Easter so that they may have their own Tet holiday," akin to recent events in Vietnam "by bombing individual homes in the Chevy Chase area," the elegant Maryland redoubt of the elite. This proposed withdrawal was little more than "foolishness,"[20] he spat out. Kensington was within brisk walking distance of Chevy Chase but a close observer had spotted an "armed camp" within range: "Baltimore was relatively quiet until it was observed that the plunderers and arsonists in Washington were virtually untouchable" and it was disintegrating. He blamed the District version of "Neville Chamberlain" since "appeasement at any price is merely forestalling the day of reckoning...."[21]

Silver Spring, too, was nearby and Richard Morauer who described himself as a "businessman...[and] a property owner in Montgomery County, Prince Georges and Charles County plus in the District"; his class position established, he stated revoltingly the obvious, he was of like mind, charging that those in the streets were "act[ing] like

19. Ben Gilbert, et.al., *Ten Blocks from the White House*, 125, 149, 158, 171, 173, 178, 182, 188, 224.

20. Mike Manatos to President Johnson, 11 April 1968, Box 20, Human Rights Gen HU2 Ex HU2/FG 216, *Johnson Papers*.

21. Attorney George Ballman to Congressman Machen, circa April 1968, Box 11., *Harvey Machen Papers*.

animals" and, thus, "should be treated as such," meaning "looters and arsonists should be shot."[22]

By 12 April, ructions continued to percolate. An agent of the District watched as "white policemen were confronted by angry Negroes in front of the Peoples Drugstore at 14th and U streets N.W...trouble started after several hundred persons gathered outside of the [SCLC, Dr. King's group] offices...." Julius Hobson ruffled feathers when he proclaimed, "'the next Negro to advocate nonviolence should be torn to bits by the black people.'" A hilltop student in tune with the temper of the times argued, "'if the white man does not accept the Negro on an equal basis, the U.S. will be like Rome—it will crumble!'" Observers had to tread carefully after reporter, Bill Greenwood was beaten and robbed on 14th Street by about a dozen Negroes.[23]

By 15 April matters in the District remained unsteady and that meant Attorney General Ramsey Clark; Deputy Attorney General Warren Christopher; Mayor Walter Washington; elite scholar James M. Burns; and others assembled to sort through what still was unwinding. They acknowledged that it was "very difficult to infiltrate many militant groups and to keep them under surveillance," a harbinger of the reversal that was to come. Yet surveillance focused like a laser beam not in the first instance on groups but an individual (which was easier): "what Stokely Carmichael was doing" was scrutinized obsessively along with "what was happening in the schools," meaning the hilltop and, specifically "what was happening at the Howard University rally" as blazes leapt uncontrollably. There was "no substitute for helicopter surveillance," quickly becoming routine in Christopher's spread-out Los Angeles. "SNCC and several African groups," again at Howard, were targeted; the former had "been very active in setting up 5 man cells and linking into PRIDE,"[24] Marion Barry's shop. But this was déjà vu all over again. About four years earlier White House aide, Lee White, was wringing his hands about a "possible riot in D.C."; indeed, he warned on 13 August 1964, there was "likely to be a riot tonight" beginning at that reliable standby, "14th and U Streets," N.W., still a flashpoint in April 1968. Instead of Carmichael, then it was said

22. Richard Morauer to Congressman Machen, 10 April 1968, Box 11.

23. Report, 12 April 1968, Box 1, RG 23, *Office of Emergency Preparedness Records re:...Demonstrations, Civil Disturbances and Special Events, 1965, 1968-1978, Municipal Archives of Washington, D.C.*

24. Minutes of Meeting, 15 April 1968, Box 20, Human Rights, Gen HU 2, Ex HU2/FG 216, *Johnson Papers.*

"out-of-town people probably associated with Malcolm X were going to create an incident...."[25]

Marion Barry was the other target of inquisitors in 1968 and by 23 April he was summoned to a special congressional hearing at Cardozo High School. The future mayor was "wondering a little bit," addressing "Mr. Hechinger," scion of a retail and real estate empire, "why we have so many policemen outside...." Then, he warned heatedly, "if the city is rebuilt the same way it was, it is going to be burned down again...." He found it outrageous that "many landlords" were "charging $125 for a $55 apartment," looting his constituency and guaranteeing yet another revolt.[26]

Holding a hearing at a high school may have been a response to these teenagers' increased activism; thus, in May 1968 12 youth from Memphis—site of the murder of Dr. King—came to Ballou High School in the District to discuss the Poor People's Movement but were rebuffed by the principal, providing an abject lesson to youth of the actual nature of the First Amendment and how Washington was poised to deliver uniquely this tutorial.[27]

Instead, these strains led to a mass revolt, which encompassed suspects thought to be unlikely. Days after 4 April President Johnson was told by the Civil Service Commission that "20 persons who are currently employed by the Federal Government in the Washington metropolitan area...have been charged with serious offenses"; admittedly, these were "low grade employees, such as messengers and laborers" but they often had access to the corridors of power, suggesting a chink in the hegemonic armor.[28]

SNCC was well aware of these class tensions; an undated report by them found the District to be a "curious city...composed either of persons in poverty...or established and comfortable"; the Hatch Act acted as a restraint as it sought to constrain activism by federal

---

25. Lee White to President Johnson, 13 August 1964, Box 20, Human Rights Gen HU2 ExHU2/FG 216, *Johnson Papers,*

26. Rehabilitation of District of Columbia. Areas Damaged by Civil Disorders. Hearings Before the Subcommittee on Business and the Subcommittee on Business and Commerce of the Committee on the District of Columbia, U.S. Senate, 90th Congress, 2nd Session, 18, 30 April and 20, 28, 29 May 1968, *Historical Society of Washington,*

27. *Washington Post,* 22 May 1968.

28. Civil Service Commission to President Johnson, 25 April 1968, Box 20, Human Rights Gen HU 2 ExHU2/FG216, *Johnson Papers, Johnson Presidential Library.*

employees. Thus, it was said "Non-involvement is the watchword. The white community is less burdened by this fear."[29]

However, it was likely that these "low grade employees" who seized the opportunity to turn the tables. Recalled nervously by Congress was an article in the *Star* about an effort to "solicit money from white merchants, sometimes under threat of burning down their stores," pointing to an enterprise "in the 1800 block of 7th Street," N.W.; the shopkeeper "waved a pistol at one such solicitor...."[30] The demand arose for stricter laws on "extortion."[31] This class then began to organize for, it was said with a sinister twist, "better protection" from "militant minorities."[32]

Al Lannon, Jr., son of a Communist maritime worker, was more conciliatory, as he loftily spoke of "we in the white community" who were "silent" about the atrocities visited upon Blacks—e.g., the Emmett Till case—but this only demonstrated that "our silence showed our racism" and "now that we have birthed an angry black backlash, we are scared...."[33]

Capitol Hill was startled by this turn of events although they had been monitoring the District for decades. By mid-May 1968 Congressman B.F. Sisk of California, while noting that the police chief was conferring with Pentagon officials as early as 3 p.m. on Friday, 5 April, in a bloodcurdling remark observed "frankly I know a lot of other people"—besides himself—"who were very upset because that had not been done," i.e., "going out and mowing people down with machine guns..." This spine-chilling remark was made though by his count of the 8,000 arrests over a eleven day period, most were for curfew violations, implying applying the death penalty for minor transgressions. Congressman John Dowdy of Texas was unhappy to hear of the demand that stores were being requested to close within a few days—on Malcolm X's birthday—"or probably get burned out...." A Maryland Congressman "saw the police disarm a group of men who had machetes... [on] upper 14th Street...."

George Kalavitinos, a District businessman, was symptomatic of the angst and anger of capital after absorbing a shock. "Our police forces" are "politically neutralized" he charged accusingly, meaning

29. Summary Report, no date, Box 56, *James Forman Papers*.
30. *Washington Star*, 26 April 1968.
31. *Washington Star*, 20 May 1968.
32. *Washington Star*, 2 May 1968.
33. *Washington Star*, 10 May 1968.

a "complete breakdown of law and order...." Verbalizing the obvious, he told Congress, "I am now damn mad...." He was upset with
the "liberals," whose pusillanimity, he thought, had delivered this
parlous state of affairs. They tolerated James Forman of the SNCC,
whose "contacts" with "Fidel Castro's Cuba" were notorious.
Instead of praising the dead, he dismissed Dr. King as a "figure-
head" in any case and a kind of political "speculator" capitalizing
on unrest. Naturally, Carmichael and his comrade H. "Rap" Brown,
were lashed: "demagogues," he said, with a "'mafia' approach," little more than "black racists" enmeshed in a "criminal conspiracy
in this city." Marion Barry's comrade, Rufus Mayfield, came in for
assault, too. That the speaker was a self-described "slumlord" did
not upset Congressman Larry Winn, Jr., a Republican from Kansas,
who extended class solidarity: "You and I are in the same boat. I am
a landlord. I own 365 units...." But the Greek land baron was concerned about doings in the bedrooms, grumbling that "many white
women have black boyfriends" and, worse, "they carry their boyfriends' guns in their purses...same applies to black women who
have white militant boyfriends...." Like his congressional interloc-
utors, he was ready to shed blood—that of his adversaries: "these
punks, demagogues, animals, militants, beatniks and other queer
ducks would have long been exterminated from their rat holes"
with more resoluteness. Harking to events in Athens, he demanded
a "Junta" like "Greece" be put in charge, i.e., neo-fascism. He, too,
was worried about a spate of bank robberies, though one grabbed
his attention in that the purloiners were all teenagers, ranging from
15 to 16, but they "used a shotgun and handguns...." Bellowing, he
added, "this city and the suburbs" were "becoming armed camps,"
as "many are arming themselves" in that "application[s] for gun
permits in the suburbs since April 4, 1968 have risen from a monthly
average of 1,350 to a total of 2,500." Though alarmist, his tormented
words were mirrored by those of Hilliard Schulberg, former Director of the District Retail Liquor Dealers Association, who claimed
that "35 stores were totally destroyed and 150 others damaged and
looted"; while Abe Liss of the Midtown Business Association argued
apocalyptically that the insurrection in the District "has caused insecurity across the country...."[34]

---

34. Civil Disturbances in Washington...Hearings Before the Committee on
the District of Columbia. House of Representatives. 90th Congress, 2nd Session. Investigating the April 1968 Rioting, Looting, Damages and Losses and
Police Actions and HGR 16941 and HR 16948. May and June 1968, Washington, D.C.: GPO, 1968, *Historical Society of Washington*. See also *Washington*

Intriguingly concurring was the Black woman attorney who thought that during April 1968 "felt as though the whole world had come to an end."[35] There were 388 liquor stores in the city but nearly half were unable to reopen in the short term. Even the opening of baseball season, a bonanza for beer sellers, was impacted.[36] Certainly, the insurance industry seized the opportunity to increase rates, which did not necessarily aid security.[37] This had backfiring consequences. The "Daily Intelligence Summary" reported that an "official for Richard Nixon's inauguration denied...that it was refused insurance against riots during the January 20th event. G. Dewey Arnold, Chairman of the Inaugural's Insurance Committee said that we have all the insurance we intended to acquire"—however, the overriding point was the nervousness about a "riot" even as the "law and order" candidate was about to be sworn in.[38]

Given the pulse of the times, the inauguration organizers prepared for the worst. According to the *Star*, on the scene were "more than 400 medical personnel including about 100 physicians" amounting to the "most extensive medical organization for a presidential inauguration"; there were "32 medical aid stations and 55 ambulances," plus a "mobile coronary intensive care unit for possible cases of heart attack, the first time heart resuscitation equipment has been available at the scene" of this quadrennial event.[39]

Rushing not to be overcome by events, in early May 1968, as the spearhead of the late Dr. King's Poor People's Movement was about to arrive en masse at "Resurrection City," an encampment from which Congress would be pressed, White House aides again assembled. The theme was "Washington...Riot and Future Planning" and present were Joseph Califano, Warren Christopher, and Mayor Washington, among others. Califano who was to serve as a weighty member of the Cabinet, was "reflecting concern about the loss of confidence in the community, in Congress, and in the press about the ability of the Government to maintain law and order in Washington," no small matter and a painful admission besides. Christopher was fretting that "our facilities can detain up to 10,000 prisoners but they will be overtaxed if many arrests are made on the same day...."

Post, 2 July 1968: "1,338 cases of curfew violations arising from the April riot...about one third of the 4,050 arrested during the disorders...."
35. Dovey Johnson Roundtree, *Mighty Justice*, 219.
36. *Washington Daily News*, 11 April 1968.
37. *Washington Star*, 21 April 1968.
38. Daily Intelligence Summary, 31 December 1968, Box 9, RG 23.
39. *Washington Star*, 17 January 1969.

The FBI pledged to make "certain intelligence material available to the District of Columbia police" and their being based in Washington demonstrated the steep incline protesters had to surmount. Mayor Washington gave an opportunistic nod to affirmative action when he claimed that the "best intelligence reports are coming from young Negro agents in Army Intelligence who are cooperating very well with the District and FBI officials...." Yet, the consensus seemed to be that "we know very little about what the militants are doing, but they appear to be very active...." The beat went on since "2,000 anti-war demonstrators from New York are expected on May 25th" not to mention the imminence of the Poor People's Campaign, at the core of the King legacy. "We have agents and Community Relations with each group," it was said. Despite routing the Reds in the previous decade, there was inordinate focus on a "person named Blackwell, an alleged Communist...[who] is also with one of the groups," unspecified. The District "only" had "2,900 policemen," a real worry since there were "rumors of plans to hit places like Connecticut Avenue," within hailing distance of legations and opulent residences.[40]

Reports from ground zero of protest were hardly reassuring. Daniel Flores described himself as "the only Hispanic working in the 10th district" of the city and he recalled a force of "1,800" not 2,900; "now we have 3,800," he said in 1986, part of a general upgrade in that April 1968 "changed law enforcement" bringing the force "out of the dark ages into modern times" as "we began to get more money" and equipment. Thus, "crime has gone down more here than it has nationwide" as stability of the center of power became more of a priority. Still, he assessed that "the '68 riots didn't really stop until the '70s," the percussiveness "went on and on" and only slowed down "when we got out of Vietnam" in 1975. He recalled that "wherever you went in the city you would find Jewish landlords, business owners" with a "credit type of system"; a number of protesters "wanted to burn those IOUs" showing debits, meaning "selective looting"—"not everybody was looted," he insisted. As he remembered things, "fires didn't start until 2 or 3 days after the beginning," not a universally shared view.[41]

What was agreed upon was that firefighters were overmatched by arsonists; at one point 35 percent of Montgomery County's force

40. Minutes of "Washington, D.C. Riot and Future Planning," 7 May 1968, Box 20, Gen HU 2 Ex HU 2/FG 216, *Johnson Papers*.
41. Oral History, Daniel Flores, 29 July 1986, *Historical Society of Washington, D.C.*

were across the border in the District, leaving this affluent enclave terribly exposed.[42] As early as 7 April, the *Post* was reporting that "hostile bystanders hamper firefighters" as "hundreds of new and rekindled fires" emblazoned the sky. The "weary firemen" were barely holding on, though "under police and military protection...." The "1,419 man force was placed on a special three platoon schedule under which two platoons were on duty at all times...." At one harried point, the force "were faced with 40 fires at one time," while "late yesterday the total number reported in the city had passed the 500 mark," while "16 firemen had been treated for injuries," most hit by projectiles tossed by "taunting teenagers." Molotov cocktails were a specialty then. Near 1515 F Street N.E. there was a danger that the neighborhood would have to be evacuated if a storage facility had caught fire and released noxious ammonia gas. Fire department brass were bewildered by the hostility they faced.[43]

Still, they were not too buffaloed to recommend a ban on the sale of gasoline in containers, essential for proliferating Molotov cocktails, endangering firefighters' lives, banned alongside sales of firearms.[44] The next day, 12 April, in stylish Silver Spring, Maryland, "Atlantic Guns" reopened as the county lifted its temporary ban on sale of firearms—and they were overrun with customers, including an army major and a lieutenant in full battle dress.[45]

They should have taken seriously the prattling and prating of District police captain John B. Lofton, who before April—perhaps after having watched too many football games—suggested that his forces should tolerate minor infractions to avert a larger catastrophe, akin to the "prevent" defense on the gridiron.[46] However, as too many Monday morning quarterbacks have advised, this defense often "prevents" your side from prevailing as the opposition gains momentum, a description of what began to unfold in the streets of Washington.

Clyde Garriott, a self-described "Washington, D.C. fireman," residing in Forestville, Maryland, who "worked in the recent civil disturbance" was "disgusted" by what he witnessed to the point where he advised that "less fatalities would have occurred and a 'riot' would never have developed had total force been used and immediate action and any means necessary been taken to quell the

---

42. *Washington Star*, 10 May 1968.
43. *Washington Post*, 7 April 1968.
44. *Washington Daily News*, 11 April 1968.
45. *Washington Daily News*, 12 April 1968.
46. *Washington Post*, 20 February 1968.

troublemakers."[47] Unnervingly, the congressman replied, "I agree completely with your views on the riots..."[48]

Congressman Machen was also responding to more delirious constituents. Pauline Davidson of Landover—even before 4 April—was "trembling" in her "home with the doors lock[ed]," as she contemplated that the "Negroes are planning to massacre us," as if 1864 had returned. "I don't go into the beautiful capital anymore," she wailed.[49] Therese Ann Olson of Hyattsville, found her homeland to be the "laughingstock of the world" and, besides, "the Negroes" in the streets are "barbarians of the highest order," congruent with "our own nation...in a state of anarchy"; all the while "our American boys are dying in Vietnam...." The result, as far as she was concerned was "abject fear of the Negro minority...."[50]

The hotbed of racism that was Hyattsville also contained Henry Bowen who knew that the "rebellion was obviously not spontaneous"; anyway, "participants" included "college graduates, librarians and civil servants" and "their motive was evil" in that "it was the Black Power motive to cripple the United States through disruption." Indeed, there was "heartbreaking visible parallelism between the policy of the American authorities and the policy of the Hindenburg government in Germany," meaning Negro fascism was nigh. Actually, the "Black Power movement is unquestionably following the Bolshevik-Fascist-Nazi technique" and "using the same language." For Black Power "is force to the utmost and it can be broken only by 'force without stint or limit' as President Wilson, the nemesis of Negroes, said of Berlin in 1917." "There will be no peace in this land until Black Power has been broken," he squawked, "and that will require force and sacrifice...."[51]

David Lawrence, columnist, alarmed his already worried readership by painting a desperate portrait of a "reign of terror [that] prevails in the capital of the United States," while the "police force is inadequate," emblematic was that "property losses in Washington were $13 million" as of late May 1968, likely an underestimate.[52] (A

47. Clyde Garriott to Congressman Machen, 16 May 1968, Box 13, *Harvey Machen Papers*. Emphasis in original.

48. Congressman Machen to Clyde Garriott, 13 June 1968, Box 13.

49. Pauline Davidson to "Dear Sir," 19 March 1968, Box 11, *Harvey Machen Papers*.

50. Therese Ann Olson to "Dear Sir," circa 1968, Box 11.

51. Henry Bowen to Congressman Machen, 11 April 1968, Box 11.

52. *Washington Star*, 29 May 1968.

congressional estimate from the same time was $57.6 million, closer to accuracy.)[53]

Estimated accurately was the precipitous drop in tourist revenues, perhaps the city's most sizable source of private revenue, meaning substantial tax losses and a resultant drop in city services.[54] This troubling trend was evident as early as 11 April.[55] Not reassuring to potential tourists was the point made in early June 1968 by the Commander of the National Guard, Major General C.L. Southward, who demanded a "team of marksmen...with orders to shoot to kill any sniper."[56] Tourism in a potential war zone was unwise.

Indicatory of the unsettledness then was that a constituent element of capital, the District Bankers' Association upped the ante in a "unanimous vote" by demanding "1,000 men from the military" to augment the police force, meaning an increase of 177 percent, it was said; their immediate issue was the recent sharp increase in bank robberies,[57] as if certain activists were snatching funds with expansive ambition in mind. The "Daily Intelligence Summary" of 25 May 1968 reported morosely that "robberies in the District mount...involving banks" particularly.[58]

Basil Winstead, division manager at Safeway's in the District, a grocery chain, anticipated this trend in March 1967 when he pointed out that "monetary loss from robberies and holdups" were "on the increase."[59] Earlier, David Paulos of the District had "been robbed 3 times in six months at gunpoint," though there was a "bank across the street," a lusher target; he was "robbed so frequently" that he "closed up,"[60] shuttered his business. This was a trend: "Outgoing merchants seek Negroes as new owners" read one headline as

---

53. Riots, Civil and Criminal Disorders. Hearings Before the Permanent Subcommittee on Investigations of the Committee on Government Operations. U.S. Senate. 1st Session. 27 and 28 May 1969, *Historical Society of Washington, D.C.*

54. *Washington Post*, 1 June 1968.

55. *Washington Daily News*, 11 April 1968.

56. *Washington Star*, 10 June 1968.

57. *Washington Post*, 16 June 1968.

58. Daily Intelligence Summary, 25 May 1968, Box 5, RG 23, *Office of Emergency Preparedness Records*.

59. Remarks of Basil Winstead, 3 March 1967, Box 1, ACC. No. 2014-3, *Records of the History of the University of Maryland, University of Maryland-College Park*.

60. David Paulos to Congressman Machen, 3 May 1965 [sic], Box 11, *Harvey Machen Papers*.

the middle class was a clear beneficiary of the revolt.[61] Rather than emulate Paulos, John Elliott, president of the Amalgamated Transit Union, demanded that buses not carry cash in order to "remove the possibility for robbery."[62] But that only shifted the crisis to cabbies who worried that a transition to scrip on buses would send robbers in their direction.[63]

Charles W. Hawkins also was decomposing psychologically, even before 4 April indicating that something more than the murder of Dr. King as a trigger was afoot. He worked for D.C. Transit and spoke of "over 100 robberies since the first of January. Six operators have been attacked with knives and guns. Four have received broken noses and jaws; one a split disk due to be being kicked in the back"; he demanded the "death penalty for anyone" who "rob[bed] another with a gun and a knife...."[64]

Michael Eisenberg, Vice President of South Capital Liquors, sited at 4654 Livingston Road, S.E. ascertained the presence of "desperation, anxiety and defiance" (the latter word was repeated repetitively by quite a few), then he pivoted, as he was anxiously "waiting for the moment when someone walks into my place of business and demands either by oral threat or armed threat, for all my money, my life or both....."[65] Nat Hauser of Cheverly, a Maryland suburb, derided "undesirables in the District," observing that "starting a few years ago the enforcement of law became a farce"; there was a rise, he veritably shouted, of "muggings-rapes-assaults-killings!" His "business...[was] located off a main highway, the Washington-Baltimore Parkway at Maryland [Route] 202...." It was an "Esso station" and his pocketbook was hit by the tumult; he had "never seen travel curtailed as drastically as it has been since the April riots" and the same held true for "thousands" of other enterprises.[66]

Off the parkway in Baltimore, 18 signatories of elite John Hopkins University, from their elevated post, thought the nation was akin to pre-1917 Russia with the Czar (Johnson?) being too weak and now a "minority of the population has taken to revolution" (Negroes as Bolsheviks?). On the other hand, they counselled sagely

---

61. *Washington Post*, 5 July 1968.

62. Report, 23 January 1968, Box 1, RG 23, *Office of Emergency Preparedness Records*.

63. *Washington Star*, 4 August 1968.

64. Charles W. Hawkins to Congressman Machen, 30 March 1968, Box 11.

65. Remarks by Michael Eisenberg, 6 May 1968, Box 1, ACC. No. 2014-3.

66. Nat Hauser to Congressman Machen, 23 May 1968, Box 1, ACC. No. 2014-3.

that "effective far reaching reforms" must be "enact[ed]" to "preserve our nation from an imminent civil war…one from which it will never recover…."[67]

Alarmingly, the idea of Negroes acting like Bolsheviks in the citadel of power was not a chimera. The notion was co-signed by columnist Drew Pearson who said that "Carmichael's real goal…is the overthrow of the United States Government…." His apparent source was the FBI, which prepared a "report on black militants" sketching the "underground black nationalist movement" and their "plan to take over the Nation's Capital…."[68] But then Pearson received a kind of comeuppance when he was said to be "accosted and beaten" at Resurrection City. The *Post* was apoplectic, booming that "hatred against whites…recently has become much intensified" amounting to a "real danger in this country…." Instantaneously, Black Conservative relic, George Schuyler, termed it "Insurrection City" and "planned pandemonium." Yet even the *Post* could not deny that this legacy of the Dr. King crusade "helped pry loose more than $200 million in surplus food" for the hungry and "speeded up the [fair] housing bill…."[69]

Max Burns of 7949 Pennsylvania Avenue S.E. was a 15 minute drive from Eisenberg but closer in sentiment, beseeching that "Riots are caused by a rising tide of black racism," he emphasized as he saluted the "courageous stance assumed by" Governor Agnew and Senator Robert Byrd of West Virginia who was similarly censorious. Anticipating the 45th U.S. president, he chose to "deplore the demagogic approach…by such people as 'little' Bobby Kennedy…."[70] The woman who identified herself as "Mrs. Karl Wirth" of College Park also castigated RFK (though not poking fun at his diminutiveness) and for good measure added that "most of us are fearful of the so called Poor Peoples March," meaning "we have all avoided going to Washington."[71]

The latter campaign infuriated many suburbanites—officialdom, too. By late April 1968, an official report gloated that it had "fallen flat…SCLC appears to be disorganized…a meeting with Dean Rusk at State Department had no one show up except 1 priest…[and]

---

67. Statement from Johns Hopkins to Congressman Machen, 8 April 1968, Box 11, *Harvey Machen Papers*. Emphasis in original.

68. *Washington Post*, 31 July 1968.

69. *Washington Post*, 27 July 1968.

70. Max Burns to Congressman Machen, 14 April 1968, Box 11, *Harvey Machen Papers*.

71. Mrs. Karl Wirth to Congressman Machen, 9 May 1968, Box 11.

another meeting with Secretary of Agriculture Orville Freeman proved the same—no representatives...."[72]

Kenneth Dorn of Bowie, Maryland seemed to be on the verge of a nervous breakdown, typical of the times. As of 22 May he was a worker at the Government Printing Office—"responsible for the printing of the Congressional Record that is on your desk promptly each and every day," was his message to Congressman Machen—but "for the past 6 weeks I have feared for my life," feared "being attacked, knifed, shot, yoked, robbed, beat up, not to mention being killed!"[73] John Williams of Beltsville, seemed to have lost mental acuity as well; he was "sickened by fear and disgust" and mortified by "fear...fear...fears"; an "ill wind" was whistling filled with "bitterness and distrust," as if there were "two worlds" involved; then he began to ramble about "monsters...troublemak-ers...insurrectionists" and an "insidious plot" to "overthrow our government...."[74]

A resident of Oxon Hill chose not to share his name, perhaps because of the flagrant words he shared: protesters were "terroriz-ing...with impunity..." as the "spectacle of armed U.S. soldiers in our Capital City," enraged. There was the "burnt offerings of white people and their businesses," as if the distant past had intruded, all publicized by the "bleating press and their clerical allies...." There was no Civil Rights Movement, there was a "Black Bowel Move-ment...while the blackbirds thus sing...." Congress "is again being blackmailed and bullied into another Civil Riots Act" because of "blackbird coddling...." Wickedly, it was added, "I don't ask for suppression! I ask for execution—summary execution of all rioters, all looters, all murderous arsonists...."[75]

Like battalions of others, Calvin Patton of the militaristic Amer-ican Legion thought that fighting this war at home involved a revamping of armed forces—or so he informed the Civil Defense Director of the U.S. Army. Surveying the charred landscape on 18 April he said, "during the latest civil disorder" it was "obvi-ous that our present telephone system is totally inadequate during

72. Report, 29 April 1968, Box 2, RG 23, *Office of Emergency Preparedness Records*

73. Kenneth Dorn to Congressman Machen, 22 May 1968, Box 1, ACC. No. 2014-3.

74. John Williams to Congressman Machen, 9 April 1968, Box 11.

75. Unknown to Congressman Machen, 10 April 1968, Box 11, *Harvey Machen Papers.*

emergency situations"; it was "forty five minutes before one could hear a dial tone."[76]

Near the same time, Stanley Asrael of the Greater Washington Waste Dealers, noticed a "burglary and holdup problem that has besieged" the authorities: "25 percent of our membership has within the past nine months suffered either daylight holdup and/or repetitious nocturnal burglary...."[77]

Then John Macbryde of the Building Congress of the District found that among "construction equipment distributors," it was "routine within our repair department to have to go into the field and repair construction equipment that has been vandalized," while "cases of thievery" were "constant...."[78] Yes, it was possible that these men were gaslighting so as to bolster phony tax and insurance claims, but other kinds of evidence bolster their claims.

Next door in Maryland, as the District was proving itself to be utterly combustible, a gubernatorial election of national import was proceeding. According to the *Post*, "white conservatives" who were authoritative in the Democratic Party were touting George Mahoney who, it was said, "campaigned primarily on an anti-open housing platform," which led many Negroes to defect to the banner of his main competitor: Spiro Agnew—"by margins as large as 50 to 1 in some precincts...." Energized Black activists proceeded to display bullwhips and Klan sheets as campaign symbols. During the zenith of the April 1968 revolt, said the *Post*, "white merchants and politicians criticized [Governor] Agnew because no looters were not being shot." Spooked, the Greek American executive issued a statement deflecting responsibility to Washington for this perceived policy of timidity. But it did not take long for Agnew to seize the spirit of the times, which led him to become a loose-tongued U.S. Vice President within months, by lecturing Black "dandiprats," along with "'ready-mix, instantaneous, circuit riding, Hanoi visiting, caterwauling, riot inciting, burn-America-down type[s].'"[79] As so-called "urban riots and the crime problem," as the *Star* odoriferously put it became a major issue during the 1968 campaign, Senator Daniel Brewster of

---

76. Calvin Patton to Civil Defense Director, 18 April 1968, Box 1, ACC. No. 2014-3.
77. Stanley Asrael to Congressman Harvey Machen, 16 March 1967, Box 1, ACC. No. 2014-3.
78. John Macbryde to Congressman Machen, 15 May 1967, Box 1, ACC. No. 2014-3.
79. *Washington Post*, 16 April 1968.

Maryland was left exposed[80] and plunged to defeat, tarred as he was by the backwash afflicting Resurrection City.

As if he were auditioning to be "Nixon's Nixon" or prime hatchet man, as the Poor Peoples Campaign was assembling, Agnew—who had run as a kind of "liberal" in 1966—spotted "'a lot of Cadillacs over there,'"[81] a trope designed to capitalize on racist theories of "welfare queens" or Negroes looting public coffers. Reflective of how a counter-revolutionary impulse was unfurling—a noticeable trend in the republic—sharply shifting the political spectrum rightward, Agnew countered by averring, "'I have never felt more liberal now than I ever did in my life.'" This utterance was made as he denounced the campaigners for government aid to the poor as "'lobbyists for opportunism.'"[82] His constituent, Henry Miller of Riverdale, Maryland was against this activism of the poor since it barely masked "plans afoot by the Negro hoodlum element to turn the march into a violent demonstration…."[83] The woman who signed her name "Mrs. Everett Pyle," also of Maryland, wondered pensively, "why should I have to drive through the streets" of the District "with my car doors locked and windows rolled up, even in the heat of the summer…." Why should she "turn my diamond to the inside of my head in the bright sunlight to avoid a thief…."[84]

As can be inferred, there was a basis for the governor ripping off his mask and baring his filed and sharpened teeth. Prominent scandal mongering columnists, Drew Pearson and his comrade, Jack Anderson, found a link among student revolts at Howard, Columbia—and College Park. It was "spelled out very carefully" at the latter campus at a meeting of the Students for a Democratic Society: there was "some suspicion that Chinese Communists are behind…the student militants." (Apparently, Moscow agents were busy elsewhere.)[85] Then Pearson and Anderson, "after extensive research" (of course) were "able to report that there is an international student conspiracy" with Columbia's Mark Rudd at the helm.[86]

---

80. *Washington Star*, 26 May 1968.

81. *Washington Post*, 16 June 1968.

82. Clipping, circa 21 June 1968, Series II, SS 2, Box 3, *Spiro Agnew Papers, University of Maryland-College Park*.

83. Henry Miller to Congressman Machen, 7 May 1968, Box 11, *Harvey Machen Papers*.

84. Mrs. Everett Pyle to Congressman Machen, 9 May 1968, Box 11.

85. *Washington Post*, 30 April 1968.

86. *Washington Post*, 14 June 1968.

District authorities kept tabs on Rudd's Students for a Democratic Society, monitoring their meeting at Georgetown University where they were planning a "children's march...aged 6 to 18" to Capitol Hill.[87] By July 1968, local intelligence was monitoring the SDS march in the capital provocatively honoring Che Guevara, Fidel Castro, and Simon Bolivar.[88] With more sobriety the news column of the *Wall Street Journal* scrutinized "campus militants" and the "turmoil" they were said to have unleashed.[89]

Libby Landsman of neighboring Prince George's County, soon to undergo a stunning demographic transformation converting it into a bastion of the Black working and middle classes, disparaged the "riots" as nothing but "bare acts of theft, arson and defiance...." The remedy? "We need more men like Governor Agnew," to "ask Congress to declare martial law" or suspending civil liberties "for at least six months."[90]

E.B. Hayden, Jr. of nearby Lanham, Maryland also sought "martial law," i.e., "shoot the legs out from under the looters and rioters on sight...[and] don't force the citizens to arm themselves for protection."[91] D.F. Ward, also of hyperbolic Lanham, demanded "martial law" and wondered "why were not the rioters, looters and burners shot," an appropriate memorial to that "demagogue...Dr. King..." along the lines of Hitler and Father Charles Coughlin, a true demagogue of the past. "Anarchy prevails," he implored and "why must a share of my tax dollars be spent to support Howard University," where "the American flag no longer flies...." He was "moved to tears" as he confessed to voting for President Johnson—but never again.[92] More soberly, F.E. Wood of College Park argued that the "ghettos" in the District were the "direct result of Negroes being unable to find adequate housing outside the District,"[93] but his was not a voice consulted often.

Even the *Post* days before the King murder, headlined, "Slum Landlords buy up Shaw Houses," driving up rents and forcing Blacks elsewhere.[94]

---

87. Report, 29 June 1968, Box 1, RG 23, *Office of Emergency Preparedness Records*.
88. Report, 25 July 1968, Box 7, RG 23, *Office of Emergency Preparedness Records*.
89. *Wall Street Journal*, 14 February 1968.
90. Libby Landsman to Congressman Machen, 3 May 1968, Box 1, ACC. No. 2014-3.
91. E.B. Hayden, Jr. to Congressman Machen, 9 April 1968, Box 11, *Harvey Machen Papers*.
92. D.F. Ward to Congressman Machen, 7 April 1968, Box 11.
93. F.E. Wood to Congressman Machen, 9 April 1968, Box 11.
94. *Washington Post*, 24 March 1968.

Congressman Harvey Machen with close links to College Park set an example for Agnew to follow. Days before 4 April 1968, he was in exhortatory mode: "Major crime" in the District is "at an all time high and rising steadily"; intriguingly, he demanded gun control on the premise that Blacks had too many weapons, a view that was to shift dramatically in coming decades.[95]

By November 1968 Richard M. Nixon was swept into the White House on a platform that pressed demagogically the matter of crime with his vice presidential nominee—Spiro T. Agnew—supposedly providing expert testimony as to how this manifested at the seat of power. Clifford Barrow of Brentwood, Maryland argued that the combined vote for the GOP ticket and segregationist George Wallace in Prince George's County—"where I live"—prevailed in a land-slide. The "great majority of the federal workers in the District," he said, "live in nearby Maryland and Virginia largely because of the 1954 school decision" mandating school desegregation and generat-ing a severe counter-reaction: flight and fight. He was contemptuous of "Mayor' Washington," a title Barrow held with tongs as if it were poisonous: "by reason of his genetic inheritance [he] is unable to see beyond his own race" and, thus, "wants to disarm the police" and that "will ultimately result in the complete banishment of white people" and "require the use of large numbers of federal troops... to enable white people safely to continue to work in the District..." As he saw things, the affluent "Hechinger" family, real estate bar-ons, were primary victims of the April revolt, i.e., "principally his Jewish brethren who have suffered most at the hands of the crimi-nal elements...." Scorned were Fauntroy and his comrade Channing Phillips and the allied Black United Front, since their statements on police killings should have been "cause for their prosecution and incarceration." Hailed were politicos like Maryland's Larry Hogan and Virginia's Joel Broyhill. [96]

Across the border on the hilltop a sampling of votes revealed that the victorious Nixon-Agnew ticket received 1 percent of the support while their main opponent, Hubert H. Humphrey got 78 percent[97]—presumably the remainder went to third party candi-dates, e.g., Peace & Freedom Party nominee and Black Panther Party leader, Eldridge Cleaver—then being touted as the master of revolt.

---

95. Machen Report, 17 March 1968, Box 1, ACC. No. 2014-3, *Records of the History of the University of Maryland, University of Maryland-College Park.*
96. Clifford Barrow to President-Elect Richard M. Nixon, 21 November 1968, Box 1, *History of the University of Maryland, ACC. No. 2014-3.*
97. *The Hilltop,* 1 November 1968.

Chapter 22

Aftermath of Revolt, 1968-1971

Joseph Hicks of Beltsville, Maryland epitomized a gathering sentiment locally and nationally in the aftermath of April 1968. It "sickens me," he expectorated, "to think that one dollar of my tax money might be spent to support Howard University and to help propagate the blatant racism displayed by most of the spectators and Howard players during the playing of our national anthem...." Attached to his missive to Congressman Machen was a *Post* article detailing students at a football game with rival, Fisk, raising clenched fists during the playing of the national anthem in order to back sprinters Tommy Smith and John Carlos who during the Mexico Olympics protested similarly on a global stage the rancid oppression of African Americans.[1] On cue the House Un-American Activities Committee proposed "detention centers" for dissidents, an announcement highlighted on campus.[2]

"Resurrection City," too, was not long in being as its very presence encapsulated for many suburbanites the trauma they thought they had experienced in April 1968; this legacy of Dr. King's memory had a brief lifespan of six weeks and a peak population of 2,000 as it was muddied by incessant rains and persistent defamation.[3] This encampment was bound to attract attention in light of the preceding tumult. Premier District cop, Patrick Murphy, expressed the consensus when he announced that the "'entire world will be focused on Washington during the coming weeks.'"[4]

Yet during that time, it attracted considerable publicity to the cause of uplifting the poverty-stricken and attracting celebrities, e.g.,

---

1. Joseph Hicks to Congressman Machen, 29 October 1968, Box 11, *Harvey Machen Papers*. See also *Washington Post*, 29 October 1968.
2. *The Hilltop*, 10 May 1968.
3. Ben Gilbert, et.al., *Ten Blocks from the White House*, 197.
4. *Washington Post*, 29 April 1968.

the singer-actor, Eartha Kitt, who gave a guided tour there.[5] Still, the often lurid headlines about events there may have discouraged city-wide participation. By July an "aide" was "beaten in [a] sex rebuff... the men demanded homosexual relations. When he refused...they beat him over the head with a chair...."[6] (Assuming the accuracy of the reportage, this troubling incident was an aspect of a larger tableau. There was a Black gay bar, Nob Hill, but the Mattachine Society of Washington was largely monochromatically "white" though the District was challenging San Francisco as the "Gay Capital" of the nation[7]—contrastingly, the H.U. campus organ was not above using the offensive term "fags.")[8]

But then, almost gleefully, intelligence began to issue one more doomsaying report after another: "tenseness...appears to be increasing" at the encampment; "a firebomb was thrown onto a platform which was built for the solidarity march"; thus, "police are arming themselves with teargas."[9] The next day circulating throughout the political elite was the "rumor" of a "plan to firebomb any U.S. govt. bldg. [sic]" in the vicinity of Resurrection City.[10] In a sense this was payback in that weeks earlier there were threats to bomb police headquarters.[11]

The report of the National Capital Planning Committee exposed why the word trauma was tossed around so casually after the uproar of April 1968: 645 buildings were damaged with 10 percent substantially damaged with commercial buildings being especially hit hard. Seventh Street N.W., 14th Street N.W. and H Street N.E. bore the brunt of the damage.[12] The City Council—after detailing a $3 million tax loss, absorbable in retrospect—launched a counter-offensive finding that the "Black Separatist" voices were "most startling" in April, accompanied—shockingly—by the "suspicion of white motives...." Even in rebuilding, some of these same voices

---

5. Report, 19 June 1968, Box 5, RG 23, *Office of Emergency Preparedness Records*.

6. *Washington Post*, 9 July 1968.

7. David K. Johnson, *The Lavender Scare*, 193. See also James Kirchik, *Secret City*, 446: Racist bias in gay clubs was part of the District milieu.

8. *The Hilltop*, 10 April 1970.

9. Report, 20 June 1968, Box 5, RG 23, *Office of Emergency Preparedness Records*.

10. Report, 21 June 1968, Box 5, RG 23.

11. *Washington Daily News*, 11 April 1968.

12. "Civil Disturbances in Washington, D.C.," 4-8 April 1968, "Riots-Pamphlets," *Special Collections of Washington, D.C. Public Library*.

insisted that this be done under Black aegis and control. "Under severe attack were white suburban owners of inner city businesses," i.e., Congressman Machen's infuriated constituents. If U.S. foreign aid mandated indigenous ownership, why not extend this domestically—underlining the point that increasingly there were those who saw African Americans as an internal colony. Thus, of the 388 "Class A" liquor licenses, "only a handful" were held by Negroes.[13]

On the ideological front, another counter-offensive ensued, as arriving at the hilltop campus to lecture was Negro conservative, Thomas Sowell, publicized in a full page advertisement with the caption that there would be held a "summer intensive training program in Economic Theory"—meaning capitalism—"supported by the Rockefeller Foundation."[14]

Many students were in no mood to compromise with conservatives, however. By 26 April 1968 a campus reporter was watching as "an occupation army marched and rode through the streets of Washington, D.C. and guarded shops and street corners...." Despite damage to outlying areas and nationally, "the nation's capital was the city hardest hit by looting, fires and armed force...." The District's approximate 2,000 cops were bolstered by about 12,000 armed forces including "regular Army troops, D.C. National Guard, Marines and Paratroopers" and the usual array of auxiliary forces, e.g., forces guarding Capitol Hill.[15] Like self-styled revolutionaries anywhere, those on the hilltop sought to export their example, dispatching cadre to Columbia University as that Harlem facing campus encountered bumpiness. Of course, columns of the paper were peppered by words of wisdom from Mao Zedong.[16] Local hero, Stokely Carmichael, was accorded front page coverage in *The Hilltop* as he embraced yet another icon of Black Power: boxer, Muhammad Ali. As militants of all sorts walked up the steep hill leading to the campus in search of allies and resources, metaphorically heading in the opposite direction was Frank Snowden, leaving administration for greener research pastures.[17]

In a possibly related item campus activist Steve Able was indicted in May 1968 for arson, i.e., tossing firebombs at the homes of

---

13. "Report of City Council...Public Hearings on the Rebuilding and Recovery of Washington, D.C...from the Civil Disturbances of April 1968," "Riots-Pamphlets," *Special Collections of Washington, D.C. Public Library.*
14. *The Hilltop*, 17 May 1968.
15. *The Hilltop*, 26 April 1968.
16. *The Hilltop*, 3 May 1968.
17. *The Hilltop*, 10 May 1968.

Snowden and Nabrit—though the accused said that he was "framed by [Philip] Reese—closest companion and trusted friend."[18] This controversy was preceded by another when Nabrit spoke to 700 on campus and 125 students walked out—accompanied by faculty, including Nathan Hare—leaving in their wake rancorous denunciations of "Uncle Toms"[19]

When cadre was dispatched northward to Morningside Heights in Manhattan, it was under the aegis of "Ujaama," a hilltop grouping that ran candidates for student government. Their name, an invocation of the East Central African lingua franca that was Swahili and meaning unity and family—and allied definitions—was resonant of the rising consciousness of the continental homeland that was an aspect of the mounting Black Power ideology. Lewis Myers, who went on to become a stalwart attorney with the National Conference of Black Lawyers and on behalf of the Nation of Islam, was elected Student Council president on the Ujaama ticket.[20] Gaining valuable political experience, it was later asserted that his victory and that of his comrades was akin to a "bloodless coup."[21]

An aghast *Post* reporter then told his readers that twenty Howard students "forced their way past two policemen into a meeting of University trustees," dropping a "written statement" before the assembled, "outlining their criteria for a new president," as "shoving and shouting" reigned: "they have suggested the appointment of Kwame Nkrumah, deposed president of Ghana" as their preferred choice.[22]

Per usual, local spies monitored carefully events on campus including collecting student propaganda; for example one leaflet read, "Support!!! Student Strike...Saturday night Howard University male and female students were tear-gassed by racist D.C. police in front of...campus...." Yet the students were sufficiently oriented to underline an important factor: "...our brothers and sisters from Federal City College," recently inaugurated, "support us...."[23] There were hundreds at this rally including Communist presidential candidate, Charlene Mitchell. However, Charles Cassell of the Black United Front set the tone—according to a wary gumshoe—as he "told the students to get guns to defend themselves against the

18. *The Hilltop*, 24 May 1968.

19. *Washington Star*, 20 September 1967.

20. *The Hilltop*, 17 May 1968. *The Hilltop*, 24 May 1968.

21. *The Hilltop*, 4 October 1968.

22. *Washington Post*, 23 October 1968.

23. Report, 4 November 1968, Box 2, RG 23, *Office of Emergency Preparedness Records re:...Demonstrations, Civil Disturbances and Special Events.*

police. He said that the Black United Front would be holding rallies to raise money to buy guns" and then "at a closed meeting…[he] advocated that Negroes use guns to change the present social and economic systems…."[24]

Doubtlessly the organizers garnered worthy learning from sampling the ample wares at Drum and Spear Bookstore where Malcolm X's autobiography was a bestseller.[25] With a touch of yeast, founder Charlie Cobb boasted of the 10,000 volumes resting on shelves, perhaps overly stimulated by the electric presence there in the flesh of the two Howard alumni, Carmichael, and the Poet Laureate of Black Power, Le Roi Jones/Amiri Baraka.[26]

It was well for Ujaama to export their example since signals from other campuses were disturbing, meaning they might need external support too: thus, Cheyney State in Pennsylvania, another Historically Black College/University, purged nine members of the Black Student League, an analogue to Ujaama.[27] In return an advertisement touting "Official Harvard Strike Shirt" was placed in the organ of Howard students.[28]

It was at a Ujaama rally in October 1968 that Irving Ray of Ujaama announced portentously, "'You have a Cold War between Black people and white people'" afoot. What prompted this analysis was the slaying of Elijah Bennett, 22, of 752 Gresham Place N.W. by a motorcycle cop, David Roberts, after the deceased had jaywalked. This father of four was married and his spouse gave birth to their fifth child after he expired. The lesson, said Ray, was "'when you get off this campus, you are just another [n-word].'"[29] According to journalist, C. Sumner Stone, in 1967 "'four Blacks were killed by white cops. So [far] this year, seven more'" fell victim at their hands,[30] a perilous trend. Also perilous for the city itself was another remarked upon incident; on 31 July 1967 a fire at 7th Street N.W. blazed as hundreds gathered before being rousted.[31]

The Bennett slaying outraged the Black United Front and inflamed the press accounts that recounted their reaction. "Carmichael

---

24. Report, 4 November 1968, Box 2, RG 23.
25. *The Hilltop*, 20 September 1968.
26. Clipping, 31 May 1968, Box 3, RG 23, *Office of Emergency Preparedness Records*.
27. *The Hilltop*, 6 December 1968.
28. *The Hilltop*, 3 October 1969.
29. *The Hilltop*, 11 October 1968.
30. *The Hilltop*, 25 October 1968.
31. J. Samuel Walker, *'Most of 14th Street is Gone,'* 31.

harangued a street rally of 200 Negroes," according to the *Star* in launching what had become a customary denunciation of this latest bete noire. He was speaking on 14th Street between V and W, then a Black fortification but soon to be gentrified—predictably. His quoted words were hardly soothing: "'We just organize and kill some white cops...more honorable to kill a honky cop than a Vietnamese [while] above ground we push for control. Underground, we do what he have to do....'"[32] Carmichael's presence was an insignia of his frayed relations with SNCC and his leapfrog to the embattled BUF.[33] An exasperated Front was cited for the proposition that "slaying of police...[is] justifiable...." [34]

This tinderbox was exposed when Mayor Washington was taunted and jeered by a Black crowd, rebuked as the "colonial governor." Appearing Zelig-like at the police precinct at 1620 V Street N.W. was Carmichael who drove the assembled to a fever pitch when the former philosophy major at Howard—and master of syllogism—announced, "'There is no right or wrong about killing. If any of these young Black brothers were sent to Vietnam, he would be given a medal for killing Vietnamese. If a Black brother kills a honky cop, the Black community should give him a medal,'"—as the crowd cheered.[35]

Just before this flaming incident the woman who called herself "Mrs. Herbert Mitchell" of Landover Hill, Maryland laid down the law: Carmichael "should be arrested for sedition, treason and for advocating anarchy."[36] Since 90 percent of those arrested in April were Black men, he would have been in familiar company.[37]

Creatively, the Front studied the concept of a "Self Defense Unit" which would supplant numerous functions of the police in Black neighborhoods.[38] Correspondingly, at Howard it was proposed that students and staff alike be trained in the art of self-defense, use of weaponry and demolition and that the school develop what was called "a Revolutionary Guerilla Warfare Program."[39]

---

32. *Washington Star*, 13 October 1968.
33. *Washington Post*, 24 July 1968.
34. *Washington Post*, 6 July 1968.
35. *Washington Post*, 13 October 1968. See also *Washington Star*,13 October 1968.
36. "Mrs. Herbert Mitchell" to Congressman Machen, 26 August 1968, Box 11, *Harvey Machen Papers*.
37. J. Samuel Walker, *Most of 14th Street is Gone'*, 103.
38. *Washington Post*, 15 August 1968.
39. *The Hilltop*, 22 November 1969.

By July 1968 the *Post* found the "situation" in the District was "explosive…lid could blow off at any time…."[40] As so often happens, at one juncture it seemed the "lid" would "blow" internally—at least that's what the *Star* suggested when their reporter ambled into Canaan Baptist Church at 1607 Newton N.W. where first tense Euro-Americans were unceremoniously ejected, then Carmichael was blasted as a "hypocrite" for unclear reasons; then a straggling Euro-American woman was "shoved and struck several times by two Negro women" revealing the inter-racial friction within this gender. Then the displeased Carmichael exclaimed "'You want [to] jump in my chest…brother?'" This was more a veiled threat than a request and, thus, he, his newlywed—Miriam Makeba—and the challenged "brother" stepped outside where the latter hurriedly explained he would rather spar with the older C. Sumner Stone or the similarly physically unimposing, Sterling Tucker.[41]

This confrontation was minor compared to a volley of gunfire directed at the SNCC office—2208 14th Street N.W.[42] —the third attack in as many days. The *Post* saw this as a power struggle between nascent Panthers versus the so-called "Black Man's Army of Liberation" versus Marion Barry and his legions.[43]

Whatever the case, the *Star* stumbled onto the truth when it announced in November 1968 that Washington "has become a Black Power capital" with both Carmichael and his comrade, H. Rap Brown, using the city as a base for forays nationally.[44] Although the charter of the Central Intelligence Agency ostensibly barred domestic surveillance, local intelligence reported on Election Day 1968—perhaps understandably from their viewpoint—that the CIA "ops center called for situation report."[45] Similarly, Attorney General Ramsey Clark formed a so-called "Interdivisional Information Unit" to monitor recalcitrant Negroes particularly, not easy since then the FBI had 40 Negro agents out of a total of 6,300.[46]

Moreover, as the youthful reporter, Carl Bernstein, reported in the *Post*, "the city's 2,700 man police force" would be supplemented by "the Pentagon and the Justice Department"; the District building, "would be the command centers for restoring order" in case there

---

40. *Washington Post*, 23 July 1968.
41. *Washington Star*, 2 August 1968.
42. *Washington Star*, 9 September 1968.
43. *Washington Post*, 9 September 1968.
44. *Washington Star*, 3 November 1968.
45. Report, 5 November 1968, Box 9, RG 23.
46. J. Samuel Walker, *'Most of 14th Street is Gone,'* 41.

was a "serious eruption of violence." Thus, protesters were confronting the might of the entire state—and why not the intelligence arm too? The Guard in the District was deemed to be too small—an estimated 2,000—which contributed to a situation that distinguished Washington further from its urban peers.[47]

Quite telling was the maneuverings of Cyrus Vance, who became Secretary of State in 1977, but in early April in the midst of turmoil in the District, left his post as an advisor to Mayor Washington and began negotiating peace in Vietnam—as if the former was training for the latter.[48]

Bernstein's report was in early March, four weeks later the press reported that even before the King assassination and concomitant conflagration, the District was receiving intelligence reports from the FBI and related agencies.[49] The recruiting of federal muscle was part of the all-hands-on-deck approach to securing the capital with suburban communities dispatching 70 pieces of firefighting equipment.[50]

More agencies and governments involved in detention likely increased the hassles. A paper maze ensued whereby some detainees were "lost" in a Kafkaesque roundabout. Some cops had to sign their names 27 times in processing a single arrest with excessive red tape being much too mild a descriptor. There was a sudden surge of arrests from 10 p.m. on 4 April to midnight on 10 April, but the reverberations extended over months.[51] Yet, "Chocolate City" demonstrated why some thought "Neapolitan" would be a more acceptable flavor in that by July 1968 the U.S. Attorney's office had failed to convict anyone on a felony charge emerging from the April unrest,[52] as juries were balking. Not unrelated is the news that just before April foreclosures were ensnaring what the *Star* termed as those who were "relatively poor and ignorant" or those more likely to be moved to take to the streets in frustration[53] or as a juror look sympathetically at the accused.

Judge Harold Greene thought he was the one who suffered, after presiding over what he considered "two separate civil disorders,"

---

47. *Washington Post*, 2 March 1968: alert readers may have noticed the varying estimates of the size of the police force; it is likely that pre-April it was less than 3,000.

48. *Washington Daily News*, 11 April 1968.

49. *Washington Star*, 4 April 1968.

50. *Washington Post*, 12 April 1968.

51. *Washington Star*, 18 May 1968.

52. *Washington Daily News*, 24 July 1968.

53. *Washington Star*, 2 February 1968.

April and June, with the volatility brought by Resurrection City. "Some of the looting was visible from the very windows of the courthouse," he said reflectively, while the "stench" and "smoke" assaulted the olfactory senses—and, perhaps, the judgment of jurists—as the air in "the courthouse, the courtrooms and the judges' chambers" was subject to an alien invasion.[54]

It was also on election day that students protested outside the White House because of a dearth of "meaningful choice" in the presidential election. Still, there was heavy turnout locally with estimates ranging to 90 percent of the electorate voting and befitting "Chocolate City," registered Democrats outnumbered Republicans by five-to-one and Independents by ten-to-one; according to United Press International, these were the "first elections for local officials since 1874," no balm to the right-wing which realized that home rule was creating—as expected—a left-leaning fortress.[55]

Then at an election day rally at George Washington University, blows were exchanged between Barry's former comrade, Rufus Mayfield, and a heckler.[56] A few weeks later the man who also answered to the nickname "Catfish," became the 501st and perhaps final person indicted as a result of the April 1968 revolt.[57]

The era seemed to demand ever more inflammatory rhetoric, often unmoored to a sober analysis of the actual balance of forces, which brought more cameras—and more negative attention from the authorities. Thus before his exchange with the heckler, Mayfield warned of an impending "'bloodbath'" in that the "'Black Revolution is in a new phase...there will be a bloodbath in this city with the red blood of the police and black warriors if something isn't done...black brothers out here have the stuff (weapons) and they're ready....'" He taunted—accurately—police reminding all of the time when they "'ran up to Congress and said 'I don't want to ride with no nigger' when integrated squad cars were first proposed," leaving hanging the implication that Black officers remained stung by this slight and could be adjudged to be unreliable politically.[58]

Yet the press observed that the "majority of businessmen" in the District and thereabouts "feel the urban riots were organized by outside

---

54. Judge Harold Greene, "D.C. Bar Journal," August-September 1968, "Riots-Pamphlets," *Special Collections of Washington, D.C. Public Library.*
55. *United Press International,* 5 November 1968, Box 9, RG 23.
56. *Washington Post,* 5 November 1968.
57. *Washington Post,* 10 December 1968.
58. *Washington Daily News,* 10 August 1968.

forces,"[59] mandating the slamming down of the iron fist, meaning heightened incarceration—leaving a number of activists wholly unprepared, as their rhetorical volleys outstripped their actual strength.

One of the weaknesses of this emerging Black Power movement was their seeming inability to conduct an analysis that took into account the actual white supremacist history often renounced in general terms but often accompanied by a major ideological concession: obeisance to founding myths about the hyped U.S. Constitution and/or ignoring how problematic the origins of the republic was for Africans. This double-barreled concession ill-prepared this movement to conduct an analysis that took into account global forces—especially the role of Moscow, which these forces either ignored or castigated.[60]

There was observance of the complex matter of desegregation—"Blacks lose jobs as schools integrate" was a telling headline at Howard[61]—but this insight could not compensate for overall ideological weakness.

Even at College Park, site of Maryland's flagship university, sharp growing pains were the result when Black students were admitted in the midst of cyclonic unrest. By October 1968 the controversy centered on four coeds rejected as participants in the Home Economics Department; they were told by Professor Lillian C. Butler that since Negroes were different in biological makeup, their participation in a social science experiment would introduce a statistical variable in a nutritional study that could not be subject to a control group.[62] Emulating Howard, 150 Black students held a two hour rally.[63]

Fisticuffs in the streets were becoming an accepted part of the landscape, a thinly disguised form of class struggle. In mid-October 1968 for the third time in as many days, teenagers—and sub-teens—blocked traffic, broke a number of store windows, soliciting police teargas, along the H Street corridor; what sparked their mini-revolt was—again—a rumor, this one being the slaying of singer, James Brown, by a "white sniper."[64] "Soul Brother Number 1" had jetted

---

59. *Washington Star*, 1 May 1968.
60. See e.g., Gerald Horne, *The Counter-Revolution of 1776: Slave Resistance and the Origins of the United States of America*, New York: New York University, 2014.
61. *The Hilltop*, 31 October 1969.
62. Black Student Union to "Dear Dr. Martin," 14 October 1968, Box 1, RG 17, Series-Student Organizations, *Student Affairs Records, University of Maryland-College Park*.
63. *Washington Post*, 23 October 1968.
64. *Washington Post*, 16 October 1968.

into town from Boston in April where he had been seeking to douse yet another brushfire.[65]

Days earlier a number of fires were set at George Washington University within an eight hour period; blame was affixed to a group calling itself "Red and Black," calling for "revolutionary action" with these intellectual radicals quoting both the novelist, Stendahl, and—again—Mao Zedong.[66] Simultaneously, a fire blazed at Selective Service headquarters at 1724 F Street, N.W., as a Molotov cocktail was casually tossed by an arsonist.[67]

By early November 1968 intelligence detailed what was becoming normative: "mid-day disorder on [14th] Street...sparked by the wounding of two women by a policeman"; symptomatically, "Negro youths" were "hurling rocks and bottles at passing automobiles. The principal targets were any white people who ventured by car...."[68] The *Star* noticed a trend exemplified by this stormy November; whereas in April the fury often targeted stores and buildings but gradually the targets became "white people," i.e., "Negroes sought out and inflicted punishment on whites"; on one day just before the pivotal 1968 election, "nearly 20 cars and some trucks" carrying Euro-Americans were attacked. "For more than an hour, white persons were assaulted"; even "several light skinned Negro motorists had their windows broken before somebody shouted 'He's a brother'"! The spark was yet another rumor, this one asserting yet another Black youth was shot by cops, leading to mimicking of James Brown's anthem: "'I'm Black and I'm proud.'"[69] Such outbursts caused Councilman Joseph Yeldell to make his own ebullition, alleging that someone must be "'programming'" youth to revolt.[70]

The Black United Front facilitated a burst of affirmative action in hiring spies and agents when they demanded, said U.S. intelligence, that "white persons and members of the press be put out of the meeting" they were holding.[71] That was in July. By October the man identified as "security specialist Lacey of Howard" was said to have "reported" on both Carmichael and Black Panther leader, Eldridge Cleaver, and was slated to address same at yet another overflow

---

65. *Washington Daily News*, 11 April 1968.

66. *Washington Post*, 4 October 1968.

67. Report, 3 October 1968, Box 8, RG 23.

68. Daily Intelligence Summary, 4 November 1968, Box 8, RG 23: Note the reports from the Office of Civil Defense within these records.

69. *Washington Star*, 3 November 1968.

70. *Washington Daily News*, 17 October 1968.

71. Daily Intelligence Summary, 25 July 1968, Box 7, RG 23.

crowd at Cramton Auditorium on the hilltop—the implication being that campus administration was cooperating with the authorities in surveillance.[72]

However, the case of Willie Ivery, dead at 25, might have halted a rush to the agent recruiting office. He was an undercover agent for the police but was killed by two fellow officers who mistook him for something else; he was shot through the head by one of six bullets fired because he failed to obey the order to drop his pistol. Consistent with his job, he was unshaven and wearing old clothes; by mid-November 1968 there had been 174 homicides and 127 by firearms and Ivery was collateral damage in this bloody process.[73]

An alarmed "Police Wives Association" instructed the mayor to halt "'socializing between top officials of his administration and leaders of the Black United Front....'" They also claimed that the centrists— NAACP, Urban League—were too conciliatory toward BUF too, especially the latter's critique of gun control legislation—i.e., a "'white racist way of taking guns for self-defense from Black people....'"[74]

Responsively, the "Daily Intelligence Summary" prepared for regional authorities noted that in late May 1968 "200 residents of uneasy Salisbury, Maryland," not far distant from Cambridge, wracked with instability, "organized march with placards calling for law and order"—the dominant buzzwords along with "white backlash,"[75] all designed to obfuscate the acceleration of the Black Scare.

Promptly, Hobson urged Blacks to arm and practiced what he preached by buying a relative popgun, a 22. Caliber rifle and two boxes of ammunition in protest of a recently ratified District gun control law. Hobson was irate since this bill "'poses restrictions on city residents while whites in the suburbs are arming themselves and using church basements as classrooms on the use of guns,'" leaving African Americans as sitting ducks cooped in the city,[76] with the Front agreeing with this pungent analysis.[77]

On campus diverse ideological currents continued flowing. Max Stanford outlined the concept of a separate Black nation in North

72. Report, 18 October 1968, Box 8, RG 23.

73. *Washington Post*, 16 November 1968.

74. *Washington Post*, 11 August 1968.

75. Daily Intelligence Summary, 25 May 1968, Box 5, RG 23, *Office of Emergency Preparedness Records*.

76. Clipping, 11 August 1968, Box 1, RG 23, *Offices of Emergency Preparedness Records re:...Demonstrations, Civil Disturbances and Special Events, 1965, 1968-1978, Washington, D.C. Municipal Archives*.

77. *Washington Post*, 10 August 1968.

America—amid tight security—on behalf of the Republic of New Africa. The Elijah Bennett killing gave impetus to a theme raised during Stanford's appearance: "The Blacks in Washington are colonized...."[78] The ideological smorgasbord that students could sample included Julius Hobson who confessed that he was a socialist, as he appeared on a platform with Communist Party presidential candidate, Charlene Mitchell, and historian, Lerone Bennett, who addressed a "small crowd."[79]

In sharpened contrast, alumnus and Black Power embodiment, Stokely Carmichael, addressed 1,900 on campus as he delivered the opening address of the "Towards a Black University Conference." "It was a night worth remembering," said a glowing commentator. Carmichael's sturdy presence was indicative of another trend that was transforming the campus. He had Trinidadian roots and by the time of his well-received appearance there had been a large increase of the Anglo-Caribbean or "West Indian" presence on campus; suggestively, the Caribbean Student Association was formed in December 1945 after a visit to the hilltop by Norman Manley of Jamaica and their membership had ballooned since with estimable ideological impact in that as migrants from sovereign states they had diplomatic weight to convey that could benefit the overall Black population.[80]

Continuing to bring political savvy to campus was the region that produced Walter Rodney, among other luminaries. Howard's star soccer team was started—again—by Jamaican students in 1947, just one more indicator of their positive presence. The hilltop squad had begun in 1929, but because of Jim Crow, the only opponents who would deign to play them were teams from various embassies—as opposed to local universities.[81]

Once again, Howard tended to receive succor from "foreigners" when supposed compatriots turned their collective back. But as a sign of changing times, by 1969 the soccer team had players from 16 different nations, an outgrowth of the school continuing to have one of the nation's largest foreign enrollments; symptomatically, at one critical game, a steel band played, often associated with Trinidad and Tobago.[82]

---

78. *The Hilltop*, 18 October 1968.
79. *The Hilltop*, 8 November 1968.
80. *The Hilltop*, 15 November 1968. According to local intelligence, the venue where Carmichael spoke—Cramton—had a capacity of 1,508: Report, 18 October 1968, Box 8, RG 23, *Office of Emergency Preparedness Records*.
81. *The Hilltop*, 7 November 1969.
82. *The Hilltop*, 24 and 31 October 1969.

Ewart Brown technically was not from the Caribbean. But this future Bermudian leader was often grouped with them and as president of the student assembly his lofty post showed mass support on campus. It was he, along with future film impresario, Anthony Gittens, who addressed the ongoing 1968 crisis on the hilltop. They were utterly serious about what it meant to "'begin to move towards becoming a black university,'" meaning a revamping of culture and curriculum. In that context, Nabrit and Dean Snowden had to go and students fired for "'political activism'" had to be reinstated. Yes, they "disrupted" Charter Day, a solemn occasion ordinarily, but desperate times required desperate tactics.[83]

This overall Black population needed all the external aid that could be mustered. For as Carmichael was in the process of addressing adoring fans, President-elect Nixon was accepting kudos for backing Walter Washington for yet another term as the District's mayor; he was also supported by "leading business and civic people," according to Carl Shipley, Republican National Committeeman for the city. Like others, he was "fearful of the consequences of any change at this time," given the uproars of recent months. Moreover, "our people," speaking of revolting capital, "are absolutely demanding that law and order be reinstated at once" and, given the racial dynamics, he did "not think that a white public safety officer can contain this town in the present atmosphere"—not to mention a "white" mayor,[84] the presumed preferred option.

Daniel Patrick Moynihan, a Nixon comrade, who was to soar to the U.S. Senate based in no small measure on pummeling Africans of whatever stripe, told the president that the "amount of crime in the District is genuinely alarming," with the accent on a "certain amount of arson and looting" which was continuing—as of early 1969—"on a sporadic basis."[85] The outgoing Johnson regime paved the path by focusing heavily on crime in the District.[86]

Not to be left behind, Senator Barry Goldwater of Arizona, failed GOP nominee for the White House in 1964, took careful note of a

---

83. Ewart Brown, "What Happened at Howard University: The Chronology of a Crisis," 8 May 1968, *University of Virginia-Charlottesville*.

84. Carl Shipley to President-elect Nixon, 14 December 1968, Box 3, *White House Central Files, Subject Files, Richard M. Nixon Presidential Library, Yorba Linda, California*.

85. Daniel Patrick Moynihan to President-elect Nixon, 9 January 1969, Box 3, *White House Central Files*.

86. See Material on Crime in the District, Box 117, *Office Files of Charles Horsky, Johnson Presidential Library*.

congressional staff study which claimed that "nowhere in the nation is the crime rate more drug related than it is in Washington, D.C.,… [a] center for narcotics traffic" with this odious commerce "no longer exclusive to the ghetto," as it was "moving into the white community," notably the "so-called hippie community" abutting "Du Pont Circle and Georgetown…." Plus, "after the 1968 riots Washington was flooded with stolen goods, pushing the price for hot [sic] merchandise way down" since, it was posited, addicts have to steal more to feed their habit.[87] Whatever the case, Senator Goldwater was behind the so-called "District of Columbia Comprehensive Drug Abuse and Narcotics Crime Control Act of 1969." Therein it was maintained that "drug abuse, illegal trafficking in controlled drugs and drug related crimes are rapidly increasing in the [District]" and then flowing into suburbia, Maryland and Virginia,[88] the redoubt of Congresspersons and military brass. As matters evolved, stifling drug trafficking became yet another rationale for imprisoning more Black folk, with the residual "benefit" of reducing protesters in the streets. Contemporaneously, William K. Scheirer, president of the Kalorama Citizens Association, neck-and-neck with Georgetown as the chicest neighborhood in the District, warned Senator Goldwater that the city was "becoming increasingly a welfare city," yet another rationale for accentuating a prison-industrial complex and heightening the Black Scare.[89]

But Kalorama and their ilk thought they had legitimate concerns, an issue punctuated in 1969 when the *Post* worriedly reported that "dozens of militant demonstrators roamed through Georgetown… stopping traffic, setting fires in curbside trash cans and skirmishing periodically with police…[these] mostly white militants in Georgetown could ultimately bring retributive punishment on poor blacks," they argued with unctuous insincerity.[90]

Hitting the ground running—like a paratrooper in Southeast Asia—Nixon shortly after taking office conferred with the conservative press and made it clear that the District would be spotlighted in a centerpiece of domestic policy—crimefighting. The *Washington Daily News*, he intoned, was "rendering a public service with its front

---

87. Staff Study on Drug Abuse in Washington, D.C. U.S. Senate, 91st Congress, 1st Session, 1969, Box 145, *Barry Goldwater Papers, Arizona State University-Tempe.*
88. Crime Bill, S3071, 27 October 1969, Box 145, *Barry Goldwater Papers.*
89. Statement by William K. Scheirer, 20 February 1969, Box 252, *Barry Goldwater Papers.*
90. *Washington Post*, 17 November 1969.

page highlighting of the D.C. crime problem...." Nixon, the gauleiter as chief executive, made it evident that he was "cracking the whip on the Justice Department and every other department of government" to make sure they responded in a way he deemed appropriate.[91] He may have had personal reasons for "cracking the whip." His spouse was departing a luncheon at Du Pont Circle in early May 1969 when a suspected thief wounded a District cop and killed a father of six children in a gun battle.[92]

As so often happened, Nixon was traversing ground prepared by his Democratic predecessor: as the dust was clearing post April 1968, it was President Johnson who sought to add 1,000 more cops to the local force, raising their numbers—by one account—to 4,100 and as the *Post* bragged, "giving Washington by far the largest number of policemen per citizen of any city in the nation...."[93] This troubling announcement came on the same day that Dr. King's successor—the Reverend Ralph Abernathy—and Chicano folk hero, Reies Tijerina, embraced at Resurrection City,[94] marking a landmark in Black-Brown relations and demonstrating Washington's special role of forging coalitions with national reach. In a remarkable metronome, Secretary of State Rusk promptly met with a Chicano delegation—this after they had demonstrated at the diplomatic entrance at Foggy Bottom—to discuss the continuing viability of the Treaty of Guadalupe Hidalgo, settling the 1848 denuding of Mexico, which supposedly guaranteed equality for the nationals of the vanquished and their descendants stuck on this side of the border.[95] Then the heroic Tijerina headed to Manhattan to confer with United Nations Secretary General U Thant. According to the U.S. intelligence, the purpose was "to discuss the group's land claims in the Southwest."[96]

Feeding off these protests, Iranian students sought to picket the White House; according to the "Daily Intelligence Summary," they were "protesting the renewed aid to Iran when we should be feeding our own poor people,"[97] illustrating the symbiosis between the domestic and the global. Joining the fray were Nigerian secessionists

---

91. President Nixon to Richard Hollander, 5 February 1969, Box 1, *White House Central Files, Subject Files.*
92. Report, 7 May 1969, Box 10, RG 23.
93. *Washington Post,* 28 May 1968.
94. *Washington Post,* 28 May 1968.
95. *Washington Post,* 8 June 1968.
96. Daily Intelligence Summary, 28 June 1968, Box 6, RG 23.
97. Daily Intelligence Summary, 12 June 1968, Box 5, RG 23, *Office of Emergency Preparedness Records.*

known as Biafrans, who amassed at the State Department and the British legation since both were deemed insufficiently supportive of their campaign.[98] Possibly related was the story about two Nigerian embassy cars that were set on fire—with gasoline—in the wee hours of the morning.[99]

In sum, a temblor began to vibrate wildly in Washington post April 1968 whose shockwaves were magnified by the presence of other causes and controversies in a relatively small space.

In tandem, the Supreme Court was besieged over Indigenous fishing rights as, said the *Post*, "five windows of the building were smashed with rocks...."[100] Then the authorities reported that a "large group of people marched across 17th Street throwing bottles...at the Park Police...."[101]

Post April 1968 there seemed to be a tsunami of revolt ascending. By July the military authorities reported a "rumor" about the Poor People's Movement marching militantly to Capitol Hill then Selective Service headquarters. (Routinely, these reports were distributed to "police," "intelligence," and "mayor" guaranteeing that often poorly sourced details would receive wider circulation, leading to unbalanced reaction.)[102]

Yet it was understandable why there would be bipartisan support for police expansion. By May 1968 so-called "riot phones" were installed in senatorial offices on Capitol Hill so that jittery legislators could more easily summon police if their offices were invaded—the domestic analogy to the "hotline" linking Moscow and Washington at times of crisis—or so it was explained.[103]

Senator Gordon Allott, a Colorado Republican, sensed the outlines of this dilemma. He was "extremely concerned about the potentially explosive situation with which we are confronted here in the Nation's Capital"; for "even though we are capable of communicating from Paris to Moscow with no problem these days, in an emergency in the United States...we can't communicate to a point 3 blocks away," an advantage for insurrectionists. Thus, during the Detroit revolt in 1967 there were "four different communications systems going on

---

98. Report, 1 August 1968, Box 7, RG 23.
99. Report, 25 September 1967, Box 8, RG 23.
100. *Washington Post*, 30 May 1968.
101. Report, 20 June 1968, Box 5, RG 23, *Office of Emergency Preparedness Records*.
102. Report, 10 July 1968, Box 5, RG 23, *Office of Emergency Preparedness Records*.
103. *Washington Post*, 22 May 1968.

at the same time"—federals, National Guard, state highway patrol, and city cops—with Washington even more overlaid with various militarized agencies than most cities these doughnut gorgers, Maxwell Smart wannabes, and would-be Rambos could hardly avoid stumbling over each other.[104]

* * *

Howard University continued to set the pace for student activists nationally but, likely, had more impact since they were sensitively close to the esophagus of the beast at the White House. By early 1969, law school students—tossing career concerns to the four winds—began to boycott because of what were called "'deplorable'" conditions in the building where they attended class.[105] The *Hilltop* did not help matters when its headline quoted student leader, Lewis Myers, as saying that he was threatening to "'meet violence with violence,'" when actually he said, "'violence begets violence'"[106]—although both iterations were expressive of a troubled era; unusually, after Myers objected to this organ's "'sheer sensationalism,'" their editorial apologized.[107] Medical students, perhaps even more career conscious, launched a protest because of objections to various actions of Dr. W. Montague Cobb, a District man through and through, alumnus of Dunbar High School and the Medical School at Howard. His ouster from his perch teaching anatomy was won by protesters[108] and the attempt to rehabilitate him by administrators ran aground.[109] The dominos continued to fall when Joseph Applegate was ousted as African Studies Director, as students yearned for a display in the classroom of what they were demonstrating in the streets.[110]

Ditto for law students: future Cabinet member and U.S. ambassador, Patricia Roberts Harris, resigned her deanship after a one month tenure.[111] She said it was due to a conflict with President Nabrit, then pivoted to defending in court Billy Austin, accused of killing two

---

104. *Congressional Record*, 16 May 1968, Box 5, RG 23, *Office of Emergency Preparedness Records*.
105. *The Hilltop*, 14 February 1969.
106. *The Hilltop*, 21 February 1969.
107. *The Hilltop*, 28 February 1969.
108. *The Hilltop*, 7 February and 21 February 1969.
109. *The Hilltop*, 26 September 1969.
110. *The Hilltop*, 24 October 1969.
111. *The Hilltop*, 28 February 1969.

FBI agents.[112] Ironically, it was at that juncture that former Attorney General, Ramsey Clark, joined the law school faculty.[113] The contagion spread when Fine Arts students joined the boycott wave.[114]

Then the Caribbean Students Association journeyed to the British legation to protest the invasion of tiny Anguilla, after London refused to invade secessionist Rhodesia in 1965. "All students are asked to meet on main campus...to be transported to the British Embassy" was the message.[115] Then as if Howard amounted to a Pan-African U.N., the leadership of the island came to campus to outline the nature of the protest.[116]

Acolytes of "Col. Hassan Jeru Ahmed," added to his portfolio, which had included the "Black Man's Army of Liberation" as he became both president and executive director of the "United Moorish Republic"; still, he claimed now to be fighting "dope" while advocating methadone, a step forward from some of his previous views.[117] By 1971 the questionable Colonel was conferring with kleptocratic representatives of both Zaire (Congo) and the kakistocracy that was the Shah's Iran.[118]

Congresswoman Shirley Chisholm of Brooklyn and Barbadian roots then arrived at the hilltop but what got students' passions racing was the appearance of Congressman Adam Clayton Powell—or so said the student organ; the tall, stemwinding orator "excites crowd with black rhetoric"; this was the takeaway—though "only" 540 appeared (about three times as many showed up for Carmichael in Cramton, where the pastor spoke). He vowed to "personally serve an injunction" against any college president who moved to halt federal scholarship aid to students "convicted of disruptive acts" on campus. The "enthusiastic audience" also appreciated his cry to "'Get out of Vietnam'" and attend to domestic matters. "The audience responded with a loud applause,"[119] justifiably. Later yet another member of the Congressional Black Caucus, a growing force on Capitol Hill—speaking of Louis Stokes of Cleveland—addressed hundreds of Howardites at a local park named for Malcolm X at a vigorous antiwar rally.[120]

---

112. *The Hilltop*, 9 July 1969.
113. *The Hilltop*, 10 October 1969.
114. *The Hilltop*, 7 March 1969.
115. *The Hilltop*, 21 March 1969.
116. *The Hilltop*, 25 April 1969.
117. *The Hilltop*, 10 October 1969. See also *The Hilltop*, 29 October 1971.
118. *The Hilltop*, 12 November 1971.
119. *The Hilltop*, 2 May 1969.
120. *The Hilltop*, 17 October 1969.

Then after a now repetitive article on purported "student apathy,"[121] the energized matriculants among them chose to "paralyze" the campus, placing barricades at the gates to campus, chairs mostly. Social Anthropology students led the seizure of six campus buildings, just as the School of Social Work entered its third week of boycott.[122] A campus editorialist was furious about the reaction to this activism. These "whitewashed house niggers (known to some as faculty and administrators are sitting atop a powder keg—and the fuse has already been lit...." What stirred their anger was "last week's arrest and incarceration of 21 Howardites...follow[ing] the law 'n' order dictates of their 'massa' in the Big House" at 1600 Pennsylvania Avenue.[123] (Perhaps because Howardites were converting the entrance to the White House into a new headquarters, the Department of Interior issued restrictions for the sidewalk fronting this edifice with no permits granted to groups numbering more than 100.)[124] After to and fro in the courts, Supreme Court Chief Justice Earl Warren, beleaguered himself, reinstated the curbs on picketing the White House after the Department of Justice carped angrily about the "'ravages of a huge mob.'"[125]

By July President Nabrit was summoned to Capitol Hill to explain what was happening on campus, with the threat of budget cuts ever present.[126]

Detained students remained on tenterhooks throughout the summer until September when Judge Gerhard Gesell ruled in favor of 15 hilltoppers who had been arrested and two others pled guilty—and received two weeks behind bars.[127]

At that juncture, it seemed that the District and the nation it ostensibly led were sitting atop dynamite about to ignite. But, alas, Black Power muscle flexing in "Chocolate City" was one thing but certain activists did not seem to realize that their longevity and string of victories would have had more of a chance to continue if they there had been more ideological rigor.

---

121. *The Hilltop*, 2 May 1969.
122. *The Hilltop*, 9 May 1969.
123. *The Hilltop*, 16 May 1969.
124. Lawrence Speiser to David Silvergleid, President-National Postal Union, 8 July 1968, Box 131, *Joseph Rauh Papers*.
125. *Washington Star*, 3 May 1969.
126. *The Hilltop*, 9 July 1969.
127. *The Hilltop*, 19 September 1969.

Chapter 23

The Struggle Continues, 1968-1971

By 1969 the transition away from the ideological likes of Alphaeus Hunton and Doxey Wilkerson and their comrades and toward "Black Power," represented by Howard's Carmichael, was virtually completed. To be sure, this latter movement had many virtues, including militancy, especially in opposing the Vietnam war and confronting domestic antagonists. However, the 1968 election of Nixon—and his Marylander vice president, Agnew—along with the startling popularity north and south of the Mason-Dixon line of Alabama's pro-Jim Crow governor, was a sign of the actual balance of forces. Moreover, even at Howard, going back to the days of Pentagon contractors, intelligence agencies recruiting on campus, support for ROTC, the subsequent trajectory of students like Togo West (becoming a prime U.S. military official), etc., all were evidentiary of the point that not only did Black Power militancy face a retrograde Euro-American majority across class lines but hardly had nailed down unanimous support among African Americans (across class lines). Internationally, this movement was—at most—agnostic toward the forces headed by Moscow during the Cold War though more forthcoming to socialism's allies, e.g., Cuba. Similarly, although they were favorable toward Tanzania, they were not necessarily positive toward the ultimately triumphant forces in Angola and, importantly, South Africa.[1]

Because of an inadequate understanding of history[2] which—to be fair—was hardly unique and encompassed over-confident Communist forces too, there was little recognition that because of the

---

1. Gerald Horne, *White Supremacy Confronted: U.S. Imperialism and Anticommunism vs. the Liberation of Southern Africa, from Rhodes to Mandela*, New York: International, 2019.
2. See e.g., Marcus Baram, *Gil Scott-Heron: Pieces of a Man*, New York: St. Martin's, 2014: The subject of this biography and an intermittent resident of the District, was more advanced ideologically than most but in his prototypical

resonance of the counter-revolutionary impulse among settlers, progress domestically involved global alliances,[3] which this new movement was not in a position to inspire. This meant setbacks particularly for the Black Panther Party, which was at the tip of the spear and more globally minded than many of their ostensible comrades, meaning they were bound to be knocked down for the count—given aforementioned reaction at home and a paucity of global links abroad.[4]

The first full year of the Nixon regime—1969—seemed to be a continuation of the storminess of the previous year. Medical students on the hilltop continued their strike, for example.[5] By December 1969, according to the *Star*, the "entire 99 member sophomore class" at the medical school was boycotting classes since they demanded that Dr. Albert Harden resign. The student leader, Ewart Brown, purportedly sought to "reduce white enrollment," so that the "number of whites at Howard should parallel the number of blacks admitted to the University of Alabama Medical School."[6]

The security figure identified as "Captain Lacey" continued to report to the campus administration—"Cramton Auditorium was filled to capacity...no incidents to report...."[7] Earlier, James Garrett—said by the *Post* to represent the "more radical black point of view"—was across town at Federal City College,[8] where Trinidadian titan, C.L.R. James, was settling in. The FBI found it curious that at F.C.C., Claude Lightfoot, high ranking Black Communist, was lecturing on "Marxism & Black People," while Julius Hobson was speaking on "Introduction to the Communist World...."[9] Soon the FBI was even more concerned when chaos rocked this campus with firearms flashing.[10]

---

song, "Winter in America," speaks—albeit ambiguously—of the U.S. Constitution as "noble" in a "free society."

3. Gerald Horne, *Negro Comrades of the Crown: African-Americans and the British Empire Fight the U.S. Before Emancipation*, New York: New York University Press, 2012.

4. See also Gerald Horne, *Armed Struggle? Panthers, Communists and Black Nationalists in Southern California During the 1960s*, forthcoming.

5. *The Hilltop*, 5 December 1969.

6. *Washington Star*, 2 December 1969.

7. Report, 22 September 1969, Box 2, RG 23, *Office of Emergency Preparedness Records*.

8. *Washington Post*, 14 November 1968.

9. FBI Source of Report, 23 May 1969, Box 12, RG 23.

10. *The Hilltop*, 20 November 1970.

The presence of Lightfoot and Charlene Mitchell was evidentiary of a shift in the political spectrum. It gave ballast to the FBI contention that Communists were to blame for spreading unrest in the District[11]—rather than poverty, racism, police terror, unemployment and the like. Policy nationally and District-wide had been to oust from influence the likes of Hunton and Wilkerson, i.e., Communists with global backup. This left two major ideological strands: liberalism, not immune to anticommunism and, thus, wars—cold and hot—abroad, e.g., the NAACP, and "Black Power" advocates who were certainly and thankfully militant, but were seemingly incapable of conducting an analysis of forces at home and abroad leading to the development of a winning strategy. But then the case of Angela Y. Davis exploded on the scene: the self-confessed Communist was ousted from her post at UCLA, then placed on trial for her life, accused of complicity in a Marin County courthouse shootout[12]—she added a dollop of armed struggle to the political mix because of her ties to the Panthers, in contradistinction to the hegemonic non-violence, a philosophy which was in many ways contrary to the trajectory of settler colonialism's triumph and, thus, hard for many to accept.

Her case was attuned to the proliferating militancy at the hilltop, as campus editorialists praised her,[13] as did the Reverend Jesse Jackson who sought to adopt the mantle of the slain Dr. King.[14] A rally on her behalf was held in front of Douglass Hall.[15] The well-connected fraternity, Kappa Alpha Psi, spoke in her defense and were prominent among the hundreds at the rally.[16] Dean Paul Miller of the law school aided her defense and sought to link her to a previous glorious history: "'The whole civil rights movement started here at Howard,'" he contended fairly, "'and practically all those involved have their roots at Howard....'"[17]

In College Park Davis' arrival on the scene brought more discord. "Had enough" asked one leaflet rhetorically; "known Communists like Angela Davis supply criminals with guns to turn courtrooms into battlefields," but hark, for "now at U. of Md. you can work with

---

11. J. Samuel Walker, 'Most of 14th Street is Gone, 27.

12. Angela Davis, An Autobiography, Chicago: Haymarket, 2021.

13. The Hilltop, 16 October 1970.

14. The Hilltop, 23 October 1970.

15. The Hilltop, 30 October 1970.

16. The Hilltop, 13 November 1970.

17. The Hilltop, 12 December 1971.

other students to smash the leftist treason machine," ending with the infamous call—"America Awake!"[18]

Davis' ascendancy opened the door for the arrival on campus of Shirley Graham Du Bois, erstwhile Communist and widow of W.E.B. Du Bois; she addressed an impressive crowd of 700.[19]

The embrace of Davis was an example of a growing militancy. Just before the spring semester ended in 1969 gasoline was found on the hilltop campus, i.e., two gallons in containers near the Home Economics Building, and a mere one gallon in a container at Douglass Hall and one more gallon at Locke Hall—for reasons unclear but likely involved mayhem.[20] Army Intelligence thought it had reason to believe that just before the first anniversary of Nixon's 1968 election victory, the "Secret Service reported they heard of a car with a mortar or rocket launcher" was spotted as "1,000 people" were "regrouping on Constitution Avenue, between 8th and 9th...."[21] Then "Michael Harris...notified [the] FBI that he had picked up a hitchhiker on P Street N.W." and was told to "avoid Ellipse on 9 May [1970] since students would set off dynamite...as a diversion for a rush on north front of White House...."[22] Making it to public conversation was the petrifying reality that bomb threats at Howard were becoming as common as protest marches.[23]

It would not be unfair to infer that the authorities were bewildered by mass protests and this lubricated their imaginations, allowing for pre-emptive bludgeoning of activists, as they pursued ghosts bizarrely. Thus when "Lynn Fink" of the Venceremos Brigade, a pro-Cuban formation arrived in the area, it was reported anxiously that "members are trained in use of explosives,"[24] which was not necessarily accurate. There was also the distinct possibility of misinformation leaking into raw intelligence reports of the kind involved in this chapter. Thus, along with "Lynn Fink," a "Miss Nancy Timmons from Women's Strike for Peace at Columbia, [Maryland] called the FBI...and told them that many protesters who are coming to D.C." for an antiwar protest, "have guns and intend to use them at

18. Leaflet, 1970, Box 1, *History of the University of Maryland, Campus Unrest, University of Maryland-College Park.*

19. *The Hilltop,* 11 December 1970.

20. Report, 12 May 1969, Box 10, RG 23.

21. Report from Army Intelligence, 4 November 1969, Box 18, RG 23.

22. Report, 9 May 1970, Box 20, RG 23.

23. *The Hilltop,* 15 January 1971.

24. Report, 9 May 1970, Box 20, RG 23.

the White House and monument ground...."[25] (WSP maintained a well trafficked office at 1822 Massachusetts Avenue N.W.)[26]

Likewise, local intelligence observed in May 1970 that "an individual known at Case Western University...as 'Uncle Fester' who is reported to be an expert in incendiaries departed evening hours of 8 May with two associates" headed for the District and "alleged to be carrying Molotov cocktails...."[27] "Uncle Fester" may have been expected to join unnamed "hippies" on 4 July who—it was said—planed to "roam street[s] downtown after fireworks display," then "overthrow cars and break windows."[28]

Perilously, People's Drug Store at 14th Street and New York Avenue told the police that their entire stock of "oven cleaner had been sold," not necessarily to dutiful housecleaners but to those who appreciated the flammability of this product.[29]

Flammability of another sort was provided by Vice-President elect Agnew who also in 1969 referred indecorously to a "Fat Jap," then a "Polack," and capped it off by asserting "when you've seen one slum, you've seen 'em all...."[30]

Disorder was flaring at local high schools too, in sympathy with Howard protests as leaflets read: "'When the man moves on Howard...the high schools of D.C. shall fully support our brothers and sisters....'"[31] Earlier, the rumor arose that high school students were "considering taking over the schools" in an occupation.[32] They may have been inspired by the Nixon inauguration which was greeted, said intelligence, by "200 colored children age 12-15" 14th and H streets N.W., who were busily "throwing rocks and bottles and rolling trash cans into the street blocking the traffic...."[33]

Thus, Black college organizers visited McKinley, Roosevelt, Coolidge, and Wilson high schools passing out leaflets and encouraging students to march to the White House and, as local intelligence

25. Report, 9 May 1970, Box 20, RG 23.
26. Hearing, House Un-American Activities Committee, 87th Congress, 2nd Session, 13 December 1962, Box 2, *Women's Strike for Peace Papers, American University*: Leader, Dagmar Wilson resided at 1413 29th Street N.W.
27. Report, 9 May 1970, Box 22, RG 23.
28. Report, 4 July 1970, Box 24, RG 23.
29. Report, 20 January 1969, Box 14, RG 23.
30. Report, 18 January 1969, Box 14, RG 23.
31. Report, 8 May 1969, Box 11, RG 23.
32. Report, 20 February 1969, Box 15, RG 23.
33. Report, 20 January 1969, Box 15, RG 23.

put it, "through the White House...."[34] Apparently, the message to Coolidge resonated since "info from under-cover agent" averred that "guns are being brought into this group...."[35] By May 1970 almost 4,000 high school students from Eastern, Chamberlain, and Anacostia were marching toward Capitol Hill,[36] headed down East Capitol Street, then on to the White House.[37] Days later "juveniles stoned a car, then turned it over."[38]

College students had not relinquished the idea of banding together in that by May 1970 representatives from Georgetown, G.W.U., and Catholic universities were mulling the idea of joining with their H.U. peers in a march to Capitol Hill.[39] By October, 86 Black students from H.U. and Georgetown departed for Alabama in solidarity with protests there.[40]

The "Daily Intelligence Summary" noted that hilltoppers were incensed because of the "killings of six Negroes on Monday, 11 May in Augusta, Georgia [and] have scheduled a rally on campus...followed by a march to Capitol Hill to hold conferences with their congressmen," to be joined by other area students.[41] Hundreds gathered at Douglass Hall on the hilltop, which also protested slaying of two Black students at Jackson State in Mississippi, indicative of the iron fist then hammering activism. As was often the case, Howard was in the vanguard with the Atlanta University complex voting on a H.U. proposal to suspend classes or close for the remainder of the semester. Violence erupted at Morgan State in Baltimore when the authorities attempted to lower the "Black flag of liberation."[42] Scores more protesters at Howard assembled in front of the Fine Arts Building demonstrating solidarity with the slain at South Carolina State University.[43]

President James Cheek of H.U. felt compelled to send a telegram to his ally in the White House, Richard Nixon, to request a meeting to discuss the slayings[44] but this milquetoast appeal likely inflamed more than it calmed.

---

34. Report, 15 October 1969, Box 12, RG 23.
35. Report, 15 October 1969, Box 12, RG 23.
36. Report, 8 May 1970, Box 13, RG 23.
37. Report, 8 May 1970, Box 13, RG 23.
38. Report, 11 May 1970, Box 13, RG 23.
39. Report, 15 May 1970, Box 13, RG 23.
40. *The Hilltop*, 30 October 1970.
41. Report, 15 May 1970, Box 20, RG 23.
42. *The Hilltop*, 20 May 1970.
43. *The Hilltop*, 20 February 1970.
44. *The Hilltop*, 20 May 1970.

It was not just the bobbysoxers and their immediate elders who had beefs, said the *Post*: "Teachers angrily walked out at two more of Washington's junior high schools...in protest against the school board's new ban against suspending unruly students...." Thus, "50 teachers left Shaw Junior High School" and a "half dozen or so left Hart Junior High School" and, inevitably, "students at the two schools trailed their teachers out of the classrooms" and instinctively, "yelled jubilantly as they left...." This display was prompted when "25 unruly eighth graders had tossed milk and jello around the lunchroom...."[45]

As the first anniversary of the assassination of Dr. King approached, intelligence asserted that an "unidentified Negro female" was sighted at a "fire in Hahn Shoe Store" at 14th and Irving, N.W. who with comrades "were going to burn out Irving Street and start throwing rocks at whites...."[46]

As the tenor of women's liberation waxed women were becoming more active. The City Council was hosting riotous meetings and at one notable session a woman with a pistol seized the microphone, accompanied by those depicted as "disrupters" and "propagandists"; an ashtray was tossed expertly; violence surged as a call was made for police backup.[47]

On the actual day of the assassination anniversary, Tony Cox, also known as Vernon Cox—"believed to head United Black Brothers"—was expected to "go to Meridian Hill" and "throw white man off [a] platform."[48]

So far, so militant.

But those paying closer attention may have noticed contrary signals. By early 1970 there was big time gambling taking place on campus, a "lumpen" diversion of which there were many, draining time from political organizing meetings.[49] When journalist, Leroy Giles, arrived at Dunbar High School in 1969, the crème de la crème of secondary education, he was "appalled" in this "visit to the old alma mater" to see that "students were gambling" and hearing that "profanity replaced polysyllables ."[50] Medical students may have gone on strike but prominent Negro surgeon, Dr. Thomas Matthew, repudiated the Poor People's Campaign in no uncertain

45. *Washington Post*, 10 May 1969.
46. Report, 3 April 1969, Box 16, RG 23.
47. *Washington Post*, 14 September 1969.
48. Report, 4 April 1969, Box 16, RG 23.
49. *The Hilltop*, 6 February 1970.
50. *The Hilltop*, 24 April 1970.

terms.[51] According to Howard student, Reg Hildebrand—soon to be a professor in Chapel Hill—the highly regarded History Department was "in turmoil,"[52] not normatively a precondition for bright ideas and progress. A like condition prevailed at the Government Department, then under the misrule of chairman, George Kousoulas. "Student gripes" proliferated and the fact that "most of the faculty" was defined as "white" led to "heated, emotional conflict between students, faculty and the chairman,"[53] detracting from campus-wide organizing.

Sterling Tucker had been consorting incessantly with Black Power types, but by 1969 he was being hailed in the retrograde pages of the *Star*, in words deemed worthy of retaining by Senator Goldwater of Arizona. The bespectacled intellectual was congratulated for critiquing "'the failure of black leadership to speak out' against the [so-called] criminal element in this city," i.e., the "principal offenders are youthful blacks...number of robberies here in July [1969] and again in August, was greater than the yearly totals for 1960, 1961, 1962 and 1963," meaning more admittees to the prison-industrial complex[54]—and more defectors to the Black Scare cabal.

In November 1968 at the hilltop homecoming, the crowd gave— said an observer—a "Black Power salute during the playing of the National Anthem" in support of the heroized Tommy Smith and John Carlos, sprinters who had protested on the victory stand at the Mexico City Olympics, the plight of Black folk north of the border. But by 1969 at this same event, "the theme of Blackness was overshadowed by the crowd's festive spirit."[55] Similarly—according to the *Post*—two Panthers sought vainly to sell copies of the party organ, as the correspondent asserted happily: "yesterday was not a day for Black Power...."[56]

I will spare readers the seamy details, but shortly thereafter there was a "panty raid" on campus, featuring about 300 students participating, for which some readers expressed disdain, it is true.[57]

The crossroads that had been reached was brought sharply into dramatic relief when a hilltop reporter began to sketch the

51. *Washington Post*, 28 April 1968.
52. *The Hilltop*, 27 February 1970.
53. *The Hilltop*, 6 March 1970.
54. *Washington Star*, 28 October 1969, Box 252, *Goldwater Papers*.
55. *The Hilltop*, 7 November 1969.
56. *Washington Post*, 2 November 1969.
57. *The Hilltop*, 14 November 1969.

"psychological problems which confront Howard students [that] seem to be on the rise...." One reason? Hilltoppers had to "determine whether he [or she] will join in all the protests and rallies," of which there were many, or "run the risk of being called a 'Tom'" or sellout, all of which meant "the new morality is also taking its toll...."[58] But it was not just hilltop students who were enduring emotional stress: by September 1969, 15 year old Greg Rogers of Fairfax County, Virginia committed suicide at Capitol Hill, as he was distraught about the recent death of his brother-in-law at Vietnam.[59]

In terms of contradictory trends, few were more pronounced that was occurring in the antiwar movement. Local intelligence reported with seeming enthusiasm that "the two predominantly black campuses, Howard...and [Federal City College] are not participating" in a Fall 1969 antiwar demonstration with organizers saying that "Negroes have traditionally stayed clear of anti-war protests, preferring to work on their own problems."[60] This may have been wishful thinking for at the same time mainstream leader, Sterling Tucker, was wondering why the U.S. was demanding "'free elections'" in Vietnam but not the District,[61] rhetorically adding strength to antiwar forces. Hilltoppers had the advantage of having on campus Professor Bernard Fall, who one analyst termed "the principal source for the American public of detailed information and analysis" of Southeast Asia.[62]

Of course, it is folly in this nation to ever downplay the iron fist of repression in evaluating events—though the authorities could argue they were only responding to an escalation from the other side of the barricades. Two H.U. students were outraged when FBI agents entered their apartment without a warrant and with guns drawn on the premise that they had killed a cop in 1967—which Michael Harris and Buddy Wilson of the 3000 block of 16th Street N.W. denied adamantly.[63] By May 1969, near the hilltop was an armory holding— said an intelligence report—"45,000 rounds of .22 rifle ammunition" for reasons that were not evident.[64] Then intelligence spotted a "crowd on Howard campus...total crowd numbers about 700 people;

---

58. *The Hilltop*, 5 December 1969.

59. *Washington Star*, 3 September 1969.

60. Daily Intelligence Summary, circa October 1969, Box 12, RG 23.

61. *The Hilltop*, 12 December 1969.

62. Leonard Liggio on Professor Fall, no date, Box 5, *Myra MacPherson Papers, American University*.

63. *The Hilltop*, 10 April 1970.

64. Report, 8 May 1969, Box 11, RG 23.

seem very hostile; overheard discussing gas and weapons. Each building held, has a number of students on roof…gates at 4th Street and 6th Street are barricaded. Group of students overheard to say, 'When do we use the gas?'"[65] Later, it was said, "gasoline has been set on fire in front of women's dorm—deliberately spreading fire," only "extinguished by students…."[66] There were "threats of burning at Howard…all gates are locked and any fire apparatus responding should use extreme caution,"[67] euphemistic phrasing.

"HU appears to be well-armed with weapons," was the considered opinion of local intelligence.[68] They also were bolstered by deftly placed fists— "white student was beaten, police responded & cars were stoned"[69]—and adroitly placed stones: "marshals requested 60 to 70 metro police because of the rock throwing by students…."[70]

Even the staid NAACP, which had long since made its peace with U.S. rulers, angrily denounced "harassing telephone calls" that had "intensified to the point where they disrupt the orderly proceedings of the office…on April 22 [1969] we were subjected to a continuing series of these calls for approximately 40 minutes…."[71]

Also, by May 1969 upheaval at Howard made the front page of the *Star*. "U.S. marshals clear Howard" was the essence: "100 helmeted" of them, along with "600…National Guardsmen" were "standing by at the Armory" perhaps uneager to spring into action since the marshals were greeted by "barrages of rocks, bottles and other missiles…three white newsmen were roughed up…." There was only "one major campus fire," a "wooden structure used for ROTC classes…." Naturally, a responding firetruck was promptly set afire, forcing occupants to flee for their lives. A motorcycle cop fired twice at reputed suspects on the eastern fringes of the campus…." Illuminatingly, the command post for activist students was plastered with a headline from the Nation of Islam newspaper: "'Old World Going out; New World Coming in.'"[72]

---

65. Report, 8 May 1969, Box 11, RG 23.
66. Report, 8 May 1969, Box 11, RG 23.
67. Report, 8 May 1969, Box 12, RG 23.
68. Report, 8 May 1969, Box 12, RG 23.
69. Report, 8 May 1969, Box 12, RG 23.
70. Report, 9 May 1969, Box 12, RG 23.
71. J. Francis Polhaus to C&P Telephone, 23 April 1969, Box IX: 229, *NAACP Papers*.
72. *Washington Star*, 9 May 1969.

This religion was embraced while there was an attempt to set afire the School of Religion—oriented toward Christianity.[73] Another source spoke of students "pelting cars with rocks...and banning all white persons from the campus."[74] The *Post* was unrestrained, aping the *Star* on the front page: "ROTC Hall burns in Howard siege... firemen, police cars are stoned...."[75]

What was at issue, according to protesters, was that "students are occupying university buildings in defiance of a federal court order because the carbon copy white folk who run Howard refuse to deal with the changes to make Howard an important part of the black community" and, thus, they were "threatened with head-cracking and eviction by D.C. police and U.S. soldiers...."[76]

Ideologically influential was the increasing critique of traditional religion exemplified when local intelligence bird-dogged a Black United Front demonstration at Arlington churches and synagogues as the militants demanded 15 percent of their budget be allocated to the local Black community, as a "'down payment of conscience for past injustice.'"[77] The Front was ever active—and perpetually surveilled—as when after their Arlington protest, they planned on recruiting Black mothers who lost sons in the war to engage in civil disobedience at the headquarter of the Selective Service.[78]

As a possible warmup, police reported in early 1969 that a "bottle was thrown" into their building and "considerable damage was done...."[79] As 4 July 1970 approached, the Front pledged to plot a "'dishonor America day,'" with Douglas Moore at the controls.[80] The Front further demanded that Howard's James Cheek and the NAACP's Roy Wilkins ignore the holiday rally planned by GOP comedian, Bob Hope, and evangelist, Billy Graham, terming it contemptuously "'Honor White Racism Day.'"[81]

By June 1969 the ubiquitous "Captain Lacey" was elaborating on a "rumor that some HU students plan to stage a walk off during

73. *Washington Post*, 9 May 1969.
74. *United Press International*, 8 May 1969, Box 11, RG 23.
75. *Washington Post*, 9 May 1969.
76. Leaflet from Howard, circa May 1969, Box 12, RG 23.
77. Daily Intelligence Summary, circa September 1969, Box 10, RG 23.
78. Report, 14 October 1969, Box 10, RG 23.
79. Report, 18 January 1969, Box 14, RG 23.
80. *Washington Star*, 30 June 1970.
81. Report, 1 July 1970, Box 23, RG 23.

graduation ceremonies" and that was sufficient to mobilize "Metro police…a total of 43 guards" and also "guards from Freedmen's Hospital and private security" since "10,000 people are expected."[82] By June 1969 the dialectic between repression and resistance was embodied when Nathan Hare and four other hilltop professors were allowed to sue for dismissal during the 1967 unrest, just as 1969 unrest was cresting.[83]

By 1970 Howard remained in an uproar. Hundreds of students marched from the hilltop to the White House protesting a "possible" U.S. intervention in Trinidad; some did what a reporter described as "calypso steps" en route; others carried placards with barbed messages: "'Yankee Go Home,'" "'Yankee Get Out,'" and "'Black Power in Trinidad and Tobago.'"[84]

The Hilltop counted "700 Howard students" in this impressive display, which spotlighted the supposed perfidy of former hilltop professor, then Prime Minister Eric Williams, a "lackey of western imperialism…." The slogan they found moving was "Send the troops to Rhodesia; send the troops to South Africa; send the troops to hell." The route, appropriately, "went along a route which took them by the hulks of burnt out buildings, remnants of the April 1968 riots…" The marchers "sang a piece from Le Roi Jones' poem, 'Who Shall Survive America'…very few niggers and no crackers at all'…." Courtney Boxill, president of the sponsoring Caribbean Students Association, was moved to announce, "the people of Trinidad will be 'motivated strongly when they know that Black brothers and sisters of the world are with them.'"[85]

Subsequently, the Ethiopian Union of North America marching and chanting in the scores headed north on Connecticut Avenue toward the legation of their homeland.[86] They were followed by Iranian students, of which a number were to be found at the hilltop; 60 of them marched—and according to a commentator—as they were "seeking the support of Blacks in America for the Palestinian… movement," as they denounced the regal Shah.[87] They were knocking on an open door since earlier at All Souls Church at 16th and Harvard, three speakers—just back from a month with the

---

82. Report, 4 June 1969, Box 2, RG 23, *Office of Emergency Preparedness Records*.
83. Daily Intelligence Summary, 18 June 1969, Box 10, RG 23.
84. *United Press International*, 6 May 1970, Box 12, RG 23.
85. *The Hilltop*, 24 April 1970.
86. Report, 28 December 1970, Box 25, RG 23.
87. *The Hilltop*, 15 January 1971.

Palestinian movement—addressed a lively audience.[88] (The leading Iranian architect, Kamran Diba, was trained at the hilltop.)[89]

As of 1969 H.U. had the largest percentage of international students on a U.S. campus—15 percent of the student body—with many having roots in Africa and the Caribbean, which continued to resonate domestically and globally. (Interestingly, Ernest Wilson, who coordinated this influx travelled to Salisbury, Rhodesia under the aegis of an outlaw regime on behalf of the State Department.)[90]

By September 1970 hilltop students ratified what had been obvious, as they were described as exiting the "'Ebony Tower'" and forming a "D.C. Project," i.e., "community involvement programs" formalized by spending of almost $4 million on this outreach.[91] Soon H.U. students were headed to Cairo, Illinois, site of fierce anti-racist struggle, as they vindicated their role as youthful firefighters.[92]

Awakening from a deep slumber, administrators at American University in mid-1969 began to try to recruit Black faculty. F.J. Piotrow, Dean of the School of International Service, told his superior, "your concern about the slow pace of recruitment of black faculty members" was being tackled. He seemed strangely proud to underscore that his shop "counts among its faculty one of the two black members on the [A.U.] faculty"; they were interested in Dr. Ronald Walters—who went on to a distinguished career at Howard and at College Park—but, with the usual dodge were concerned about his "qualifications."[93] By September 1969 in an appropriate District twist, a symposium on repression with 750 present at American University was menaced by the Nazi Party and surveilled by local intelligence.[94]

The College Park campus appeared to be experiencing a different trajectory. Whereas Howard had been battling and absorbing blows—and dishing out a share—for decades and, at times, becoming exasperated and bedraggled in the process, Black students across the border were relatively recent arrivals in sizable numbers and, thus, arrived with a burst of energy. As Howard's 1969 homecoming

---

88. Leaflet, 1970, Box 1, *History of the University of Maryland-Campus Unrest, University of Maryland-College Park*.
89. Andrew Friedman, *Covert Capital*, 275.
90. *The Hilltop*, 13 November 1970.
91. *The Hilltop*, 25 September 1970.
92. *The Hilltop*, 11 December 1970.
93. F.J. Piotrow to President George Williams, 9 June 1969, Box 3, *George Williams Papers, American University-Washington, D.C.*
94. Report, 13 September 1969, Box 7, RG 23.

was being adjudged as a retreat from "Black Power," the administration across the border in Maryland concluded—seemingly without satisfaction—that "Black Student protest is not a myth; violent demonstrations have occurred on several college campuses" and, said this official body, "we believe that black student disruptive demonstrations can, and very likely might occur at the University of Maryland in greater intensity than experienced thus far"—the gift of prophecy for certain. Expected were "property destruction, bodily harm," even "kidnapping...building takeovers, office takeovers...."[95] In an undated response, George Ware, Jr., resonated with 1968 when he exhorted, "We will change the system—destroy it—or die...."[96]

By late 1969 the pot of student unrest was boiling over. There was "'polarization'" at a "student government meeting," such was the message to a local cop. "'The room was packed...at least 3 times as should have been [present] with 50-75 blacks,'" an extraordinary number for this campus. "'Emotions were raging in the form of foul, screaming language...blacks took the position that no one was leaving until their budget had been dealt with,'" and just in case, "'the doors were being blocked by blacks....'" The informant stressed, "'I did not hear any individual threats nor see any knives, guns, or chains,'" unexpectedly so. There was some "shoving and a [press] photographer was roughed up a bit...." Expectedly, "the white backlash went into effect as rumors spread," which was spreading like a fungus nationally in any case. One reason? "'Black faces scared some folks,'" problematizing any protest, no matter how mild or simple.[97]

The backlash appeared to envelope a professor at the campus laboratory for Radiation and Polymer Science who—amidst denunciations of the "Black Nazi" and the "hoodlum element"—termed what was happening on his beloved campus a "disgrace" as College Park had "become a sanctuary for the felon" and was "held for ransom by the sadist...."[98]

Local intelligence received a report "from someone who said he was a ham radio" operator and informed that College Park "students

95. "Report of Ad Hoc Committee on Black Student Demonstrations," November 1969, Box 1, RG 17, *Student Affairs Records, Series-Student Organizations, University of Maryland-College Park.*

96. Undated Message from George Ware, Box 1, RG 17.

97. Ralph Swinford to Dr. J. Winston Martin, 6 December 1969, Box 1, RG 17.

98. Professor J. Silverman to President Wilson Elkins, 7 October 1969, Box 1, RG 17.

are using citizen band…talkies to coordinate disruptive activities" with their "base [station] reported to be in [the] chapel…."[99]

By 1970 the Regents of the University of Maryland endured a chaotic four hour meeting with a main agenda item being how to "increase the number of Negro students in the university's professional schools," which had been fought relentlessly for decades but was now being pressed via duress: these incompetents, said a commentator, were "interrupted frequently by questions and heated arguments…."[100]

Miles away at American University similar plaints were heard. "A group of concerned students" expressed dedicated "interest" in "putting an end to the revolutionary elements" on campus, referring to Mike Spiegal of SDS, an "admitted Communist" and those in his milieu, i.e., "several black students who were at the meeting tonight had guns. Others had machetes and switchblades."[101] Likewise, Donald Williamson, Jr., warned that "this university…is in grave danger of destruction," because of "openly subversive organization…controlled and manipulated by Communists." The remedy? "Kick the SDS off campus. Expel any students found to be members of SDS…don't let overguilt [sic] for the McCarthy period (Joe that [is]) paralyze you from taking action."[102]

Someone—perhaps President Williams himself—was reacting badly to the mushrooming unrest. When the *Post* ran a headline—"AU President Favors More Authority"—scribbled alongside was "sissy appeasement."[103]

The *Post* was pleased when fraternity boys and jocks forcibly ousted SDS protesters occupying an administrative building in their attempt to emulate Howard.[104] But this vigilantism also was backed by conservative guru, Richard Viguerie, then sited not far away in a posh building at 1825 Connecticut Avenue N.W. He was "shocked" to "read of your disapproval" of the ejection, he said, in his finger-wagging rebuke of President Williams that denounced the "Communist dominated SDS" and heaped praise on the

---

99. Report, 6 May 1970, Box 13, RG 13.
100. *Baltimore Sun*, 21 November 1970, *Vertical File, Admissions/Negroes, University of Maryland-College Park.*
101. Letter to President Williams, 25 February 1969, Box 12, *George Williams Papers.*
102. Donald Williamson, Jr. to President Williams, 26 April 1969, Box 12, *George Williams Papers.*
103. *Washington Post*, 6 March 1969, Box 12.
104. *Washington Post*, 25 April 1969.

"anticommunist students...nothing but contempt for you and praise for the students...."[105] President Williams took note when neighboring George Washington University hired Harry Gagelin, a former leader of the Secret Service, to direct campus security as the mood shifted to a crackdown on obstreperous students.[106]

Yet despite the roughing up, progressive students stood their ground: as masses streamed into the District galvanized by the New Mobilization Committee to End the War in Vietnam, from their office at 1029 Vermont Avenue N.W., organizers told President Williams cordially, "We have been deeply touched by the willingness of students to assist in meeting the sleeping requirements" of protesters by arranging lodging.[107] This concession by the administration reflected the residual strength of progressive forces. By the Spring of 1970 local intelligence found "tear gas" to be "very heavy in the air," as A.U. students "are continuing to be pushed back onto the campus by police...."[108]

Even George Washington University acted similarly, providing as administration put it, "facilities...for day and evening meetings, seminars, lectures" plus working with the "Food Liberation Committee" on feeding the masses arriving for an antiwar manifestation.[109] This mostly peaceful demonstration notwithstanding, the State Department alleged that "explosives are rumored" with "possible violence against Vietnam Embassy...2251 R St. N.W."[110] This report did not detract from a headline days later: "Largest rally in Washington history" surpassing the March on Washington of 1963—though noted was the point that "militants resume evening violence...."[111]

The following May, 1970, an antiwar demonstration was accompanied by ten windows broken at the Department of Justice and 64 of same at the National Guard Association—hundreds all told. Two vehicles were completely destroyed by fire at 2010 H Street N.W. and at 21st and Eye, with five officers injured.[112]

---

105. Richard Viguerie to President Williams, 28 April 1969, Box 12, *George Williams Papers*.

106. *Washington Star*, 19 October 1970, Box 13, *George Williams Papers*.

107. NMCTEWV to President Williams, 10 November 1969, Box 14, *George Williams Papers*.

108. Report, 6 May 1970, Box 13, RG 23.

109. Office of the President, GWU to GWU Mobilization/Moratorium Committee, 5 November 1969, Box 11, RG 23.

110. Report from State Department, 4 November 1969, Box 18, RG 23.

111. *Washington Post*, 16 November 1969.

112. Report, 19 May 1970, Box 22, RG 23.

Why George Washington escalated in the security realm was revealed when the effervescent SDS seized the building housing the Institute for Sino-Soviet Studies in protest of their "anti-communist activities," while being accused of vandalism and rifling of files.[113] (The head of the Black Student Union on campus, Jim McQueen, chimed in and termed the school "'an enemy of Black people in D.C.'"[114]) McQueen led a demonstration at the central office of the AFL-CIO because of their "lack of commitment to striking hospital workers in Charleston," South Carolina, then met with Lane Kirkland, then an aide to labor boss, George Meany[115]—who eventually took his place. So pressured, G.W.U. chose to sever ties with what was described as an "army research unit."[116] Then G.W.U. and A.U. students collaborated in picketing the Internal Security Committee of the U.S. Senate, a fearsome anticommunist body.[117]

Georgetown was unexempt. While visiting at Catholic University, Mayor Joseph Alioto of San Francisco recounted with dread his recent experience at the home of the Hoyas. "'There was fighting, switchblades were in evidence; women, who were guests of the University, were screaming...students block a doorway, take over a corridor....'"[118] Inexorably, the "Daily Intelligence Summary" reported in the Spring of 1969 that the "National Socialist White People's Party" traded blows in Georgetown with what was depicted as a "crowd of hippies."[119]

Students for a Democratic Society were also active in College Park. At a September 1969 rally jocks and fraternity boys—a kind of Young Fascist League—ripped down a "Vietcong flag" as outbreaks of fighting involving more than a dozen students, including few young women; the spark seemed to be the presence of high-profile SDS leaders Bill Ayers and Jeff Jones.[120] SDS made a big splash on campus when they coordinated a 48-hour fast for peace in Vietnam, starring 13 students—eight men and five women.[121] Then came

---

113. *Washington Post*, 28 April 1969.
114. *Washington Star*, circa 25 April 1969, Box 11, RG 23.
115. *Washington Post*, 3 May 1969.
116. *Washington Post*, 11 April 1969.
117. Report, 13 March 1969, Box 11, RG 23.
118. *Washington Post*, 4 May 1969.
119. Daily Intelligence Summary, 14 April 1969, Box 12, RG 23.
120. *Washington Post*, 25 September 1969.
121. *Baltimore Sun*, 16 February 1965, *Vertical File-Campus Unrest, University of Maryland-College Park*.

a sit-in protest against CIA recruitment on campus.[122] By mid-1970 there was more than $90,000 in damage as a result of a campus fire in the central administration building; arson was suspected and the governor declared a state of emergency and imposed a curfew.[123] Formerly this flagship, like its lesser peers, was derided as a somnolent "cow college," but now bulging at the seams with 33,000 students, 500 of them had just been arrested with 100 injured in various protests. Tear gas was unleashed on antiwar activists after a lengthy protest that gained headlines.[124] Wiping away the compelled tears, 1,000 students marched on the ROTC/Air Force armory on campus and many yelled approval as some 45 militants smashed furniture, broke windows, trashed records, and burned uniforms. Then they moved on to Route 1, blocking traffic and launching stones at the 140 state police assembled, while others burned the U.S. flag amid cries of "'Fascist Pigs.'"[125]

A few days later Terrapins were among other area students who closed schools, blocked highways—and plotted a general strike because of the war; twelve students were arrested near American University. Catholic University students flocked to College Park to join the Terrapins,[126] for at this wracked campus there was a teach-in bluntly termed "'Foreign Affairs Student Day'" which supplanted regular classes.[127]

By 1970 the beset Regents also had to contend with protest at what was then called Maryland State College, "almost all rural and black," sited in Princess Anne, pockmarked said an observer with "deteriorated buildings and mud paths," a real "cow college...." In the late 1940s the total budget was a skimpy $187,000 and the entire campus consisted of three buildings, three telephones, and one car—this is what passed for higher education for Negroes, an intended insult meant to underline their presumed inferiority. After a building seizure by enraged students, the name of the campus was changed to the University of Maryland-Eastern Shore, as cosmetic makeover took precedence over substantive reform.[128] Shaken by the riotous commotion, police intelligence frantically

---

122. *Baltimore Sun*, 31 October 1967.
123. "Cecil Whig," 3 June 1970, *Vertical File, Campus Unrest, University of Maryland-College Park*.
124. *Washington Star*, 2 May 1970.
125. *Washington Star*, 2 May 1970.
126. *Washington Star*, 6 May 1970.
127. "University Record," 6 May 1970, *Vertical File, Campus Unrest*,
128. *Washington Star*.

inquired about a new organization, "Government Employees for a Democratic Society," as if they were an equivalent of SDS.[129]

It did seem that a legacy of the Red Scare was to marginalize class struggle trade unionism, creating a vacuum then filled by energized students, particularly Black students. However, the Black working class in the District—possibly inspired by their children, nieces and nephews—were inspired too by the spirit of the era. Inexorably, H.U. was leading the way, campaigning against "second rate pay," said to attract "second rate instructors."[130]

And they too were surveilled. Thus, in late July 1970, the "Daily Intelligence Summary" focused on "Black D.C. transit drivers," who it may be recalled, had an uphill climb to be hired in the first place. Their hardline detractors had not surrendered but simply retreated to the next barrier as management then began to support a "'white only' employee recreation association through which promotions often are made while systematically discriminating against blacks in promotion...." At that point "about two thirds of company's three thousand drivers are black," meaning that this was truly a proposed apartheid policy designed to benefit a minority defined as "white."[131]

Near the end of the year, the Daily Intelligence Summary took note: the "predominantly black National Alliance of Postal and Federal Employees will hold a rally...to protest against racial discrimination of Washington area black federal workers," with the purported firebrand, Julius Hobson, to speak.[132] Teamsters Local 639 then sought to represent 2,000 non-academic workers at Georgetown University, backed by the Black Student Alliance.[133]

Black workers of fair income faced problems that their poorer brethren knew all too well. James Ford was 46 in 1969 and had toiled as an agricultural expert for the government in Brazil, along with his spouse and two children. His comfortable abode was a three bedroom beachfront house in an upmarket section of Rio de Janeiro. Yet when he returned home to Washington he was unable to buy anything remotely comparable, though he was searching in suburban Maryland—racism was the suspected reason.[134]

---

129. Report, 9 July 1969, Box 5, RG 23, *Office of Emergency Preparedness Records*.
130. *The Hilltop*, 2 October 1970.
131. Daily Intelligence Summary, 27 July 1970, Box 24, RG 23.
132. Daily Intelligence Summary, 11 November 1970, Box 25, RG 23.
133. *Georgetown Voice*, 6 June 1969, *Unions Archive Record File, Georgetown University-Washington, D.C.*
134. *Washington Post*, 13 March 1969.

There were also workers being recruited whose main job was repressing the Black working class. Egil "Bud" Krogh informed his fellow henchman for Nixon, John Ehrlichman, that the District police force was recruiting and unsurprisingly, "90% of all applicants are white"; though "much recruiting went on [in] the Middle South and Deep South previously," replete with African Americans, "most of our candidates" as of early 1970 were "coming from the military" and "will provide almost 3,000 applicants" capable of doubling the force.[135] There was an ineffective stab at a kind of community policing, so as to camouflage the iron fist. But yet another Nixon henchman, Martin Anderson, found the "police pilot project board election" to be the "biggest phony." Why? Marion Barry "and about 20 of his hoodlum PRIDE group took over the election room" using "cursing and obscene threats...." The future mayor and "his tough-ies" were the problem, he said as they executed "crooked voting," said to be a harbinger of what home rule portended.[136]

There were other workers with different complaints, firefighters in the first instance. By December 1970 at 1945 Calvert, an alarm was sounded but when the firefighters arrived, they were assaulted and police were called to protect them—but then two buckets of paint were tossed at the men in blue, as five arrests were made.[137]

Again, as Nixon prepared for re-election in 1972, anti-racist and radical forces thought they were prepared to meet the challenge. But the wily chief executive pulled a fast one, opening ties with China, which at once discombobulated those who had looked long-ingly to Mao Zedong for sustenance—the Black Panthers in the first instance—as it destabilized the forces that relied on Moscow, especially those in Southern Africa. The upshot? The rise of Ronald Reagan and a deft counter-offensive against radicalism at home and abroad.

---

135. Bud Krogh to John Ehrlichman, 9 March 1970, Box 7, *White House Central Files, Nixon Presidential Library.*

136. Martin Anderson to Hon. Joel Broyhill, 12 February 1970, *SMOF, White House Central Files, Nixon Presidential Library.*

137. Daily Intelligence Summary, 3 December 1970, Box 25, RG 23.

Chapter **24**

Black Panthers Roar, 1968-1972

"For Howard the sixties have been catastrophic," such was the considered opinion of a student journalist while digressing on the attainments of "Howard figures [such] as Stokely Carmichael and Rap Brown," not accidentally the embodiments of an ascending "Black Power."[1] It was Brown who in 1967 counselled Jersey Citians that "'if you loot, loot a gun store'" as he was becoming as notorious as the better known Carmichael.[2] Later, 1969 was termed "perhaps the most chaotic year that the University has ever experienced."[3]

Truly, to the extent that these sweeping words dripped with veracity, it had something to do with the iron fist of the authorities, who took seriously the hilltop's strategic position within walking distance of the White House and Capitol Hill and containing students and staff not unwilling to mosey to either site. For as was said of the graduating class of 1971—entering in 1967—"activism…had made Howard one of the most famous campuses in the country…."[4]

Student columnist and top editor, Robert "The Black" Taylor, observed in April 1971 that "Washington, D.C. undercover agents have increased their surveillance activities" on campus. Helpfully, he reminded that "the first three license plates of a police undercover car are 775 and the antenna of the car is located on the upper middle part of the car trunk."[5]

There was an extraordinary ideological struggle unwinding at the hilltop with national, if not global, significance (indubitably, "Stokely" and "Rap" as they were familiarly called, were not

---

1. *The Hilltop*, 19 December 1969.
2. Bryan Burrough, *Days of Rage: America's Radical Underground, the FBI and the Forgotten Age of Revolutionary Violence*, New York: Penguin, 2015. 41.
3. *The Hilltop*, 1 October 1971.
4. *The Hilltop*, 23 April 1971.
5. *The Hilltop*, 2 April 1971.

simply local figures). The forces at play were encased not only in the former two personalities but, as well, the Nation of Islam and the Black Panther Party (with the latter at times appearing to be a stalking horse for the once weighty Communist Party, decimated by the Red Scare but making a comeback with the pre-eminence of Angela Davis; even the arrival as a teacher at Howard and F.C.C. of Trinidadian radical, C.L.R. James, ostensibly an ideological foe, was seen as a boon to the Reds).[6] Her currency was on display in 1971 when Howard decided not to have a Homecoming Queen and chose instead to "show support of Angela Davis' struggle for Black Liberation."[7] In turn she was named as "Queen Mother," a high honor in the African mythos then in motion—which elicited a number of criticisms.[8] *The Hilltop* cited approvingly an account from Liberia that "condemns us for treatment of Angela Davis."[9]

Remarkably, the chairman of the Homecoming festivities was future Congressional Black Caucus potentate, Elijah Cummings of Baltimore,[10] whose columns were placed strategically adjacent to her appeals.[11] This Maryland neighbor continued to exert considerable influence at the hilltop, as the leader of Afro-American Studies, Russel Adams, had roots in Baltimore too.[12]

The Panthers had difficulty in establishing a viable chapter in the District, not least because of the overweening influence of NAACP-style centrism and the liberalism from the emerging Congressional Black Caucus, along with the persistence of various forms of Black Nationalism. For example, when the Panthers were bogged down in siege warfare, the Urban League in 1968 crowed that "during the past year...membership grew to an unprecedented 17,000. Our staff reached nearly 100"—and this was just in the District.[13]

In October 1968. when the nation was aflame, Panther spokesman, Eldridge Cleaver, said bluntly that there was no Panther chapter in the District and activist poet Gaston Neal concurred[14]—and the authorities strained to insure they were not proven to be wrong. Actually, local intelligence thought that there were Panthers in the

---

6. *The Hilltop*, 30 April 1971.

7. *The Hilltop*, 8 October 1971.

8. *The Hilltop*, 15 October 1971.

9. *The Hilltop*, 10 March 1972; *Liberian Age*, 27 February 1972.

10. *The Hilltop*, 8 October 1971.

11. *The Hilltop*, 10 December 1971.

12. *The Hilltop*, 5 November 1971.

13. Urban League Newsletter, January 1968, Box IX: 228, *NAACP Papers*.

14. *The Hilltop*, 11 October 1968.

District but leaders—e.g., Huey P. Newton and David Hilliard—were unimpressed by them.[15]

The Howard student organ thought it knew why: the party, it said, had been "slowly, carefully but very assuredly eradicated" in that as of October 1969 "46 top officials" were "under arrest," while the "press has refused to deal with the Panthers" credibly.[16] Yet, because of their militancy and their attempt to form global alliances, while not carrying the negative baggage affixed to Communists over the decades, the BPP presented a formidable challenge—until they were mowed down systematically and imprisoned. "Black Panthers vs. The Police—The Rising Toll," was a Howard headline in late 1969 that spoke volumes,[17] that a rally at the Social Work Building accentuated.[18]

For various reasons, the Panther presence was felt deeply in Baltimore.[19] In 1970 the chapter there announced heatedly that Ochika Young "was made into the first victim of Baltimore's fascist courts" as the "stage was set for Baltimore's largest murder trial"; at 567 Mosher Street "massive arrests were made, doors kicked in, people tossed out of their beds and tossed into jail...."[20] As of April 1970, eleven Panthers in Baltimore were arrested.[21]

The comedian and actor, Tommy Davidson, grew up in the vicinity and later observed that "to me, Baltimore was the most racist city in the world"; in the 1970s, if he was "on the bus sitting by a window and a white man saw me, he would start yelling at me and cursing me"; once a "police officer stopped me in one of the housing project hallways and put his gun barrel in my mouth. Another police officer had a vicious dog that he held in my face...." The Baltimore born actor, Charles Dutton, was part of this milieu; before arriving at the leafy Yale School of Drama he killed a man and served seven years for manslaughter.[22]

---

15. Report, 28 November 1970, Box 24, RG 23, *Office of Emergency Preparedness Records*.

16. *The Hilltop*, 3 October 1969.

17. *The Hilltop*, 12 December 1969.

18. *The Hilltop*, 19 November 1969.

19. Marshall "Eddie" Conway, *Marshall Law: The Life and Times of a Baltimore Black Panther*, Oakland: AK, 2011.

20. Leaflet, 1970, MS0848, *Johns Hopkins University-Baltimore,*

21. National Committee to Combat Fascism/Organizing Bureau of the Black Panther Party to "The People of Washington, D.C.," 30 April 1970, Box 1, *History of the University of Maryland-Campus Arrest.*

22. Tommy Davidson, *Living in Color: What's Funny About Me*, New York: Kensington, 2020, 16, 169.

It was only in 2017 that monuments to the traitorous secessionist slaveholders were removed from the Baltimore landscape—and it was only in 2022 that they were shipped westward to a Los Angeles "art space,"[23] removing sustenance for those who hounded the likes of Davidson and may have infuriated Dutton.

As Davidson was dodging mayhem, local intelligence in Washington saw "about six Black Panther agitators in [a] crowd of...350 demonstrators at 20th & N N.W." Of course, police were "sent to break up [the] crowd," as it was claimed that the "Panthers [were] trying to get people to burn down Francis Jr. High School."[24] A few months later, the nascent Panther formation in the District was strangled in the crib: perhaps appropriately, it was the evening of 4 July when, said defenders, their office was "the victim of an unprovoked raid by the police"; they broke in while shouting "'I'm gonna kill me a nigger tonight!'" "They seemed to go wild, chasing the people all over the building with axes and wrecking hammers in their hands, dragging them down the stairs and beating them indiscriminately...for around twenty minutes...then the officers ran amuck in the office, destroying tape recorders, radios, record players, cabinets, mattresses, chairs," while their sticky fingers meant "nine hundred dollars" disappeared.[25] Blandly, the raid at 17th and U streets was reported officially as "1 officer injured" with "3 prisoners."[26]

Also perhaps appropriately, it was on 4 July that intelligence saw "2 carloads of Panthers stoning police headquarters" at 1620 V Street N.W. in apparent retaliation for the losses they had suffered.[27]

Their embryonic office was near Du Pont Circle but instantaneously, said a spokesperson, there was "an inexcusable, illegal raid" engrossed by "lies and distortions" including an allegation in the *Post*, designed to inflame: the party was said to have a stash of a "'large assortment of machine guns and shotguns and handguns....'"[28] Backing up the reporter, local intelligence was said to have recovered "a large cache of weapons" while making "15

---

23. *Washington Post*, 24 August 2022.
24. Report, 9 May 1970, Box 22, RG 23, *Office of Emergency Preparedness Records*.
25. Statement by Committee to Defend the Panthers, 24 September 1970, Box 1, *History of the University of Maryland-Campus Unrest*
26. Report, 4 July 1970, Box 24, RG 23, *Office of Emergency Preparedness Records*.
27. Report, 4 July 1970, Box 24, RG 23.
28. Statement by Committee to Defend the Panthers, 24 September 1970, Box 1.

arrests...."[29] Sadly from 1346 Connecticut Avenue, #1021, came the affecting message that the missing $900 was "to be used for the Free Breakfast Program for Children as well as Liberation Schools...."[30]

Unflinchingly, as others were marking a festive Thanksgiving, Panthers and their comrades were gathering at All Souls Church at 16th and Harvard—where the martyr James Reeb had once served[31]—for a "Constitutional Convention." Local intelligence was unimpressed though noticing "2,000 persons have registered," though fortunately "no info on any Panther officials being in town except 'Big Man,'" a reference to the dauntingly nicknamed Elbert Howard.[32]

To prepare for this event, the party had an office at 2327 18th Street N.W.[33] The ever present Howard security official known as "Captain Lacey" informed the FBI that a "rich Jewish wom[a]n had agreed to put the money up for the Panthers['] extravaganza.[34] By then Howard student journalists were engaged in rhetorical combat with the party, coolly noting the presence of "5,000...mostly young white radicals" at a church at 16th and Newton. Again, their report-age expressed distinct unease with party allies, particularly the "Gay Liberation Front," which was "'singing such songs as two, four, six, eight, gay is just as good as straight.'" The "Women's Liberation Movement was also present," while the party "rock group, 'The Lumpen' entertained."[35]

When paramount leader, Huey P. Newton, arrived at the air-port—"met by Jane Fonda and together they will go to the rally to speak"—the espying agent seemed about to dissolve into connip-tions.[36] He may have been heartened by the assailing of Newton at Howard, especially after he cancelled for the third time when slated to speak. He was also attacked for his denunciation of local hero, Carmichael, and "forming coalitions with the Students for a Democratic Society and the Gay Liberation Movement."[37] Newton came in for another battering when he termed "Pan-Africanism"

---

29. Report, 4 July 1970, Box 24, RG 23.
30. Statement by Committee to Defend the Panthers, 15 July 1970, Box 1.
31. Dorothy Gilliam, *Trailblazer*, 141.
32. Report, 27 November 1970, Box 24, RG 23.
33. Leaflet, 9 June 1970, Box 5, *Radical Left Wing Publication Collection, George Washington University.*
34. Report, 27 November 1970, Box 24, RG 23.
35. *The Hilltop*, 4 December 1970.
36. Report, 27 November 1970, Box 24, RG 23.
37. *The Hilltop*, 20 November 1970.

the "highest expression of cultural nationalism," unintended as a compliment.[38] But this broad indictment swept within its ambit, the popular Chicago poet, then known as Don L. Lee, then teaching at Howard.[39]

This fit of frenzy may have been exported to others arriving in town. Twelve men were arrested following a scuffle at a cocktail lounge on Wisconsin Avenue, with the assailants said to be part of the "Gay Liberation Front" with whom the BPP enjoyed comradely relations. Beer bottles were tossed, however, when they were refused service and told to depart forthwith.[40] Days later there was a front page editorial in Howard's student organ, castigating "our blond blue-eyed homosexual brothers and friends," meaning BPP allies.[41]

Eldridge Cleaver, born in Arkansas but raised in Southern California,[42] reflected the utter seriousness of the challenge—signaled by the audacity of holding a "Constitutional Convention"—when asked in April 1970 if he was trying to overthrow the central government in Washington, D.C. His response seemed to say "of course," but his quoted words were his rationale for same: "'Because that's where the seat of power is.'"[43] Quite perilously, he defined his party as "'Marxist-Leninist'" then further told his German interlocutor that "we have the terrain to fight...the United States has more mountains than...Cuba or...Vietnam...at the same time dissatisfaction in the ranks of the [U.S. Army] is at an all-time peak."[44]

When an author claimed threateningly that the Panthers "are not Black...they are Red," Cleaver's bravado was turned against him.[45]

African Americans as a whole were a "Black Trojan Horse," he said,[46] as he continued to inflame sensitive nerves reaching back to

---

38. *The Hilltop*, 20 November 1970.

39. *The Hilltop*, 8 October 1971.

40. *United Press International*, 28 November 1970, Box 24, RG 23.

41. *The Hilltop*, 4 December 1970.

42. Justin Gifford, *Revolution or Death: The Life of Eldridge Cleaver*, Chicago: Lawrence Hill, 2020.

43. *The Black Panther*, 11 April 1970.

44. Interview with Cleaver, circa 1970 in G. Louis Heath, ed., *The Black Panther Leaders Speak: Huey Newton, Bobby Seale, Eldridge Cleaver and Company Speak out Through the Black Panther Party's Official Newspaper*, Metuchen: Scarecrow Press, 1976, 59.

45. Julian Williams, "The Black Panthers are not Black...they are Red," Tulsa, 1970, *University of Maryland-College Park*.

46. *The Black Panther*, 20 September 1969.

the era of slavery when U.S. Negroes were enmeshed in more bed-
lam and plotting than at the time of Cleaver's provocative remarks.[47]

By November 1968, Cleaver had arrived in the District speaking
to a crowd of 1,500 at American University. Yes, he said, "'Right here
in the Bay of Pigs.'"[48] By September 1969, about 1,700 arrived for a
Panther ally at Du Pont Circle, then 200 to Meridian Park.[49] However, by October 1971 Cleaver had been tossed a curveball that left
him—and others—baffled. "'The Chinese invitation to President
Nixon to visit Peking,'" said the disoriented verbal gymnast, "'has
thrown the revolutionary movement into disarray [and] is a cause
for alarm....'"[50] That it was. The BPP had become reliant ideologically on China but then was wrongfooted when they allied with
U.S. imperialism against Moscow, leaving party cadre disoriented
and strengthening the assisted trend that it was perilous for African
Americans to rely on global forces when actually the opposite was
the case.

As the foregoing suggests, the "victors" in the ideological struggle
in Black America were assisted mightily by the incessant assaults on
the BPP. It is accurate, however, to assert that the party's diplomacy
could have withstood improvement.

By early 1970 BPP leader, David Hilliard and his attorney, Charles
Garry of San Francisco, were addressing Howard law school students
in a room filled to capacity. "'Stokely ain't got no damn sense,'" was
the flagrant insult tossed at one of the hilltop's favorite sons. Then
he was off on a tangent excoriating increasingly popular "cultural
nationalists" who bequeathed the still popular Kwanzaa holiday.
Hilliard was unimpressed, gruffly instructing the assembled that
"'the most beautiful cultural nationalis[m] is having an AK-47 in
your hand and making use of it.'"[51]

Since Howard still was producing a disproportionate number of
Black attorneys,[52] this Hilliard denunciation carried extra weight.

The campus columnist, Pearl Stewart, was unimpressed with Hilliard's exhibition. She was "disappointed" by his "childishly rant

---

47. Gerald Horne, *The Counter-Revolution of 1776: Slave Resistance and the Origins of the United States of America*, New York: New York University Press,
2014.
48. *Washington Free Press*, 15 November 1968, Box 1, *History of the University
of Maryland-Campus Unrest.*
49. *Washington Post*, 13 September 1969.
50. *The Hilltop*, 15 October 1971.
51. *The Hilltop*, 27 February 1970.
52. *The Hilltop.* 1 October 1971.

and rave [against] the Black Muslims" and sketching "what's wrong with Stokely Carmichael"; then there were the infantile epithets: why say "'scurvy-assed mothafuckas.'" It all wreaked of invidiousness: "I was not satisfied with Hilliard's explanation of how Cleaver's work in Algeria," to which he had fled only recently, "is so much more important than Stokely's work in Ghana...." She also felt "that what the Black Muslims did to Malcolm was wrong. I distinctly remember hearing Muhammad Ali call Malcolm a faggot two years ago in Cramton," but that hardly excused Hilliard's tirade.[53]

Unmoved, Hilliard returned in April addressing a respectable crowd of 800 in Cramton. But again an observer heard his undiplomatic outburst "critical of the emerging Pan African movement," while he defended Marxism, likely undermining this philosophy simultaneously. He did not seem to blemish Carmichael's reputation at his alma mater for he too appeared on campus in April 1970; the last time he was there in November 1968 he drew an overflow crowd of more than 1,900.[54] This time he spoke to more than 1,500—which could be seen as a decline from the recent past or almost double those who had come to hear Hilliard. He received a standing ovation when he denounced the "dope racket [as] a trick of the oppressors to stifle political awareness," but he too ran aground on tricky political reefs when a "lively question and answer period followed with Carmichael at one point emerging into a heated debate with a Biafran student"—referencing a then ongoing secessionist movement in Nigeria— "over Nkrumah's political objectives...."[55] Well after this contretemps Miriam Ikejani contended that the Ghanaian leader "supported Biafra," but by then the campus had moved on to other debates.[56]

However, what was at stake was a battle of ideas with Hilliard and the BPP unfurling the tattered banner of socialism, bludgeoned during the Red Scare and the recrudescence of ideologies once associated with Marcus Garvey, who had purchase on campus in the 1920s but had declined in the wake of an ill-fated alliance with a vanquished Tokyo.[57] As the state bludgeoned the BPP and continued to harass Communists, this ideology had difficulty in gaining adherents—Angela Davis notwithstanding. Then there was the

53. *The Hilltop*, 27 February 1970.
54. *The Hilltop*, 10 April 1970.
55. *The Hilltop*, 24 April 1970.
56. *The Hilltop*, 1 May 1970.
57. Gerald Horne, *Facing the Rising Sun: African-Americans, Japan and the Rise of Afro-Asian Solidarity*, New York: New York University, 2020.

liberal alternative pursued by the NAACP and delegates on Capitol Hill; in this era of fiery militancy, they could offer a more fruitful career but did not necessarily get the pulse racing. After Hilliard and Carmichael, arriving to address students was Julian Bond, late of SNCC but subsequently a long-time Chairman of the NAACP Board. The student observer thought that the Atlantan "disappoints those seeking ideology," an oblique reference to Hilliard and Carmichael's flamethrowing. Yet he was speaking in an inauspicious climate as classes had been suspended from noon until 2 p.m. so that students could address expansion of the war into Cambodia, along with what was depicted as the Panther "controversy and nationwide student dissent...."[58] Similarly, a lackadaisical reception was granted to the Reverend Andrew Young, an alumnus, former top aide to Dr. King and future United Nations Ambassador.[59]

The conflict between Hilliard and Carmichael, thusly, occupied much mental space on campus to the detriment of competing ideas.[60] Students continued to mimic Carmichael, heading to Dixie—Mississippi by 1971—to campaign, just as he earlier had headed to Alabama.[61]

However, organizationally speaking a long term victor of the scrap between Hilliard's and Carmichael's ideas was represented by the speaker who spoke to what was described as a "meager 700-800" at Cramton. The representative of the Nation of Islam—Minister Louis "Farakan [sic]" (the inability to spell his name properly was telling)—unloosed his own kind of tirade, which on its face was insulting to the audience: "having established the fact that we're a pitiful people," he proceeded, said the observer, to tell the audience that "he—or Elijah [Muhammad] can solve the problem." Just below this article was the headline "Angela [Davis] captured" and an account of a campus appearance by Michael Tabor of the Panthers but her—and his—ideology, too, in coming decades were to recede as the Nation's rose.[62]

The Nation had the local advantage of having within its ranks, Dr. Lonnie Shabazz, a graduate of Dunbar High School and of Lincoln University in Pennsylvania—where Langston Hughes, Thurgood Marshall, and Nkrumah all had matriculated—but also holding an advanced degree from M.I.T. and doctorate from Cornell. He had

58. *The Hilltop*, 8 May 1970.
59. *The Hilltop*, 10 December 1971.
60. *The Hilltop*, 13 November 1970.
61. *The Hilltop*, 29 October 1971.
62. *The Hilltop*, 16 October 1970.

been a "Marxist," according to the Howard newspaper, then in September 1950 he heard Elijah Muhammad denounce collard greens and he was convinced to follow him and by December 1970 the University of Islam which he had helped to build in the District educated hundreds of students beginning with the third grade, with the study of Arabic and Spanish being integral to the curriculum. But even Dr. Shabazz ran into biting verbal gales when he castigated Malcolm X as "'the worst hypocrite'" which, it was reported, was the "source of some very heated and often violent debates"[63]—which the Nation was able to overcome eventually.

As Dr. Shabazz was enjoying success, like a seesaw the BPP was declining. By early 1971 the already weakened chapter was on the fast track to extinction. "They have never had enough members to make their work in the community effective," said Barbara Womack, thus "telephones have been disconnected" and "the Free Breakfast Program has been discontinued...."[64]

Womack, the resident party critic, found Huey Newton to be an "egotistical, opportunist faggot whose only revolutionary act was to teach his white lover to cook chitterlings"; by then there was an incipient dispute between him and Cleaver and she heaped praise on the latter; as for the Nation, she claimed that it had "withered" after Malcolm's murder.[65]

As the BPP was disappearing over the horizon, the Nation was flexing. Minister Farrakhan—his name still misspelled though this would not last much longer—made his second appearance at Howard during the 1970-71 academic year, dubbed "an unprecedented feat in the ten year history of Project Awareness," which had been bringing controversial speakers to campus for years. The Minister was named "Outstanding Speaker" for the series and this time a hefty 1,100 came to hear him. This time he called his audience "dumb"— a demotion over his previous characterization: "pitiful"—and had choice words for Malcolm X as he, too, was degraded and devalued. Dr. King's non-violent philosophy was termed too conciliatory and Carmichael's "Black Power" as filled with more anger than wisdom. The observer was struck that "his sharpest attack came against revolutionaries who adopted Marx," a reference to Angela Davis and the BPP and for good measure he "rejected 'broken wrist' men as unfit for any nation," meaning their Gay Liberation Front allies.[66]

---

63. *The Hilltop*, 11 December 1970.
64. *The Hilltop*, 28 February 1971.
65. *The Hilltop*, 2 April 1971.
66. *The Hilltop*, 12 March 1971.

By late 1971, the Minister had demoted his audience further, pictured as delivering an "angry, dramatic address" at a "moderately filled Cramton," those assembled were now seen as a "'sick group of black brothers and sisters; faggots, freaks, pimps, whoremongers, reefer smokers, dope users....'"; the fulminating cleric claimed that parents would be "better off sending your daughter to a house of prostitution...."[67] rather than the capstone of Black higher education. Criticism followed: "the Honorable Minister has not investigated the sexual lives of Howard women," said a dissenting editorial according "all respect to Black women and Pan-African Power,"[68] but organizationally, the Nation was gaining altitude, nonetheless.

Robert "The Black" Taylor, top campus editor at H.U., found it noteworthy that the Nation journal was carrying articles attacking Carmichael "and his Pan African ideology" as they pressed their advantage.[69] As for Taylor, he argued that the "Sudan conflict pits Arabs against Africans,"[70] which decades later led to the secession and creation of the independent nation of South Sudan.

The Minister was having an impact; he was followed in this round-robin of verbal masters by Carmichael whose audience had been moved to the gymnasium in order to accommodate a crowd of 3,000. Yet the commentator found that he "failed to measure up to the Carmichael of the past"—or, perhaps, Black Power absent organization was hardly compelling. He amped up the verbiage in response, asserting "'There is no room for compromise or peaceful coexistence,'" a jab at Moscow and their domestic allies but, still, his talk was found wanting: "too short and too repetitious."[71] Despairing or maybe being realistic, the "advice" given to "young activists" was clear: "Get your passport,"[72] prepare for exile, which is what Carmichael did. Yet Carmichael may have been enticed to exit because of the extended scrutiny he continued to receive. By early 1971 the FBI kept an eye on his latest speech at Cramton, with Pan-Africanism as the topic: "expects full attendance and no trouble," it was said.[73]

The influence of the Nation can possibly be detected when Deborah Allen, Vice President of the Spanish Club, joined by others

---

67. *The Hilltop*, 10 December 1971.
68. *The Hilltop*, 17 December 1971.
69. *The Hilltop*, 30 April 1971.
70. *The Hilltop*, 5 November 1971.
71. *The Hilltop*, 12 March 1971.
72. *The Hilltop*, 26 March 1971.
73. Report, 8 March 1971, Box 25, RG 23.

demanded a purge of the Department of Romantic Languages, focusing on "'suckers of black blood [and] destructive parasites....'"[74]
Correspondingly, the Panther trend was being eclipsed. By October 1971, when victims of the drive toward incarceration rebelled
at Attica, a prison in upstate New York, Howard Moore—Angela
Davis' attorney—was described as speaking to a "small" campus rally.[75] Weeks later an editorial lamented the "apolitical nature and lack
of serious study which afflicts perhaps the overwhelming majority
of [hilltop] students."[76]

What "The Black"—campus editor—had noticed was little more
than the cutting edge of a still destabilizing trend. Earl Caldwell,
the Black reporter for the *New York Times* tasked with covering the
Panthers, exposed a glaring reality when he confessed to hilltoppers
that he was "'not the white world's spy on the Black community'"[77];
he could have added that deflationary pressures had hit this market
for there were so many already employed in this dubious venture.
The Law Enforcement Assistance Administration came into being in
1968 as part of the Department of Justice—a sprightly amble from
the hilltop—and by the time of Taylor's writing was the fastest growing federal outfit in spending on all aspects of criminal justice; their
budget tripled between 1968 and 1985, a greater increase than seen
in any other budgetary outlay. They had so much to spend that they
allowed their creativity to take flight, leading to the formation of a
Police Operations Combat Center that held so-called "war games"
in "Mao-land" (Baltimore) and Georgetown University. The ultimate
result of these antics was a shocking acceleration of incarceration
that ensnared especially young Black men—perceived as the instigators of unrest.[78] Unwittingly, the Black Panthers had contributed to
the Black Scare, the motive force behind this deviltry.

By the summer of 1970, Senator Joseph Tydings of Maryland was
discussing with his easily convinced peer, Senator Ernest Hollings
of South Carolina, a chamber of horrors, otherwise known as
"Crime Legislation" for the District, garlanded with authorization
of "'No Knock'" search warrants and massive pre-trial detention.[79]

---

74. *The Hilltop*, 2 April 1971.
75. *The Hilltop*, 1 October 1971.
76. *The Hilltop*, 25 October 1971.
77. *The Hilltop*, 23 October 1970.
78. Stuart Schader, *Badges Without Borders*, 138, 183.
79. Senator Tydings to Senator Hollings, 17 July 1970, Box 128, *Ernest Hollings Papers*. For a copy of this bill, see Box 511, *Edward Brooke Papers, Library of Congress-Washington, D.C.*

Ingratiatingly, the silver-thatched Carolinian, harumphed and found this bill "constitutionally sound and not an extension of existing procedural safeguards...."[80]

More prosaically, Congressman Thomas Abernethy of the Magnolia State, speaking as a "resident of this city," meaning the District, rued the perceived reality that "in the past several years" this lovely capital had "been literally torn to shreds by a bunch of hoodlums."[81]

A gauge of the emergent "Southern Strategy" of the Nixon regime was the point that this draconian rewriting of the law was not just backed by Dixiecrats, it was pushed by the Department of Justice headed by the New Yorker cum Detroiter, John Mitchell. DOJ propaganda argued that "'No Knock' provisions...[were] recommended by the Department to the Congress in the District of Columbia Court Reorganization Bills" and, besides, was backed by the District "government, the [District] Bar Association" and the resident U.S. Attorney.[82] They all subscribed to the approach that undergirded this subversion, i.e., "a crime crisis grips the Washington area" making the thriving capital a "virtual ghost city by night...." Remarkably, the rationale focused laser-like on "Chocolate City," stressing that "this bill is the only local crime legislation Congress can enact for any particular jurisdiction in the continental United States...provisions of this bill will apply only in [D.C.]—nowhere else."[83]

In other words, a decade or so earlier, District dynamics—heavily Black city forced to accommodate to African legations—helped to force desegregation locally then nationally, but now the worm had turned: District dynamics (racist hysteria about crime) would be used for a laboratory experiment—Washington as guinea pig—to be exported nationally, perhaps globally. To put it another way, the right wing—as had been their wont at least since 1776[84]—waved the bloody flag of the "Black Scare," frightening Euro-Americans across class lines.

What Capitol Hill was reacting to in part was an increased and more militant activism, especially on campuses. Federal City College, whose student body came heavily from a roiled and disquieted

80. Senator Hollings to Betty Nash, 23 July 1970, Box 128.
81. Congressman Abernethy to Raymond Ross, 7 February 1969, Box 317, *Thomas Abernethy Papers*.
82. DOJ Press Release, 14 May 1970, Box 204, *Edward Brooke Papers, Library of Congress-Washington, D.C.*
83. "Draft Statement of the Managers on the Part of the Senate...Regarding S. 2601," 1970, Box 511, *Edward Brooke Papers*.
84. Gerald Horne, *The Counter-Revolution of 1776*.

District, was beginning to challenge hilltoppers for the esteemed role as the vanguard. A group of them contacted Dr. King's successor, the Reverend Ralph Abernathy, after watching a well-publicized television special on hunger. "We saw children starving before our very eyes," they cried, referring to "the appalling conditions of hunger in America, the richest country in the world, is in itself a crime...." Sure, "the people who work for the government in Washington, D.C. consider themselves very fortunate" while "those of us who are Black... wonder: if the government continues to permit starvation anywhere in the United States, how long can we enjoy the security of our government." Their view? "The needy and low income people everywhere should be fed, regardless of their lack of the purchase price."[85]

Howard was deemed worthy of scrutiny because—ideologically—many of the students had strayed far beyond the mainstream of opinion. An editorial argued that "only when Black people come to realize that they are a domestically colonized African people within the racist-capitalist American society...it is ludicrous and 'negro-ish' for us to consider ourselves Americans," an unavoidable assessment given centuries of polecat status.[86]

As such, the student organ sought to build bridges abroad in order to countervail potent domestic foes, circulating in the Caribbean, the Soviet Union, Canada, Cuba, Canada, Great Britain, and China. As ever, on their triumphant soccer team, there was only one U.S. national but, instead, was stocked with athletes from the Caribbean and Africa.[87]

By 1970 many of the latter were encountering problems that had not disappeared magically with the passage of the 1964 Civil Rights Act. Zambia, a frontline state housing liberation movements from Namibia, Angola, Zimbabwe, South Africa, and other conflicted nations, found opposition when it sought to convert an old mansion at 2419 Massachusetts Avenue N.W. into an office.[88] Again, the State Department won few friends in Dixie when it stood alongside the Africans and against Euro-American opponents when it harpooned the objections since these detractors were "'making the United States look silly in the eyes of the world...as ridiculous as saying you can't put a clothing store at 13th and F streets.'"[89]

---

85. FCC Students to the Reverend Abernathy, 19 February 1969, Box 204, *SCLC Papers, Emory University-Atlanta.*
86. *The Hilltop*, 12 November 1971.
87. *The Hilltop*, 19 November 1971.
88. *Washington Post*, 16 October 1970.
89. *Washington Star*, 24 October 1970.

Police were not necessarily in accord. When Howard's African Studies professor, Zuberi Muamba of Tanzania—another frontline state—had a parking violation on campus, he was arrested and not allowed to call his legation.[90]

The potential neighbors of the Zambians thought they had reason to object to their presence. In August 1970 there was a terrifying bomb blast at the legation of the outlaw regime of Rhodesia, 2852 McGill Terrace N.W. A neighbor identified as "Mrs. John Jackson" residing at 2840 McGill Terrace, told the press. "'the house shook...I never heard such a noise in all my life....'" There was also a blast at the legation of Portugal—a key ally of the outlaw regime and the colonizer, inter alia, of Angola and Mozambique—and they too were located in a fancy neighborhood, 2125 Kalorama Road N.W.: though, "only" windows were broken. Bombings in Washington were becoming too frequent for comfort and were becoming bipartisan. In January 1967 the Yugoslav chancery was hit and as of August 1970, there had been five such bombings at legations—with more expected.[91]

As for the bombing on McGill Terrace, investigators could have been excused if they had inferred that hilltop fingerprints were apparent. A note was left stating, "'We are an African people and we are at war with all...that conduct and support...exploitation and oppression of African people around the world. Angola, Mozambique and Zimbabwe shall and will be freed." This missive was signed by "the Revolutionary Action Party" and "attached to the card was a button with green, black and red stripes...."[92]

Their edict was echoed by a Howard editorial wherein it was "decided to take an ideological stand. And that ideology is Pan-Africanism...[and] we are an African people and not Americans...."[93]

Then the bombers turned to the patrons of colonizers, meaning a bomb blast "in the Senate wing of the Capitol today came on the 17th anniversary of a wild shooting fray in the House chambers...[by] Puerto Rican nationalists"[94]—or so it was pronounced.

Howard continued to entertain a visiting array of African dignitaries, giving coherence to this widespread idea that "We are an African people." The latest in this cavalcade was General Sangoule Lamizana, leader of the nation to be known as Bourkina Faso.[95] Then

---

90. *The Hilltop*, 26 March 1971.
91. *Washington Post*, 31 August 1970; *Rhodesia Star*, 29 August 1970.
92. *Washington Post*, 31 August 1970.
93. *The Hilltop*, 24 September 1971.
94. Report, 1 March 1971, Box 26, RG 23.
95. *The Hilltop*, 23 October 1970.

President Cheek toured Ghana and Nigeria, suggesting that a kind of Pan-Africanism was not unique to students but resonated with Black Capital of which he was a leading delegate.[96] The hemisphere was not absent for then touring the campus was Rahman Gajraj, a leader of Guyana.[97]

Customarily, the NAACP did not accept these ideological shifts with equanimity. They had lambasted the Communists and now their chief, Roy Wilkins, was deriding "[Black] militants [as] 'pip-squeaks.'"[98] Fortunately, there were contrary trends: because of the growing affluence of the region, i.e., desegregation allowing for more income for certain African Americans: thus, Washington was becoming an ATM for visiting politicians, including Richard Hatcher—who became the first Black mayor of Gary, Indiana and hosted an important Black Power assembly thereafter.[99] President Cheek of Howard was known to be close to the Nixon White House and his campus, along with other Negroes, were applying busily for licenses to operate radio stations, which—at the time—seemed to be a license to print money. Initially, H.U. was blocked because their "application" was "mutually exclusive" with that of the Pacifica Foundation, a sturdy entity of the left but, as things evolved, both prevailed.[100]

Howard's trustees included Chicago based magazine mogul, John H. Johnson, of "Ebony-Jet" fame and Dr. Kenneth Clark of New York City, well-connected in the lush field of philanthropy with both being able to generate capital.[101]

What was occurring was an unavoidable amount of instability as the region and nation transitioned from an apartheid society to—officially—a society where the status quo ante was seen as illegitimate. As reflected in previous pages, this occurred because of a complex calculation involving African and Caribbean liberation combined with a devastating Red Scare—however, then as now, the idea was that what was occurring was the U.S. supposedly returning to the principles of its founding, a kind of blinkered thinking that handicapped severely an ability to craft an analysis that could guide steps forward.

---

96. *The Hilltop*, 6 November 1970.

97. *The Hilltop*, 6 November 1970 and 20 November 1970.

98. *Washington Daily News*, 22 June 1970.

99. *Washington Post*, 26 April 1971.

100. Ben Waple of Federal Communications Commission to President Cheek, 4 February 1970, Box 449, *Edward Brooke Papers*.

101. *The Hilltop*, 1 May 1970.

The resultant turbulence was manifested most graphically on campuses, replete with youngsters seeking to understand these complexities and often unwilling to swallow comforting cant. College Park was in the unenviable position of bordering a tempestuous District though responsible to a distinctly Dixie discourse. The expansion of the war in the spring of 1970, as elsewhere, led to interminable rallies, including one with the provocative come-on, "This Is It," which culminated with an attack on the armory and ROTC, accented by Molotov cocktails and fire bombs.[102] ROTC was also the target at H.U. as "arson" was charged, though the "fire was confined to the...storeroom, where there was major damage" caused by a combination of "turpentine & lighter fluid," according to local intelligence.[103] In 1972, the campus was at the center of ever more disruptive antiwar activism, culminating in vicious police attacks upon students. Five years earlier students had organized one of the first demonstrations nationally against Marine recruiters and on one occasion more than 8,000 demonstrated against ROTC and fought pitched battles with state, county, and campus police and National Guardsmen. This was followed by an infestation of spies, informers, undercover cops, and agents all bent on a different kind of disruption.[104] Governor Marvin Mandel had issued an "emergency proclamation" designed to further impose order on this unruly campus with little obvious effect.[105]

Then 300 students doffed their dungarees in favor of more formal attire and trooped to Capitol Hill to lobby Congress to pass a measure that would require the latter's approval of further spending in support of the expansion of the war into Cambodia.[106]

Then dungarees were once more embraced as protests soared as the reactionary comic mogul, Bob Hope, was slated to appear at Cole Field House amidst credible rumors that the notorious

102. Narrative, 1 May 1970, *History of the University of Maryland-Campus Unrest'*, Box 1, 88-274, ACC: 2002-137, *University of Maryland-College Park*. In this collection, see also Michael Fincham, "Chronology of Dissent on University of Maryland Campus, May 1970. At the same site, see also Doris Plumer, RN, "University of Maryland, 1969-1971: One Student's Memories." 103. Report, 28 June 1971, Box 25, RG 23.
104. Newsletter of "Md-DC Committee to Oppose Political Repression," October 1972, Box 2, *History of the University of Maryland-Campus Unrest,*
105. "Joint Statement by Chancellor C.E. Bishop and General Edwin T. Warfield..." et.al., 2 May 1972
106. Narrative, 6 May 1970.

"Weathermen," a dissident split-off from SDS, were coming from the District with disruption in mind.[107]

SDS proper remained consistently active in College Park. Their issues included the "numerous coeds raped on campus" and the misdeeds of various professors, including "Drs. MacEntire and Davis of our Psych Department" who "are helping the army breed and select scout dogs for Vietnam," i.e., "attack dogs" that "could also be used against students."[108]

The ultra-right was not dormant. On 4 September 1970 they claimed that "Marxist oriented rabble rousers", i.e., "leftist thugs" with "half baked theories" were on the march. "Only you can save the University of Maryland! Now the radicals claim they have explosives...they have threatened 'on[e] building for each student expelled'" and, now "they must be forcefully stopped. If our government is too weak to do it," said the National Action Party, "then the citizenry must...."[109]

Ultimately, the National Guard was invited to campus to restore order but this outraged many, including Karen Liebert, a teaching assistant in the History Department. She was "shocked" by their arrival and easily envisioned "gassing, shooting and/or using dogs on students"; this was an "unnecessary provocation," which she decried and presented a "danger to both sides (as Kent State made more painfully obvious),"[110] a reference to yet another campus tragedy.

Actually, the National Guard occupied the campus from 14 May to 6 June 1970, but 1971 saw no surcease as phony bomb scares during class hours became fashionable.[111] By the time of her writing in 1971 violent confrontations between demonstrators and police were common. At one notable march, 3,000 protesters were driven off Route 1 by police using clubs, tear gas, and an aggressive K-9 corps.[112]

As at Howard, the trigger was the presence of ROTC on campus; eventually 5,000 demonstrators were counted and outsiders spotted

---

107. Narrative, 9 May 1970.

108. Leaflet, Circa 1970, Box 1, *History of the University of Maryland Campus Unrest, University of Maryland-College Park.*

109. Leaflet, 4 September 1970, Box 1, *History of the University of Maryland-Campus Unrest.*

110. Karen Liebert to C.E. Bishop, Chancellor, 7 May 1971, Box 12, Series V, RG 28, *Office of the Chancellor Records, University of Maryland-College Park.*

111. *Baltimore Sun*, 12 January 1971.

112. Report, 6 May 1971, *Vertical File-Campus Unrest, 1971, University of Maryland.*

included Rennie Davis—noted antiwar activist—and Hosea Williams, a Georgia comrade of the late Dr. King.[113] They were outshone
by Jane Fonda of Hollywood wattage who arrived earlier in support
of the antiwar movement.[114] Though official reports had stated that
Blacks were indifferent to the antiwar movement, this was belied in
early 1971 when there was a teach-in on the war at Howard, then
a march to Lafayette Park—fronted by Marion Barry and Julius
Hobson—to confront the White House.[115] George Murphy, scion of
the family that simultaneously was a Black press barony, continued
to crusade for peace.[116]

College Park shared Prince George's County with a proliferating
Black community buoyed by desegregation and erosion of Jim Crow
barriers, placing more money in more pockets—and more confidence too. Black teachers there formed their own group since they
were "'appalled'" by a countywide teachers' vote that rejected a plan
to desegregate two all Black secondary schools; about 15 percent of
the county's 7,200 teachers were Black—and now they were able to
develop a treasury and initiatives without the constraints of their
less progressive peers.[117]

By 1 May 1971, protest in the District reached a crescendo when
what was billed as the "biggest mass arrest" in the nation's history occurred in the midst of an antiwar demonstration. The
District's top cop, Jerry Wilson, was straight from an audition in
Hollywood—6' 4" inches tall with North Carolina roots, he was
squaring off against activists sited at their office at 1029 Vermont
Avenue. Supposedly, he was seeking to reverse the edict from years
past that mandated that his force could be no more than 15 percent
Black to the point when the Secret Service needed a hand, the message sent was "'Send white officers only,'" arguably compromising
national security. Middle class Negroes were not exempt from their
depredations as the home of then H.U. president, James Nabrit,
was attacked in 1968 by inebriated cops firing shots. This was the
atmosphere to which antiwar campaigners arrived, threatening to
disrupt the 14th Street bridge to Virginia—the longest such artery
in the world, said wags, insofar as it connected Africa [the Dis-
trict] with Europe [suburbs]. This artery was chosen purposefully
since it was thought to deposit suburbanites to the Department of

---

113. *Washington Post*, 6 May 1971.
114. *Washington Post*, 23 May 1970.
115. *Washington Post*, 28 March 1971.
116. *Daily World*, 30 November 1977.
117. *Washington Post*, 27 April 1970.

Justice and did not inconvenience the Black working class. Thus, 7,000 were arrested though the District could only handle 2,700 in about 14 precinct jails—with a whopping 14,000 detained altogether. This—in a sense—marked the end of the tumult of the 1960s and the onset of a new era.[118]

---

118. Lawrence Roberts, *Mayday 1971: A White House at War, a Revolt in the Streets and the Untold History of America's Biggest Mass Arrests*, Boston: Houghton Mifflin, 2020, xxiii, 56, 82, 83, 125, 161, 245, 324.

Chapter 25

Home Rule—or Who Shall Rule at Home? 1970-2022

As the 1970s unspooled, Dorothy Gilliam—one of the few Black journalists on the staff of the *Post*—was motoring along in her career but dissatisfied with the overall climate there and in the city where she served. As of early 1972 she counted a mere nine Black reporters at this premier periodical, leading to a lawsuit. Even Ben Bradlee, the top editor, conceded that the paper had a "'redneck streak.'" But this bluntness did him few favors since, she said, "Ben was seen as too close to the black community, because he heard and understood our concerns." C. Sumner Stone, local activist and former aide to Congressman Adam Clayton Powell, called this eminent journal "'a paper for white Washingtonians.'" Even Gilliam acknowledged that "so many black Washingtonians still thought of [the *Post*] as a white newspaper in a black city." On a brighter note, she found the defeat of Congressman John McMillan of South Carolina—Bilbo's successor as Dixie's overseer in the District—to be a possible sign of things to come.[1] As to be expected, hilltop students worked assiduously to oust him.[2]

Before he was dislodged, Congressman McMillan was under siege, battling his peers on Capitol Hill, led by Congressman Charles Diggs of Detroit, a founding member of the Congressional Black Caucus. Diggs was among those who objected to "establishment of subcommittees with no defined jurisdiction...inequitable and arbitrary distribution of bills to subcommittee...arbitrary reassignment and withdrawal of bills from subcommittee[s]...required monthly meetings not called...special meetings and executive sessions called without notice and with inadequate notice...no advance notice of any agenda...committee members not given time to file dissenting

---

1. Dorothy Butler Gilliam, *Trailblazer*, 158, 159, 168, 181, 205, 209, 206.
2. *The Hilltop*, 17 March 1972.

493

or supplemental views to committee reports...official committee reports written to reflect the chairman's viewpoint regardless of committee action...committee reports and reported bills unavailable to House members until the moment of floor consideration... conference committee appointees selected irrespective of rank on committee, subcommittee membership or position on legislation... subcommittees arbitrarily refused permission to conduct hearings... full committee not permitted to discuss or approve committee investigations...legislative requests of the District of Columbia government ignored...."[3]

In short, District governance was shambolic but it was inconsistent with the growing militancy of Black residents, leading to the ousting of Congressman McMillan. Eventually, Congressman Ronald V. Dellums of the Black Caucus would lead the District committee, a turnabout in that since 1808 leadership had been in the hands of those akin to McMillan; and yet the latter served during a time of tumult and responded accordingly, "sponsoring or authoring more enactments relating to the District" than any of his predecessors— or so he said—which boomeranged spectacularly when Black folk engineered his political demise,[4] by arriving in droves in his district and campaigning against him.

The demise of McMillan marked the end of an era; he had ruled the District from 1949 to 1972 in the manner of a feudal baron in his personal fiefdom or as the master of a plantation.[5] He also added a dollop of modernity by arguing that Home Rule was a Communist ruse,[6] meaning that his unseating marked a turning point and the onset of a new dispensation.

The Reverend Fauntroy was a beneficiary of his own activism, helping to dislodge McMillan then catapulting himself into Congress as a District delegate, albeit non-voting, by 1973. However, his organization—the Southern Christian Leadership Conference, founded by the sainted Dr. King—had fallen on hard times. By 1975, the District chapter was told that their "presence...leaves much to be desired" in that their "existence in D.C. does not make one bit of difference. The national office does not receive any

---

3. Congressman McMillan to "Dear Colleague," 1 February 1971, Box 3, *Cornelius Gallagher Papers, University of Oklahoma-Norman.*
4. Legislation Relating to the District of Columbia, Summary Report, 18 October 1972, Box 6, *John McMillan Papers, University of South Carolina-Columbia,*
5. *Afro-American,* 22 September 1979. See also Box 4, *Ronald V. Dellums Papers, Oakland African American Museum & Library.*
6. *Regardies,* May 1989, Box 4, *Dellums Papers,*

information from you in regards to matters on [Capitol] Hill which should demand our attention...we simply have a paper presence in D.C...."[7] The recipient of this rebuke, Henry Silva, fired back with similar gusto at this "rather nasty letter," while the chapter was busily "undoing the negative impression SCLC has left in this town since 1968" and Resurrection City, perceived by some as a fiasco. This "has not been easy," he said; besides, "you don't know this city. You don't do things here from an organizational point of view as you would in the Gulf Coast of Mississippi...."[8] This energetic riposte may have served to arrest District decline as far as SCLC was concerned. By 1983 the Reverend Joseph Lowery, then leader, was told that "in Washington, D.C. we have a D.C. Metro chapter and a clandestine chapter" at Howard,[9] perhaps unwilling to stick its head above the parapet during the backsliding of the Reagan years. Tellingly, picketing restrictions at the White House had been imposed in 1976, when the California governor first chose to make a bid for the presidency.[10]

The odyssey of Congressman Fauntroy, a small and wiry man who had served as pastor at New Bethel Baptist Church—a SCLC man through-and-through—exposed the debilities of his organization when he got into financial difficulties then fled the country, only returning in 2016.[11] His comrade Sterling Tucker, got into a tiff with his employer, the Urban League, and he thought that this was their "latest step in a contrived yet transparent plan to separate me" from the group[12]; that was in 1972 and by 1974, Vernon Jordan, then an Urban League boss just before decamping to a fabulously lucrative career as an investment banker and influencer, as doors were flung open widely for him, accepted Tucker's "formal resignation."[13]

It was Jordan, one of the principal monetary beneficiaries of the anti-Jim Crow movement and a supple fixer, who maneuvered to place Walter Carrington, a Negro and future envoy to Nigeria, into a strategic post on the hilltop. By 1981 and the advent of the Reagan

---

7. Fred Taylor, Director of Chapters and Affiliates to Henry Silva, D.C. Metro Chapter, 18 December 1975, Box 332, *SCLC Papers, Emory University-Atlanta.*
8. Henry Silva to Fred Taylor, no date, Box 332.
9. J.C Saunders to the Reverend Lowery, 18 March 1983, Box 322,.
10. Picketing Restrictions of 1976, Box 131, *Joseph Rauh Papers.*
11. Carl Bernstein, *Chasing History*, 316, 334.
12. Sterling Tucker to Harold Sims, 7 January 1972, Box III: 351, *National Urban League Papers.*
13. Vernon Jordan to Sterling Tucker, 30 May 1974, Box III: 385, *National Urban League Papers.*

regime, the counter-revolutionary impulse had asserted itself and the unrest that had rocked the campus previously was not as intense. It was then that Carrington, with Jordan's assist, who was "overseeing everything Howard does internationally," as radical energy was co-opted into mainstream advance. "Howard, by its history and geography," said Carrington "ought to be the foremost American university interacting with nations overseas. I hope to make it that,"[14] admirable on the surface but a far cry from what those like Carmichael had envisioned years ago.

It is true that activism at varying levels has continued on the hilltop, most prominently in 1989 where luminaries—then students—e.g., as future Newark mayor, Ras Baraka and future mega-entrepreneur, Sean Combs, were involved.[15] But it is equally true to assert that the conditions of the 1960s were utterly unique—Cold War pressures intersecting with African independence in the first place—making this latter decade difficult to duplicate.

Marion Barry, elected mayor for the first time in 1979, assayed subsequently that 1974 was "our very first election under Home Rule," the culmination of years of relentless struggle—though it then raised the companion issue: Who Shall Rule at Home? Others determined that only statehood would deliver democracy to the District.[16] In the prelude to Barry's victory, the District had an estimated two-thirds Black majority but this population, despite economic advance, held about three percent of government contracts: Barry was sworn to overturn this status quo, which did not win many plaudits in traditional business circles. One beneficiary of the Barry regime was R. Donahue "Don" Peebles, of late in the top ten of wealthiest Black Americans with a net worth approaching $1 billion. Born in the District, he was appointed by Barry to the city's Board of Equalization and Review, where he learned the innards of real estate development. However, after raising funds for campaigns of Bill Clinton and Barack Obama and serving as Chair of the Congressional Black Caucus Foundation, he became a devoted supporter of Donald

---

14. Walter Carrington to Vernon Jordan, 8 June 1981, Box III: 253, *National Urban League Papers*.

15. Joshua M. Myers, *We are Worth Fighting For: A History of the Howard University Student Protest of 1989*, New York: New York University Press, 2019.

16. *Wall Street Journal*, 27 November 2022: The attempt by policymakers to expand voting rights in the District sparked an editorial that claimed that this would mean "staff at the Chinese Embassy" would soon be casting ballots in elections.

J. Trump,[17] as his class interests asserted itself, unsurprisingly in essence. Peebles had been preceded by William Syphax, descendant of an old regional family, who expired in 1989 after a career building homes for Negroes in Northern Virginia.[18]

Peebles and Syphax represented a developing industry in the region based on real estate, which often swept aside history in reckless abandon in search of profit. By 1974, when Barry was marking what he deemed to be the onset of a new chapter in Home Rule, the idea was afloat to demolish Dunbar High School, once the companion of Howard in developing generations of leaders and intellectuals. Roscoe Brown, Jr., a former Tuskegee Airman, then college president in The Bronx, was among those who expressed "shock and personal dismay" since this school was "probably the most outstanding Black secondary school in the country"—which was accurate though floating the notion of seeking to "provide a new football field for the new Dunbar High" was, sadly, more in accord with priorities then.[19] So urged, the City Council blocked the Dunbar demolition.[20]

By 1982, one of the outstanding sons of Dunbar—then M Street High—and Howard, Rayford Logan, passed from the scene. Unlike many subsequent Black intellectuals, he was highly active internationally, his still relevant and signature book concerned one of the most important events in Pan-African history, the Haitian Revolution and its relations with the U.S.[21] Logan did not go gently into decline, continuing to rail against changes at Howard, which should have brought him more positive attention from the similarly skeptical press but typical of the skewed politics of the time, he found that the *Post* had been "hostile to Howard University for some time."[22] "I of course repudiate the very idea of a 'Black University,'" he said in 1968.[23] His "opposition" to now anodyne terms, e.g., "'Black'" and "'Afro-American'" was unsparing.[24] (Although the record is unclear, it would be unsurprising if Logan had been among the troglodytes who at one time barred the Music Department from instructing in

---

17. *Washington Post*, 22 December 2010 and 10 February 2022; *Charlotte Observer*, 12 August 2016.
18. *Washington Post*, 6 March 1989.
19. Roscoe Brown, Jr. to James Banks, Housing Officer, 17 January 1974, Box 426, *Edward Brooke Papers*,
20. *Washington Post*, 2 April 1974.
21. Funeral Program, 1982, Box 219-5, *Merze Tate Papers*.
22. Entry, 8 January 1977, Box 7.
23. Entry, 24 March 1968, Box 7, *Logan Papers*.
24. Entry, 9 January 1970, Box 7.

the music called "Jazz," compelling world-class drummer, Billy Hart, then an engineering student on the hilltop, to learn this art form elsewhere.[25])

Of course, there were stressors that may have clouded his thinking. A bomb was tossed at the home of President Nabrit in late 1967, then a Molotov cocktail was thrown through the window of the home of then Dean Snowden. Then in a final telling signal Sterling Brown was committed to St. Elizabeth's, a resting place for those undergoing mental strain: it was "clear to me," said Logan, that "he was deranged...."[26] When the campus newspaper observed that the school was "known for its disagreeable and often negatively superior attitudes of its personnel toward its students,"[27] they may have had Logan in mind.

Dunbar may have survived but its companion on the hilltop continued to endure jeopardizing difficulties. By 1972 the student organ carried the slogan "the largest and best known Black student publication in the world,"[28] which was not puffery. The Nation of Islam tended to gain traction; the poet once known as Sonia Sanchez spoke to 300 at Rankin Chapel under the name "Sonia 5X."[29] As ever, there were external factors that were shaping the internal scene. "For the past four years," said a 1972 editorial, "we have been able to observe that a drug culture mentality has been spreading on campus. The tragic deaths of two students this academic year" was a result, along with a kind of music—they singled out the wildly popular "Funkadelics"—which "reinforces the drug culture mentality."[30] (Celebrated instead were alumnus, Roberta Flack; and former students, Curtis Mayfield and Donny Hathaway.)[31]

The erstwhile Black National who called himself "General Hassan Jeru-Ahmed, the Commanding Officer of the Black Man's Volunteer Army of Liberation spoke to a small audience at Rankin," said the student organ, addressing "why he is becoming a congressional candidate on the Republican ticket"; unmasking himself thoroughly after years of militant posturing, he "hope[d] that Nixon will be re-elected so that he can have Nixon's ear'" and listen to a "Moor" like himself.[32]

---

25. *Washington Post*, 27 March 2022.
26. Entry, 26 February 1968, Box 7, *Rayford Logan Papers*.
27. *The Hilltop*, 10 March 1972.
28. *The Hilltop*, 28 January 1972.
29. *The Hilltop*, 28 January 1972.
30. *The Hilltop*, 18 February 1972.
31. *The Hilltop*, 28 April 1972.
32. *The Hilltop*, 25 February 1972

The self-described "Moor" was not the only person on Georgia Avenue with an interest in the ancestral continent. Scores of students picketed the Portuguese embassy after an aerial strike inside Tanzania because of that nation's backing of fighters from neighboring Mozambique.[33] Then Guinean leader, Sekou Toure, who had embraced an exiled Alphaeus Hunton, reported the sad news of the expiration of Nkrumah[34]; Carmichael who reportedly had taken the name "Chaka Zulu" in homage to the South African combatant,[35] then took the names of the two West African giants.

Figures like the self-designated "General" seemed to be inserted on campus in order to spark disarray, of which Howard had a surplus already. Students were heavily involved in the "National Black Political Convention" in Gary, Indiana in 1972 but their participation, said a commentator, "generated a flurry of hostile reactions from several community organizations" who thought these matriculants were over-represented.[36] *The Hilltop* editorialized sharply against the then prevailing praxis of busing younger students for purposes of desegregation—it "defrauded the Black Nation"—but this was hardly a universally shared view.[37]

Just as the high school was spared, the Howard Medical School was complaining about facing bias in the increasingly lucrative business that was kidney transplants, though they had performed more successful operations than its competitors—Georgetown and George Washington.[38] Despite the obstacles, Howard's medical arm continued to be pursued by non-Blacks, including Dr. Weissbluth, who in 1980 lobbied John Jacob of the Urban League—soon to become an executive in the beer industry—for aid in gaining admittance for his son, Jay, there—he was then enrolled at a medical school in Manila.[39]

In other words, Peebles notwithstanding, ordinary members of the Negro elite continued to encounter manifold problems. It did seem, however, that the teething problems of adjusting to an influx of African envoys had eased by the late 1970s, as officialdom showed that they could adapt to what once seemed unfathomable. By 1977,

---

33. *The Hilltop*, 28 April 1972.
34. *The Hilltop*, 12 May 1972.
35. *The Hilltop*, 21 April 1972.
36. *The Hilltop*, 3 March 1972.
37. *The Hilltop*, 17 March 1972.
38. *Washington Post*, 21 May 1975.
39. Dr. Jack Weissbluth to John Jacob, 17 June 1980, Box III: 253, *National Urban League Papers*.

the *Post* posted an admiring profile of Ambassador Tiothee Ahoua of the Ivory Coast and his spouse as they hosted an elaborate affair for author, Alex Haley, after both had read his book *Roots* along with his Malcolm X autobiography. Reflecting the tightened trans-Atlantic tie, they had rearranged their schedules for the eight evenings when the televised version of *Roots* was broadcast, a cultural landmark. Earlier they had entertained singer James Brown and the *Post* opined that since the recent crisis over Angola, whereby the U.S. found itself isolated in league with apartheid South Africa, the State Department and U.S. elite had embarked on a charm offensive with Africans. Said the ambassador, "'For Africa it's very late and history moves very fast.'"[40]

Developing Negro billionaires was far from being the warp and woof of the mayor's doings. Besides, said Barry, "Washington was also still a police state when I got into office," barely eluding the previous era when Negro cops "couldn't arrest white folks. He could only detain them," policies designed to maintain the status quo in the purported fortress of democracy.[41] Barry had been present for the April 1968 revolt—"the Army had M-16 rifles with bayonets attached," in what he termed a "real mess."[42] A repetition of this history he too sought to alter, again incurring wrath.

Barry's press aide, Florence Tate, added that most high-level District governmental posts were not held by Blacks at the time of his election—and that promptly began to change, inflaming passions. The same could be said for Mayor Barry's decision to continue the BPP tradition—says Tate, "Marion was one of the first politicians in the country to support gay rights."[43] By 1979, in a landmark, Barry was sworn in as mayor of the nation's 12th largest city and carrying a $2 billion budget.[44]

---

40. *Washington Post*, 26 February 1977.
41. Marion Barry, Jr., *Mayor for Life*, 127, 140, 194.
42. Marion Barry, Jr., *Mayor for Life*, 135.
43. Florence L. Tate and Jake-Ann Jones, *Sometimes Farm Girls Become Revolutionaries: Notes on Black Power, Politics, Depression and the FBI*, Baltimore: Black Classic, 2021, 214, 216.
44. *New York Times*, 3 January 1979, Box 74, *James Forman Papers, Library of Congress-Washington, D.C.* Also see, Shahan Mufti, *American Caliph: The True Story of a Muslim Mystic, a Hollywood Epic and the 1977 Siege of Washington, D.C.*, New York: FSG, 2022, 266: President Jimmy Carter was on the verge of declaring martial law in the city, illustrating once more the peril endured by African Americans residing in the capital.

Barry barely made it to high office. In 1977 he was shot in the chest and Maurice Williams, a 22 year old reporter at the hilltop radio station was slain. This occurred as a group described as "Hanafi Muslims" invaded the equivalent of City Hall, wounding 13, taking scores hostages as they demanded that comrades held in 1973 slayings be freed, among other grievances; a large number were also held in the B'nai B'rith building.[45]

That brush with death was a bad omen for his mayoralty for the hostility to him and his regime congealed in the office of U.S. Attorney, Joseph di Genova, who admitted that Washington was a "small southern town" and "not a northern town" with all the historical weight that carries, exacerbated by his characterization of the District as "sixty two square miles of gossip," realities that Barry flaunted, contributing to his arrest and imprisonment after being caught on camera sampling illicit narcotics. The U.S. Attorney accused Barry and his cronies of "stealing from people" and mounting a "very bad local government" that he was sworn to dismantle.[46]

What historically had contributed heavily to District militancy was its role as a capital, attracting diverse forces with various agendas adding to the overall mix. Such was the case in 1972 when about 800 Native American activists and allies occupied the Bureau of Indian Affairs for six days: they simply walked in and refused to depart—until the victorious reelection campaign of President Nixon caused his aide, Leonard Garment, to raise about $66,000 in cash for the occupiers to return home but not after analysts termed it "'the most important act of Indian resistance since the defeat of Custer at the Little Big Horn....'"[47]

As the acute journalist, Dorothy Gilliam, also pointed out, those who delivered the news were making news. It was in March 1972 that Black reporters at the *Post* filed a complaint with the Equal Employment Opportunities Commission, a legacy of the anti-Jim Crow movement. Of the 310 employees involved with the newsroom, only 37 were Black, including 13 reporters, one editorial writer, two Metro desk editors, one columnist, and two photographers. The architect

---

45. *New York Times*, 10 March 1977. See also *New York Post*, 10 March 1977: Apparently, beheadings were threatened as the perpetrators wanted boxer, Muhammad Ali and others be turned over to them.

46. Oral History, Joseph di Genova, 30 September-18 December 2003, *Historical Society of Washington, D.C.*

47. *Washington Post*, 25 January 2021.

of this far-reaching initiative was the Black District attorney, Clifford Alexander, who was to resign from the EEOC after coming into conflict with the Nixon regime.[48]

Nixon was elected in 1968 on a restoration platform, that he would check supposed Black marauding and restore "law and order," as he deftly invoked the Black Scare. Purportedly, by 1972 there had been a still astonishing 1,900 domestic bombings in the U.S.—but then these detonations began to sputter and flicker out. A number were conducted by Euro-American radicals, outraged both by the war and domestic racism and saw themselves as emulating the antebellum radical, John Brown.[49]

At his first press conference as president in 1969 he beat the drum incessantly about a supposed crime wave in the District and how he was warned by the Secret Service not to dream about taking a walk in the streets.[50] The District as the "Crime Capital of the Nation" was his calling card and, as suggested, by 1970 the city was regarded as the only jurisdiction nationally with a preventive detention law, as Washington became an experimental laboratory. The city had the highest ratio of prisoners to population of any jurisdiction in the nation, as the *Post* and *Star* bayed for more.[51] Fortunately, by 1972 Senator Edward Brooke was pushing legislation to ban the death penalty in the District.[52]

Still, by 1974, not least because of a proliferation of small arms, the number of murders in the District reached a new high and gun violence because the leading cause of death for men under 40.[53] It was near that same time that a *Post* reporter went to the home of Chief Justice Warren Burger, seeking a comment on a matter of national interest, and the jurist greeted him with weapon in hand, a long barreled steel monstrosity. Although the purported crime wave was also laid at the doorstep of Black Washington, from 1974-1984 the number of federal officials convicted of federal crimes rose from

48. *Washington Post*, 9 July 2022. See also *Washington Star*, 26 March 1972: According to Sterling Tucker, 37 of the 397 *Post* employees were Black at this point, 13 of whom were reporters.

49. Bryan Burrough, *Days of Rage*, 5, 68.

50. John Norris, *Mary McGrory: The Trailblazing Columnist who Stood Washington on its Head*, New York: Penguin, 2016, 131.

51. *D.C. Gazette*, November 1977, Box 200, *James Forman Papers, Library of Congress-Washington, D.C.*

52. Senator Adlai Stevenson to Senator Brooke, 5 July 1972, Box 521, *Edward Brooke Papers*.

53. Kyle Sommers, "'I Believe in the City,'" 269.

43 in 1975 to 429 in 1984—not including the sprawling Iran-Contra scandals and cover-up.[54]

This real crime wave also underscored the importance of a Black presence on juries, the counterpoint to the gentrification that was changing the city's demography,[55] but then by 2021 a pandemic intervened, leading to the headline: "D.C. white population fell... reversal of trend after a long climb...falls for first time in nearly 20 years." Furthermore, "many of the region's close-in suburbs also lost [white] residents than at a much higher rate than previously, including Montgomery County, as well as Fairfax and Arlington counties and the city of Alexandria in Virginia." However, "the District's Black population...also dropped more precipitously between 2020 and 2021" though "[white] people...make up only 37 percent of the [District's] population...."[56]

Jill Nelson, who formerly toiled for the *Post*, says that the city's designer, Pierre L'Enfant, "had the city laid out in circles to keep the unruly mob from the houses of government"; thus, "if you are poor and Black and live in Southeast Washington, there is no reason to leave your Bantustan at all" with the "Anacostia River" the equivalent of the "Red Sea before Moses...." Fanning the flames of racism, she said, was their columnist, Richard Cohen, who was writing that "it's okay to lock [your] shop door and not buzz in Black males," all of which contributed to the demonizing and mass incarceration of this beleaguered group.[57]

After the pardoning of Nixon by his successor, Gerald Ford, the importance of jury composition was highlighted, according to former U.S. Attorney for the District, "there were a huge number of acquittals in the Superior Court because jurors felt that that [it] was unfair that the former president should have been held accountable legally for his conduct" and jurors were "simply refusing to convict young felons of just about anything." In this "truly unique city," he says, "there is much more scrutiny of what goes on in Superior Court than there is in other major cities...."[58]

---

54. Ben Bradlee, *A Good Life*, 321.

55. Sabiyha Prince, *African Americans and Gentrification in Washington, D.C.: Race, Class and Social Justice in the Nation's Capital*, Burlington, Vermont: Ashgate, 2014.

56. *Washington Post*, 2 July 2022.

57. Jill Nelson, *Volunteer Slavery: My Authentic Negro Experience*, Chicago: Noble, 1993, 3, 31, 59.

58. Oral History, Joseph di Genova. 30 September; 11 November; and 18 December 2003, *Historical Society of Washington, D.C.*

However, what some of his voters had not bargained for was that this crackdown in the District would include lawlessness of government itself, encapsulated in a mélange of scandals denoted as "Watergate." Nixon was fighting back by purging the Department of Justice in what was called the "Saturday Night Massacre" of 1973, leading the *Post*'s Leonard Downie to wonder, along with others, if "there would be tanks on the streets downtown" as the right-wing upsurge exerted its wicked logic.[59] Intriguingly, what led directly to the downfall of Nixon was Frank Wills, an $80 a week Black security guard—operating then on five hours of sleep and living in a $14 per-week room—in June 1972, who managed to detect operatives burglarizing the Democrats' office: this triggered multiple investigations—and scandals, forcing a presidential resignation about two years later.[60]

This militancy included a complement of labor militancy, which brought discipline and savvy. This was especially the case at Georgetown University, where by 1972 a union organizing drive unfolded at the medical school and hospital, spearheaded by District 1199 of today's Service Employees International Union (full disclosure: I once worked with this union at its Manhattan headquarters). Ambitiously, the union sought to organize as well the medical complex at George Washington University; Cafritz Hospital; Children's Hospital; Columbia Hospital for Women; Providence Hospital; Walter Reed Hospital. To a degree this drive came up short, but it also left behind a positive class struggle unionism.[61]

This could be seen on the campus at large. The towering basketball coach, John Thompson, an African American raised in the District, recalled a time in the late 1960s, as the flames of unrest were shedding light, and "Charlie Deacon, the Dean of Admissions... realized that Georgetown had a responsibility to Black people in Washington and helped launch a program to admit more Black students...." Still, by the 1970s there were fewer than 100 Black students in the entire undergraduate population of more than 4,000—though to watch Thompson's talented athletes, overwhelmingly of African descent and bringing a fortune in filthy lucre to the school's coffers, one could be easily misled otherwise.[62] Meanwhile, the Jesuits who

---

59. Leonard Downie, *All About the Story*, 98.
60. See e.g., *Woodward & Bernstein Collection, University of Texas-Austin. Washington Post*, 17 June 2022.
61. See e.g., "Mid-Week Report," 4 April 1972; *The Hoya*, 17 March 1972; *Georgetown Voice*, 5 September 1973; *1199 D.C. Weekly News Report*, 6 September 1972 all in Box 1, *Union Collection, Local 1199-D.C., Georgetown University*.
62. John Thompson with Jesse Washington, *I Came as a Shadow*, 100.

sold 272 enslaved men, women, and children in 1838 to Louisiana plantations in order to preserve the solvency of the university, by 2022 had fallen behind on their pledge to raise $100 million for a so-called "reconciliation initiative."[63]

The Black working class—unpaid and otherwise, antebellum and postbellum—found it difficult to rest in peace. By late 2020 headstones from the Columbia Harmony Cemetery, a historic African American burial ground that was dug up and relocated in 1960 to make way for commercial development and, thus, became the site of the Rhode Island Avenue-Brentwood Metro Station and encircling shops and condos, had begun to wash up downstream in Virginia. Among the 37,000 buried there between 1859 and 1960 were relatives of Frederick Douglass. The noted anthropologist, Michael Blakey of the College of William and Mary, termed what had occurred as "'dehumanizing'" in that "'racism is about dehumanizing people so that they can be dealt [with] without empathy.'"[64] This was becoming a trend. In late 2022 a dispute emerged in Montgomery County concerning a historic Black cemetery buried beneath a parking lot.[65] The ugly fate of the Black deceased was a metaphor for the abuse of the Black living.

Still, the working class remained torn in the District. It was also in the 1970s when workers at the Library of Congress split when the decision was made to select an AFL-CIO local as the bargaining agent: Black workers, who numbered over 400, were outvoted by the majority who were heavily Euro-American.[66] On the other hand, the NAACP continued cooperation with the AFL-CIO as they both became pillars of the Democratic Party establishment nationally. The union federation extended support to Congressman Parren Mitchell of the Black Caucus, a close relative of the Association's Clarence Mitchell. The latter Mitchell was concerned that the "black community" was unaware of "progress that is being made in organizing various establishments in the Baltimore area," though admittedly there was rough sledding: "even the Holiday Inn presents problems...."[67] Baltimore continued to supply proletarian vigor and spine to the region with strong contingents of

63. *Washington Post*, 20 August 2022.
64. *Washington Post*, 26 October 2020.
65. *Washington Post*, 7 October 2022.
66. *D.C. Gazette,* June 1976, Box 200, *James Forman Papers,*
67. Clarence Mitchell to Andrew Biemiller, AFL-CIO Department of Civil Rights, 6 March 1972, Box 58, RG9-003, *AFL-CIO Records, University of Maryland-College Park.*

Teamsters; Seafarers; Iron Workers; Printers; Operating Engineers; Stevedores—and more.[68] Yet Baltimore was enduring in the 1970s the pain of "de-industrialization" with Communists arguing that there was a connection between the city having the highest cancer rate in the nation and the epidemic of same at the reeling Bethlehem Steel.[69]

As steelworkers reeled, so did their brethren in the District, especially during the epochal 1975-1976 pressmen's strike at the *Post*, wherein management bared their fangs. Katharine Graham, the heralded publisher, conferred with owners of the *Star*, against their mutual union foe, a putative restraint of trade and antitrust violation. (However, she adds that the *Star*...took every advantage there was to take...the *Star* was doing everything it could to hurt us....") "Scabs" were recruited and, as she recalled, there was a "constant threat of violence" with "powerful air gun[s] firing metal pellets... roughness on the picket line became habitual...flat tires caused by nails...spouses were regularly called and threatened violently and obscenely...." As she saw things, the union collaborated with a "hitman for the Mafia...." Despite her whingeing, she admitted that it was "one of the pressmen" that "committed suicide."[70]

Her chief lieutenant, Ben Bradlee, offered the opinion that Washington "isn't and never was a labor town," not entirely accurate but he was determined to make his wish a reality. He confessed that the police backed management, not atypically as the police chief himself "walked innocently up to another striker, put his left elbow in the man's stomach and then slammed his right fist into the palm of his left hand. The picketer dropped to the sidewalk in agony. And we all cheered." The strike began in October 1975 and by late December, says Bradlee, "the paper handlers, a union of predominantly black men who load the huge rolls of newsprint into the presses and maintain the press room, announced they were going to settle with the *Post*...[since] the lily white pressmen's union had never done anything for them," as—once again—both wings of labor were damaged by a dearth of inter-racial unity.[71]

By the 1990s the paper had moved strategic infrastructure into Virginia; according to editor, Leonard Downie, this was done "to avoid union problems and labor strikes that had plagued the *Post* in the

---

68. Ed Miller, President of Hotel and Restaurant and Bartenders International Union to Michael Belfoure, circa 1972, Box 58, RG9-003.
69. *Daily World*, 12 January 1977.
70. Katharine Graham, *Personal History*, 539, 543, 555, 558, 569, 571.
71. Ben Bradlee, *A Good Life*, 415, 416, 417.

past,"[72] which was also an indicator that the capital's alignment with the Slave South, which had caused for it to be sited there in the first instance had eroded with the rise of the anti-Jim Crow movement.

According to U.S. Attorney Joseph di Genova, the newspaper was split between a news and editorial sections that "don't talk to each other"; besides they were "worried about advertising and the view of them in the African American community" in a "very racially divided" city where the police were "in disarray...one of those sad stories" that afflicted Blacks disproportionately—all of which contributed to a paper in disarray.[73] *Post* editor, Leonard Downie, agrees, recalling that the publisher felt the paper "was about Woodward and Bernstein," star reporters, "but also about Woodward and Lothrop... the paper's largest advertiser," this at a time when uber-capitalist, Warren Buffet, controlled 20 percent of the corporation.[74]

More to the point, Jill Nelson, a Black reporter on the paper's staff in the strike's aftermath, was wholly indifferent to the alleged charms of the vaunted Bradlee, depicting him as a "short, gray, wrinkled gnome" and the staff over which he presided: "two white males running the Metropolitan desk in a 70 percent Black city that is also the nation's capital" in an enterprise "in a constant state of intrigue." Thus, she was elected "Unit Chair of the Baltimore-Washington Newspaper Guild...at the 'Washington Post'" and, consequently, as she later wrote, "on July 13, 1988 the unit filed a complaint with the D.C. Office of Human Rights charging the 'Post' with discrimination based on age, race, sex and national origin going back to 1877, when the paper was founded"[75]—and accelerating post-1976 when the pressmen were defeated. But the competitive market for journalists was about to be transformed by the rise of the Internet and even articles drafted with artificial intelligence.[76] In 1964 the *Star* had a circulation of 258,167 and the *Daily News* had 193,013 but by the time of Nelson's labor activism, the *Post*, which then had a circulation of 408,701, stood alone.[77]

The decade of the 1970s was overflowing with transformations and this included the impending demise of the *Washington Star*, which found it increasingly difficult to compete. By 1977 the paper

72. Leonard Downie, *All About the Story*, 330.
73. Oral History, Joseph di Genova, 30 September-18 December 2003.
74. Leonard Downie, *All About the Story*, 328.
75. Jill Nelson, *Volunteer Slavery*, 137.
76. Kai-Fu Lee, *AI Super-Powers: China, Silicon Valley and the New World Order*, New York: HMH, 2018.
77. *New York Times*, 20 April 1964.

was hemorrhaging 70,000 dissatisfied readers annually—clearly unsustainable. Soon the *Post* was selling more than 600,000 copies daily propelled by its prize-winning Watergate coverage and the *Star* was limping along with 320,000 readers. Soon this declining journal was slated to lose $20 million annually, largely from a decline in advertising and sooner still, it was defunct—a monument to a paper, which refused to acknowledge that right-wing populism was incongruent with a rising tide of Black militancy and even Black affluence.[78] The paper's decision to die rather than adapt was seen just before its expiration when Black journalist and activist, C. Sumner "Chuck" Stone, was sacked after writing on national— and not just Negro—issues.[79]

However, there was understandable dissension in the union movement, given the AFL-CIO's foreign policy particularly, which leaned toward neo-colonialism, undermining their own membership; thus, when Governor Marvin Mandel of Maryland held a 1971 fundraiser with hundreds of friendly construction workers, tens of thousands of dollars were raised—but the event was picketed by other unions.[80]

Miles away in College Park, authorities continued seeking to restrain demonstrators. By 1972 Chancellor C.E. Bishop was reassuring Senator J. Glenn Beall that this had led to a clampdown in that "one of those who had been apprehended is an alien and there was another who played a leading role in the demonstrations... deportation proceedings are being processed,"[81] a dampening signal to nearby Howard where international students, too, had been in the forefront of protest. Also viewed with suspicion was a "Radical Guide to the University of Maryland," published contemporaneously wherein the authors thanked the Communist Party for "cartoons and pictures."[82]

The authorities in College Park should have recognized that obsession with the Communist Party was a distraction from other

---

78. John Norris, *Mary McGrory*, 178, 192, 292. The Italian American journalist, Gay Talese, blamed the scandals that engulfed the administration of President Bill Clinton on Irish American journalists—Maureen Dowd (formerly of the *Star*); Tim Russert; Pat Buchanan and, of course, the *Star's* McGrory, who in "Washington often did function as a clan."

79. *D.C. Gazette*, May 1979, Box 200, *James Forman Papers*.

80. *Baltimore Sun*, 20 April 1971.

81. C.E. Bishop to Senator Beall, 11 May 1972, Box 12, Series V, RG 28, *Office of the Chancellor Records, University of Maryland-College Park*.

82. "Radical Guide....", Box 11, Series III, *Records of League of Women Voters of Prince George's County, University of Maryland-College Park*.

pressing matters. They should have been focused more on the legacy of Jim Crow; in 1962 civil rights groups there were telling James Hill of the faculty senate of the university that his employer was "condoning segregated housing" and "not providing for equal facilities" for all.[83]

By 2021, Lakeland was the only place in this college town that Blacks could reside for the longest time. Only one square mile and once containing 150 single family homes, by the early 1980s it had disappeared virtually due to "urban renewal"—or Negro removal—as 104 of these residences were bulldozed. Yes, the City Council of College Park apologized much later and bruited the notion of reparations. However, today where Lakeland once thrived, there now stands apartment towers filled with university faculty and students—as the school's depredations of the past still resonate.[84]

The struggle continued, nonetheless. At the same time, workers and students were coming together by 1972—possibly prompting a divisive focus on "aliens"—leading to pressure on Governor Mandel, touted by certain unions, who had said "no to pay raise" and "paid hospitalization" and "collective bargaining" more generally. The American Federation of State, County and Municipal Employees pressed the case.[85]

Contributing to the good riddance category was the departure of the baseball team, the Washington Senators, in 1960 for Minnesota, then a newer franchise of the same name left in 1971. It did seem that major entities found it difficult to adjust to a new order featuring Black militancy and affluence and either folded—or left. Speaking in 1978 in Waseca, Minnesota, Calvin Griffith of the earlier baseball team said he moved to this midwestern state after he "'found out you only had 15,000 Blacks....'"[86] Griffith then told another reporter that "'Black people don't go to ball games, but they'll fill up a rassling ring and put up such a chant it'll scare you to death. We came here because you've got good hard-working white people here.'" The trailblazing Black reporter, Sam Lacy, who recounted this story also accused racist pitchers of beaning—or plunking fastballs

---

83. Committee on Housing, CORE of Prince George's County to James Hill, 13 October 1962, Box 1, RG 17, *Series-Student Organizations, Student Affairs Records*.

84. *Washington Post*, 3 November 2021.

85. Poster, 5 April 1972, Box 11, Series III, *Records of League of Women Voters of Prince George's County*.

86. *Wall Street Journal*, 23 February 2021.

with malice aforethought—into the head, torso, and limbs of Black sluggers, e.g., Frank Robinson of the Baltimore Orioles.[87]

These departures were part of an elongated process of yanking the District away from the most horrific putridity of Jim Crow to a different status quo. This was part of the process of the District adapting to a post-Jim Crow reality. This was followed by an effort to install statehood for the District or at least provide a vote for the lone congressional delegate. Senator Brooke was among those who formulated a constitutional amendment to correct this latter defect.[88] Skeptics argued that this would form an unwanted precedent compelling like representation for Guam, Puerto Rico, and other "territories"[89]—i.e., colonies. Senator Barry Goldwater received a sharp reprimand from a (former) Dixie supporter as a result: "You are a disgrace," said William Wright of Greenville, North Carolina, since "you vote to make D.C. a state...because you want the Negro vote. When are you going to think of the white vote?" Wright was irate, instructing the Arizonan chauvinistically, "Step down and let a man take over."[90]

There was a long road en route to parity and equity, however, as exemplified by the revelation that at a time in the 1970s when the District was overwhelmingly Black, the National Gallery, the Smithsonian, and the other pillars of the Cultural Establishment, were accused credibly of ignoring this racial reality in their staffing and programming.[91]

The fact remained, however, that the District had changed tremendously in past decades—but, admittedly, not enough. Arguably, the city and nation had yet to recover from the Red Scare which sabotaged class based organizations and the critique of capitalism and imperialism that was manifested in long-gone figures, e.g., Howard professors, Doxey Wilkerson and W. Alphaeus Hunton. Yet, such thinker-activists grew organically from horrifying conditions as much as anything else, meaning that inevitably the vacuum of their absence would be filled. Thus, by 1980 Maurice Jackson, leader of District Communists—and African American intellectual—was

---

87. Sam Lacy with Moses J. Newsom, *Fighting for Fairness*, 86, 158.

88. SJ Res 65, 18 May 1977, Box 154, *Barry Goldwater Papers*.

89. Staff Briefing Paper on House Joint Resolution 554, Box 154, *Barry Goldwater Papers*.

90. William Wright to Senator Goldwater, 23 August 1978, Box 405, *Barry Goldwater Papers*.

91. *Village Voice*, 12 November 1970, Box 74, *James Forman Papers, Library of Congress-Washington, D.C.*

running for local office backed by George Murphy, billed not as part of the celebrated Baltimore press barony but, instead, as campaign manager for Du Bois when he ran for the U.S. Senate from New York state in 1950.[92]

He received 8,000 votes in his race for the City Council[93] and then leapfrogged to graduate school, becoming a premier professor at Georgetown University, a school which not so long ago was renowned for its slave trading. Even as Jim Crow was crumbling all about in the 1960s, snooty Georgetown had fewer than 20 African American undergraduates with the bulk, saying then student, Wendell Robinson, feeling "isolated and unwanted." Even Patricia Harris, who served on the board after a stint leading Howard's law school, by 1971 felt that Black students were "'alienated, not so much angry as hurt and rejected. They appear to have retreated into a shell.'" However, as unrest spread, the administration was compelled to respond and by 1973 they had seen fit to allow 170 Black undergraduates to enroll.[94]

The ampler point to be digested was that despite the conspicuous presence of revolting fascists, as indicated by 6 January 2021, the struggle for economic and political democracy continued unabated.

---

92. *Daily World*, 8 October 1980.

93. *Daily World*, 18 November 1980.

94. Robert Emmett Curran, *A History of Georgetown University: The Rise to Prominence, 1964-1989*, Washington, D.C.: Georgetown University Press, 2010, 125, 76, 77.

Index

About the Author

Gerald Horne is Moores Professor of History & African American Studies at the University of Houston. He has published more than three dozen books including *White Supremacy Confronted: US Imperialism & Anticommunism vs the Liberation of Southern Africa from Rhodes to Mandela, The Apocalypse of Settler Colonialism: The Roots of Slavery, White Supremacy and Capitalism in 17th Century North America and the Caribbean* and *The Counter Revolution of 1836: Texas Slavery & Jim Crow and the Roots of U. S. Fascism.*